MANUAL OF BUSINESS SPANISH

The **Manual of Business Spanish** is the essential companion for all who use Spanish for business communication.

The *Manual* is divided into five sections covering all the requirements for business communication, whether written or spoken. Fully bilingual, the *Manual* is of equal value to the relative beginner or the fluent speaker.

Features include:
- 40 spoken situations, from booking a ticket to making a sales pitch
- 80 written communications covering memos, letters, faxes and résumés
- facts and figures on the countries that use the language
- a handy summary of the main grammar points
- a 5000-word two-way glossary of the most common business terms

Written by an experienced native and non-native speaker team working in business language education, this unique *Manual of Business Spanish* is an essential one-stop reference for all students and professionals studying or working in business and management where Spanish is used.

Michael Gorman and **María-Luisa Henson** are Senior Lecturers in Spanish at the School of Languages and European Studies, University of Wolverhampton.

RELATED TITLES PUBLISHED BY ROUTLEDGE

Modern Spanish Grammar
Christopher Pountain and Juan Kattán-Ibarra

Modern Spanish Grammar Workbook
Juan Kattán-Ibarra

España a tu alcance
Spanish skills for Intermediate Students
Michael Truman, Concha Pérez Valle and Peter Furnborough

Así somos los españoles
Spanish skills for Advanced Students
Michael Truman, Concha Pérez Valle and Peter Furnborough

Manual of Business French
Stuart Williams and Nathalie McAndrew Cazorla

Manual of Business German
Paul Hartley and Gertrud Robbins

Manual of Business Italian
Vincent Edwards and Gianfranca Gessa Shepheard

Further details are available on our website: **www.routledge.com**

MANUAL OF BUSINESS SPANISH

A comprehensive language guide

**Michael Gorman
and
María-Luisa Henson**

London and New York

In the preparation of the Business Situations and Business Correspondence sections of this handbook every effort was made to avoid the use of actual company names or trade names. If any has been used inadvertently, the publishers will change it in any future reprint if they are notified.

First published 1996
by Routledge
2 Park Square, Milton Park, Abingdon, Oxon, OX14 4RN

Simultaneously published in the USA and Canada
by Routledge
270 Madison Ave, New York NY 10016

Reprinted 2001

Transferred to Digital Printing 2006

Routledge is an imprint of the Taylor & Francis Group

© Michael Gorman and María-Luisa Henson 1996

Typeset in Rockwell and Univers by Solidus (Bristol) Ltd

British Library Cataloguing in Publication Data
A catalogue record for this book is available from the British Library

Library of Congress Cataloguing in Publication Data
A catalogue record for this book has been requested

ISBN 0–415–09264–7 (hbk)
ISBN 0–415–12903–6 (pbk)

Publisher's Note
The publisher has gone to great lengths to ensure the quality of this reprint but points out that some imperfections in the original may be apparent

Contents

Business Situations

How to use the Business Situations

The spoken situations which follow are intended to cover a wide range of business interactions, from the brief and informal through to the more formal and prolonged exchange typical of the negotiating or interview situation. The user is encouraged not simply to read the situations together with their parallel English version, but to attempt, individually or in group work, with the help of the recording if applicable, the following exploitation exercises:

- using the original situations as models, construct dialogues on similar lines with the available vocabulary
- use the situations, or sections of them, as the basis for role-play exercises
- interpreting practice Spanish/English, English/Spanish
- practice in oral summary (i.e. listen to the recorded Spanish version, and then summarize the content, in English or in Spanish)
- oral paraphrase: listen to one version, then recount it using different expressions, but attempting to keep the same meaning
- transcription/dictation practice from the recording
- translation practice Spanish/English, English/Spanish

The material in the situations is intended as a basis for further expansion and exploitation, and is ideal for use in in-house training programmes, or in open-learning centres, as well as for individual use.

Primera parte
Section I

Por teléfono
On the telephone

1 Making an enquiry

(a) Can I visit?

Maureen Simmons	Good morning. Robinson's Motors.
Mr Lewis	Hello, my name is Lewis. I've just seen your advert for the Riva 25s available on fleet terms. We've been looking for half a dozen vehicles at the right price for a while and your offer interests us.
Maureen Simmons	Fine. Would you like me to send you more information?
Mr Lewis	No, thanks. I'd rather come down to your salesroom this afternoon with a colleague to discuss the matter with you.
Maureen Simmons	No problem, sir. My name is Maureen Simmons and I'll be available from 2.30. Can you give me your name again and your company, please?
Mr Lewis	Of course. It's Alan Lewis, from Stafford Electronics. I know where your office is, so we'll be there for 2.30. See you then, goodbye.
Maureen Simmons	Thanks, see you later.

(b) Sales enquiry

Telephonist	Preece and Pritchard. Good morning.
James Davies	Good morning. Could you put me through to Sales?
Telephonist	Certainly. Just a moment.
Sales Department	Sales, good morning. Can I help you?
James Davies	My name is James Davies, from Goodright Inc. I'm ringing to enquire if you sell water pumps.
Sales Department	Yes, we do. Industrial and domestic.
James Davies	Can you send me a copy of your catalog and price list?
Sales Department	Certainly, just give me your address and we'll get it off to you later today.

1 Pidiendo información

(a) ¿Puedo pasar a verle?

Marisa Sanz	Buenos días.[1] Automóviles Ramírez.
Sr Linares	Buenos días. Me llamo[2] Linares. Acabo de ver el anuncio referente a la flota de los Riva 25 que tiene disponibles. Hace algún tiempo que llevamos buscando unos cuantos automóviles[3] a precio competitivo, y por consiguiente estamos interesados en su oferta.
Marisa Sanz	Vale. ¿Quiere que le envíe más información?
Sr Linares	No, gracias. Prefiero acercarme hasta la sala de exposición con un colega esta tarde, y hablar del asunto con usted.
Marisa Sanz	Sin problema alguno, señor. Pregunte por Marisa Sanz, que soy yo, y estaré a su disposición a partir de las dos y media. ¿Quiere darme su nombre y el de su empresa?
Sr Linares	Por supuesto. Alfonso Linares, de Electrónica San Fermín. Ya sé dónde está ubicado su negocio, así que pasaremos por ahí a las dos y media. Hasta luego. Adiós.
Marisa Sanz	Gracias y hasta luego.

1 In Latin America: variously *¡Aló!* or *¿Hola?* or *¿Bueno?*, depending upon the country.
2 In Latin America more likely: *Mi nombre es. . . .* A further alternative to both is *Soy* + first and surname.
3 Likely to be abbreviated in speech to *autos* (also *coches* in Spain, or *carros* in Latin America).

(b) ¿Vende usted . . . ?

Telefonista	Buenos días. Pérez y Pintor.
Jaime Dávila	Buenos días. ¿Podría conectarme[1] con el departamento de ventas?
Telefonista	Sí, cómo no.[2] Un momento, por favor.
Ventas	Buenos días. Ventas. Dígame.[3]
Jaime Dávila	Le habla Jaime Dávila de Gomera S.A. Le llamo para preguntarle si venden bombas de agua.
Ventas	Por supuesto que sí. Para uso doméstico e industrial.
Jaime Dávila	¿Podría enviarme una copia de su catálogo junto con la lista de precios?
Ventas	No faltaría más.[4] Deme su dirección, y se las enviaremos esta misma tarde.

1 This verb is especially common in Latin America; more frequent in Spain is *poner con*.
2 Literally, 'how not' (meaning, 'why not?'/'yes'), and sometimes written with question marks.
3 Literally, 'Tell me' (the most frequent response on answering a ringing phone), and sometimes written with question marks.
4 Literally, 'It would not lack more' (idiomatic term).

2 Ordering

(a) Placing an order

Tracy	DIY Stores, Tracy speaking. How can I help you?
Customer	I should like to order some plywood please.
Tracy	Certainly sir, putting you through.
Wood Department	Wood Department. Can I help you?
Customer	I would like to order quite a large quantity of plywood.
Wood Department	Certainly sir. Do you know what quality or can you tell me what it is for?
Customer	It's to make shelving and the quality should be good enough to hold books.
Wood Department	Right, then I would suggest three-ply 1½ cm thickness. How many metres do you want to order?
Customer	I need 150 metres. Is there a discount for quantity?
Wood Department	There are progressive discounts starting from 50 metres.
Customer	Very good. I will give you my address and you can tell me when your earliest delivery date is and what invoicing procedure you operate.

(b) Changing an order

Colin Pine	Please put me through to Steve Jones in Sales. . . . Hello, Steve. Colin here. I've had a think about what you suggested yesterday regarding the photocopier we ordered. We've decided to change our order from the CF202 to the FC302. I think that will meet our requirements better. Shall I send you a new order?
Steve Jones	That would be a good idea. Please send it with a note cancelling the initial order.
Colin Pine	Thanks, Steve. Bye.

2 Pedidos

(a) Solicitando un pedido

Trini	Bricolaje. Al habla Trini. Dígame.
Cliente	Quisiera que me sirvieran un pedido de contrachapado, por favor.
Trini	Por supuesto, señor; ahora le conecto.
Depto. de maderas	Maderas. Dígame.
Cliente	Quisiera que me sirvieran un pedido bastante grande de contrachapado.
Depto. de maderas	Sí, señor. ¿De qué calidad? o ¿Para qué es?
Cliente	Es para estanterías, y la calidad tiene que ser lo suficientemente buena como para aguantar peso de libros.
Depto. de maderas	Bueno, entonces le sugiero el de tres láminas y de un centímetro y medio de grosor. ¿Cuántos metros quiere?
Cliente	Necesito ciento cincuenta metros. ¿Hacen descuento[1] según la cantidad?
Depto. de maderas	Hacemos descuento progresivo sobre pedidos a partir de cincuenta metros.
Cliente	Muy bien. Le voy a dar mi dirección, y dígame la fecha del próximo reparto junto con el modo de pago . . .[2]

1 *Hacer descuento*: to give discount.
2 More formally: *modo de facturación*.

(b) Cambiando un pedido

Carlos	Por favor, póngame[1] con Esteban López, de Ventas. . . . Hola, Esteban. Soy Carlos.[2] He estado pensando sobre lo que me comentabas ayer respecto a la fotocopiadora que pedimos. Hemos decidido cambiar el pedido de la CF202 por la FC302. Pienso que cubrirá mejor nuestras necesidades.[3] ¿Quieres que te envíe un pedido nuevo?
Esteban	Me parece una idea muy buena. Haz el favor de enviármelo adjuntando una nota que cancele el anterior.
Carlos	Gracias, Esteban. Adiós.

1 The *por favor* component is equally frequent before and after the verb, which is naturally an *usted* command. In Latin America *comuníqueme* is most widely used.
2 The informal greeting is used. *Soy Carlos* (literally, 'I am Carlos') means 'It's Carlos' in this particular context.
3 *Cubrir necesidades*: to cover needs.

(c) Cancelling an order

Store manager	Hello, Sandhu's Wholesale.
Customer	Morning. It's Mrs Wilson here, of Lomas Supermarket. I'm ever so sorry, but my brother has got our order wrong this week. Do you mind if we change it over the phone?
Store manager	No, madam, as long as there's nothing perishable that we've had to order specially. Can you give me the order number?
Customer	Yes, it's SCC 231. We only put it in three days ago and it's all packaged catering goods. What we want is to cancel the soft drinks and the cereals, and have instead another 15 large boxes of Mercury. Is that all right?
Store manager	I've found your order and the invoice. We can change that before you call tomorrow and I'll make you out another bill. Will you pay on the spot?
Customer	Yes, by cheque as usual. Thanks for your help. See you tomorrow.

(d) Confirming receipt of an order

Telephonist	Klapp and Weaver. Good morning.
Julie Little	Morning. Can I speak to Mr Rees, please?
Telephonist	Yes, putting you through now.
George Rees	Hello, Rees here.
Julie Little	Morning Mr Rees. Julie Little here. I'm ringing to confirm receipt of our order number B/397/386.
George Rees	The radial tyres?
Julie Little	Yes, that's them. They arrived today. You asked me to confirm receipt as soon as possible.
George Rees	Well, thanks for letting me know.
Julie Little	We'll get your invoice processed in the next few days.
George Rees	Fine. Thanks for ringing. Goodbye.
Julie Little	Goodbye.

(c) Anulando un pedido

Jefe de Almacén	Mayoristas Sánchez. Dígame.
Clienta	Buenos días. Soy la señora Vicente, del supermercado Solysombra. Siento que esta semana mi hermano se haya equivocado con nuestro pedido. ¿Le molesta que lo cambiemos ahora por teléfono?
Jefe de Almacén	Pues no, señora, si no incluye productos perecederos pedidos urgentemente por nosotros. ¿Me da[1] el número del pedido, por favor?
Clienta	Claro, es el SCC231 (dos tres uno). Lo solicitamos hace tan sólo tres días y consiste en comestibles ya embalados. Lo que pasa[2] es que queremos anular los refrescos y los cereales y pedir en su lugar quince cajas grandes más de Mercurio. ¿Está bien?
Jefe de Almacén	Aquí tengo su pedido y la factura. Sí que lo podemos anular, y así cuando venga usted mañana le pasaré[3] la nueva factura. ¿Prefiere pagar en el momento?
Clienta	Sí, señor. Pagaré con cheque, como de costumbre. Gracias por todo. Hasta mañana.

1 A commonly used alternative (as interrogative) to the command.
2 *Lo que pasa es que*: a frequently used expression in popular speech to precede the recounting or explanation of events.
3 *Pasar*: to hand over (here).

(d) Confirmando recibo de un pedido

Telefonista	Buenos días. Hermanos Cepillo.
Julia Lagos	Buenos días. ¿Podría hablar con el señor Ruiz, por favor?
Telefonista	Sí, un momento que le conecto.
José Ruiz	Diga. Al habla Ruiz.
Julia Lagos	Buenos días, señor Ruiz. Soy Julia Lagos. Le llamo para confirmarle el pedido[1] número B/397/386.
José Ruiz	¿Los neumáticos radiales?
Julia Lagos	Sí, ése. Han llegado hoy. Me pidió que le confirmara recibo de los mismos[2] lo antes posible.
José Ruiz	Bien. Gracias por comunicármelo.
Julia Lagos	Le tramitaremos la factura dentro de unos días.
José Ruiz	Bueno. Gracias por llamar. Adiós.
Julia Lagos	Adiós.

1 The notions of 'receipt of' and 'our' are implied.
2 The tyres.

(e) Clarifying details of an order

Edward   Good afternoon, DIY Stores, Edward speaking.

Customer Hello, I am ringing about an order I made on the 27th. My name is Jones.

Edward   Just a moment . . . 24 litres of paint to be delivered on the 4th, in the name of Mr B Jones?

Customer Yes, that's the order but I would like to change a couple of details if possible.

Edward   Certainly, Mr Jones. Go ahead.

Customer I originally ordered six litres of eggshell blue matt, I would like to change that to sky blue vinyl silk. Is that OK?

Edward   Yes, that is all right. We have it in stock. Anything else?

Customer Just the delivery address. Could you deliver the paint to the site, 34 Western Way, on the 4th as agreed?

Edward   No problem, sir.

(e) Aclarando detalles sobre un pedido

Eduardo   Bricolaje. Buenas tardes. Eduardo al aparato.[1]

Cliente   Oiga.[2] Le llamo acerca de un pedido que hice el día veintisiete. Le habla Jiménez.

Eduardo   Un momentito . . .[3] ¿veinticuatro litros de pintura para ser despachados el día cuatro a nombre del señor B. Jiménez?

Cliente   Efectivamente, ese es el pedido, pero a ser posible me gustaría cambiar un par de cosas.

Eduardo   ¿Cómo no? Usted dirá.[4]

Cliente   En principio pedí seis litros mate, colorido azul cáscara de huevo. Me gustaría cambiarlo por la pintura vinílica brillante azul celeste. ¿Puede ser?

Eduardo   Por supuesto que sí. La tenemos en almacén. ¿Alguna otra cosa?

Cliente   Sólo la dirección de adónde enviar el pedido. ¿Podrían enviarlo a la Avenida de la Cruz, número treinta y cuatro, para el día cuatro, según lo acordado?[5]

Eduardo   Sin ningún problema, señor.

1 A further way of answering the phone.
2 Literally, 'Listen'; formal singular command frequently used in conversation and on the telephone.
3 Typical diminutive, to indicate brevity of time kept waiting.
4 Literally, 'You will say'.
5 Literally, 'according to the agreed'.

3 Making an appointment

Receptionist	Good morning, Chiltern International. Can I help you?
Paul Wignall	Good morning, I would like to speak to Mrs Mills's secretary.
Receptionist	One moment, please.
Secretary	Sue Jones.
Paul Wignall	Good morning, Ms Jones. My name is Wignall, from Whitnash Industries. I shall be in your area next week and would like to discuss product developments with Mrs Mills. The best day for me would be Tuesday or Wednesday.
Secretary	Just let me have a look at Mrs Mills's diary. She could see you Wednesday morning at 10.
Paul Wignall	That would be fine. Thank you very much.
Secretary	Thank you.
Paul Wignall	Goodbye.
Secretary	Goodbye.

3 Llamada concertando una entrevista

Recepcionista	Buenos días, Corona Internacional S.A. Dígame.
Pablo Valle	Buenos días. Quisiera hablar con la secretaria de la señora Mola.
Recepcionista	Un momentito, por favor ...
Susana Gil	Susana Gil al habla.
Pablo Valle	Buenos días, señorita Gil. Soy el señor Valle de Industrias Obando. Pasaré por esa zona la semana que viene, y me gustaría hablar con la señora Mola sobre el desarrollo de productos. A mí me vendría mejor[1] el martes o el miércoles.
Susana Gil	Espere que eche un vistazo a la agenda de la señora Mola. Podría verse con[2] usted el miércoles a las diez de la mañana.
Pablo Valle	Está bien. Muchas gracias.
Susana Gil	Gracias a usted.[3]
Pablo Valle	Adiós.
Susana Gil	Adiós.

1 Literally, 'It would come better to me'.
2 Literally, 'to see herself with'.
3 A standard way to repay gratitude just expressed.

4 Invitation to attend a meeting

Secretary   Hello, Mr Anguita?

Director   Yes, speaking.

Secretary   Javier Clemente here. I'm secretary to Lucía Ordóñez, public relations manager at Agencia Rosell, Barcelona.

Director   Oh, yes. We met last week at the trade fair in Tarragona. She mentioned that your agency could perhaps assist my company.

Secretary   That's right. Well, since then she has been in touch with a number of local firms who wish to set up joint projects elsewhere in Europe. A meeting has been scheduled for Tuesday, 6 October, at our offices here in Barcelona. Lucía has written to invite you. I'm ringing now to give you advance warning.

Director   That's very kind. I'll check my diary and either way I'll get my secretary to ring you before the weekend. Will you thank Ms Ordóñez and tell her I hope I will be able to make it on the 6th?

Secretary   I will. Thank you, Mr Anguita. By the way, our number is 3516784.

Director   Sorry, I nearly forgot to ask you! Send her my regards, and thanks again. Goodbye.

Secretary   Good afternoon.

4 Invitación para asistir a una reunión

Secretario	Oiga. ¿Está[1] el señor Anguita?
Director	Sí, al habla.
Secretario	Le habla Javier Clemente. Soy el secretario de Lucía Ordóñez, jefa de relaciones públicas de la Agencia Rosell, de Barcelona.
Director	Ah, sí. Nos conocimos la semana pasada en la feria de muestras, en Tarragona. La señorita Ordóñez mencionó que su agencia quizás pueda ayudar a mi empresa.
Secretario	Eso es.[2] Desde entonces la señorita Ordóñez se ha puesto en contacto con varias empresas locales que desearían establecer co-proyectos en Europa. Se ha programado una reunión para el martes, seis de octubre, en nuestras oficinas, aquí en Barcelona. Lucía le ha escrito invitándole a que asista. Le llamo ahora para advertírselo[3] por adelantado.
Director	Es usted muy amable. Consultaré mi agenda; de un modo u otro mi secretaria se pondrá en contacto con usted antes del fin de semana. ¿Podría darle las gracias a la señorita Ordóñez y decirle que espero poder asistir el día seis?
Secretario	Así lo haré.[4] Gracias, señor Anguita. A propósito, nuestro número es el 3516784.
Director	Perdone, casi me olvido de preguntárselo. Bueno. Dele recuerdos de mi parte, y gracias una vez más. Adiós.
Secretario	Buenas tardes.

1 *Estar* used here for: 'Is X in?'.
2 A standard conversational way of confirming the previous statement.
3 To warn you (*se* for *le*) of it (*lo*); *lo* refers to the fact of the meeting having been arranged.
4 Literally, 'Thus I will do it'.

5 Apologizing for non-attendance

(a) At a future meeting

Mary Galton	Mary Galton.
Patrick Herman	Morning, Mary. Patrick Herman here.
Mary Galton	Hello, Patrick, how are you?
Patrick Herman	Fine thanks. Look, I've just received notice of the sales meeting called for next Tuesday.
Mary Galton	Yes, is there a problem?
Patrick Herman	Afraid so. I'll have to send my apologies. I'm already committed to a trade fair trip.
Mary Galton	OK. I'll pass on your apologies. Can you send someone in your place?
Patrick Herman	I've a colleague who can probably come. Her name is Susie Rogerson. She'll get in contact with you later today.
Mary Galton	Fine. Well, have a nice trip. I'll see you when you get back.

5   Excusándose por no poder asistir

(a) A una futura reunión

Marta Gallardo	Marta Gallardo, dígame.
Patricio Herrera	Buenos días, Marta. Soy Patricio Herrera.
Marta Gallardo	Hola, Patricio ¿qué tal?[1]
Patricio Herrera	Bien, gracias. Mira,[2] acabo de recibir notificación de la reunión sobre ventas, convocada para el martes.
Marta Gallardo	Sí, ¿pasa algo?[3]
Patricio Herrera	Sí. Siento decir que no voy a poder ir. Ya estoy comprometido a asistir a una feria de muestras.
Marta Gallardo	Bueno. Les diré que te excusen. ¿Puedes mandar a alguien en tu lugar?
Patricio Herrera	Tengo una colega que a lo mejor puede ir. Se llama Susana Rastro. Se pondrá en contacto contigo hoy, más tarde.
Marta Gallardo	Bueno. Pues, feliz viaje. Te veré a la vuelta.

1 Standard conversational Spanish. Alternatives: *¿cómo está(s)?, ¿qué hay?, ¿cómo anda(s)?* amongst others.
2 Command to attract the attention, physical or intellectual.
3 Colloquial. Literally, 'Is anything happening?'

(b) At a meeting that has already been held

George	Could you put me through to the Managing Director, please.
Secretary	Certainly, sir. One moment.
Henry	Hello, George. We missed you yesterday.
George	I am calling to apologize. I didn't write to you because I intended to come, but was prevented at the last moment.
Henry	I gather there's a spot of bother in the Gulf.
George	Oh you've heard. Bad news travels fast. Yes, we have a container ship on its way there and there are rumours of war.
Henry	What will you do? Send it somewhere else pro tem?
George	Yes, but don't worry – I'll sort it out. Meanwhile how did your 'do' go?
Henry	Very well. All the important people came. Barry Clerkenwell from the BOTB was asking for you. I said you'd give him a bell.
George	Will do, and sorry again that I couldn't make it.

(b) A una reunión ya celebrada

Jorge	Por favor, ¿podría conectarme con el director gerente?
Secretaria	Por supuesto. Un momentito, por favor.
Enrique	Hola, Jorge. Ayer te echamos de menos.[1]
Jorge	Llamo para pedirte disculpas. No te escribí porque tenía intención de ir, pero a última hora me fue imposible.
Enrique	Tengo entendido[2] que hay algo de dificultad en el Golfo.
Jorge	Ah, lo has oído. Las malas noticias corren como el fuego. Sí, tenemos un portacontenedores que se dirige hacia allí, y se rumorea que están en guerra.
Enrique	¿Qué vais[3] a hacer? ¿Mandarlo a algún otro lugar por ahora?
Jorge	Sí, pero no tienes por qué preocuparte. Lo resolveré. Entretanto, ¿cómo resultó vuestra recepción?
Enrique	Muy bien. Estuvo presente toda la gente importante. Mauricio Ortiz, del Ministerio, me preguntó por ti. Le dije que le darías un telefonazo.[4]
Jorge	Lo haré, y perdona una vez más que no fuera.

1 Idiomatic Spanish. Literally: 'we threw you of less'.
2 Literally, 'I have (it) understood'.
3 You plural (*vosotros*); form not used in Latin America.
4 The augmentative (-*azo*) refers to the action carried out with the instrument in question.

6 Making a complaint

Mr Russell	Service Department, please.
Assistant	Service Department. Can I help you?
Mr Russell	Hello, my name's Russell, from Littleborough Plant & Equipment. Item IP/234 was ordered by us two weeks ago and has still not been delivered. I rang on Wednesday and was promised delivery by 5 p.m. yesterday. But we're still waiting for it.
Assistant	I'm sorry, Mr Russell, let me check . . . I'm sorry to say they still haven't sent the part to us. It's still on order from the manufacturer.
Mr Russell	Look, I'm not interested in all that. I just want to know when we'll get the part. It's highly likely I'll lose a good customer if I don't repair his machinery. If I don't get the part today, I'll go to another supplier.
Assistant	I'll chase up the manufacturer and see what I can do. I'll get back to you by 1 o'clock and let you know what the situation is.

6 Expresando una queja

Sr Rosell	Póngame con el Departamento de Mantenimiento, por favor.
Empleado	Departamento de Mantenimiento. Dígame.
Sr Rosell	Soy el señor Rosell de Equipos Bach, de Lérida. Le hicimos el pedido de una pieza IP/234 hace dos semanas y todavía no nos la han entregado. Llamé el miércoles y prometieron que la tendríamos para las cinco de la tarde de ayer. Pero todavía seguimos esperándola.
Empleado	Perdone, señor Rosell, permítame que lo compruebe . . . Siento decirle que dicha pieza todavía no nos la han enviado. Estamos esperando que nos la envíe el fabricante.
Sr Rosell	Mire usted.[1] No me importa en absoluto todo eso. Lo que me interesa es saber cuándo dispondremos de[2] la pieza. Es muy probable que pierda un buen cliente si no reparo la maquinaria. Si no me envían la pieza hoy mismo,[3] recurriré a otro distribuidor.
Empleado	Le meteré prisa[4] al fabricante, y a ver qué pasa.[5] Le llamaré a usted a la una y le informaré de cuál es la situación.

1 A popular expression in Spanish for asking someone to take note.
2 *Disponer de*: to have available.
3 *Mismo* serves to emphasize the urgency ('this very day').
4 Literally, 'I will put haste into him'.
5 Colloquial: 'and we'll see how it goes'.

7 Reminder for payment

Tardy customer	Good day. Paul Erskine speaking.
Supplier	Hello, Mr Erskine. It's Bankstown Mouldings here. Did you receive a letter from us last week reminding you about the outstanding account you have with us?
Tardy customer	No, can't say I did. Mind you, that's no surprise when you see the state of this office. We've just moved from the middle of town.
Supplier	Oh. Sorry to hear that. Well, it's an invoice for $2,356 which we sent out on 17 April; it probably arrived on the 19th or 20th.
Tardy customer	Can you remind me what it was for?
Supplier	Of course. We supplied you in March with several hundred wood and plastic ceiling fittings for the houses you were working on at the time. The invoice code is QZ163P.
Tardy customer	OK. I'll ask my wife to have a good look for it. In the meantime, what about sending me a copy so that we can pay up at the end of the month even if we can't trace the original?
Supplier	That's no problem. I'll fax it to you this afternoon if you have a machine.
Tardy customer	Don't bother about faxing. I haven't seen ours since we moved! Send it by post to this address: Unit 12, Trading Estate, Pacific Highway. We'll settle up as soon as we get it. Sorry for the hassle.
Supplier	I'll post a copy today, and rely on you to keep your word.

7 Recordando efectuar un pago

Cliente	Buenas tardes. Paco Escribano al habla.
Distribuidor	Hola, señor Escribano. Le llamo de Moldes Sen. ¿Recibió usted una carta que le enviamos la semana pasada recordándole que tienen un pago pendiente con nosotros?
Cliente	No, no te[1] puedo decir que la he recibido. Bueno, no es de extrañar,[2] si vieras cómo está esta oficina. Acabamos de mudarnos de una del centro de la ciudad.
Distribuidor	Lamento saberlo. Bueno, se trata de una factura por valor de 235.600 pesetas que le enviamos el diecisiete de abril y que probablemente la recibirían el diecinueve o el veinte de abril.
Cliente	¿Puedes recordarme de qué era?
Distribuidor	¿Cómo no? En el mes de marzo les suministramos varios cientos de accesorios de plástico y de madera para los techos de las casas que estaban construyendo por aquel entonces. El número de la factura es el QZ163P.[3]
Cliente	Vale. Le diré a mi mujer que la busque bien. Entretanto ¿qué te parece[4] si me mandas una copia, y así podemos pagarte a finales de mes, incluso si no encontramos la original?
Distribuidor	Sin problema. Si tiene fax, se la enviaré esta tarde.
Cliente	¡No te molestes por lo del fax![5] Lo he perdido de vista desde que nos mudamos aquí. Envíala a esta dirección: Unidad 12, Parque Comercial, Carretera de la Costa. Desembolsaremos en cuanto la recibamos. Disculpa las molestias ¿eh?
Distribuidor	Le enviaré una copia hoy, y confío en que cumpla lo prometido.[6]

1 Note immediate informal address used by the client.
2 Literally, 'it is not to surprise'.
3 Probably conveyed over the phone as follows: *ku, theta, uno, seis, tres, pe.*
4 Literally, 'what does it seem to you?'
5 *Lo de*: 'the matter of'.
6 Literally, 'the promised'.

8 Enquiry about hotel accommodation

Telephonist	Good morning, Hotel Brennan. Can I help you?
Customer	Hello. Can you put me through to Reservations?
Telephonist	Certainly. Putting you through now.
Reservations Desk	Reservations. Can I help you?
Customer	Morning. Could you tell me if you have a double room free from 14 to 16 May, or from 18 to 20 May?
Reservations Desk	Just a moment. I'll check for you. Yes, we do. On both dates.
Customer	What's the price?
Reservations Desk	The price per night, with bath and including breakfast, is £160. That includes service and VAT. Do you want to make a reservation?
Customer	I'll get back to you on it. Goodbye.
Reservations Desk	Goodbye.

8   Pidiendo información sobre alojamiento en un hotel

Telefonista	Buenos días. Hotel Palace. Dígame.
Cliente	Oiga. ¿Puede ponerme con Reservas?[1]
Telefonista	Por supuesto. Ahora mismo le conecto.
Recepcionista	Reservas, dígame.
Cliente	Buenos días. ¿Podría decirme si van a tener libre alguna habitación[2] doble del catorce al dieciséis de mayo, o del dieciocho al veinte?
Recepcionista	Un momento, por favor. Voy a ver lo que nos queda. Sí, tenemos libres[3] para ambas fechas.
Cliente	¿Qué precio tiene?
Recepcionista	El precio por noche, en habitación con baño, e incluyendo el desayuno, es de veinte mil (20.000) pesetas. Van[4] incluidos el servicio y el IVA.[5] ¿Quiere que se la reservemos?
Cliente	Le volveré a llamar. Adiós.
Recepcionista	Adiós.

1 In Latin America: *Reservaciones.*
2 In Latin America: *pieza.*
3 *Habitaciones* is understood.
4 The use of verb *ir* for *estar* or *ser* is frequent in Spanish.
5 *Impuesto al Valor Agregado/Impuesto sobre el Valor Añadido.*

9 Changing an appointment

Susana López	Hello. May I speak to Elena Aznar?
Elena Aznar	Yes, that's me. How can I help you?
Susana López	This is Susana López. I rang yesterday to see if I could visit the Ministry on Friday to discuss with your staff the new plans for tax reforms in the recent Budget. Unfortunately, my boss has just told me that the time we fixed is no good as I have to attend an urgent meeting with him. Could we possibly change our appointment?
Elena Aznar	I'm sorry that's happened, but don't worry. When do you think you can come?
Susana López	Any chance of the following week, maybe Tuesday afternoon?
Elena Aznar	It looks unlikely, I'm afraid. How about Thursday at about 10.30? All the key staff should be here then.
Susana López	If you can give me a moment, I'll check . . . Yes, that's fine as long as you don't mind me leaving by 1 p.m. – my boss has to fly to the States in the afternoon.
Elena Aznar	That will suit us. When you arrive, please inform the security staff and they will direct you to the relevant department, which is on the fourth floor. OK?
Susana López	Many thanks for being so helpful. Until the 8th then?
Elena Aznar	Till then. Goodbye.

9 Cambiando horario para asistir a una cita

Susana López	Oiga. ¿Puedo hablar con Elena Aznar?
Elena Aznar	Sí, soy yo. ¿Qué desea?[1]
Susana López	Aquí Susana López. Llamé ayer para ver si podía visitar el Ministerio el viernes: para hablar con su personal sobre los nuevos planes del reciente Presupuesto para reformar los impuestos. Por desgracia, mi jefe me acaba de decir que la hora que fijamos no es conveniente ya que tengo que asistir con él a una reunión urgente. ¿Habría posibilidad de cambiar la cita?
Elena Aznar	Siento lo que ha pasado, pero no se preocupe.[2] ¿Cuándo podría venir?
Susana López	¿Podría ser la semana siguiente, quizás el martes por la tarde?
Elena Aznar	Me parece que no,[3] lo siento. ¿Qué le parece el jueves a eso de las diez y media? A esa hora estará aquí todo el personal pertinente.
Susana López	A ver,[4] un momento que voy a mirar . . . Sí, me viene bien, con la condición de que no le importe si salgo a la una: mi jefe tiene que coger un vuelo[5] a los Estados Unidos por la tarde.
Elena Aznar	Eso nos viene bien a nosotros. Cuando llegue, haga el favor de informar a los de seguridad, quienes se encargarán de dirigirle al departamento apropiado, que está en el cuarto piso. ¿Vale?
Susana López	Gracias por su cooperación. Hasta el día ocho.
Elena Aznar	Hasta entonces. Adiós.

1 Less brusque in Spanish than its direct English equivalent.
2 A standard way in Spanish to calm others' concern; more colloquially, *tranquilo,* or even *tranqui* can be used.
3 Literally, 'It seems to me that not'.
4 Literally, 'To see . . .'.
5 In Latin America *tomar* rather than *coger*: 'to take (a flight)'.

10   Informing of a late arrival

James Cannon	James Cannon.
Paul Alexander	Morning, James, Paul here.
James Cannon	Hi, Paul. Where are you?
Paul Alexander	Still at Heathrow – my flight has been delayed.
James Cannon	So you'll be late for the meeting.
Paul Alexander	Afraid so! I'm now due to arrive at Düsseldorf at 11.15. I should be with you about 12.
James Cannon	Don't worry. We'll push the start of the meeting back to 11.30 and take the less important agenda items first.
Paul Alexander	Fine. Thanks for that. Look, I'd better dash – they've just called the flight.
James Cannon	OK. See you later. Bye.
Paul Alexander	Bye.

11   Ordering a taxi

Taxi firm	Hello.
Customer	Hello, is that A & B Taxis?
Taxi firm	Yes, dear. What can we do for you?
Customer	We would like a cab straightaway to take our Sales Manager to the airport.
Taxi firm	Birmingham Airport?
Customer	Yes, the new Eurohub. It's quite urgent. He has to be at the check-in in 35 minutes.
Taxi firm	Don't worry, we'll get him there. Give me your address and a cab will be with you in 5 minutes.

10 Notificando retraso en la llegada

José Carmona	Aquí José Carmona.
Pablo Alejandro	Buenos días, José. Soy Pablo.
José Carmona	Hola, Pablo. ¿Dónde te encuentras?
Pablo Alejandro	Todavía en Barajas,[1] han retrasado el vuelo.
José Carmona	Entonces llegarás tarde a la reunión.
Pablo Alejandro	Así es.[2] Llegaré a Sevilla a las once y cuarto. Estaré con vosotros a eso de las doce.
José Carmona	No empezaremos la reunión hasta las once y media, y presentaremos primero los puntos menos importantes del orden del día.
Pablo Alejandro	Bueno. Te lo[3] agradezco. Mira, tengo que marcharme; acaban de anunciar el vuelo.
José Carmona	Bueno. Hasta más tarde. Adiós.
Pablo Alejandro	Adiós.

1 The name of Madrid's airport.
2 Literally, 'Thus it is'.
3 *Lo*: José's delaying of the agenda items.

11 Llamada al servicio de taxis

Servicio de Taxis	Diga.
Cliente	Oiga. ¿Es el servicio de taxis A y B?
Servicio de Taxis	Sí, querida.[1] Diga.
Cliente	Nos gustaría que mandaran un taxi ahora mismo para llevar a nuestro Director de Ventas al aeropuerto.
Servicio de Taxis	¿Al aeropuerto de Barcelona?
Cliente	Sí, a la nueva terminal[2] del Puente Aéreo Europeo.[3] Es bastante urgente. Tiene que estar en facturación dentro de treinta y cinco minutos.
Servicio de Taxis	No se preocupe usted, que le llevaremos. Deme su dirección, que dentro de cinco minutos llegará ahí el taxi.

1 The taxi operator uses a frequent, if over-familiar, greeting to the unknown caller (here assumed to be female).
2 In Latin America: *el terminal*.
3 Literally, 'European Air Bridge'.

12   Checking flight information

Travel agent	Russell's Travel, good morning.
Customer	Could you confirm my travel details for me, please?
Travel agent	Certainly, sir. Do you have your ticket? Can you give me the details?
Customer	My flight number is EA739 to Prague next Wednesday and then on to Bratislava the next day.
Travel agent	Flight EA739 leaves Heathrow at 11.35 a.m. and arrives in Prague at 15.05. Flight CZ417 leaves Prague at 16.30 and gets to Bratislava at 17.20. Is it an open ticket?
Customer	No, it's an Apex ticket.
Travel agent	That's fine, then. You must check in one hour before departure.
Customer	Thank you very much for your help.
Travel agent	Don't mention it.

12 Comprobando información sobre un vuelo

Agente de Viajes	Agencia de Viajes Turinsa. Buenos días.
Cliente	¿Podría confirmarme la información de mi viaje, por favor?
Agente de Viajes	Sí, señor. ¿Tiene ahí el billete?[1] ¿Quiere darme los pormenores?
Cliente	El número de vuelo es el EA739, a Caracas para el próximo miércoles, que después continúa a Lima al día siguiente.
Agente de Viajes	El vuelo EA739 sale de Heathrow a las once treinta y cinco,[2] y tiene la llegada a Caracas a las veinte cero cinco. El vuelo EA417 sale de Caracas a las veintidós treinta, y llega a Lima a las veintitrés cincuenta. ¿Es un billete normal?
Cliente	No, es un billete Apex.
Agente de Viajes	Está bien. Debe presentarse en facturación una hora antes de la salida del vuelo.
Cliente	Muchísimas gracias.
Agente de Viajes	De nada.[3]

1 In Latin America the ticket would be referred to as *pasaje* or, possibly, *boleto*.
2 The 24-hour clock is used in Spain, even in speech, when discussing travel arrangements. It is also used in official language.
3 The typical response to thanks; also *no hay de qué*.

13   Booking a flight

Customer	Hello. Sunline Air Services?
Airline clerk	Yes, madam. This is Anthony Lawrence. Can I help you?
Customer	Thank you. My name is Robertson. I'd like to book a direct flight to Antigua. How many times a week do you offer Luxury Class travel on your flights?
Airline clerk	There are departures from London on Monday afternoons and Thursday mornings. In addition, there are flights on other days with different airlines, but our tariffs are very competitive.
Customer	Yes, that's what they told me at the travel agency, but I wanted to check for myself. Could you quote me for two return tickets leaving on Thursday, 7 May?
Airline clerk	Can we first check flight details and then look again at prices?
Customer	Yes, fine. So how does the 7th look?
Airline clerk	There are several pairs of seats still available on the 9.30 departure; for your return journey you can make arrangements at the other end. Shall I pass you over to my colleague, Janet, who can give you more information on prices? Everything else will be dealt with by her, including your personal details, form of payment and delivery of tickets to you.
Customer	Thank you for your help.
Airline clerk	My pleasure. Goodbye.

13 Reservando un vuelo

Clienta	Oiga. ¿Es Aérolíneas Sol?
Empleado	Sí, señora. Aquí Antonio Lara. Dígame.
Clienta	Ah, gracias. Soy la señora Rodríguez. Me gustaría reservar un vuelo a Cuba. ¿Cuántas veces por semana se puede viajar en primera clase en sus vuelos?
Empleado	Hay vuelos desde San Juan todos los lunes en[1] la tarde y los jueves en la mañana. Además, también hay vuelos otros días con otras compañías, pero nuestros precios son muy competitivos.
Clienta	Sí, eso fue lo que me dijeron en la agencia de viajes, pero quería comprobarlo yo misma. ¿Podría darme precio de dos pasajes[2] de ida y vuelta para salir el jueves siete de mayo?
Empleado	¿Podemos comprobar primero la información y después vemos los precios?
Clienta	Sí, bien. ¿Qué le parece el siete?
Empleado	Todavía hay pares de asientos libres para el vuelo de las nueve treinta; para el vuelo de regreso usted puede hacer los trámites una vez allí. ¿Quiere que le ponga con mi colega, Juana? Ella podrá darle más información sobre precios.[3] Pues del resto se encarga ella, incluso lo referente a la información personal de ustedes, la forma de pago y el envío de los pasajes.
Clienta	Muchas gracias por ser tan amable.
Empleado	De nada. Adiós.

1 Latin American usage; in Spain, *por* (*la tarde/mañana*) more normal.
2 In Spain: *billetes.*
3 Alternatives: *tarifas, costos, gastos.*

14   Thanking for hospitality

Joy Viney	Joy Viney.
Rachel Crisp	Hello, Ms Viney. Rachel Crisp here, from Galway plc.
Joy Viney	Hello, Mrs Crisp. Did you have a good flight back?
Rachel Crisp	Yes, very good thanks. I'm ringing to thank you for your hospitality last night. It was a very enjoyable evening, and it was very kind of you to ask us all round – particularly at such short notice!
Joy Viney	I'm pleased you found it enjoyable. It was very interesting for me to meet you all.
Rachel Crisp	It really was kind of you. So thanks once again. If you ever come over here with James, you must visit us.
Joy Viney	Yes, I'll do that. Thanks for ringing.
Rachel Crisp	And thank you. Goodbye.
Joy Viney	Bye.

14 Agradeciendo la hospitalidad brindada

Yolanda Vega	Yolanda Vega. Diga.
Raquel Crespo	Hola, señora Vega. Aquí Raquel Crespo, de Galán S.A.
Yolanda Vega	Hola, Raquel. ¿Qué tal[1] el vuelo de regreso?
Raquel Crespo	Muy bien, gracias. Le llamo para darle las gracias por la hospitalidad que nos brindó anoche. Fue una velada[2] muy agradable, y le agradezco mucho que nos invitara a todos; especialmente con tan poca antelación.
Yolanda Vega	Me complace saber que lo habéis pasado bien. Fue verdaderamente interesante el conoceros a todos.
Raquel Crespo	Usted fue muy amable. Gracias una vez más. Si alguna vez pasa por aquí con Jaime, tiene que venir a visitarnos.
Yolanda Vega	Sí, lo haré. Gracias por llamar.
Raquel Crespo	Gracias a usted. Adiós.
Yolanda Vega	Adiós.

1 The expression *¿Qué tal?* is applicable to objects and events as well as to people. Here Sra Vega is addressed formally by a younger business acquaintance, whom she in turn treats more informally.
2 A social evening.

15 Invitations

(a) Accepting

John Brown	Hello, this is John Brown of International Tool & Die. I am calling to accept your invitation to the lunch in honour of Mr Aspley.
Chamber of Commerce Employee	You are only just in time Mr Brown. I am fixing the final number of guests at 12 noon today.
John Brown	I'm sorry I did not reply sooner and in writing. I have just come back from a business trip. I wouldn't want to miss this occasion.
Chamber of Commerce Employee	A lot of people think highly of our Euro MP. There's going to be a good turnout.
John Brown	I am pleased to hear it. Mr Aspley has certainly helped my business to get into the EC market. Are any bigwigs coming?
Chamber of Commerce Employee	The Lord Mayor is coming and so is the president of the European Parliament. I don't know about our local MPs.
John Brown	Anyway, you've got me on your list?
Chamber of Commerce Employee	Yes, Mr Brown. You are on the list.

15 Invitaciones

(a) Aceptando

Juan Barranco	Oiga. Aquí Juan Barranco de Herramientas Internacional S.A. Llamo para decirle que acepto la invitación al almuerzo en honor del señor Asturias.
Empleado de la Cámara de Comercio	Llama usted en el momento oportuno, señor. Decidiré el número final de invitados hoy al mediodía.
Juan Barranco	Siento no haberle contestado[1] antes por escrito. Acabo de regresar de un viaje de negocios. No quisiera perder esta ocasión.
Empleado de la Cámara de Comercio	Hay mucha gente que sí aprecia a nuestro eurodiputado. Va a haber un gran número de asistentes.
Juan Barranco	Me alegra saberlo. El señor Asturias ha hecho mucho para que mi empresa entrara en el mercado comunitario. ¿Viene algún pez gordo?[2]
Empleado de la Cámara de Comercio	Estará presente el Alcalde, y también el Presidente del Parlamento Europeo. No sé si vendrá algún otro diputado regional.
Juan Barranco	En todo caso, figuro en la lista yo, ¿verdad?
Empleado de la Cámara de Comercio	Sí, señor Barranco, usted figura en ella.

1 Literally, 'I regret not to have replied to you'.
2 Literally, 'fat fish'; cf. colloquial English ('big fish') with slightly different connotations.

(b) Declining

John	Hello, Michael. This is John Gregory from Car Products International. We've organized a trip to the Indycar road race at Long Beach for our most valued clients. It's taking place the last weekend of April. Would you be interested in coming?
Michael	Let me check my diary. I'm sorry, John, but I'm down to go to a company sales convention in Malta that weekend. I'm afraid there's no way I can get out of that.
John	That's a pity. It would have been great to get together again. If you would like to send one of your staff, don't hesitate to let me know.
Michael	Will do. Goodbye.
John	So long.

16   Travel enquiry

(a) Rail

Passenger	Good afternoon. Could you tell me if there is a train out of Seville in the early afternoon going to Madrid?
Booking clerk	Do you mind how long the journey takes?
Passenger	Well, I have to be at a conference in the capital by 6 o'clock in the evening.
Booking clerk	There's a high-speed train which leaves every day at 12 midday. You'll be there by mid-afternoon.
Passenger	That sounds fine. Can I purchase my tickets by phone?
Booking clerk	No, I'm sorry, you have to come and pay in person.
Passenger	I suppose a colleague or my personal assistant couldn't make the purchase for me?
Booking clerk	Yes, sir, of course.
Passenger	Very well. I shall be travelling on Friday of this week and will require two singles. How much is that?
Booking clerk	34.000 pesetas in first class or 21.000 in second.
Passenger	Fine. Thanks for your help.

(b) Rechazando

Juan	Oye,[1] Miguel. Aquí Juan Gárate de Productos Internacionales del Auto. Hemos organizado un viaje a las carreras de Indycar, en Long Beach, para nuestros clientes más estimados. Tendrá lugar el último fin de semana de abril. ¿Te interesa venir?
Miguel	Espera un momento que mire la agenda. Lo siento, Juan. Me he apuntado para asistir a un congreso de ventas en Malta ese fin de semana. No tengo más remedio que ir.
Juan	Es una lástima. Hubiera sido estupendo reunirnos de nuevo. Si quieres que vaya alguien de la plantilla,[2] no dejes de decírmelo.
Miguel	Lo haré. Adiós.
Juan	Adiós.

1 The informal equivalent of *oiga* (listen).
2 Also, 'team', 'workforce'.

16   Pidiendo información

(a) Sobre trenes

Pasajero	Buenas tardes. ¿Puede decirme si hay un tren de Sevilla a Madrid que salga mañana a primeras horas de la tarde?
Empleado	¿Le importa el tiempo que tarda[1] en llegar?
Pasajero	Bueno, tengo que asistir a una conferencia en la capital a las seis de la tarde.
Empleado	Hay un tren diario de alta velocidad[2] que sale a las doce del mediodía. Usted estará allí hacia las tres y media de la tarde.
Pasajero	Me parece bien. ¿Se pueden comprar los billetes por teléfono?
Empleado	Lo siento; tiene que venir a pagar personalmente.
Pasajero	Supongo que un colega o mi ayudante podría comprármelos ¿no?
Empleado	Por supuesto, señor.
Pasajero	Muy bien. Voy a salir de viaje este viernes; pues, quisiera dos billetes de ida. ¿Cuánto cuestan?
Empleado	Son treinta y cuatro mil pesetas en primera clase o veintiún mil en segunda.
Pasajero	Bueno. Gracias a usted.

1 *Tardar*: 'to take (time)', 'delay'.
2 The AVE (Alta Velocidad Española) is Spain's first high-speed train, running between Madrid and Seville.

(b) Ferry

Booking clerk	Speedline Ferries. Can I help you?
Customer	Yes, I'm taking my car over to France next week, from Dover to Calais. Can you give me the times of the crossings?
Booking clerk	Well, they're very frequent. About what time do you want to leave?
Customer	About 8 a.m.
Booking clerk	Well, there's one at 8.45, and another at 10.45.
Customer	Is there an earlier one?
Booking clerk	Yes, but that one goes at 6.
Customer	And what's the return fare?
Booking clerk	Your vehicle and how many passengers?
Customer	Only me.
Booking clerk	The fare is £185.
Customer	That's fine. Can I book by phone using my credit card?
Booking clerk	Certainly, sir.
Customer	Thanks for your help. Goodbye.
Booking clerk	Thank you for calling.

(b) Sobre ferrys

Empleado   Ferrys Rápido. Diga.

Pasajero   Quiero ir con coche de Algeciras a Tánger la semana que viene. ¿Podría decirme el horario del ferry?

Empleado   Bueno, son muy frecuentes. ¿A qué hora quiere salir aproximadamente?

Pasajero   A eso de las ocho de la mañana.

Empleado   Bueno, pues hay uno a las nueve menos cuarto y otro a las once menos cuarto.

Pasajero   ¿Hay otro más temprano?

Empleado   Sí, pero sale a las seis.

Pasajero   Y, ¿cuánto vale el billete de ida y vuelta?[1]

Empleado   El coche, y ¿cuántos pasajeros?

Pasajero   Sólo yo.

Empleado   El coste[2] es de veintidós mil (22.000) pesetas.

Pasajero   Bueno. ¿Puedo hacer la reserva por teléfono y pagar con tarjeta de crédito?[3]

Empleado   Sí señor, cómo no.

Pasajero   Gracias. Adiós.

Empleado   Gracias por llamar.

1 Literally, 'of gone and returned'.
2 In Latin America: *costo*.
3 Frequently reduced to *tarjeta* (*de crédito* understood).

17 Arranging delivery of goods

Customer   Hello, Mr James? You wanted me to ring you back.

Supplier   Thanks for calling. I wanted directions to the factory for the delivery of parts that we are making on Monday.

Customer   Ah, right, this will be your first delivery. Well, take the motorway north. Come off at exit 27 and head towards Northam.

Supplier   How do you spell that? N-O-R-T-H-A-M?

Customer   That's it. After five miles take the Eastfield road at a big roundabout.

Supplier   E-A-S-T-F-I-E-L-D?

Customer   Yes. After two miles you meet the ringroad, clearly indicated, at a traffic light. Go straight ahead and go through the next two traffic lights.

Supplier   One roundabout, two miles and three traffic lights . . .

Customer   At the fourth traffic light you turn left and then second right. This is Alverton Road and our premises are 150 yards down on the left.

Supplier   Thanks very much; our lorry will be there on Monday.

17   Tramitando la entrega de mercancías

Cliente	Oiga, señor Jamones. Usted quería que volviera[1] a llamar.
Abastecedor	Gracias por la llamada. Quisiera que me indicara la dirección de la fábrica donde debemos entregar las piezas el lunes.
Cliente	Ah vale, ésta será la primera entrega ¿no?[2] Entonces, coja la autovía hacia el norte. Después coja la salida veintisiete y diríjase[3] hacia Navarrete.
Abastecedor	¿Cómo se escribe eso? ¿N-A-V-A-R-R-E-T-E?
Cliente	Eso es. Cuando haya recorrido ocho kilómetros, coja la carretera hacia El Castello al llegar a la gran rotonda.
Abastecedor	¿E-L C-A-S-T-E-L-L-O?
Cliente	Sí. Después de unos tres kilómetros de recorrido entre en la circunvalación: está señalizada en el semáforo. Siga todo recto[4] y pase dos semáforos más.
Abastecedor	Una glorieta, tres kilómetros y tres semáforos ...
Cliente	Al llegar al cuarto semáforo, doble a la izquierda y luego es la segunda a la derecha. Esa[5] es la Calle Alarcón; nuestro almacén está a ciento cincuenta metros, bajando la calle, a la izquierda.
Abastecedor	Muchas gracias. Llegará nuestro camión el lunes.

1   Literally, 'You wanted that I should ring again'.
2   Now in frequent use in Spain as an alternative to *¿verdad?*, having been typically Latin American in origin.
3   One of nine instances of the *usted* command, used during this conversation; from *dirigirse a*: 'to head for'.
4   In Latin America: *todo derecho*.
5   Literally, 'That one' (street).

Segunda parte
Section II

Cara a cara
Face to face

18 Arriving for an appointment

Receptionist   Good morning, can I help you?

Ms Jones   Good morning, my name is Claire Jones. I have an appointment with Mrs Leslie at 10.

Receptionist   One moment, please. Mrs Leslie's secretary will come down to meet you. Please take a seat.

Ms Jones   Thank you.

Receptionist   Would you like a coffee while you are waiting?

Ms Jones   Yes, thank you.

Receptionist   Please help yourself, the coffee machine and the cups are on your left.

18   Llegada a una cita

Recepcionista	Buenos días, ¿Qué desea?
Srta Germán	Buenos días. Me llamo Clara Germán. Tengo una cita con la señora Ledesma a las diez.
Recepcionista	Un momento, por favor. La secretaria de la señora Ledesma bajará a verla. Siéntese,[1] por favor.
Srta Germán	Gracias.
Recepcionista	¿Quiere tomar un café mientras espera?
Srta Germán	Sí, gracias.
Recepcionista	Sírvase usted misma,[2] la máquina y las tazas están a la izquierda.

1   The standard way of inviting a visitor (formal) to sit down.
2   Literally, 'Serve yourself'.

19 Arranging further contacts with a company

Mr Calder	Thank you very much for your help this morning, Mr Wallace. I think we've made a lot of progress on the matter of financing the deal.
Mr Wallace	Yes, I agree. It's been useful to clear the air in view of the initial difficulties we experienced. Presumably, this will not be our last meeting as we must await the final decision and then act quickly.
Mr Calder	Indeed. Do you know when that will be?
Mr Wallace	I've been promised an answer by the end of June, so if we say early July there will still be a couple of weeks before we close for the summer vacation.
Mr Calder	Fine. How about Monday the 3rd?
Mr Wallace	I can't make the morning, but I shall be free all afternoon. More importantly, the main people involved will be able to work on the final proposals that week. If we need to develop our plans further, bringing in other companies or arranging further contacts, there should be time enough to do that.
Mr Calder	So, shall we say 2 p.m. here? In the meantime we can still explore the possibilities or value of involving other parties both within and outside our companies.
Mr Wallace	Very well. I'll get that organized. I'll give you a ring by the 14th to confirm everything we might know by then.
Mr Calder	Right. Thanks again. .... Can I get to the carpark by going straight down in the elevator?
Mr Wallace	Yes. First floor, first door on the left. See you in July if not before.

19 Tramitando más contactos con una empresa

Sr Caldas Muchas gracias por ayudarme esta mañana, señor Velasco. Pienso que hemos hecho muchos progresos en lo que se refiere a[1] la financiación del proyecto.

Sr Velasco Sí, estoy de acuerdo. Ha sido útil aclarar la situación en vista de las dificultades que se nos planteaban[2] al principio. Probablemente esta no sea la última reunión, ya que tenemos que esperar a que se tome la decisión definitiva para luego actuar con rapidez.

Sr Caldas Por supuesto. ¿Sabe usted cuándo será?

Sr Velasco Han prometido darme respuesta para finales de junio, así que si decimos que será a primeros de julio nos quedarán dos semanas antes de que cerremos por vacaciones.

Sr Caldas Bueno. ¿Qué le parece para el lunes día tres?

Sr Velasco Por la mañana no puedo, pero estaré libre toda la tarde. Aun más importante es que los principales participantes podrán trabajar en las propuestas finales esa semana. Si tenemos que desarrollar más nuestros planes, introduciendo otras empresas o haciéndonos con otros contactos, tendremos tiempo suficiente para ello.

Sr Caldas Entonces, ¿quedamos[3] aquí para las dos? Entretanto podemos todavía explorar las posibilidades o el valor de participación de terceros,[4] bien sean de dentro o de fuera de nuestras empresas.

Sr Velasco Muy bien. Lo organizaré. Le llamaré por teléfono antes del catorce y le confirmaré lo que se sepa entonces.

Sr Caldas Bien. Gracias de nuevo. ¿Se puede llegar al aparcamiento[5] bajando en el ascensor?

Sr Velasco Sí. Planta baja, primera puerta a la izquierda. Le veré en julio si no es antes.

1 Literally, 'in that which refers to'; a standard expression.
2 *Plantear* (*problemas, dificultades*): 'to pose', 'present'.
3 Literally, 'we remain'; meaning 'we agree on ...'.
4 Literally, 'thirds'.
5 Also *el parking*; in Latin America, *el estacionamiento*.

20 Presenting a proposal

Helen	Morning, John. Do come in and take a seat.
John	Morning, Helen. Thanks.
Helen	You wanted to see me about our new product launch?
John	Yes, I think we should try to bring it forward to December.
Helen	That might be a bit tight. Any particular reason?
John	Well, we'd catch the important Christmas business, and we'd be ahead of the opposition.
Helen	I'm not sure that our production people could handle it.
John	Not a major problem. Our plant in Wellington can take on more of the production. We have spare capacity there.
Helen	Have you discussed this with your people there?
John	Yes, and they're convinced they can deal with it.
Helen	We can't risk any slip-up on this – the launch is very important. And what about the advertising schedule?
John	That's OK. The advertising copy is virtually ready. The ads could be pulled forward to December.
Helen	Look, there's some advantage in doing this, but I'll have to check it with the board first. There's a meeting tomorrow at 2. Can you make it?
John	I've got one or two things on, but I can reshuffle them.
Helen	Fine. Look, I've another meeting now, but I'll catch up with you later.
John	OK. See you later.

20 Presentando una propuesta

Elena	Buenos días, Miguel. Pasa y siéntate.[1]
Miguel	Buenos días, Elena. Gracias.
Elena	Quieres hablar conmigo sobre el lanzamiento de nuestro nuevo producto ¿verdad?
Miguel	Sí, creo que lo deberíamos adelantar para diciembre.
Elena	Vamos a andar cortos de[2] tiempo. ¿Por qué, entonces?
Miguel	Bueno, podríamos captar el importante negocio navideño, e ir por delante de los competidores.
Elena	No estoy segura de que los que están a cargo de la producción puedan tenerlo listo.
Miguel	No es un gran problema. Nuestra fábrica en Burgos puede encargarse de más producción. Allí tenemos capacidad de sobra.
Elena	¿Lo has hablado con los de allí?
Miguel	Sí, y están seguros de poder hacerle frente.
Elena	No podemos arriesgar a equivocarnos en esto . . . El lanzamiento es muy importante. ¿Y qué me dices del programa publicitario?
Miguel	Está bien. La redacción publicitaria está casi terminada. Los anuncios podrían adelantarse a diciembre.
Elena	Mira, hay alguna ventaja en hacerlo para entonces, pero antes tengo que comprobarlo[3] con la junta de administración.[4] Mañana hay reunión a las dos. ¿Vas a ir?
Miguel	Tengo algunas cosas por hacer, pero puedo reorganizarme.
Elena	Bien. Mira, ahora tengo otra reunión, pero te veo más tarde.
Miguel	Bueno. Hasta luego.

1 The standard informal invitation to sit down.
2 Literally, 'to walk'/'go short of'.
3 *Lo* refers to the matter of earlier publicity.
4 Alternatives: *consejo de administración, junta directiva*.

21 Exploring business collaboration

Visitor	Pleased to meet you, Mr Mendoza, and thank you for arranging my hotel.
Local Businessman	The pleasure is mine, Mr Sanders. I understand that you want to discuss possible joint ventures with us.
Visitor	Yes, we are both in building and civil engineering. We want to expand into Europe, and you might find it beneficial to have us as partners.
Local Businessman	It's a pity we didn't have these discussions three months ago; we recently wanted to bid for a stretch of motorway in this region but we did not quite have the resources.
Visitor	Was there no local company you could combine with?
Local Businessman	Unfortunately we are the only firm in the region with the necessary expertise. We would have been good partners – we've made a study of your past projects.
Visitor	And we have studied yours, of course. We were thinking of the proposed port development just down the road.
Local Businessman	You are really on the ball, Mr Sanders. We have just received the detailed specifications and were contemplating a tender.
Visitor	And I have the spec in English in my briefcase! Shall we roll our sleeves up and work out a joint tender?

21   Explorando colaboración comercial

Visitante inglés	Encantado de conocerle,[1] señor Mendoza, y le quedo muy agradecido por organizarme lo del[2] hotel.
Hombre de negocios	Es un placer, señor Sanders. Tengo entendido que usted quiere hablar sobre posibles empresas conjuntas con nosotros.
Visitante inglés	Sí, nuestras dos empresas se dedican a la construcción y a la ingeniería civil. Queremos introducirnos al mercado europeo, y tal vez podamos beneficiarnos mutuamente si nos asociamos.
Hombre de negocios	Es una lástima que no tratáramos de este asunto hace tres meses, pues hace poco quisimos presentar una oferta para un tramo de autovía en esta región, pero apenas nos quedaban los recursos necesarios.
Visitante inglés	¿No había ninguna otra empresa con la que asociarse?
Hombre de negocios	Por desgracia somos la única empresa experta de esta zona. Hubiéramos sido buenos socios: hemos llevado a cabo[3] un estudio de sus proyectos anteriores.
Visitante inglés	Y nosotros de los suyos, por supuesto. Teníamos en mente[4] el proyecto portuario que propusieron a poca distancia de aquí.
Hombre de negocios	A usted no se le escapa ni una,[5] señor Sanders. Acabamos de recibir las especificaciones detalladas; estábamos pensando presentarnos a la licitación.
Visitante inglés	¡Y en mi maletín las tengo en inglés! ¿Nos ponemos de mangas y preparamos una oferta conjunta?

1 A conventional mode of greeting, both formal and informal.
2 *Lo de*: 'the matter of'. The neuter pronoun embraces certain prior information or understood surrounding circumstances.
3 Literally, 'we have brought to an end' (i.e. carried out).
4 Literally, 'We had in mind'.
5 Literally, 'Not one escapes you . . .'.

22   At the travel agent's

(a) Enquiry/booking

Customer   Could you give me details of flights to Wellington, New Zealand, please?

Assistant   When do you wish to fly?

Customer   The first week of June.

Assistant   Let me see. Which day do you want to depart?

Customer   Tuesday, if possible.

Assistant   There's a flight leaving Sydney at 8 a.m. which gets into Wellington at 1 p.m. Do you want to make a booking?

Customer   How much is the flight?

Assistant   It's 725 Australian dollars return.

Customer   OK. Go ahead.

(b) Changing a booking

Customer   I'd like to change a flight reservation for Mr David Street.

Assistant   Could you give me the flight details?

Customer   BY567 to Rome on 21st March. Would it be possible to change it to 23rd March?

Assistant   I'll just check. That's OK. The flight's at the same time. I'll issue a new ticket and send it to you later today.

Customer   Thank you.

22   En la agencia de viajes

(a) Información/reserva

Cliente	Por favor, ¿podría darme información sobre vuelos a Santiago?
Empleada	¿Cuándo quiere viajar?
Cliente	La primera semana de junio.
Empleada	Voy a mirar. ¿Qué día prefiere salir?
Cliente	A ser posible, el martes.
Empleada	Hay un vuelo que sale de Miami a las ocho[1] de la mañana y que llega a Santiago a la una de la tarde. ¿Se[2] lo reservo?
Cliente	¿Cuánto es?
Empleada	Setecientos veinticinco dólares americanos (US$725) ida y vuelta.
Cliente	Bueno. Resérvemelo.[3]

1   24-hour clock references are equally likely in this context.
2   *Se* for *le*: you (*usted*). When two pronouns beginning with the letter 'l' follow each other, the former (indirect) changes to *se*.
3   In affirmative commands the pronouns are attached to the end of the verb (NB they precede negative commands).

(b) Cambiando una reserva

Cliente	Me gustaría cambiar la reservación[1] del vuelo del señor David Calles.
Empleado	¿Quiere darme la información del vuelo?
Cliente	Vuelo AV567 a San José para el veintiuno de marzo. ¿Podría cambiarlo por el veintitrés de marzo?
Empleado	Voy a mirar. Sí, vale. El vuelo es a la misma hora. Le expediré otro pasaje[2] y se lo mando[3] hoy más tarde.
Cliente	Gracias.

1   Latin American usage.
2   Latin American term; in Spain, *billete*.
3   Present tense used to express future in conversation.

(c) Flight cancellation

Customer	I'm ringing on behalf of Mrs Mary Thomas. She was due to fly to Cape Town next Thursday, but she has unfortunately fallen ill.
Assistant	I see.
Customer	Can she get her money back?
Assistant	How did she pay?
Customer	By cheque, I think.
Assistant	If she took out travel insurance she will be able to get her money back, if her doctor signs a certificate.
Customer	I'd better ask her if she took out any insurance and then I'll get back to you.

23   Checking in at the airport

Assistant	Good evening, sir. Can I have your ticket and passport?
Passenger	Certainly.
Assistant	Are you travelling alone?
Passenger	Yes, that's right.
Assistant	How many items of luggage are you checking in?
Passenger	Just this case.
Assistant	Can you put it on the belt, please? Did you pack it yourself?
Passenger	Yes.
Assistant	Are there any electrical items in it?
Passenger	No, they're in my hand baggage.
Assistant	What are they?
Passenger	An electric shaver and a lap-top computer.
Assistant	That's fine. Smoking or non-smoking?
Passenger	Non-smoking, please.

(c) Anulando un vuelo

Clienta	Llamo de parte de la señora María Tomás. Iba a salir en avión hacia Asunción el jueves próximo, pero por desgracia ha caído enferma.
Empleada	¡Vaya![1]
Clienta	¿Podrían devolverle el dinero?
Empleada	¿Cómo efectuó el pago?
Clienta	Creo que con cheque.
Empleada	Si sacó seguro de viaje, le devolverán el dinero si su médico firma un certificado.
Clienta	Será mejor que le pregunte si sacó algún seguro y después le[2] volveré a llamar.

1 A multipurpose term, here implying surprise/sympathy: 'Oh dear!'
2 In this case *le* refers to the speaker, not the sick passenger.

23 En la facturación de equipajes: aeropuerto

Empleado	Buenos tardes, señor. ¿Quiere darme su billete y el pasaporte?
Viajero	Cómo no.
Empleado	¿Viaja solo?
Viajero	Sí, eso es.
Empleado	¿Cuánto equipaje va a facturar?
Viajero	Sólo esta maleta.
Empleado	Póngala en la cinta, por favor. ¿Hizo[1] usted la maleta?
Viajero	Sí.
Empleado	¿Lleva en ella algún aparato eléctrico?
Viajero	No, los llevo en la bolsa.
Empleado	¿Qué son?
Viajero	Una maquinilla de afeitar y un ordenador portátil.[2]
Empleado	Está bien. ¿Fumadores o no fumadores?
Viajero	No fumadores, por favor.

1 *Hacer la maleta*: to pack a suitcase.
2 In Latin America: *computador portátil*.

24 Checking in at a hotel

Receptionist	Good afternoon, madam.
Guest	Good afternoon. I have a reservation in the name of Battersby.
Receptionist	A single room for two nights?
Guest	Wasn't that changed to a double room? My husband is due to join me later this evening.
Receptionist	I'll just check. Oh, yes, there is a note to that effect. Will you be having dinner here at the hotel?
Guest	Yes, dinner for one. Can I also order an early call tomorrow morning and can I have a newspaper?
Receptionist	At 6 o'clock, 6.30?
Guest	That's too early. Let's say 7 o'clock. And could we have a copy of *The Times*?
Receptionist	I am sorry but we will not have the London *Times* until tomorrow afternoon. Would you like the *Herald Tribune* or perhaps a Spanish newspaper?
Guest	No, thank you. I'll leave it. Can you call me a taxi for half an hour from now? And what time is dinner by the way?

24 Inscribiéndose en un hotel

Recepcionista	Buenas tardes, señora.
Clienta	Buenas. Tengo hecha una reserva a nombre de Berral.
Recepcionista	¿Una individual[1] para dos noches?
Clienta	¿No la cambiaron por una doble? Mi marido se reunirá conmigo más tarde esta noche.
Recepcionista	Voy a comprobarlo. Ah, sí, hay un aviso aquí a ese respecto. ¿Van a cenar aquí en el hotel?
Clienta	Sí, cena para una persona. ¿Podrían despertarme pronto mañana, y subirme un periódico?
Recepcionista	¿A las seis, a las seis y media?
Clienta	Eso es demasiado temprano. Digamos que a las siete. ¿Y nos podrían subir un ejemplar del *Times*?
Recepcionista	Lo siento, pero el London *Times* no nos llegará hasta mañana por la tarde. ¿Le gustaría el *Herald Tribune* o tal vez un periódico español?
Clienta	No, gracias. Déjelo.[2] ¿Podría llamarme un taxi para dentro de media hora? Y, a propósito, ¿a qué hora se cena?

1 *Una (habitación) individual.*
2 *Lo* can refer to the paper or, more likely, to the matter of a paper being supplied.

25 Checking out of a hotel

Guest	I would like to check out now.
Receptionist	Certainly, sir. What is your room number?
Guest	324.
Receptionist	Mr Lawrence? Did you make any phone calls this morning? Have you used the mini-bar?
Guest	No, I haven't made any calls since yesterday evening. Here is my mini-bar slip.
Receptionist	Thank you. Would you be so kind as to fill in the hotel questionnaire while I total your bill? How do you wish to pay?
Guest	By credit card.
Receptionist	Fine. I'll just be a minute. There you are, Mr Lawrence. Thank you very much.

25 Pagando la cuenta y marchándose de un hotel

Cliente	Quisiera pagar ahora e irme.
Recepcionista	Vale, señor. ¿En qué habitación está?
Cliente	En la tres dos cuatro (324).[1]
Recepcionista	Señor Lawrence, ¿hizo usted alguna llamada esta mañana? ¿Tomó algo del minibar?
Cliente	No. No he llamado por teléfono desde la tarde[2] de ayer. Aquí tiene la tarjeta del minibar.
Recepcionista	Gracias. ¿Sería tan amable de rellenar este cuestionario del hotel mientras le preparo la cuenta? ¿Cómo va a pagar?
Cliente	Con tarjeta de crédito.
Recepcionista	Bien. Un momentito, por favor. Aquí tiene, señor Lawrence. Muchas gracias.

1 The number could also be given as: *trescientos veinticuatro.*
2 *Tarde*: no clear distinction is made in Spanish between afternoon and evening, except by reference to the time.

26 Ordering a meal

Waitress	Good afternoon, madam. Would you like the menu?
Customer 1	Yes, thank you. And may we have a dry white wine and a pint of lager whilst we are choosing our meal?
Waitress	Certainly. Here is the menu; we also have a chef's special set meal at 15 dollars.

* * *

Customer 1	Would you like to have a look first?
Customer 2	No: I'll have what you recommend as you know the local cuisine far better than I do. But I'm looking forward to my lager.
Customer 1	Fine. Here come the drinks, anyway. May we have two hors d'oeuvres? Then for the first course two pepper steaks with vegetables and roast potatoes. I think we'll also have a bottle of house red with the steak.
Waitress	A bottle of red, two hors d'oeuvres and two pepper steaks; how would you like the steaks cooked?
Customer 2	Well done for me, please.
Customer 1	Medium for me.

* * *

Waitress	Have you enjoyed your meal?
Customer 1	Yes, it was fine, thank you. I think we'll skip the sweet as we are running a bit late. Just two black coffees and the bill, please.

* * *

Waitress	Your coffee and the bill, madam. Could you pay the head waiter at the till when you leave?
Customer 1	Of course. And this is to thank you for having looked after us so well.
Waitress	Thank you, madam. I'm glad you enjoyed your meal.

26 Pidiendo una comida

Camarera	Buenas tardes, señora.[1] ¿Quiere el menú?
Clienta 1	Sí, gracias. ¿Y quiere traernos[2] un blanco seco y una jarra de cerveza mientras seleccionamos la comida?
Camarera	Por supuesto. Aquí tiene el menú; también tenemos el menú especial, a quince (15) dólares, recomendado por el jefe de cocina.

* * *

Clienta 1	¿Quieres mirar tú primero?
Cliente 2	No. Yo voy a tomar lo que tú recomiendes puesto que conoces la cocina local mejor que yo. Sin embargo, estoy deseando tomarme[3] la cerveza.
Clienta 1	Bueno. Aquí nos traen las bebidas. ¿Puede traernos dos entremeses? De primero, dos filetes a la pimienta con verduras mixtas y patatas salteadas. Creo que también nos vamos a tomar una botella de tinto de la casa con el filete.
Camarera	Una botella de tinto, dos entremeses y dos filetes a la pimienta. ¿Cómo quieren los filetes?
Cliente 2	Para mí, bien pasado.
Clienta 1	Medianamente pasado para mí.

* * *

Camarera	¿Les ha gustado la comida?
Clienta 1	Sí, estaba buena, gracias. Creo que vamos a pasar del postre ya que se nos está haciendo[4] algo tarde. Sólo dos solos[5] y la cuenta, por favor.

* * *

Camarera	Señora, su café y la cuenta. Por favor, al salir, ¿quiere pagar en caja al camarero jefe?
Clienta 1	Por supuesto. Con esto quiero darle las gracias por habernos atendido tan bien.
Camarera	Gracias a usted, señora. Me es grato saber que les ha gustado la comida.

1 If the customer had called the waitress she might have used the command *¡Oiga!*; in Spain this is not regarded as brusque, though many might also adopt the practice of addressing the waiter/waitress as *¡Señor!/¡Señorita!* The latter approach is more normal in Latin America, whilst in Chile and Argentina *¡Garzón!* is often used.
2 *¿Quiere traer . . . ?* is a standard mode of requesting food and drink in a restaurant.
3 Reflexive (*me*) to emphasize his thirst. Here the speaker uses the verb *tomar* in reference to drinking only, which is normal in Latin America; in Spain the verb is applicable to both eating and drinking, whilst in Latin America *comer* is only used to refer to eating.
4 Literally, 'it is making itself a bit late to us'.
5 *Cafés* is understood. In Latin America black coffee is called *tinto* (not to be confused with red wine in Spain).

27 Verifying a bill

Waiter	Yes, sir? Did you enjoy your meal?
Customer	Yes, but can I check the bill with you?
Waiter	Certainly – is there a problem?
Customer	I think there might be a mistake – we had four set menus at £15 a head and also the aperitifs and the wine.
Waiter	Yes?
Customer	But what's this item here?
Waiter	Four whiskies, sir. £10.
Customer	But we didn't have any!
Waiter	Just a moment, sir, I'll go and check it. . . . Sorry, my mistake. I'll get you an amended bill at once.
Customer	Thank you.

27 Comprobando una cuenta

Camarero   Diga, señor. ¿Le gustó la comida?

Cliente   Sí, pero ¿podría comprobar la cuenta con usted?

Camarero   Claro. ¿Hay algún problema?

Cliente   Creo que hay un error: eran cuatro menús a tres mil (3.000) pesetas, junto con los aperitivos y el vino.

Camarero   Sí.

Cliente   Pero, esto ¿qué es?

Camarero   Cuatro whiskis, señor. Dos mil (2.000) pesetas.

Cliente   ¡Pero si no tomamos ninguno![1]

Camarero   Un momentito, por favor, que voy a comprobarlo . . . Perdone, es culpa mía.[2] Ahora mismo le rectifico la cuenta.

Cliente   Gracias.

1 Literally, 'But if we didn't have any!'
2 Literally, 'it's my fault'.

28 Drawing up a schedule of visits for reps

Senior representative	Thanks for coming to this meeting. I thought it would be useful to discuss the areas we will be visiting in the autumn quarter.
Representative 2	Conveniently enough the schedule of leads and follow-up visits shows a roughly equal split between the northwest, northeast and southwest regions.
Representative 3	We need to consider what to do about the lack of interest in our products in the southeast.
Senior representative	There is also a scattering of trade fairs that one or other of us should attend, including one in Marseilles in mid-September.
Representative 2	Perhaps we should all be there to work out a strategy for the southeast. And we could all be at the Paris Salon des Arts Ménagers in early November.
Representative 3	Good idea. I have some contacts that might help. Shall we proceed as originally suggested? Me in Bordeaux, George in Lille and Alf in Strasbourg?
Senior representative	That all seems OK. Are you happy, Alf? Apart from the Marseilles and Paris fairs we can each plan our own regional fairs individually.
Representative 2	I am happy with that. Same budget as last year?
Senior representative	I am glad you asked. The operating budget has been increased by a meagre 5 per cent. Any requests for increased staffing need to be justified by increased business.
Representative 3	So what else is new? Let's get those dates in our diaries.

28 Preparando un programa de visitas para los representantes

Representante de categoría superior	Gracias por asistir a esta reunión. Pensé que sería útil tratar de las zonas que vamos a visitar en el trimestre del otoño.
Representante 2	Se da la casualidad de que[1] el programa de primeras y consecuentes visitas está dividido equitativamente entre las regiones del noroeste, las del nordeste y las del sudoeste.
Representante 3	Tenemos que pensar en lo que hay que hacer acerca de la falta de interés por nuestros productos en el sureste.
Representante de categoría superior	Además hay toda una serie de ferias de muestras a las que alguno de nosotros debería asistir, incluyendo una que se celebra en Marsella a mediados de setiembre.
Representante 2	Tal vez debiéramos asistir todos, y preparar una estrategia para ponerla en marcha en el sureste. Y de esta manera podríamos ir todos a la Exposición Menaje Hogar de París a principios de noviembre.
Representante 3	Buena idea. Tengo algunos contactos que podrían ser útiles. ¿Vamos a actuar según lo sugerido?[2] ¿Yo en Burdeos, Jorge en Lille y Alfredo en Estrasburgo?
Representante de categoría superior	Todo eso parece razonable. Alfredo ¿qué te parece? Además de las ferias de Marsella y París, cada uno de nosotros podemos programar nuestras respectivas ferias regionales por separado.
Representante 2	Estoy de acuerdo con eso. ¿Con el mismo presupuesto que el año pasado?
Representante de categoría superior	Me alegro que lo hayas preguntado. El presupuesto de explotación[3] lo han incrementado un escaso cinco por ciento. Cualquier petición de aumento de personal debe de justificarse con el incremento del negocio.
Representante 3	Entonces, ¿hay alguna novedad?[4] Anotemos esas fechas en nuestras respectivas agendas.

1 Literally, 'The chance gives itself that ...'
2 'Originally' from the English version is conveyed by the use of *lo* + past participle here.
3 In Latin America: *costos de operación*.
4 Literally, 'Is there any novelty?'; obvious irony intended.

29 Conducted visit of a department

Guide	Before I show you round the department, come and meet my deputy, Frederick Fallon.
Miss Lomas	Pleased to meet you, Mr Fallon.
Frederick Fallon	Welcome to the department, Miss Lomas.
Guide	Frederick is responsible for the day-to-day running of the department. I'll take you round now. This is the general office, with Mrs Conway looking after reception and PC operators.
Miss Lomas	How many secretaries work for Mrs Conway?
Guide	Normally five. One is currently on sick leave and one on holiday. . . . This is the overseas sales office. They have their own fax machines and deal directly with our agents in Europe. . . . And this is the design section. Most of their work is now done by CAD/CAM. They've got some of the most sophisticated computer equipment in the company. David, can I introduce Miss Lomas.
David Carter	Pleased to meet you, Miss Lomas.
Guide	David has four designers working for him. And finally, this is Ted Stolzfuss, who is over here from our American parent company. Ted, meet Miss Lomas. Ted is with us to look at the way we operate in Europe.

29   Visita dirigida a un departamento

Gerente	Antes de enseñarle el departamento, venga que quiero presentarle a mi suplente,[1] Federico Fente.
Srta Lozano	Mucho gusto, señor Fente.
Federico Fente	Bienvenida al departamento, señorita Lozano.
Gerente	Federico es responsable de la gestión cotidiana del departamento. Ahora le llevaré a enseñárselo. Esta es la oficina general, con la señora Costa, encargada de recepción y mecanografía.
Srta Lozano	¿Cuántas secretarias trabajan para la señora Costa?
Gerente	Por regla general, cinco. Una de ellas está ausente por enfermedad y otra por vacaciones. . . . Esta es la oficina de ventas al extranjero.[2] Tienen sus propias máquinas fax, y hacemos todas las transacciones directamente con nuestros agentes europeos. . . . Y esta es la sección de diseño. La mayor parte del trabajo se lleva a cabo con el CAD/CAM. El material de ordenadores que tenemos aquí es de lo más actualizado de la empresa. David, te presento a la señorita Lozano.
David Castro	Encantado, señorita Lozano.
Gerente	David está al frente de[3] cuatro diseñadores que trabajan para él. Por último, éste es Ted Stolzfuss: viene de nuestra empresa matriz de los Estados Unidos. Ted, te presento a la señorita Lozano. Ted está con nosotros para estudiar cómo dirigimos la empresa en Europa.

1   Also *subdirector, director adjunto*.
2   Note that *al extranjero* implies movement **to** foreign countries, whilst *en el extranjero* refers to location **in** them.
3   Literally, 'is at the front of'.

30 Informal job interview

Personnel manager	Good morning, Ms Jiménez, and welcome. I hope you had no trouble getting here.
Gloria Jiménez	Good morning. Thank you, it was nice of you to invite me in for a chat.
Personnel manager	First, let me introduce you to Pepe Romero, who is in charge of advertising. As you can see, he's always snowed under with work, eh Pepe? Gloria Jiménez, Pepe Romero.
Pepe Romero	Pleased to meet you. Don't take her too seriously, Gloria, you'll see for yourself when you start next week.
Gloria Jiménez	How many staff do you have in this department?
Pepe Romero	Seven of them are fulltimers and a couple of others are freelance and help out when we have special projects on.
Gloria Jiménez	It looks a friendly set-up, anyway.
Personnel manager	Yes, you're right. They are one of our most efficient and successful departments. Would you like to meet Fernando, with whom you will be working most closely? He is our art director.
Gloria Jiménez	Fine. Has he been with the company for a long time?
Personnel manager	No, he was brought in recently when the company merged. Oh, it looks as if he's in a meeting, so we'll wait here and talk a bit more about you. How did you get into commercial design?
Gloria Jiménez	When I finished university I realized that there were good prospects for young people with ideas in the field of design and advertising, so I took a course in Seville not long before the World Fair was awarded to the city.
Personnel manager	Did you actually work on the project?
Gloria Jiménez	Yes, my first job was with a Japanese agency that was promoting its high-tech industries, and I carried on until the Fair closed.
Personnel manager	That sounds just the sort of experience we are looking for. Ah, here comes Fernando...

30   Entrevista a un puesto de trabajo: informal

Directora de Personal	Buenos días, señora Jiménez, y bienvenida. Espero que no haya tenido inconveniente en acercarse hasta aquí.
Gloria Jiménez	Buenos días. Gracias por invitarme a venir a hablar con usted.
Directora de Personal	En primer lugar, le presento a Pepe Romero, que está encargado de la publicidad. Como podrá observar, está siempre atiborrado de trabajo, ¿verdad, Pepe? Gloria Jiménez, Pepe Romero.
Pepe Romero	Mucho gusto.[1] No la tome demasiado en serio, Gloria; ya verá cuando empiece a trabajar la semana que viene.
Gloria Jiménez	¿Cuántos empleados trabajan en este departamento?
Pepe Romero	Siete de ellos están fijos, y otros dos que trabajan por cuenta propia[2] y que nos ayudan cuando tenemos un proyecto especial.
Gloria Jiménez	De todos modos, parece que hay buen ambiente.
Directora de Personal	Sí, es verdad. Forman parte de uno de los departamentos más eficientes y exitosos de nuestra empresa. ¿Le gustaría conocer a Fernando, con quien va a estar más ligada[3] en el trabajo? Es nuestro director de diseño.
Gloria Jiménez	Bueno. ¿Hace mucho que trabaja para esta empresa?
Directora de Personal	No, entró cuando se fusionó la empresa. Ah, me parece que está en una reunión, así que vamos a quedarnos aquí y hablar algo más acerca de usted. ¿Cómo es que escogió diseño comercial?
Gloria Jiménez	Cuando terminé la carrera me di cuenta de que había buenas perspectivas para los jóvenes que tienen imaginación en el campo del diseño y de la publicidad, y así hice un curso en Sevilla poco antes de que la nominaran ciudad en la que se iba a celebrar la Exposición Universal.
Directora de Personal	¿Trabajó usted en el proyecto?
Gloria Jiménez	Sí. Mi primer trabajo lo[4] hice para una agencia japonesa que promocionaba industrias de alta tecnología, y seguí allí hasta que la Feria finalizó.
Directora de Personal	Ese tipo de experiencia es precisamente lo que buscamos. Ah, ahí viene Fernando . . .

1 A standard response on being introduced.
2 Literally, 'by their own account'.
3 Literally, 'linked'.
4 *Lo* refers directly back to *trabajo*; such repetition by means of the pronoun is characteristic of Spanish usage.

31   Formal job interview

Part 1

Personnel officer   Do come in, Ms Martin, and take a seat.

Ms Martin   Thank you.

Personnel officer   Well, if I can make a start, can you tell us why you want this particular post?

Ms Martin   As I said in my application, I'm working with quite a small company at the moment. My promotion prospects are limited because of that.

Personnel officer   So that is your main reason?

Ms Martin   Not just that. I've been with the company for five years now, and although I found the work interesting at first, I now feel that I want a more varied post which is more challenging.

Personnel officer   And you feel that you'll find that here?

Ms Martin   Yes, I think so. You're a big company in the process of expansion, and the department I'd be working in would give me much more variety.

Personnel officer   Do you think that moving from a small department to a much larger one would be a problem?

Ms Martin   It would be rather new at first, but I worked with a big company before my present job, and I do integrate well. I'm confident that I can make the change.

31   Entrevista formal

Primera parte

Jefa de Personal	Adelante,[1] señorita Martínez, y siéntese.
Srta Martínez	Gracias.
Jefa de Personal	Bueno. Para empezar ¿podría decirnos por qué ha solicitado este puesto?
Srta Martínez	Como dije en mi solicitud, en la actualidad trabajo para una empresa bastante pequeña. Por eso, las perspectivas de ascenso son limitadas.
Jefa de Personal	Entonces, ¿es esa la principal razón?
Srta Martínez	Esa no es la única. Llevo con la empresa desde hace cinco años y, aunque al principio el trabajo era interesante, ahora me gustaría obtener un puesto más variado y estimulante.
Jefa de Personal	¿Y le parece que lo encontrará con nosotros?
Srta Martínez	Así lo creo.[2] Ustedes son una empresa en expansión, y el departamento en el que trabajaría ofrecería mucha más variedad.
Jefa de Personal	¿Piensa que será problemático cambiar de un departamento pequeño a otro mucho más grande?
Srta Martínez	Al principio sería bastante nuevo, pero antes de trabajar para la empresa actual trabajaba en una grande; además, me integro bien en mi trabajo. Estoy segura de que podré ajustarme al cambio.

1 Used when inviting somebody to come forward; hence also 'come in'.
2 Literally, 'Thus I believe it'.

Part 2

Director	As you know, we're a multinational organization, and that means that one of the things we're looking for in this post is a competence in languages.
Ms Martin	Yes, well, as you'll see from my CV, I studied German and Spanish at school, and I've lived and worked in France for several years.
Director	How would you describe your language competence?
Ms Martin	My French is fluent, and I can still remember the basics in German and Spanish.
Director	What if we were to ask you to take further language training?
Ms Martin	I'd welcome that. I feel that it's important to get them to as high a level as possible.
Director	Fine. On another issue: if we were to offer you the post, when could you take it up?
Ms Martin	In two months. I'm working on a project in my current post, and I'd like to see that through first. Would that be a problem?
Director	I don't think so, but I'd have to check with the department before confirming, of course. Well now, are there any questions you want to ask us?
Ms Martin	Just two: you mention your management training programme in your particulars. Can you tell me more about it?
Director	Yes, we expect all our middle managers to try to reach their full potential through self-development. We help them in that by running a series of in-house residential training courses.
Ms Martin	How often is that?
Director	Three or four times a year, and we expect everyone to attend them, as far as possible.
Ms Martin	That's fine. One other question, if I may?
Director	Certainly.
Ms Martin	When will I hear if I've got the post?
Director	We'll be contacting the successful candidate by phone this evening, and we'll be writing to the others.
Ms Martin	Thanks very much.
Director	Well, thank you for coming to interview, Ms Martin. Goodbye.
Ms Martin	Goodbye.

Segunda parte

Director adjunto	Como usted sabe, formamos parte de una organización multinacional, lo que implica que una de las cosas que buscamos en este puesto de trabajo es ser competente en lenguas.
Srta Martínez	Sí, bien; como se observa de mi currículum,[1] estudié alemán y francés en el instituto, y he vivido y trabajado en Italia durante varios años.
Director adjunto	¿Cómo definiría su competencia lingüística?
Srta Martínez	Domino el italiano y todavía recuerdo lo básico del alemán y del francés.
Director adjunto	¿Y si fuéramos a pedir que se volviera a dedicar al estudio de las lenguas?
Srta Martínez	Eso me gustaría mucho. Pienso que es importante elevar el nivel cuanto más mejor.
Director adjunto	Bueno. Otro asunto. Si le ofreciéramos este puesto ¿cuándo estaría dispuesta a incorporarse?
Srta Martínez	Dentro de dos meses. En mi puesto actual estoy trabajando en un proyecto que primero quisiera dar por terminado. ¿Eso sería problemático?
Director adjunto	Creo que no, pero por supuesto que primero tendría que consultarlo[2] con el departamento. Bueno, pues ahora ¿tiene algo que preguntarnos?
Srta Martínez	Sólo dos cosas. En su folleto con los detalles hace mención al programa de formación administrativa. ¿Puede darme información más amplia a este respecto?
Director adjunto	Por supuesto. Esperamos que todos nuestros directivos que ocupan puestos intermedios consigan alcanzar escalas más elevadas[3] a través del autodesarrollo. Nosotros les apoyamos en esa iniciativa por medio de una serie de cursos de perfeccionamiento a cargo de la empresa.
Srta Martínez	¿Con qué frecuencia son?
Director adjunto	Tres o cuatro veces al año, y esperamos que, en la medida posible,[4] todo el mundo asista a ellos.
Srta Martínez	Me parece bien. ¿Puedo hacerle otra pregunta?
Director adjunto	Cómo no.
Srta Martínez	¿Cuándo me notificarán si he conseguido el puesto?
Director adjunto	Nos pondremos en contacto con la persona seleccionada por teléfono esta tarde, y escribiremos a los demás.
Srta Martínez	Muchas gracias.
Director adjunto	Bueno, gracias a usted por haber asistido a la entrevista, señorita Martínez. Adiós.
Srta Martínez	Adiós.

1 The second word (vitae) is rarely used. 2 *Lo* refers to the question of her starting two months later. 3 A slight paraphrase: 'manage to reach higher scales'. 4 Literally, 'in the measure of the possible'.

Part 3

Carol Martin	Hello. Carol Martin.
Personnel officer	Good evening, Ms Martin. Barbara Carter here, from Keystone Engineering. I'm ringing to offer you the post here.
Carol Martin	Really? Well, thank you very much!
Personnel officer	I suppose the first question has to be whether or not you wish to accept the post.
Carol Martin	Yes, I do. Thank you.
Personnel officer	The starting salary, as we agreed, would be £25,000, with a salary review after your first six months.
Carol Martin	Yes, that's fine.
Personnel officer	When could you start?
Carol Martin	As I explained at the interview, there is a project I'm working on at the moment that I'd like to see through. Therefore, if possible I'd like to start in two months.
Personnel officer	Shall we say the 1st of June, then?
Carol Martin	Probably. I'll just need to discuss things with my present employer first. I'll do that after I get your offer in writing, and then ring you.
Personnel officer	You'll need to get down here a few times before, of course, to meet one or two people and get the feel of the place.
Carol Martin	Yes, certainly. I'd like to do that.
Personnel officer	Well then, I'll get my colleagues to send the formal written offer to you. That should be with you in a couple of days.
Carol Martin	Thank you for offering me the post.
Personnel officer	Look forward to working with you. Bye.
Carol Martin	Goodbye.

Tercera parte

Srta Martínez	Conchita Martínez. Diga.
Jefa de Personal	Buenas tardes, señorita Martínez. Le habla Bárbara Cebrián de Ingenieros Pardo. Le llamo para ofrecerle el puesto con nosotros.
Srta Martínez	¿De verdad? Estupendo,[1] y muchísimas gracias.
Jefa de Personal	Supongo que la primera pregunta que debo hacerle es si desea o no aceptarlo.
Srta Martínez	Por supuesto que sí. Gracias.
Jefa de Personal	El sueldo inicial, como lo acordamos, ascenderá a cinco millones de pesetas al año, con revisión salarial al cabo de seis meses.
Srta Martínez	Sí, vale.
Jefa de Personal	¿Cuándo podría incorporarse?
Srta Martínez	Como dije en la entrevista, ahora estoy trabajando en un proyecto que quiero terminar. Por consiguiente, a ser posible, me gustaría empezar a trabajar con ustedes dentro de dos meses.
Jefa de Personal	Entonces, ¿para el primero[2] de junio?
Srta Martínez	Es probable. Primero tengo que tratar de algunas cosas con mi jefe actual. Esto lo[3] haré cuando haya recibido confirmación escrita de su oferta, y después le llamaré.
Jefa de Personal	Desde luego que antes va a tener que pasar por aquí alguna vez para conocer a una o dos personas y ambientarse un poco con el lugar.
Srta Martínez	Sí, cómo no. Me gustaría que así fuera.[4]
Jefa de Personal	Bueno, pues entonces notificaré a mis colegas para que le envíen la oferta formal por escrito. Le llegará dentro de unos días.
Srta Martínez	Gracias por ofrecerme el puesto.
Jefa de Personal	Tenemos muchas ganas de que empiece a trabajar con nosotros. Adiós.
Srta Martínez	Adiós.

1 Great!, super!, brilliant!.
2 In Latin America, *el uno de . . . .*
3 *Lo* repeats the preceding word (*esto*) partly for emphasis and partly due to the needs of the syntax.
4 Literally, 'I'd like that it were thus'.

32   Planning a budget

Managing director	All right, if I can open the meeting. This need not be too formal but I hardly need to say how important it is. And, for a start, the balance sheet for last year is for our eyes only.
Director 2	It makes very pleasant reading, 11 per cent growth on the preceding year.
Managing director	Don't get carried away, Derek. I've looked at our orders and would suggest that we should not count on more than 5 per cent growth in the coming year.
Director 2	Does that mean an average 5 per cent increase in expenditure all round?
Director 3	Most of the increase will be forced on us. We have got to give the staff a cost of living increase, fuel for the vans is bound to increase by at least 5 per cent.
Managing director	We certainly cannot recruit extra staff at this point so I agree with that. Is there any equipment we need to replace, Derek?
Director 2	The production stuff is in good nick and we have at least 20 per cent spare capacity. The vans are OK, not too much mileage.
Director 3	Rosemary needs a new printer and we could all do with a higher spec photocopier. We probably need to up our marketing effort.
Managing director	I am relying on you to watch the monthly cash flow like a hawk, Marcia. Most of my time is taken looking for new business. What about production costs, Derek?
Director 2	I reckon we can increase production by 10 per cent with hardly any extra cost and no danger. How about that!
Managing director	And the bank is happy with the state of our overdraft. That all looks fairly satisfactory. As long as we continue to work flat out!

32 Planificando un presupuesto

Director gerente	Vamos a ver, amigos, que quiero empezar la reunión. Esta no tiene que llevarse a cabo de manera formal, pero ni qué decir tiene que[1] es importante. Y, para empezar, la hoja de balance del año pasado no debe salir de estas cuatro paredes.[2]
Director 2	Es agradable observar un incremento del once por ciento al del año anterior.
Director gerente	No te emociones, Daniel. He estudiado nuestros pedidos y sugeriría que no contásemos con más del cinco por ciento de crecimiento para el año próximo.
Director 2	¿Significa esto un promedio del cinco por ciento en todo tipo de gastos?
Directora 3	La mayoría de los incrementos serán forzosos. Tenemos que proveer a nuestro personal de un incremento salarial, el carburante para nuestras furgonetas es casi seguro que subirá por lo menos un cinco por ciento...
Director gerente	Está claro que por ahora[3] no podemos aumentar la plantilla, así que estoy de acuerdo con eso. Daniel, ¿necesitamos reponer algún material?
Director 2	Lo referente a[4] la producción va bien, y disponemos, por lo menos, de un veinte por ciento de capacidad sobrante. Las furgonetas marchan bien; no tienen demasiado kilometraje.
Directora 3	Rosa tiene que hacerse con una nueva impresora y nos vendría bien a todos una fotocopiadora de alta calidad. Probablemente tendremos que elevar nuestro esfuerzo en lo que al márketing se refiere.
Director gerente	Confío en que no pierdas de vista el cash-flow mensual, Guillermina. La mayor parte del tiempo de que dispongo yo la paso buscando nuevas iniciativas. ¿Y qué hay respecto a los gastos de producción, Daniel?
Director 2	Pienso que podemos incrementar la producción en un diez por ciento sin casi ningún gasto extra y sin riesgo. ¿Qué os parece?
Director gerente	Y el banco está satisfecho con el estado del saldo deudor de nuestra cuenta. Todo eso parece bastante satisfactorio. ¡Con tal que sigamos trabajando sin tregua![5]

1 *Ni qué decir tiene que*: 'it goes without saying that ...'.
2 Literally, 'must not leave these four walls'.
3 For the time being.
4 *Lo referente a*: 'the matter of'.
5 Literally, 'without truce'.

33 Organizing a product launch

Director 1   My suggestion is that we hire a river cruiser and take our key accounts for a cruise and dinner. After dinner we can unveil our new range of services.

Director 2   Do you think that'll be enough?

Director 1   Well, when we've informed the key accounts, we can do some promotion in the trade press – some ads and, if possible, a press release. The key accounts managers will just have to keep in touch with their clients. We'll have to wait and see what response we get from the trade journals.

Director 2   OK. Let's go ahead with this. Do you want me to get Jim started on the arrangements?

Director 1   Yes, you might as well. By the way, what about hospitality for the press? Couldn't we invite them to the Clubroom for a special presentation?

Director 2   Good idea! I'll get Jim to see to it.

33 Organizando el lanzamiento de un producto

Director 1	Mi sugerencia es que alquilemos un crucero por el río e invitemos a nuestros clientes principales a una cena en crucero. Después de la cena podremos dar a conocer[1] nuestra nueva gama de servicios.
Director 2	¿Piensas[2] que eso será suficiente?
Director 1	Bueno, cuando les hayamos informado a estos clientes principales, podemos hacer promoción en la prensa comercial: algunos anuncios y, si es posible, un comunicado de prensa. Los encargados de cuentas importantes tendrán que estar en contacto con sus clientes. Sólo nos quedará esperar y ver qué tipo de respuesta nos da la prensa comercial.
Director 2	Vale. Arranquemos con esto. ¿Quieres que yo me encargue de que Jaime se responsabilice de estos trámites?
Director 1	Sí, a ello.[3] A propósito, ¿cómo vamos a recibir a la prensa? ¿No podríamos invitarles a que asistieran al Club para hacerles una presentación especial?
Director 2	Buena idea. Le diré a Jaime que se encargue de ello.

1 Literally, 'to give to know'.
2 Informal address between peers in a formal setting.
3 Literally, 'to it'.

34   Contacting official agencies

(a) Chamber of Commerce

Roberto Comas   How do you do? I'm Roberto Comas, from Textiles Paloma.

Arturo Castro   Pleased to meet you. Arturo Castro. My staff told me you were going to call in this morning. How can we help?

Roberto Comas   We are thinking of expanding the business, especially to focus on the '30 to 50' market, and were advised to seek your views on how and where best to establish retail outlets for our fashion products.

Arturo Castro   Well, Sr Comas. I hope you will join the Chamber as and when you set up in the city, but for the time being you are welcome to our assistance.

Roberto Comas   Yes, I understand, but right now we are keen to obtain some information on local retail figures, the competition, some data on the local population, available premises and so on.

Arturo Castro   That's no problem. We can provide you with what you request and much more. Are you likely to be creating any jobs through your new initiative?

Roberto Comas   I think it's inevitable that we will take on new staff, both in the factory and in the local shops. Do you happen to have a good contact at the Jobcentre?

Arturo Castro   Yes, of course. If you'd like to come through to my office, we'll have a coffee and get down to business on this one.

34 Contactando con agencias oficiales

(a) La Cámara de Comercio

Roberto Comas	Encantado de conocerle. Soy Roberto Comas, de Textiles Paloma.
Arturo Castro	Arturo Castro. Encantado. Mis empleados me dijeron que iba a venir esta mañana. ¿En qué podemos serle útil?
Roberto Comas	Estamos contemplando la expansión del negocio, concentrándonos especialmente en el mercado de 'los treinta a los cincuenta', y se nos ha aconsejado que nos asesoren ustedes respecto a cómo y dónde es la mejor manera de hacernos con[1] minoristas que vendan nuestras modas.
Arturo Castro	Bien, señor Comas, espero que se haga socio[2] de la Cámara cuando establezca su negocio en la ciudad, pero por ahora estamos encantados de poder ayudarle.
Roberto Comas	Sí, lo comprendo, pero lo que nos interesa ahora es obtener información sobre cifras de ventas en esta localidad, la competencia,[3] el número de habitantes, la disponibilidad de locales etcétera.
Arturo Castro	No hay problema. Nosotros podemos proporcionarle lo que solicita y mucho más. ¿Piensa usted que creará algún puesto de trabajo con su nueva iniciativa?
Roberto Comas	Creo que es inevitable que contratemos a personal nuevo, tanto en la fábrica como en los establecimientos locales. ¿Tiene usted buenos contactos con la Oficina de Empleo?
Arturo Castro	Claro que sí. Si quiere pasar por mi despacho, tomaremos un café y nos pondremos manos a la obra.[4]

1 Here: 'to obtain', 'make contact with' (retailers).
2 *Hacerse socio de*: to become a member of.
3 *Competencia* also means 'competence' ('ability') and in Spain it is also used to allude to administrative power(s).
4 Literally, 'put (our) hands to the work'.

(b) Customs and Excise

Customs and Excise officer	Good morning, sir.
Retailer	Hello, I have a query regarding the import of meat products. I wonder if you can help me.
Customs and Excise officer	Certainly. Can you explain?
Retailer	We're a meat retailer based here in Dover, and we're intending to import a range of cooked meats and sausages from a German supplier. So far we've only been supplied by British companies. I need to know what the regulations are.
Customs and Excise officer	It's rather difficult and complex to explain briefly. There is a range of regulations and restrictions. They're all contained in our information brochures. When are you intending to import?
Retailer	We'll get the first shipment in a couple of weeks.
Customs and Excise officer	Then you'd better move fast. I'll collect all the information for you. The best thing is for you to read it and then, if you have any queries, come back to us.
Retailer	Fine. I'll get down to it.

(b) Aduanas e Impuestos

Oficial de Aduanas	Buenos días, señor.
Detallista	Oiga, quisiera hacerle una pregunta acerca de la importación de productos cárnicos. Me pregunto si usted podría informarme.
Oficial de Aduanas	Cómo no. ¿Quiere explicármelo?
Detallista	Somos detallistas[1] de productos cárnicos aquí en Irún, y pretendemos importar un surtido de carnes precocinadas y salchichas procedentes de un distribuidor alemán. Hasta ahora sólo nos han surtido empresas españolas. Necesito saber cuál es el reglamento al respecto.[2]
Oficial de Aduanas	Es un poco difícil y complejo para explicárselo de forma breve. Hay una serie de reglamentos y restricciones; toda la información está recogida en nuestros folletos explicativos. ¿Cuándo tienen intención de importar?
Detallista	Dentro de un par de semanas recibiremos el primer envío.
Oficial de Aduanas	Entonces tendrá que darse prisa. Yo me hago cargo de recogerle la información necesaria, y lo mejor es que, una vez leída y en caso de duda,[3] se ponga en contacto con nosotros de nuevo.
Detallista	Bueno. Lo haré ahora mismo.

1 Alternative: *minorista(s)*.
2 Literally, 'to the respect'.
3 Both phrases (*una vez leída* and *en caso de duda*) are typical of the economy of expression possible in Spanish.

35 Presenting company policy

(a) Location

Managing director	As you know, the company's policy is based on setting up new plants in areas which offer the most advantages. For this reason the liquid detergent plant here will close as soon as the new plant is operational in the south-east. There are both economic and social benefits in doing it this way.
Journalist	What about the people currently working at the plant? What will happen to them? Will they be made redundant?
Managing director	That's not the way we do things here. We'll look to natural wastage and early retirements throughout the company – nobody will be made redundant because of this. Clearly, some people will have to be redeployed and there may be possibilities at the new plant for some of the specialist technicians if they are willing to relocate.
Journalist	How will you reorganize the remaining staff? Would they qualify for removal assistance if they agreed to move?
Managing director	Clearly we will offer them a relocation package if they are prepared to move; that's standard practice here.

35   Exponiendo la política de una empresa

(a) Ubicación

Director gerente   Como sabe, la política de la empresa se basa en la creación de nuevas instalaciones en zonas que ofrecen más ventajas. Por esta razón la planta de detergente líquido, que tenemos aquí, cerrará tan pronto como la nueva esté en funcionamiento en el sudeste. Hay beneficios tanto económicos como sociales haciéndolo[1] de esta forma.

Periodista   ¿Y qué me dice[2] respecto a los empleados que trabajan en la instalación? ¿Qué les pasará? ¿Perderán el puesto de trabajo?

Director gerente   Aquí no actuamos de esa forma. Estudiaremos las bajas vegetativas[3] y las jubilaciones anticipadas por toda la compañía; nadie perderá su puesto de trabajo debido a esta causa. Está claro que algunos tendrán que ser trasladados, y puede que haya posibilidades en la nueva instalación para ciertos técnicos especialistas si ellos están dispuestos a cambiarse.

Periodista   ¿Cómo reorganizará usted al resto de la plantilla? ¿Tendrán derecho a remuneración por traslado si están de acuerdo con éste?

Director gerente   Por supuesto que les ofreceremos un paquete para volver a colocarlos si están de acuerdo con el traslado; eso es lo que se hace aquí por regla general.

1   Gerund has force of 'by . . .ing'.
2   A conversational addition, with a hint of criticism.
3   Literally, 'vegetative losses'.

(b) Development

Personnel manager	So, as we have seen during the last half-hour, the prospects for the next few years are quite encouraging. We now need to consider precisely how we are going to develop policies to benefit the firm and its employees.
Managing director	Can I just add before you continue, Alan, that the Board will be taking very seriously whatever conclusions are drawn by this group today. So it is essential that people speak their mind.
Personnel manager	Thanks for confirming that, Vicky. Frankly, recent EU legislation means that our profit margins can be increased as long as we take into account from the start matters like Health and Safety, employee compensation, maternity benefits etc. These items, that normally and quite properly cost us a percentage of raw profits, can be reclaimed if fully documented.
Financial director	Well, that's good news as in the past we've never been able to prepare very well for covering this sort of cost to the company.
Personnel manager	I am proposing, therefore, that we create a small unit within the company to cover the full range of benefits that can accrue to us under the new provisions. In addition to this, we should be able to demonstrate to the workforce that by our observing these criteria, they too will have an enhanced status. Before I continue with my next subject, are there any questions?
Sales manager	Alan, can anyone guarantee that our current level of sales is sustainable? What you are saying about the interests of the workforce and those of the company as a whole being convergent seems to me a rather optimistic interpretation.
Personnel manager	We've commissioned a report on this very question, so as long as everybody is prepared to wait for a week or two longer I should be able to give you an honest answer. Frankly, whatever the precise outcome of that report, we have to make plans for a future in which we balance the financial well-being of the firm with that of all the individuals who work in and for it.

(b) Desarrollo

Director de Personal
Bueno, tal y como hemos visto durante la pasada media hora, la perspectiva para los próximos años es bastante alentadora. Ahora necesitamos plantearnos precisamente cómo vamos a desarrollar una política que beneficie[1] a la empresa y a sus empleados.

Directora Gerente
Alonso, antes de que sigas, quisiera añadir que la Junta Directiva tomará muy en serio cualquiera de las conclusiones acordadas por el grupo en el día de hoy. Por lo tanto es esencial que los aquí presentes hablen claro.

Director de Personal
Victoria, gracias por confirmarlo. Francamente, la reciente legislación comunitaria[2] significa que nuestros márgenes gananciales pueden incrementarse con tal que se consideren, desde un principio, asuntos como la seguridad y sanidad, la retribución[3] a empleados, los beneficios de maternidad etcétera. Todos estos pagos, que por lo general y en verdad suponen un porcentaje de nuestras ganancias brutas, pueden reclamarse bajo documentación apropiada.

Director de Finanzas
Bueno, esa es una buena noticia ya que en el pasado nunca hemos podido, en esta empresa, prepararnos muy bien para cubrir este tipo de costes.

Director de Personal
Propongo, por lo tanto, que dentro de la empresa creemos una pequeña unidad que cubra todo tipo de beneficios que se nos vayan acumulando según las nuevas disposiciones. Además de esto, debemos ser capaces de demostrar a la plantilla que, al cumplir estos criterios nosotros, los mismos empleados verán mejor protegida su posición. Antes de pasar al próximo tema, ¿hay alguna pregunta?

Directora de Ventas
Alonso, ¿puede alguién garantizar que nuestro nivel de ventas sea ininterrumpido? Lo que dices acerca de intereses convergentes de la plantilla y de la empresa en general me parece un juicio bastante optimista . . .

Director de Personal
Hemos pedido un informe sobre este mismo asunto; por lo tanto, siempre que todos estén dispuestos a esperar una o dos semanas más, podré daros una respuesta franca. Sinceramente, sea cual fuere[4] el resultado exacto del informe, tenemos que planear un futuro en el cual equilibremos el bienestar financiero de la empresa con el de todos los individuos que trabajan en ella y para ella.

1 The first of numerous examples of the subjunctive in this conversation; predictable because future developments are being discussed. 2 Adjective derived from *Comunidad* (*Europea*). 3 Both meanings of compensation (American English: 'salary', British English: 'indemnity') are covered by *retribución*; if only 'salary' is intended the alternatives are: *salario/sueldo/remuneración*. 4 Literally, 'be it what it will be': a formal expression, including the (rare) future subjunctive *fuere*.

(c) Staffing

Personnel manager	I've called you in to tell you about our proposed staff changes.
Trade union representative	Yes, I know. I've heard that you're planning compulsory redundancies.
Personnel manager	No, that's not the case, but we do need to rationalize.
Trade union representative	Can you tell me why?
Personnel manager	Everyone knows why: production costs have been increasing because of outmoded plant. We've taken the decision to close one of our older plants.
Trade union representative	Has it been decided which one?
Personnel manager	We have a choice of either Sheffield or Gloucester. The precise figures are being worked out.
Trade union representative	And what happens to the workforce?
Personnel manager	We'll propose voluntary redundancies and early retirements. That should alleviate the problem considerably.
Trade union representative	But not fully. You'll have to lay people off.
Personnel manager	We don't think so. The staff remaining after redundancies and early retirement can be relocated. We have other plants within 20 miles of either Sheffield or Gloucester. It's a case of streamlining production, not cutting it back.
Trade union representative	So what will be the total reduction in the workforce?
Personnel manager	In the region of 200 to 250.
Trade union representative	And when are the changes being made?
Personnel manager	We're hoping to have them complete by the end of January.
Trade union representative	Has it been discussed at board level yet?
Personnel manager	Of course – the board gave its approval last week. That's why we're moving on it now.

(c) Personal

Director de Personal	Le he llamado para informarle acerca de los cambios propuestos para el personal.
Representante sindical	Sí, ya lo sé. He oído que usted propone bajas forzosas.
Director de Personal	No, ese no es el caso, aunque sí tenemos que racionalizar.
Representante sindical	¿Puede explicarme el por qué?
Director de Personal	Todo el mundo sabe el por qué: los costes[1] de producción han ido en aumento[2] debido a la anticuada instalación. Hemos decidido cerrar una de nuestras plantas más antiguas.
Representante sindical	¿Han decidido cuál de ellas?
Director de Personal	Podemos escoger entre la de Segovia y la de Avila. Se están estudiando las cifras con exactitud.
Representante sindical	¿Y qué va a suceder con la plantilla?
Director de Personal	Vamos a proponerles el paro[3] voluntario y la jubilación anticipada, lo que puede aliviar el problema sustancialmente.
Representante sindical	Pero no por completo. Ustedes tendrán que despedir a empleados.
Director de Personal	Pensamos que no es así. Al resto de los empleados les volveremos a colocar. Tenemos otras plantas, ambas a veinte kilómetros de Segovia o Avila. Se trata de hacer más eficiente la producción, no recortarla.
Representante sindical	Entonces, ¿cuál será la reducción total de la plantilla?
Director de Personal	Entre los doscientos (200) y los doscientos cincuenta (250).
Representante sindical	¿Y cuándo se efectuarán los cambios?
Director de Personal	Esperamos completarlos para finales de enero.
Representante sindical	¿Ya se ha tratado a nivel de reunión?
Director de Personal	Evidentemente: el Consejo de Administración dio su aprobación la semana pasada. De ahí que[4] ahora vaya adelante.

1   In Latin America: *costos*.
2   Literally, 'have been going in increase'.
3   In Latin America *paro* refers to a strike; in Spain to unemployment and unemployment benefit, as well as to a strike.
4   Literally, 'From there that . . .'.

(d) Sales

Chairman	I am pleased to open this first Board Meeting following our change of parent company. The first item on the agenda is sales policy, Charles.
Charles	Thank you, Mr Chairman. I am instructed by the main board of our parent company to plan, with you, the introduction of a new sales policy.
Director 2	What view is taken of our existing policy? Too expensive?
Charles	In a nutshell, yes. The company's product lines are mostly good but the sales operation could be improved.
Director 2	I am not surprised. I have thought for some time that we have too large a sales force in too many regions.
Charles	That brings us to one of the proposals I want to make. To redraw the regions and slim down the workforce.
Director 2	By redundancy or natural wastage?
Charles	A bit of both will probably be necessary. Also, some concern has been expressed about the size of the advertising budget.
Director 3	Hear, hear. For a company with good products we do a hell of a lot of advertising.
Charles	I gather it is proposed, subject to this board's approval, to appoint a top class Marketing Manager with a view to reviewing the whole operation.
Director 2	Is a system of dealerships on the cards?
Charles	Nothing is excluded based on the premise of a need to rationalize the sales operation.

(d) Ventas

Presidente	Tengo el placer de dar comienzo a esta primera reunión de la Junta Directiva tras los cambios acaecidos en nuestra casa matriz. Carlos, el primer asunto a tratar en el orden del día es la política de ventas.
Carlos	Gracias, Presidente. La junta principal de nuestra casa matriz me ordena planificar, con ustedes, la introducción de una nueva política de ventas.
Directora 2	¿Cuál es la opinión de la actual política? ¿Demasiado cara?
Carlos	En resumidas cuentas, sí. Nuestra gama de productos es en general buena, pero las operaciones de ventas podrían mejorarse.
Directora 2	No me sorprende. Llevo mucho tiempo pensando que en demasiadas regiones nos sobran vendedores.
Carlos	Eso nos lleva a una de las propuestas que quiero hacer. Volver a trazar las regiones y reducir el número de empleados.
Directora 2	¿Por despidos o por bajas vegetativas?
Carlos	Probablemente será necesario un poco de los dos. También se ha expresado preocupación acerca del tamaño del presupuesto publicitario.
Director 3	¡Ya lo creo![1] Como empresa con buenos productos, hacemos muchísima publicidad.
Carlos	Tengo entendido que se propone, si lo aprueba la Junta Directiva, nombrar a un Director de Márketing de óptima reputación con vistas a revisar toda la operación.
Directora 2	¿Se prevé una red de concesionarios?[2]
Carlos	Basándose uno en la necesidad de racionalizar la operación de ventas, no se descarta[3] nada.

1 Literally, 'Now I believe it'; I should think so!
2 More accurately: 'dealers'.
3 *Descartar*: 'to rule out', 'discard'.

36 Visiting the bank manager

Bank Manager   Good morning, Mrs Ansell. I'm pleased to see you again.

Mrs Ansell   Good morning, Mr Donald. I have come to discuss our business plan with you. Our turnover has risen by 40 per cent over the last three years and our products have been selling really well. We'd like to open another shop in Loughborough.

Bank Manager   Well, Mrs Ansell, I have followed the success of your company with interest. This bank has been very happy to support its development and you've always stayed within your overdraft limits. How might we help you now?

Mrs Ansell   We're having to plough back most of our profits into the business in order to finance our growth. We've had market research done in Loughborough and are convinced that it will be a success, particularly as Loughborough is a university town. What I've come to discuss is a loan to finance the lease of a shop and to buy start-up stock.

Bank Manager   I'm sure the bank will be willing in principle to finance your business's future growth. If you send me your proposal for the shop in Loughborough, specifying the amount you wish to borrow, along with cash-flow projections – you know, all the usual information – I will consider it as quickly as possible.

Mrs Ansell   Thank you very much. I'll send you our proposal in the next few days.

36 Haciendo una visita al director de un banco

Director de Banco	Buenos días, señora Arias. Me complace volver a verla.
Sra Arias	Buenos días, señor Domingo. He venido a tratar de nuestros planes comerciales con usted. Nuestra facturación[1] ha aumentado en un cuarenta por ciento durante los últimos tres años, ya que los productos se están vendiendo muy bien. Nos gustaría ya abrir otra sucursal[2] en Salamanca.
Director de Banco	Bien, señora Arias, he seguido con interés el éxito de su empresa. Este banco siempre ha querido apoyar sus iniciativas, y ustedes han permanecido dentro de los límites de su saldo deudor. ¿Cómo podemos ayudarles ahora?
Sra Arias	Nos vemos obligados a reinvertir la mayoría de nuestras ganancias con objeto de financiar nuestra expansión. Hemos llevado a cabo un estudio de mercado en Salamanca y estamos convencidos de que será un éxito puesto que Salamanca es ciudad universitaria. De lo que he venido a tratar es sobre un préstamo para financiar el alquiler de una tienda y comprar las existencias necesarias para ponerla en marcha.
Director de Banco	Estoy seguro que, en principio, el banco no tendrá inconveniente en financiar la futura expansión de su negocio. Si me envía la propuesta para la tienda de Salamanca, especificándome la cantidad que desea que le prestemos, junto con la proyección del flujo de fondos – ya sabe, la información acostumbrada – la estudiaré tan pronto me sea posible.
Sra Arias	Muchísimas gracias. Le enviaré nuestra propuesta en los próximos días.

1 Note same term is used for invoicing and for checking in (travel).
2 'branch'.

37 Selling a service to a client

Teresa Flowers	Good morning, Mr Tolson. I'm Teresa Flowers from P and G Computer Maintenance Services. You answered one of our ads in the *Evening Mail*, so I have come to fill you in on what we have to offer small businesses.
Mr Tolson	Ah yes, thank you for coming so soon. As you can see, we recently purchased a computer system to maximize our efficiency in dealing with orders.
Teresa Flowers	I assume that you have an initial service contract on the machines, but once that runs out you would be best advised to take out a plan like ours. We can provide a 24-hour breakdown cover, three-monthly servicing, immediate replacement of faulty equipment, regular updating of your software and a free consultancy service for the duration of the contract.
Mr Tolson	It sounds a good deal, but what are the conditions of payment? Is it possible to pay monthly via a standing order or does it have to be a lump sum?
Teresa Flowers	You can pay either way, as long as your bank can guarantee that your account will bear it. Let me leave you some brochures to read at your leisure; you'll be able compare our prices and conditions with others, though I can assure you that it's the most favourable deal available at present.
Mr Tolson	OK, fair enough. Can you give me a ring in about a week and I'll let you know what I think.
Teresa Flowers	No problem. Give me your number and I'll contact you early next week.

37   Vendiendo un servicio a un cliente

Teresa Flores	Buenos días, señor Torres. Soy Teresa Flores, del Servicio de Mantenimiento de Ordenadores P y G. Usted contestó a uno de nuestros anuncios que figuraban en el *Correo de la Tarde*; así que he venido a informarle sobre lo que ofrecemos al pequeño comerciante.
Sr Torres	Ah, sí. Gracias por venir tan pronto. Como podrá observar, recientemente compramos un sistema informatizado[1] para potenciar al máximo nuestra eficacia cuando se trata de pedidos.
Teresa Flores	Me figuro que usted tendrá un contrato inicial de servicio para la maquinaria, pero una vez que éste caduque le aconsejaríamos que sacara un seguro como el nuestro. Nosotros proporcionamos un seguro de cobertura de avería de veinticuatro (24) horas al día, servicio de mantenimiento trimestral, repuesto inmediato de material defectuoso, actualización constante del software y servicio gratuito de asesoramiento mientras dure el contrato.
Sr Torres	Parece una buena oferta, pero ¿cuáles son las condiciones de pago? ¿Se puede efectuar el pago mensual por orden permanente[2] o tiene que pagarse una suma fija?
Teresa Flores	Puede pagarse de cualquier forma con la condición de que su banco garantice que su cuenta puede correr con los gastos.[3] Le daré unos folletos que puede leer detenidamente; podrá comparar nuestros precios y condiciones con otros, aunque le aseguro que es el contrato más favorable de que disponemos en la actualidad.
Sr Torres	Vale. ¿Podría darme un telefonazo dentro de una semana aproximadamente? Le diré lo que pienso.
Teresa Flores	Sin problema. Deme su número y contactaré con usted a principios de la semana que viene.

1   'Computerized'.
2   'Standing order': (*la*) *orden permanente de pago*.
3   Literally, 'to run with the costs'.

38 Selling a product to a client

Salesman	This motor is very good value, sir, if you prefer not to buy new.
Customer	It certainly looks to be in immaculate condition. About two years old, is it?
Salesman	Eighteen months. It only has 6,000 miles on the clock.
Customer	That's unusual, isn't it? Who was the previous owner?
Salesman	It's been a demonstration model. That explains the complete lack of any dents and no rust, of course.
Customer	What sort of discount could I have? Can you offer a hire purchase deal?
Salesman	We are offering a 5 per cent discount off the list price and you could repay over one or two years.
Customer	That sounds quite interesting. And you would offer me the trade-in price for my present car that we discussed earlier?
Salesman	Yes indeed, sir. Would you like to go for a spin?

38 Vendiendo un producto a un cliente

Vendedor   Señor, si no quiere comprarse un carro[1] nuevo, éste está muy bien de precio.[2]

Cliente   Desde luego que parece estar en perfectísimas condiciones. Tendrá dos o tres años ¿verdad?

Vendedor   Tiene dieciocho (18) meses. El cuentakilómetros marca sólo diez mil (10.000) kilómetros.

Cliente   Eso es poco corriente[3] ¿verdad? ¿Quién fue su último propietario?

Vendedor   Ha sido el carro de demostración. Claro, así se explica por qué no tiene ni abolladuras ni corrosión.

Cliente   ¿Qué tipo de descuento me haría? ¿Y podría comprarlo a plazos?[4]

Vendedor   Ofrecemos un cinco por ciento de descuento del precio del catálogo, y podría pagarlo en un plazo de uno o dos años.

Cliente   Esa oferta es interesante. ¿Y usted me restará también del precio lo que vale mi coche actual, según lo acordado antes?

Vendedor   Por supuesto, señor. ¿Le gustaría ir a dar una vuelta?

1 The Latin American term; in Spain (*el*) *coche*.
2 *Está bien de precio*: idiomatic usage.
3 Literally, 'little current'.
4 'In instalments'.

39 Giving an informal vote of thanks

Speaker   Ladies and gentlemen, I'd like to take this opportunity of thanking
Leonard White and his colleagues for arranging the seminar over
the last few days. I'm sure we've all found it most interesting and
stimulating, and we all have good ideas to take back with us.

I'd also like to thank Leonard White and his colleagues for their
hospitality over the last two evenings, and I'm sure I speak for all of
us when I say that the seminar has been a great success.

As you all know, we intend to hold a similar seminar next year at
our headquarters, and that will give us the opportunity to return the
hospitality. Thanks again, Leonard and colleagues, for a most
successful event.

39 Dando las gracias: forma no ceremoniosa

Oradora   Señoras y señores: quisiera aprovechar esta oportunidad para darles las gracias a Leonardo Blanco y a sus colegas por haber organizado el seminario durante los últimos días. Estoy segura de que ha sido interesante y estimulante y que todos[1] nos llevaremos de vuelta muy buenas ideas.

También me gustaría darles las gracias a Leonardo Blanco y a sus colegas por la hospitalidad que nos brindaron durante las dos últimas veladas, y estoy segura de que en nombre de todos puedo decir que el seminario ha tenido un éxito rotundo.

Como saben, tenemos la intención de celebrar un seminario semejante en nuestra oficina central el año próximo, y tendremos la oportunidad de devolver la hospitalidad. Gracias una vez más a Leonardo y colegas por este acontecimiento[2] de lo más exitoso.

1 Although the speaker is female, she uses masculine adjectives in referring to a group in which the genders are mixed, a normal linguistic practice.
2 'Event'.

40 Discussing contracts

(a) Sales conditions

Client   I'm pleased to inform you that we are prepared to include your company as one of our suppliers. Before we sign an agreement, we need to agree on terms and conditions.

Supplier   We're delighted. What in particular do we need to agree?

Client   Firstly, our terms of payment are 20 per cent on receipt of the goods and the remainder within 90 days.

Supplier   We normally expect to be paid in full within 60 days, but if we can have a two-year agreement, we could accept that.

Client   Fine. We also want a 10 per cent discount for orders of over 5,000 parts. Deliveries must also be made by the specified date, with penalties for late delivery. I think you've already been given some details.

Supplier   Yes, and I can assure you that we are accustomed to just-in-time delivery. I'm sure that you know already that we offer good service at a good price. We're ready to sign.

Client   That's good. I have the agreement here.

40 Debatiendo un contrato

(a) Condiciones de venta

Cliente	Me complace informarle que estamos dispuestos a incluir a su empresa como una de nuestros distribuidores. Antes de firmar un convenio, pues, hay que ponerse de acuerdo sobre las condiciones.
Distribuidor	Nosotros estamos encantados. En concreto, ¿qué tenemos que acordar?
Cliente	En primer lugar, nuestras condiciones son efectuar el pago del veinte por ciento del valor de las mercancías al recibo de éstas,[1] y el resto en un período de noventa días.
Distribuidor	Por lo general esperamos que nos efectúen el pago completo en un período de sesenta días, pero si nos hacemos un contrato de dos años, podríamos aceptar eso.
Cliente	Está bien. También queremos que nos hagan un descuento del diez por ciento en pedidos de más de cinco mil (5.000) piezas. Las entregas deben efectuarse también en la fecha especificada, penalizando los retrasos. Tengo entendido que ya les[2] han dado algunos de los pormenores.
Distribuidor	Sí, y le aseguro que estamos acostumbrados a efectuar las entregas a tiempo. Estoy seguro que ya son conscientes de que ofrecemos buen servicio a buen precio. Estamos dispuestos a firmar.
Cliente	Estupendo. Aquí tengo el acuerdo.

1 *Éstas* refers to the goods.
2 *Les*: 'you' plural (in spite of one-to-one conversation).

(b) Payment conditions

Client   When will I be required to complete the payment of the instalments on the new equipment?

Supplier   There are several plans under which you have maximum flexibility of conditions. Obviously, you can pay the full amount in a one-off sum, which would mean a substantial saving overall as interest costs are always high in the transport sector.

Client   Suppose I could pay you 50 per cent of the total cost now, what sort of arrangements would best suit us both for the other half over a couple of years?

Supplier   That would depend on how we structure our own borrowing requirement, but in principle there is no reason why payments cannot be adjusted exactly to suit your circumstances.

Client   Fine. Can you give me a few days to discuss this with my accountant? If the bank is willing to lend me more than I had first thought, it may be possible to buy it outright.

Supplier   Why not? With general interest rates as they are it could be worth risking a big outlay. Remember: either way we can help as our own finances are secured by the parent company.

Client   Thanks for the reassurance. I'll let you know ASAP.

(b) Condiciones de pago

Cliente   ¿Cuándo tendré que completar el pago a plazos[1] del nuevo
material?

Distribuidor   Hay diversidad de planes según los cuales usted dispone de una
gran flexibilidad de condiciones. Por supuesto, puede pagar la
suma total de una vez, lo que supondría un ahorro general
considerable, ya que en el sector del transporte los intereses son
siempre altos.

Cliente   Suponiendo que le pudiera pagar el cincuenta (50) por ciento del
coste total ahora, ¿qué tipo de arreglo podríamos acordar, y que
nos viniera bien a ambas partes, para pagar la otra mitad en un
período de dos años?

Distribuidor   Eso dependería de la forma en que estructuremos nuestras
necesidades de préstamo, pero en principio no existe razón por la
que los pagos no puedan ajustarse a sus circunstancias.

Cliente   Bien. ¿Puedo disponer de unos días para tratar de esto con mi
contable?[2] Si el banco está dispuesto a prestarme más de lo que
había pensado en un principio, tal vez fuera posible comprarlo en
su totalidad.

Distribuidor   Cómo no. Según están los tipos[3] de interés, valdría la pena
arriesgar un desembolso grande. Recuerde usted: comoquiera
que sea, podremos echarle una mano ya que nuestros fondos
vienen garantizados por la empresa matriz.

Cliente   Gracias por su promesa tranquilizadora. Se lo comunicaré lo
antes posible.

1 Also *mensualidades*; in Latin America *cuotas*.
2 In Latin America: *contador*.
3 In Latin America: *tasas de interés*.

(c) Breach of contract

Client   Well, here we have the order contract that you wanted to discuss.

Supplier   Yes, thanks. The paragraph I wanted to look at was this one, 9b.

Client   Is there a problem?

Supplier   It indicates that unless we deliver within three days of the date indicated, we are in breach of contract and the order can be cancelled.

Client   It's part of our normal contract. Would you have a problem with that?

Supplier   I find it a bit unusual.

Client   We've had to introduce it because in the past we had lots of problems with suppliers missing the delivery dates by weeks. We lost a lot of customers because of that. Since we introduced the modified contract we've had far fewer problems with delays.

Supplier   Is it possible to vary it a little?

Client   In what way?

Supplier   Well, I find three days very restrictive. We'd be much happier with one week.

Client   I'm sure you would! Any particular reason? Have you run into difficulties meeting dates in the past?

Supplier   Only rarely, but it does happen. And it's usually because a supplier has let us down. I'd like to modify that paragraph a bit, to give us a little more time.

Client   Let me check it out with our manager. I'll get back to you in the next 24 hours.

Supplier   Thanks.

(c) Infracción

Cliente Bien, aquí está el contrato del pedido que usted quería debatir.

Distribuidor Sí, gracias. El párrafo que quería examinar es éste, el 9b.

Cliente ¿Hay algún problema?

Distribuidor Señala que a no ser que efectuemos la entrega dentro de los tres días estipulados, hay infracción de contrato, y el pedido puede anularse.

Cliente Eso constituye parte de nuestro contrato habitual. ¿Les plantearía algún problema?

Distribuidor Pues, lo considero un poco extraño.

Cliente Hemos tenido que incluirlo, ya que en el pasado tuvimos muchos problemas con los distribuidores, los cuales pasaban por alto[1] las fechas de entrega durante semanas. Debido a ello perdimos a muchos clientes. Desde que hemos introducido la modificación en el contrato, nos hemos encontrado con poquísimas dificultades de tipo retrasos.

Distribuidor ¿Es posible reformarlo un poco?

Cliente ¿De qué forma?

Distribuidor Bueno, pienso que es muy restrictivo lo de tres días. Estaríamos más satisfechos con una semana.

Cliente ¡Ya lo creo que estarían![2] ¿Por alguna razón en concreto? ¿En el pasado se han tropezado con dificultades a la hora de cumplir con las fechas?

Distribuidor En muy raras ocasiones, pero sí ocurre; y es probable que un distribuidor nos haya dejado plantados.[3] Me gustaría modificar un tanto ese párrafo para disponer de un poco más de tiempo.

Cliente Déjeme que lo consulte con nuestro director. Contactaré con usted en las próximas veinticuatro horas.

Distribuidor Gracias.

1 *Pasar por alto*: 'to miss', 'ignore'.
2 Literally, 'Now I think you would be!'
3 *Dejar plantado*: 'to leave in the lurch', 'let down'.

41   Meeting a visitor at the airport

Mr Parker	Messrs Martin and Bertot from Toulouse?
M. Martin	Are you Mr Parker from Perkins Industrial?
Mr Parker	Yes, indeed. I am glad to hear that you speak English, I was trying to remember my schoolboy French on the way to the airport.
M. Martin	My colleague Bertot cannot speak English I am afraid, so you may need to try out some of your schoolboy French, or perhaps get the help of an interpreter when we come to discuss the contract.
Mr Parker	Right, I'll see to it. Are these your bags? My car is just outside. Did you have a good journey?
M. Martin	We had a fairly good journey. For some reason our plane from Toulouse to Paris was delayed so we nearly missed the Paris–Birmingham flight.
Mr Parker	I am sure our Chairman will be pleased that you made it. We have high hopes for our proposed deal. Would you like to have a coffee before we set off?
M. Martin	Don't worry, we had a meal during the flight.
Mr Parker	Before we get back to talking shop can I just ask you what time you need to check in for this evening's return flight?

41 Recibiendo a visitas en el aeropuerto

Sr Pajares   ¿Los señores Martin y Bertot de Tolosa?

M. Martin   ¿Es usted Pajares, de Enfisa?

Sr Pajares   Efectivamente. Me complace saber que habla castellano; de camino al aeropuerto trataba de recordar el francés que aprendí en el instituto.

M. Martin   Siento decirle que mi colega Bertot no habla castellano, así que tal vez tenga que poner en práctica el francés que usted aprendió en el instituto, o quizá servirse de un intérprete cuando tratemos de lo referente al contrato.

Sr Pajares   Bien, me encargaré de ello.[1] ¿Son éstas sus maletas? Tengo el coche fuera, ahí mismo. ¿Qué tal[2] les fue el viaje?

M. Martin   Hicimos el viaje bastante bien. Por no sé qué razón el avión de París a Tolosa se retrasó, así que casi perdimos el vuelo Tolosa–Valencia.

Sr Pajares   Estoy seguro que a nuestro presidente le agradará saber de su llegada. Tenemos puestas[3] grandes esperanzas en el trato que vamos a proponerles. ¿Les gustaría tomar un café antes de que empecemos?

M. Martin   No se moleste. Comimos algo durante el vuelo.

Sr Pajares   Antes de que volvamos a hablar de negocios, quisiera preguntarles, ¿a qué hora tienen que estar en el aeropuerto esta tarde para coger el vuelo de regreso?

1 *Ello*: the arrangements for an interpreter.
2 *¿Qué tal...?* used to refer to a variety of phenomena (here, the flight, and including a verb).
3 Literally, 'We have great hopes placed ...'.

Business Correspondence

Spanish commercial correspondence – general notes

The business letter in Spanish is subject to certain conventions in respect of its layout, its language register and its contents. There are also differences between practice in Spain and in the many Spanish-speaking countries of Latin America. Apart from a tendency in the latter area to continue with expressions or formulae now regarded as rather outmoded in Spain itself, there is naturally an American influence in commercial correspondence and it should be noted that there are minor variations in practice between individual countries. However, by observing what is current practice in Spain (and here too there is an increasing flexibility due to influence from EU nations and the USA), writers and readers of business correspondence should not experience difficulty in dealing with Latin American contacts.

Style of letter-writing

First, it must be said that spoken registers rarely appear in such correspondence, as is also the case elsewhere in the world; second, the phenomenon of 'formality' in Spanish-language expression is established primarily via the use of *usted/ustedes* (as opposed to *tú/vosotros*) and thereafter by the use of certain syntactic mechanisms, verb forms and lexical items. For example, subject pronouns referring directly to those involved in the transaction are avoided, the impersonal *se* expressions (with third person verb forms) frequently replacing them; the use of first person plural verbs and pronouns, as opposed to the singular, suggests corporate responsibility (and therefore more *gravitas*); the use of the complicated subjunctive mood is very widespread in business correspondence; a more abstract and perhaps lengthier item of vocabulary will appear even where there is a quite acceptable alternative. Sentence structure can therefore sometimes be lengthy and dense, conveying at best a necessary gravity or respect for detail, and at worst pomposity or obscurity. Equally, there are business letters that reduce their message and length almost to a telex format.

Company names

Most Spanish companies use stationery with a printed letterhead (*el membrete*) which includes its logo, name, address and telephone number; fax, telex and VAT numbers may also appear here. The name of the company is frequently followed by the letters S.A. (*Sociedad Anónima*), which indicate that it is an entity closely resembling a plc. These letters are sometimes incorporated into the company's name (e.g. Enfisa, Matesa); other cases, usually smaller companies, are S.L. or S.R.L. (*Sociedad de Responsabilidad Limitada*), *y Co* or *y Cía* ('and Company'), *e hijos/y hermanos* ('and sons/brothers'). In the *membrete,* or more likely at the foot of the company stationery, may appear the names of the directors, branch addresses and the company's official registered number. The main company information might appear at the top left of the page rather than in the top centre part of it.

Letter layout

Explained schematically, the rest of the letter would be as follows if observing the conventions (not necessarily the norm):

Left-hand side of page

Your Reference (*Su Referencia*): letters or numbers etc.
Our Reference (*Nuestra Referencia*): letters or numbers etc.
(The main terms might be printed on the stationery and might appear in reverse order from the one above.) Equally this information might appear below the address of the recipient.

The date:	Place	–	Day	–	of	–	Month	–	of	–	Year
e.g.	Almería		11		de		mayo		de		199-

The date can also appear on the right-hand side of the page, well above the body of the text. The place of origin is sometimes omitted if it is obvious from the *membrete*; the actual date details are sometimes reduced to figures only.

The name and address of the person/company to receive the letter (also known as the 'inside address') is allotted one line per item:

- Title (*Sr/Sra/Srta/Dr*) + first name/initials + surname(s)
- Role in company
- Company name
- Street/road name followed by numbers of building and floor
- City/town name (plus code)
- Province (plus code)
- Country

The post code for each town is added to the province number (a specific number between 1 and 50), thus invariably making a five-digit full code. To phone a Spanish town from outside Spain you dial 00 + 34 + the provincial code (*minus* its initial 9) shown in international directories + the subscriber's number.

A letter can be directed to a specified person by placing below the address a statement to the effect: *Para/A la atención de . . .*; similarly, the precise purpose of the letter can be noted on the next line as follows: *Asunto . . . .* If the contents of the letter are confidential, either/both *Privado* and *Confidencial* would appear after the inside address.

Opening lines

When addressing a known person, the following salutation is customary: *Estimado Sr* + surname/*Estimada Sra* + surname. First names can be included here, but not in the form of initials. If the person is not known (and therefore the letter is probably addressed to the company in general, to a department, or to an unnamed Head of . . .) it is customary to use the more generic salutation: *Muy señor mío* ('Dear Sir')/*Muy señora mía* ('Dear Madam'). Plurals can also be used here (e.g. *Muy señores míos/Muy señoras nuestras*), suggesting a broader approach on either side. Note that it is preferable to maintain singular or plural reference, according to the salutation, throughout a given item of correspondence; in practice, however, the two are at times mixed.

Plain *Señor(es)* is frequently used to greet the unknown addressee(s), as it allows for virtually any nuance of interpretation. A letter might also be directed to *Señor/Sr Director* or *Señora/Sra Secretaria* as an unknown postholder, and when first names are included to a known person it is still possible to use the traditional title *Don/Doña* (e.g. *Sr Don Miguel Valdés*). There are several other, more official, titles available in Spanish (e.g. *Presidente, Doctora, Excelencia*), but these of course are used only in very specific contexts. Note also that after the opening salutation in Spanish a colon, as opposed to the English comma, is used (e.g. *Estimada Sra Ruiz:*).

Style

The format of most business letters in Spanish is now blocked to the left, with the opening paragraph sometimes commencing in line with the end of the salutation. This is the only systematic style occurring in the text (see examples of letters in main section). There is also a tendency to allow a wider horizontal gap between the salutation and the main body of the letter. Capital letters are not as commonly used in Spanish as in English; their use in certain abbreviations (e.g. *Vd., Sra*) has already been noted, and they appear also where a specific person, rather than just a role or title, is alluded to (e.g. *el Presidente, el Jefe de Ventas, la Directora*). However, as a sign of courtesy in a business letter, certain positions like those above may be accorded *mayúscula* (capital letter) status even where no specific individual is concerned. When accompanied by the name of a person, all titles are capitalized if that person is being addressed; proper nouns for companies, people, places, products etc., are naturally accorded initial capitals. Spelling is relatively easy in Spanish as the language is phonetic. Thus, although the appropriate register/tone for commercial correspondence requires careful cultivation, imitating the style of authentic sources is a sensible way of achieving the impersonal, courteous (and frequently euphemistic) mode of expression characteristic of most Spanish business correspondence.

Closing lines

Just as in English and other languages, the 'complimentary close' (*la despedida*) is essential; a range of typical endings is shown in the main letters section, and many are interchangeable. Clearly, however, it is important to ensure that there is a degree of compatibility between the salutation and the close. As a rule the use of *Estimado/a* in the initial greeting permits use of the adverb *cordialmente* at the close, whilst *Muy señor/a mío/a* suggests *atentamente* for the close. The basic verb used in this part of the letter is *saludar,* and invariably the writer expresses his/her greeting as a third person (*saluda*), thereby confirming the element of formality. In recent times a whole variety of expressions has emerged in both formal and informal correspondence.

Beneath the *despedida* the writer signs his/her name and the following typed version of the name usually mirrors exactly the signature, which may include initials for the first name(s) and one or both surnames, depending upon the preferences of the writer. Below this name usually appears the role or position in the organization of the sender (e.g. *Encargada de Márketing, Jefe de Personal, Director Gerente*). If the letter is signed on behalf of somebody else (p.p.) the inscription *p/o* (*por orden*) appears beside the typed name. Any copies of the letter sent to others are indicated, as in English, by c.c. at the foot of the page. Similarly, enclosures (*anexos*) in the envelope are indicated by the appearance of that word near the left margin below all other information in the letter; the word *adjunto* may also be used to indicate that there are accompanying enclosures.

Envelopes

The envelope (*el sobre*) is normally filled out exactly as the details of the addressee appear in the letter itself, and the front of the envelope may bear any one of a number of inscriptions to identify to the postal service or to the recipients the nature of the missive (e.g. *urgente, por avión, confidencial, a reexpedir, impresos*). The back flap of the envelope normally bears the surname and address of the sender (*remitente*) after the latter word itself, or *remite*, or *Rte.*

Note on translations

The documents presented here in parallel text are not a word-for-word translation of each other. Due to obvious differences in letter-writing style in Spain (and Latin America) and the business vocabulary used, it is only possible to offer an equivalent version of the Spanish letter in the English text.

1 Enquiry about a product

4 January 199-

Augustin SA
Z.I. de l'Empereur
F-19200 Ussel
France

Dear Sir/Madam

RE: TOOTHPICK MAKING & PACKAGING MACHINE

We represent a major distributor of foodstuffs and other related materials in Kenya.

We have found your name in *Kompass* under the category of suppliers of toothpick-making machinery. Our present requirement is for a special toothpick-making and packaging machine. If you do produce such equipment or can supply it we would be pleased to receive your earliest quotation CIF Mombasa, prices for this machine and its equipment, together with a stated delivery time.

Please would you also quote for the installation of this machine in the Ususu factory in Mombasa.

We look forward to your earliest reply and remain

Yours faithfully

John Mason
Technical Director

1 Solicitando información sobre un producto

Hnos.[1] Godoy
Polígono[2] Nuevo, Unidad 45
Palencia,[3] ESPAÑA.   4 de enero de 199-

Asunto: Máquina de fabricación y envasadora de palillos

Estimado/a Sr/Sra:[4]

Representamos a un importante distribuidor de comestibles y otras materias relacionadas con esta industria en Kenia.

Su nombre figuraba en *Kompass* bajo la denominación de abastecedores de maquinaria de fabricación de palillos. Necesitamos disponer de una máquina especial al objeto de fabricar y envasar palillos. Si usted[5] es fabricante de dicha maquinaria, o la abastece, le agradeceríamos nos enviara[6] lo antes posible presupuesto CIF[7] Mombasa, precios de esta máquina y material complementario, junto con la fecha de entrega.

Asimismo, sírvase[8] comunicarnos precio de instalación de la misma[9] en nuestra fábrica de Ususu, en Mombasa.

En espera de una pronta contestación, le saludamos[10] muy atentamente.

Gianni Mussini
Director Técnico

1 Abbreviation of *Hermanos* ('brothers').
2 *Polígono*: industrial/trading estate typical of economic development in Spain since the 1960s.
3 The Spanish town/city name is frequently preceded here by a five-digit code; the first two digits refer to its province.
4 Abbreviation for *Señor/Señora* ('Mr'/'Mrs') – also *Señorita* ('Ms') abbreviated to *Srta* – is normal here. *Estimado/a*: the most simple, and increasingly popular, of several virtually equivalent ways of greeting the addressee.
5 *Usted* (abbreviated to *Vd.*): formal mode of 'you' singular form of address, used with third person verbs and pronouns. In Latin America *usted* is yet more widespread; its plural (*ustedes*) is used in Latin America for any 'you' plural; whilst in Spain *vosotros* (plural of *tú*: informal) is also used, informally. *Tú* and *vosotros* would not be used in commercial correspondence.
6 Conditional tense followed by imperfect subjunctive: a complex verb structure typical of Spanish commercial correspondence.
7 CIF: English abbreviation used in Spanish, whose equivalent is *coste* ('cost'), *seguro* ('insurance'), *flete* ('freight').
8 One of several ways to say 'please' formally.
9 *La misma*: 'the aforementioned', referring back to *máquina*.
10 Plural verb ('we greet') to refer to all in firm addressed.

2   Enquiry about prices

28 February 199-

Bandani Detergenti SpA
Via A. Lamarmora 75
20093 COLOGNO MONZESE (MI)
Italy

Dear Sir/Madam

RE: QUOTATION RMS 34/16 JAN 199-/TOILET CLEANSER

On 16 January we received a quotation from your company for the supply of 4,000 litres of industrial toilet cleanser and disinfectant. We were unable to justify ordering this at the time, because we had sufficient stocks from our previous order at the end of last year.

We would like to enquire now if the prices quoted at the time are still valid for this commodity.

If you are unequivocally able to confirm that this is the case, please take this letter as an order for a further 10,000 litres. If there has been any price increase, please be so kind as to fax this to us or phone the undersigned, so that we can proceed and agree a price in due course.

Yours faithfully

Dick DeZwart
Buyer

2 Solicitando precios

Bandani Detergenti s.p.a.
Via A. Lamarmora 75
20093 Cologno Monzese
Milano, ITALIA.   28.2.199-

Asunto: Presupuesto RMS 34/16 enero 199-/detergente limpieza sanitarios[1]

Muy Sr/Sra nuestro/a:[2]

      El pasado 16 de enero recibimos de su empresa un presupuesto para el suministro de 4.000[3] litros de detergente y desinfectante industrial para la limpieza de sanitarios. Por entonces nos fue imposible aceptar su oferta ya que disponíamos de suficientes existencias restantes de nuestro pedido anterior, efectuado a finales del año pasado.

Ahora nos gustaría informarnos si los precios vigentes en aquellas fechas[4] son todavía válidos para este producto.

Si usted puede confirmarnos, sin dejar lugar a dudas, que esto es así, sírvase considerar esta carta como un pedido de 10.000 litros más. Si ha habido subida de precios, tenga a bien enviarnos los precios por fax, o llame al abajo firmante por teléfono, y así poder proceder y llegar a un acuerdo sobre el precio en su debido momento.

Reciba[5] atentos saludos.

F. Redondo
Jefe de Compras

1 Abbreviated format for presentation of main data.
2 A traditional and formal mode of introduction in commercial correspondence (also *mío/mía*): 'Our'/'My Dear Sir'/'Madam'.
3 In Spain a point is used to separate parts of a number over a thousand from one another; commas are used to indicate decimal places. In some Latin American countries the English system of points and commas is used.
4 Literally, 'on those dates'.
5 The *usted* command form of *recibir*, used with a plural object.

3 Enquiry about a company

7 March 199-

GiardinPrati SpA
Via Cassia Km 89
Val di Paglia
53040 RADICOFANI
Siena
Italy

Dear Sir/Madam

RE: ORDER LAWN-IND/CZ28

We refer to your quotation for 30 industrial mowing machines, model CZ28.

We gather that our client is now eager to proceed with finalizing the order for this equipment as we are slowly approaching spring time. As we have never placed an order with your company, we would like to receive your full audited accounts for the last four trading years.

Please ensure that the above accounts reach us within the next five working days, as we are eager not to miss the six-week delivery time which will enable us to have the equipment in our hands as soon as possible.

Yours faithfully

Lawrence Raines
Sales Department

3 Solicitando informes sobre una empresa

GiardinPrati s.p.a.
Via Cassia Km 89
Val di Paglia
53040 Radicofani
Siena
Italia.   7.3.199-

Asunto: pedido segadora[1] IND/CZ28

Estimado/a Sr/Sra:

             Hacemos referencia a su presupuesto para 30 segadoras industriales, modelo CZ28.

Le comunicamos[2] que nuestro cliente está impaciente por pasar a concluir el pedido de esta maquinaria ya que estamos aproximándonos a la primavera. Puesto que nunca hemos hecho ningún pedido a su empresa, nos gustaría recibir de la misma[3] una completa auditoría de los últimos cuatro años de ejercicio.[4]

Le rogamos que dicha auditoría nos llegue[5] en el plazo de los próximos cinco días laborables, ya que no deseamos perder las seis semanas correspondientes al período de entrega que nos permitirían tener la maquinaria en nuestro poder lo antes posible.

Atentamente le saluda,

                                                                    Lorenzo Ranura
                                                                    Encargado de Ventas

1 Full word for farm mower, harvester.
2 Included here in Spanish to enhance authenticity.
3 *La misma*: literally, 'the same', referring back to *empresa*.
4 *Ejercicio*: here meaning 'financial year'.
5 Present subjunctive after *Le rogamos que* . . .

4 Enquiry about a person

11 September 199-

ROPER Industriale
Viale San Benedetto 39–43
20084 Lacchiarella
Milano

Dear Sirs

RE: MR SAMUEL SMITH

We write to you as a fellow producer of machine tools. We have recently received an application from Mr Samuel Smith of Reading (England) who is applying for a post as technical support engineer with our company. This gentleman has given your company's name both as a previous employer and as a character referee.

From our reading of Mr Smith's CV he would appear most suitable for the post. However, we are also keen that people should fit into our factory and we are most concerned that in his early twenties Mr Smith was a very active member of the European Pro-Whale Organization. We would appreciate your comments on this, as we are keen to be better informed about this candidate.

Yours faithfully

Carlo Ruggeri
Personnel Manager

4 Solicitando informes personales

Roper Industries
Polywide Science Park
Basingstoke
Hampshire
Inglaterra.   11.9.199-

Asunto: El[1] Sr Samuel Smith

Señores:

      Nos ponemos en contacto con ustedes como cofabricantes[2] de máquinas herramienta. Ultimamente hemos recibido una solicitud del Sr Samuel Smith, de Reading, en la que nos solicita un puesto como ayudante de ingeniero técnico. Dicho señor nos ha proporcionado el nombre de su empresa para poder pedirle referencias personales y profesionales del mismo ya que fue empleado suyo.[3]

A juzgar por su currículum vitae, el Sr Smith parece ser el candidato idóneo. No obstante, tenemos mucho interés en que nuestros futuros empleados se ajusten a nuestra fábrica, y nos preocupa el hecho de que cuando el Sr Smith era veinteañero fuera un miembro muy activo de la Organización Europea en favor de las Ballenas. Les agradeceríamos nos hicieran las pertinentes observaciones acerca de este asunto, ya que tenemos mucho interés en obtener información más amplia de este candidato.[4]

Les saluda atte.[5]

Carlos Rivera Sanz
Director de Personal

1 The article El/el (or La/la) is included before a person's surname when talking **about** him/her, as opposed to **to** him/her. In abbreviated form (Sr for Señor, Sra for Señora, Srta for Señorita) the capital S of the title (equivalent to 'Mr'/'Mrs'/'Ms') is invariably retained. Where the full title is used, other than at the beginning of a sentence, the tendency is to write the initial in lower case (e.g. La señorita Gómez).
2 Cofabricantes implies joint activity; fabricante homólogo would imply only equivalent activity.
3 A paraphrase in Spanish for enhanced authenticity of expression.
4 Alternative, for most general use: aspirante.
5 Common abbreviation of atentamente.

5   Enquiry asking for a specific quote

2 April 199-

Sales Manager
OFFICE 2000
89–91 Scott Road
Olton
Solihull
West Midlands
B92 7RZ

Dear Sir/Madam

RE: LASER PHOTOCOPIER PR3000

We have been in correspondence with your company over the last six months and have in that time received a number of different quotations for different models of the industrial laser photocopying machines produced by your company. We have decided that the most suitable machine for our requirement is the PR3000.

We note, however, that your price of £4,000 is for one machine only. We are keen to purchase 20 printers of this particular model and we would therefore like to know what your discount would be on an order of this magnitude.

We would also like to know the delivery time for this equipment. If it were possible to deliver the printers in two separate batches of 10 each, we would require the first delivery in three months' time and the second some two months after that, when our new British office is completed in Cromer.

Yours faithfully

Luca Evangelista
Sales Manager

5 Solicitando presupuesto determinado

Director de Ventas, Office 2000
89–91 Scott Road
Olton, Solihull
West Midlands B92 7RZ
Inglaterra.   2.4.199-

Asunto: Fotocopiadora láser PR3000

Estimado/a Sr/Sra:

        Llevamos unos seis meses manteniendo correspondencia con su empresa, y durante ese tiempo hemos recibido diversas cotizaciones para diferentes modelos de máquinas fotocopiadoras láser, tipo industrial, fabricadas por su empresa. Hemos acordado que la más apropiada a nuestros requisitos es la PR3000.

Sin embargo, observamos que el precio de 4.000 libras esterlinas que nos dieron se refería sólo al de una máquina. Deseamos comprar veinte impresoras[1] de este determinado modelo y, por lo tanto, nos gustaría saber cuál sería[2] el descuento en un pedido de esta magnitud.

Nos gustaría saber, asimismo, la fecha de entrega de dicho equipo. Si hubiera posibilidad de entregar las impresoras en dos partidas distintas de diez envíos[3] en cada una, necesitaríamos la primera dentro de tres meses, y la segunda unos dos meses después, cuando esté[4] terminada nuestra nueva oficina ubicada en Cromer, Inglaterra.

Le saluda cordialmente.

Luis Evangelista
Director de Ventas

1 *Impresoras* is used here to refer to the copiers; it is also the generic term for 'computer printer'.
2 Accent on *cuál* indicates indirect question; conditional *sería* emphasizes speculation on this deal rather than usual discount.
3 Here *envíos* implies the ten individual machines to be sent.
4 Present subjunctive *esté* to indicate indefinite future time.

6 Soliciting an agency

4 December 199-

Erwin Page plc
Electrical Appliances & Supplies
29 Landon Place
London
SE45 9AS

Dear Sirs

We have heard from business associates that you are looking for an agency for the promotion of your products in the US. We feel therefore that we may be of assistance to you: we are a long established agency with offices in the midwest and on the west coast of the United States, and are experienced in the sale and promotion of domestic electrical equipment. We have helped several British firms to boost their US sales, and are convinced that you too could benefit from our experience. Our UK representative, Charles J Parker, would be pleased to call on you to discuss your needs further: you can contact him on 0171 745 4756. In any event Mr Parker will be visiting your locality in the coming week, and will take the opportunity of calling on you.

Yours faithfully

Peter Bowles
Director

6   Ofreciendo servicio de agencia

Ernesto Valderrama e hijos
Paseo de la Paz, 34
Quito
Ecuador.   4.12.199-

Muy señores nuestros:

De acuerdo con lo que nos han comunicado nuestros socios, ustedes buscan una agencia que se encargue[1] de la promoción de sus productos en los Estados Unidos. Por lo tanto, pensamos que nosotros podríamos serles de utilidad: nuestra agencia lleva muchos años establecida, y tenemos oficinas en la zona central de EE.UU. así como en la costa oeste del país. Tenemos experiencia considerable en la venta y promoción de electrodomésticos. Hemos ayudado a varias empresas sudamericanas a estimular sus ventas en los Estados Unidos, y estamos convencidos de que ustedes podrían beneficiarse también de nuestra experiencia. Nuestro representante en su país, Charles J. Parker, estará gustoso en hacerles una visita para tratar con más detalle sus necesidades: pueden ponerse en contacto con él llamando al 2 45475. En todo caso, el Sr Parker visitará su localidad la semana próxima, y aprovechará la ocasión para visitarles.

Sin otro particular,[2] les saluda cordialmente,

Peter Bowles
(Socio mayoritario)

1   Verb in the subjunctive because the *agencia* mentioned is (only) hypothetical at this stage.
2   A standard expression to end a business letter: 'with no more to add'.

7 Requesting information about agents

23 July 199-

Duperrier SA
24 avenue des Sylphides
Brignoles
83170 Var
France

Dear Sirs

RE: LÜTTICH GmbH

We have heard from colleagues that you have recently used the services of
Lüttich GmbH as agents for your products in Germany. We are in a different line
of business from yourselves, but we believe that Lüttich represents companies of
various kinds. We are looking for agents in Germany and Switzerland for our
stationery products. We should be grateful if you could let us have further
information on the above-named firm. Any information you send us will be
treated with the strictest confidence.

Yours faithfully

P Brandauer
Sales Department

7 Solicitando información sobre agentes

Duperrier S.A.
24 avenue des Sylphides
Brignoles
83170 Var
Francia.   23.7.199-

Asunto: Lüttich GmbH

Señores:

   Hemos sabido por unos colegas que recientemente ustedes se sirvieron[1]
de Lüttich GmbH como representantes de sus productos en Alemania. Nosotros
llevamos un negocio distinto al suyo,[2] pero nos consta que Lüttich representa a
empresas de varios tipos. Buscamos agentes comerciales que representen
nuestros productos de papelería en Alemania y Suiza. Les agradecería nos
proporcionaran más información de la empresa arriba mencionada. Toda
información[3] será tratada confidencialmente.

Atentamente les saluda.[4]

                                          Pablo Banderilla
                                          (Depto. de Ventas)

1 *Servirse de*: 'to use', 'to make use of'.
2 *Suyo* (*de usted*): 'yours'.
3 Implies 'information you send us'.
4 This final greeting can end variably: with a comma, a full stop, or nothing before the
   signature in Spanish-language correspondence.

8   Giving information about agents

8 August 199-

Herrn H Pike
Heinrich Pittmann GmbH
Ofterdingenstraße 69
6800 Mannheim
Germany

Dear Mr Pike

RE: DIETER & HELLER

Thank you for your letter enquiring about the company Dieter and Heller, who have been agents for our products for several years. This company has represented our interests in Eastern and Central Europe very effectively and our sales in those regions have been buoyant as a result. You will find their Bonn-based manager, Max Lettmann, particularly helpful, and I am sure he will be interested in co-operating with you.

If you do contact him, don't hesitate to mention my name.

Yours sincerely

Maria Fischer

8   Dando información sobre agentes

Sr R. Caminero
Farmacéuticos Ledesma S.A.
Carretera del Norte
Oviedo
España.   8.8.199-

Asunto: Dieter y Heller

Estimado Sr Caminero:

Le agradezco[1] su carta en la que pide información sobre la empresa Dieter y Heller, con la cual llevamos varios años trabajando en la promoción de nuestros productos. Dicha empresa nos ha representado eficazmente en Europa Central y del Este, y como resultado las ventas de nuestros productos en esas áreas han sido de demanda intensiva.[2] El Sr Max Lettmann, director en Bonn, le será muy útil, y estoy segura que estará muy interesado en cooperar con usted.

Si contacta con él, podrá mencionarle mi nombre con toda confianza.

Le saluda atentamente

Maria Fischer

1   First person verb, 'I thank'; note third person form in final greeting.
2   More literally, 'in great demand'.

9 Request for a business reference

11 March 199-

<u>CONFIDENTIAL</u>

Mr G Le Blanc
Sales Director
CURTAINS & BLINDS Ltd
PO Box 181
Croydon
CR0 5SN

Dear Mr Le Blanc

<u>RE: CASELLACCI SpA</u>

We would like to introduce our company as a major supplier of castors for office furniture. We have been approached by Casellacci SPA of Pisa as potential distributors of our products in the Italian market. Mr Casellacci has explained that he has been supplying your range of curtain fittings in the market for some fifteen years and has a proven track record of both successful sales and prompt payment with your company.

We are eager to proceed in the Italian market, but we wish to have some reassurance about this company, as we do not know either the company or the individuals concerned. It would appear that they are selling only high quality products and that our range of castors would fit very well into their sales range.

We would appreciate your earliest comments and thank you in advance for providing this information, which we would treat in the utmost confidence.

Yours sincerely

Steve Watwood
Export Manager

9 Solicitando información sobre un negocio

Sr G. Blanco
Director de Ventas
Cortinas y Persianas Luján
Avenida Elche, 34
Valencia
España. 11 de marzo de 199-

Asunto: Casellacci s.p.a. (Confidencial)

Estimado Sr Blanco:

Nos gustaría presentarle a nuestra empresa[1] como importante abastecedora de ruedecillas para mobiliario de oficina. Casellacci s.p.a. de Pisa se ha dirigido a nosotros para actuar como posibles distribuidores de nuestros productos en el mercado italiano. El Sr Casellacci nos ha explicado que él lleva aproximadamente quince años suministrando su gama de accesorios de cortinas, y que tiene antecedentes garantizados en el éxito de las ventas y el pago rápido con su empresa.

Estamos deseosos de introducirnos en el mercado italiano, pero queremos estar completamente seguros acerca de esta empresa ya que no conocemos a la susodicha[2] ni a sus empleados. Parece ser que sólo se dedican a la venta de productos de alta calidad y que nuestra gama de ruedecillas se ajustaría perfectamente a la suya.[3]

A este respecto,[4] le agradeceríamos su pronto comentario y le damos las gracias anticipadas por esta información que guardaríamos estrictamente confidencial.

Quedo atento y seguro servidor[5] de usted.

Steve Watwood
Director de Exportación

1 Alternatives for *empresa*: *compañía, firma, entidad, casa*.
2 *La susodicha*: 'the abovementioned' (company).
3 *La suya*: 'theirs' (i.e. their range – *gama* – of castors).
4 'In this regard'.
5 Note first person verb and use of *servidor*: 'I remain your . . . servant'.

10   Favourable reply to request for a business reference

23 March 199-

Mr S Watwood
Castassist
158–161 Cressex Estate
New Malden
Surrey
KT13 4EY

Dear Mr Watwood

RE: CASELLACCI SpA OF PISA

We thank you for your letter of 11 March, regarding the company Casellacci of Italy as potential distributors of your range of castors.

We have indeed been working with Casellacci now for 23 years and know both Andrea Casellacci and his son Antonio, who has become more active in the company over the last few years. Casellacci have a number of most competent sales personnel covering the whole of Italy and the islands and have performed most effectively for our company against our large German competitors within the market. Casellacci have over this period of time proven to be most prompt in their payment. At the time of writing I cannot recall any undue delay in the company's settlement of their bills.

I have some knowledge of your company and its products and I am quite sure they are suited to the Italian market. I trust that the Casellacci company will prove a dependable and successful distributor for your product.

We hope you find this information sufficient to your requirements. Should you need any further comments please do not hesitate to contact us.

Yours sincerely

George Le Blanc
Sales Director

10 Respuesta favorable a la petición de referencias comerciales

Sr S Watwood,
Castassist
158–161 Cressex Estate
New Malden
Surrey
KT13 4EY
INGLATERRA.   23.3.199-

Asunto: Casellacci s.p.a. de Pisa

Estimado Sr Watwood:

Le agradecemos su atta. carta del 11 de marzo, en la que nos hace referencia a la empresa Casellacci de Italia como posibles distribuidores de su gama de ruedecillas.

Por supuesto[1] que llevamos trabajando con Casellacci desde hace[2] ahora veintititrés años y conocemos a Andrea Casellacci y a su hijo Antonio, el cual juega un papel más importante en la empresa desde hace unos años.

Casellacci cuenta con un personal de ventas muy competente que se extiende por toda Italia y las islas,[3] y ha llevado a cabo una labor muy provechosa para nuestra empresa frente a nuestros grandes competidores alemanes en el mercado. Casellacci ha demostrado ser durante este período de tiempo muy puntual en efectuar sus pagos. En el momento de escribir la presente,[4] no recuerdo que la mencionada empresa se haya retrasado en la liquidación de sus facturas nunca.

Tengo conocimiento de su empresa de usted y sus productos, y estoy plenamente[5] seguro que se adaptarán bien al mercado italiano. Confío en que la firma Casellacci tendrá seriedad y éxito como distribuidora de su producto.

Esperamos que esta información sea suficiente. En caso de requerir más detalles, no dude[6] en contactarnos.

Le saluda atentamente.

Gerardo Blanco
Director de Ventas

1 Literally, 'of course'.
2 *Desde hace*: literally, 'since ago', used with present tense.
3 Referring mainly to Sardinia and Sicily.
4 *La presente* (i.e. *carta*: 'letter').
5 Literally, 'fully'.
6 Negative formal command: 'don't doubt/hesitate to . . .'.

11 Unfavourable reply to request for a business reference

23 March 199-

Mr S Watwood
Castassist
158–161 Cressex Estate
New Malden
Surrey
KT13 4EY

Dear Mr Watwood

RE: CASELLACCI SpA OF PISA

We are in receipt of your letter regarding the company of Andrea Casellacci with whom you have been discussing the potential distribution of your products in the Italian market.

We must first ask you to accept our comments on this company in the most confidential terms. We have indeed been working with Casellacci for many years, but unfortunately six months ago Mr Andrea Casellacci was detained by the Italian police and due to this certain irregularities within the company have come to light. A direct result of this situation, in our particular case, is that we have not received payment for the last three major shipments of goods to Casellacci, which were due to us at different times. We are at the moment in discussions with our solicitors who will be undertaking the appropriate action on our behalf.

As a result of this, it is our opinion that although this company has performed successfully in the past, it is obviously not in a position to continue this work on our behalf and therefore we would advise you that it would not be a suitable partner for you at this time.

Yours sincerely

George Le Blanc
Sales Director

11   Respuesta desfavorable a la petición de referencias comerciales

Sr S. Watwood,
Castassist
158–161 Cressex Estate
New Malden
Surrey
KT13 4EY, INGLATERRA.   23.3.199-

Asunto: Casellacci s.p.a. de Pisa

Estimado Sr Watwood:

                        Obra en nuestro poder[1] su atenta carta en la que nos hace
referencia a la empresa de Andrea Casellacci con la que ha tratado sobre la
posible distribución de los productos de su empresa de usted en el mercado
italiano.

En primer lugar queremos rogarle[2] acepte los comentarios que pasamos a
exponerle sobre esta empresa de forma totalmente confidencial. Llevamos[3]
trabajando con los Casellacci[4] muchos años, pero por desgracia el Sr Andrea
Casellacci fue detenido hace seis meses por la policía italiana, y debido a ello,
han sido descubiertas[5] ciertas irregularidades dentro de la empresa. La
consecuencia directa de este problema, en nuestro caso, es que no hemos
recibido el pago por los tres últimos embarques importantes de mercancías que
hemos despachado a Casellacci y que deberían haberse abonado[6] en distintas
fechas. Por ahora el asunto está en manos de nuestros abogados, quienes
tomarán las medidas necesarias en nombre nuestro.

Por lo tanto, es nuestro criterio que, aunque esta empresa haya[7] tenido éxito en
el pasado, queda patente que no está en situación de continuar esta labor en
nuestro nombre, y por lo tanto es justo advertirle que, hoy por hoy,[8] no será el
socio favorable para usted.

Atentamente le saluda,

                                                              Gerardo Blanco
                                                              Director de Ventas

1   Literally, 'It acts in our power'.
2   *Rogar*: 'to ask' (formal).
3   For true past perfect meaning: *llevábamos* plus gerund.
4   'The Casellaccis' (i.e. the family).
5   A passive verb construction.
6   *Abonar*: 'to pay' (in, for).
7   *Hubiera* (+ *tenido*) for true past perfect subjunctive.
8   'At present', 'currently'.

12   Evasive reply to request for a business reference

23 March 199-

Mr S Watwood
Castassist
158–161 Cressex Estate
New Malden
Surrey
KT13 4EY

Dear Mr Watwood

RE: CASELLACCI SpA OF PISA/ITALY

We are in receipt of your letter regarding the company Casellacci SpA with whom you have been discussing the distribution of your products in the Italian market.

Casellacci are a very reputable company, but we are concerned that they might have already stretched themselves with the selling of our products in Italy. We feel that, if they did take on your range of products, they would probably have to employ a further product manager and perhaps another half a dozen regional sales people to cover the Italian market adequately.

We trust this information is sufficient, but should you require any further comments please do not hesitate to contact us.

Yours sincerely

George Le Blanc
Sales Director

12   Respuesta evasiva a la petición de referencias comerciales

Sr S. Watwood
Castassist
158–161 Cressex Estate
New Malden
Surrey
KT13 4EY
Inglaterra.   23.3.199-

Asunto: Casellacci s.p.a. de Pisa, Italia

Estimado Sr Watwood:

Acusamos recibo[1] de su atta.[2] carta referente a la empresa
Casellacci s.p.a. con la que ha estado tratando de la distribución de sus productos
de usted en el mercado italiano.

Casellacci es una empresa de muy buena reputación, pero nos preocupa que, tal
vez, se hayan sobrepasado con la venta de nuestros productos en Italia;
opinamos que si aceptan su gama de productos probablemente tengan que
contratar a otro director más de productos y quizás a unos cuantos vendedores
regionales más para cubrir debidamente el mercado italiano.

Confiamos en que esta información sea suficiente, pero en caso de no ser así,[3]
tengan[4] a bien ponerse en contacto con nosotros.

Cordialmente le saluda,

                                                    Gerardo Blanco
                                                    Director de Ventas

1 Literally, 'We accuse receipt of ...' ('we acknowledge').
2 Abbreviation of *atenta*.
3 'If this is not the case ...': an expansion of the English version.
4 Note frequent and varied use of the subjunctive in this letter. Note also plural form of the
   verb here even though the letter is addressed to a single person.

13 Placing an order

10 October 199-

Jenkins Freeman plc
Unit 36
Heddington Industrial Estate
Birmingham
B34 9HF

Dear Sirs

We thank you for your catalogue and price list, which we read with interest. On the basis of your current prices, we wish to order the following:

50 electric drills, model 1456/CB
50 chain saws, model 1865/CH

Delivery is required by 3.11.199-, and the goods should be delivered to our warehouse in Riddington Way, Battersea. As agreed, payment will be by banker's draft.

Yours faithfully

Gillian Brookes
Purchasing Department

13   Solicitando un pedido

Jiménez y hermanos
Polígono Industrial de Toledo
Toledo
España.   10.10.199-

Señores:

Les damos las gracias[1] por su catálogo y lista de precios que estudiamos con interés. Basándonos en sus precios actuales, procedemos a hacerles el siguiente pedido:

50 taladradoras eléctricas, modelo 1456/CB
50 sierras de cadena, modelo 1865/CH

La entrega ha de[2] efectuarse para el 3.11.199-, y las mercancías deberán ser depositadas en nuestro almacén en Riddington Way, Battersea, Londres. Según acuerdo,[3] el pago deberá efectuarse por giro.

Sin otro particular, les saluda atentamente

Gillian Brookes
Departamento de Compras

1 *Dar las gracias*: a frequent alternative to *agradecer.*
2 *Ha de*: from *haber de*, implying mild compulsion (future).
3 An elliptical expression, with *nuestro* ('our') implied between the two words.

14   Cancellation of order

6 July 199-

Porzellanfabrik Hering
Langauer Allee 18
7000 Stuttgart
Germany

Dear Sirs

RE: ORDER NO. HGF/756

We recently placed an order for 60 bone china coffee sets (model 'Arcadia'). The order reference: HGF/756.

We regret that due to circumstances beyond our control, we now have to cancel the order. We apologize for any inconvenience this may cause you.

Yours faithfully

D. Grey

14 Anulando un pedido

Porcelanas Preciosas S.L.
Calle Rubina, 11
Murcia
España.   6.7.199-

Asunto: pedido No. HGF/756

Muy Sres nuestros:

En fecha reciente les hicimos un pedido de sesenta juegos de café de porcelana (modelo 'Arcadia') – no.[1] de referencia del pedido: HGF/756.

Lamentamos notificarles que debido a circunstancias ajenas a nuestra voluntad nos vemos obligados a anular dicho[2] pedido. Les rogamos sepan[3] disculparnos las molestias causadas.

Les saludamos cordialmente

D. Grey

1 Abbreviation of *número*.
2 *Dicho*: from *decir*: 'the said (order)'.
3 From *saber*: literally, 'We ask that you should know how to excuse us'.

15 Confirming a telephone order

18 January 199-

Henning & Söhne GmbH
Schillerstraße 45
4300 Essen
Germany

Dear Mr Hartmann

Following the visit of your representative Dieter Höne last week, we are pleased to confirm our telephone order for

   250 car seat covers, model AS/385/c

The total price of the order, including discount, is £4,600. Payment will follow immediately upon delivery. The covers should be delivered no later than Tuesday 3 February, to our warehouse on the Pennington Industrial Estate, Rochdale.

Yours sincerely

Derek Batty

15 Confirmando un pedido efectuado por teléfono

Henning & Söhne GmbH
Schillerstraße 45
4300 Essen
Alemania.   18.1.199-

Estimado Sr Hartmann:

Como continuación a la visita que nos hizo su representante Dieter Höne la semana pasada, nos es grato[1] confirmarle nuestro pedido telefónico de:

250 fundas de coche, modelo AS/385/c

El precio total del pedido, incluido descuento, asciende a 956.000 pesetas. El pago se efectuará inmediatamente después de la entrega del mismo.[2] Las fundas deberán entregarse para el martes día 3[3] de febrero en nuestro almacén ubicado[4] en el Polígono Industrial de Artiga, en Castellón.

Atentamente.[5]

Daniel Beltrán

1 Literally, 'it is pleasing for us'.
2 Referring to the order (*pedido*).
3 The word for day is invariably included before the date (e.g. *día* 3) in Spanish usage.
4 'Located'.
5 A minimal version of the final formal greeting.

16 Making an order for specific items of office equipment

7 July 199-

Your ref.
Our ref. HB/LP

Garzón e Hijos
Plaza de la Catedral 8
Bogotá

Dear Sir/Madam

Please supply the following items, using the Order Number E183, to the above address at your earliest convenience. Payment will be made within 14 days of receipt of your invoice and of the goods as ordered.

 6 artists' stools (aluminium)

20 sets of 5 painting brushes

10 reams of A5 drawing paper

 2 drawing tables: 2m × 1m

 1 Sanchix camera: FB4x model

 1 QRM computer: portable TGs model

Before you prepare and invoice us for these goods, please inform us by telex or phone of the cost per item, as in the past we have received unexpectedly high invoices.

We thank you in anticipation of your prompt reply.

Yours faithfully

Herberto Baza
Studio Supervisor

16   Solicitando un pedido de enseres de oficina

Garzón e hijos
Plaza de la Catedral, 8
Bogotá.   7.7.199-

Su ref.
Nuestra ref. HB/LP

Muy Sr mío/Sra mía:

        Agradeceremos que se sirvan anotar el siguiente pedido No. E183 que deberán enviar, lo antes posible, a la dirección arriba indicada. Deberá girar a nuestro cargo el importe de la remesa,[1] y el pago se efectuará catorce días después del recibo de la factura y de las mercancías.

   6 sillas de delineante (aluminio)

20 juegos de 5 pinceles

10 resmas de papel de dibujo A5

   2 mesas de delineante: 2m × 1m

   1 cámara fotográfica Sanohix: modelo FB4x

   1 ordenador QRM: modelo portátil TGs

Antes de preparar y girar a nuestro cargo el importe de la remesa, agradeceríamos nos informaran, por télex o por teléfono, del precio de cada artículo, ya que en el pasado hemos recibido facturas extremadamente[2] altas.

Confiando en su pronta entrega,[3] le doy las gracias anticipadas y le saludo[4] atentamente.

Herberto Baza
(Supervisor de Estudio)

1 Expanded from the English: 'the cost of the consignment should be charged to us'.
2 Literally, 'extremely'.
3 Implying reply about delivery.
4 Note first person verb form.

17 Acknowledgement of an order

17 September 199-

Mr Henry Putton
33 Flintway
West Ewell
Surrey
KT19 9ST

Dear Mr Putton

Thank you for your signed order given to our Advisor for a bed to be constructed to your specific requirements.

We shall now pass your order to our Design Department complete with the personal specification with which you have provided us.

Delivery time will be in approximately seven weeks and you will be advised of the exact date in due course.

Once again many thanks for your order.

Yours sincerely

Janet Craig
Customer Relations Manager

17   Acusando recibo de un pedido

Sr Henry Putton
33 Flintway
West Ewell
Surrey
KT19 9ST
Gran Bretaña.   17.9.199-

Estimado Sr Putton:

Le damos las gracias por el pedido que firmado entregó a nuestro asesor con el fin de que se le hiciera[1] una cama especial según sus requisitos.

Nos complace[2] comunicarle que dicho pedido se enviará a nuestro Departamento de Diseño junto con la especificación personal que usted nos ha proporcionado.

La entrega será aproximadamente dentro de siete semanas, aunque le notificaremos la fecha exacta a su debido tiempo.

Una vez más le agradecemos el pedido y nos despedimos[3] de usted muy atentamente.

Juanita Cabrera
Directora de Relaciones Públicas

1 Note use of reflexive *se* to express passive: 'bed to be constructed'.
2 A convention in correspondence: 'It pleases us to . . .'.
3 *Despedirse de*: 'to sign off', 'say goodbye'.

18   Payment of invoices

Letter accompanying payment

2 February 199-

Dr V Meyer
Neue Marktforschung GmbH
Kastanienallee 14
D–45023 Osnabrück
Germany

Dear Dr Meyer

I enclose an international money order to the value of 450DM as payment for the three market research reports on dairy products published by your organization this year.

As agreed during our telephone conversation on 15.1.199-, the sum enclosed includes postage.

I look forward to receiving the reports as soon as possible.

Yours sincerely

Maria Meller

Enc.

18   Pago de facturas

Carta acompañada de pago

Dr V. Meyer
Neue Marktforschung GmbH
Kastanienallee 14
D–45023 Osnabrück
Alemania.   2.2.199-

Estimado Dr Meyer:

Le adjunto[1] giro bancario internacional por valor de 450 marcos alemanes correspondiente al pago de los tres informes pertenecientes a la investigación del mercado de los productos lácteos publicados por su organización el presente año.

Según lo acordado[2] en nuestra conversación telefónica del 15.1.199-, en dicha cantidad va incluido el franqueo.[3]

Me veré muy complacida en recibir los informes cuanto antes.[4]

Sin otro particular, le saluda muy atentamente,

María Molina

Anexo

1 Note absence of article (un/el) in this typical usage of the verb adjuntar ('to enclose').
2 Lo plus past participle/adjective: a typical feature of the Spanish language – here 'that which is/has been agreed'.
3 Franquear: 'to pay postage'.
4 Alternatives: cuanto antes, lo antes posible, lo más pronto posible.

19 Payment of invoices

Request for deferral

4 March 199-

South East Finance Ltd
Alton Court
Cleeve Road
London
W11 1XR

Dear Sirs

RE: MAXITRUCK 2000

I refer to our recent agreement of 30 November 199- regarding payment for one 40-ton Maxitruck 2000.

As you will recall, we paid an initial instalment of £10,000 and agreed to 10 further monthly instalments of £3,000. The December and January instalments, as you will know, have been paid promptly.

However, owing to the serious economic situation we find ourselves in, we are at the moment unable to make payments as agreed. Because of our reduced cash flow we are unable to pay more than £2,000 a month. We would, therefore, appreciate the opportunity to discuss this matter with you and reach a mutually satisfactory arrangement.

Yours faithfully

Tom Page
Finance Manager

19   Pago de facturas

Petición de aplazamiento

South East Finance Ltd
Alton Court
Cleeve Road
London W11 1XR
Inglaterra.   4.3.199-

Estimados señores:

Hago referencia a nuestro acuerdo del 30.11.199- sobre el pago de un Maxitruck 2000 de cuarenta toneladas.

Si ustedes recuerdan,[1] abonamos[2] un pago inicial de 10.000 libras esterlinas y acordamos abonar otros diez pagos mensuales de 3.000 libras cada uno. Los pagos correspondientes a diciembre y enero, como bien saben, los efectuamos sin demora.

Sin embargo, debido a la grave crisis económica en la que nos vemos sumergidos,[3] nos es de momento imposible[4] seguir efectuando los pagos según lo estipulado. Puesto que nuestro flujo de efectivo[5] está reducido, nos vemos en la imposibilidad de abonar más de 2.000 libras mensuales. Nos gustaría poder tratar de este tema con ustedes y poder llegar a un mutuo y satisfactorio arreglo.

Les saluda atentamente,

Tomás Patalote
Director de Finanzas

1 Literally, 'If you remember'.
2 *Abonamos, acordamos, efectuamos* are all past tense forms.
3 Literally, 'in which we see ourselves submerged' – a typically vivid expression in Spanish.
4 Inverted word order, as compared with English.
5 *Efectivo*: a standard reduced form (*dinero en efectivo*). Alternatives: (*el*) *cashflow* or (*el*) *flujo de caja*.

20 Payment of invoices

Refusal to pay

19 May 199-

Johnson (Builders) Ltd
Nugget Grove
Christchurch

Dear Sirs

RE: INVOICE NO. L28/4659

We refer to your invoice No. L28/4659 regarding repairs to the roof of workshop 17 at Heath End.

In spite of the repair work carried out by your employees the roof still leaked in a number of places during the recent rains, as a result causing a shut-down of the workshop for safety reasons.

We look forward to a speedy response in order to resolve this problem and assure you that your invoice will be paid as soon as this matter has been resolved to our satisfaction.

Yours faithfully

Daniela Fellowes
Deputy Director

20   Pago de facturas

Negándose a efectuar un pago

Hermanos Jordán
Calle de la Justicia, 23
Managua.   19.5.199-

Asunto: factura No. L28/4659

Muy Sres nuestros:

Hacemos referencia a su factura No. L28/4659 relacionada con las reparaciones del tejado del taller No. 17, ubicado en la zona franca este.

A pesar de las reparaciones efectuadas por sus empleados, el tejado ha seguido goteando por varios sitios durante las últimas lluvias, lo que[1] ha dado lugar al cierre definitivo del taller por razones de seguridad.

Les agradeceríamos una pronta respuesta para resolver este problema, y les aseguramos el pago de su factura tan pronto hayan resuelto[2] este asunto a nuestra satisfacción.

Reciban un cordial saludo[3]

Daniela Fonseca
Subdirectora

1 Referring to the fact of the roof leaking.
2 Subjunctive after *tan pronto*: indefinite future time.
3 A minimal final greeting.

21 Apologies for non-payment

17 August 199-

Mr I Sahani
Michigan Lake Trading Co.
974 South La Salle Street
Chicago
Illinois 60603
USA

Dear Mr Sahani

I refer to our telephone conversation yesterday.

I must once again apologize for the fact that you have not yet received payment for order no. 072230/5310.

Payment was duly authorized by me on the 10 July, but due to staff holidays the paperwork appears to have gone astray between our sales and finance departments.

We have now traced the relevant documentation and I can assure you that the matter is being attended to with the utmost urgency.

If you have not received payment by Monday, 22 August, I would be grateful if you would contact me immediately.

I apologize once again for the inconvenience this has caused you and assure you of our best intentions.

Yours sincerely

Timothy Morton

21   Pidiendo excusas por no efectuar un pago

Sr I. Sahani
Michigan Lake Trading Co.
974 South La Salle Street
Chicago
Illinois 60603
EE. UU.   17.8.199-

Estimado Sr Sahani:

Por la presente hago referencia a nuestra conversación telefónica de ayer.

Una vez más le pido sepa excusar el hecho de que usted no haya recibido todavía el pago relacionado con el pedido No. 072230/5310.

Dicho pago fue autorizado por mí el 10 de julio, pero debido a las vacaciones de nuestro personal la tramitación del mismo parece haberse extraviado entre el departamento de ventas y el de finanzas.

Ahora ya[1] hemos localizado la documentación pertinente, y le aseguro que estamos ocupándonos de este asunto con la mayor urgencia.

Si para[2] el lunes, 22 de agosto, no ha recibido el pago, le agradecería se pusiera en contacto conmigo inmediatamente.

Le ruego una vez más perdone[3] las molestias causadas, y le aseguramos nuestros mejores propósitos.

Reciba un atento saludo,

Tancredo Morales

1   *Ahora ya*: duplication of same idea for emphasis.
2   *Para* in time expressions implies 'by'/'before'.
3   The fourth example in the letter of subjunctive required in the subordinate clause.

22   Request for payment

15 May 199-

Huron Motor Factors
6732 John Street
Markham
Ontario
Canada L3R 1B4

Dear Sir

RE: INVOICE NO. JE/17193

As per our invoice JE/17193 of 13.3.199-, we supplied your Nashlee plant with 500 litres of AVC automotive base paint, payment due 60 days after receipt of our consignment.

This period of time has now elapsed and we request immediate settlement of the above invoice.

Yours faithfully

Duane Rogers
Accounts Manager

22 Petición de un pago

Servicio Carro Lindo
Avenida del Héroe, 65–68
Monterrey
México.   15.5.199-

Muy Sr mío:

Según nuestra factura JE/17193 del 13.3.199- suministramos a su fábrica de Monterrey 500 litros de pintura base AVC para autos – importe pagadero[1] sesenta días después del recibo del envío.

El estipulado período de tiempo ya ha transcurrido, y ahora nos vemos obligados a hacer requerimiento inmediato de dicho pago.

Sin otro particular, quedamos a la espera del mismo[2] y le saludamos atentamente.

Duane Rogers
(Responsable de pedidos)

1 *Importe pagadero*: 'amount payable'.
2 I.e. 'the said payment' (*dicho pago*).

23   Overdue account

First letter

31 May 199-

Lota (UK) Ltd
93 Armstrong Road
Dudley
West Midlands DY3 6EJ

Dear Sir

<u>Arrears on Finance Agreement No. 261079</u>

I am writing to advise you that your bankers have failed to remit the April instalment of £8,373 on the above agreement and as a result the account is now in arrears.

This has incurred an additional £460.50 in interest and administration charges.

Please advise your bank to transfer £8,833.50 to our account to bring your account up to date and enable us to remove it from our arrears listing.

Yours faithfully

Rosemary Wilson
Accounts Department

23   Pago atrasado

Primera notificación

Lota (España) S.A.
Carretera del Norte, 11
Burgos
España.   31.5.199-

Asunto: Atraso en el pago según acuerdo financiero No. 261079

Estimado señor:

Le escribo para informarle que su banco no ha abonado la cuota,[1] que corresponde al mes de abril, de las 8.373 libras esterlinas según lo acordado, y por lo tanto dicho pago está ahora atrasado.

Esto ha originado gastos adicionales de intereses y de administración que ascienden a 460 libras con 50 peniques.

Le ruego informe a su banco que transfiera 8.833 libras con 50 peniques a nuestro favor con objeto de actualizar su cuenta y así poderle[2] eliminar de nuestra lista de atrasos.

Le saluda atentamente

Rosemary Wilson
(Depto.[3] de Contabilidad)

1   Instalment; also used for 'quota', 'share', 'fee', 'deposit', 'dues', 'premium'.
2   More correctly, *poder eliminarle*: 'be able to remove you'.
3   Abbreviation for *departamento*.

24   Overdue account

Final letter

12 June 199-

Lota (UK) Ltd
93 Armstrong Road
Dudley
West Midlands DY3 6EJ

Dear Sir

<u>Arrears on Finance Agreement No. 261079</u>

Our records show that despite our previous reminders, your account remains overdue.

We now insist that you clear the outstanding arrears by close of business on Friday, 26 June 199-.

If you should fail to comply with this request by the date specified, we would be obliged to rescind the contract and would take steps to recover our property.

Yours faithfully

Rosemary Wilson
Accounts Department

24 Pago atrasado

Última notificación

Lota (España) S.A.
Carretera del Norte, 11
Burgos
España.   12.6.199-

Asunto: Atraso en el pago según acuerdo financiero No. 261079

Estimado señor:

      Según apuntan nuestros registros contables, y a pesar de las notificaciones y advertencias[1] enviadas, su pago sigue pendiente.

Ha llegado el momento de insistirle que usted debe liquidar[2] dicho pago para el viernes 26 de junio de 199- para la hora de cierre.

Si no cumpliera con esta petición para la fecha y hora estipulada, nos veríamos obligados a la rescisión del contrato, y tomaríamos medidas para recuperar los pagos pendientes.[3]

Le saluda atentamente.

Rosemary Wilson
(Departamento de Contabilidad)

1 *Advertencias*: 'warnings'.
2 'To settle, to pay off'. Alternatives: *pagar, abonar, saldar.*
3 'Outstanding payments'.

25   Job advertisement

Letter to newspaper

14 December 199-

H J Marketing Services
County House
53 Stukely Street
Twickenham TW1 7LA

Dear Sir

Please would you insert the attached job advertisement in the January issues of *East European Marketing Monthly* and *Food Industry Digest*.

As usual, we would like a quarter-page ad, set according to our house style.

Please invoice payment in the usual way.

Yours faithfully

Philip Redmond
Personnel Manager

Enc.

25 Anuncio de puesto de trabajo

Carta a periódico

H.J. Marketing Services
County House
53 Stukely Street
Twickenham TW1 7LA
Inglaterra.   14.12.199-

Muy señor nuestro:

Le ruego inserte[1] en los números de enero de las revistas *East European Marketing Monthly* y *Food Industry Digest* el adjunto anuncio de puesto de trabajo.

Como de costumbre, deseamos que dicho anuncio ocupe un cuarto de página y figure según el estilo de esta empresa que le adjuntamos.[2]

Sírvase enviar factura según acostumbra.[3]

Sin otro particular, le saluda

                                                              Felipe Remedios
                                                              (Jefe de Personal)

Anexo

1 This, together with three further examples in this brief letter, well illustrates the frequency and importance of subjunctive forms in Spanish-language correspondence: where one party is requesting the other to act, the desired outcomes are expressed as hypotheses.
2 Literally, 'the style of this company which we enclose to you'.
3 Again, note the elliptical style of much correspondence, omitting words obvious to writer and addressee.

26 Job advertisement

We are now expanding our operations in Eastern Europe and require experienced people within the food processing industry who are looking for an opportunity to sell products of leading Hungarian and Bulgarian food companies. The products are of good quality and already enjoy a substantial international reputation.

Salary for the above position is negotiable dependent upon experience and qualifications. A competitive benefits package is offered.

For further details and application form please write to the Personnel Manager, EEF Ltd, 34–40 Roman Road, Epsom, Surrey, KT72 7EF, quoting reference HB/127.

Closing date: 14 February 199-.

26   Anuncio de puesto de trabajo

Con motivo[1] de la expansión de nuestras operaciones en la Europa del Este, necesitamos personal experto en el área de la industria de transformación de alimentos, e interesado en la oportunidad de vender productos procedentes[2] de importantes empresas alimenticias de Hungría y Bulgaria. Los productos, que son de buena calidad, gozan ya de sustancial reputación internacional.[3]

Salario a negociar según experiencia y cualificaciones. Se ofrece un competitivo conjunto de beneficios.

Para obtener mayor información y hoja de solicitud de empleo, sírvase escribir al Encargado de Personal, EEFSA, Calle Mayor 34–40, Sevilla, España; referencia HB/127.

Fecha de cierre: 14 de febrero de 199-

1   Expressing purpose rather than time.
2   I.e. exports from Hungary and Bulgaria.
3   Alternatively, and perhaps more likely: *tienen mucha fama.*

27 Asking for further details and application form

14 January 199-

EEF Ltd
34–40 Roman Road
Epsom
Surrey KT72 7EF

Dear Sir

REF. HB/127

I would be grateful if you could send me further details and an application form for the post of sales manager advertised in this month's issue of the journal *East European Marketing Monthly*.

Yours faithfully

Lauren Russell (Ms)

27 Pidiendo información e impreso de solicitud para un puesto de trabajo

Encargado de Personal

EEFSA
Calle Mayor, 34–40
Sevilla
España.   el 14 de enero de 199-

Ref. HB/127

Muy señor mío:

Le agradecería me enviara más información, así como impreso de solicitud, para el puesto de director de ventas aparecido en el número de este mes de la revista *East European Marketing Monthly*.

Le saluda cordialmente.

Lauren Russell (Srta)

28 Job application

25 January 199-

Black's (Automotive) Ltd
18 Dawson Street
Birmingham
B24 4SU

Dear Sir

I am applying for the post of market research officer advertised in the *Guardian* on 21 January 199-.

I graduated from Chiltern University in June with an upper second class degree in European Business. The following January I was awarded the Diploma of the Chartered Institute of Marketing. On my degree course I specialized in market research and did a one-year work placement with Cox, Paton and Taylor in London.

Since leaving university I have been employed as a market research assistant in the Quantocks Tourist Agency. I am now seeking an opportunity to apply the knowledge and skills I have acquired in a larger, more market-orientated organization.

I enclose a CV and the names of two referees. I would be grateful if you would not contact my current employer without prior reference to me.

Yours faithfully

Michael Westwood

Encs

28   Solicitud de empleo

El Director de Personal
Automotriz S.A.
Cruce Ducal, 1
Teruel
España.   el 25 de enero de 199-

Estimado señor:

Me complace solicitar el puesto de investigador de mercado, anunciado en *El País*[1] del 21.1.199-.

El pasado junio terminé mis estudios de licenciatura en la Universidad de Chiltern, donde cursé la carrera[2] de Ciencias Empresariales Europeas, obteniendo matrícula de honor. En enero del año siguiente[3] me otorgaron el Diploma del Instituto de Márketing.[4] Durante los estudios de licenciatura me especialicé en la Investigación de Mercado y trabajé, durante un año y como parte integral de mis estudios, para la empresa Cox, Paton y Taylor de Londres.

Desde que terminé mis estudios universitarios estoy trabajando como ayudante de investigador de mercado para la Agencia de Turismo Quantocks. Ahora quisiera[5] poner en práctica, sirviendo a una organización más grande y más orientada hacia el mercado, los conocimientos y las destrezas que he ido adquiriendo.

Adjunto C.V. y los nombres de dos personas que pueden proporcionarle referencias mías. Le agradecería no se pusiera en contacto con mi jefe actual sin antes contar conmigo.[6]

Le saluda cordialmente.

                                                Michael Westwood

Anexos

1 Spain's major national daily paper.
2 Literally, 'where I followed the course . . .'.
3 I.e. **this** year.
4 In Latin America the term *mercadeo* is more frequent.
5 'I would like'.
6 Literally, 'without before counting with me'.

29 Curriculum vitae

Surname:	Cording
First names:	Donald Maurice
Date of Birth:	18 March 1959
QUALIFICATIONS:	BA (Hons) Business Studies (Leeds, 1981) MBA (Warwick, 1985)
CURRENT EMPLOYMENT: (Sept. 1988 to the present)	Marketing Manager, Cockpit Industries Ltd, 8 Wendover Road, Accrington, Lancs. BB7 2RH

PREVIOUS EMPLOYMENT:

(a) Jan. 1986–Sept. 1988:	Marketing Assistant, Spurlands Ltd, 71 Misbourne Road, Northallerton, Yorks. DL5 7YL
(b) Oct. 1981–Dec. 1985:	Marketing Assistant, Tutton Enterprises Ltd, Wye House, Cores End, Wolverhampton WV6 8AE
(c) Sept. 1979–July 1980:	Sales Assistant, J V Ansell & Co., Greenaway Avenue, Leek, Staffs. ST15 4EH

29 Curriculum vitae

Apellido:[1]	Cording
Nombres:	Donald Maurice
Fecha de nacimiento:	18.03.1959
ESTUDIOS:	Licenciatura en Ciencias Empresariales, Leeds,[2] 1981
	MBA, Warwick, 1985

PUESTO ACTUAL:

Setiembre[3] 1988 –	Director de Márketing, Cockpit Industries Ltd, 8 Wendover Road, Accrington, Lancs. BB7 2RH, Inglaterra.

PUESTOS ANTERIORES:

a) Enero 1986 – Setiembre 1988:	Ayudante de Márketing, Spurlands Ltd, 71 Misbourne Road, Northallerton, Yorks. DL5 7YL, Inglaterra.
b) Octubre 1981 – Diciembre 1985:	Ayudante de Márketing, Tutton Enterprises Ltd, Wye House, Cores End, Wolverhampton WV6 8AE, Inglaterra.
c) Setiembre 1979 – Julio 1980:	Ayudante de ventas, J.V. Ansell & Co., Greenaway Avenue, Leek, Staffs. ST15 4EH, Inglaterra.

1 Spanish people, of course, have two surnames: one each from mother and father.
2 Evidently, from the University (see below, also, Warwick).
3 Also spelt *septiembre*; months in Spanish are still usually spelt in normal text with lower case initial letter.

30 Unsolicited letter of application

5 November 199-

Executive Agency plc
22 Ellison Place
London WC1B 1DP

Dear Sirs

I have recently returned to Britain after working in Canada and the Gulf States for the last 15 years.

I spent five years working in Canada as chief financial accountant of Bourges-Canada in Montreal, before moving to the Gulf. I have worked as financial director for Jenkins-Speller for the last ten years. During this period the company's number of clients as well as its turnover have quadrupled.

I have returned to Britain for family reasons and I am now seeking an appropriate position in a company that can capitalize on my expertise in financial management and strategy.

I enclose a detailed CV for your further information and look forward to hearing from you soon.

Yours faithfully

Roger Bennett

Enc.

30 Solicitando empleo no anunciado

Agencia Mérito[1]
Plaza de los Héroes, 7
Santiago de Chile.   5.11.199-

Estimados señores:

Hace poco tiempo que he regresado a Chile después de haber trabajado en el Canadá[2] y en los países del Golfo Pérsico durante quince años.

Durante cinco años trabajé en el Canadá de jefe de contabilidad para la empresa Bourges-Canadá, en Montreal, antes de trasladarme al Golfo. Durante los diez últimos años he trabajado en el puesto de director financiero para Jenkins-Speller, período en el que tanto el número de clientes como el volumen de facturación de dicha empresa se ha visto[3] cuadruplicado.

He regresado a Chile por razones familiares, y ahora busco un puesto de trabajo apropiado en una empresa, la cual pueda sacar partido de la experiencia en dirección y estrategia financiera[4] que poseo.

Para mayor información adjunto C.V.[5] detallado, y espero tener pronto noticias suyas.

Atentamente suyo,[6]

Rodrigo Benet

Anexo

1 A private employment agency.
2 Canada is one of several country names invariably accompanied in Spanish by the definite article.
3 A singular verb is frequently used where a plural might more correctly reflect two (or more) subjects.
4 Again, plural (*financieras*) would be more accurate if it refers to both *dirección* and *estrategia*.
5 In Colombia, for example, the CV is called *hoja de vida*.
6 'Yours' ('faithfully', 'sincerely').

31   Interview invitation

12 February 199-

Ms F Jones
23 Park View
Colchester
Essex CO4 3RN

Dear Ms Jones

<u>Ref. PS/2021: Personnel assistant</u>

Interviews for the above position will take place on Friday, 22 February 199-, beginning at 10 a.m.

We expect to conclude the interviews after lunch, at approximately 2.30 p.m.

Please confirm whether you will attend the interview.

Yours sincerely

Mr C Smith
Personnel Officer

31   Llamada a una entrevista

Srta F. Jarpa
Edificio Violeta Ramos
Planta 1, D, izq.[1]
Glorieta del Sol
Mendoza.   12 de febrero de 199-

Ref. PS/2021

Asunto: Ayudante de personal

Estimada Srta Jarpa:

       Las entrevistas para el puesto arriba indicado tendrán lugar el viernes, 22 de febrero de 199-, dando comienzo a las 10 de la mañana.

Esperamos terminar dichas entrevistas después del almuerzo, aproximadamente a las 14.30h.[2]

Sírvase informarnos si asistirá a la misma.[3]

Le saluda atentamente,

                                              Sra C. Salas
                                              Jefa[4] de Personal

1   '1st floor, flat D, on the left'.
2   Also expressed as *las dos y media de la tarde*.
3   *Misma*: referring to the interview (plural in antecedent). *Confirmarnos si/que*: an alternative to '*informarnos . . .*'.
4   A now commonly accepted feminine form of the masculine *jefe*.

32 Favourable reply to job application

26 March 199-

Mrs L Flint
7 Fisherman's Way
Okehampton
Devon EX12 0YX

Dear Mrs Flint

I am writing to offer you formally the position of personal assistant to the operations director at Farnbury.

As discussed at the interview the normal working hours are 8.30 a.m.–5 p.m., Monday to Friday, although the position requires a flexible approach and on occasions you will be expected to work outside these times. The annual salary is £18,000.

You will receive further details should you accept the position.

Please confirm in writing by first post, Monday 3 April at the latest, whether you accept the offer of the position.

Yours sincerely

Oliver Ross
Personnel Manager

32   Respuesta favorable a una solicitud de empleo

Sra L. Flint
7 Fisherman's Way
Okehampton
Devon EX12 0YX
Reino Unido.

26.3.199-

Estimada Sra Flint:

Le escribo para ofrecerle oficialmente el puesto de ayudante de personal de nuestro director de operaciones en Inglaterra.

Según lo acordado en la entrevista, el horario laboral es de 8.30 de la mañana a 5[1] de la tarde, de lunes a viernes; no obstante,[2] el puesto requiere flexibilidad de horario y habrá ocasiones en las que tenga[3] que trabajar horas distintas a las estipuladas. Percibirá[4] un salario de 18.000 libras esterlinas anuales.

En caso de que acepte dicho puesto, le remitiremos información más detallada.

Le ruego nos confirme por escrito, a más tardar[5] para el primer reparto del lunes 3 de abril, si acepta la oferta que le proponemos.

Sin otro particular, le saluda muy atentamente,

Orlando Ríos
(Encargado de Personal)

1   Note omission of article *las* in the times of day.
2   Literally, 'notwithstanding'.
3   The subjunctive is used because the situation alluded to is hypothetical.
4   A frequent alternative to *ganar* and *cobrar* ('to earn').
5   Literally, 'at most to delay'.

33 Unfavourable reply to job application

11 July 199-

Mr R Smith
15 Adams Way
Reading
Berks
RG23 6WD

Dear Mr Smith

RE: POSITION AS SALES DIRECTOR

I am writing to inform you that your application was unsuccessful on this occasion.

Thank you for the interest you have shown in our company and we wish you every success with your career.

Yours sincerely

Raymond Dawson
Personnel Manager

33 Respuesta desfavorable a una solicitud de empleo

Sr R. Smith
15 Adams Way
Reading
Berks
RG23 6WD
Inglaterra.   11.7.199-

Asunto: puesto de director de ventas

Estimado Sr Smith:

       Lamento[1] informarle que, en esta ocasión, su solicitud de empleo ha sido rechazada.[2]

Le agradezco el interés que usted ha mostrado por nuestra empresa y le deseo mucho éxito en su carrera.

Atentamente le saluda,

Ramón Díaz
(Encargado de Personal)

1 'I regret': paraphrased in the Spanish version.
2 The word 'rejected' is a paraphrase in the Spanish version.

34   Requesting a reference for a job applicant

Your ref. AS/
Our ref. FG/JL

1 May 199-

The Manager
First Class Bank
1–6, King's Square
BURY

Dear Mr Swift

RE: MISS STEPHANIE BOSSOM

This branch of the Safety First has recently received an application for employment as an accounts clerk from Ms Stephanie Bossom. She has quoted your name as a referee to whom we might address ourselves in the event of our wishing to interview her.

I believe that Ms Bossom has been working in your bank for several years and that her desire to change employment is prompted largely by her intention to marry and settle in this area. From her application she appears to be the ideal candidate for this company; therefore we should be most grateful if you could confirm the impression we have of her in writing (or by fax if possible) as soon as is convenient.

Please feel free to comment on any aspect of Ms Bossom's work that you deem to be of likely interest to us.

I thank you in advance for your cooperation.

Yours sincerely

Frank Graham
Branch Manager

34   Pidiendo referencias sobre una persona que solicita un puesto de trabajo

The Manager
First Class Bank
1–6, Kings Square
Bury

Su ref: AS/
Nra ref: FG/JL   1.5.199-

Estimado Sr Swift:

Esta sucursal[1] de la Safety First ha recibido recientemente de la señorita Stephanie Bossom una solicitud para un puesto de trabajo como empleada del[2] departamento de contabilidad. Dicha[3] señorita nos ha proporcionado su nombre de usted como referencia y persona[4] a quien pudiéramos[5] dirigirnos en caso de[6] querer hacerle una entrevista.

Me consta que la señorita Bossom lleva trabajando[7] varios años en su banco y que su deseo de cambiar de puesto de trabajo ha surgido principalmente en vistas a[8] su próximo matrimonio y su intención de fijar su residencia en esta zona. Según se desprende[9] de su solicitud, parece ser la candidata idónea para esta empresa; por lo tanto le agradeceríamos a usted nos confirmara[10] por escrito (o bien por fax) a la mayor brevedad posible la impresión que tenemos de ella.

No dude en hacer cualquier observación pertinente al trabajo de la señorita Bossom que le parezca nos pudiera[11] interesar.

Agradeciéndole de antemano su cooperación, le saluda atentamente

Frank Graham
(Director de sucursal)

1 The standard term for a branch of a business.
2 Alternatively, *en el* ...
3 *Dicha*: 'the above mentioned'.
4 *Referencia* alone does not necessarily imply the human nature of 'referee'; hence the inclusion of *persona*.
5 Imperfect subjunctive, expressing possibility.
6 Here, followed by the infinitive because all verbs in this clause have the same subject ('us': i.e. Safety First).
7 *Llevar* + gerund: to express continuity from past to present.
8 'With a view to', 'in view of'.
9 *Desprenderse*: 'to conclude, to infer'.
10 Imperfect subjunctive after main verb conditional tense.
11 Note: the third of three subjunctive forms in one sentence.

35 Providing a positive reference for an employee

2 April 199-

Your ref. FG/JL
Our ref. AS/MN

Mr F Graham
Safety First Assurance plc
12, Bright Street
Lancaster

Dear Mr Graham

MS STEPHANIE BOSSOM

I hasten to reply to your letter requesting a reference for Ms Stephanie Bossom. Please accept my apologies for not being able to fax my reply, but at present we are experiencing problems with the machine.

Yes, Stephanie has been an ideal employee who started with us as an office junior straight from school and has been promoted on several occasions in recognition of her work. I understand her reasons for wishing to leave and I would have promoted her again very soon, were she to have stayed with us.

You will see from her application that she has sat and passed a number of professional examinations over the last two years. During that time she has taken responsibility for supervising the progress of trainees and has been involved in new initiatives relating to our office systems.

You will find Stephanie a pleasant, willing and talented person. You can rely upon her to carry out her professional duties to the best of her ability at all times.

I hope you will be able to offer her the post, which you imply is likely in your initial letter.

Yours sincerely

Alan Swift
(Manager, Town Centre Branch)

35   Respuesta favorable a una petición de referencias

Sr F. González
Jefe de Personal
Delta S.A.
Calle del Carmen, 36
Logroño
España.   2.4.199-

Su ref. FG/JL
Nuestra ref. AS/MN

Estimado Sr González:

Me apresuro a dar contestación a su carta en la que me pedía le proporcionara referencias de la señorita Stephanie Bossom. Le ruego sepa disculpar no le haya podido enviar la contestación por fax, debido a los problemas que nos han surgido con el aparato.

Ciertamente, le confirmo que Stephanie Bossom ha sido una empleada modelo,[1] la cual empezó a trabajar con nosotros en capacidad de oficinista subalterna recién terminada su escolarización, y en reconocimiento a su trabajo ha sido ascendida de puesto varias veces. Soy consciente de las razones que la mueven a cambiarse de puesto,[2] y de haberse quedado con nosotros la hubiera vuelto a ascender muy pronto.

Por su solicitud observará que, durante los últimos dos años, la Srta Bossom ha superado una serie de exámenes y pruebas profesionales. Durante ese período de tiempo se ha responsabilizado de supervisar el progreso de las aprendices, y ha llevado a cabo nuevas iniciativas relacionadas con el sistema de esta oficina.

Usted comprobará que Stephanie es agradable, aplicada y talentosa; en ella se puede confiar el llevar a cabo sus tareas profesionales en todo momento.

Espero que usted pueda ofrecerle el puesto, según afirma de esta posibilidad en su primera carta.

Atentamente le saluda,

Alan Swift
(Director)

1   *Modelo* is a noun acting as an adjective, so it does not change to agree grammatically with *empleada*.
2   ('To leave') literally, 'to change jobs'.

36 Acceptance letter

20 July 199-

Melton's Motor Factors Ltd
63 Station Road
Thirsk
N. Yorkshire
YO9 4YN

Dear Sir

Thank you for your letter of 17 July offering me the post of parts manager.

I am delighted to tell you that I accept your offer.

Yours sincerely

Andrew Camp

36 Aceptando un puesto de trabajo

Sr S. Palacios
Coches Real S.A.
Avenida Manresa
Estepona.   el veinte de julio, 199-

Muy señor mío:

Le agradezco su atta.[1] carta del 17 de julio en la que me ofrece el puesto de gerente del departamento de piezas.

Me es grato comunicarle que acepto dicho cargo.[2]

Le saluda atentamente,

                                                            Andrés del Campo

1 Abbreviation of *atenta*.
2 *Cargo*: 'job, position'.

37   Contract of employment

Dear

Following recent discussions we are pleased to offer you employment at our Company as Area Manager on the following terms and conditions:-

Remuneration
Your salary will be £15,000 per annum plus commission on the basis we have already discussed with you. As with all our staff, your salary will be paid monthly on the last Thursday in each month, your first review being in July 199-.

Notice
As with all our staff, you will be employed for an initial trial period of six months, during which time either you or we may terminate your appointment at any time upon giving seven days' notice in writing to the other. If we are satisfied with your performance during the trial period, once it is completed we will immediately confirm your appointment as a permanent member of our staff and the seven days' period of notice referred to above, will be increased to one month.

Sickness Pay
During any reasonable absence for illness the Company, at its discretion, will make up the amount of your National Insurance Benefit to the equivalent of your normal salary, although this will be essentially relative to your length of service.

Holidays
Your normal paid holiday entitlement will be 20 working days in a full year, the holiday year running from 1 January to 31 December.

Car
We will provide you with a suitable Company car (cost circa £14,000), which is to be mainly for your business use but also for your private use. The Company will meet all normal running expenses associated with the car such as road tax, insurance, repairs, servicing and petrol.

Pensions
The Company operates a Pension Plan. You can either decide to join the Company Scheme after six months' service at the Scheme's next anniversary date (6 July 199-), or alternatively choose a Personal Pension Plan to which the Company would contribute.

Hours
Normal office hours are from 9.00 a.m. to 5.15 p.m. from Monday to Friday, with one hour for lunch. However, it is probable that additional calls will be made upon your time.

Grievance and Disciplinary Procedure
Should you wish to seek redress for any grievance relating to your employment, you should refer, as appropriate, either to the Company Secretary or to the Managing Director. Matters involving discipline will be dealt with in as fair and equitable a manner as possible.

37   Contrato de trabajo

Estimado/a

Según lo tratado[1] recientemente, nos complace ofrecerle el puesto de Director/a de Zona en nuestra empresa bajo las siguientes condiciones.[2]

Remuneración
De acuerdo con lo acordado recientemente, usted percibirá un salario de 3.120.000 pesetas anuales más comisión. El salario se le abonará, como al resto de nuestro personal, el último jueves de mes, efectuándose la primera revisión del mismo[3] en julio de 199-.

Despido/Dimisión[4]
El período inicial de prueba de empleo que se lleva a cabo con todo nuestro personal es de seis meses; durante este plazo bien usted o nosotros podemos terminar el contrato en cualquier momento, mediante previa notificación hecha por escrito siete días antes del mismo.[5] Si estamos satisfechos con el cumplimiento de su cargo durante el período de prueba, una vez cumplido éste,[6] le comunicaremos inmediatamente la inclusión permanente a nuestra plantilla,[7] y el período de notificación de cese, al que nos referíamos anteriormente, quedará prolongado a un mes.

Subsidio de enfermedad
Durante un período razonable debido a enfermedad la Empresa completará, a su discreción, la cantidad de prestaciones a la Seguridad Social equivalentes a su salario normal, aunque esto será esencialmente relativo a la antigüedad.[8]

Vacaciones
Usted tendrá derecho a veinte días laborables al año de vacaciones pagadas, estando éstas comprendidas entre el 1 de enero y el 31 de diciembre.

Vehículo
La empresa le proporcionará un automóvil adecuado (cuyo coste está estimado en aproximadamente 2.900.000 ptas), que podrá utilizar para su trabajo y uso particular. Nosotros nos haremos cargo de cualquier gasto relacionado con dicho vehículo, tal como impuesto de circulación, seguro, reparaciones, mantenimiento y gasolina.

Pensión
La Empresa dispone de un Plan de Pensiones. Usted puede acogerse al Plan de la Empresa al cabo de seis meses, es decir, el próximo 6 de julio, o por otra parte, puede escoger un Plan Personal de Pensión al que la Empresa contribuiría.

Horario
El horario laboral de oficina es de 9 de la mañana a 5.15 de la tarde, de lunes a viernes, disponiendo de una hora para el almuerzo. No obstante, es probable que tenga que trabajar horas extra.[9]

Health & Safety at Work Act

A copy of the Staff Notice issued under the Health & Safety at Work etc. Act 1974 will be given to you on the first day of your employment. Your acceptance of the appointment will be deemed to constitute your willingness to comply with these regulations.

Start Date

The date on which your employment is to commence remains to be agreed by the Company. We look forward to establishing a mutually acceptable date as soon as possible.

Would you kindly provide us with your acceptance of this offer of employment by signing and returning to us the enclosed duplicate copy of this letter.

We trust that you will have a long, happy and successful association with our Company.

Yours sincerely

B. Foster
Managing Director

Enc.

4.6.199-

Juicio de faltas y disciplina

En caso de querer desagraviar cualquier queja relacionada con su trabajo, deberá dirigirse, oportunamente, bien al Secretario de la Empresa o al Director-Gerente. Los asuntos relacionados con la disciplina se tratarán de la manera más justa y equitativa posible.

Higiene y Seguridad

El primer día de trabajo con nosotros, le será entregada una copia del libro que distribuimos a nuestro personal sobre la Ley de Higiene y Seguridad en el Trabajo (1974). El aceptar el puesto de trabajo ofrecido conlleva[10] el deseo del cumplimiento de dicho reglamento.

Fecha de comienzo de empleo

La fecha en la que ha de comenzar a trabajar con nosotros está por determinar por la Empresa, pero esperamos que usted y la Empresa acordarán dicha fecha[11] lo antes posible.

Le rogamos nos proporcione aceptación de esta oferta de trabajo firmando y remitiéndonos[12] la copia de esta carta que se adjunta.

Esperamos que su relación con esta Empresa sea larga, feliz y provechosa.

Le saluda atentamente,

B. Fernández
Director Gerente

(4.6.199-)

Anexo

1 Impersonal expression: 'that which was dealt with'.
2 In Spanish the word for 'terms' is synonymous with 'conditions' (*condiciones*); though *términos* might also be used.
3 *Mismo*: referring to *salario*.
4 *Despido*: dismissal. *Dimisión*: resignation. See *cese* (below): more generally, notice of both kinds.
5 *Mismo*: referring here to act of terminating the contract.
6 Literally, 'once accomplished this'.
7 This word can mean 'staff', 'workforce' or 'team'.
8 *Antigüedad*: in this specific context: 'years of service'; elsewhere: 'age' or 'antiquity'.
9 'Overtime'; also *horas extras*.
10 Literally, 'brings with it'.
11 'The said (i.e. agreed between both parties) date'.
12 The present participle/gerund (*firmando y remitiéndonos*) includes the amplified meaning of 'by .. -ing'.

38 Enquiring about regulations for purchase of property abroad (memo)

<u>Internal memorandum</u>

From: Terry Baddison (Customer Services)
To: Guillermo Estuardos (Legal Department)

Date: 9 September 199-

Message: I urgently need some information on current rules and regulations
concerning the purchase and renting of property in Spain. We have
some clients interested in the new complex at Carboneras, but there
seems to be doubt over whether they can sublet part of the premises
without paying local tax on the rental. Can you check this out ASAP?

P.S. I'm in the office every afternoon this week.

Terry

38   Pidiendo información sobre adquisición inmobiliaria en el extranjero (comunicado interno)

Comunicado interno

De: Terry Baddison (Servicios para el cliente)

A: Guillermo Estuardos (Asesoría[1] Jurídica)

9 de setiembre de 199-

Necesito urgentemente información sobre reglamento[2] vigente acerca de la compra y alquiler de inmuebles en España. Algunos de nuestros clientes están interesados en la nueva urbanización[3] en Carboneras, pero parece que hay dudas sobre si pueden subarrendar una parte de la propiedad sin pagar impuestos municipales en el alquiler. ¿Puedes comprobarlo cuanto antes?

P.D.[4] Esta semana estoy en la oficina todas las tardes.

Terry

1   More specifically: 'Consultancy'.
2   The omission of the article (*el*) prior to the key word (*reglamento*) would be normal in a brief communication.
3   The *urbanización*, a new housing estate for tourist or permanent accommodation, has been a typical feature of post-1950s economic development in Spain; alternatively, *complejo* for a smaller, more recent or more tourist-based location.
4   *Post data*: 'P.S.'

39 Advising of delay in delivery (telex)

TELEX:	Expofrut (Almería, Spain) to Henshaw Bros. (Wolverhampton, England)
Subject:	Delay in delivery
Sender:	Pablo López
Addressee:	Mary Henshaw
Date:	14 December 199-

Message: APOLOGIES FOR FAILING TO DELIVER USUAL ORDER THIS WEEK.

DOCKS STRIKE CALLED FROM TODAY THROUGHOUT SPAIN.

YOUR CONSIGNMENT OF FRUIT AND VEGETABLES ON QUAYSIDE. STILL POSSIBLE TO SEND GOODS BY ROAD, BUT COULD NOT GUARANTEE DELIVERY BY WEEKEND.

INFORM BY TELEPHONE (00 3451 947583) THIS P.M. IF TO PROCEED WITH ORDER BY ROAD.

REGARDS

Pablo López
(Export Manager)

39   Notificando el retraso de una entrega (télex)

TELEX

Para: Henshaw Bros (Wolverhampton, Inglaterra)
De :   Expofrut (Almería, España)

Asunto: Retraso de entrega

Remitente: Pablo López

Destinataria: Mary Henshaw

14 de diciembre, 199-

Mensaje[1]

Disculpen no entregar, como de costumbre, pedido esta semana. Retraso debido

a huelga portuaria convocada hoy por toda España.

Su consignación de frutas y verduras en el muelle. Posibilidad de enviar

mercancías por carretera, pero no garantizar entrega para fin de semana.

Notifiquen por teléfono (00 3451 947583) esta tarde si quiere pedido por

carretera.

Saludos.

Firma,[2]

Pablo López
(Director de Exportación)

---

1   As a telex, the message is expressed in elliptical terms: omitting articles and some
    verbs, in particular. The main verbs relating to the sender's actions are expressed in the
    infinitive (*entregar, enviar, garantizar*); those relating to the addressee's, in the
    command/imperative form (*Disculpen, Notifiquen*).
2   Literally, 'he signs'.

40 Seeking clarification of financial position (fax)

To: Accounts Section, MULTIBANK,
         Prince's Square, Crewe

From: John Turket, PERLOANS
         High Street, Tamworth

Date: 4 November 199-
No. of pages, including this: 1

Dear Sir

This company has been approached today by a Mr Alan Thomas, who wishes to secure a loan in order to finance a family visit to relatives living overseas. Mr Thomas has given his approval to my contacting your branch of Multibank, where he holds two accounts, in order to verify and clarify information he has already proffered about his financial position.

Once you have satisfied yourselves that Mr Thomas is willing that you divulge facts about his finances, could you please provide the following information?

1 Has Mr Thomas incurred major overdrafts since 1990?

2 Do both Mr Thomas and his wife have salary cheques paid directly each month into their current account?

3 Does your bank believe that Mr Thomas will be able to repay a £3,000 loan to Perloans over 3 years from July 199-?

We hope you are in a position to respond to our request, and thank you for your assistance in this matter.

Yours faithfully

John Turket
Loans Manager

40   Solicitando aclaración sobre situación financiera (fax)

FAX

A: Multibank, Sección de Contaduría,
          Plaza del Príncipe,
          Madrid, España.

De: John Turket, Perloans,
          High Street, Tamworth, Inglaterra.

Fecha: 4 de noviembre, 199-
No. de páginas, incluida ésta: 1

Muy Sr mío:

El Sr Alan Thomas se ha puesto en contacto con esta compañía con objeto de conseguir un préstamo[1] para financiar una visita a familiares que viven en la América Latina. El Sr Thomas está de acuerdo con que yo me ponga en contacto con su sucursal de Multibank, en la cual tiene abiertas dos cuentas, y así verificar y aclarar la información ya ofrecida por él acerca de su situación financiera.

Una vez convencidos ustedes[2] de que el Sr Thomas está dispuesto a que ustedes revelen su situación financiera, ¿podrían facilitar la siguiente información a esta casa?[3]

1   ¿Ha contraído el Sr Thomas algún saldo deudor importante desde 199-?
2   ¿A los Sres Thomas les domicilian[4] mensualmente sus salarios respectivos en su cuenta corriente?
3   ¿Piensa su banco que el Sr Thomas puede llegar a pagar a Perloans un préstamo de 3.000 libras esterlinas, por un período de tres años, a partir de julio de 199-?

Esperamos que usted se encuentre en posición de dar contestación a nuestra petición, y le agradecemos su colaboración en este asunto.

Le saluda atentamente,

John Turket
(Gerente de Préstamos)

1   Alternatives: *crédito, empréstito*.
2   Note change to plural (*ustedes*) and subsequent reversion to singular (*usted*).
3   *Casa*: 'company', 'business', 'branch'.
4   *Domiciliar*: 'to pay direct into an account', 'to lodge'. The subject of the verb here is unstated third person plural 'they', implying the Thomas's employers.

41 Reporting to client on availability of particular property (fax)

To: Lilian Topcopy
         Trendset Printers
From: Dorothy Russell
         Smith & Jones

Date: 6 September 199-

No. of pages, including this: 1

Re: Office for lease

Dear Lilian

I am faxing you urgently to let you know that office premises have just become available in the area of town you told me that you liked. The lease on a street-front shop with upstairs office has been cancelled early by another client, who is moving south. If you would like to see the property, please get back to us this afternoon and we will arrange a visit.

Best wishes

Dorothy Russell

41   Informando a un cliente sobre disponibilidad de una determinada propiedad (fax)

FAX

A: Liliana Copias
        Imprenta Progre

De: Dorothy Russell
        Smith & Jones

6/9/9-

N°. de páginas, incluida ésta: 1

Asunto: Arriendo de oficina

Estimada Liliana:

Te envío este fax urgente para que sepas[1] que acaban de quedar libres locales[2] de oficinas en la zona que me dijiste te gustaba. El alquiler de una tienda que da a la calle,[3] y con oficina en la parte de arriba, ha sido cancelado antes de tiempo por otro cliente, quien se traslada al Sur. Si quieres ver el local, llámanos esta tarde para concertar[4] una visita.

Saludos,

Dorothy Russell

1 Subjunctive after *para que* . . . .
2 *Locales*: 'premises'. The singular (*local*) is also frequent.
3 Literally, 'it gives to the street'.
4 Alternatives: *arreglar, acordar*.

42   Complaining about customs delay (fax)

To: HM Customs and Excise
                 London

From: Ordenasa, Madrid

Date: 21/2/9-
No. of pages: 1

Dear Sirs

On behalf of my director colleagues of this computer software business I wish to lodge a complaint about customs clearance at British airports.

On several occasions since October 199- materials freighted from Madrid to retailers in Great Britain have been subject to unexplained and unjustifiable delays. This company depends for success on its ability to respond quickly to market demand; furthermore, at all times the requisite export licences have been in order.

This communication by fax is prompted by the latest and most frustrating hold-up, at Gatwick Airport yesterday, which has allowed a market competitor to secure a valuable contract ahead of us.

If the Single Market is to function effectively, this is precisely the type of situation that must be avoided. I intend to contact the relevant Chamber of Commerce about this matter, but in the meantime I insist on an explanation from your officers as to why consignment AT/463 was not permitted immediate entry on 20 February 199-.

Yours faithfully

Dr. Norberto Mateos
(Managing Director)

42   Quejándose por el retraso en la Aduana (fax)

FAX

A:	HM Customs and Excise
	Londres
De:	Ordenasa, Madrid
Fecha:	21/2/9-
Nº. de páginas:	1

Distinguidos Sres:

En nombre de mis colegas, los directivos de esta empresa de software para ordenadores, deseo presentar queja[1] sobre el despacho de aduanas en los aeropuertos británicos.

En varias ocasiones, desde octubre de 199-, los materiales cargados en Madrid para los minoristas británicos han sido objeto de retrasos inexplicables e injustificados. El éxito de esta empresa depende de la rápida capacidad de respuesta a la demanda del mercado; además, los permisos indispensables para la exportación han estado, en todo momento, en regla.

Este fax es debido a la más reciente e inconcebible[2] retención, la de ayer en el aeropuerto de Gatwick, que tuvo como resultado que un competidor nuestro consiguiera un importante contrato antes que nosotros.

Si el Mercado Unico ha de[3] funcionar con eficacia, esta es precisamente la situación que debe evitarse. En lo que respecta a este asunto, pienso ponerme en contacto con la Cámara de Comercio pertinente, pero entretanto agradecería una explicación de parte de sus agentes de policía, en la que notificaran[4] por qué no le dieron entrada inmediata a la consignación AT/463 , el 20 de febrero 199-.

Les saluda atentamente,

Dr Norberto Mateos
(Director)

---

1   Indefinite article (*una*) omitted.
2   'Frustrating' (see English letter) because inconceivable.
3   An alternative for future tense, with a hint of obligation.
4   Imperfect subjunctive: 'in which they notified (me) . . .'.

43 Stating delivery conditions

1 August 199-

Your Reference: AD/LR
Our Reference: TH/PA

Sr José Escalante
Managing Director
Escalante e hijos
Avenida del Sol
San Sebastián
SPAIN

Dear Mr Escalante

Thank you for your fax communication of yesterday regarding the delivery of the chickens and other poultry ordered by you from this company in early July. As we indicated in our original quote to Mr Salas, who first contacted us, the delivery can only be guaranteed if your bank is able to confirm that debts owed to us will be cleared this week.

Please note that our drivers would much appreciate assistance with overnight accommodation and that any costs they incur should be charged directly to Langley Farm once we have completed delivery next week.

We look forward to hearing from you on both matters.

Yours sincerely

Tom Holbrook
Transport Manager

43   Confirmando condiciones de entrega

Su Referencia: JE/LR
Nuestra Referencia: TH/PA

Sr José Escalante
Director Gerente
Escalante e hijos
Avenida del Sol
San Sebastián
España.   1.8.199-

Distinguido Sr Escalante:

Le agradecemos su comunicación por fax recibida ayer respecto al suministro de pollos y otras aves, pedido que usted hizo a esta empresa a principios de julio. Según le indicamos al Sr Salas en nuestro presupuesto original, cuando contactó con nosotros por primera vez, la entrega sólo puede ser garantizada si su banco nos confirma que las deudas a nuestro favor quedan[1] liquidadas esta semana.

Sírvase tomar nota de que[2] nuestros conductores[3] le agradecerían les prestara ayuda con el alojamiento de noche, y que cualquier gasto correrá a cargo de[4] Langley Farm una vez hayamos terminado la entrega la semana próxima.

Confiando en que pueda contestar a estos dos asuntos, le saluda atentamente.

T. Holbrook
(Jefe de Transportes)

1   *Quedar* can replace the verbs *ser* and *estar* in specific contexts (e.g. with past participles or other adjectives).
2   When verbs incorporating the word *de* (e.g. *acordarse de*) are followed by a subordinate clause, the *de* is retained and it precedes *que*, as in this case.
3   In Latin America the term *camioneros* is at least as commonly used.
4   *Correr a cargo de*: literally, 'to run to the charge of' ('to be the responsibility of').

44 Confirming time/place of delivery

12 June 199-

Your Reference: RCG/LP
Our Reference: FG/JD

Dr Rosa Castro Giménez
Subdirectora
Departamento de Relaciones Exteriores
Ministerio de Industria
Quito
ECUADOR

Dear Madam

Further to our communication of 9 May in which we outlined to your department the likely oil needs of the companies we represent, it is with some concern that we have heard indirectly that your Ministry may be unable to fulfil its immediate responsibilities. We would be most obliged to hear, at your earliest convenience, that the draft agreement signed recently by our representatives remains valid.

In spite of our concern we are fully committed to the trading relations discussed and as such wish to confirm details of first delivery of manufactured goods being exchanged for the above-mentioned oil imports. Carlton Excavators plc have confirmed this week that the consignment of earthmovers and tractors bound for Constructores Velasco was loaded on Monday of this week. It should reach the port of Guayaquil by the end of the month. We will, of course, provide you with more precise details nearer the time.

Meanwhile, please accept our best wishes for the continuation of our collaborative venture as we await your confirmation regarding the deliveries of your oil to the New South Wales terminal.

Yours faithfully

Frank Gardner
SENIOR PARTNER

44   Confirmando hora y lugar de entrega

Su Referencia: RCG/LP
Nuestra Referencia: FG/JD

Dra Rosa Castro Giménez
Subdirectora
Departamento de Relaciones Exteriores
Ministerio de Industria
Quito
Ecuador.   12.6.199-

Distinguida Sra:

Hacemos referencia a nuestra comunicación del 9 de mayo, en la que explicábamos a su Departamento las posibles necesidades de crudo que tienen las compañías que representamos. Nos preocupa el haber oído indirectamente que tal vez su Ministerio no pueda cumplir sus responsabilidades más inmediatas. Les quedaríamos muy agradecidos nos comunicaran, cuanto antes, si el acuerdo de proyecto[1] firmado recientemente por nuestros representantes es todavía válido.

A pesar de nuestra preocupación estamos enteramente comprometidos a las relaciones comerciales acordadas, y de ahí que les confirmamos datos sobre la primera entrega de mercancías manufacturadas a cambio de las importaciones de crudo a las que hemos hecho referencia antes. Excavadoras Carlton S.A. ha confirmado esta semana que la consignación de excavadoras y tractores dirigida a Constructores Velasco se cargó el lunes de la presente semana. Se espera que llegue al puerto de Guayaquil para finales de mes; huelga decir que[2] les pasaremos información detallada más cerca de la fecha.

Entretanto, confiando en que sabrán[3] aceptar la continua y mutua participación en esta colaboración, esperamos nos confirme la entrega del crudo a la terminal de New South Wales.

Le saluda con toda consideración.[4]

Frank Gardner
(Socio Mayoritario)

1 Alternatives: *de borrador*, (*acuerdo*) *preliminar*.
2 Idiomatic expression: 'it goes without saying that . . . .
3 *Sabrán*: 'you will know how to' (adding formality).
4 Yet another variant of the final greeting.

45   Checking on mode of transportation

19 February 19-

Your ref. SM/MB
Our ref. TS/PU

Mr Sebastián Morán
Sales Manager
Hermanos García S.L.
Carretera Luis Viola, 24
CUENCA
Spain

Dear Mr Morán

Thank you for your letter sent on Tuesday last in which you refer to the kitchen equipment we ordered from García Brothers in December. As you know, our market has been rather depressed, although there are recent signs of improvement, and as a result we now need to receive the cupboard doors and worktops much more promptly than we had originally thought.

Can you please confirm that where necessary you would be able to deliver some items by road, or even by air if very urgent, rather than by the sea route you currently use?

We have checked that from Valencia it would be possible to airfreight at a reasonable price to East Midlands Airport on a Monday afternoon and a Thursday evening.

I would be grateful if you could send us a reply once you have been able to ascertain whether this proposal is viable.

Yours sincerely

Trevor Sharp
Warehouse Manager

45   Comprobando modo de transporte

Sr Sebastián Morán
Director de Ventas
Hermanos García S.L.
Carretera Luis Viola, 24
Cuenca
España.

Su ref. SM/MB
Nuestra ref. TS/PU   19.2.199-

Estimado Sr Morán:

Le agradezco su carta del pasado martes en la cual hace
referencia al mobiliario de cocina que pedimos de Hermanos García en
diciembre. Como saben, nuestro mercado ha estado en baja, aunque ya hay
señales[1] de mejoría, y por consiguiente necesitamos recibir las puertas de los
armarios y las encimeras mucho antes de lo que se ha solido pensar.[2]

¿Podría confirmar que si fuera[3] necesario nos entregarían alguna partida[4] por
carretera, o incluso por avión si fuera muy urgente, en vez de hacer uso de la ruta
marítima de costumbre?

Hemos comprobado que desde Valencia se podría hacer uso del transporte aéreo
al aeropuerto de la Región Central Este, el lunes por la tarde y el jueves por la
noche, a un precio razonable.

Le agradecería que, una vez haya averiguado si esta proposición es viable, nos
envíe notificación.

Sin otro particular, le saluda atentamente

                                                              Trevor Sharp
                                                          (Jefe de Almacén)

1 Alternative: *indicios*.
2 Meaning: 'much earlier than we have tended to think'. *Soler*: 'to be accustomed to'.
3 *Fuera*, imperfect subjunctive: 'if/when it were . . .'.
4 *Partida*: 'batch, consignment'.

46 Claiming for transportation damage

24 January 199-

Claims Department
Lifeguard Assurance plc
Safeside House
High Street
Bromsgove
Worcs.

Dear Sir/Madam

POLICY NO. AL 78/2139B

My letter concerns a claim I wish to make on behalf of this firm, Anchor Lighting. We have had a policy with your company for many years, and rarely have needed to call upon your services. This time, however, we have suffered a serious financial loss due to damage incurred during the transit of goods.

Last week a whole consignment of lamps and other fittings was lost when our delivery truck ran off the road and turned over. The retail value of the merchandise ruined was in the region of £7,000, a sum equivalent to an entire quarter's profit.

I would be most grateful if you could send at your earliest convenience a major claim form and some general information on your settlement procedures.

Our policy number is as follows: AL 78/2139B.

I look forward to hearing from you soon.

Yours sincerely

Brian Tomkinson
(Proprietor)

46 Reclamando daños de transporte

Departamento de Daños y Reclamos
Seguros Salvavidas S.A.
Plaza Oriente
Valencia
España.   24.1.199-

Asunto: Póliza no. AL 78/2139B

Señor/Señora:

       Por la presente hago referencia a una reclamación que deseo presentar en nombre de esta empresa, Balbica S.A. Estamos asegurados con ustedes desde hace muchos años, y en muy raras ocasiones hemos tenido que recurrir a ustedes. Ahora, sin embargo, hemos sufrido una gran pérdida financiera debido a daños incurridos en el transporte de mercancías.

La semana pasada una consignación completa de lámparas y otros accesorios fue totalmente destruida cuando nuestro camión de reparto se desbordó de la carretera y volcó. El valor al por menor[1] de las mercancías perdidas asciende a alrededor de 1.456.000 pesetas, suma equivalente a las ganancias totales de un trimestre.[2]

Le agradecería encarecidamente[3] nos enviara cuanto antes impreso de reclamación mayor, junto con información general sobre sus trámites[4] de pago.

El número de nuestra póliza es el siguiente: AL 78/2139B.

En espera de una pronta respuesta, le saluda atentamente

Bernardo Tomás
(Propietario)

1 Alternative: *al detalle*. (Wholesale: *al por mayor*).
2 Adjective: *trimestral*.
3 *Encarecer*: 'to beg' (formal).
4 Alternatives: *procedimiento, modo*.

47 Enquiring about customs clearance

5 November 199-

Your ref.
Our ref. TC/LJ

The Customs and Excise Branch
Foreign Ministry of Chile
SANTIAGO
Chile
South America

Dear Sirs

I have been advised to write to you directly by the Commercial Section of the Chilean Embassy in London. My company produces high-tech toys for the world market; at a recent trade fair in Barcelona several Chilean retailers expressed interest in importing our products, but were unable to provide information on customs formalities in your country. Similarly, the London Embassy has recommended that I consult your Branch to seek up-to-date information.

The situation is as follows: our products include computer games, remote-control toy cars, mini-sized televisions etc. It seems that goods made in the EC are subject to a customs process rather more restrictive than those from Japan or the USA. As my company is a wholly-owned subsidiary of a US parent firm, would it be easier and cheaper to export to Chile from the USA rather than from Britain?

My intention is not merely to circumvent regulations but to optimize our operations at a time when such matters as customs clearance can result in costly delays.

I thank you for your attention and look forward to an early reply.

Yours sincerely,

Thomas Carty
MANAGING DIRECTOR

47   Pidiendo información sobre mercancías pendientes de despacho en Aduana

Aduanas e Impuestos
Ministerio de Asuntos Exteriores
SANTIAGO
Chile.   5.11.199-

Nuestra ref. TC/LJ

Muy Sr mío:

El Departamento Comercial de la Embajada de Chile en Londres me ha aconsejado que me ponga directamente en contacto con usted.[1] Mi empresa se dedica a la fabricación de juguetes de alta tecnología para el mercado mundial; en una reciente feria comercial, que tuvo lugar en Barcelona, varios detallistas chilenos expresaron interés en importar nuestros productos, pero no pudieron informarnos acerca de las formalidades del despacho aduanero de su país. Asimismo, la Embajada en Londres me ha recomendado que consulte con su Sección, con objeto de ponerme al día.[2]

La situación es la siguiente: nuestros productos incluyen juegos para el ordenador, coches con mando a distancia, mini-televisores, etcétera. Parece ser que las mercancías fabricadas en la UE están sujetas a prácticas restrictivas aduaneras bastante más rígidas que las que se aplican al Japón y a los Estados Unidos. Debido a que mi empresa es una filial, propiedad por entero,[3] de una sociedad matriz,[4] norteamericana ¿resultaría más fácil y más barato exportar a Chile desde los Estados Unidos que desde Gran Bretaña?

Mi propósito no es sólo salvar[5] el reglamento sino más bien optimizar nuestras operaciones en un momento en el que tales asuntos como el despacho de mercancías pendientes en Aduana pueden convertirse en un retraso costoso.

Le agradezco su colaboración, y en espera de una pronta respuesta le saludo atentamente,

Thomas Carty
(Director Gerente)

1 Referring to the unnamed official who will handle the matter.
2 Literally, 'put myself to the day'. Alternative: *actualizar(me)*.
3 A standard expression in commercial parlance.
4 From *matriz* (womb); meaning also 'headquarters of a company'.
5 Alternatives: *evitar, sortear*.

48 Undertaking customs formalities

27 November 199–

Your ref.
Our ref. AR/AP

HM Customs and Excise
Government Offices
LONDON WC2

Dear Sir/Madam

I write to inform you of a business operation in which my company is to be involved for the first time and to request your advice in the case of any misapprehension on my part.

As sole director of Leatherlux I have recently been able to conclude a deal with a firm of suppliers in Tunisia. I imagine that as a non-EU nation Tunisia cannot trade with complete freedom from import/export levies. I wish therefore to inform you that I intend to import from Nabeul in the next fortnight the following articles:

    150 men's leather jackets
     50 pairs of ladies' leather trousers
    250 leather belts
    100 pairs of leather sandals
     50 pairs of men's leather boots

I anticipate paying approximately £3,000 for the consignment. Can you please provide me with official documentation (if required), or at least confirm, by fax if possible, that I shall be required to pay some form of duty on these imports?

I thank you in anticipation of your assistance.

Yours faithfully

Andrew Royston
Managing Director

48 Emprendiendo formalidades aduaneras

Sección de Aduanas
Ministerio de Asuntos Exteriores
Madrid.   27.11.199-

Nuestra ref. AR/AP

Distinguido/a Señor/Señora:

Le escribo con motivo de informarle sobre una operación comercial en la que mi empresa participará por vez primera,[1] y para que me asesoren[2] en caso de que esté equivocado.

Como director en exclusiva de Leatherlux, recientemente he concertado un trato con una empresa de abastecedores tunecinos. Supongo que, como Túnez no pertenece a la UE, no se le[3] permitirá comerciar sin estar sujeto a impuestos de importación y exportación. Por lo tanto, quisiera informarle que en la próxima quincena[4] tengo la intención de importar de Nabeul los artículos siguientes:

150 chaquetas de cuero[5] para caballero
50 pares de pantalones de cuero para señora
250 cinturones de cuero
100 pares de sandalias de cuero
50 pares de botas de cuero para caballero

Espero pagar aproximadamente 24.000 pesetas por la consignación. ¿Puede ser tan amable de[6] proporcionarme la documentación oficial (si ésta es necesaria) o por lo menos comunicarme por fax, si es posible, si tendré que pagar algún tipo de impuesto en estas importaciones?

Confiando en que pueda asistirme y agradeciéndole de antemano su información, le saluda muy atentamente,

Andrés Rodríguez
(Director Gerente)

1 A simple inversion: *por primera vez*.
2 Subjunctive after *para que*, expressing future intention.
3 The use of reflexive *se* and the indirect object pronoun (*le*) is typical of Spanish in rendering the passive ('will not be allowed to trade').
4 Literally, 'fifteen-day period'.
5 If it is soft leather (as in jackets/trousers), an equally appropriate word is *piel*.
6 'Please be so kind as to . . .'.

49 Informing of storage facilities

13 June 199-

Your ref. JG/TK
Our ref. JS/PI

Hurd's (International) Removals
34-36, Wesley Avenue
CROYDON
Surrey

Dear Mrs Gordon

I am pleased to inform you that the container of household goods your company contracted us to transport from Australia has now been delivered to our depot.

We will need by the end of this week to complete the official formalities, but you are welcome to pick up the unloaded contents for onward delivery to your customer from next Monday.

If you prefer to leave the goods here in store until further notice, please consult our price list (enclosed) which gives details of storage facilities and let us know your intention by fax.

As and when your driver does come to pick up the goods, he should enter the terminal by the side entrance which will lead him straight to the relevant loading area, marked DOMESTIC.

I trust these arrangements meet with your approval.

Yours sincerely

Jim Smith
Depot Manager

Enc.

49 Informando sobre facilidades de almacenamiento

Mudanzas Gómez
Zona Industrial Este
Alicante
España.   13.6.199-

Su ref. JG/TC
Nuestra ref. JS/PI

Estimada Sra Gómez:

Me complace informarle que el contenedor de artículos del hogar, para cuyo[1] transporte desde Australia nos contrató su compañía, ha sido entregado ahora en nuestro almacén aquí, en Barcelona.

Nos llevará[2] completar las formalidades oficiales hasta finales de semana, pero usted podrá pasar a recoger el contenido descargado, para que de esta forma pueda entregarlo a su cliente, a partir del lunes que viene.

Si prefiere dejar las mercancías aquí en almacén hasta previo aviso,[3] haga el favor de consultar la lista de precios (aquí incluida) que detalla las facilidades de almacenamiento, y sírvase comunicarme[4] por fax cuál es su intención.

Cuando su conductor venga a recoger las mercancías, debe de entrar en la terminal por la puerta lateral que le llevará directamente a la adecuada zona de carga señalada DOMÉSTICA.

En espera de que estas medidas[5] sean de su aprobación, le saluda cordialmente,

Juan Silvero
(Encargado de Almacén)

Anexo

1 *Cuyo*: 'whose' (i.e. the transportation).
2 *Llevar* in temporal expressions refers to length of time taken.
3 Literally, 'until prior warning'.
4 Note use of *me*: singular and plural freely interchanged in commercial correspondence.
5 'Measures'.

50 Assuring of confidentiality of information

1 November 199-

Your ref. EF/LJ
Our ref. HE/PI

Dr Ernesto Furillo
University Hospital
University of Managua
Managua
República de Nicaragua

Dear Dr Furillo

MISS ALICIA BARTOLOMÉ

Thank you for your letter of last month in which you sought confirmation that the reference you provided for Miss Alicia Bartolomé and her personal details would remain confidential.

It is the policy of the Government and of this Ministry to maintain total discretion when dealing with citizens from other countries who come to develop their professional studies. Miss Bartolomé's course begins in three weeks' time, by which time her curriculum vitae will have been duly stored on computer in this Ministry and will be accessible only to those with the due authorization.

As you will be well aware, the need for confidentiality in matters such as these is paramount, so you may rest assured that all proper measures will be taken to protect the interests of your institution and of its employees.

Yours sincerely

Hortensia Enríquez Castro
Personnel Supervisor

50   Asegurando confidencialidad en la información

Dr Ernesto Furillo
Hospital Universitario
Universidad de Managua
Managua
República de Nicaragua.   1.11.199-

Su ref. EF/LJ
Nuestra ref. HE/PI

Asunto: Srta Alicia Bartolomé

Distinguido Dr Furillo:

        Le agradezco su carta del mes pasado en la[1] que solicitaba que la referencia y la información personal que usted proporcionó de la señorita Alicia Bartolomé se mantuvieran[2] confidenciales.

Tanto la política estatal como[3] la de este Ministerio es guardar discreción total cuando trata con ciudadanos de países extranjeros quienes vienen a ampliar sus estudios profesionales. El curso de la Srta Bartolomé dará comienzo dentro de tres semanas, y para entonces su currículum vitae[4] habrá sido archivado en el ordenador de este Ministerio, al cual sólo tendrán acceso aquellas personas previamente[5] autorizadas.

Como usted bien sabe, es primordial mantener confidencialidad en asuntos de esta índole;[6] por lo tanto puede estar seguro que se tomarán todas las medidas adecuadas para proteger los intereses de su institución y del personal de la misma.

Me despido[7] con saludos cordiales.

Hortensia Enríquez Castro
(Supervisora de Personal)

1   The *la* is repeated in reference to *carta*.
2   Imperfect subjunctive after a past tense (*solicitaba*) in the main clause.
3   *Tanto . . . como*: 'both'.
4   Frequently abbreviated to *currículum*.
5   Literally, 'previously'.
6   This word can be used to mean 'type', 'kind', 'nature'.
7   Literally, 'I say goodbye'.

51   Informing a client on conditions of loans/mortgages available

14 July 199-

Your ref. GB/LK
Our ref. EF/VE

Mr G Bernard
Managing Director
MultiCast
Floor 11
Forum House
Dukeries Avenue
Mansfield

Dear Mr Bernard

Since receiving your letter of 23 June we have been making enquiries on the matter of financing that you raised; please accept our apologies, nevertheless, for the delay. You will find enclosed three leaflets containing information about properties you may find interesting. We shall await your reaction to them.

More pressing, perhaps, is the question of finance. Having consulted local banks as well as our own finance broker, we have concluded that you would do best to arrange a meeting with the latter, Gilbert Cross, who will be pleased to outline for you in general terms a variety of mortgage as well as short-term loan plans.

All four major banks in town offer facilities for loans, so you may prefer to try them before or after meeting Mr Cross. However, it certainly appears that our broker can secure more favourable conditions if you are interested principally in a short-term loan.

Please contact our broker, whose address is below, about the kind of information you require:

Element Financial Services, Star Chambers, High Street, Worksop, Nottinghamshire.

Yours sincerely

Edward Fenton
Customer Liaison

Encs

51   Informando a un cliente sobre condiciones de préstamo/créditos hipotecarios

Sr G. Bernal
Director Gerente, Multivisión
Planta 11, Edificio Gil
Carrera 7/61
Bogotá, COLOMBIA.   14.7.199-

Su ref: GB/LK
Nuestra ref: EF/JU

Estimado Sr Bernal:

Desde que recibimos su carta del pasado 23 de junio hemos estado pidiendo informes sobre el asunto financiero al que usted se refería; no obstante, le pedimos nos disculpe por el retraso.

Le adjuntamos tres folletos que contienen información sobre inmuebles que pueden interesarle. Son muy fáciles de entender dichos folletos, y esperamos su comentario sobre los mismos.

Quizás[1] sea más urgente el asunto financiero. Habiendo consultado con los bancos locales, así como con nuestro agente financiero, llegamos a la conclusión de que sería mejor organizar una reunión con el Sr Gilberto Cruz, el cual[2] le explicará gustoso,[3] y en términos generales, la variedad de créditos hipotecarios, así como los planes de préstamo a corto plazo.

Los cuatro bancos principales de esta ciudad conceden facilidades de préstamo; por lo tanto quizá[1] usted prefiera consultar con ellos antes o después de la reunión con el Sr Cruz. No obstante, es casi seguro que nuestro agente financiero pueda conseguirle condiciones más favorables si usted está interesado principalmente en un préstamo a corto plazo.

Sírvase solicitar a nuestro agente, a la dirección abajo indicada, cualquier tipo de información que desee;

Asesoramiento[4] Financiero Cruz, Calle Medina 27, Lima, Perú.

Suyo atentamente

Eduardo Fuentes
(Servicio Clientes)

Anexos

1 Subjunctive form follows both variants of the word (*quizá*/*ás*).
2 Alternatives: *quien* or *que*; *el cual* is more specific.
3 Adjective replacing adverb (*gustosamente*).
4 'Advice', 'consultancy'.

52 Circulating local businesses with property services available

10 March 199-

Our ref. CE/MB

To: Directors of all businesses in the Castilla-León region

Dear Colleague

I take the opportunity to write to you on behalf of myself and my partner, Ana Martiarena, in order to publicize as widely as possible the property services we can make available to businesses in the region.

Since establishing our company here in 1976 we have gradually expanded our range of activities and clients. Most recently we have opened a free advice centre in Puentenorte for any member of the public to obtain up-to-date information on the property market.

As regards the needs of business, we offer the following services:

- a weekly guide to premises for rent and sale
- a direct link to sources of finance
- rent-collection service
- legal and insurance consultancy
- assistance in securing mortgages
- technical support in planning space and furbishment
- computer database linked to the national property network

These and many more services are available from us, and all are on your doorstep. Don't hesitate – call us today on 234 56 71 or come in person to 69 Calle Balbita, Puentenorte, where you can be sure of a warm welcome.

Yours sincerely

Carlos Estévez

52 Difundiendo información a empresas locales sobre servicios inmobiliarios

A: Los Sres Directores
    de todas las empresas
    de La Comunidad Autónoma de
    Castilla-León.   10.3.199-

Nuestra ref. CE/MB

Estimado colega:

En mi nombre, y en el de mi colega Ana Martiarena, le escribo para dar la máxima publicidad posible a los servicios inmobiliarios que tenemos disponibles a las pequeñas[1] empresas de esta Autonomía.

Desde que se estableció aquí nuestra compañía en 1976, hemos ido ampliando progresivamente nuestra gama de servicios y clientela; hace poco hemos inaugurado un consultorio gratuito en Puentenorte, cuyo objeto es poner al día al público en general sobre asuntos relacionados con el mercado inmobiliario.

Teniendo en cuenta[2] las necesidades de las empresas, ofrecemos los siguientes servicios:

- guía semanal de locales en alquiler y en venta
- contacto directo con fuentes financieras
- servicio de recaudación de renta
- asesoramiento legal y de seguros
- ayuda hipotecaria
- ayuda técnica en la planificación y renovación del espacio
- base de datos conectada a una red inmobiliaria nacional

Disponemos de esta y mucha más información, toda ella al alcance de su domicilio.[3] No lo dude,[4] llámenos[5] hoy al 234 56 71, o venga personalmente a la Calle Balbita 69, Puentenorte, donde le aseguramos una cordial bienvenida.

Le saluda muy atentamente,

Carlos Estévez (Socio Superior)

1 Small and medium-sized businesses in Spain often are referred to collectively as PYMES: *Pequeñas y Medianas Empresas*.
2 *Tener en cuenta*: 'to take into account'.
3 'Your home'.
4 Literally, 'don't doubt it'.
5 Polite command to one person: 'call us'.

53 Advertising maintenance services available for office equipment

30 January 199-

Your ref.
Our ref. TC/JI

To: Office Managers:
     Motor Sales businesses
     in South London area

Dear Colleague

You may be aware from press advertising that the above firm offers a new service to the motor trade, particularly to maintain equipment used in processing stores supplies. Most large dealerships with service and accessories departments have installed a fully-integrated system that reduces drastically the need for large numbers of warehousemen.

The service charge is £350 per quarter, irrespective of visits made or problems solved; this figure also includes a component of insurance that covers both the dealership and ourselves against major breakdowns.

In recent months we have signed such service contracts with more than 40 dealerships whose names we are happy to supply if you are interested in checking our claims.

Thank you for your attention. Please do not hesitate to ring or fax us this week if the enclosed leaflet information is relevant to your needs.

Yours sincerely

Tom Cardinal
Managing Director

Enc.

53   Anunciando servicios de mantenimiento para equipos de oficina

Para: los directores administrativos de pequeñas empresas de venta de automóviles en el área del oeste de Barcelona.

Nuestra ref. TC/JI   30.1.199-

Estimado colega:

Tal vez[1] haya visto en los anuncios de la prensa que la empresa que figura en el membrete de esta carta ofrece un nuevo servicio a la industria del automóvil, especialmente con miras[2] a conservar en buen estado la maquinaria y el equipo utilizados[3] en el procesamiento de suministros de almacén.

La mayoría de las grandes concesiones[4] que disponen de departamento de servicio y de accesorios han[5] instalado un sistema completamente integrado que reduce drásticamente la necesidad de un gran número de almaceneros.

El coste del servicio es de 72.800 pesetas trimestrales,[6] sean cuantas sean[7] las visitas efectuadas o los problemas que se resuelvan; esta cantidad incluye asimismo un seguro que cubre tanto al concesionario[8] como a nosotros contra fallos importantes.

De pocos meses acá[9] hemos firmado tales contratos de servicio con más de cuarenta concesiones, cuyos nombres le facilitaremos gustosos si usted estuviera[10] interesado en comprobar nuestras declaraciones.

Le quedamos muy agradecidos por su atención y le rogamos no dude en telefonearnos o enviarnos un fax esta semana si la información especificada en el folleto adjunto está relacionada con sus necesidades.
Le saluda cordialmente

Tomás Cardenal
(Director Gerente)

Anexo

1 'Perhaps' (followed by subjunctive).
2 'With a view' (to).
3 Masculine plural adjective for feminine and masculine nouns.
4 *Concesiones*: 'franchized businesses', 'dealerships'.
5 Plural verb (*han instalado*) for (collective) singular subject.
6 'Quarterly' (adjective).
7 *Sean . . . sean*: subjunctive, 'be they . . . they might be'. The notion recurs in '*problemas . . . resuelvan*', otherwise expressed.
8 Refers to the dealer (*concesionario*) who runs the franchise.
9 Literally, 'from few months (to) here', i.e. in recent months.
10 Imperfect subjunctive: 'if you were (interested)'.

54 Arranging a meeting for further discussions

5 November 199-

Our ref: TSS/EHK

Mr Angelo Ricasso
Cuscinetti SpA
Via Alessandro Manzoni, 32
20050 Triuggio (MI)
Italy

Dear Mr Ricasso

RE: THRUST BEARINGS

In 1989 we had discussions with you regarding the addition of our thrust bearings to the Dudley range for sale in your country.

We regret that due to many changes which have occurred in this company and in our parent company no progress was made with our arrangements, and we understand that it must have been disappointing for you not to have heard from us for such a long time.

We are now willing to try again, if you have not made other arrangements, and we would like to arrange a meeting with you at the Hardware Fair in Cologne next March.

We look forward to hearing from you,

Yours sincerely

Thomas Stone
SALES DIRECTOR

54   Concertando una reunión para tratar de un tema con más detalle

Nuestra Ref: TSS/EHK

Sr Angel Ricote
Ricote y Bermúdez S.A.
Zona Industrial No.3
Cartagena
España.   5.11.199-

Asunto: Cojinetes de empuje

Estimado Sr Ricote:

En 1989 tratamos con[1] usted acerca de incluir cojinetes de empuje a la gama Dudley, con objeto de venderlos en su país.

Debido a los numerosos cambios acaecidos[2] en esta empresa y en nuestra casa matriz, lamentamos informarle que no hemos progresado en nuestros acuerdos, y somos conscientes de que le habrá defraudado que no haya tenido noticias nuestras desde hace[3] tanto tiempo.

Ahora estamos dispuestos a intentarlo de nuevo, si usted no tiene otro compromiso,[4] y nos gustaría concertar una entrevista con usted en la Feria de Muestras de la Ferretería que se celebra en Colonia el próximo marzo.

En espera de sus prontas noticias, le saluda atentamente

Thomas Stone
(Director de Ventas)

1   *Tratar con*: 'to deal with'.
2   From *acaecer* (formal): 'to happen'.
3   Literally, 'since ago', used with present tense.
4   The same word can be used to mean: 'commitment', 'obligation', 'arrangement', 'agreement'.

55 Reservations

Enquiry about hotel accommodation (fax)

23 April 199-

Hotel Lucullus
Amadeusplatz 27
Hannover
Germany

Dear Sirs

I am attending the trade fair in Hanover in May with two colleagues, and we require rooms for three nights. Please could you confirm availability and price of the following:

three single rooms with bath/shower from 3 to 6 May.

Yours faithfully

Fred Garner

55 Reservas

Pidiendo información sobre alojamiento en un hotel (fax)

Hotel Lucrecia
Calle Mayor, 23
León
España.   23.4.199-

Estimados Sres:

Asistiré, junto con[1] otros dos colegas, a la Feria Comercial que se celebra en León en mayo y necesitamos alojamiento[2] para tres noches. Le ruego me comuniquen si tienen vacantes[3] y precios de:

tres habitaciones[4] individuales con baño/ducha[5] para los días del 3 al 6 de mayo.

Sin otro particular, le saluda cordialmente

Fred Garner

1 *Junto con*: '(along) with'.
2 'Accommodation', 'lodging(s)'.
3 *Vacante (la)*: 'vacancy' in hotel or company.
4 In much of Latin America *pieza* is preferred (in Mexico, *recámara*).
5 In Latin America bathroom facilities are described as *servicios*.

56 Reservations

Confirmation of reservation (fax)

30 October 199-

Ms G Cole
Ledington Parker plc
Moreton Avenue
Birmingham
B37 9KH

Dear Ms Cole

ROOM RESERVATION 15–18 NOVEMBER

We are pleased to confirm that we are able to offer the following accommodation for 15–18 November:

Four single rooms with shower/WC @ £150 per night, inclusive of breakfast and service.

We should be grateful if you could confirm the booking in writing as soon as possible.

Yours sincerely

H Japer
Manager

56 Reservas

Confirmando una reserva (fax)

Srta G Cole
Ledington Parker plc
Moreton Avenue
Birmingham
B37 9KH
Reino Unido.   30.10.199-

Asunto: Reserva[1] de habitaciones, 15–18 de noviembre

Estimada Srta Cole:

Nos complace confirmarle reserva de habitaciones del 15 al 18 de noviembre, y que[2] estamos gustosos de ofrecerle:

cuatro habitaciones individuales con ducha/WC al precio de 30,000 pesetas por noche, incluidos desayuno y servicio.

Le agradeceríamos confirmara por escrito,[3] y tan pronto le fuere[4] posible, dicha reserva.

Le saluda atentamente

E. Jabones (Sra)
Gerente

1   In Latin America, more frequently *reservación*.
2   The *que* follows from *Nos complace confirmarle*.
3   'In writing'.
4   A future subjunctive, rarely used except in documents or formal correspondence.

57   Reservations

Change of arrival date

11 March 199-

Ms J Hinton
Hotel Bonner
46 Southampton Way
London
SE39 8UH
England

Dear Madam

We have today received your confirmation of our booking of three single rooms from 18 to 23 March.

Unfortunately, we have had to change our plans, and shall not now arrive in London until the morning of 20 March. We would be grateful if you could change the reservation accordingly.

Yours faithfully

Henry Sands

57 Reservas

Cambio de la llegada al hotel

Srta J Hinton
Hotel Bonner
46 Southampton Way
London
SE39 8UH
Inglaterra.   11.3.199-

Estimada Srta:

Obra en nuestro poder[1] la confirmación de la reserva de tres habitaciones individuales para la fechas 18 a 23 de marzo.

Por desgracia, hemos tenido que cambiar de planes, y ahora no llegaremos a Londres hasta el 20 de marzo por la mañana. Le agradeceríamos cambiara dicha reserva tal y como sea posible.[2]

Sin otro particular, le saluda atentamente

Enrique Saenz

1 The use of this expression precludes reference to today as the time of receipt.
2 More literally, 'however it may be possible'; *tal* (*y*) *como* can be used with or without the link word.

58 Reservations

Request for confirmation of reservation

14 July 199-

Ms J Petersen
45 Dorrington Terrace
Bradford
Yorkshire
England

Dear Ms Petersen

You made a telephone reservation one week ago for a single room for two nights (20–22 July). We indicated to you when you made the reservation that we would hold it for one week, but that we required written confirmation.

If you still wish to reserve the room, could you please confirm by fax within 24 hours, or we shall have to reserve the room for other clients.

Thank you for your cooperation.

Yours sincerely

Victoria Palmer

58 Reservas

Pidiendo información sobre confirmación de una reserva

Srta J Petersen,
45 Dorrington Terrace
Bradford
Yorkshire
Inglaterra.

14.7.199-

Estimada Srta Petersen:

Hace una semana nos hizo una reserva, por teléfono, de una habitación individual para dos noches (20–22 de julio). Cuando habló con nosotros le dijimos que dicha reserva le quedaba hecha[1] para una semana, y que necesitábamos confirmación de la misma[2] por escrito.

Si todavía desea que dicha reserva sea en firme,[3] sírvase confirmárnoslo[4] por fax antes de veinticuatro horas, ya que de no ser así,[5] la reserva pasaría[6] a otro cliente.

Gracias por su cooperación y reciba un atento saludo

Victoria Palomar
(Secretaria)

1 Literally, 'remained made for you'.
2 The reservation.
3 *En firme*: 'firm(ly)'.
4 The *lo* refers to the client's desire to have a firm reservation.
5 *De no ser así*: 'if it is not the case'.
6 Conditional tense where future seems more logical.

59 Insurance

Request for quotation for fleet car insurance

1 July 199-

Hartson Insurance Services
24 Westbury Way
Sheffield
S12 9JF

Dear Sirs

We understand from colleagues that you specialize in insurance for company fleet cars. We have a large fleet of executive saloons, and are currently obtaining quotations for insurance cover.

If you are interested in giving us a quotation, could you please contact Ms Helen Bridges, our fleet manager, who will give you the appropriate details.

Yours faithfully

D J Spratt

59 Seguro

Solicitando presupuesto para asegurar flota de vehículos

Seguros López y Garrido
Calle de la Estación, 3–6
Pamplona
España.   1.7.199-

Muy señores nuestros:

Tenemos entendido, según colegas nuestros, que ustedes se especializan en los seguros de flotas de coches de empresa. La nuestra es una flota importante de turismos[1] para directivos y estamos solicitando actualmente presupuestos para asegurar dichos vehículos.

Si están interesados en ofrecernos su presupuesto, sírvase[2] ponerse en contacto con la señorita Elena Basuabla, encargada de nuestros vehículos, la cual le proveerá la información necesaria.

Les saluda atentamente

Diego Sebastián

1 'Saloon' is best rendered in Spanish as *turismo*, but it also implies a private car.
2 Note use of singular verb, immediately after plural in *están*.

60 Insurance

Reminder of overdue premium

2 June 199-

Mr R Collins
45 Delta Road
Stoke-on-Trent

Dear Mr Collins

Your vehicle, registration no. H351 AWL, is currently insured by us. We sent you several days ago a reminder that the insurance renewal premium was due. We have still not received this from you. We have to write to inform you that unless we receive payment within 72 hours, the insurance cover will lapse. Please send payment directly to our office in Gower Street, London.

Yours sincerely

Reginald Lawton
Customer Services

60 Seguro

Aviso de vencimiento de prima

Sr R. Collar
Comunicaciones A1
Calle 2 de Agosto, 65
San Sebastián
España.   2.6.199-

Estimado Sr Collar:

Hacemos referencia a su vehículo, matrícula N°. H351 AWL, que tiene asegurado con nosotros. Hace varios días le enviamos aviso de renovación de prima[1], pero todavía no hemos recibido pago de la misma. Nos ponemos en contacto con usted para informarle que, de no recibir dicho pago[2] en un período de, a más tardar, setenta y dos horas, daremos por anulado[3] el seguro de cobertura.[4] Sírvase enviar pago directamente a nuestras oficinas de la Calle Gower, en Londres.

Le saluda atentamente

Reginald Lawton
(Servicios al cliente)

1 Alternatively, *notificación de renovación de prima.*
2 Payment of the new premium.
3 *Dar por anulado*: 'to take as cancelled'.
4 'Cover(age)' of all kinds.

61 Insurance

Submission of documents to support claim

4 April 199-

Darton Insurance Services
59 Tristan Road
Uttoxeter
Staffordshire

Dear Sirs

I submitted to you several days ago a claim form under the terms of my motor vehicle insurance (policy number CDF 9486756 UY 94766). Your head office has since requested from me the original policy document. I regret that this is no longer in my possession, and I enclose herewith a photocopy. I trust that this will meet your requirements.

Yours faithfully

A Lightowlers

Enc.

61   Seguro

Presentando documentos para apoyar una reclamación

Asprilla y Rincón Cía. de Seguros
Edificio Monumental
Plaza de los Reyes
Madrid.   4 de abril, 199-

Muy señores míos:

Hace varlos días les presenté un impreso de reclamación según las condiciones de seguro de mi vehículo (póliza Nº CDF 9486756 UY 94766). Ahora la oficina central de su empresa me ha pedido el documento original de dicha póliza. Lamento informarles que éste ya no obra en mi poder, y por lo tanto les adjunto una fotocopia del mismo,[1] que espero sea admisible.[2]

Atentamente les saluda

                                                          Alejandro Latilla

Anexo

1   Referring to the policy document.
2   Also acceptable: *adecuado*.

62 Insurance

Taking out third party vehicle insurance

11 October 199-

Uxbridge Insurance
Grosvenor House
12b Weston Terrace
Bournemouth
Hants

Dear Sirs

RE: QUOTATION RC28FO

With reference to the above quotation, I confirm that I wish to take out Third Party car insurance, and enclose the appropriate fee in the form of a cheque.

I should be grateful if you could send me confirmation and the policy certificate as soon as possible.

Yours faithfully

Julie Vincent

62   Seguro

Seguro de vehículo a terceros

Uxbridge Insurance
Grosvenor House
12b Weston Terrace
Bournemouth
Hants.
Inglaterra.   el once de octubre de 199-

Asunto: Presupuesto Nº RC28FO

Estimados señores:

De acuerdo con[1] el presupuesto recibido, les comunico que desearía asegurar mi vehículo a terceros,[2] por lo que adjunto, a tales efectos,[3] cheque por valor de la cantidad presupuestada.

Les agradecería me notificaran recibo[4] de dicho cheque y me enviasen asimismo la póliza lo antes posible.

Sin otro particular, les saluda atentamente

Julia Venegas

Anexo

1   Literally, 'in accordance with'.
2   Fully comprehensive (as opposed to third party, *a terceros*) would be: *contra todo riesgo*.
3   Formal: 'for this purpose'.
4   'Receipt': in this case not the document, but the act of receiving.

63 Insurance

Refusal to meet claim

9 April 199-

Ms D Leach
29 Janison Avenue
York

Dear Ms Leach

RE: CLAIM NO. JH 8576/HY

We acknowledge receipt of your claim form (reference JH 8576/HY) concerning water damage to your stock on the night of 27 March. We regret, however, that we are unable to meet the claim, as our policy (section 3, paragraph 5) specifically excludes this form of damage, particularly since the premises were unoccupied for a period of two weeks before the damage occurred.

Yours sincerely

Peter Ardley

63   Seguro

Negándose a saldar un reclamo

Srta L. Vicario
Prendas Sporty
Centro Comercial El Yate
Gerona
España.   9.4.199-

Asunto: Reclamación JH 8576/HY

Estimada señorita Vicario:

Acusamos recibo de su reclamación (referencia JH 8576/HY) concerniente a los daños que el agua ocasionó a sus existencias en la noche del pasado[1] 27 de marzo. Sentimos informarle que no podemos abonarle[2] el pago de dicha reclamación, ya que la sección 3, apartado 5, de dicha póliza excluye este tipo de daño, debido especialmente a que los locales estuvieran[3] vacíos durante dos semanas antes de haber ocurrido los daños.

Le saluda muy atentamente

Pedro Ardiles

1   When referring to dates in the recent past this (redundant) term is frequently included in correspondence.
2   *Abonar*: 'to credit', 'pay out'.
3   Also *estuvieron* (indicative past tense); the use of imperfect subjunctive can be determined by the preceding *debido a que*.

64 Considering legal action

24 May 199-

Cabinet Rossignol
4 rue des Glaïeuls
75009 Paris
France

For the attention of Maître Patelin

Dear Maître Patelin

Your name was given to us by Robert Mackenzie of Canine Crunch Ltd for whom you acted last year.

We have a complaint against the newspaper *La Gazette du Samedi* who have, in our opinion, seriously defamed us in the enclosed article dealing with the closure of our plant at Roissy-en-France.

We would wish to take legal action against the said journal but before taking this step would like to have your professional advice on the strength of our case. Could you also, at the same time, let us know how long such a case might run and the likely scale of our legal costs.

Yours sincerely

Lionel E Bone
Managing Director

Enc.

64 Asesoramiento legal: daños

Cabinet Rossignol
4 rue des Glaïeuls
75009 París
Francia.

24 de mayo de 199-

Para la atención del Maître Patelin

Estimado Señor Patelin:

Su nombre nos fue proporcionado[1] por el señor Rodrigo Mendoza de Hermanos Ibarra, a quien usted representó el año pasado.

Deseamos presentar una queja[2] contra el diario *La Gazette du Samedi*, que en nuestra opinión nos ha calumniado gravemente en el artículo que le adjunto, y que se trata del cierre de nuestra fábrica de Roissy-en-France.

Quisiéramos entablar demanda[3] contra el mencionado diario, pero antes de proceder a ello[4] nos gustaría nos proporcionara asesoramiento jurídico sobre el peso de nuestro caso. Asimismo, le agradeceríamos nos notificara la posible duración del mismo[5] y a lo que pueden subir los honorarios jurídicos.

Le saluda muy atentamente

Leonardo Duarte
Director Gerente

Anexo

1 *Proporcionar*: 'to provide', 'supply'. (See also below *nos gustaría nos proporcionara*: 'we would like that you should provide').
2 The standard expression for lodging of complaints.
3 Alternatives: *demandar a, llevar a juicio.*
4 *Ello*: i.e., the bringing of the lawsuit.
5 'The case in question'.

65   Requesting information on setting up a plant abroad

23 May 199-

Office Notarial
84 rue du Grand Pineau
85000 Olonnes sur Mer
France

Dear Sirs

Our company is proposing to set up a dairy produce processing plant in western France and we would like you to find us a suitable site.

We need either freehold or leasehold premises of 2,000 square metres on a plot with easy access for large vehicles.

Can you help us in finding the site and act for us in its acquisition? This is our first venture into France so we would appreciate all additional information about property purchase or leasing.

Yours faithfully

Arthur Sturrock
Managing Director

65 Asesoramiento legal: compra de bienes

Hernández y socios
Calle Luis de León, 76
Salamanca
España.   23 de mayo de 199-

Muy Sres míos:

Nuestra empresa se propone instalar una fábrica para la elaboración de productos lácteos en el oeste de España, y nos gustaría encargarles[1] a ustedes que nos buscaran[2] un lugar adecuado.

Necesitamos disponer de una nave[3] de dos mil metros cuadrados con fácil acceso para vehículos de gran tonelaje, bien sea[4] de adquisición absoluta[5] o para arrendar.[6]

¿Podrían ustedes buscarnos un solar y representarnos en la adquisición del mismo? Este es nuestro primer negocio en España, y por lo tanto les agradeceríamos todo tipo de información adicional sobre compra o alquiler de propiedades.

Aprovecho[7] gustoso para saludarles atentamente.

Arthur Sturrock
Director Gerente

1 *Encargar*: 'to entrust'.
2 Imperfect subjunctive after conditional form in main clause.
3 Technical term: 'premises' (e.g. *nave industrial*). The word can also mean 'ship'.
4 *Bien sea*: 'whether it be'.
5 'Outright purchase'.
6 'To rent'.
7 *Aprovechar*: 'to take advantage', 'take the opportunity'.

66 Complaint about delay in administering a bank account

8 September 199-

Société Bancaire Générale
4 boulevard Leclerc
76200 Dieppe
France

For the attention of the Manager

Dear Sir

RE: ACCOUNT NO. 654231

We have received the July statement of our above account no. 654231 and are surprised that the balance shown is so low.

We have been assured by two of our major customers, Alligand SA and Berthaud Etains, that they settled large outstanding invoices by bank transfer to that account four weeks and five weeks ago respectively.

Will you please check very carefully and let us know by fax the exact balance of our account. If, as we think, work is being processed by you in a dilatory fashion, please could you let us know the reason for this.

Yours sincerely

Eric Smith
Finance Director

66 Queja sobre demora en la gestión de una cuenta bancaria

Banco Mediterráneo
Calle Calderón, 67
Reus
España.   8 de setiembre de 199-

Para la atención del Sr Director

Muy Sr mío:

Hemos recibido el estado[1] de nuestra cuenta (No. 654231) perteneciente al mes de julio, y nos sorprende saber que el balance sea[2] tan bajo.

Dos de nuestros importantes clientes, Alimate S.A. y Bernabeu Martín, nos aseguran que han saldado[3] las facturas importantes que tenían pendientes por medio de transferencia bancaria a dicha cuenta, hace cuatro y cinco semanas respectivamente.

Sírvase revisar meticulosamente el balance exacto de nuestra cuenta, y envíenoslo[4] por fax. Si, como pensamos, usted va retrasado en esta gestión,[5] tenga a bien comunicarnos la razón de ello.

Atentamente,

Eric Smith
Director de Finanzas

1 *Balance* might also be used here, if it were not to be quoted just after with the more specific meaning of 'cash in credit'.
2 Subjunctive after a verb of emotion (surprise).
3 Alternatives: *liquidar, pagar.*
4 An *usted* command: 'send it to us'.
5 'Action', 'running', 'procedure'.

67   Complaint about mail delivery

19 November 199-

The Central Post Office
Place Centrale
53000 Laval
France

Dear Sirs

We have made some enquiries here in England concerning delays we have experienced in the delivery of our mail to our subsidiary in Cossé le Vivien and have been informed that these are being caused at the Laval sorting office.

Since our business is being seriously inconvenienced by postal delays we would be most grateful if you could look into the matter.

It should not take 10 days for orders and invoices to get from us to our colleagues in Cossé. We therefore enclose a sample mailing on which the dates are clearly marked.

Yours faithfully

Jeremy P Johnson
Director

Enc.

67 Queja sobre reparto de correo

Le Bureau de Poste
Place Centrale
53000 Laval
Francia.

19 de noviembre de 199-

Señores:

Les notificamos que hemos pedido información aquí en España acerca de los retrasos existentes en el despacho del correo a nuestra filial en Cossé le Vivien, y nos comunican que las causas de éstos[1] corresponden a[2] la oficina de distribución del correo de Laval.

Puesto que los retrasos postales están causando grandes inconvenientes a nuestro negocio, les agradeceríamos investigaran este asunto.

Los pedidos y las facturas que circulan entre nosotros y nuestros colegas de Cossé no deberían tardar diez días; de ahí que[3] les remitimos[4] una muestra de correo en la cual figura, con toda claridad, la fecha del matasellos.[5]

Sin otro particular, les saludamos atentamente

María José Forlán (Srta)
Directora

Anexo

1 The delays.
2 *Corresponder a*: 'to relate to', 'concern'.
3 Literally, 'hence'.
4 *Remitir*: 'to send' (of mail, in particular).
5 'Postmark', 'date stamp'.

68 Complaint about wrong consignment of goods

1 September 199-

Dessous Dessus
14 rue Legrand
80000 Amiens
France

For the attention of Mr A Malraux

Dear Mr Malraux

RE: INVOICE NO. 13322/08/92

We regret to inform you that the garments you sent us in your consignment of 25 August were not what we had ordered.

Please refer to our order (copy enclosed) and to your invoice (no. 13322/08/92). You will note that the briefs, slips and bras are mostly the wrong sizes, colours and materials.

We are at a loss to explain this departure from your normally reliable service. Will you please contact us immediately so that we can put matters right?

Yours sincerely

Fred Smith
Manager

Enc.

68 Queja sobre entrega errónea de mercancías

Vestisa
Polígono Industrial El León
Sabadell
España.   1 de setiembre de 199-

Para la atención del Sr A. Maldonado

Asunto: Pedido Nº 13322/08/92

Estimado Sr Maldonado:

Lamentamos informarle que las prendas que nos envió en la remesa del 25 de agosto no eran las que habíamos pedido.

Sírvase hacer referencia a nuestro pedido (cuya copia le adjuntamos) y a su factura (no. 13322/08/92). Comprobará[1] que las bragas, las enaguas y los sujetadores, en su mayoría, no corresponden ni[2] en las tallas, ni en los colores, ni en la composición del tejido.

Nos sorprende la alteración[3] de este servicio hasta ahora digno de crédito.[4] Le agradeceríamos se pusiera en contacto con nosotros inmediatamente, con objeto de resolver este asunto.

Atentos saludos

Fred Smith
Gerente

Anexo

1 *Comprobar*: 'to check'. Alternatives: *verificar, revisar; chequear* in parts of Latin America.
2 *Ni ... ni ... ni ...*: neither, nor, nor.
3 Alternatives: *cambio, modificación* (deliberate); *alteración* here is unlikely to imply an intentional change in practice.
4 Formal: 'worthy of credit', 'creditable'.

69   Complaint about damage to goods

3 April 199-

Transports Transmanche SA
Quai des Brumes
14000 Caen
France

For the attention of Mr Gérard Dispendieux

Dear Monsieur Dispendieux

We have received a complaint from John Ferguson of Amex Insurance concerning his company's removal to Beauvais three weeks ago. You will remember that we subcontracted this removal to your company.

Mr Ferguson claims that several of the items of furniture and office equipment were damaged on arrival at the premises in Beauvais.

Although he complained there and then to your deliverymen, he has still not heard from you. In the interests of our future business relations I would be grateful if you could clarify this situation.

Yours sincerely

Gerald Wagstaffe
French Area Manager

69   Queja sobre artículos dañados

Mudanzas Garranzo
Bulevar Las Hayas, 35
Badajoz
España.

3 de abril de 199-

Para la atención del Sr Jorge Deva

Estimado Sr Deva:

Hemos recibido una queja del señor John Ferguson, de Seguros Amex, concerniente al[1] traslado de su firma[2] a Badajoz hace tres semanas. Si recuerda, subcontratamos a su empresa para efectuar dicha mudanza.[3]

El Sr Ferguson afirma que algunos de los muebles y enseres de oficina estaban estropeados a su llegada al local de Badajoz.

A pesar de que el Sr Ferguson se quejó a los transportistas en el acto,[4] usted todavía no se ha puesto en contacto con él. En beneficio de seguir, en el futuro, la buena relación entre ambas compañías, le agradecería aclarara esta situación.

Le saluda atentamente

Gerald Wagstaffe
Gerente de la Zona Española

1 Alternatives: *relativo a, relacionado con, en cuanto a, en lo que se refiere a, respecto a.*
2 It is the firm, rather than just Mr Ferguson, that has moved.
3 *Mudanza* is more specifically the removal of goods on a fairly permanent basis; *traslado* can apply simply to the transfer of personnel.
4 Literally, 'on the spot'.

70 Informing customers that a company has been taken over

24 July 199-

Produits Chimiques SA
89 rue Jules Barni
80330 Longueau
France

Dear Sirs

Thank you for your order dated 17 July. We have to inform you, however, that our company has been taken over by a larger concern, INTERNATIONAL CHEMICALS Inc.

As a result of this, we have to tell you that we no longer produce the polymers that you request at this site. We have, however, passed on your order to our parent company and are confident that you will be contacted soon.

In the interests of our future business relations we enclose the latest catalogue of our total range of products, indicating which subsidiary manufactures which product.

Yours faithfully

Frederick Herriot
Plant Director

Enc.

70   Informando sobre cambios en una empresa: adquisición

Químicos Vascos S.A.
Zona Industrial de Andoaín
País Vasco
España.   24 de julio de 199-

Muy Sres nuestros:

Les agradecemos su pedido fecha[1] 17 de los corrientes.[2] Debemos informarles no obstante, que una empresa mayor, Químicos Internacionales S.A., ha absorbido la nuestra.[3]

Además de ello,[4] les comunicamos que en este lugar ya no fabricamos los polímeros que ustedes piden. Sin embargo, hemos enviado el pedido a nuestra empresa matriz y confiamos que se pondrán en contacto con ustedes en breve.

En beneficio de seguir manteniendo futuras relaciones comerciales, adjuntamos el último catálogo que ilustra la gama completa de nuestros productos, así como[5] el nombre de las filiales y el nombre de los productos que fabrica cada una de ellas.

Sin otro particular, les saludamos atentamente.

Frederick Herriot
Director de Fábrica

Anexo

1 Omission of *de* or *con* before the key word (*fecha*) is normal in commercial correspondence.
2 Because the month of July appears in the heading, this term (meaning 'the current days') can be used in reference to 17 July, and is typical in this context.
3 *La nuestra*: 'ours' (company).
4 *Ello*: 'all the above-mentioned information' ('it').
5 Literally, 'thus as' ('as well as').

71 Informing customers of change of name and address

EUROPEAN COMMERCIAL INSURANCE Ltd
47 Broad Walk
Preston
Lancashire United Kingdom

(Formerly PRESTON INSURERS Inkerman Street, Preston)

1 June 199-

The Export Manager
Nouveaux Textiles
342 chaussée Baron
59100 Roubaix
France

Dear Sir

RE: CHANGE OF COMPANY NAME AND ADDRESS

We are writing to all our valued customers to inform them that Preston Insurers has changed both its registered name and its address.

We are still located in Preston and operating as commercial insurers as before. However, we have acquired new partners who have invested fresh capital in the business.

It is our intention to increase our European business, hence the new name. Enclosed is our brochure setting out our range of services and tariffs. Do not hesitate to contact us if you have any queries about these changes.

Yours faithfully

Nancy Wilton
Customer Liaison Manager

Enc.

71 Informando sobre cambio de nombre de una empresa

European Commercial Insurance Ltd
(Formerly Preston Insurers, Inkerman Street, Preston)
47 Broad Walk
Preston
Lancashire
Reino Unido.
Tel. +44 772 345217
Fax +44 772 345192

La Directora Gerente
Cosmética Ayala de Ruch
Paseo de la Concha, 12
Santander
España.   1 de junio de 199-

Asunto: Cambio de nombre de empresa y de dirección

Estimada señora:

Por la presente[1] notificamos a todos nuestros estimados clientes que hemos cambiado de nombre comercial y de dirección.

Todavía seguimos ubicados en Preston y, como antes, seguimos dedicándonos a los seguros comerciales. Sin embargo, hemos adquirido a socios nuevos que han invertido capital en el negocio.

Tenemos pensado expansionar nuestros negocios con Europa y de ahí que haya surgido[2] el nuevo nombre. Adjunto le enviamos nuestro catálogo en el que figura nuestra gama de servicios y precios. Si tiene alguna duda sobre estos cambios, no deje de[3] contactar con nosotros.

Cordialmente le saluda

Nancy Wilton
Encargada de Relaciones Públicas

Anexo

1 Formal: 'by the present (letter)', 'in writing'.
2 *Surgir*: 'to spring', 'derive'. Alternatives: *provenir, originar*.
3 *Dejar de*: 'to omit to', 'fail to'. In this case, a polite command.

72 Informing customers of increased prices

12 November 199-

Epicerie Fine
9 rue Dutour
72100 Le Mans
France

Dear Monsieur Olivier

In reply to your letter of the 5th I am sending you a new price list.

You will note that all of our prices have increased by some 6.3 per cent. This was unfortunately made necessary by our continuing inflation as well as the British Chancellor's recent decision to increase the general rate of VAT to 17.5 per cent.

I hope that the quality of our produce will continue to engage your loyalty. It is also the case that the pound sterling has reduced in value – thanks to the Chancellor!

Yours sincerely

Michael McDermott
Marketing Manager

Enc.

72 Informando sobre cambios de precios

AliDeliSA
Calle de la Fuente, 45–47
La Coruña
España.
                                            12 de noviembre de 199-

Distinguidos Señores:

En contestación a su carta del cinco de los corrientes, adjunto remito[1] la nueva lista de precios.

Observará que todos nuestros precios han aumentado en un 6,3%.[2] Este aumento ha sido debido tanto a la continua inflación como a la reciente decisión tomada por nuestro Ministro de Hacienda de aumentar al 17,5% el tipo[3] de interés general del IVA.

Espero que la calidad de nuestros productos alimenticios continúe siendo de su agrado.[4] También se da el caso de[5] que la libra esterlina ha disminuido de valor. ¡Le daré las gracias de su parte al Ministro de Hacienda!

Sin otro particular, aprovecho para saludarle gustoso.

Michael McDermott
Director de Márketing

Anexo

1 Literally, 'I send attached'.
2 Note comma rather than full point in decimal figure. Percentage references are preceded in Spanish by *en* or *por*.
3 In Latin America *tasa* is preferred to *tipo*.
4 The Spanish is simplified from the slightly ironic English.
5 *Darse el caso* (*de*): 'to arise', 'come about'.

73 Requesting information about opening a business account

23 October 199-

The Manager
Crédit Mercantile
89 rue Béranger
69631 VÉNISSIEUX
France

Dear Sir

We are proposing to open an office and refrigerated storage facility at Vénissieux in the new year and would appreciate it if you would send us some information about opening a bank account at your branch.

Initially we would be transferring funds to finance the setting up of our new business premises. Thereafter we would expect to use the account to receive payments from French customers and to pay local suppliers etc.

We would be most grateful if you could inform us of all the formalities that we need to observe, both public and particular, to Crédit Mercantile. Could you also inform us of your charges on business accounts?

Yours faithfully

Alfred Sanger
Commercial Manager

73 Solicitando información sobre la apertura de cuenta bancaria

El Director
Banque de Crédit Mercantile
89 rue Béranger
69631 Vénissieux
Francia.
                                                    23 de octubre de 199-

Muy señor nuestro:

A primeros del año que viene[1] nos proponemos abrir una oficina y un depósito de almacenaje refrigerado en Vénissieux, por lo que les agradeceríamos nos enviaran información sobre la apertura de una cuenta bancaria en su sucursal.[2]

En principio trasladaríamos fondos para financiar la puesta en marcha de un nuevo local comercial; luego haríamos uso de dicha cuenta para que nuestros clientes franceses nos abonaran pagos a nuestro favor y para efectuar[3] pagos a los abastecedores locales etcétera.

Le agradeceríamos encarecidamente nos informaran de todas las formalidades que debemos cumplir, tanto las públicas como las que correspondan al Banque de Crédit Mercantile. Asimismo sírvase informarnos de los gastos bancarios cobrados a empresas.

Sin otro particular, aprovechamos esta ocasión para saludarle atentamente.

Alfonso Sabio
Director Comercial

1 Alternatives: *año nuevo, año próximo.*
2 *Agencia* can also be used.
3 Infinitive here (cf. *abonaran*) because continuation of main clause.

74 Requesting information about opening a personal bank account

4 November 199-

The Manager
Banque Nationale
146 boulevard Haussmann
75016 Paris
France

Dear Sir

My British employers are posting me to their French subsidiary as of the beginning of next January. I will therefore be moving to Paris with my family and I expect to be resident in France for two years.

Will you please send me information about opening a personal current account at your bank? My salary would be paid into the account and both my wife and I would wish to draw money from it and to pay bills by cheque etc. We may also wish to transfer money to a bank account in England.

Please send me any documentation you have. By the way, I *can* read French though I am not very good at writing it.

Thank you in advance for your assistance.

Yours faithfully

Stuart Smith

74   Solicitando información sobre apertura de cuenta corriente

El Director
Banque Nationale
146 boulevard Haussmann
75016 París
Francia.   4 de noviembre de 199-

Muy señor mío:

A primeros de enero próximo mi compañía va a trasladarme de España a la filial francesa. Por lo tanto me voy a mudar[1] a París con mi familia, y espero fijar[2] mi residencia en Francia por dos años.

Sírvase enviarme información sobre apertura de cuenta corriente personal en su banco. Mi sueldo se abonará directamente en la cuenta; tanto mi esposa como yo retiraríamos fondos de ella y abonaríamos facturas por medio de cheque bancario etcétera. Es probable que también queramos[3] transferir dinero a una cuenta bancaria en España.

Le agradecería me enviara la información pertinente. Nótese[4] que leo el francés, aunque no lo escribo muy bien.

Reiterándole las gracias anticipadas,[5] le saluda atentamente

Sergio Castro Escudero

1   *Mudarse* (*de casa*): 'to move' (house).
2   *Fijar la residencia*: 'to take up (permanent) residence'.
3   Subjunctive after '*Es probable que . . .*'.
4   A polite/formal reminder to the bank manager.
5   'Thanks in advance', with repetition implied.

75 Letter re overdrawn account

9 March 199-

J H Jameson
47 Narrow Bank
Lichfield
Staffordshire

Dear Mr Jameson

We regret to inform you that your account, number 62467840, is overdrawn by
£21.09.

We would appreciate your rectifying this situation as soon as possible, since you
have no overdraft arrangement with us.

Yours sincerely

F E Jones
Manager

75 Carta en relación con estado de cuenta en números rojos[1]

Sr Alberto Ferrer
Calle Contreras, 27 4, izq.[2]
San Sebastián
País Vasco
España.   9 de marzo de 199-

Distinguido[3] Sr Ferrer:

           Lamentamos informarle que su cuenta No. 62467840 arroja un saldo[4] de veintiuna libras esterlinas con nueve peniques, cantidad a nuestro favor.[5]

Le agradeceríamos rectificara esta situación lo antes posible, ya que usted no dispone de acuerdo con nosotros a este respecto.[6]

Le saluda atentamente,

                                                    F E Jones
                                                    Director

1 Literally, 'in the red'.
2 4th floor, on the left. Presumably there are only two apartments on this floor (to the right and to the left).
3 A rather complimentary form of address in view of the nature of the letter.
4 Literally, 'throws up a balance'.
5 *Cantidad a nuestro favor*: 'debit balance'. See also *saldo deudor/negativo*: 'debit balance'.
6 I.e. regarding overdrafts.

76 Informing a customer of a bank deposit

2 May 199–

Mr Bernard J Mann
4 Beauchamp Mews
London
England

Dear Mr Mann

We are writing to inform you that we have today received a cheque payable to you for the sum of $124,035.00 and sent by J et P Barraud Notaires, 307 rue du Château, Luxembourg.

Can you please confirm as soon as possible whether you were expecting this deposit and let us know your instructions concerning it?

Enclosed is a photocopy of this cheque and its accompanying letter.

Yours sincerely

Amélia Dupont
Head Cashier

Encs

76 Notificando al cliente sobre transferencia a su favor

Sr Arturo Pérez
Impex S.L.
Calle Dolores Butraga, 87
Lugo
España.   2 de mayo de 199-

Distinguido Sr Pérez:

Nos es grato comunicarle que hoy hemos recibido un cheque a su favor, por la cantidad de 124.035 dólares, enviado por los notarios J. y P. Barraud de Rue du Château 307, Luxemburgo.

Sírvase confirmar, lo antes posible, si usted tenía previa notificación[1] de que dicho cheque iba a ser abonado aquí, y sus instrucciones a este respecto.

Adjunto[2] envío fotocopia del cheque y de la carta que acompañaba al mismo.

Sin otro particular, y en espera de sus instrucciones,[3] le saluda

Amélie Dupont
Cajera en jefe

Anexos

1 Literally, 'prior notification'.
2 Here used as an adverb; 'I send enclosed . . .'.
3 A typical, if gratuitous, inclusion here.

77   Enquiry about banking

Letter from the Ombudsman

4 April 199-

Monsieur J. Delor
Président-Directeur Général
Mouton-Poulenc
7 rue du Trocadéro
Paris 3 Cedex
France

Dear Sir

In response to your general query about banking in England, there are two main types of bank, merchant banks and commercial banks. The former are very numerous and deal with companies generally. The latter are mainly the four big groups: Lloyds, National Westminster, Barclays and Midland.

The enclosed leaflet will give you further details, including information about banking in Scotland. Our office is mainly concerned with complaints about banks.

In addition you should note that The Post Office also has some banking and money transfer facilities.

Yours faithfully

C D Prettyman
For the Ombudsman

Enc.

77   Solicitando información sobre la banca

Carta del Defensor

Dr Alonso Torrete
Apartado Aéreo 341[1]
Buenos Aires
República de Argentina.   4 de abril de 199-

Distinguido Doctor:

Doy contestación a la duda general que tiene usted sobre la banca[2] en Inglaterra. Existen dos tipos de bancos: los mercantiles[3] y los comerciales. Los primeros son muy numerosos y, en general, negocian con las empresas. En los segundos van incluidos los cuatro grupos[4] principales: Lloyds, National Westminster, Barclays, y el Midland.

El folleto adjunto le informará más detalladamente, incluso[5] sobre la banca escocesa. Nuestra oficina se dedica, en particular, a las quejas relacionadas con los bancos.

Le advertimos que Correos también tiene a la disposición de los clientes servicio[6] bancario y de transferencia.

Le saluda atentamente

C. D. Prettyman (Srta)
De parte del Defensor

Anexo

1   'PO Box'; used mainly, as the name implies, for air mail.
2   'The banking system'.
3   Also *banco de negocios*.
4   *Grupo*: group of banks; also applicable to individual banks.
5   'Even' ('including').
6   Note lack of article before *servicio*.

78 Enquiry about post office banking facilities

2 February 199-

La Poste Centrale
Place Général De Gaulle
16000 Angoulême
France

Dear Sirs

I am intending to open a second business in Angoulême and would like to enquire what services you offer to small businesses.

I have in mind giro banking, and I was wondering if you could tell me how your post office bank accounts work. Secondly, is it to you that I should apply to have a telephone? And finally, do you have special rates for business mail?

I would be most grateful for any information you can send me.

Yours faithfully

Mostyn Evans
Proprietor

78   Correos: solicitando información sobre operaciones bancarias

Servicio de Correos
Plaza 23 de Febrero
Marbella
España.   2 de febrero de 199-

Señores:

Tengo el propósito de abrir un segundo negocio en Marbella y quisiera me enviaran información sobre los servicios que ustedes ofrecen a la[1] pequeña empresa.

Tengo pensado efectuar operaciones bancarias por giro postal,[2] y me pregunto si pudieran proporcionarme información sobre los tipos de cuentas que ustedes ofrecen. En segundo lugar, ¿es a ustedes a quienes[3] debo de solicitar la instalación de un teléfono? Y por último, ¿disponen de tarifas especiales para la correspondencia de empresas?[4]

Les agradecería cualquier información que pudieran enviarme, y les saludo cordialmente.

Mostyn Evans
Propietario

1   A standard way of referring to the whole sector.
2   Specifically: 'by money order'.
3   Rather involved syntax: 'Is it to you to whom ...?'.
4   Alternatives: *correspondencia comercial* or *empresarial* (though *comercial* obviously has broader meaning).

79 Enquiry about opening a post office account

8 March 199-

Bureau Central
Postes et Télécommunications
Paris
France

Dear Sirs

I do not know exactly who to address this letter to and hope that it will reach the right service.

I wish to obtain information about opening a Post Office account, to enable my French customers to settle my invoices in France and permit me to pay certain of my French suppliers by cheque.

Would you please be kind enough to inform me of your formalities and send me the necessary forms?

Yours faithfully

Eric Clifford
Managing Director

79   Solicitando información sobre apertura de cuenta por giro postal

Bureau Central
Postes et Télécommunications
París
Francia.   8 de marzo de 199-

Distinguidos señores:

No sé exactamente a quien dirigirme con la presente,
aunque[1] espero que llegue al servicio apropiado.

Deseo obtener información sobre cómo abrir una cuenta en Correos, con objeto
de que mis clientes franceses salden[2] mis facturas en Francia y que yo pueda
abonar con cheque a varios de mis abastecedores de dicho país.

Tengan la amabilidad[3] de enviarme información sobre los trámites a seguir, junto
con la solicitud necesaria para abrir dicha cuenta.

Atentamente les saluda,

                                                        Julián Bakero
                                                        Director Gerente

1 'Although'.
2 Subjunctive after *con objeto de que*; note that *pueda* is also governed by the same
   phrase.
3 *Tener la amabilidad de*: 'be so kind as to'.

80 Opening poste restante

18 April 199-

La Poste Centrale
Place Bellecour
69001 Lyon
France

Gentlemen

We are in the process of moving our French subsidiary from Villeurbanne to Saint Priest; the move should be completed some time in the next month.

Could we ask you on receipt of this letter and, until further notice, to retain all mail addressed to us poste restante at your central office?

Please inform us if there are any other formalities to observe. Enclosed is an addressed envelope and international reply coupon for your reply.

Thank you in advance.

Arthur T Goldberg
On behalf of Software Supplies Inc.

Encs

80 Retención de correspondencia en lista

El Director
Servicio de Correos
Gran Vía, 3
Valladolid
España.   18 de abril de 199-

Estimado Señor:

Estamos en vías de trasladar nuestra filial española de
Valladolid a Salamanca, traslado[1] que se efectuará durante el mes próximo.

Les agradeceríamos que cuando reciban esta carta, y hasta próximo aviso,[2]
retengan[3] en su oficina central todo el correo dirigido a nuestro nombre.

Sírvanse también informarnos sobre si debemos cumplir algún otro requisito.[4]
Adjunto les remitimos sobre con nuestro nombre y dirección[5] y cupón
internacional de respuesta para que nos den contestación.

Dándoles[6] las gracias anticipadas, les saludamos atentamente,

                                                Arthur T. Goldberg
                                    De parte de Software Suppliers Inc.

Anexos

1 No article as 'traslado' is held to be in apposition to previous information.
2 Literally, 'until next warning'.
3 The subjunctive here, after agradeceríamos, acquires the force of a polite request.
4 'Requirement', 'prerequisite'.
5 Alternative: domicilio.
6 A present participle/gerund, typically used to round off a letter (cf. 'thanking you',
   'requesting you', 'reminding you' . . .).

Business Practice

1 Addressing people

When speaking to somebody you do not know, or whom you know in a formal context only, it is customary to use *usted* (plural: *ustedes*) as the term meaning 'you'; these forms are often abbreviated to *Vd.* and *Vds.* in writing. The use of *usted* and *ustedes* means, in turn, that third person forms of the verb and related pronouns are required (e.g. *¿Tiene Vd. tiempo para . . ?* or *¿Les interesa a ustedes . . .?*).

Once you are well acquainted with the person concerned it is increasingly likely that you would address each other as *tú* (plural: *vosotros*); *tú* and *vosotros* are, of course, the normal ways of addressing any 'second person(s)' whom you know well. In the great majority of Latin American countries *ustedes* is used for **all** plural second person relationships and in general *usted* is also more frequently used than in Spain, where social informality, even in business, has become widespread since the advent of democracy in the mid-1970s.

As regards titles, *Señor/Señora/Señorita* (Mr/Mrs/Miss) are the terms used to address directly your contact, accompanied by his or her surname; note that Hispanic people have two surnames (from both parents and/or from marriage), of which the first given is the one to be used in social and business relations. In written form the abbreviations *Sr/Sra/Srta* are frequently used, accompanied by the surname; however, the full spelling/pronunciation is retained when addressing a person without using her/his surname (e.g. *Sí, señorita* or *Buenos días, señor*). It is common to address plural business contacts as *señores* (abbreviated in writing to *Sres*); occasionally in a business context the full title may be followed by a first name only (e.g. *Señorita Carmen*). If you refer to a person in the 'third party' sense (as opposed to addressing him/her), then the definite article (*el/la*) precedes the title, for which lower case initial is used in writing (e.g. *Ayer hablaba con el señor Ruiz y la señorita Paredes*). If a business contact is well known to you first-name terms are normal.

Useful phrases

On meeting or taking leave of somebody it is customary to shake hands and to say *Hola/¿Qué tal?* or *Adiós/Hasta luego*. On first meeting, and especially in a business context, both parties would probably say *Encantado(a)/a de conocerle* (Pleased to meet you). Among good friends kissing on both cheeks is normal upon meeting. To attract somebody's attention, *Perdóneme, señor* or *Por favor, señora* are typical expressions. *Lo siento* is used to apologize, *¿Como?* to request clarification, *Gracias* to express thanks, *¿Me puede . . .?* to solicit assistance.

2 Communicating with people (phone/fax/telex/mail)

Telephone

Spain's telephone service is run by the Telefónica from Madrid. Public booths (*cabinas telefónicas/cabinas de teléfonos*) are plentiful in Spain; most bars, restaurants and hotels also make the facility available. Hispanic people are invariably very sociable, a fact reflected by the heavy use to which the telephone service is put. Five, 25 and 100 peseta coins may be used, and from most booths calls can be made to local, national and international subscribers. Each of the 50 national provinces has its own two- or three-digit code (*prefijo*), whose first digit is 9.

A directory enquiries (*Información*) service is available (national, dial 009; provincial, dial 003) and, as long as you have the name of the person or company and of the town, the service can provide a number; for business purposes there is a Yellow Pages (*Páginas Amarillas*) directory. Other services, including Police (091) and Ambulance (227 20 21) for the two major cities, are listed in the main directory (*guía telefónica*), as are all the international codes. International directory enquiries can be obtained by dialling 005. Predictably, it is cheaper to make long-distance calls in the evening and more expensive to call from hotel rooms; it is also worth noting that there can be differences between UK and Spanish time during certain months.

Telephone numbers within Spain normally comprise seven digits; in informing somebody orally of your number you can present each of the seven individually or can present the last six in pairs, preceded by the single initial digit. In spelling out words on the telephone each letter is 'named' individually, sometimes accompanied by well-known names that begin with the particular letter (e.g. B de Barcelona, F de Francia, R de Ramón).

Making a call

On lifting the receiver you soon hear a continuous dial tone. After dialling the number, either the ringing tone (single, spaced) or the engaged tone (rapid, continuous) is obtained unless the phone is out of order. On answering, the person at the end of the line usually says '*Dígame*' or '*¿Sí?*', or if speaking for a company (s)he will give the company name and possibly her/his own. On hearing with whom you are speaking you would normally greet the person (*Buenos días*, *Buenas tardes*) and introduce yourself (*Habla/Soy/Aquí* + name), saying whom you wish to contact (*Póngame, por favor, con el señor X*). *Un momento, que le conecto* is a likely response if the person is available; if (s)he is not, then *Lo siento, señor/a/ita, no está/no contesta* might be the reply. To leave a message you would say simply *Quisiera dejarle un recado/mensaje, por favor* and then go ahead with the information. To complete the call, whether successful or not: *Gracias (por su atención), adiós*.

A few helpful expressions to avoid problems on the telephone are:

¿Me oye bien?	Can you hear me?
¿Me hace el favor de repetirlo?	Can you please repeat it?
Perdone, no entiendo lo que dice.	Sorry, I don't understand.
¿Me podría ayudar?	Could you help me?
Volveré a llamarle mañana.	I'll call you back tomorrow.

Fax

Many companies and institutions have their own fax facility, though the Post Office (*Correos*) offers Burofax, a telex service via the telephone or by post, to those without access to a private fax machine. Local Chambers of Commerce (*Cámaras de Comercio*) also operate a sending and receiving fax service for their members. The *Guía para usuarios de los servicios de Correos y Telégrafos* (cf. Post Office Guide) includes in its list of services Telefax, a high speed facsimile facility (see also Mail below). The format of the standard fax document shows company letterhead (*membrete*), date and time (*fecha y hora*), addressee (*destinatario/a*), sender (*remitente*), number of pages (*número de páginas, incluida ésta*), the subject (*asunto*), plus the message itself and probably a final greeting.

Telex

International telegrams and international telex both provide businesses with the conventional forms of rapid communication. The body responsible for Spanish postal and telecommunications services (*Correos y Telecomunicaciones*) offers a variety of telex-based facilities to companies, for many of whom the telex is preferable to both telephone and letter for reasons such as cost, security and accuracy. The tendency in Spain is to avoid excessive abbreviation, though the omission of high-frequency, or 'function', words is normal.

Mail

Airmail between Spain and other countries is often subject to delays, though the average delivery time within Europe is approximately four days. International postal services are summarized in the *Guía para usuarios de los servicios de Correos y Telégrafos*: these include Cash on Delivery, Reply Paid, Express Mail, PO Box and Advice of Delivery facilities. Post offices in Spain are usually open from 8 a.m. until 1 p.m. on weekdays; on Saturday there is no service to the public except at the main *Correos* in Madrid and Barcelona, which offer the usual morning hours. The purchase of stamps is done by most Spaniards at their local *estanco*, which combines minor post office facilities with those of a tobacconist.

3 Appointments and punctuality

In Spain it is frequently the case that appointments (*citas*) are made and meetings (*reuniones*) are called at short notice. If a meeting **has** been arranged well in advance it is advisable to ring a few days before the proposed date to confirm details. In Latin America the term *hora* is often used for an appointment, whilst in Spain the more generic *compromiso* implies obligation to be somewhere at a given time. A request for an appointment should be made by letter if the matter is weighty, but for more routine business matters a telephone call will suffice. A similar procedure might be adopted in order to cancel an appointment. This practice perhaps reflects the fact that the oral mode predominates over the written in Hispanic business culture.

In contrast with customs in some other parts of the world, Hispanic culture does not emphasize punctuality: it is not uncommon to be kept waiting by your host, especially if (s)he is a very busy or senior person; equally, however, that person may not be offended by your own late arrival. Hispanic people are possibly more aware of the social, as opposed to the specifically transactional, dimensions of business relations; on the other hand, smart dress in business has become the norm – especially in Spain – since the studiedly casual days of its transition to democracy. On actually meeting, it is normal to shake hands, to exchange greetings and to engage briefly in conversation not directly related to your business purpose. The modernization of the Spanish economy and business practices has not meant that the traditional value placed on personal trust and compatibility in business dealings has been diminished. The possible frustration experienced by foreign executives in wishing to move quickly to a decision has to be set against the Spanish preference for a more personal and less time-constrained relationship (see Business entertainment, below).

4 Business cards and gifts

It is normal practice in Spain to exchange business cards (*tarjetas de visita*) whenever the opportunity arises, and certainly at the beginning of meetings with clients or potential partners. The typical Spanish card bears the same information as in Britain and businesspeople are recommended to keep an ample supply available. The most obvious situation in which a gift might be made is on being invited to the home of a Spanish business client or partner. Because such an invitation is still not the norm it would imply a very close or important level of contact and it should never be refused. Most appropriate would be flowers, sent with a visiting card to the home of the host and his wife before your visit; a card sent a day or two after the dinner, to thank the hostess, would also be a logical follow-up action. Evidently, when companies have special promotions or are celebrating special events they may offer selected clients some form of corporate memento, just as happens in other countries. Overt or frequent exchanging of gifts in business is not typical of Spain, whereas offering hospitality clearly is (see Business entertainment).

5 Business entertainment

As already suggested, Hispanic people have always placed great importance on the concept of hospitality, whatever the area of human relations. Whilst visits to cultural events or to leisure facilities may form part of some companies' entertainment budget, by far the most common practice is an invitation to dine or have lunch out with colleagues. Many large firms now have their own dining rooms where working lunches can be taken. Neither here nor in restaurants is service likely to be available before 2 p.m., though in the latter the meal is unlikely to be finished before 4 p.m. and will no doubt require a strong constitution on the part of the guest. Naturally, on hosting a meal for business colleagues in a country so renowned for its food and drink it is essential to ensure a high standard of cuisine, beverages and service. An invitation to dine out in a restaurant, with respective spouses, is a popular way of making business relations more sociable whilst avoiding the extremes of a sandwich lunch in the office and the set-piece dinner at home.

As in the case of lunch, dinner is taken fairly late: the invitation might be for 10 p.m., and before going to the restaurant or hotel a visit might be made to one or two *tapas* bars to stimulate the appetite (*abrir el apetito*) and to loosen tongues a little. The Spanish in particular enjoy dressing smartly to go out in the evening and are usually well informed about the political and economic life of their country; on both accounts they would wish their guests (or hosts) to share their interest. As elsewhere, payment for the meal would be by credit card or by cash, or perhaps directly on the company account. As a guest, you would run the risk of offending your host if you sought to pay for pre-dinner drinks; likewise if, as the host, you expected your guest to pay. Moreover, if no service charge were included in the restaurant bill, it would be standard practice to leave a tip of between 10 per cent and 15 per cent. There is still in Hispanic societies an emphatic desire to be 'honourable' in social situations and many will view others' social and personal conduct as a good pointer to their integrity or their worth in business.

6 Office and shop hours

The working day in Spain normally lasts eight hours, from 9 a.m. until 7 p.m., with as much as a two-hour break at lunchtime. However, an 8 a.m. start, flexitime over half-hours, or staying late till 8 p.m. for meetings are increasingly observable as Spain adjusts to the demands of the European and world markets in which its economy has become so prominent. Between June and September it is now common to follow the *horario intensivo*, from 8 a.m. to 3 p.m. without a main break, but actually working only seven hours. However, few offices are open on Saturdays, whilst leaving early on a Friday to make the most of a weekend is popular. Schools also work a minimum eight-hour day, making arrangements for working parents relatively straightforward.

Most shops are open from 9.30 a.m. to 1 p.m. or 1.30 p.m. The large stores (*almacenes*) usually start at 9 a.m., but like other shops they close for a couple of hours before 4 p.m. From 4 p.m. until 8 p.m. all shops do brisk trade. The public therefore have access from Monday to Saturday inclusive and have two lengthy periods of time per day to shop. Many general foodshops (*supermercados* or *autoservicios*) also offer a Sunday morning service, whilst on most weekdays and in most towns there is a thriving covered market up to lunchtime. Bars are open from early in the morning, to serve a breakfast of coffee (often laced with brandy) and rolls/buns, through lunchtime and the afternoon, and thereafter until well after midnight. Restaurants are usually open from 1 p.m. until 4 p.m. and then from 8.30 p.m. until 12 midnight or later. To see a whole family eating late at night in a restaurant is not unusual, nor is it for the family to be up early next day for work/school!

Since the early 1980s the rapid rise of hypermarkets (nickname: *los hiper*) has changed retailing and consumer habits, as well as moving retail sites to the edges of towns and concentrating the market in the hands of a very small number of chains. More recently have come the new shopping centres (*centros comerciales*), some on prime sites back in city centres. The Spanish in particular are eager consumers: shopping for personal goods, eating out and entertainment are regarded as normal activities by all social classes as long as they are in employment. However, the 1990s have seen an overall unemployment rate of almost 20 per cent, which has gravely affected the economy as well as social harmony, in a country that had until then experienced a generation of almost uninterrupted economic growth.

7 Business organizations

The legal basis and background to business organization and organizations in Spain are considered briefly below, followed by a look at the nature and functions of key Spanish organizations at home and abroad. In conclusion, some processes and bodies that can facilitate trade with Spain in particular are noted.

Companies

All companies in Spain, barring sole traders (*comerciantes*) but including foreign concerns wishing to establish branches (*sucursales*) there, must be formally registered at the Mercantile Register (*Registro Mercantil*) in the capital of the province where their head office is situated. Since the return of democracy in the 1970s increasing attention has been paid to the public accountability of business enterprises, though the hectic economic changes of most recent years have not been free of high-profile scandals. Spain's membership of the EU, huge foreign investment in the country and various indigenous factors meant that the *Sociedad Anónima* (plc) became the most widespread company status, almost irrespective of size, market or capital holdings. Nevertheless, the limited company (*Sociedad de Responsabilidad Limitada: SL* or *SRL*), general partnership (*Sociedad Regular Colectiva: SRC*), cooperatives (*cooperativas*), and joint ventures (*uniones temporales* or *agrupaciones de empresas*) are viable alternatives for those companies not permitted S.A. status since July 1992 (see below: Types of Company) or whose interests are best served by such other categorizations.

Professional associations

Professional associations (*colegios profesionales*) have long been able to defend the interests of their members at national and at provincial level. In addition, they engage in advisory, consultancy and monitoring capacities subject to Constitutional Law and other regulations specific to certain Ministries. Employers' associations (*asociaciones empresariales*) have been numerous in the past, though are not of long standing; in 1977 the CEOE (*Confederación Española de Organizaciones Empresariales*) was founded to bring together over a million members and now exerts an influential role in the political as well as economic life both of the country and of the European Union. Clearly, its major task is to represent the interests of employers; those of employers and others engaged in small and medium-sized businesses are in some cases subsumed by the CEOE, though the owners of these PYMES (*Pequeñas y Medianas Empresas*) do retain a degree of independence at national and regional level. It is, however, the Chambers of Commerce (*Cámaras de Comercio*) that on a day-to-day basis provide, in every provincial town around Spain, the services to businesses normally associated with such organizations in most other countries. The Chambers are coordinated by the Consejo Superior de Cámaras in Madrid. Membership of the local Chamber is automatic and the latter collects from its local businesses, as a fee, a small percentage of their taxable trading profit in order to fund its services.

In 1982 the Instituto de Comercio Exterior (ICEX) – Institute for Foreign Trade – was established to promote and to coordinate activities beneficial to Spanish foreign trade within the framework of Government economic policy. It offers Spanish exporters a wide range of services and publishes a daily bulletin (BISE) on computer for its domestic subscribers; in addition, it organizes trade missions to Spain for foreign importers and provides them with information on Spanish market requirements.

Entering the Spanish market

In considering an incursion into the Spanish market, a foreign firm might begin by identifying a member of staff with the ability to research that market and who might possess the necessary language skills. Finance would need to be ascribed to preparing publicity material in the foreign language, to recruiting a local agent or lawyer, and to paying for a trade mission visit. An alternative that could prove less costly, if perhaps more risky, would be to ally with a Spanish company of similar size or activity in order to pool expertise, time and even finance on a small initial project; obviously, full joint ventures, mergers and takeovers are far more serious undertakings. ICEX and the Spanish Chambers have been working with the PYME sector to facilitate closer relations between companies which without their support would lack the resources or commitment to look beyond a traditional market or product. Moreover, the possibility of accessing EU funds for such an initiative between countries would enhance the prospects for all.

The following addresses may be useful:

Instituto Español de Comercio Exterior (ICEX) (Institute for Foreign Trade)	Paseo de la Castellana 14, 28046 Madrid Tel. (91) 431 1240
Instituto de la Mediana y Pequeña Empresa (Medium-Sized and Small Companies Institute)	Paseo de la Castellana 141, 28046 Madrid Tel. (91) 582 9300
Registro Mercantil (Company Registry)	Príncipe Vergara 94, 28006 Madrid Tel. (91) 411 3758
Cámara Oficial de Comercio e Industria de la Provincia de Madrid (Madrid Chamber of Commerce)	Huertas 13, 28012 Madrid Tel. (91) 429 3193
Comisión Europea (European Commission)	Serrano 41, 5a Planta, 28001 Madrid Tel. (91) 435 1700
AECE: Asociación Española de Comercio Exterior (Foreign Trade Association)	Velázquez 109, 28006 Madrid Tel. (91) 262 4147
Cámara Oficial de Comercio e Industria de Barcelona (Barcelona Chamber of Commerce)	Paseo de Gracia 11, 08007 Barcelona Tel. (93) 317 3220

8 Banks and other financial institutions

Banks (*bancos*) are open in Spain from 9 a.m. until 2 p.m., Monday to Friday, and from 9 a.m. until 1 p.m. on Saturday. The savings banks are usually open from 8 a.m. until 1 p.m., Monday to Friday only. Naturally, money can be changed outside these hours at an exchange bureau (*oficina de cambio*) and cash can be obtained from wall dispensers made available nationwide by virtually all banks. Europe-wide cards issued in Britain can be used in some dispensers.

The Spanish banking system

The banking system as a whole (*la banca*) has traditionally been a powerful influence in national economic life; its activities are overseen by the central issuing bank, the Banco de España, located in the capital. Responsibility for overseeing all financial institutions and much Government economic policy lies with the Ministerio de Economía y Hacienda. Since the late 1970s, but especially since 1986, there has been a great deal of change in the structure of the banking industry owing to such factors as economic recession and expansion, heightened levels of public interest in its operations, competitive pressures, mergers, liberalization, diversification of services, internationalization, etc. The original 'Big Seven' banks, traditionally run by idiosyncratic presidents who lent to their bank a certain image or reputation, have been obliged to change or lose ground to new competition in the financial markets. Nevertheless, even in the mid-1990s the *visto bueno* ('approval') of the banking sector remains a most valuable asset for governmental plans to 'modernize' Spain.

Expressed in very schematic terms, the main participants in the Spanish financial system are as follows:

1 Bank of Spain.
2 State-owned banks; Spanish private banks; foreign banks; savings banks; (rural) credit cooperatives.
3 Finance companies.
4 Investment institutions.
5 Brokers.
6 Insurance and reinsurance companies.

The private banks and savings banks are especially important within Spain owing to their volume of business and their involvement in all sectors of the economy. Most Spanish banks offer a full range of services to both corporate and private customers, including collections and payments outside Spain via their organizations abroad. Some fifty foreign banks also have offices within Spain, handling much of the business of foreign companies operating there; such companies established in Spain have access to the financial system under the same conditions applying to Spanish ones.

As regards the savings banks (*Cajas de Ahorros*): for a long time they have attracted a high volume of private savings and logically they prefer to lend to private customers (for mortgages etc.); they represent approximately a third of all deposits and a quarter of all loans. Since the early 1990s they have been involved in mergers and changes of status to protect or enhance their position within the Single Market and in the Spanish market, where they now compete with the big private banks. Naturally, the rural credit cooperatives focus their attention on the agricultural sector within Spain.

The handful of state-owned banks (*Entidades Oficiales de Crédito*) are mainly involved in supporting major projects, in promoting new ventures and in export financing. These bodies receive funds via the Instituto de Crédito Oficial (ICO) which has funds allocated from the annual state budget via the Ministry. The Banco Exterior de España (Overseas Trade Bank) is funded in part by the state and in part by shareholders; its purpose is self-evident. In 1991 the Government created the Corporación Bancaria de España (CBE) in order to match the state banking sector in other EU countries, a move regarded with suspicion by banks and which has been a factor in various mergers between private banks. In that same year was created the Banco Central Hispanoamericano (BCH) from two former banks (the Central and the Hispanoamericano), which became Spain's largest private bank.

Two years later the new 'fluidity' of the banking system in Spain was again demonstrated by the imminent collapse of the mighty Banco Español de Crédito (Banesto), which brought to light serious mismanagement and led to its being absorbed by the Banco de Santander to create the new giant, Santander-Banesto. The other two of the four major private banking groups currently operating are Banco Bilbao Vizcaya (BBV) and Argentaria. In total there are around 150 different private banks, with an overall average of some 100 branches apiece; they hold three-fifths of all deposits and make about a half of all loans. The largest of them are heavily involved in the ownership of or major shareholding in key economic sectors and companies, mainly at home, but increasingly abroad in areas like Latin America which in recent years have opened their markets to foreign investment.

Many foreign banks have bought outright, bought shares in or have gone into partnership with existing smaller Spanish banks which, like their major domestic counterparts, have had a large network of branches. However, in pursuit of efficiency and competitiveness, they and their domestic counterparts in Spain are now focusing on quality as opposed to quantity of operations. The private banks in general are the main source of financing for industry and, although they can be grouped under 'industrial' and 'commercial' headings, the latter predominate, sometimes having an industrial affiliate. Working capital needs can be satisfied variously: loans, overdraft facilities and bills of exchange (*letras*) are most widespread. Loans are usually granted for three- to six-month periods, but can be extended to a year. This is the normally negotiated period for overdrafts, whose rate of interest is fixed quarter by quarter; medium-sized firms frequently raise finance via bill discounting.

Spanish banking long endured a reputation for delay and obscurity in transactions. However, great advances have been achieved. For example, cheques are now credited to accounts after two days in normal circumstances and banks are now required, under threat of complaint to the Bank of Spain, to disclose the reasons for their charges to customers. The advent of electronic banking has made for both speed and efficiency; exchange control regulations are now freer but also more effective than in the past; payments abroad must be made through a legally established bank in Spain and any taxes on such transactions duly paid; many banks are now members of the SWIFT network which ensures international payments are made as promptly as possible. On the subject of credit: references can be obtained via specialist organizations and the use of bills of exchange has meant that 90 or 120 days are regarded as normal credit periods. Imports and exports can be covered by the Compañía Española de Seguro de Crédito a la Exportación for several years against various types of risk. It is now necessary to obtain from the Ministry or its Trade Office the official import documents for goods worth over half a million pesetas before money may be remitted abroad in payment.

These few illustrations cannot hide the fact that there is still a frustrating element of bureaucacy to be faced in Spain (see Section 16 – Red Tape), but it is equally important to acknowledge that many procedures have been made worthwhile rather than symbolic and that Spain has adapted very quickly to changes. Other financial institutions or players in the financial system also bear witness to those changes. The stock markets – based on the four Exchanges (*bolsas*) in Madrid, Barcelona, Bilbao and Valencia – were reformed in 1989 in order to modernize and thereby meet the needs of the fast-growing national economy. The Madrid Exchange dominates in terms of business activity, and foreign investment has been a powerful instrument for expansion and change. The issuers are mainly state agencies, leading private Spanish companies, and banks; foreign companies' shares can also be quoted following legislation passed in time for the advent of the Single Market in 1992/3.

The insurance sector

A whole range of other bodies and institutions is active in the field of finance, many in the money market, in investment and in brokerage; but one in particular merits special attention for its development since 1986 – the insurance (*seguros*) sector. Traditionally, private insurance was not a prominent consideration amongst Spaniards, probably for cultural as well as economic reasons. Increasing prosperity, closer attention to individual responsibility, and international influence have seen company and/or personal pension schemes, plus proper security for corporate enterprises turn this sector into a very profitable and attractive one for Spanish banks (which bought up small existing companies), and for major foreign insurance companies taking advantage of new freedoms under EU legislation. The latter have formed subsidiaries or branches or have bought existing Spanish-run companies. Vehicle and medical insurance, life assurance and insurance on exports have become prominent areas of such activity.

9 Legal practitioners

The Spanish legal system

The Spanish legal system is based on civil, as opposed to common, law. The sources of legal regulation are legislation, custom and general principles of law, in that order. Laws come into force 20 days after their publication in the *Boletín Oficial del Estado* (*Official State Gazette*). Judges and magistrates are independent as a judiciary, but neither they nor state attorneys may hold other public offices or belong to political parties or trade unions. The governing body of judges and magistrates is the Consejo General del Poder Oficial, comprising its president and 20 members appointed by the king. This body guarantees the independence of the judiciary *vis-à-vis* the other powers of the State, including the Ministry of Justice. The Attorney General (*Fiscal General del Estado*) is also appointed by the King after consultation with the *Consejo* over the person proposed by the Government. Spain also has the office of *Defensor del Pueblo* (Ombudsman), whose role is to oversee the conduct of the public administration and to ensure citizens' rights *vis-à-vis* government.

The legal profession

Lawyers in Spain are generally called *abogados*, and their professional association is the Colegio de Abogados. They are also called by the traditional names of *licenciados* and *letrados*; lawyers' offices are frequently known as *bufetes*. The functions of lawyers are defined by a Royal Decree of 1982, and they have the right to exercise their profession in courts and tribunals. Normally, petitions have to be signed by a lawyer. The case of litigants in court is usually presented by a *procurador* ('procurator'), who acts for the parties and the lawyers they have engaged. A third type of legal practitioner is the *notario*, at once legal professional and public servant, who authorizes public documents, acts, wills etc. In certain contracts and other legal matters the involvement of *notarios* is mandatory: they act as witnesses to contracts, they draw up official documents and in effect oversee the organization of public records in the legal field. At present it is necessary to be of Spanish nationality in order to practise as a lawyer in Spain.

10 Accountants and auditors

Like the banking system and other areas of economic activity, financial reporting in Spain has been subjected to considerable reform since 1986. The Código de Comercio (Commercial Code) is the basis of mercantile legislation, which in 1989 was brought into line with (then EC) EU practices. Two more specific items of legislation have been central to accounting (*contabilidad*) and auditing (*auditoría*) since the late 1980s: the Plan General de Contabilidad of 1990 and the Ley de Auditoría of 1988. The former systematized accounting principles, valuation rules and methods of drawing up annual accounts. In 1991 its provisions were refined by a further decree to cover consolidated accounts. The 1990 decree also established ICAC (Instituto de Contabilidad y Auditoría de Cuentas) to regulate both activities, the second of which saw the introduction of compulsory auditing of accounts and a general harmonization with EU norms. According to new rules established in 1989 the Registro Mercantil (see above) should receive the annual accounts (*cuentas anuales*) of all companies registered in Spain. These accounts comprise the balance sheet (*balance de situación*), profit and loss account (*cuenta de pérdidas y ganancias*) and notes to the account (*memoria*). These must be accompanied by the directors' report (*informe de gestión*) and the auditors' report (*informe de los auditores*).

Annual accounts

Companies and groups must make available to shareholders the annual accounts, which consist of: the directors' annual report, the end-of-year balance sheet, the profit and loss account, a statement of the proposed distribution of profits. Shareholders then have to approve them within six months of the end of the financial year. Spanish law requires that independent auditors report to the shareholders on whether the accounts demonstrate a 'true and fair' view of the company's activities. Those auditors are now frequently international accounting firms like Arthur Andersen. The early 1980s saw friction between the Colegio de Economistas and the Auditors' Institute (*Instituto de Censores Jurados de Cuentas de España*) over which practitioners were entitled to carry out the increasingly lucrative auditing work in Spain. The Spanish Accounting and Business Administration Association (AECA), including experts from companies, accounting firms, universities, professional organizations and Ministerial representatives, has been involved since the mid-1980s in the revision of the National Chart of Accounts. This is now applicable to companies quoted on the stock exchanges, banks and other financial institutions, companies supplying goods and services to or obtaining the same from government, amongst others appearing on the Registro Mercantil. When the auditors, whatever their origin or status, are fully satisfied that a 'true and fair' view has been provided by the company accountants (*contables*), they issue an unqualified report (*informe sin salvedades*); where they have doubts, the report is *con salvedades*, so the shareholders and/or public authorities have to decide on what action, if any, is appropriate. As has been the case elsewhere in the EU, the heightened awareness of the potential of business has seen rapid growth in the numbers aspiring to work in the field of financial reporting in Spain.

11 The advertising media

A wide range of national and international advertising agencies operate in Spain, focused largely on Madrid and Barcelona, and among these there are many that specialize in market research, direct marketing or graphic reproduction. There had been a strong American presence in the field since the 1950s, but European and national agencies or media groups have in the last 20 years become prominent. An average growth level of 20 per cent per annum in the Spanish advertising industry was registered between 1988 and 1993, though economic recession has most lately reduced such figures to more rational proportions. Foreign investment in the Spanish media as a whole (television, radio, various press sources) had increased almost tenfold between 1988 and 1989 alone! By 1993 the dominant multimedia groups in Spain, in which famous international names have shareholdings, were Prisa, Godó, Zeta and Correo. Whilst the media generally, and advertising (*publicidad*) in particular, have been affected by the economic climate, their situation has not reached crisis proportions. Of all of them television has proved the most durably popular, followed by magazines and radio in roughly equal measure, and finally newspapers: some 90 per cent of Spaniards over 14 are regular television watchers, nearly 60 per cent read magazines, over 50 per cent listen to the radio, but only 35 per cent read newspapers.

Given that all the media depend at least in part on advertising revenue, cutbacks in spending on advertising as a result of recession have had negative effects on those media. The case of the popular weekly magazine *Panorama*, which was first published in the heady days of 1987, well illustrates the situation. When its last issue appeared in late August 1993 the editor noted that it was one of eight such weeklies, whilst its average sales of 50,000 plus compared with a print run of

125,000 in a market of around 200,000 buyer/readers. In fact, spending on advertising in the Spanish media as a whole dropped in 1993 for the first time in ten years: the seminal year of 1992 had seen a peak of 593,101 million pesetas spent on all forms of advertising. The drop of 7 per cent was spread over television, radio, the printed media (*prensa escrita*) and other areas such as street hoardings (*vallas*), cinemas and public transport. A key organization concerned with advertising, the Asociación Española de Anunciantes (AEA), identified magazines as the worst hit (15 per cent drop), then Sunday papers (11 per cent) and daily papers (5.5 per cent). Radio and television registered only a 4 per cent drop, but the television channels had offered very favourable discounts in order to maintain and increase their output of advertising. Patently, the 'oral' media are favoured in Spain, as elsewhere, and advertisers generally are keen to target the largest audience possible for their wares. Private television channels – recent additions to the media market – have been very active, often with strong foreign backing. Two useful addresses:

AEAP: Asociación Española de Agencias de Publicidad,
        Velázquez 64–66, 28001 Madrid. Tel. (91) 435 6983

AEPE: Asociación Española de Publicidad Exterior,
        Alberto Alcocer 40, 28016 Madrid. Tel. (91) 250 5028

12 Holidays

Annual holidays are taken by most people in business during the month of August, 30 calendar days being the minimum agreed allowance. There is some overlap between July and August, and in certain organizations staff and management agree to phase holidays over the two months to permit at least a skeleton service to operate throughout the period. Nevertheless, little serious business is done in mid-summer; even between June and September, when the seven-hour *jornada intensiva* is often worked, those who have a second home in the mountains or on the coast are unavailable from some point on Fridays. City-dwellers who do not take their main vacation by the sea or in the mountains often return to their family's village of origin for several weeks or, increasingly, are taking holidays abroad. Vacation periods for schools usually comprise July, August and the first half of September; the universities have a further month before the students begin classes. The length of summer holidays has much to do with climate in Spain, in contrast to the longish breaks at Christmas and Easter taken by some Europeans, which in Spain are rare.

On the other hand, the Spanish enjoy a good number of individual public holidays spread throughout the year. Each region has its own festival days, but the 11 celebrated nationally leave only three, of the official 14, for specifically regional use. When public holidays fall on a Tuesday or a Thursday many Spanish people take the Monday or Friday from their annual holiday allowance in order to have a long weekend; this practice is known as *hacer puente*. It could mean that in early December, for example, when there are two national public holidays (the 6th and 8th), a business could be inaccessible for an entire week.

The working week itself consists of a maximum 40 hours, with at least one and a half days rest per week. Spanish citizens are also permitted time off for special events such as marriages and funerals, and recent EU legislation makes provision for maternity and paternity leave, which each member state interprets according to local conditions.

13 Trade unions

During the Franco dictatorship opposition to the regime most frequently came from banned workers' organizations operating as the syndical arm of the also banned Socialist and Communist parties. With democracy came legalization and the emergence of two major trade unions: the Unión General de Trabajadores (UGT), linked to the Labour Party (PSOE) in government since 1982, and the Comisiones Obreras (CC.OO.), which is regarded as the trade union of the Communist Party even though the union prefers to play an independent role. Relations between the unions, which have tended to represent different sectors of the working population (UGT in the smaller and medium-sized concerns, CC.OO. in the large public-sector ones), have often been strained by rivalry over political affiliation and over membership; but the fact remains that union membership is generally low (about 20 per cent of the working population), the unions have little financial power and the UGT's links with the Government since 1982 have proved to be as much a burden as a bonus for it. Other, smaller unions exist at national and regional level, but it is the big two that have gained 'most representative' status and that have therefore benefited most from legislation conferring rights on organizations established to protect workers' interests.

However, a whole range of factors – the trade unions' role in the consolidation of democracy in the 1970s, the nature of the Spanish economy with its multiplicity of small and medium-sized firms, the streamlining (*reconversión*) of major industries in the 1980s, accession to the (then) European Community in 1986, 'modernization' of Spanish society since 1982, economic recession in the 1990s – have all combined to ensure that even the occasional day-long general strikes have been accepted with relative equanimity by all concerned in the process of running Spanish public life. The apparently comfortable relationship between the Socialist government and employers or other capitalists has proved a bitter pill for some trade unionists, who had perhaps not recognized that modernization of the economy could lead to a diminution of their own power and influence. The consensus approach to labour relations, with Government, employers and unions sharing responsibilities, has been expressed in a series of pacts and agreements since 1977; the 1984 Acuerdo Económico y Social (Economic and Social Agreement) was the most comprehensive in its bid to bring rational even-handedness into the industrial relations arena with its provisions on pay, productivity, training, health and safety etc. At individual company level the employees are represented on company committees by delegates who may or may not be union members. These committees are kept informed of matters relating to the performance of the company, they monitor employment policy and can comment on company strategy.

For many years the official Spanish labour market had been inflexible, though an informal economy (*economía sumergida*) has always been in operation. From the mid-1980s, however, European approaches to employment have been introduced; the Single Market has further emphasized the need for more part-time work, fixed-term contracts, better training schemes, early retirement, etc., very often facilitated by government grants and concessions. By 1992 over 30 per cent of all employees were on temporary contracts (*contratos eventuales/temporales*), a situation that the Government regarded as responsible for the creation of new jobs. With a massive youth unemployment problem on its hands, the Government has invested heavily in new-style apprenticeships, training centres and new technology, as well as reforming the education system to encourage more to stay on at school and university and to learn new skills there. For those actually in work there is a minimum wage scheme (*salario mínimo interprofesional*) and the social security system covers all employees, employers and self-employed people as well as civil servants, the military and students. Employers and employees contribute according to salary levels for particular occupations, and the contributions of employers can be reduced or exempted by their taking on given categories of high-priority social groups. It is worth remembering that it has taken some two decades of steady application to achieve most of the progress noted, and that trade unions have figured prominently in the negotiations.

14 Business taxes

General levels of taxation

Taxes are levied in Spain at national, regional and local/municipal levels. There are two major direct taxes: personal, ranging between 10 per cent and 56 per cent, and company income tax at 35 per cent. Capital tax is also levied in cases where it is appropriate. The main indirect tax is, of course, VAT: in Spain it is called IVA (*Impuesto sobre Valor Añadido*), it is charged at 12 per cent on most goods sold in Spain, and prices are quoted inclusive of this tax. One half of this rate is charged on certain necessities, whilst major luxuries are levied at nearly three times the standard rate. A key exemption is on exports, with limited exemptions applicable to a variety of social activities and to a minority of financial ones; examples of other indirect taxes are transfer tax and import duties.

Personal income tax, levied on individuals who reside for more than half the days of the year in Spain, is deducted by employers from earnings and the return has to be made by the middle of the following year. A wealth tax is also applicable to high earners, whose personal and wealth tax burden is 70 per cent of the combined total income. Inheritance tax and social security payments are levied on individuals, as are special taxes on all consumers of tobacco, alcohol and petrol. Transfer of property (land and real estate) is taxed at 12 per cent for commercial holdings and at 6 per cent for residential and agricultural; a low percentage tax rate is charged for urban land use and on increases in land value, as well as a 0.5 per cent charge for stamp tax.

Business

In the exclusively business sphere, companies are liable to pay tax in Spain if they are formed according to Spanish company law, have their head office in Spain or have their administration and management in the country. As such, they are deemed to be resident in Spain, and resident corporations are taxed on their worldwide income. Taxable income includes capital gains, income from investments not related to regular business and profits from operations. Operating losses, meanwhile, can be carried forward for as much as five years for tax purposes. Companies non-resident in Spain are taxed only on income generated by operations within the country, of course. The tax year for companies corresponds to the accounting year, and the former are required to file an annual tax return within 25 days of their balance sheet and accounts being approved by shareholders at the AGM. This return is usually drawn up by companies and their advisors, and accompanying it would be the required tax payment, minus an advance figure paid in October equivalent to 30 per cent of the previous year's tax liability.

Tax concessions

The advent of double taxation treaties has proved very helpful for foreign companies in Spain, the USA and the EU nations being most prominent in such agreements. Actual tax concessions and incentives to foreign investors since the mid-1980s have become as generous as those for indigenous companies. These opportunities emanate both from the Spanish Government and from the EU: general incentives include non-returnable subsidies of a percentage of the value of an investment, relief against national taxes, and loans from EU bank sources. More specific tax-concession areas are as follows:

- credits for investment and employment
- promotion of new technology
- reductions for investment in specified industries and locations (e.g. a *Zona de Urgente Reindustrialización* in Asturias or Murcia)
- reductions for investment in firms under productivity agreements
- benefits on mergers and spin-offs
- local concessions
- benefits for joint ventures and regional industrial development corporations
- benefits granted to certain industries

The regional incentives comprise reductions in local taxes to establish or expand industrial plants and initial reduction of the business licence tax, plus subsidies on loans and reductions in social security contributions. For information on tax treatment of different company formations in Spain, see below (Types of company).

15 Types of company

As noted briefly in the earlier section on business organizations, the most common and most prestigious form of legal entity under Spanish mercantile law is the *Sociedad Anónima* (S.A.), which corresponds closely to the plc or limited liability company. It can exist in either private or public sector, and can range from a large stock-exchange corporation to a modest family business, but it must have a minimum capital of ten million pesetas. The *Sociedad de Responsabilidad Limitada* (S.R.L. or S.L.) has certain common characteristics with the former, but its stockholders cannot exceed 50 and its minimum capital is half a million pesetas. Additionally, there is no maximum capital requirement, it does not have shares and the capital is divided among the stockholders. This type of company is frequently found in the service and retail sectors. Partnerships (*Sociedad Regular Colectiva* and *Sociedad en Comandita*) are not numerous in Spain, but do have legal status; the two types noted differ in respect of their partners and of the extent of their liability. The creation and development of cooperatives (*Cooperativas*) have been government policy for a number of years, especially in agricultural areas. A high proportion of businesspeople in Spain are registered as *comerciantes* ('sole traders') and operate across a variety of sectors including retail, catering and services; there are formal regulations to be observed, but such traders do enjoy relative freedom within their chosen field of enterprise.

Establishing a company in Spain

Foreign companies wishing to establish in Spain can effectively choose either branch or subsidiary status. Unlike the S.A. or the S.L., the branch (*sucursal*) is not a legal entity in Spain, but must nevertheless register at the Registro Mercantil and present the requisite documents authorized by a notary. Factors influencing a decision over status are commented upon below. A *Sociedad Anónima*, the most widespread type of business enterprise for a subsidiary, must have a minimum of three shareholders, who may be companies or individuals of any nationality. The shareholders or their representatives are required to appear before a notary who carries out the relevant public deed of incorporation. The capital stock must be fully subscribed and at least 25 per cent of it must be paid at the time of incorporation. The Registro Mercantil issues a certificate to permit use of the company name, the Directorado General de Transacciones Extranjeras (DGTE) normally gives clearance to the projected investment within a month, and the whole deed of incorporation is executed, as indicated above, by a public notary who should have at his disposal the various documents of approval.

If such a process is to be effected outside Spain the Spanish consul in the country normally acts in place of the public notary. A number of other, preparatory steps also have to be taken before the company can be formally granted S.A. status according to the procedure outlined above. The costs of establishing the company include the notary's fee, a transfer tax equivalent to 1 per cent of the capital figure, a fee for filing the company on the Registro Mercantil, and some minor taxes. In all, the costs might amount to some 3 per cent of the company's capital.

Subsidiaries and branches

In considering subsidiary or branch status, it is liability to taxation, rather than initial costs, that will most likely prove decisive. Although the corporation tax rate of 35 per cent applies to both, a branch lacks separate legal status, which means that the remittance of the profits generated by a branch to its parent company is not taxed in Spain. Yet the foreign tax credit provided under Spanish legislation is in principle not available to branches; interest on loans from the foreign parent company to its Spanish branch is in principle not tax-deductible for branches, whereas it usually is for subsidiaries. The distribution of dividends from the latter, however, is taxable at 25 per cent (or, perhaps, at a reduced double-taxation treaty rate to non-resident companies), but branches are immune. Clearly, such provisions require close consideration and no doubt the guidance of a Spanish-speaking tax expert (see Business taxes section).

Shares and joint ventures

Two other major ways in which foreign companies or individuals might enter the Spanish market are by acquiring shares in existing corporations and by participating in the increasingly popular joint ventures. In the former case DGTE approval has to be obtained if the foreign holding is to comprise 50 per cent or more of the capital of the Spanish company, but if the investment is less than 25 million pesetas such authorization is not necessary. The transfer of shares must normally be attested by a Spanish authenticating official (notary public, stockbroker, Spanish consul) or possibly by a brokerage agency. Documentation similar to that required for establishing a company is required on the part of those wishing to make the purchase. Fees, too, are similar to those obtaining for the above purpose, though transfer tax is not normally applicable in these transactions. When one non-resident shareholder sells shares in a Spanish company to another non-resident, the formal procedures are reduced to each party's informing the DGTE of the transaction. However, it is preferential tax provisions which seem to have attracted many foreign companies to try joint ventures in Spain, of which there are four main types:

Sociedad de empresa: a minimum of three participants – whether individuals, S.A.s or S.L.s – who constitute a separate legal entity. They can bring to the venture different types of asset, but the overall holding of each cannot exceed 30 per cent of their own capital. Such schemes have been prominent in manufacturing and sales operations, often aimed at expansion or modernization projects.

Agrupación de empresa: a grouping of companies which agree to collaborate over common-interest matters, but without constituting themselves as a separate legal entity.

Unión temporal de empresa: a business agreement for a specific period of time intended to perform a particular service or complete a specific project.

Cesión de unidades de obra: a subcontracting arrangement by which the partners engage third parties to do some or all of a job.

Whatever the field or type of business activity, logic suggests acquiring the services of specialists to ensure good and proper practice where complex regulations and financing are concerned.

16 Red tape

Spanish bureaucracy during and prior to the Franco period is legendary, not only because civil servants placed self-interest above public service, but also because the type of State authoritarianism embraced by Franco encouraged dependency and delay, which in turn permitted corruption and indolence. The inefficiency of government administration led in Spain (and in Latin America) to the establishment of *gestorías administrativas*, agencies which charge individuals for completing on their behalf all the routine tasks associated with State–citizen relations.

The new PSOE Government of 1982 made a concerted effort to modernize all branches of the administration, often in spite of resistance from its own employees. Moreover, attempts to modernize fiscal policy and the penal code, for example, to create a more just system that befitted a democratic society, were often met with scepticism by those they were designed to help, so strong was Spaniards' mistrust of officialdom. On the strictly business front, the tight regulation of much of the Franco period has gradually given way to a more pragmatic approach that recognizes that progress and profit depend on decision-making at all levels, even though foreign businesspeople can also find dealing with Spanish officialdom a frustrating experience. In the private sector, for example, the family control of many businesses can mean that responsibility for decisions is not delegated. However, the securing of contacts, often known as *enchufes* ('plugs') in Spain and *palancas* ('levers') in Latin America, has long been regarded as an acceptable means to an end. At worst the practice suggests corruption, at best it reflects the fact that Hispanic people place considerable emphasis on the personal or social dimension of doing business.

Spanish entry into the then EC in 1986 and the advent of the Single Market in 1992 have necessarily opened up business practices to outside influences. Whilst far more simple than they were in the period up to 1986, such matters as exchange controls, foreign investment in 'sensitive' industries, work permits, patenting, debt collection, import documentation, exporting of capital etc., still require patience from all concerned. The fact remains that if business opportunities are to be taken, then foreign interests must adapt in part to local conditions, whether those conditions can be categorized as 'red tape' or simply the business culture prevalent in that country. In Spain large and small businesses rely quite heavily on *gestores* ('local agents'), whose *gestoría* acts as an advice centre on legal, financial and bureaucratic matters. Foreign companies therefore should do likewise, to ensure good relations with trading partners and the relevant institutions.

Reference Grammar

This grammar summary is only a brief guide to the basics of Spanish grammar. For additional explanations and a comprehensive list of regular and irregular verbs, it is well worth investing in a good Spanish grammar book.

1 The definite article

In the singular the masculine form is **el** and the feminine form **la**. Objects as well as living things are divided into masculine and feminine 'genders', with no obvious reason for inanimate objects taking one or the other: for example, a hotel (**el hotel**) is masculine, whilst a company (**la empresa**) is feminine. The only foolproof way of remembering which is the gender of a noun is to learn the noun with its article:

Masculine		*Feminine*	
el hotel	the hotel	**la agencia**	the agency
el grupo	the group	**la empresa**	the company

It is useful to know that nouns ending in **-o** are generally masculine whilst those ending in **-a** are generally feminine, but there are exceptions: **el minorista, el sistema, la mano, la foto.**

Note usage: **Juan es *el* secretario**: John is *the* secretary (a particular secretary), but **Juan es secretario**: John is *a* secretary (his job).

Señor, señora. Note also that when speaking *to* a person you say **Señor Evans** (Mr Evans) or **Señora Evans** (Mrs Evans), but when speaking *about* a person you say **el señor Evans, la señora Evans.**

The contractions al and del

A + el becomes **al**: 'to the', 'at the'

Vamos al aeropuerto el domingo.

De + el becomes **del**: 'of the', 'from the' (except when **El** begins with a capital letter)

Los disquetes son del jefe.   **Se venderán obras de El Greco.**

2 Omission of subject pronouns

These are generally omitted in both spoken and written Spanish because the verb endings make them largely superfluous. However, they can be used to avoid confusion, e.g. in the third person (**él, ella, usted**) and for emphasizing who is doing an action.

3 The verb 'to be'

Spanish has two verbs, **ser** and **estar**, which in different circumstances mean 'to be'.

	Ser	*Estar*	
yo	soy	estoy	I am
tú	eres	estás	you are (fam. sing.)
él	es	está	he is, it is
ella	es	está	she is, it is
usted	es	está	you are (pol. sing.)
nosotros-as	somos	estamos	we are
vosotros-as	sois	estáis	you are (fam. pl.)
ellos	son	están	they are (masc.)
ellas	son	estáan	they are (fem.)
ustedes	son	están	you are (pol. pl.)

It is essential to understand clearly the different uses of **ser** and **estar** from the outset.

Ser indicates *who* and *what*: i.e. identity, nationality, permanent and inherent characteristics, and occupation:

El señor Brown es inglés.	Mr Brown is English.
Somos analistas.	We are analysts.
Soy aplicado.	I am hardworking.

Estar indicates *where* and *how*: i.e. position, condition and temporary state:

| **Robert está en su oficina.** | Robert is in his office. |
| **Están pendientes.** | They are pending. |

4 The polite form of 'you'

Vd. is short for **usted**; similarly, in the plural **Vds.** for **ustedes. Usted** and **ustedes** are used (rather than **tú** and **vosotros**) except when addressing children, relatives, close friends and colleagues of similar standing.

5 Plural of the definite article

The masculine plural form of 'the' is **los** and the feminine plural is **las**:

| **los beneficios** | the profits | **las acciones** | the shares |
| **los libros** | the books | **las cifras** | the figures |

Note that the definite article, whether singular or plural, must be included before a noun used in its generic sense: e.g. **Las inversiones son necesarias.**

6 Plural of nouns and adjectives

Those ending in a vowel add **-s** to form the plural, whilst those ending in a consonant normally add **-es**:

préstamo:	**préstamos**	loans
carpeta:	**carpetas**	files
hotel:	**hoteles**	hotels

Note that words ending in **-ión** drop the accented **ó** in the plural:

habitación   **habitaciones**
excursión   **excursiones**

This is because the stress automatically falls on the newly formed penultimate syllable.

7 The indefinite article

'A' ('an'), is expressed by **un** (masc.) and by **una** (fem.). The plural forms, **unos** and **unas**, mean 'some' or 'a few'.

un balance	a balance sheet
unos balances	some (a few) balance sheets

Note: **unos** and **unas** meaning 'some' are frequently omitted, particularly after the verb **tener** ('to have').

Tenemos plazas vacantes.	We have some places vacant.

8 Position and agreement of adjectives

Adjectives may be placed either before or after the noun: e.g. **bonitas alfombras**, **vino bueno**. When the adjective comes first it implies greater emphasis, whilst placing the adjective *after* the noun emphasizes the noun rather than the adjective. Exceptions to note are numbers and other adjectives implying quantities and amounts, which are always placed *before* the noun. All adjectives must agree in number (singular or plural) and gender (masculine or feminine) with the noun they describe:

un despacho moderno   una carta breve   unas buenas ofertas

Remember that those adjectives which do not end in **-o** remain the same in the singular for both genders, except for adjectives of nationality:

e.g. **español**	**española**
japonés	**japonesa**

9 The verb tener 'to have'

tengo	I have
tienes	you (sing.) have
tiene	he/she/it has (+ you: **usted**)
tenemos	we have
tenéis	you (pl.) have
tienen	they have (+ you: **ustedes**)

Expressions with tener

Spanish uses **tener** where English uses 'to be' in expressions such as:

tener prisa	to be in a hurry
tener sed	to be thirsty
tener ganas	to be willing (wish)
tener dudas	to be doubtful
tener razón	to be right

10 How to express obligation

There are three principal ways of using verbs to express obligation in Spanish:

Tener que	indicates something that one has to or needs to do
Hay* que	indicates a more impersonal obligation
Deber	indicates a less strong obligation, as if one were giving advice and telling somebody that (s)he ought to do it

These three verbs are followed by the infinitive of the verb which identifies the action:

No puedo salir ahora porque tengo que terminar esta carta.

Hay que revisar las cuentas una vez al mes.

El jefe me ha dicho que debo trabajar más.

*Note: the impersonal **hay** alone means 'there is', 'there are'.

11 Todo **and** todos

As a noun **todo** means 'all' or 'everything', whilst **todos** means 'everybody', 'everyone'. The adjectives are **todo** (masc. sing.), **toda** (fem. sing.), **todos** (m. pl.), **todas** (f. pl.):

todo el día	all (the) day
todas las empleadas	all (the) female staff

12 The infinitive

The verb in its infinitive form behaves like a noun, and as such can be the subject of a sentence:

Esperar más tiempo no tiene sentido.

It can also be the object of a verb:

Prefiero no hablar de ello.

It can also follow a preposition:

Fue a Barcelona sin decir nada a nadie.

13 Verbs

Present tense of regular verbs

1st conjugation, infinitive ending in -**ar**

Mirar to look (at)

(yo)	**miro**	(I look, I am looking)
(tú)	**miras**	
(él/ella/Vd.)	**mira**	
(nosotros)	**miramos**	
(vosotros)	**miráis**	
(ellos/ellas/Vds.)	**miran**	

The two forms of the present tense in English, e.g. 'I look' and 'I am looking', can be expressed by the one form in Spanish: e.g. **miro**.

2nd conjugation, infinitive ending in -**er**

Comer to eat

como	(I eat, I am eating)
comes	
come	
comemos	
coméis	
comen	

Irregular verb hacer: 'to do', 'to make'

In the present indicative this verb is irregular only in the first person singular. It is an important verb as it is the basis for many idiomatic phrases.

Hacer

hago	(I do, I am doing)
haces	
hace	
hacemos	
hacéis	
hacen	

Hacer is used in expressions relating to the weather:

Hace frío.	It is cold.
Hace calor.	It is hot.

but **Tener** is used for persons:

Tengo calor	I am hot.

3rd conjugation, infinitive ending in -ir
These verbs have the same endings as the **-er** verbs, except for the 1st and 2nd persons plural.

Escribir to write

escribo	(I write, I am writing)
escribes	
escribe	
escribimos	
escribís	
escriben	

Irregular verb Ir: 'to go'
This is a completely irregular verb which should be learned by heart from the start.

voy	(I go, I am going)
vas	
va	
vamos	
vais	
van	

When using the verb **ir** to indicate destination or purpose, the preposition **a** must follow the verb:

Voy a Madrid.	I am going to Madrid.
Van a escribir una carta.	They are going to write a letter.

Expressing a future idea or intention using Ir
The construction **ir** + **a** + infinitive is used to express a future intention, and corresponds with the English 'to be going to' + infinitive: **Ellos van a salir de Santiago mañana**.

Irregular verbs: present tense
(a) Verbs which change their stem from **-e-** to **-ie-**

ar	er	ir
pensar	**querer**	**preferir**
pienso	**quiero**	**prefiero**
piensas	**quieres**	**prefieres**
piensa	**quiere**	**prefiere**
pensamos	**queremos**	**preferimos**
pensáis	**queréis**	**preferís**
piensan	**quieren**	**prefieren**

Other verbs which follow the same pattern are **empezar, cerrar, comenzar, despertarse, sentarse**, etc.

(b) Verbs which change their stem from -o- to -ue-

ar	er	ir
encontrar	poder	dormir
tnencuentro	puedo	duermo
encuentras	puedes	duermes
encuentra	puede	duerme
encontramos	podemos	dormimos
encontráis	podéis	dormís
encuentran	pueden	duermen

Other verbs which follow the same pattern are **almorzar, costar, volver, llover, morir**, etc.

(c) Verbs which change their stem from -e- to -i-

This change only applies to verbs of the 3rd conjugation, in **-ir**

pedir

pido
pides
pide
pedimos
pedís
piden

Other verbs which follow the same pattern are **impedir, medir, despedir, reír,** etc.

Verbs which are irregular in the 1st person singular

Infinitive	1st pers. sing.
conocer	conozco
traducir	traduzco
conducir	conduzco
producir	produzco
hacer	hago
poner	pongo
salir	salgo
dar	doy
ver	veo
saber	sé
traer	traigo
decir	digo
tener	tengo
venir	vengo

Reflexive verbs

These are very commonly used in Spanish. They are formed by placing the reflexive pronoun **me, te, se, nos, os, se** in front of the inflected verb:

lavarse

me lavo
te lavas
se lava
nos lavamos
os laváis
se lavan

With infinitives the reflexive pronoun remains attached to the end of the verb; it also attaches to present participles and affirmative commands.

Se as a substitute for the passive voice

When the subject of the action is not expressed or is not important, the reflexive pronoun **se** is often used with the 3rd person singular or plural of the verb:

Se **habla español.**

14 Tenses

Present continuous

In Spanish the present continuous is formed using the verb **estar** + present participle. The present participle is formed by adding **-ando** to the stem of **-ar** verbs, and **-iendo** to **-er** and **-ir** verbs:

hablar	**Jorge está hablando.**
vender	**Estamos vendiendo productos de alta calidad.**
escribir	**Están escribiendo a clientes extranjeros.**

There are some verbs which form their participle irregularly:

ir	**yendo**
construir	**construyendo**
sentir	**sintiendo**
decir	**diciendo**

Present perfect

The present perfect is formed with the present tense of the verb **haber** followed by the past participle of the verb in question. Its use, as in English, is to describe what *has* happened.

haber	+	*past participle*
he		**hablado**
has		**andado**
ha		**comido**
hemos		**leído**
habéis		**salido**
han		**venido**

The past participle is formed by adding **-ado** to the stem of **-ar** verbs and **-ido** to the stem of **-er** and **-ir** verbs:

Antonio ha hablado con su homólogo francés.
No hemos leído el periódico de ayer.
Han venido a la reunión.

There are a number of irregular past participles such as **dicho, hecho, puesto, vuelto, muerto,** etc.

The future

The future tense of all regular verbs is formed in the same way, by simply adding **-é, -ás, -á, -emos, -éis, -án** to the infinitive of the verb:

ar	*er*	*ir*
hablar	**vender**	**vivir**
hablaré	**venderé**	**viviré**
hablarás	**venderás**	**vivirás**
etc.	etc.	etc.

Some verbs are irregular in the future. The irregularity occurs in the stem of the verb, not in the ending, e.g.

poner:	**pondré**	**salir:**	**saldré**
decir:	**diré**	**hacer:**	**haré**
tener:	**tendré**	**saber:**	**sabré**

The conditional

The conditional of all regular verbs is formed in the same way. Simply add **-ía, -ías, -ía, -íamos, -íais, -ían** to the infinitive of the verb.

ar	*er*	*ir*
hablar	**vender**	**invertir**
hablaría	**vendería**	**invertiría**
hablarías	**venderías**	**invertirías**
etc.	etc.	etc.

Those verbs that are irregular in the future are also irregular in the conditional. Simply add the conditional endings to the irregular future stem:

e.g. **saber (sabré) sabría**

The past tense

This tense describes an action completed in the past at a particular time. It is often used in conjunction with certain adverbial phases of time, such as **ayer, la semana pasada, anteayer, hace una hora.**

(a) Regular -ar verbs

These are formed by adding the following endings to the stem of the verb:
-é, -aste, -ó, -amos, -asteis, -aron.

hablar

hablé
hablaste
habló
hablamos
hablasteis
hablaron

(b) Regular -er and -ir verbs

These are formed by adding the following endings to the stem of the verb:
-í, -iste, -ió, -imos, -isteis, -ieron.

comer	vivir
comí	viví
comiste	viviste
comió	vivió
comimos	vivimos
comisteis	vivisteis
comieron	vivieron

Irregular verbs

Here are some of the more common ones:

ir	fui	fuiste	fue	fuimos	fuisteis	fueron
dar	di	diste	dio	dimos	disteis	dieron
hacer	hice	hiciste	hizo	hicimos	hicisteis	hicieron
saber	supe	supiste	supo	supimos	supisteis	supieron
ser	fui	fuiste	fue	fuimos	fuisteis	fueron
poder	pude	pudiste	pudo	pudimos	pudisteis	pudieron

Note: **ser** and **ir** have the same forms in this past (*pretérito*) tense.

The imperfect tense

This tense is more common in Spanish than in English and refers to a continuing or repeated action in the past. It can be expressed in English by 'was/were doing' or 'used to do'.

Regular -ar verbs

These add the following endings to the stem of the verb:
-aba, -abas, -aba, -ábamos, -abais, -aban.

hablar

hablaba
hablabas
hablaba
hablábamos
hablabais
hablaban

Regular -er and -ir verbs

These add the following endings to the stem of the verb:
-ía, -ías, -ía, -íamos, -íais, -ían.

vender	escribir
vendía	escribía
vendías	escribías
vendía	escribía
vendíamos	escribíamos
vendíais	escribíais
vendían	escribían

15 How to give orders/the imperative

To give orders and to tell people to do things the imperative (command) mood of
the verb is used. When addressing people in the imperative one can either use
the informal (**tú/vosotros**) or the formal/polite (**usted/ustedes**) form.

Singular

The informal imperative is normally formed using the third person singular of the
verb in the present tense:

ar	er	ir
hablar	**comer**	**escribir**
habla	**come**	**escribe**

The following verbs have irregular informal imperatives:

tener:	ten	hacer:	haz
venir:	ven	salir:	sal
ir:	ve	poner:	pon
decir:	di	ser:	sé

The formal imperative is formed by adding -e to the stem of the first person
singular of the present tense of -ar verbs and -a to the stem of the first person
singular of the present tense of -er and -ir verbs:

ar	er	ir
hablar	**comer**	**escribir**
[habl] – hable	**[com] – coma**	**[escrib] – escriba**
tomar	**tener**	**construir**
[tom] – tome	**[teng] – tenga**	**[construy] –**
		construya

The following verbs, amongst others, have irregular formal imperatives:

> **dar: dé   estar: esté   ser: sea   ir: vaya   saber: sepa**

Plural

The plural of the informal and formal imperative is formed as follows.

Informal imperative: replace **-r** of the infinitive with **-d**

> **contar: contad   vender: vended   venir: venid**

Formal imperative: add **-n** to the singular formal imperative:

> **tome: tomen   tenga: tengan   vaya: vayan**

Negative commands

To express a negative informal command or instruction in the singular, simply add an **-s** to the formal imperative command and **no** before the verb:

> **tome: no tomes   coma: no comas   vaya: no vayas**

In the plural add **-is** to the singular formal imperative and add an accent over the preceding vowel:

> **tome: no toméis   coma: no comaís   vaya: no vayaís**

To express a negative formal command or instruction in both singular and plural, simply put **no** before the formal imperative command:

> **dé: no dé**   **escriba: no escriba**   **tomen: no tomen**
> **tengan: no tengan**   **vayan: no vayan**

16 The subjunctive

The subjunctive (as opposed to the indicative) is a form of the verb used to express the result of commands and wishes. The 'polite form' (**usted/ustedes**) of the imperative, it should be remembered, is the same as the third person of the subjunctive:

> **Venga aquí.**   Come here.
> **Que vengan.**   Let them come.

Form of the present subjunctive

To form the present subjunctive of an **-ar** verb, take the first person singular of the present indicative (e.g. **miro**), remove the vowel ending and then substitute the endings **-e, -es, -e, -emos, -éis, -en**.

To form the present subjunctive of an **-er** or **-ir** verb, take the first person singular of the present indicative (e.g. **como, vivo**), remove the vowel ending and then substitute the endings **-a, -as, -a, -amos, -áis, -an**.

mirar	comer	vivir
mire	coma	viva
mires	comas	vivas
mire	coma	viva
miremos	comamos	vivamos
miréis	comáis	viváis
miren	coman	vivan

In a radical-changing verb the change normally occurs in the present subjunctive in the same persons as for the present indicative.

poder

pueda
puedas
pueda
podamos
podáis
puedan

The exception to this is **-ir** verbs (which change **e** to **i**) where the radical change takes place throughout the present subjunctive.

pedir

pida
pidas
pida
pidamos
pidáis
pidan

Uses of the subjunctive

The present subjunctive replaces the present indicative in certain cases and circumstances. It is used:

(a) **after verbs of wanting and wishing**

Quiere que yo le visite en Madrid.
He wants me to visit him in Madrid.

No quiero que me esperes en la estación.
I don't want you to wait for me at the station.

(b) after verbs of emotion

Estoy contento de que puedas venir.
I'm glad you can come.

(c) after verbs of commanding or instructing

Nos piden que paguemos la cuenta.
They ask us to pay the bill.

(Note the **u** which is inserted into the present subjunctive of verbs ending in **-car** and **-gar** in order to keep the sound of the **c** and **g** hard: e.g. **buscar – busque; llegar – llegue.**)

The subjunctive is used in all the above cases when the subject of the verb in the subordinate clause is different from that in the main clause and in some way depends upon it. Note the difference in the following examples:

Quiero visitar Madrid.	I want to visit Madrid.
Quiero que visites Madrid.	I want you to visit Madrid.
Estoy contento de poder venir.	I am happy to be able to come.
Estoy contento de que puedas venir.	I am happy that you can come.

(d) after a negative or indefinite antecedent

No encuentro a nadie que le conozca.
I can find nobody who knows him.

Busco alguien que sepa hacerlo.
I am looking for someone who can do it.

No hay nada que podamos hacer.
There is nothing we can do.

(e) after certain impersonal verbs and expressions

es mejor que	it is best that
más vale que	"
es preciso que	it is necessary that
es menester que	"
es necesario que	"
es posible que	it is possible that
es imposible que	it is impossible that
puede ser que	it may be that

Más vale que no venga.
It is best for him not to come.

Es posible que lo tenga.
It is possible that he has it.

Es preciso que llegues mañana.
It's necessary for you to arrive tomorrow.

Note: expressions of certainty such as **es cierto que** (it is certain that) do not require the subjunctive except when used negatively.

(f) after the following conjunctions:

a fin de que	so that (purpose)
a no sea que	unless
aunque	even if, even though (concession)

Volvió a España a fin de que su hijo pudiera explicárselo.
He returned to Spain so that his son could explain it to him.

Aunque compre acciones, no le van a beneficiar.
Even if he buys shares, they won't help him.

but

Aunque el banco cierra a las dos, ha salido ya.
Although the bank closes at two, he has already left.

(g) following the expression **por . . . que**, unless it expresses an absolute certainty

Por grande que sea, no lo quiere.
However big it is, he does not want it.

but

Por mucho que traté, no pude hacerlo.
However much I tried, I could not do it.

(g) in certain fixed expressions such as:

sea lo que sea	be that as it may
haga lo que haga	whatever he may do
pase lo que pase	whatever may happen
sea quien sea	whoever he may be
diga lo que diga	whatever he may say

The imperfect subjunctive

All verbs form this tense in the same way, by taking the third person plural of the past tense, removing the ending **-ron** and replacing it by the endings **-ra, -ras, -ra, -ramos, -rais, -ran,** *or* **-se, -ses, -se, -semos, -seis, -sen.**

venir	**viniera**	or	**viniese**
decir	**dijera**	or	**dijese**
comer	**comiera**	or	**comiese**
ir	**fuera**	or	**fuese**
hablar	**hablara**	or	**hablase**
oír	**oyera**	or	**oyese**
hacer	**hiciera**	or	**hiciese**

The imperfect subjunctive is used in the same circumstances as the present subjunctive, but when referring to past time:

Quería que yo fuese a España con él.
He wanted me to go to Spain with him.

Les dije que lo hicieran en seguida.
I told them to do it at once.

17 Personal a

The personal **a** is used before a direct object of a verb (except **tener**) when the object is a noun indicating a definite or particular person, personified thing, well-loved place or pet.

El médico visita a la encargada de ventas.

Visito a Madrid.

18 Adjectives

(a) Possessive

These agree in gender and number with the thing possessed, and they precede the noun.

Singular	Plural	
mi	mis	my
tu	tus	your
su	sus	his, her, its, your (**Vd.**)
nuestro/a	nuestros/as	our
vuestro/a	vuestros/as	your
su	sus	their, your (**Vds.**)

Nuestro hotel es moderno.
Mi banco está cerrado.
Sus cuentas no tienen fondos.

If there is any doubt regarding to whom **su** refers, the forms **de él, de ella, de Vd., de ellos, de ellas, de Vds** may be added.

El ingeniero y sus amigos van a su taller de él.

(b) Demonstrative

The Spanish use three forms, in contrast with the English two:

este, esta, estos, estas	this, these (near the speaker)
ese, esa, esos, esas	that, those (near the listener)
aquel, aquella, aquellos, aquellas	that, those (over there)

The masculine/feminine and singular/plural features are clear.

19 Pronouns

(a) Demonstrative

These are identical to the demonstrative adjectives, except that they bear an accent (as they replace the noun):

éste, ésta. éstos, éstas	this one, these (ones)
ése, ésa, ésos, ésas	that one, those (ones)
aquél, aquélla, aquéllos,as	that one, those (ones)

Note: neuter forms **esto, eso, aquello** are used when the gender is uncertain. They do not have accents, and the one form expresses both singular and plural notions:

¿Qué es eso?
Aquello de ayer me lo contó tu secretaria.
Estop no está muy claro.

(b) Possessive

These agree in number and gender with the noun they represent. The article may be omitted only after the verb **ser**.

el mío, la mía, los míos, las mías	mine
el tuyo, la tuya, los tuyos, las tuyas	yours
el suyo, la suya, los suyos, las suyas	his, hers, its, yours (**Vd.**)
el nuestro, la nuestra, los nuestros, las nuestras	ours
el vuestro, la vuestra, los vuestros, las vuestras	yours
el suyo, la suya, los suyos, las suyas	theirs, yours (**Vds.**)

Tengo mi choche y tienes el tuyo.
No es su revista, es mía.
¿Dónde están los suyos?

Where the exact meaning of **suyo** is not clear, the forms **de él, de ellas**, etc., may be added.

La máquina es suya de él, pero las fotografías son suyas de ella.

(c) Direct and indirect object pronouns

Direct	Indirect
me	**me**
te	**te**
lo	**le**
la	**le**
nos	**nos**
os	**os**
los	**les**
las	**les**

Direct and indirect pronouns are normally placed before the verb. These pronouns are used to substitute for nouns when we already have referred to the latter by their full name:

¿Quién tiene los informes?
Los tiene la secretaria.

¿Por qué está Juan tan contento?
Porque el jefe le ha subido el sueldo.

However, object pronouns are attached to the end of infinitives, present participles and affirmative commands, although in the first two cases they may also precede the main verb:

¿Qué haces con esa carta?
Voy a abrirla.

¿Qué hago con los libros?
Póngalos encima de la mesa.

(d) Verbs used with indirect pronouns

Certain verbs in Spanish are always used with an indirect object. These verbs include **gustar, encantar, agradar, parecer, sorprender, doler**, etc.

gustar

me gusta
gusta   **(pasar muchas horas en la oficina)**
le gusta
nos gustan
os gustan   **(los nuevos empleados)**
les gustan

20 Comparatives and superlatives

(a) Comparison of superiority

To form the comparative of adjectives, the following construction is used:

más + adjective + **que**
Mi cartera es más nueva que la tuya.

When the comparative is followed by a number the construction **más de** is used instead of **más que**:

La empresa tiene más de cien empleados.

Four adjectives have irregular forms for the comparative. These are:

bueno:	**mejor**
malo:	**peor**
grande:	**mayor**
pequeño:	**menor**

El Hotel España es mejor que el Quijote.

(b) Comparison of equality

To form the comparative of equality of adjectives the following construction is used:

tan + adjective + **como**

Banesto es tan fuerte como Caja de Madrid.

Note: to express a comparison of inferiority it is possible to use the construction

menos + adjective + **que**

María es menos aplicada que su jefa.

but it is more normal to use a negative verb with a comparison of equality:

María no es tan aplicada como su jefa.

(c) Superlative of adjectives

To form the superlative of adjectives the following construction is used:

más + adjective + **de**

However, one of the forms of the definite article (**el, la, los, las**) is always placed before **más**, and agrees with the noun being described:

Esta firma es la más débil del sector.

The same rule applies for the irregular adjectives described above:

El Hotel Madrid es el mejor de todos.

21 Negative and interrogative

(a) The negative

A statement or question is made negative by inserting **no** before the verb:

El cliente tiene razón.	The customer is right.
El cliente no tiene razón.	The customer is wrong.

(b) The interrogative

If a subject is included, the question is normally formed by inverting subject and verb. Note that all Spanish questions are preceded by an inverted question mark. (The same principle applies to exclamations: **¡Enhorabuena!**)

Statement:	**El director es Alonso.**	Alonso is the director.
Question:	**¿Es Alonso el director?**	Is Alonso the director?

Note also the position of the adjective in a question:

¿Es viejo el edificio?	Is the building old?

(c) The negative interrogative

In a negative question the Spanish **no** remains in front of the verb.

¿No es abogado?	Is he not a lawyer?

Finally, when an answer begins with 'yes' or 'no', the comma and the pause are important:

Sí, es arquitecto.	Yes, he's an architect.
Sí es arquitecto.	He certainly is an architect.
No, es arquitecto.	No, he is an architect
No es arquitecto.	He is not an architect

22 Prepositions

Por/para

Both of these words have various uses and can express English 'for'. It is important, however, to distinguish between them. **Para** indicates *purpose* and *destination*, whilst **por** indicates *reason* and *exchange*.

Producimos para vender.
Hay un paquete para Vd.

¿Por qué lo hizo?
Gracias por su carta.
Le di cien pesetas por su billete.

Note the following expressions:

por la mañana	in the morning
por ejemplo	for example
por supuesto	of course

A

(a) place:

El teléfono está a la derecha.

(b) motion:

Teresa va a Sevilla.

Con

(a) togetherness:

Café con azúcar.

(b) the means or way of doing something:

Escribo con rotulador.

De

(a) possession:

La agenda es de Roberto.

(b) material:

La cartera de cuero.

(c) origin:

Peter Smith es de Inglaterra.

Pronouns after prepositions

Normally, the forms used after prepositions are **mí, ti, él, ella, Vd., nosotros, vosotros, ellos, ellas, Vds.**

El regalo es para ella.
No me gusta ir sin ellos.

However, after the pronoun **con** the following unusual forms are used: **conmigo** with me, **contigo** with you, **consigo** with himself, herself, themselves.

Trabajan conmigo.
Contamos contigo.

23 Numerals

1	uno	11	once	30	treinta
2	dos	12	doce	40	cuarenta
3	tres	13	trece	50	cincuenta
4	cuatro	14	catorce	60	sesenta
5	cinco	15	quince	70	setenta
6	seis	16	dieciséis	80	ochenta
7	siete	17	diecisiete	90	noventa
8	ocho	18	dieciocho	100	cien
9	nueve	19	diecinueve	1.000	mil
10	diez	20	veinte	1.000.000	un millón

24 Dates

In Spanish the cardinal numbers are used for dates, although an ordinal number is normally used for the first day of each month. When speaking, the article **el** must be used before the number, although this is omitted when writing the date:

el primero de enero de 1995 *or* **1 de enero de 1995**

Days of the week and months of the year

lunes	Monday
martes	Tuesday
miércoles	Wednesday
jueves	Thursday
viernes	Friday
sábado	Saturday
domingo	Sunday

enero	January	**julio**	July
febrero	February	**agosto**	August
marzo	March	**setiembre**	September
abril	April	**octubre**	October
mayo	May	**noviembre**	November
junio	June	**diciembre**	December

Remember, the days of the week and the months of the year are written with *lower-case* initial letters in Spanish. The days of the week are also preceded by the article **el** or **los**.

Voy a ir a Madrid el lunes.
No trabajamos los sábados.

25 Greetings and farewells

Buenos días.	Good morning.
Buenas tardes.	Good afternoon/evening.
Buenas noches.	Good night.

More colloquial expressions are:

¿Qué tal?	How are you?
Adiós	Goodbye
Hasta la vista	See you again
Hasta luego	Goodbye (till later)

Business Glossary

Key to glossary

Grammatical abbreviations

abbr	abbreviation
adj	adjective
adv	adverb
conj	conjunction
det	determiner
n	noun
nf	feminine noun
nfpl	plural feminine noun
nm	masculine noun
nmpl	plural masculine noun
pp	past participle
pref	prefix
prep	preposition
vb	verb

Symbols

* denotes slang term
(US) term particular to USA
(GB) term particular to Great Britain
(LAm) term particular to Latin American country/countries

NB: Contexts are given in parentheses after term and part of speech or before multiple translations

Parts of speech are provided for all headwords and for translations where appropriate. Subterms are only supplied with parts of speech where it is considered necessary to indicate gender or to avoid ambiguity

Latin American variants are given after main Spanish term. Multiple Latin American variants are separated from each other by semicolons. The part of speech is always provided for Latin American variants of Spanish terms where the part of speech differs from that of Spanish term. Where there is no part of speech indicated for a Latin American variant, the part of speech is the same as that of Spanish term

Spanish–English

abandonar *vb* abandon *vb*, quit *vb*
abandono *nm* neglect *n*, withdrawal *n*, desertion *n*
abastecedor, -ora *nm,f* supplier *n*
abastecer *vb* supply *vb* **abastecer algo a crédito** supply sth on trust
abogado, -ada *nm,f* solicitor *n*, lawyer (US) *n* **abogado que actúa únicamente en el juicio oral** barrister *n*, lawyer (US) *n*
abogar *vb* defend *vb*, champion *vb* **abogar por** advocate
abolición *nf* abolition *n*
abolir *vb* abolish *vb*
abonar *vb* pay *vb* **abonar algo en una cuenta** credit sth to an account, pay sth into an account
abreviación *nf* abbreviation *n*
abreviado *adj* abbreviated *adj*
abreviar *vb* abbreviate *vb*
abreviatura *nf* abbreviation *n*
abrir *vb* (market) open *vb*, open up *vb* **abrir una cuenta** open an account
absentismo *nm* absenteeism *n*
absoluto *adj* absolute *adj*, total *adj*
absorber *vb* absorb *vb* **absorber existencias sobrantes** absorb surplus stock
absorción *nf* takeover *n*
abundancia *nf* abundance *n*, wealth *n*
abusar *vb* abuse *vb* **abusar de** abuse *vb*
abuso *nm* abuse *n* **abuso de confianza** abuse of confidence **abuso de poder** abuse of power
acabar *vb* complete *vb* (end) turn out *vb* **acabar con un proyecto** kill a project
acápite *nm* (LAm) heading *n*, paragraph *n*, section *n*
acatar *vb* comply *vb*, obey *vb* **acatar las normas** observe the rules
accesibilidad *nf* accessibility *n*
acceso *nm* access *n*
accidente *nm* accident *n* **accidente laboral** industrial accident
acción *nf* action *n*, share *n* **acción cotizada** listed share, listed stock (US) **acciones** *nfpl* stocks and shares **acciones cotizables en bolsa** listed securities **acciones que se cotizan en Bolsa** quoted shares, quoted stocks (US) **acciones emitidas sin aumento de capital** watered capital **acción industrial, paro** (LAm) industrial action **acción nominativa** registered share **acción ordinaria** ordinary share, ordinary

stock (US) **acción al portador** bearer share **acción de Tesoro** government bond
accionista *nmf* shareholder *n*, stockholder *n* **accionista apoderado, -ada** nominee shareholder
aceleración *nf* acceleration *n*
acelerar *vb* accelerate *vb*, expedite *vb*
aceptación *nf* acceptance *n* **aceptación de mercado** market acceptance **aceptación por parte del consumidor** consumer acceptance **aceptación con reservas** qualified acceptance
aceptar *vb* accept *vb* **aceptar la entrega de** accept delivery of
aclarar *vb* (sort out) resolve *vb*, clarify *vb*
aconsejar *vb* recommend *vb*, warn *vb* **aconsejarle a alguien sobre algo** advise sb about sth
acordado *adj* agreed *adj*
acotación *nf* limit *n*
acreedor, -ora *nm,f* creditor *n* **acreedor, -ora hipotecario, -ria** mortgagee
acta *nm* record *n* **el acta de la reunión** the minutes of the meeting **actas de conferencia** conference proceedings
activo *nm* asset *n* **activo circulante** floating assets **activo congelado** frozen assets **activo disponible** liquid assets, quick assets **activo fijo** capital assets, fixed assets **activo intangible** intangible asset **activo material** tangible asset **activo neto** net(t) assets **activo nominal** nominal assets **activos ficticios** fictitious assets **activos financieros** financial assets **activos ocultos** hidden assets **activo tangible** tangible asset
actuación *nf* (behaviour) performance *n*, action *n*
actual, moderno (LAm) *adj* up-to-date *adj*
actualizar *vb* (records) update *vb*
actuar *vb* act *vb*
actuario, -ria *nm,f* actuary *n*, Clerk of Court *n* **actuario de seguros** (insurance) actuary
acudir *vb* attend *vb*, come *vb* **acudir a una cita** keep an appointment
acuerdo *nm* agreement *n*, treaty *n*, understanding *n* **de acuerdo con** in accordance with **acuerdo entre caballeros** gentleman's agreement **acuerdo comercial** commercial treaty, trade agreement **acuerdo de cuotas** quota agreement **acuerdo de pago de suma única** lump sum settlement **acuerdo no**

escrito verbal agreement **acuerdo fiduciario** trust agreement **acuerdo global** package deal **acuerdo laboral** working agreement **Acuerdo Monetario Europeo (AME)** European Monetary Agreement (EMA) **acuerdo mutuo** compromise **acuerdo oficial** formal agreement **acuerdo salarial** wage(s) agreement, wage(s) settlement **por acuerdo tácito** by tacit agreement **acuerdo de trueque** barter agreement **acuerdo verbal** verbal agreement **de común acuerdo** by mutual agreement

acumulación *nf* accrual *n* **acumulación de trabajo atrasado** backlog

acumulado *adj* accumulated *adj*

acumular *vb* accumulate *vb*, hoard *vb*

acuñar *vb* mint *vb*

acusar *vb* accuse *vb* **acusar recibo de algo** acknowledge receipt of sth, confirm receipt of sth

adaptación *nf* adaptation *n*, adjustment *n*

adaptar *vb* adjust *vb*, (adapt) tailor *vb*

adecuado *adj* (price) keen *adj*, appropriate *adj*

adelantar *vb* (salary) advance *vb*, bring forward *vb*

adelanto *nm* (on salary) advance *n*, cash advance *n*, progress *n*

adeudar *vb* (account) debit *vb*, owe *vb*

adición *nf* (LAm) bill *n*

adjuntar *vb* enclose *vb*

adjunto *adj* attached *adj*, enclosed *adj*, deputy *adj*

administración *nf* administration *n*, government *n* **administración de aduanas e impuestos sobre el consumo** the Board of Customs and Excise **administración de empresas, gestión** (LAm) management **administración pública** civil service

administrador, -ora *nm,f* administrator *n*, bailiff *n*, bursar *n*

administrar *vb* administer *vb*, manage *vb*

administrativo, -iva *nm,f* clerical worker *n*, white-collar worker *n*

adquirido *adj* vested *adj*, acquired *adj*

adquirir *vb* acquire *vb*, purchase *vb*, (company) take over *vb*

adquisición *nf* acquisition *n*, buy-out *n*, purchase *n*, takeover *n* **adquisición apalancada de empresas** LBO (leveraged buy-out) *abbr* **adquisición de una empresa por sus propios directivos** management buy-out

aduana *nf* customs *npl*

aduanero, -era *nm,f* customs inspector *n*, customs officer *n*

advertencia *nf* reminder *n*, warning *n*

advertir *vb* warn *vb*

aeropuerto *nm* airport *n*

afán *nm* keenness *n*, effort *n* **con afán de lucro** for pecuniary gain

afectado *adj* affected *adj* **muy afectado** hard-hit

afilado *adj* (competition) keen *adj*

afiliación *nf* affiliation *n*, membership *n* **afiliación sindical** union membership

afirmación *nf* statement *n*

aflojar *vb* (market) weaken *vb*

afueras, colonias (LAm) *nfpl* suburbs *npl*

agencia *nf* agency *n* **agencia de colocaciones** employment agency, Jobcentre (GB), Job centre, job shop **agencia de empleo** employment agency **agencia exprés** express agency **Agencia Federal** Federal Bureau (US) **agencia de informes comerciales** credit agency **agencia inmobiliaria** estate agency, real estate agency (US) **agencia de prensa** news agency **agencia de publicidad** advertising agency **agencias generales** general agencies (US) **agencia de trabajo** employment agency **agencia de transporte, agencia de fletes** (LAm) forwarding agency **agencia de venta de localidades** ticket agency **agencia de viajes** travel agency

agenda *nf* agenda *n*, timetable *n*, diary *n*

agente *nmf* agent *n*, representative *n* **agente de bolsa** commission broker, jobber, stockbroker **agente de cambio** foreign exchange dealer **agente comercial** broker, sales representative **agente de despacho, agente de flete de mercancías** (LAm) forwarding agent **agente expedidor** shipping broker **agente fiscal** fiscal agent **agente general** general agent **agente de importación** import agent **agente inmobiliario, -ria** estate agent, real estate agent, realtor (US) **agente al por mayor** (buyer of debts) factor **agente mediador, -ora** dealer **agente oficial** authorized dealer **agente que recibe una comisión elevada porque garantiza el pago** del credere agent **agentes de bolsa** brokerage firm **agente de seguros** insurance agent, insurance broker, insurance representative **agente de transportes, agente fletero** (LAm) forwarder, forwarding agent, freight forwarder, transport agent

agotamiento *nm* depletion *n*, exhaustion *n*

agotar *vb* (reserves) exhaust *vb*

agrario *adj* agrarian *adj*

agricultura *nf* agriculture *n*, farming *n*

agrimensor, -ora *nm,f* surveyor *n* **agrimensor colegiado** chartered surveyor

agroindustria *nf* agribusiness *n*

agrónomo, -oma *nm,f* agronomist *n*

agrupación *nf* syndicate *n* **agrupación temporal de empresas** collaborative venture, joint venture

ahorrar *vb* save (time, money) *vb* **que ahorra tiempo** time-saving

ahorro *nm* saving *n* **ahorro neto** net(t) saving **ahorros** savings

aire *nm* air *n*, look *n* **con aire acondicionado** air-conditioned

ajustar *vb* adjust *vb* **ajustar las cifras** adjust

the figures **ajustar el presupuesto** balance
the budget
ajuste *nm* adjustment *n* **ajuste definitivo**
final settlement **ajuste por suma fija** lump
sum settlement
albañil *nmf* bricklayer *n*, builder *n*
alcance *nm* range *n*, reach *n* **de gran
alcance** wide-ranging **de largo alcance**
long-range
alcista 1. *adj* upward *adj* **2.** *nmf* (stock
exchange) bull *n*
alguacil *nmf* bailiff *n*
aliciente *nm* incentive *n*
aliviar *vb* moderate *vb*, relieve *vb*
almacén, bodega (LAm) *nm, nf* warehouse *n*
en almacén ex factory/works, ex store/
warehouse, in stock **almacén de depósito**
bonded warehouse **grandes almacenes,
tienda de departamentos** (LAm)
department store
almacenaje *nm* warehousing *n* **almacenaje
de datos** information storage
almacenamiento *nm* storage *n*
alojamiento *nm* accommodation *n*
alojamiento hotelero hotel
accommodation
alquilar, arrendar; rentar (LAm) *vb* hire *vb*
(property) let *vb* (house, office) rent *vb* **se
alquila, se arrienda; se renta** (LAm) for
hire
alquiler, arriendo (LAm) *nm* hire *n*, hire
charges *npl*, rent *n*, rental *n* **alquiler de
maquinaria** plant hire, tool hire
alza *nf* (in bank rate) rise *n* **alza de la
demanda** boom in demand
amarrar *vb* moor *vb*, fasten *vb*
ambiente *nm* atmosphere *n* **ambiente
laboral** working environment
ámbito *nm* terms of reference *npl*, ambit *n* **de
ámbito nacional** nationwide *prep*
amigable *adj* user-friendly *adj*
amo, ama *nm,f* boss *n*, owner *n*
amortización *nf* amortization *n*, depreciation
n, redemption *n*
amortizar *vb* amortize *vb*, depreciate *vb*,
redeem *vb*, write down *vb*
ampliación *nf* expansion *n*
ampliar *vb* enlarge *vb*, expand *vb* **ampliar la
capacidad** expand capacity **ampliar la
gama** extend the range
amplio *adj* comprehensive *adj*, wide-ranging
adj
análisis *nm* analysis *n* **análisis de cifras** (of
figures) breakdown **análisis coste-
beneficio** cost-benefit analysis **análisis de
costes, análisis de costos** (LAm) cost
breakdown **análisis económico** economic
analysis **análisis funcional** functional
analysis **análisis horizontal** horizontal
analysis **análisis de mercado** market
analysis **análisis de mercados** market
research **análisis de necesidades** needs
assessment **análisis numérico** numerical
analysis **análisis de riesgos** risk analysis

análisis de sistemas systems analysis
análisis de tendencias trend analysis
analista *nm* analyst *n* **analista de sistemas**
systems analyst
analizar *vb* analyze *vb* **sin analizar**
(unprocessed) raw
anexo *nm* enclosure *n*, appendix *n*
anfitrión, -ona *nm,f* host *n*
año *nm* year *n* **al año** per annum **por año**
per annum **año fiscal** financial year, fiscal
year, tax year
anotar *vb* note *vb*, record *vb*
antecedentes *nmpl* record *n*, track record *n*
antedatar *vb* backdate *vb*
antedicho *adj* above-mentioned *adj*
antelación *nf* notice *n*, priority *n*
anticipar *vb* anticipate *vb*, advance *vb*
anticuado *adj* obsolete *adj*, out-of-date *adj*
antigüedad *nf* seniority *n*
anual *adj* yearly *adj*
anualidad *nf* annuity *n*
anulación *nf* annulment *n*, cancellation *n*,
write-off *n*
anular *vb* rescind *vb* (debts) write off *vb*
anular un contrato cancel a contract
anular un pedido cancel an order
anunciar, hacerle réclame (LAm) *vb*
advertise *vb*, announce *vb*
anuncio, aviso; réclame (LAm) *nm*
advertisement *n*, bulletin *n* **anuncio por
palabras, aviso clasificado** (LAm)
classified advertisement **anuncio
publicitario, aviso** (LAm) newspaper
advertisement **anuncios clasificados,
avisos clasificados** (LAm) small ads
aparato *nm* machine *n*, appliance *n* **aparato
estatal** machinery of government
aparecer *vb* appear *vb*, come out *vb*
apartado *nm* box *n*, section *n* **apartado de
correos, apartado postal; casilla postal**
(LAm) box number, PO box
apelación *nf* appeal *n*
apelar *vb* appeal *vb*
aplazado *adj* (tax) deferred *adj*, postponed
adj
aplazar *vb* adjourn *vb*, postpone *vb*, defer *vb*
(to next period) hold over *vb*
aplicación *nf* enforcement *n*
aplicar *vb* (policy) enforce *vb* **aplicar por**
(LAm) apply for
apoderado, -ada *nm,f* (power) proxy *n*, agent
n
aportación *nf* contribution *n* **sin
aportaciones por parte del empleado**
non-contributory
aportar, hacer aportes (LAm) *vb* contribute
vb
apostador, -ora *nm,f* stakeholder *n*
apoyar *vb* support *vb*
apoyo *nm* backing *n*
apreciación *nf* appreciation *n*
apremiante *adj* urgent *adj*
aprendiz, -iza *nm,f* apprentice *n*, trainee *n*
aprendizaje *nm* apprenticeship *n*, training *n*

aprendizaje asistido por ordenador (CAL), aprendizaje asistido por computadora (LAm) computer-aided learning (CAL)

apretón nm handshake n, hug n apretón de manos handshake

aprobación nf approval n, endorsement n, seal n

aprobar vb approve vb, vote vb

apropiación nf appropriation n

apropiado adj relevant adj, suitable adj

aprovechar vb exploit vb, make use vb aprovechar un mercado tap a market

aprovecharse vb benefit vb, take advantage of vb aprovecharse de la ocasión seize an opportunity

aproximadamente adv approximately adv

aproximado adj approximate adj

aptitud nf ability n

apuntar vb write down vb apuntar algo make a note of sth

arancel nm tariff n

arbitraje nm arbitrage n, arbitration n arbitraje laboral industrial arbitration

arbitrar vb arbitrate vb

arbitrario adj arbitrary adj

árbitro, -tra nm,f arbitrator n, referee n

archivador, archivero (LAm) nm filing cabinet n

archivar vb file vb

archivo nm computer file n, file n, record n, register n

área nf área de la bodega hold area área de trabajo working area

argumento nm argumentos arguments, reasoning argumentos de venta sales talks

aritmética nf arithmetic n

arreglar vb repair vb, resolve vb, arrange vb

arreglo nm (agreement) arrangement n

arrendador, -ora, hacendado, -ada (LAm) nm,f landlord n, lessor n

arrendamiento nm leasehold n, rent n, rental n arrendamiento de medios de producción equipment leasing

arrendar, rentar (LAm) vb hire vb, lease vb (house, office) rent vb se arrienda, se renta (LAm) for hire

arrendatario, -ria nm,f leaseholder n, lessee n, tenant n

arriendo nm hire n, hire charge n, income (LAm) n

artículo nm item n artículo de gancho loss leader artículo líder market leader artículo de mayor venta market leader artículos consignados, mercaderías en consignación (LAm) goods on consignment artículos defectuosos faulty goods artículos de importación, mercaderías de importación (LAm) import goods artículos de lujo luxury goods artículos de mercería dry goods artículos perecederos, mercaderías perecederas (LAm) perishable goods

artículos de primera necesidad staple commodities artículos de producción en serie, mercaderías a granel (LAm) bulk goods artículos de venta rápida, mercaderías de venta rápida (LAm) fast-selling goods

artificial adj man-made adj

asalariado, -ada nm,f wage earner n, paid employee n

ascender vb (person) promote vb, upgrade vb ascender a amount to

ascenso nm (of person) promotion n

aseguradora nf insurance company n

asegurar vb indemnify vb, insure vb, warrant vb (risk) underwrite vb asegurar la marcha de la empresa keep the business running

asesor, -ora nm,f adviser/advisor n, consultant n asesor comercial marketing consultant asesor económico economic adviser asesor de empresas business consultant, management consultant asesor financiero financial consultant asesor de inversiones investment adviser asesor de seguros insurance representative

asesoramiento nm advice n

asesorar vb consult vb asesorarle a alguien sobre algo advise sb on sth

asesoría nf consultancy n, consultancy work n, consulting (US) n asesoría financiera financial consultancy

asiento nm seat n, entry n asiento contable ledger entry asiento final final entry

asignación nf appropriation n, allowance n asignación de fondos funding

asignar vb allocate vb, assign vb, budget for vb, commit vb

asistencia nf aid n, attendance n asistencia económica al exterior foreign aid asistencia social welfare

asistir vb attend vb, help vb asistir a una entrevista attend for interview

asociación nf partnership n asociación comercial trading partnership asociación de estudiantes, gremio (LAm) students' union Asociación Europea de Libre Comercio EFTA (European Free Trade Association) asociación general general partnership asociación limitada limited partnership

asociado, -ada nm,f associate n, partner n, joint vendor n

aspirante nmf (for job) candidate n aspirante a un puesto directivo trainee manager

astillero nm dockyard n, shipyard n

asumir vb assume vb asumir responsabilidad de algo take responsibility for sth

asunto nm matter n, subject n Asunto re asunto urgente a matter of urgency

ataque nm offence n, offense (US)

atasco nm bottleneck n, obstruction n

atender vb attend to vb atender una reclamación meet a claim

atenerse a *vb* abide by *vb*
atestiguar *vb* witness *vb* **atestiguar una firma** witness a signature
atrasado *adj* in arrears *adj*, overdue *adj*
atrasarse *vb* be late *vb*, fall behind *vb* **atrasarse en los pagos** fall/get into arrears
atraso *nm* **atrasos** arrears *npl* **atrasos de sueldo** back pay
atribución *nf* **atribuciones** allocations, attributions **atribuciones y responsabilidades** terms of reference
auditor, -ora *nm,f* auditor *n*
auditoría *nf* audit *n* **auditoría externa** external audit **auditoría interna** internal audit
auge *nm* increase *n* **en auge** booming
aumentar *vb* boom *vb*, enlarge *vb*, escalate *vb*, expand *vb* (prices) bump up *vb*, improve *vb*, mark up *vb*, rise *vb* **aumentar la producción** increase output **aumentar de valor** gain in value
aumento *nm* boost *n*, mark up *n* (in earnings, inflation) rise *n* **aumento de capital** expansion of capital **aumento del coste de vida, aumento del costo de vida** (LAm) increase in the cost of living **aumento rápido de la demanda** boom in demand **aumentos de productividad** productivity gains **aumento de sueldo** pay increase/rise **aumento de ventas** sales growth
ausente *adj* absent *adj*, absentee *adj*
autoedición *nf* desk-top publishing *n*
autoevaluación *nf* self-assessment *n*
autofinanciación *nf* self-financing *n*
autogestión *nf* self-management *n*
automático *adj* automatic *adj*
automatización *nf* automation *n*
autónomo *adj* autonomous *adj*, self-employed *adj*
autoridad *nf* (official) authority *n*
autorización *nf* approval *n*, attestation *n*, licence *n*, warrant *n*
autorizar *vb* accredit *vb*, approve *vb*, authorize *vb*, license *vb*
autoservicio *nm* cash and carry *n*, supermarket *n*
autosuficiente *adj* self-sufficient *adj*
auxiliar *adj* auxiliary *adj*, junior *adj*
avalúo *nm* (LAm) appraisal *n*
avance *nm* (on salary) advance *n*, progress *n* **avance importante** breakthrough
avanzar *vb* (research, project) progress *vb*
avería *nf* fault *n* **avería importante** serious fault
averiado, descompuesto (LAm) *adj* out-of-action *adj*
avión *nm* aeroplane *n* **avión de carga** freighter
avisar *vb* notify *vb*, warn *vb* **avisar de algo** give notice of sth
aviso *nm* (suggestion) tip *n* warning *n*, advertisement (LAm) *n* **aviso por adelantado** advance notice **aviso de envío** advice note **aviso de expedición** advice

note, remittance advice **aviso previo** advance notice **hasta nuevo aviso** until further notice
ayuda *nf* backing *n* **ayuda financiera** financial aid
ayudante *nmf* assistant *n* **ayudante de dirección** assistant manager
ayudar *vb* help *vb* **ayudar a salir de un apuro** tide over
ayuntamiento *nm* town council *n*, town hall *n*
azar *nm* chance *n*, random *n* **al azar** at random
baja *nf* (economic) decline *n* redundancy *n*, termination of employment *n* **a la baja** downward **baja por enfermedad, licencia por enfermedad** (LAm) sick leave
bajar *vb* decrease *vb*, (price, interest rate) lower *vb*
bajista *nmf* (stock exchange) bear *n*
bajón *nm* (economic) downturn *n*
balance *nm* stocktaking *n*, balance *n* **balance final** final balance **balance financiero** financial balance **balance fiscal** fiscal balance **balance general** balance sheet, financial statement **balance de situación** balance sheet
balanza *nf* balance *n*, scale *n* **balanza comercial** balance of trade, trade balance **balanza comercial favorable** favourable balance of trade **balanza comercial negativa** adverse balance of trade **balanza de pagos** balance of payments **balanza de pagos favorable** favourable balance of payments
banca *nf* banking *n*, banking system *n* **banca de depósito** commercial bank **banca electrónica** electronic banking
bancario, -ria *nm,f* (LAm) bank clerk *n*
bancarrota *nf* bankruptcy *n* **en bancarrota** bankrupt
banco *nm* bank *n* **banco central/de emisión** central bank **banco comercial** clearing bank, commercial bank **banco comercial de negocios** acceptance house **banco de compensación** clearing bank **banco de datos** data bank **banco de depósito** commercial bank **banco de direcciones** mailing list **banco emisor** bank of issue, issuing bank **Banco Europeo de Inversiones (BEI)** European Investment Bank (EIB) **banco extranjero** foreign bank **banco fundado antiguamente por cédula real** chartered bank **banco mercantil** commercial bank, merchant bank **Banco Mundial** World Bank **banco de negocios** merchant bank
banda *nf* band *n*, scale *n* **banda impositiva** tax bracket
bandeja *nf* pallet *n*
banquero, -era *nm,f* banker *n* **los banqueros suizos** the Gnomes of Zurich
barato *adj* (price) low *adj*, cheap *adj*
barco *nm* ship *n* **barco de carga** cargo ship

barrera *nf* barrier *n* **barrera arancelaria** tariff barrier, trade barrier, tariff wall **barrera comercial** trade barrier **barrera contra la inflación** hedge against inflation **barrera a la importación** import barrier

barrio *nm* **barrios** *nmpl* districts, suburbs **barrios residenciales de las afueras** outer suburbs

base *nf* base *n*, basis *n* **base de conocimientos** knowledge base **base de datos** data base **base de evaluación** basis of assessment

beneficiar *vb* benefit *vb*

beneficiario, -ria *nm,f* payee *n*, recipient *n*

beneficio *nm* benefit *n*, dividend *n* **beneficios, utilidades** (LAm) *nm* profits *n*, earnings *n*, proceeds *n* **beneficio extra** (formal) perquisite **beneficio ficticio** paper profit **beneficio inesperado** windfall profit **beneficio neto** net(t) profit **beneficio nulo** nil profit **beneficio no realizado** paper profit **beneficios contables/en libros, utilidades contables** (LAm) book profit **beneficios de explotación, beneficios de operación** (LAm) operating profit **beneficios extraordinarios** extra profit **beneficios extrasalariales** fringe benefits

bianual *adj* biennial *adj*

bien *nm* **bienes** chattels *npl*, goods *npl* **bienes de capital** capital assets, capital goods **bienes duraderos** durable goods **bienes de equipo** capital goods **bienes ocultos** hidden assets **bienes raíces** real estate

bienestar *nm* welfare *n*

bienhechor, -ora *nm,f* benefactor *n*

bilateral, de doble mano; de doble vía (LAm) *adj* two-way *adj*

billete, pasaje; boleto; tiquete (LAm) *nm* ticket *n* **billete de abono, boleto de abono** (LAm) season ticket **billete de banco** banknote **billete de ida, pasaje sencillo; boleto sencillo** (LAm) (rail/flight) single/one-way ticket **billete de ida y vuelta** return ticket, round-trip ticket (US)

bimensual *adj* bimonthly *adj*

bloque, cuadra (LAm) *nm,nf* block *n*

bloquear, tapar (LAm) *vb* block *vb*, blockade *vb*

bloqueo *nm* blockade *n*

bodega *nf* stowage *n*, cellar *n*, hold *n*, warehouse (LAm) *n*

boicot *nm* boycott *n*

boicotear *vb* boycott *vb*

boletería *nf* (LAm) box office *n*

boletín *nm* bulletin *n*, journal *n* **boletín informativo** newsletter **boletín interno de la empresa** house journal/magazine

boleto *nm* coupon *n*, ticket (LAm) *n*

bolsa *nf* Stock Exchange **bolsa de empleo** Jobcentre, job shop **Bolsa de Nueva York** NYSE (New York Stock Exchange) **bolsa de valores** Stock Exchange, stock market

bombo *nm* hype *n*

bonificación *nf* bonus *n*, discount *n*, weighting *n* **bonificación recibida al concluir un seguro** terminal bonus

bonista *nmf* bondholder *n*

bono *nm* bond *n*, debenture *n*, voucher *n* **bono amortizable** redeemable bond **bono de fidelidad** fidelity bond **bono no garantizado** unsecured bond **bono sin intereses** fiat bond **bonos de financiación** funding bonds **bonos municipales** municipal bonds **bonos del Tesoro** gilts **bono de yen** yen bond

boom *nm* boom *n* **boom económico** economic boom

borrador *nm* draft *n*

botar *vb* (LAm) dismiss *vb* **botar del trabajo** dismiss from job, axe*

botín *nm* spoils *npl*

brecha *nf* gap *n*

brevedad *nf* brevity *n* **a su mayor brevedad posible** at your earliest convenience

británico *adj* British *adj*

bruto *adj* before tax *adj*, gross *adj*

buque *nm* ship *n* **en buque** ex ship **buque de carga** freighter **buque mercante** merchant ship

burocracia *nf* bureaucracy *n*, red tape *n*

burócrata *nmf* bureaucrat *n*

burocrático *adj* bureaucratic *adj*

buscar *vb* seek *vb* **buscar trabajo** look for work

cabeza *nf* head *n* **a la cabeza de** at the head of

cabina, casilla; caseta (LAm) *nf* booth *n*, cabin *n* **cabina de teléfonos** telephone box, telephone booth (US)

CAD (diseño asistido por ordenador) *nm* CAD (computer-aided or assisted design) *abbr*

cadena *nf* chain *n* **cadena hotelera** hotel chain **cadena de minoristas** retail chain **cadena de montaje** assembly line, production line **cadena de producción** production line **cadena de tiendas** chain of shops

caducado, vencido; perimido (LAm) *adj* out of date *adj*

caducar *vb* expire *vb*

caducidad *nf* expiry *n*, obsolescence *n*, termination *n*, expiration (US)

caer *vb* (market) weaken *vb* **caer en desuso** fall into abeyance **caer en picado** slump *vb*

caída *nf* (of economy) collapse *n* **caída bursátil** collapse on stock market **caída repentina** slump *n*

caído *adj* fallen *adj* **caído en desuso** obsolete

caja *nf* cash desk *n* **caja de ahorros** savings bank

cajero *nm* **cajero automático** automatic cash dispenser/machine, cashpoint

cajero, -era *nm,f* cashier *n* **cajero de banco** teller **cajero jefe** chief cashier

calculadora *nf* calculator *n*

calcular *vb* assess *vb*, calculate *vb*, estimate

vb, measure *vb* **calcular el coste de un trabajo, calcular el costo de un trabajo** (LAm) cost a job

cálculo *nm* assessment *n*, calculation *n*, estimate *n*

calendario *nm* timescale *n*, calendar *n*

calidad *nf* quality *n* **de baja calidad** shoddy* **de calidad superior** high-grade **en mi calidad de presidente** in my capacity as chairman

calificación *nf* (LAm) qualification *n*, bond *n*

calificado *adj* (LAm) qualified *adj*

calificar *vb* label *vb*

cámara *nf* camera *n*, chamber *n* **Cámara de Comercio** Board of Trade, Chamber of Commerce **cámara de compensación** clearing house

cambiar *vb* (market) turn *vb*, (money) change *vb* **cambiar de domicilio** change address **cambiar impresiones** compare notes **cambiar radicalmente** reverse

cambio, vuelto; vueltas (LAm) *nm, nm; nfpl* (from purchase) change *n*, bureau de change *n*, foreign exchange dealings *npl*, shift *n*, swap *n*, turnabout *n* **a cambio** in return **cambio comprador** buying price **cambio favorable** favourable exchange **cambio de futuros** futures exchange **cambio de moneda extranjera** foreign exchange

cambista *nmf* exchange broker *n*, foreign exchange dealer *n*, money trader *n*

camino *nm* route *n*, way *n*

campaña *nf* campaign *n* **campaña dirigida a** targeted campaign **campaña de publicidad** advertising campaign **campaña publicitaria** advertising campaign, publicity campaign **campaña de reclutamiento** recruitment campaign **campaña de ventas** sales campaign

campo *nm* countryside *n* **campo editorial** publishing **campo de trabajo** working area

cancelación *nf* cancellation *n*

cancelar *vb* (contract) repudiate *vb*, liquidate *vb*, rescind *vb*, withdraw *vb*, cancel *vb*, write off *vb*

candidato, -ata *nm,f* (for job) candidate *n* nominee *n*

candidatura, postulación (LAm) *nf* nomination *n*

canje *nm* swap *n*

canjear *vb* swap *vb*

cantidad *nf* amount *n*, quantity *n*, volume *n*

capacidad *nf* ability *n*, volume *n* **capacidad de almacenaje** storage capacity **capacidad de almacenamiento** storage capacity **capacidad excesiva** excess capacity **capacidad de ganar dinero** earning capacity/power **capacidad industrial** industrial capacity **capacidad de memoria** memory capacity **capacidad de negociación** negotiating skills **capacidad de pago** creditworthiness **capacidad de producción** manufacturing

capacity **capacidad de rendimiento** earning capacity **capacidad no utilizada** idle capacity

capacitación *nf* training *n* **capacitación avanzada** advanced training

capacitado, calificado; capacitado (LAm) *adj* qualified *adj*, skilled (LAm) *adj*

capacitar *vb* (staff) train *vb*, authorize *vb*

capataz *nmf* foreman/forewoman *n*

capaz *adj* able *adj*, capable *adj* **capaz de realizar cálculos aritméticos elementales** numerate

cápita *nf* per cápita per capita, per head

capital *nm* capital *n* **capital certificado** registered capital **capital circulante** capital funds, trading capital, working capital **capital desembolsado** paid-up capital **capital disponible** capital assets **capitales de fuga** flight capital **capital de especulación** risk capital **capital de explotación** trading capital **capital fijo** fixed capital **capital inicial** initial capital **capital invertido** invested capital **capital a largo plazo** long-term capital **capital limitado** limited capital **capital líquido** liquid capital **capital nominal** nominal assets, registered capital **capital operativo** capital funds, working capital **capital de puesta en marcha** start-up capital **capital de riesgo** venture capital, risk capital **capital social** equity capital, share capital **capital de vendedor, -ora** vendor capital

capitalismo *nm* capitalism *n*

capitalista *nmf* backer *n*, capitalist *n*

capitalizar *vb* capitalize *vb*

captación *nf* gaining *n*, raising *n* **captación de datos** data capture

carácter *nm* character *n* **caracteres pequeños** small type **carácter numérico** numeric character

carestía *nf* scarcity *n*, high cost *n*

carga *nf* bulk cargo *n*, cargo *n*, freight *n*, load *n* (consignment) shipment *n*, charge *n* **carga aérea** air freight **carga a granel** bulk cargo **carga paletizada, mercaderías empaletizadas** (LAm) palletized freight **cargas fiscales** taxation **carga de trabajo** workload **carga útil** (of vehicle) payload

cargamento *nm* cargo *n*

cargar *vb* (account) debit *vb*, charge *vb*, load *vb* **cargar algo** charge for sth **cargar algo a una cuenta** charge sth to an account **cargar un ordenador, cargar una computadora** (LAm) boot a computer

cargo *nm* debit *n*, office *n*, official *n* **altos cargos** top management **cargo de administrador** trusteeship

carguero *nm* cargo ship *n* **carguero de graneles** bulk carrier

caridad *nf* charity *n*

carné *nm* card *n*, permit *n* **carné de identidad** identity card

carnero, -era *nm,f* (LAm) (worker) scab* *n*

carpeta *nf* file *n*, folder *n*

carrera *nf* career *n*, course *n*

carretera *nf* road *n*, highway *n* **por carretera** by road

carta *nf* letter *n* **carta certificada, carta registrada; carta recomendada** (LAm) registered letter **carta de crédito** letter of credit **carta de crédito irrevocable** irrevocable letter of credit **carta de crédito revocable** revocable letter of credit **carta de recomendación** letter of introduction **carta de solicitud** letter of application **carta verde, permiso de residencia y trabajo** (LAm) green card

cartel *nm* cartel *n* (advertising) poster *n*

cartera *nf* briefcase *n*, portfolio *n*, wallet *n* **cartera de pedidos** order book **cartera de valores** holding, investment portfolio **cartera de valores en divisas** foreign exchange holdings **cartera de valores extranjeros** foreign holdings

casa *nf* establishment *n*, household *n* **casa de cambio** bureau de change **casa financiera** acceptance house **casa de la moneda** mint

casco *nm* hull *n*

casilla, caseta (LAm) *nf* box *n*, pigeonhole *n*, booth (LAm) *n* **casilla de la consigna automática, locker de la consigna** (LAm) left-luggage locker

caso *nm* case *n* **caso que sienta jurisprudencia** test case

categoría *nf* category *n*, quality *n* **de primera categoría** top-level

causar *vb* cause *vb* **causar daños graves** cause extensive damage

CE (Comunidad Europea) *abbr* EC (European Community) *abbr*

ceder *vb* yield *vb* **ceder en arriendo** lease

celebrar *vb* celebrate *vb* **celebrar una reunión** hold a meeting

cenit *nm* zenith *n*

censor, -ora *nm,f* auditor *n* **censor de cuentas interior** internal auditor

centralita *nf* telephone switchboard *n* **centralita de teléfonos, conmutador** (LAm) switchboard

centralización *nf* centralization *n*

centralizar *vb* centralize *vb*

centro *nm* centre *n*, center (US) *n* **centro de almacenaje y distribución** entrepôt **centro ciudad** town centre **centro comercial** business centre, shopping mall, shopping centre **centro de coste, centro de costo** (LAm) cost centre **centro financiero** business centre **centro financiero de Nueva York** Wall Street **centro de formación** training centre **centro informático** computer centre

cero *nm* nil *n*, zero *n* **bajo cero** below zero

cerrado *adj* closed *adj*

cerrar *vb* (informal) shut up shop *vb*, close *vb* **cerrar una cuenta** close an account **cerrar una empresa** close a business **cerrar un trato** call it a deal, clinch a deal, close a deal

certificado *nm* certificate *n* **certificado de empleo** certificate of employment **certificado de haber efectuado el despacho de aduana** clearance certificate **certificado de matrimonio** marriage certificate **certificado de origen** certificate of origin **certificado de propiedad** certificate of ownership **certificado de seguros** insurance certificate

certificar *vb* certificate *vb*, certify *vb*

cesante *adj* (LAm) unemployed *adj*, jobless *adj*

cesantía *nf* (LAm) unemployment *n*, strike *n*

cese *nm* (strike) stoppage, *n* redundancy *n*, shutdown *n*, termination *n*, termination of employment *n*

cesión *nf* assignment *n*, transfer *n* **cesión por el gobierno de la acción recaudatoria a un particular** particular farming of taxes

cesionario, -ria *nm,f* assignee *n*

cesta *nf* basket *n* **cesta de la compra** foodstuffs **cesta de monedas, canasta de divisas** (LAm) basket of currencies

chanchullo *nm* racket *n*

chantaje *nm* blackmail *n*

chatarra *nf* (metal) scrap *n*

checar *vb* (LAm) check *vb*

cheque *nm* cheque *n*, check (US) *n* **cheque abierto** open cheque **cheque bancario** bank draft **cheque en blanco** blank cheque **cheque cruzado** crossed cheque **cheque no cubierto** dud cheque **cheque descubierto** bad cheque **cheque en divisas** exchange cheque **cheque sin fondos** bad cheque, dud cheque **cheque impagado** unpaid cheque **cheque negociable** negotiable cheque **cheque al portador** bearer cheque **cheque de tesorero** treasurer check (US) **cheque por valor de cien libras** a cheque for the amount of £100 **cheque de viajero/de viaje** traveller's cheque, traveler's check (US)

chequear *vb* (LAm) check *vb*

chequera *nf* cheque book *n*

chévere *adj* (LAm) great *adj*, brilliant *adj*, keen *adj*

ciclo *nm* cycle *n* **ciclo económico** economic cycle, trade cycle

cien *nm* hundred *n* **cien por cien** one hundred per cent

ciencias *nfpl* sciences *npl* **ciencias empresariales** business studies

ciento *nm* hundred *n* **por ciento** per cent

cierre *nm* seal *n* **cierre de una empresa** closure of a company **cierre patronal, paro patronal** (LAm) (of strikers) lockout

cif (coste, seguro y flete) *abbr,nm* c.i.f. (cost, insurance and freight) *abbr*

cifra *nf* figure *n*, sum *n* **cifra de facturación** turnover **cifras de ventas** sales figures

cinta *nf* tape *n* **cinta magnética** (DP) magnetic tape

circulación *nf* circulation *n*, movement *n* **en circulación** in circulation **circulación en la carretera, tránsito en la carretera** (LAm) road traffic

circular *nf* (letter) circular *n*

círculo *n* circle *n*

circunstancia *nf* circumstance *n* **circunstancias ajenas a nuestra voluntad** circumstances beyond our control **circunstancias imprevistas** unforeseen circumstances

circunvalar *vb* bypass *vb*

cita, hora (LAm) *nf* (to meet) engagement *n*, appointment *n*

clase *nf* kind *n* **de alta clase** high-class **clase preferente** (plane) business class

clasificación *nf* classification *n*, placing *n* **clasificación crediticia** credit rating

cláusula *nf* (in contract) clause *n* **cláusula de excepción** escape clause **cláusula de exclusión** exclusion clause **cláusula de incumplimiento** neglect clause **cláusula de negligencia** negligence clause **cláusula de opción** option clause **cláusula de protección**, hedge clause (US) **cláusula de renuncia** waiver clause **cláusula de salvaguardia** escape clause

cliente, -nta *nm,f* buyer *n*, client *n*, customer *n* **cliente de la casa** regular customer **cliente habitual** regular customer

clientela *nf* clientele *n*, goodwill *n*, patronage *n*

climatizado *adj* air-conditioned *adj*

cobertura *nf* cover *n* **cobertura a plazo** forward cover **cobertura del seguro** insurance cover

cobrable *adj* chargeable *adj*

cobrar *vb* charge *vb*, receive *vb* **cobrar por algo** charge for sth **cobrar de más** overcharge **cobrar un cheque** cash a cheque **cobrar comisión** charge commission **cobrar una deuda** collect a debt **cobrar el sueldo** earn a living **cobrar honorarios** charge a fee **cobrar impuestos** levy taxes **cobrar interés** charge interest **cobrarle de menos a alguien** undercharge

cobro *nm* (of debt) recovery *n*, payment *n* **cobro por cancelación** cancellation charge **cobro a la entrega** COD (cash on delivery) *abbr* **cobro en metálico** encashment **cobro de morosos** debt collection **cobro al recibo de mercancías** cash on receipt of goods

codicioso *adj* acquisitive *adj*, greedy *adj*

código *nm* code *nm* **código de barras** bar code **código fiscal** tax code **código postal** post code, zip code (US) **código de práctica** code of practice

coeficiente *nm* coefficient *n* **con alto coeficiente de mano de obra** labour-intensive **coeficiente de expansión, tasa de expansión** (LAm) rate of expansion **coeficiente de gastos** expenditure rate

cohecho *nm* bribe *n*, bribery *n*

coima *nf* (LAm) bribe *n*

coimear *vb* (LAm) bribe *vb*

coincidir *vb* concur *vb*, tally *vb* **coincidir con** tally with *vb*

cola *nf* queue *n* **cola de comunicantes** hold queue, hold line (US)

colaborar *vb* collaborate *vb*

colega *nmf* associate *n*, colleague *n*

colgar, cortar (LAm) *vb* (telephone) hang up *vb*

colonia *nf* **colonias** (LAm) suburbs, housing complex

coloquio *nm* colloquium *n*

combinación *nf* combination *n* **combinación de medios de márketing** marketing mix **combinación de productos** product mix

comentario *nm* comment *n*, observation *n*

comercial *adj* commercial *adj*, marketable *adj*

comercializable, mercadeable (LAm) *adj* marketable *adj*

comercialización, mercadeo (LAm) *nf* merchandizing *n* **comercialización de futuros** futures marketing

comercializar *vb* market *vb*, merchandise *vb*

comerciante, feriante; puestero, -era (LAm) *nmf, nmf; nm,f* dealer *n*, merchant *n*, trader *n* **comerciante al por mayor** wholesaler

comerciar *vb* trade *vb* **comerciar con alguien** trade with sb **comerciar como** (name) trade as

comercio *nm* business *n*, commerce *n*, dealing *n*, trade *n*, trading (US) *n* **comercio de acciones** equity trading **comercio armamentístico** arms trade **comercio bilateral** bilateral trade **comercio de exportación** export trade **comercio exterior** foreign trade, overseas trade **comercio de futuros** futures trading **comercio internacional** international trade **comercio al por mayor** wholesale trade **comercio al por menor** retail outlet, retail trade **comercio minorista** retail trade **el comercio textil** (informal) the rag trade **comercio de ultramar** foreign trade, overseas trade

comestible 1. *adj* edible *adj* 2. *nm* food *n*

cometer *vb* commit *vb* **cometer un error** make a mistake

comicios *nm* election *n*, general election *n*

comisión *nf* commission *n*, committee *n*, fee *n*, tribunal *n*, brokerage *n* **comisión asesora** advisory committee **Comisión de Bolsa y Valores** SEC (Securities and Exchange Commission) *abbr*, SIB (Securities and Investment Board) *abbr* **Comisión Consultiva Europea** European Advisory Committee **comisión de control** watchdog committee **comisión ejecutiva** executive committee **Comisión Europea** European Commission **comisión de**

fábricas factory board **Comisión de Monopolios y Fusiones** Monopolies and Mergers Commission
comisionista *nmf* broker *n*, commission agent *n*, commission broker *n*
comité *nm* committee *n* **comité de empresa** works committee **comité de supervisión** supervisory board
compañero, -era *nm,f* companion *n* **compañero de trabajo** workmate
compañía *nf* company *n* **compañía asociada** sister company **compañía constituida legalmente** incorporated company (US) **compañía de crédito comercial** finance company **compañía fiduciaria** trust company **compañía limitada** limited company **compañía naviera** shipping line **compañía en un paraíso fiscal** offshore company **compañía registrada** registered company **compañía de seguros** insurance company **compañía de transportes** haulage/road haulage/transport company **compañía de venta por correo** mail-order house
comparativo *adj* comparative *adj*
compartir *vb* share *vb* **compartir las responsabilidades** share the responsibilities
compatible *adj* compatible *adj*
compensación *nf* compensation *n*, quittance *n* **compensaciones por enfermedad** health benefits
compensar *vb* (cheque) clear *vb*, equalize *vb* **compensar por** compensate for
competencia *nf* competition *n*, expertise *n*, jurisdiction *n*, qualification *n*, terms of reference *npl* **competencia desleal** unfair competition **competencia encarnizada** cut-throat competition **competencia extranjera** foreign competition **competencia fuerte/intensa** tough competition **competencia internacional** international competition **competencia leal** fair competition **competencia de mercado** market competition
competidor, -ora *nm,f* competitor *n*
competir *vb* compete *vb* **competir con un/una rival** compete with a rival
competitividad *nf* competitiveness *n*
competitivo *adj* competitive *adj* (price) keen *adj*
complejo 1. *adj* complex *adj* **2.** *nm* **complejo habitacional/de viviendas, colonia** (LAm) housing complex, housing estate, housing tenement (US) **complejo de viviendas subvencionadas** housing project
complemento *nm* allowance *n*
completamente *adv* wholly *adv*
complicado *adj* complex *adj*
compra *nf* acquisition *n*, buy-out *n*, purchase *n* **una buena compra** a good buy **compra de cupos** quota buying **compra ficticia** fictitious purchase **compra a plazos** hire purchase **compras hechas sin salir del**

hogar home shopping **compra de tierras** land purchase
comprador, -ora *nm,f* buyer *n*, vendee *n*
comprador de vivienda home buyer
comprar *vb* purchase *vb*, bribe *vb* **comprar algo caro** buy sth at a high price **comprar algo a crédito** buy sth on credit **comprar en grandes cantidades** buy in bulk **comprar a granel** buy in bulk **comprarle su parte a** buy out **comprar algo al por mayor** buy sth wholesale **comprar algo a plazos** buy sth by instalments **comprar algo de segunda mano** buy sth second hand
compraventa *nf* buying and selling *n*
comprensión *nf* understanding *n*
comprobación *nf* proof *n*
comprobante *nm* voucher *n*
comprobar, chequear; checar (LAm) *vb* check *vb*
comprometer *vb* commit *vb*
comprometerse *vb* give one's word *vb*, undertake *vb*
compromiso *nm* (to meet) appointment *n*, engagement *n*, commitment *n*, obligation *n*, undertaking *n*
computadora, computador (LAm) *nf, nm* computer *n*
común *adj* common *adj* **en común** jointly *prep*
comunicación *nf* communication *n*
comunicado *nm* bulletin *n*, communication *n* **comunicado a la prensa** press release
comunicar *vb* inform *vb*, transmit *vb* **comunicar la reacción** give feedback **comunicarse con alguien** (phone) get through to sb
comunidad *nf* community *n* **Comunidad Europea del Carbón y del Acero** ECSC (European Coal and Steel Community) *abbr* **Comunidad Europea (CE)** European Community
conceder *vb* grant *vb* **conceder una desgravación** grant a rebate **conceder en franquicia** franchise **conceder indemnización** pay compensation **conceder un permiso** license, furlough (US) **conceder un préstamo** grant a loan
concepto *nm* concept *n*, idea *n* **bajo ningún concepto** under no circumstances
concertar *vb* arrange *vb*, plan *vb* **concertar una cita, pedir una cita** (LAm) make an appointment
concesión *nf* franchise *n* (patent) grant *n* **concesión de franquicias** franchising
concesionario, -ria *nm,f* franchisee *n*, licensee *n*, authorized dealer *n*
concluir *vb* wind up *vb*, end *vb*
conclusión *nf* winding-up *n*, end *n*
concurrir *vb* concur *vb*
concurso, licitación (LAm) *nm, nf* tender *n*
condición *nf* condition *n* **condiciones de compra** conditions of purchase **condiciones de crédito** credit terms

condiciones de pago conditions of payment **condiciones de trabajo** working conditions **condiciones de venta** conditions of sale **condiciones de vida** living conditions

conducta *nf* conduct *n* **conducta del consumidor** consumer habits **mala conducta** misconduct

conducto, ducto (LAm) *nm* pipeline *n*

conectar *vb* (phone) put sb through to sb (machine) turn on *vb*

conexión *nf* connection *n* **en conexión directa con el ordenador central** on-line *adj* **conexiones comerciales** (LAm) business contacts

confederación *nf* confederation *n* **Confederación de Sindicatos** Trades Union Congress

conferencia *nf* conference *n* **conferencia personal** person-to-person call

conferir *vb* confer *vb*

confiable *adj* (LAm) reliable *adj*

confianza *nf* confidence *n* **de la máxima confianza** gilt-edged

confidencial *adj* confidential *adj*

confirmación *nf* confirmation *n*

confirmar *vb* confirm *vb* **sin confirmar** unconfirmed

confiscación *nf* forfeit *n*, forfeiture *n*, repossession *n* **confiscación de acciones** forfeit of shares

confiscar *vb* impound *vb*, repossess *vb*

conflicto, diferendo (LAm) *nm* dispute *n* **conflicto colectivo** industrial dispute **conflicto laboral** industrial dispute, labour dispute

conforme *adj* consistent *adj*, satisfied *adj* **conforme a** in accordance with

congelación *nf* (on prices, wages) freeze *n* **congelación salarial** wage(s) freeze

congelar *vb* (prices, wages) freeze *vb*, peg *vb*

conglomerado *nm* conglomerate *n*

congreso *nm* conference *n*, congress *n*

conjunto 1. *adj* joint *adj* **2.** *nm* unit *n*

conocer *vb* meet *vb*, know *vb* **conocer a alguien** make the acquaintance of sb **conocer algo a fondo** have a thorough knowledge of sth

conocido 1. *adj* well-known *adj* **2.** *nm,f* **conocido, -ida de negocios** business acquaintance **conocidos de negocios, conexiones comerciales; palancas** (LAm) business contacts

conocimiento *nm* knowledge *n* **conocimiento de embarque** bill of lading **conocimiento de embarque de exportación** export bill of lading **conocimientos** expertise, knowledge **conocimientos básicos** working knowledge **conocimientos y experiencia** know-how **con conocimientos de informática** computer literate

consecución *nf* accomplishment *n*, achievement *n*

consecuencia *nf* consequence *n* **consecuencias** outcome

conseguir *vb* (capital, loan) raise *vb*, accomplish *vb*, achieve *vb*, gain *vb*, obtain *vb*, win *vb* **conseguir buen precio** get value for one's money **conseguir crédito** obtain credit

consejero, -era *nm,f* adviser/advisor *n*, director *n*

consejo *nm* advice *n*, council *n* **consejo de administración** board of directors **consejo de administración fiduciaria** (bank) trustee department **Consejo Británico** British Council **Consejo de Europa** Council of Europe **consejo de la fábrica** factory board **consejo de obreros** works council **consejo práctico** (suggestion) tip

consentimiento *nm* agreement *n*, consent *n*

consentir *vb* consent *vb*

conservar *vb* retain *vb*

consideración *nf* (for contract) consideration *n*

consigna *nf* left luggage *n*, left luggage office *n*, slogan *n*

consignación *nf* consignment *n*, shipment *n*

consolidación *nf* consolidation *n*

consolidar *vb* consolidate *vb*

consorcio *nm* consortium *n*, syndicate *n*

construcción *nf* construction industry *n*, building *n* **construcción naval** shipbuilding

cónsul *nmf* consul *n*

consulado *nm* consulate *n*

consultar *vb* consult *vb*, look up *vb*

consultivo *adj* advisory *adj*

consultor, -ora *nm,f* consultant *n* **consultor de empresas** management consultant

consultoría *nf* consultancy *n*, consulting (US) *n*

consumidor, -ora *nm,f* consumer *n* **consumidor final** end consumer

consumismo *nm* consumerism *n*

consumo *nm* consumption *n* **consumo global** world consumption

contabilidad *nf* accountancy *n*, book-keeping *n* **contabilidad comercial trimestral** quarterly trade accounts **contabilidad financiera** financial accounting **contabilidad general** general accounting **contabilidad gerencial** management accounting

contable *nmf* accountant *n*, book-keeper *n* **contable colegiado, -ada, contador, -ora público, -ica** (LAm) chartered accountant

contactar *vb* contact *vb* **contactar con** contact

contacto *nm* **contactos** connections, contacts **contactos comerciales, conexiones comerciales** (LAm) business contacts, business connections

contado *adj* few *adj*, numbered *adj* **al contado** for cash, in cash

contador, medidor (LAm) *nm* meter *n*

contar *vb* count *vb*, relate *vb*

contenedor *nm* container *n*
contener, postergar (LAm) *vb* (not release) hold back *vb*
contestación *nf* answer *n* **en contestación a su carta de** in reply to your letter of...
contestador *nm* answering machine *n* **contestador automático** answering machine **contestador telefónico** Ansaphone (R)
contestar *vb* answer *vb*
contrabandear *vb* smuggle *vb*
contracción *nf* contraction *n*
contraerse *vb* shrink *vb*
contrario *adj* contrary *adj*, opposite *adj* **contrario a la ética profesional** unprofessional
contraste *nm* contrast *n*, hallmark *n* **en contraste con** in contrast to
contratación *nf* (to a position) appointment *n*, recruitment *n* **contratación de empleados/de personal** employee recruitment
contratante *adj* contracting *adj* **las partes contratantes** the contracting parties
contratar *vb* employ *vb*, hire *vb*, recruit *vb*, retain *vb*
contratista *nmf* builder *n*, contractor *n*, entrepreneur *n* **contratista de la construcción/de obras** building contractor **contratista de transporte por carretera** haulage contractor
contrato *nm* contract *n* **contrato de alquiler, contrato de arriendo** (LAm) hire contract **contrato en firme** formal contract **contrato de futuros** futures contract **contrato hipotecario** mortgage deed **contrato a plazo fijo** forward contract **contrato de préstamo** loan agreement **contrato de seguros** insurance contract **contrato-tipo** standard agreement **contrato de trabajo** employment contract
contravenir *vb* contravene *vb*
contribución *nf* contribution *n* **contribuciones municipales, tasas** (LAm) (tax) rates **contribución territorial rústica** land tax
contribuir *vb* contribute *vb*, subscribe *vb*
contribuyente *nmf* taxpayer *n*
control *nm* (customs) inspection *n* **control de aduana** customs check **control de calidad** quality control **control de crédito** credit control **control de divisas** exchange control **control de existencias** stock control, inventory control (US) **control financiero** financial control **control de finanzas** financial control **control de gastos** expense control **control de importaciones** import control **control de producción** production control **control público de existencias, Dirección General Impositiva; Impuestos Internos** (LAm) inventory control
controlador, -ora *nm,f* controller *n* **controlador aéreo** air traffic controller

convalidar *vb* validate *vb*
convenido *adj* agreed *adj*
convenio *nm* agreement *n*, covenant *n*, treaty *n* **convenio colectivo** collective agreement **convenio de compensación de cambio** exchange clearing agreement **convenio internacional** international agreement **convenio sobre los precios mínimos de venta al público** fair-trade agreement **convenio salarial** wage agreement, wage(s) settlement
convenir *vb* agree *vb*
conversación *nf* conversation *n* **conversaciones comerciales** trade talks **conversación sobre ventas** sales talk
conversión *nf* conversion *n* **conversión al sistema métrico** metrication
convidar *vb* invite *vb*, offer *vb*
convocar *vb* call *vb*, convene *vb* **convocar una reunión** call/convene a meeting
cooperativa *nf* collective *n*, cooperative *n*
copia *nf* copy *n* **copia de la factura** duplicate invoice
copiar *vb* (photocopy) copy *vb*
copropiedad *nf* joint ownership *n*, timeshare *n*
corona *nf* crown *n* **corona danesa** (Danish) krone **corona noruega** (Norwegian) krone **corona sueca** (Swedish) krona
corporación *nf* corporation *n*, guild *n*
corporativo *adj* corporate *adj*
corredor, -ora *nm,f* broker *n* salesperson, agent **corredor de Bolsa, corredor** (LAm) floor broker, stockbroker **corredor marítimo** shipping broker **corredor de parquet** floor broker **corredor de seguros** insurance agent, insurance broker
corregir *vb* amend *vb*, correct *vb*
correo *nmf* courier *n*, mail *n*, post *n* **correo aéreo** airmail **correo certificado, correo recomendado** (LAm) registered mail **correo certificado con acuse de recibo** recorded delivery **correo electrónico** electronic mail, email **por servicio de correo** by courier service
correr *vb* run *vb*
correspondencia *nf* correspondence *n*
corresponder *vb* correspond *vb*, concern *vb* **nos corresponde** the onus is on us to...
corretaje *nm* brokerage *n*
corriente *adj* going *adj* **muy al corriente, muy interiorizado** (LAm) well-informed
corrupción *nf* corruption *n*
cortar *vb* cut *vb*, (phone) hang up (LAm) *vb*
corte *nf* court *n*
corto *adj* short *adj* **corto plazo** short term
coser *vb* sew *vb* **coser a máquina** machine sew
cosignatario, -ria *nm,f* cosignatory *n*
coste, costo (LAm) *nm* cost *n* **coste adicional** extra cost **coste de capital** capital cost **coste de explotación** operating cost, running cost **coste indirecto** indirect cost **coste marginal**

marginal cost **coste neto** net(t) cost **coste original** original cost **costes de administración** administrative costs **costes corrientes, costos de operación** (LAm) running costs **costes de manipulación** handling charges **costes de explotación** operating expenditure, operating expenses **costes fijos** fixed costs **costes fiscales** fiscal charges **costes judiciales** legal charge **costes de la mano de obra** labour costs **costes de mantenimiento** maintenance costs **costes de reparación** costs of repair **costes de transporte** carriage costs, forwarding charges **costes variables** variable costs **coste total** full cost **coste total de los salarios** wage(s) bill **coste de transporte** carrying cost **coste unitario, costo por unidad; costo unitario** (LAm) unit cost **coste de vida** cost of living

cotitular *nmf* joint holder *n*

cotización *nf* price *n*, quotation *n* **cotización de apertura** opening price **cotizaciones de la bolsa** stock exchange prices **cotizaciones a la Seguridad Social, aportes a la seguridad social** (LAm) social security contributions

coyuntura *nf* trend *n*, point in time *n*

creación *nf* establishment *n*, creation *n* **creación de empleo** job creation

crecer *vb* thrive *vb*, grow *vb*, increase *vb*

crecimiento *nm* growth *n* (in unemployment) rise *n* **crecimiento cero** zero growth **crecimiento económico** economic growth **crecimiento regido por las exportaciones** export-led growth

crédito *nm* cash advance *n*, credit *n*, goodwill *n*, loan *n* **crédito abierto** open credit **crédito en condiciones desventajosas** hard loan **crédito congelado** frozen credits **crédito al consumidor** consumer credit **crédito a la exportación** export credit **crédito extranjero** foreign loan **crédito fijo** fixed credit **crédito sin garantía** unsecured credit **crédito ilimitado** unlimited credit **crédito a largo plazo** long-term credit **crédito personal** personal loan **crédito puente** bridging loan, bridge loan (US)

crianza *nf* farming *n*, rearing *n*

crimen *nm* crime *n* **crimen organizado** racketeering

crisis *nf* (economic) depression *n* **crisis económica** economic crisis, financial crisis

criterio *nm* criterion *n*

criticar *vb* find fault with *vb* (disparage) knock *vb*

cronometraje *nm* timing *n*

crudo *adj* (unprocessed) raw *adj*, crude *adj*

cuadra *nf* (LAm) block *n*

cuadrar *vb* tally *vb*, tally up *vb*

cuadro *nm* table *n*, chart *n* **cuadros** leaders **cuadros medios** middle management

cualificación, calificación (LAm) *nf*

qualification *n* **cualificaciones necesarias** necessary qualifications **cualificación profesional** professional qualification

cualificado, calificado; capacitado (LAm) *adj* qualified *adj* (worker) skilled *adj*

cualitativo *adj* qualitative *adj*

cuantitativo *adj* quantitative *adj*

cuanto *adv* as much as *adv* **en cuanto a** with regard to... **cuanto antes** a.s.a.p (as soon as possible) *abbr*

cuasicontrato *nm* quasi-contract *n*

cuasingresos *nmpl* quasi-income *n*

cuenta, adición; rubro (LAm) *nf, nf; nm* bill *n* tally *n* **cuenta de ahorros** deposit account **cuenta bancaria** bank account **cuenta bloqueada** blocked account **cuenta de caja de ahorros** savings account **cuenta corriente** current account **cuenta de crédito** charge account **cuenta de ejercicio** trading account **cuenta de explotación** trading account **cuenta de gastos de representación** expense account **cuenta nueva** new account **cuenta en participación** joint account **cuenta de pérdidas y ganancias** operating statement, profit and loss account **por cuenta propia** freelance **cuenta rebasada** overdrawn account **por cuenta y riesgo del comprador** at the buyer's risk **las cuentas** the books **cuentas a cobrar** accounts receivable **cuentas definitivas** final accounts **cuentas a pagar** accounts payable

cuestión *nf* matter *n*, question *n* **cuestión principal** key question

cuestionario *nm* questionnaire *n* **cuestionario para realizar investigaciones de mercado** market research questionnaire

culpa *nf* blame *n*, fault *n* **culpa concurrente** contributory negligence **culpa grave** gross negligence

cultivo *nm* farming *n* **cultivo comercial** cash crop

culto *adj* knowledgeable *adj*, educated *adj*

cumplir *vb* accomplish *vb*, carry out *vb* **cumplir sus compromisos** meet one's obligations **cumplir formalidades** observe formalities **cumplir con las leyes** comply with legislation **cumplir su palabra** keep one's word **cumplir el reglamento** comply with the rules

cuota *nf* instalment *n*, quota *n*, share *n*, effect *n*, payment *n*, toll *n* **cuota de comisión** commission fee **cuota fija, tasa de interés fija** (LAm) flat rate **cuota inicial, pie** (LAm) down payment **cuota de licencia** licence fee **cuota de mercado** market share **cuotas fijas** standing charges

cupo *nm* quota *n* **cupo arancelario** tariff quota **cupo de importación** import quota **cupo de ventas** sales quota

cupón *nm* coupon *n*

currículum *nm* curriculum vitae *n*

currículum vitae (CV) curriculum vitae (CV), résumé (US)
cursar vb send vb, study vb
cursillo nm short course n **cursillo de actualización** training course
cursiva nf italic type n
curso nm process n, course n, direction n **curso de reciclaje, plan de recapacitación** (LAm) retraining programme, retraining program (US)
curva nf curve n **curva de la experiencia** experience curve **curva de rendimiento** yield curve
dañar vb damage vb
daño nm damage n **daños por accidente** accidental damage **daños materiales** damage to property **daños sufridos por mercancías durante el transporte** damage to goods in transit
dar vb give vb **dar cuentas de** account for **dar instrucciones** brief **dar interés** bear interest **dar orden de no pagar** cancel an order **dar su palabra** give one's word **dar por perdido** (debts) write off **dar por terminado un asunto** (informal) shut up shop **dar la vuelta a, voltear; dar vuelta** (LAm) turn over
dato nm fact n **datos** data, information **datos de prueba** test data **datos tabulados** tabulated data
deber 1. nm obligation n **2.** vb owe vb
debido adj appropriate adj, due adj **debido aviso** due warning
debido a adv due to adv **debido a circunstancias imprevistas** due to unforeseen circumstances **debido a un error** due to an oversight
debilitarse vb (market) weaken vb
débito nm debit n
decidirse vb make a resolution vb
declaración nf statement n **declaración de aduana** customs declaration **declaración jurada** affidavit **declaración de tonelaje** bill of tonnage
declarar vb declare vb **sin declarar** (goods) undeclared **declararse en huelga, ir al paro; declararse en paro** (LAm) strike **declarar siniestro total** (vehicle) write off
declive nm decline n **declive económico** economic decline
dedicar vb dedicate vb **dedicarse al negocio de** (informal) be in the trade
deducción nf deduction n **deducción impositiva** tax allowance
deducible adj deductible adj
deducir vb deduct vb
defecto nm defect n, fault n **sin defecto** zero defect **defecto grave** serious fault **defecto menor** minor fault **defecto oculto** hidden defect
defectuoso adj defective adj
defender vb defend vb **defenderse bastante bien en algo** have a working knowledge of sth

defensor, -ora nm,f defender n **defensor del pueblo** ombudsman
deficiencia nf deficiency n
deficiente adj deficient adj, unsatisfactory adj
déficit nm deficit n **déficit de la balanza de pagos** balance of payments deficit **déficit comercial** trade gap **déficit presupuestario, déficit presupuestal** (LAm) budgetary deficit
deflación nf deflation n
deflacionista adj deflationary adj
DEG (derechos especiales de giro) abbr SDRs (special drawing rights) abbr
dejar vb abandon vb, lend vb **dejar de** quit **dejar atrás** (resign from) leave **dejar flotar** (currency) float **dejar pasar** overlook
delegación nf delegation n **delegación de poderes** delegation
delegado, -ada nm,f delegate n **delegado sindical** shop steward, union representative
delegar vb delegate vb, farm out vb
delito nm offence n, offense (US) n
demanda nf legal action n, demand n **demanda de aumento salarial** wage claim **demanda de consumo** consumer demand **demanda máxima** peak demand **con demanda que supera a la oferta** over subscribed **haber mucha demanda** be in hot demand
demandante nmf claimant n
democracia nf democracy n **democracia industrial** industrial democracy
demografía nf demography n
demora nf delay n, holdup (LAm) n
demorar vb delay vb
departamento nm department n **departamento de comercialización** marketing department **Departamento de Comercio y Exportación** Board of Trade **departamento de control de prácticas comerciales** Trading Standards Office (US) **Departamento de Estado** Federal Bureau (US) **departamento de exportación** export department **departamento de importación** import department **departamento de márketing** marketing department **Departamento Nacional de Investigación Económica** National Bureau of Economic Research (US) **departamento de personal** personnel department **departamento de reclamaciones** claims department, complaints department **Departamento del Tesoro** the Treasury Department (US)
dependiente, -nta, corredor, -ora; empleado, -ada de tienda (LAm) nm,f salesperson n, shop assistant n
depositar vb deposit vb
depositario, -ria nm,f depository n
depósito, bodega (LAm) nm, nf entrepôt n, warehouse n, warehousing n, deposit (down payment) n **en depósito aduanero** in bond **depósito aduanero, bodega aduanera** (LAm) bonded warehouse, customs

warehouse **depósito de contenedores**
container depot **depósito a largo plazo**
long deposit
depreciación nf depreciation n, write-off n
depreciar vb write down vb
depreciarse vb depreciate vb, lose value vb
depresión nf slump n
derecha nf (politics) right n
derecho nm (customs) duty n law n, right n **el
derecho a algo** the right of sth **derecho
civil** civil law **derecho consuetudinario**
common law **derecho contractual** law of
contract **el derecho a hacer algo** the right
to do sth **derecho de importación** import
duty **derecho internacional** international
law **derecho laboral** employment law,
labour law **derecho mercantil** commercial
law **derecho de paso** right of way **derecho
penal** criminal law **derecho público** public
law **derecho a recurrir** right of recourse
derechos sobre el activo equity
derechos adquiridos vested rights
derechos de aduana customs charges
derechos de amarre mooring rights
derechos de autor copyright **derechos de
dársena** harbour dues **derechos
exclusivos** sole rights **derechos de
muelle** quayage **derechos portuarios**
harbour dues, harbour fees **derechos de
reproducción** copyright **derecho de
suscripción de nuevas acciones** warrant
derecho de voto voting right
deriva nf drift n **deriva de ingresos** earnings
drift
derivado nm by-product n
derogación nf abolition n
derrochar vb squander vb
desaceleración nf slowdown n
desaceleración económica economic
slowdown
desacelerar vb slow down vb
desagraviar vb make amends vb
desahucio nm eviction n
desarrollar vb (research, project) progress
vb, develop vb
desarrollo nm expansion n, growth n,
development n **desarrollo económico**
economic development/growth **desarrollo
profesional** career development
descansar vb take a break vb
descargar vb unload vb
descargo nm quittance n
descendente adj downward adj
descenso nm decrease n
descompuesto adj (LAm) out-of-action adj
descomunal adj king-size(d) adj
descontado adj discounted adj, reduced adj
descripción nf description n **descripción
del puesto de trabajo** job description
descuento nm deduction n, discount n,
rebate n **con descuento** at a discount
descuento por grandes cantidades
quantity discount **descuento por pago al
contado** cash discount **descuento por**

volumen volume discount
descuido nm oversight n
desechable adj (not for reuse) disposable
adj
desechos nm waste n, spoilage n **desechos
industriales** industrial waste
desembalar, desempacar (LAm) vb unpack
vb
desembolsar vb disburse vb
desembolso nm expenditure n
desembolsos outgoings
desempleado, cesante (LAm) adj jobless
adj, redundant adj, unemployed adj **los
desempleados, los cesantes** (LAm) the
jobless
desempleo, cesantía (LAm) nm, nf
unemployment n **desempleo masivo,
cesantía general** (LAm) mass
unemployment
desequilibrio nm imbalance n **desequilibrio
demográfico** population gap
desfalco nm embezzlement n
desgaste nm wastage n
desglosar vb itemize vb
desglose nm breakdown n, itemization n
desglose de estadísticas (of figures)
breakdown
desgravable adj deductible adj, tax-
deductible adj
desgravación nf deduction n, exemption n,
rebate n **desgravación fiscal** tax allowance
desgravar vb deduct vb
deshacer vb unpack vb, dissolve vb
deshacerse vb break up vb **deshacerse de**
unload
desintegración nf breakup n
desintegrar vb break up vb, split vb
desocupado adj idle adj, vacant adj **los
desocupados, los cesantes** (LAm) the
jobless
despachar vb (goods) dispatch vb **sin
despachar** (customs) uncleared **despachar
algo por aduana** clear sth through customs
despacho nm office n **despacho de aduana**
customs office **despacho de billetes,
boletería** (LAm) ticket office
despedir, botar (LAm) vb (employee)
dismiss vb, axe* vb, sack vb, ax vb, fire (US)
vb **despedir a alguien por reducción de
plantilla** make sb redundant **despedirse
de alguien** take leave of sb **despedir
temporalmente** (workers) lay off
desperdicio nm wastage n, waste n
despido nm redundancy n, termination of
employment n **despido injusto** unfair
dismissal, wrongful dismissal
despilfarrador adj spendthrift adj
despilfarrar vb squander vb, waste vb
desplazamiento nm shift n
desplome nm (of economy) collapse n
despreocupado adj negligent adj
destinar vb assign vb **destinar fondos** fund
vb
destinatario, -ria nm,f addressee n,

consignee *n*, recipient *n*, sendee *n*
destrozar *vb* wreck *vb*
detallar *vb* itemize *vb*
detener *vb* (delay) hold up *vb*, arrest *vb* **detener el pago de un cheque** stop a cheque
determinar *vb* govern *vb*, determine *vb*
deuda *nf* borrowing *n*, debt *n* **deuda consolidada** funded debt **deuda fiscal** tax liability **deuda incobrable** bad debt **deuda nacional** national debt **deuda pendiente** outstanding debt **deudas a largo plazo** fixed liabilities
deudor, -ora *nm,f* debtor *n* **deudor hipotecario** mortgagor
devaluación *nf* devaluation *n*
devengar *vb* earn *vb*, yield *vb* **que no devenga interés** non-interest-bearing **devengar interés, intereses** bear interest
devolver *vb* refund *vb*, repay *vb*, send back *vb* **devolver un cheque** refer a cheque (to drawer) **devolver la llamada, devolver el llamado** (LAm) (on phone) call back *vb*
día *nm* day *n* **al día, moderno** (LAm) up-to-date **día festivo, día feriado; fiesta patria** (LAm) bank holiday **día laborable** workday (US) **día libre** day off work **día de liquidación** (stock exchange) Account day
diagrama *nm* diagram *n* **diagrama de flujos** flow chart
diario *nm* newspaper *n*, daily newspaper *n* **diario hablado** news bulletin
dictar *vb* dictate *vb* **dictar un mandato judicial** issue a writ
dieta *nf* allowance *n* **dieta para gastos de alojamiento** accommodation allowance
difamación *nf* libel *n*
diferendo *nm* (LAm) dispute *n*
diferido *adj* (tax) deferred *adj*
dificultad *nf* difficulty *n* **dificultad financiera** financial difficulty
digital *adj* digital *adj*
digno *adj* worthy *adj* **digno de notarse** noteworthy
diluir *vb* water down *vb*
dimisión *nf* resignation *n*
dimitir *vb* leave *vb*, resign *vb* **dimitir el cargo** resign from office
dinámica *nf* dynamics *npl*
dinámico *adj* dynamic *adj*, high-powered *adj*
dineral, platal; lanón (LAm) *nm* (money) bundle *n*, packet *n*
dinero, plata (LAm) *nm, nf* cash *n*, money *n* **dinero caliente** hot money **dinero caro** dear money **dinero de curso forzoso** fiat money **dinero en efectivo, plata** (LAm) cash **dinero especulativo** hot money **dinero fraccionario** fractional money **dinero en mano** spot cash **dinero en metálico** hard cash **dinero público** public money **dinero a la vista** call money
Dios *nm* God *n* **a la buena de Dios, a la sanfasón** (LAm) hit-or-miss
diputado, -ada *nm,f* Member of Parliament (MP) (GB) *n*

dirección *nf* administration *n*, fronting *n*, leadership *n* (of business) operation *n* **alta dirección** senior management, top management **Dirección General Impositiva** (LAm) Inland Revenue **sin dirección** zero address **dirección comercial** business address, business management, sales management **dirección financiera** financial management **dirección general** general management, management, regional office **dirección hotelera** hotel management **dirección de información** information management **dirección lineal** line management **dirección por objetivos** management by objectives **dirección de oficina** office management **dirección particular** home address **dirección de personal** personnel management **dirección portuaria** harbour authorities **dirección privada** home address **dirección registrada** registered address **mala dirección** mismanagement
directamente *adv* directly *adv*, first-hand *adv*
directivo, -iva *nm,f* director *n*
directo *adj* direct *adj*, non-stop *adj*
director, -ora *nm,f* director *n*, executive *n*, manager *n*, supervisor *n* **director adjunto** associate director, deputy director **director de banco** bank manager **director de campo** field manager **director de contabilidad** head accountant **director ejecutivo** managing director **director de fábrica** plant manager, works manager **director de finanzas de la empresa** company treasurer **director general** chief executive, general manager **director gerente** managing director **director de márketing, mercadeo** (LAm) marketing director **director obrero** worker-director **director de planta** plant manager **director regional** area manager **director de sucursal** branch manager **director técnico** technical director
dirigir *vb* (department) head *vb*, administer *vb*, be head of *vb*, manage *vb* **dirigir un hotel** run a hotel **dirigirse a** address, head for
disco *nm* disk *n* **disco duro** hard disk **disco flexible** floppy disk **disco magnético** magnetic disk
discrepancia *nf* variance *n*, disagreement *n*
diseñado *adj* designed *adj* **una máquina bien/mal diseñada** a machine of good/bad design
diseñador, -ora *nm,f* (commercial) designer *n*
diseñar *vb* design *vb*
diseño *nm* design *n* **diseño asistido por ordenador (CAD), diseño asistido por computadora** (LAm) computer-aided design (CAD) **diseño de cuestionarios** questionnaire design
disminución *nf* abatement *n*, decrease *n*, depletion *n*, reduction *n*, slowdown *n*

disminuir *vb* abate *vb*, decrease *vb*
disparar *vb* (gun) fire *vb*
dispensable *adj* non-essential *adj*
disponer *vb* arrange *vb*, provide *vb*, have available *vb*
disposición *nf* (stipulation) provision *n* **de acuerdo con las disposiciones** according to the regulations **disposiciones aduaneras** customs regulations **disposiciones de liquidación** winding-up arrangements
disputa, diferendo (LAm) *nf, nm* dispute *n*
disquete *nm* disk *n*
distancia *nf* distance *n* **a distancia** long-range
distribución *nf* distribution *n* **distribución de noche** overnight delivery
distribuidor, -ora *nm,f* distributor *n* **distribuidor autorizado** authorized dealer
distribuir *vb* (payments) spread *vb*, distribute *vb*
distrito *nm* district *n* **distrito postal** postal area
diversificación *nf* diversification *n*
diversificarse *vb* diversify *vb*
diverso *adj* wide-ranging *adj*
dividendo *nm* dividend *n* **dividendo de fin de año** year-end dividend
dividir *vb* split *vb*, divide *vb*
divisa *nf* (foreign) currency *n* **divisa débil** soft currency **divisa de reserva** reserve currency **divisas** foreign currency, foreign exchange **divisas forzosas** forced currency **divisas fuertes** hard currency
división *nf* (of company) division *n* **división del mercado** market segmentation **división del trabajo** division of labour **división triple** three-way split **división por zonas** zoning
divulgar *vb* broadcast, *vb* (document) circulate *vb*
doble *adj* double *adj*, two-way *adj* **de doble mano/de doble vía** (LAm) two-way
documento *nm* document *n* **documento de trabajo** working paper
dólar, verde (LAm) *nm* buck* (US) *n* **el dólar de Hong Kong está vinculado al dólar norteamericano** the HK dollar is pegged to the US dollar
domiciliación *nf* bank payment *n*, bank details *npl*
domicilio *nm* home *n* **domicilio social** HO (Head Office), headquarters, registered address, registered office
dominar *vb* govern *vb* **dominar los principios básicos de algo** have a working knowledge of sth
donación *nf* bequest *n*, donation *n*
dotación *nf* endowment *n* **dotación de personal** staffing
ducto *nm* (LAm) pipeline *n*
dueño, -eña *nm,f* owner *n*, proprietor *n* **dueño de casa** householder **dueño de hacer lo que quiera** free agent

duplicado *nm* duplicate *n*
echar *vb* fire *vb*, throw *vb* **echarse a perder** go to waste **echar por tierra** wreck **echar del trabajo, botar del trabajo** (LAm) sack, fire* (US)
econometría *nf* econometrics *n*
economía *nf* (system) economy *n* economics *n*, savings *npl* **economía avanzada** advanced economy **economía global** global economy **economía libre** free economy **economía de mercado** free market economy, market economy **economía de mercado libre** free market economy **economía mixta** mixed economy **economía nacional** national economy **economía nueva** young economy **economía planificada** planned economy **economías de escala** economies of scale **economía subdesarrollada** underdeveloped economy **economía sumergida, economía informal; economía paralela** (LAm) black economy **economía en vías de desarrollo** developing economy
económico *adj* economical *adj*, financial *adj*, economic *adj*, (price) low *adj*
economista *nmf* economist *n*
ecu (European Currency Unit) *nm* ECU (European Currency Unit) *abbr*
editorial *nf* publishing house *n*
efectivo *nm* cash *n*, hard cash *n*
efecto *nm* effect *n*, toll *n* **efecto bancario** (financial) draft **efecto indirecto** spin-off **efectos financieros** financial effects **efectos negociables** commercial paper **efecto a la vista** sight draft
eficaz *adj* efficient *adj*
eficiencia *nf* efficiency *n*
eficiente *adj* efficient *adj*
EFTA (la) *nf (abbr)* EFTA (European Free Trade Association) *abbr*
egresado, -ada *nm,f* (LAm) graduate *n*
ejecución *nf* enforcement *n*, foreclosure *n* **ejecución de un juicio hipotecario** foreclosure
ejecutar *vb* (policy) enforce *vb*, carry out *vb*
ejecutivo, -iva *nm,f* executive *n*
ejemplo *nm* example *n*, sample *n*
ejercer *vb* exercise *vb*, practice *vb*
ejercicio *nm* exercise *n*, (financial) year *n* **ejercicio comercial** trading year **ejercicio financiero** financial year **ejercicio fiscal** fiscal year, tax year
elaboración *nf* making *n*, preparation *n*
elaborar *vb* process *vb* **elaborar un informe, hacer un reporte** (LAm) draw up a report **elaborar el presupuesto** draw up a budget
elasticidad *nf* elasticity *n* **elasticidad de demanda** elasticity of demand **elasticidad de ingresos** income elasticity **elasticidad de producción** elasticity of production
elección *nf* election *n*, option *n* **elecciones generales** general election **elecciones**

municipales local election
electrónico adj electronic adj
elevar vb raise vb
eliminación nf elimination n
elogioso adj complimentary adj
embajada nf embassy n
embalaje nm package n, packaging n
embalar vb pack vb **embalar algo** box sth up
embarcarse vb go aboard vb
embargar vb impound vb
embargo nm embargo n **embargo comercial** trade embargo
embolsar vb net(t) vb
embotellamiento nm bottleneck n
emergencia nf emergency n
emigración nf emigration n
emisión nf broadcast n, flotation n **emisión de derechos** rights issue **emisión fiduciaria** fiduciary issue **emisión de nuevas acciones** share issue, stock issue (US)
emitir vb (notes) issue vb broadcast vb, transmit vb **emitir una factura** issue an invoice
empleado, -ada nm,f clerk n, employee n **empleado de tienda** (LAm) shop salesperson **empleado de banco, bancario** (LAm) bank clerk **empleado de oficina** clerical worker, white-collar worker **empleados** staff
emplear vb employ vb, spend vb, utilize vb
empleo nm employment n, utilization n **empleo eventual, trabajo temporario** (LAm) temporary employment **empleo fijo** permanent employment **empleo remunerado** gainful employment
emprender vb undertake vb
empresa nf (project) enterprise n business n, company n, corporation n, undertaking n **empresa que comercia con otra** trading partner **empresa conjunta** collaborative venture, joint venture **empresa constructora** builder, building firm **empresa de creación reciente** new business **empresa donde los trabajadores no tienen obligación de afiliarse** open shop **empresa que emplea exclusivamente a trabajadores sindicados** closed shop **empresa envasadora** packing house (US) **empresa estatal** government entreprise, state-owned entreprise **empresa exterior** foreign company **empresa extraterritorial** offshore company **empresa familiar** family business, family corporation **empresa ficticia** phoney* company **empresa filial** branch company, subsidiary **empresa ilimitada** unlimited company **empresa líder del mercado** market leader **empresa líder del sector** market lead **erempresa matriz** parent company **empresa mediana** medium-sized firm **empresa multinacional** multinational corporation

empresa de primera clase blue-chip company **empresa privada** private enterprise **empresa de propiedad pública** state-owned enterprise **empresa pública** government enterprise **empresa rival** competing company **empresa de tamaño mediano** medium-sized firm **empresa de transporte por carretera** haulage company, freight company (US) **empresa de transportes** carrier, transport company **empresa de transportes urgentes** express carrier **empresa de utilidad pública** public utility **las grandes empresas** big business
empresarial adj corporate adj, entrepreneurial adj
empresario, -ria nm,f employer n, entrepreneur n
encabezamiento, acápite (LAm) nm heading n
encabezar vb be head of vb
encargado, -ada nm,f foreman/forewoman n **encargado de compras** buyer
encargar vb farm out vb, place an order vb **encargar a alguien con algo** charge sb with sth
encargarse vb undertake vb **encargarse de** (deal) handle
encargo, comisión (LAm) nm, nf commission n, job n, request n
encender vb light up vb, switch on vb
enchufe nm **enchufes, conexiones comerciales; palancas** (LAm) business contacts
encierro nm sit-in protest n **encierro en señal de protesta** (strike) sit-in
encomendar vb charge vb, entrust vb
encontrar vb find vb **encontrarse con** meet
encuentro nm meeting n
encuesta nf survey n **encuesta familiar** household survey
endeudado adj indebted adj
endeudamiento nm debt n **endeudamiento de una sociedad** corporate debt
endeudarse vb get into debt vb
endosar vb (cheque) endorse vb
enfermedad nf illness n **enfermedad profesional** occupational disease
enfermo, -rma nm,f patient n **enfermo fingido** malingerer
enlace nm link n **enlace sindical** shop steward
enmendar vb amend vb
enmienda nf amendment n
ensayo nm test n **ensayo y error** trial and error
enser nm **enseres** equipment, fittings **enseres domésticos** domestic goods, household goods
entablar vb begin vb, institute vb **entablar juicio hipotecario** foreclose **entablar negociaciones** begin negotiations **entablar un pleito** take legal action
entender vb hear vb, understand vb

entenderse con alguien relate to sb
entendimiento *nm* understanding *n*
entidad *nf* institution *n* **entidad caritativa** charitable trust **entidad crediticia** lender **entidad financiera** financial company, financial institution
entrada, pie (LAm) *nf, nm* deposit *n*, down payment *n* **entrada gratuita/libre** free entry **entrada para mercancías exentas de derechos de aduana, entrada para mercaderías exentas de derechos de aduana** (LAm) entry for free goods **entrada en vigor, entrada a vigor** (LAm) entry into force
entrar *vb* enter *vb* **entrar en** access **entrar a acceso** access **entrar en dársena** dock **entrar en déficit** be in the red **entrar en liquidación voluntaria** go into voluntary liquidation
entrega *nf* delivery *n* **entrega contra reembolso** cash on delivery (COD) **entrega a domicilio** home delivery **entrega futura** future delivery **entrega general** general delivery (US) **entrega gratuita/incluida en el precio** free delivery **entrega insuficiente** short delivery **entrega urgente** express delivery
entregar *vb* (goods) deliver *vb*, file *vb*, hand over *vb* **entregar por servicio de mensajero** deliver by courier
entrevista *nf* interview *n*
entrevistar *vb* interview *vb*, hold an interview *vb*
envasar *vb* pack *vb*
envase *nm* package *n*, packaging *n*
enviar *vb* (goods) dispatch *vb*, forward *vb*, send *vb* **enviar por fax** fax
envío *nm* consignment *n*, forwarding *n*, remittance *n* **envío parcial** part shipment
época *nf* season *n*, period *n*
equilibrar *vb* balance *vb* **equilibrar el presupuesto** balance the budget
equilibrio *nm* equilibrium *n*
equipamiento *nm* equipment *n*
equipar *vb* equip *vb*
equiparación *nf* comparison *n* **equiparación de cargas** equalization of burdens
equipo *nm* computer hardware *n*, equipment *n*, kit *n* **equipo de investigación** research team **equipo de oficina** office equipment **equipo de trabajo** working party **equipo de vídeo** video facilities
equivocación *nf* mistake *n*
equivocarse *vb* make a mistake *vb*
ergonomía *nf* ergonomics *n*
error *nm* mistake *n* **error de cálculo** miscalculation **error de copia** clerical error **error tipográfico** typing error
escala *nf* scale *n* **escala móvil** sliding scale a **escala nacional** nationwide **sin escalas** non-stop **escala salarial** salary/wage scale **escala de tiempo** timescale **a gran escala** large-scale
escalada *nf* (prices) escalation *n*, increase *n*

escalera *nf* staircase *n* **escalera mecánica** escalator
escalonar *vb* graduate *vb*, (holidays) stagger *vb*
escasez *nf* deficiency *n*, lack *n*, scarcity *n*, shortage *n*
escindirse *vb* split *vb*
esconder *vb* hide *vb*, hoard *vb*
escribir *vb* write *vb* **escribir a máquina, tipear** (LAm) type *vb*
escrito *adj* written *adj* **escrito a mano** handwritten *adj*
escritura *nf* (law) deed *n* **escritura de propiedad** title deed **escritura de transferencia** deed of transfer **escritura de venta** deed of sale
escudo *nm* escudo *n*
esfuerzo *nm* effort *n* **esfuerzos** labour, effort, labor (US)
eslogan *nm* slogan *n*
espacio *nm* room *n*, space *n* **espacio disponible en un muelle** quayage **espacio para maniobrar** room for manoeuvre
especialidad *nf* speciality *n*
especialista *nm,f* consultant *n*, specialist *n* **especialista en idiomas** language specialist
especializado, capacitado (LAm) *adj* (worker) skilled *adj*
especializar *vb* specialize *vb*
especificación *nf* specification *n*
especulador, -dora *nm,f* speculator *n*
especular *vb* profiteer *vb*, speculate *vb* **especular al alza** (stock exchange) bull *vb*
esperar *vb* (wait) hang on *vb* (on phone) hold on *vb* **esperando para hablar** (on phone) on hold
espiral *nm* spiral *n* **espiral inflacionista** inflationary spiral
espónsor *nmf* sponsor *n*
estabilidad *nf* stability *n* **estabilidad financiera** financial stability
estable *adj* (economy) stable *adj*
establecer *vb* establish *vb* **establecer un fideicomiso** set up a trust
establecimiento *nm* establishment *n*, institution *n*
estación *nf* season *n* **estación de autobuses, estación de micros/omnibuses/colectivos** (LAm) bus station
estacional *adj* seasonal *adj*
estadística *nf* statistic *n* **estadísticas** statistics **estadísticas de la balanza comercial** trade figures **estadísticas consolidadas** consolidated figures
estado *nm* government *n*, state *n* **estado asistencial/benefactor** welfare state **estado de cuenta** bank balance, statement of account **estado de cuentas** bank statement **estado financiero** financial statement
estafa *nf* fraud *n*, racket *n*, swindle* *n*
estafador, -ora *nm,f* swindler* *n*, racketeer *n*

estafar vb defraud vb
estafeta nf sub post office n
estancamiento nm stagnation n
estandarización nf standardization n
estar vb be vb **estar de acuerdo** agree
  estar a la cabeza de (department) head
  estar desempleado, estar en cesantía
  (LAm) be out of work **estar al día** (events)
  keep up with **estar dispuesto a dar**
  referencias sobre act as referee **estar**
  encargado be in charge **estar**
  encomendado de algo hold sth in trust
  estar exento de IVA be zero-rated for VAT
  estar insolvente be bankrupt **estar**
  necesitado de be in need **estar en**
  números rojos be in the red **estar en**
  paro, estar en cesantía (LAm) be out of
  work **estar en plantilla, estar en planilla**
  (LAm) be on the payroll **estar**
  pluriempleado moonlight*
estatuto nm statute n
esterlina nf sterling n
estimar vb estimate vb
estimular vb stimulate vb **estimular la**
  producción boost production
estipulación nf requirement n **de acuerdo**
  con sus estipulaciones in accordance with
  your requirements
estoc nm (goods) stock n, inventory (US) n
  en estoc in stock
estraperlo nm black market n
estrategia nf strategy n **estrategia de**
  crecimiento growth strategy **estrategia**
  de desarrollo development strategy
  estrategia económica economic strategy
  estrategia de exportación export strategy
  estrategia financiera financial strategy
  estrategia de inversión investment
  strategy
estratégico adj strategic adj
estrés nm stress n **estrés profesional**
  executive stress
estropear vb damage vb
estructura nf structure n **estructura**
  financiera financial structure
estudiar, revisar (LAm) vb examine vb,
  study vb
estudio nm research n, study n, workshop n
  estudio económico economic survey
  estudio de mercado consumer survey,
  market research, market research survey
  estudios sobre el terreno field work
  estudio del trabajo work study **estudio**
  de viabilidad feasibility study
etapa nf stage n **por etapas** in stages
etiqueta nf label n **etiqueta del precio** price
  ticket
etiquetar vb label vb
eurobono nm eurobond n
eurocapital nm eurocapital n
eurocheque nm eurocheque n
eurocracia nf eurocracy n
eurócrata nmf eurocrat n
eurocrédito nm eurocredit n

eurodiputado, -ada Member of the
  European Parliament (MEP) n
eurodivisa nf eurocurrency n
eurodólar nm eurodollar n
euroescéptico adj eurosceptic n
eurofondos nmpl eurofunds npl
eurofusión nf euromerger n
euromercado nm euromarket n
euromoneda nf euromoney n
europeo adj European adj
evadir vb avoid vb, evade vb
evaluación, avalúo (LAm) nf, nm appraisal
  n, assessment n, evaluation n **evaluación**
  de puestos de trabajo job analysis
  evaluación del rendimiento performance
  appraisal
evaluador, -dora nm,f referee n
evaluar vb assess vb
evasión nf evasion n **evasión fiscal/de**
  impuestos tax avoidance/evasion
evitar vb avoid vb
exactitud nf accuracy n
exacto adj accurate adj
exagerar vb exaggerate vb **exagerar los**
  méritos de oversell
examen, revisación (LAm) nm, nf
  examination n
examinar vb examine vb, inspect vb
excedencia, licencia (LAm) nf leave of
  absence n
excedente nm surplus n **excedente de**
  financiación financing surplus **excedente**
  de importaciones import surplus
excesivo adj exorbitant adj, redundant adj
exceso nm surplus n **exceso de equipaje**
  excess luggage **exceso de personal**
  overmanning **exceso de peso** excess
  weight **exceso de reservas** excess
  reserves
excluir vb exclude vb
exención nf exemption n, waiver n **exención**
  fiscal concedida a una nueva empresa
  tax holiday
exento adj exempt adj **exento de**
  impuestos tax-exempt, tax-free, zero rate/
  rating
exhibición nf (of goods) display n (exhibition)
  show n
exhibir vb display vb, exhibit vb
exigir vb call for vb, demand vb, insist on vb
  exige el contrato que it is a requirement
  of the contract that... **exigir el pago**
  inmediato de un préstamo (loan) call in
existencia nf existence n, stock n
  existencias (goods) stock, inventory (US)
  existencias acabadas finished stock **con**
  las existencias agotadas out of stock **de**
  existencias disponibles ex stock
  existencias pendientes outstanding stock
  existencias de reserva reserve stock
éxito nm achievement n, success n
exoneración nf exemption n
expandir vb expand vb
expansión nf expansion n, growth n

expansión del comercio expansion of
trade expansión económica economic
expansion expansión industrial industrial
expansion expansión del mercado market
growth expansión urbana descontrolada
urban sprawl en fuerte expansión booming
expectativa nf expectation n expectativas
del consumidor consumer expectations
expedición, flete de mercancías (LAm) nf,
nm forwarding n, dispatch n
expedidor, -ora nm,f dispatcher n, shipper n
expedir vb (tickets) issue vb expedir un
recibo issue a receipt
expeditar vb expedite vb
experiencia nf experience n con
experiencia experienced experiencia
laboral work experience
experimentar vb experience vb
experto, -rta nm,f expert n
expiración nf expiry n, expiration (US) n
explicar vb explain vb explicarse
claramente make oneself clear
explotación nf exploitation n, operation n
explotado adj overworked adj
explotador, -ora nm,f shark* n
explotar vb exploit vb, operate vb explotar
recursos tap resources
exponer vb display vb, exhibit vb
exportación nf export n exportación de
capitales export of capital exportaciones
de capital capital exports exportaciones
invisibles invisible exports exportaciones
mundiales world exports exportaciones
visibles visible exports
exportador, -ora nm,f exporter n
exportar vb export vb
exposición nf (of goods) display n exhibition
n exposición universal world fair
expresar vb express vb expresar una
objeción make/raise an objection
expropiación nf expropriation n
expropiar vb expropriate vb
extender vb (cheques/shares) issue vb
extender un cheque make out a cheque
extender un recibo issue a receipt
extender un contrato extend a contract
exterior adj external adj, foreign adj,
overseas adj
externo adj external adj
extorsión nf extortion n
extra adj extra adj
extracción nf extraction n
extragrande adj king-size(d) adj
extranjero adj foreign adj, overseas adj
f.a.b. (franco a bordo) abbr FOB (free on
board) abbr
fábrica nf works n, factory n fábrica piloto
pilot plant
fabricación nf manufacture n, production n
de buena fabricación well-made
fabricación asistida por ordenador
(CAM), fabricación asistida por
computadora (LAm) computer-aided
manufacture (CAM) fabricación en

cadena flow line production, flow
production fabricación en serie mass
production
fabricado adj made adj, produced adj
fabricado en Francia made in France
fabricante nmf manufacturer n, producer n
fabricar vb manufacture vb, produce vb
fácil adj easy adj fácil acceso accessibility
fácil de utilizar user-friendly
facilidad nf facility n
facsímil nm facsimile (fax) n
factible adj feasible adj, workable adj
factor nm factor n factor limitativo limiting
factor factor de producción factor of
production
factura nf bill n, invoice n factura definitiva
final invoice factura negociable negotiable
bill factura sin saldar unpaid bill factura
de venta bill of sale
facturación nf invoicing n, turnover n, check-
in n facturación de activo fijo fixed asset
turnover
facturar, voltear; dar vuelta (LAm) vb turn
over vb
faena nf task n
fallar vb (negotiations) fail vb
fallo nm failure n fallo de poca
importancia minor fault
falsificación nf counterfeit n, falsification n,
forgery n falsificación de cuentas
falsification of accounts
falsificar vb counterfeit vb
falso adj fictitious adj, phoney* adj
falta nf default n, fault n, lack n, shortage n
falta de actividad (laxity) slackness n a
falta de datos in the absence of
information falta de entrega non-delivery
a falta de información in the absence of
information falta de inversión lack of
investment
fama nf reputation n
fanático, -ica nm,f fanatic n, supporter n
favor nm favour n
fax nm facsimile (fax) n
fe nf faith n de buena fe bona fide
fecha nf date n sin fecha not dated fecha
de caducidad best-before date, expiry date,
termination date fecha de entrega delivery
date fecha de expedición date of dispatch
fecha objetivo target date fecha tope
time limit fecha de vencimiento expiry
date, expiration (US)
federación nf federation n
federal adj federal adj
feria nf (exhibition) show n feria de
muestras trade fair
feriante nm,f (LAm) operator n
ferrocarril nm railway n, railroad (US) n
fiabilidad nf reliability n
fiable adj (LAm) reliable n
fiacún, -una nm,f (LAm) shirker n
fianza nf bail n, caution money n, collateral n
fianza fiduciaria fiduciary bond
fichar vb sign vb fichar a la entrada al

trabajo, checar tarjeta al entrar al trabajo (LAm) clock in **fichar a la salida del trabajo, checar tarjeta al salir del trabajo** (LAm) clock out
ficticio *adj* fictitious *adj*
fidedigno, fiable; confiable (LAm) *adj* reliable *adj*
fideicomisario, -ria *nm,f* trustee *n*
fideicomiso *nm* trusteeship *n*
fidelidad *nf* accuracy *n*, fidelity *n* **fidelidad a un establecimiento** customer loyalty
fiesta *nf* holiday *n*, festival *n* **fiesta nacional, día feriado; fiesta patria** (LAm) bank holiday (GB)
figura *nf* figure *n*
fijar *vb* fix *vb* **fijar el precio** fix the price **fijarse una meta** set a target
fijo *adj* built-in *adj*, fixed *adj*
filial *nf* subsidiary company **filial de entera propiedad** wholly-owned subsidiary
fin *nm* end *n*, purpose *n* **fin de año fiscal fye** (fiscal year end) *abbr* **sin fines de lucro** non-profitmaking
final 1. *adj* terminal *adj* **2.** *nm* end *n*
financiación *nf* financing *n*, funding *n* **financiación de acciones** equity financing **financiación de déficit** deficit financing **financiación de valores** equity financing
financiar *vb* finance *vb*, fund *vb*
financiero *adj* financial *adj*
financiero, -era *nm,f* financier *n*
finanzas *nfpl* finance *n* **las altas finanzas** high finance
fingido *adj* phoney* *adj*
firma *nf* signature *n*
firmante *nmf* signatory *n* **los firmantes del contrato** the signatories to the contract
firmar *vb* sign *vb* **firmar un cheque** sign a cheque **firmar un contrato** sign a contract
fisco, Dirección General Impositiva; Impuestos Internos (LAm) *nm, nf; nmpl* the Inland Revenue, The Internal Revenue Service (IRS) (US)
fletador, -ora *nm,f* freighter *n*
flete, flete de mercaderías (LAm) *nm* freight *n*, forwarding *n*
flexibilidad *nf* (of prices) flexibility *n*
flexibilizar *vb* (market) open up *vb* (restrictions) relax *vb*
flojonazo, -aza *nm,f* (LAm) shirker *n*
florín *nm* guilder *n*
fluctuación *nf* fluctuation *n* **fluctuaciones de ventas** fluctuation in sales
fluctuante *adj* (prices) volatile *adj*
fluctuar *vb* fluctuate *vb* (market) turn *vb*
fluido *adj* fluid *adj*
flujo *nm* flow *n* **flujo de caja** cash flow **flujo de caja descontado** discounted cash flow (DCF) **flujo de caja negativo** negative cash flow **flujo de fondos** funds flow **flujo de ingresos** flow of income
folleto *nm* leaflet *n* **folleto informativo** prospectus **folleto publicitario** brochure, prospectus

fomentar *vb* boost *vb*, promote *vb* **fomentar la demanda** boost demand
fondo *nm* fund *n* **en el fondo** at the bottom **fondo de amortización** redemption fund **fondo de comercio, llave** (LAm) goodwill **fondo de custodia** trust fund **fondo de emergencia** emergency fund **Fondo Europeo de Cooperación Monetaria (FECM)** European Monetary Cooperation Fund (EMCF) **Fondo Europeo de Desarrollo (FED)** European Development Fund (EDF) **Fondo Europeo de Desarrollo Regional (FEDR)** European Regional Development Fund (ERDF) **fondo de fideicomiso** trust fund **fondo de inversión mobiliaria, costo por unidad; costo unitario** (LAm) unit trust **Fondo Monetario Internacional (FMI)** International Monetary Fund (IMF) **fondo de pensiones** pension fund **fondo de seguros** insurance fund **fondos para invertir** capital funds **fondos mutuos, costo por unidad; costo unitario** (LAm) unit trust, mutual fund (US) **Fondo Social Europeo (FSE)** European Social Fund (ESF) **fondos públicos** public funds
forma *nf* form *n*, means *npl*, (printed) form (LAm) *n* **forma de pago** method of payment
formación *nf* instruction *n*, training *n* **formación de capital** capital formation **formación de directivos** management training **formación de empleados** employee training
formal *adj* businesslike *adj*, formal *adj*, reliable *adj*, responsible *adj*
formalidad *nf* reliability *n* **formalidades aduaneras** customs clearance **formalidades aduaneras/legales** customs/legal formalities
formar, capacitar (LAm) *vb* (staff) train *vb*, constitute *vb*
formulario, impreso de aplicación (LAm) *nm* form *n*, application form *n* **formulario de pedido** order form
fortuna *nf* fortune *n*
fotocopia *nf* photocopy *n*
fotocopiadora *nf* photocopier *n*, Xerox (R) *n*
fotocopiar *vb* (photocopy) copy *vb* photocopy *vb*, xerox *vb*
fracasar *vb* (attempts) fail *vb*
fracaso *nm* failure *n*, write-off *n*
fracción *nf* fraction *n*
fraccionamiento *nm* split division *n*
fraccionario *adj* fractional *adj*
frágil *adj* fragile *adj*, handle with care *vb*
franco 1. *adj* free *adj*, frank *adj* **franco a bordo** free on board (FOB) **franco a domicilio** carriage paid, franco domicile **franco en fábrica** ex factory/works **franco en muelle** FAS (free alongside ship) *abbr*, free on quay **franco de porte, franco de flete** (LAm) carriage paid, free of freight **franco de precio** franco price **2.** *nm* franc

n **franco belga** Belgian franc **franco francés** French franc **franco suizo** Swiss franc

franquear *vb* frank *vb*, exempt *vb*

franqueo *nm* postage *n* **franqueo pagado** Freepost (R) (GB) *n*

franquicia *nf* franchise *n*, franchise outlet *n*

fraude *nm* fraud *n* **fraude fiscal** tax evasion

fraudulento *adj* fraudulent *adj*

frecuencia *nf* frequency *n*

frenar *vb* (inflation) halt *vb*

frenarse *vb* slow down *vb*

frontera *nf* frontier *n*

fuente *nf* (of a product) origin *n* source *n*

fuerte *adj* (competition) keen *adj* well-made *adj*, strong *adj*

fuerza *nf* power *n* **con fuerza jurídica** legally binding **fuerza laboral** workforce **fuerzas del mercado** market forces

fuga *nf* escape *n*, flight *n* **fugas de existencias** stock shrinkage

función *nf* (role) function *n* **funciones ejecutivas** executive duties

funcionamiento *nm* (of machine) operation *n*

funcionario, -ria *nm,f* civil servant *n*, official *n* **funcionario de aduana** customs officer

fundación *nf* (of company) formation *n* **fundación benéfica** charitable trust

fundador, -ora *nm,f* founder *n*

fundamental *adj* main *adj*, basic *adj*

fundar *vb* found *vb* **fundar una empresa** found a company

fusión *nf* amalgamation *n*, merger *n* **fusión horizontal** horizontal integration

fusionarse *vb* amalgamate *vb*, merge *vb*

futuro *nm* future commodity **futuros** futures

gama *nf* (of products) range *n* **gama de productos** product line

ganado *adj* earned *adj*, gained *adj*

ganancia, utilidad (LAm) *nf* profit *n*, benefit *n* **ganancias** earnings, proceeds **ganancias y pérdidas** profit and loss **una parte de las ganancias** a share in the profits

ganar *vb* earn *vb*, gain *vb*, win *vb* **ganarse apoyo** win support **ganarse la vida** make a living

ganga, pichincha (LAm) *nf* bargain *n*

garante, garantía (LAm) *nmf* backer *n*, guarantor *n*

garantía *nf* caution money *n*, collateral *n*, guarantee *n*, pledge *n*, warranty *n*, backer (LAm) *n* **bajo garantía** under warranty **garantía de calidad** quality guarantee **garantía colateral** collateral security

garantizar *vb* warrant *vb*

gas *nm* gas *n* **gas natural** natural gas

gastar *vb* spend *vb*

gasto *nm* cost *n*, expenditure *n*, expense *n* **gasto complementario, costo adicional** (LAm) extra cost **gasto indirecto, costo indirecto** (LAm) indirect cost **gasto público** state expenditure **gastos** expenditure, outgoings, spending **gastos**

de administración, costes de administración (LAm) administrative costs **gastos bancarios** bank charges **gastos en capital** capital expenditure **gastos de capital** capital outlay **gastos de envío** delivery charges **gastos de estiba** stowage **gastos de explotación, costos de operación** (LAm) business expenses, operating expenditure, running costs **gastos de fábrica, costos de fábrica** (LAm) factory costs **gastos generales** overheads **gastos generales de fabricación** factory overheads **gastos del hogar** household expenditure **gastos indirectos** indirect expenses, overhead costs **gastos menores** incidental expenses **gastos de representación** entertainment expenses **gastos de tramitación, costos de manipulación** (LAm) handling charges **gastos de viaje** travelling expenses, travel expenses (US) **gastos de transporte** carriage charges

GATT (Acuerdo General sobre Aranceles Aduaneros y Comercio) *nm* GATT (General Agreement on Tariffs and Trade) *abbr*

generación *nf* generation *n* **generación de ingresos** income generation

generar *vb* generate *vb* **generar ingresos** generate income

género *nm* **géneros** merchandise **géneros futuros** future goods

generosidad *nf* generosity *n*

geografía *nf* geography *n* **geografía económica** economic geography

gerencia *nf* management *n* **gerencia de personal** personnel management

gerente *nmf* manager *n* **gerente regional** area manager

gestión *nf* (of business) operation *n* **gestión de deudas de otras compañías con descuento** (of debts) factoring **gestión de empresas** business management **gestión financiera** financial management **gestión ministerial, ministerio; secretaría** (LAm) ministry **gestión de recursos humanos (GRH)** human resource management (HRM) **gestión de riesgos** risk management **gestión de tareas** task management **gestión del tiempo** time management **gestión total de calidad** TQM (Total Quality Management) *abbr* **gestión de transacciones** transaction management **gestión de ventas** sales management

gestionar *vb* address *vb*, negotiate (LAm) *vb*, manage *vb*

girar *vb* (cheque) draw *vb* **girar en descubierto** overdraw **girar en descubierto una cuenta** overdraw on an account

giro *nm* (financial) draft *n* remittance *n*, turnabout *n* **giro bancario** bank draft **giro positivo** upturn **giro postal** money order

global *adj* global *adj*, net(t) *adj*, worldwide *adj*

globalización *nf* globalization *n*
gobernar *vb* govern *vb*
gobierno *nm* government *n*
gordo *nm* jackpot *n*
grado *nm* level *n*, grade *n* **de alto grado**
high-grade **grado de rendimiento** earning
capacity, earning power
graduar *vb* graduate *vb*
gráfico *nm* chart *n*, graph *n* **gráfico de**
barras bar chart **gráfico sectorial** pie chart
gráficos de ordenador computer graphics
grande, gran *adj* large *adj*, great *adj* **Gran**
Bretaña, La Gran Bretaña (LAm) Great
Britain
gratificación *nf* gratuity *n*, perk *n*
gratificación por fin de servicio golden
handshake, golden parachute **gratificación**
por méritos merit payment
gratis *adv* free of charge *adv*
gratuito *adj* free of charge *adj*
gravar *vb* (tax) levy *vb* **gravar con un**
impuesto impose a tax
gremio *nm* guild *n*, syndicate (LAm) *n*
grueso *adj* thick *adj*
grupo *nm* group *n*, (of goods) batch *n* **grupo**
de países group of countries **grupos**
socioeconómicos socio-economic
categories
guardamuebles *nm* depository *n*, furniture
storage *n*
guardar *vb* keep *vb*, store *vb* **guardarse**
(goods) keep *vb* **guardarse dinero** (money)
keep back *vb*
guardián, -ana *nm,f* (fig.) watchdog *n*
guerra *nf* war *n* **guerra comercial** trade war
guerra de precios price war
guía *nf* handbook *n* **guía comercial** trade
directory **guía de fabricantes y**
comerciantes trade directory **guía**
telefónica, directorio telefónico (LAm)
telephone directory **guía de turismo**
courier, tourist guide
h. *abbr* (hour) h *abbr*
habilidad *nf* ability *n*, skill *n*
habitación *nf* room *n* **habitación libre**
vacancy
hablar *vb* speak *vb*, talk *vb* **hablar mal de**
(disparage) knock **hablar de negocios** talk
business **hablar en serio** talk business
hablar del trabajo (informal) talk shop
hacendado, -ada *nm,f* (LAm) landlord *n*
hacer *vb* make *vb*, do *vb*, wage *vb* **hace un**
dineral he/she mints money **hacemos**
referencia a nuestra carta de we refer to
our letter of... **hacer aportes** (LAm)
contribute **hacer la caja** cash up **hacer**
una campaña run/wage a campaign **hacer**
caso take notice **hacer circular** (document)
circulate **hacer la competencia** compete
hacer cuadrar las cuentas balance the
books **hacer la cuenta** tally up **hacer un**
curso de reconversión, hacer un curso
de recapacitación (LAm) retrain **hacer**
dinero make money **hacer factoring**

(debts) factor **hacer una fortuna** make a
fortune **hacer frente a sus obligaciones**
meet one's obligations **hacer un gran**
avance make a breakthrough **hacer**
huelga, ir al paro; declararse en paro
(LAm) strike *vb* **hacer huelga de celo,**
trabajar a reglamento (LAm) work to rule
hacer impresión (credit card) take an
imprint **hacerle un favor a alguien** do sb
a favour **hacerle propaganda a, hacerle**
réclame a (LAm) advertise **hacer una**
oferta, licitar (LAm) bid **hacer un pedido**
place an order **hacer planes** make plans
hacer progresos make headway **hacer**
público (policy) issue **hacer reformas en**
refurbish **hacer una reserva, hacer una**
reservación (LAm) make a reservation
hacer responsable a alguien hold sb
liable/responsible **hacerse con** acquire
hacerse buena reputación make a
reputation **hacerse cargo de** take charge of
sth **hacerse con clientes** win customers
hacerse conocer build a reputation
hacerse rico make a fortune **hacerse un**
seguro take out insurance **hacer**
transbordo (transport) transfer **hacer uso**
de algo make use of sth **hacer una visita**
visit
hacia *prep* towards *prep* **hacia abajo**
downward **hacia arriba** upward
Hacienda, Dirección General Impositiva;
Impuestos Internos (LAm) *nf, nf; nmpl* the
Inland Revenue, The Internal Revenue
Service (IRS) (US), tax office **Hacienda**
Pública (la) the Treasury
hecho *adj* made *adj*, done *adj* **hecho a**
mano handmade **hechos ciertos** known
facts **los hechos puros y duros** the hard
facts
heredar *vb* inherit *vb*
herencia *nf* inheritance *n* **herencia**
fiduciaria trust estate
hermético *adj* (fig.) watertight *adj*
hidroelectricidad *nf* hydroelectricity *n*
hierro *nm* iron *n* **hierro en lingotes** pig iron
hiperinflación *nf* hyperinflation *n*
hipermercado *nm* hypermarket *n*
hipoteca *nf* mortgage *n*
hipótesis *nf* hypothesis *n*
historial *nm* record *n* **historial de empleo,**
historia profesional (LAm) employment/
work history
hogar *nm* household *n*
hoja, forma (LAm) *nf* (document) form *n*
hoja de cálculo spreadsheet **hoja de**
instrucciones instruction sheet **hoja de**
solicitud, impreso de aplicación (LAm)
application form
homenaje *nm* testimonial *n*
homólogo, -oga *nm,f* opposite number *n*
honor *nm* honour *n* **de honor** honorary
honorario 1. *adj* honorary *adj* **2.** *nm* fees *npl*
honorarios por asesoría consultancy fees,
consulting fees (US)

hora *nf* hour *n*, appointment (LAm) *n* **por hora** hourly, per hour **a la hora** per hour **hora cero** zero hour **hora de cierre** closing time **hora extra(s), sobretiempo** (LAm) overtime **hora de Greenwich** GMT (Greenwich Mean Time) *abbr* **hora punta, hora pico** (LAm) rush hour **horas de oficina** business hours, office hours **horas punta** peak period, busy hours (US) **horas de trabajo** business hours **a última hora** at short notice

horario *nm* schedule *n*, timetable *n* **fuera del horario de trabajo** after hours **horario de atención al público** opening times **horario bancario** banking hours **horario fijo** fixed hours **horario flexible** flexitime, flextime (US) **horario normal de venta al público** normal trading hours **horario de oficina** business hours, office hours **horario de trabajo** working hours

hostelería *nf* hotel industry/trade *n*

hotel *nm* hotel *n* **hotel de cinco estrellas** five-star hotel

huelga, paro (LAm) *nf, nm* industrial action *n*, strike *n*, strike action *n* **huelga de advertencia** token strike **huelga no autorizada** unofficial strike **huelga autorizada por el sindicato, paro oficial** (LAm) official strike **huelga general, paro general** (LAm) general strike **huelga ilegal** unofficial strike **huelga oficial, paro oficial** (LAm) official strike **huelga pasiva, trabajo a reglamento** (LAm) (strike) go-slow **huelga salvaje, paro incontrolado; paro imprevisto** (LAm) wildcat strike

huelguista, trabajador, -ora en paro (LAm) *nmf, nm,f* striker *n*

huso *nm* **huso horario** time zone

identificación *nf* identification *n* **identificación por marca** family branding

idioma *nm* language *n* **idioma de trabajo** working language

igualar *vb* equalize *vb*

igualdad *nf* equality *n*, parity *n* **igualdad salarial** equal pay

ilegal *adj* illegal *adj*

imagen *nf* image *n* **imagen de marca** brand image **imagen pública de la empresa** corporate image

impago *nm* non-payment *n*

impedir, tapar (LAm) *vb* block *vb*, forestall *vb*

imponer *vb* (tax) levy *vb* **imponer un embargo** impose an embargo **imponer un límite a algo** put a ceiling on sth

importación *nf* import *n*, importation *n* **importaciones** imports **importaciones invisibles** invisible imports

importador, -ora *nm,f* importer *n*

importancia *nf* importance *n*

importante *adj* leading *adj*, weighty *adj* **más importante** major

importar *vb* (be of importance to) concern *vb* import *vb*

importe *nm* amount *n* **importe neto** net(t) amount **importe a pagar** outstanding amount **importe a pagar todavía** unpaid balance

imposición *nf* (of tax) imposition *n*, deposit *n*, taxation *n* **imposición del 0% del IVA** zero rate/rating for VAT **imposición de sociedades** corporate taxation

impreso, forma (LAm) *nm, nf* (document) form *n* **impreso de aplicación** (LAm) application form **impreso de reclamación** claim form

imprudencia *nf* imprudence *n* **imprudencia temeraria** gross negligence

impuesto *nm* tax *n* **antes de deducir impuestos** before tax **después de deducir impuestos** after tax **impuesto sobre beneficios extraordinarios** excess profit(s) tax **impuesto directo** direct tax **impuesto elevadísimo** supertax **impuesto a la exportación** export tax **impuesto indirecto** indirect tax **impuesto de lujo** luxury tax **impuesto sobre el patrimonio** wealth tax **impuesto sobre la(s) plusvalía(s)** capital gains tax **impuesto sobre la propiedad residencial** house duty (US) **impuesto sobre la renta, impuesto a los réditos** (LAm) income tax **impuesto sobre la renta a cuota fija, impuesto a los réditos a cuota fija** (LAm) flat-rate income tax **impuesto sobre la renta personal** income tax **impuestos sobre gastos** expenditure taxes **impuestos internos** (LAm) Inland Revenue **impuestos locales** local taxes **impuesto de sociedades** corporation tax **impuesto territorial** land tax **impuesto de transferencia** transfer duty **impuesto sobre transferencias** transfer tax **impuesto sobre el valor agregado/añadido (IVA)** value-added tax, sales tax (US) **impuesto sobre la venta** excise duty **impuesto sobre las ventas al detalle** retail sales tax **impuesto sobre el volumen de ventas y negocios** turnover tax **incluidos impuestos y gastos en entrega** inclusive of tax and delivery costs **van incluidos los impuestos** taxes are included

impulso *nm* boost *n*

inactivo *adj* idle *adj*

inadecuado *adj* inadequate *adj*, inappropriate *adj*

incentivo *nm* incentive *n* (formal) perquisite *n* **incentivos** fringe benefits **incentivos financieros** financial incentive

inclinar *vb* lean *vb*, incline *vb*

incompetente *adj* inadequate *adj*, inefficient *adj*

incondicional *adj* unconditional *adj*

inconveniente 1. *adj* inconvenient *adj* **2.** *nm* inconvenience *n*

inconvertible *adj* non-convertible *adj*

incorporado *adj* built-in *adj*

incrementar *vb* (value) enhance *vb* (prices, taxes) increase *vb* (price, interest rate) raise *vb* **incrementar aranceles** raise tariffs **incrementar las ventas** boost sales
incremento *nm* (in inflation) rise *n* **incremento salarial** pay rise, wage increase
incumbir *vb* concern *vb*, be incumbent *vb* **nos incumbe...** the onus is on us to...
incumplimiento *nm* neglect *n* **incumplimiento de contrato** breach of contract
incumplir *vb* default *vb*
incurrir *vb* incur *vb* **incurrir en** (expenses) incur
indemnidad *nf* indemnity *n*
indemnización *nf* compensation *n*, recompense *n*, reparation *n* **indemnización por despido** golden handshake, golden parachute, severance pay
indemnizar *vb* indemnify *vb* **indemnizar por** compensate for
indicar *vb* indicate *vb*, specify *vb*
índice *nm* index *n* **índice de acciones** share index **índice del coste de la vida, índice del costo de la vida** (LAm) cost of living index **índice de cotización de acciones** Thirty-Share Index **índice de cotización bursátil del 'Financial Times'** FT Index (Financial Times Index) **índice de crecimiento** growth index **índice Dow Jones** Dow-Jones average (US) **índice ponderado** weighted index **índice de precios** price index **índice de rotación de existencias** turnover rate
indicio *nm* indication *n*, sign *n*
indirecto *adj* indirect *adj*
industria *nf* industry *n* **industria del acero** steel industry **industria aeroespacial** aerospace industry **industria de asistencia médica** health care industry **industria del automóvil** automobile/motor industry **industria automovilística** motor industry **industria clave** key industry **industria de la construcción** building/construction industry **industria de construcción de viviendas** housing industry **industria familiar** family industry **industria farmacéutica** pharmaceutical industry **industria hotelera** hotel industry/trade **industria minera** mining industry **industria nacional** home industry **industria pesada** heavy industry **industria petrolera** oil/petroleum industry **industria del plástico** plastics industry **industria química** chemical industry **industria de servicios** service industry **industria textil** textile industry **la industria del turismo** the tourist trade **la industria del vestido** (informal) the rag trade
industrial *adj* industrial *adj*
industrialización *nf* industrialization *n* **de reciente industrialización** newly-industrialised

ineficiente *adj* inefficient *adj*
inesperado *adj* unexpected *adj*
inestabilidad *nf* instability *n*
inestable *adj* (prices) volatile *adj*
infalible *adj* (fig.) watertight *adj*
inferior *adj* (goods) inferior *adj*
inflación *nf* inflation *n* **inflación de demanda por cambio de estructura** bottleneck inflation **inflación galopante** galloping inflation **inflación nominal** nominal inflation **inflación provocada por la demanda excesiva** excess demand inflation
inflacionista *adj* inflationary *adj*
influencia *nf* patronage *n*, influence *n*
información *nf* data *npl*, feedback *n*, information *n*, information desk *n* **información clasificada como secreta** classified information **información concreta** hard news/information **información confidencial acerca del mercado** market tip
informado *adj* knowledgeable *adj*
informar *vb* brief *vb*, inform *vb*, notify *vb*
informática *nf* information technology (IT) *n*
informe *nm* briefing *n*, reference *n*, report *n* **informe de calidad** quality report **informe sobre la calidad** quality report **informe financiero** financial report
infracapitalizado *adj* undercapitalized *adj*
infracción *nf* contravention *n*, offence *n*, offense (US) *n*
infraestructura *nf* infrastructure *n* **infraestructura económica** economic infrastructure
infrasegurado *adj* underinsured *adj*
infrautilizado *adj* underemployed *adj*
infravalorar *vb* undervalue *vb*
infringir *vb* contravene *vb*
infructuoso *adj* unprofitable *adj*
ingeniería *nf* engineering *n* **ingeniería de caminos** civil engineering **ingeniería civil** civil engineering **ingeniería eléctrica** electrical engineering **ingeniería marina** marine engineering **ingeniería mecánica** mechanical engineering **ingeniería de precisión** precision engineering
ingresar *vb* deposit *vb* **ingresar algo en una cuenta** credit sth to an account
ingreso *nm* entry *n*, payment into *n* **de altos ingresos** high-income **ingreso fiscal** fiscal receipt **ingreso real** real wages **ingresos** earnings, income, financial means, revenue, takings **ingresos básicos** basic income **ingresos brutos** gross income **ingresos disponibles** disposable income **ingresos de explotación, ingresos de operación** (LAm) operating income **ingresos de los factores** factor income **ingresos familiares** family income **ingresos fijos** fixed income **ingresos franqueados** franked income **ingresos gravables** taxable income **ingresos marginales** marginal revenue **ingresos netos** net(t)

earnings/income **ingresos de publicidad**
advertising revenue
iniciado, -ada *nm,f* insider *n*
iniciar *vb* initiate *vb* **iniciar una moda** set a
trend
iniciativa *nf* (project) enterprise *n* **iniciativa
del gobierno** government enterprise
iniciativa privada private enterprise
inicio *nm* start-up *n*
inmovilizado *nm* fixed assets *npl*
inmovilizar *vb* (capital) tie up *vb*
inoportuno *adj* inconvenient *adj*
inquilino, -ina *nm,f* lessee *n*, occupant *n*,
tenant *n*
insatisfactorio *adj* unsatisfactory *adj*
insistir *vb* insist *vb* **insistir en** insist on *vb*
insolvencia *nf* bankruptcy *n*, insolvency *n*
insolvente *adj* bankrupt *adj*, insolvent *adj*
inspeccionar *vb* inspect *vb* **inspeccionar
algo, chequear; checar** (LAm) make a
check on sth
inspector, -ora *nm,f* inspector *n* **inspector
de fábrica** factory inspector
instalación *nf* facility *n*, installation *n*
instalaciones amenities **instalaciones
fijas y accesorios** fixtures and fittings
instalaciones portuarias harbour facilities
instalar *vb* establish *vb*, instal(l) *vb*
institución *nf* institution *n* **institución
crediticia** credit institution
instituto *nm* institute *n*
instrucción *nf* instruction *n*, statement *n*
insuficiente *adj* deficient *adj*, inadequate *adj*
integración *nf* integration *n* **integración
económica** economic integration
integración vertical vertical integration
integrar *vb* amalgamate *vb*
intensificarse *vb* escalate *vb*
intensivo *adj* intensive *adj* **intensivo en
capital** capital-intensive
intento *nm* bid *n*
intercambiar *vb* swap *vb*
intercambio *nm* swap *n*
intercesión *nf* intervention *n*
interconectar *vb* network *vb*
interés *nm* appeal *n*, interest *n*, takeup *n* **sin
interés** ex interest, interest-free **interés
acumulado** accrued interest **interés bruto**
gross interest **interés compuesto**
compound interest **intereses en títulos**
equity interests **interés fijo** fixed interest
interés nacional national interest **interés
neto** net(t) interest **interés personal** vested
interest **interés de tipo flotante, interés
de tasa flotante** (LAm) floating rate interest
interés trimestral quarterly interest
interesar *vb* appeal *vb* (be of importance to)
concern *vb*
interino, provisorio (LAm) *adj* interim *adj*
interior *adj* inland *adj*, inner *adj*
intermediario, -ria *nm,f* jobber *n*,
middleman *n*
intermedio *adj* interim *adj*, intermediary *adj*,
median *adj*

internacional *adj* international *adj*
interrelación *nf* interface *n*
interurbano *adj* long-distance *adj*
intervención *nf* intervention *n* **intervención
del estado** state intervention
intervenir *vb* intervene *vb*
interventor, -ora *nm,f* auditor *n*, inspector *n*
interventor de cuentas auditor
intransferible *adj* non-transferable *adj*
introducir *vb* (product) launch *vb*, introduce
vb **introducir legislación** introduce
legislation
inutilizable, descompuesto (LAm) *adj* out
of action *adv/prep*
invendible *adj* unmarketable *adj*, unsaleable
adj
invendido *adj* unsold *adj*
inventario *nm* inventory *n* **inventario por
cierre de ejercicio** year-end inventory
inventario de existencias stocktaking
inversión *nf* investment *n*, stake *n* **inversión
bruta** gross investment **inversión de
capital** capital expenditure **inversión
cotizada** quoted investment **inversión de
empresa** corporate investment **inversiones**
investment **inversión exterior** foreign
investment **inversión financiera** financial
investment **inversión neta** net(t)
investment
inversionista *nmf* investor *n*
inversor, -ora *nmf* investor *n*, stakeholder *n*
invertir *vb* (money) invest *vb*, reverse *vb*
investidura *nf* installation *n*, investment *n*
investigación *nf* enquiry *n*, research *n*
investigación de campo field
investigation, field research **investigación
sobre el consumo** consumer research
investigación y desarrollo (I&D) research
and development (R&D) **investigación de
mercado** market research, market research
survey
invisible *adj* invisible *adj*
invitación *nf* invitation *n*
invitado, -ada *nm,f* visitor *n*
invitar *vb* invite *vb* **invitar a un cliente**
entertain a client
ir *vb* go *vb* **ir por buen camino** be on the
right track **ir camino de** head for **ir
contracorriente** buck a trend **ir al
extranjero** go abroad **ir recortando**
(stocks) run down **irse** leave **irse al
extranjero** go abroad **ir tirando** tick over
irrecuperable *adj* (loss) irrecoverable *adj*
irrevocable *adj* irrevocable *adj*
isla *nf* island *n* **Islas Británicas** British Isles
itinerario *nm* itinerary *n*
**IVA (impuesto al valor agregado,
impuesto sobre el valor añadido)**
abbr,nm VAT (value added tax) *abbr*
jefe, -efa *nm,f* boss *n*, manager *n* **jefe de
contabilidad** chief accountant **jefe de
departamento** head of department **jefe
ejecutivo** chief executive **jefe de finanzas**
chief financial officer **jefe de gobierno**

head of government **jefe de línea** line
manager **jefe de taller** works manager
jerarquía nf (corporate) hierarchy n
   jerarquía de datos data hierarchy
   jerarquía de dirección executive hierarchy
   jerarquía de necesidades hierarchy of
   needs
jingle nm jingle n **jingle publicitario**
   advertising jingle
jornada nf day's work n **a jornada completa**
   full-time **a jornada reducida** part-time
jubilación nf retirement n, retirement
   pension n **jubilación anticipada** early
   retirement
jubilarse vb retire vb
judicial adj judicial adj
jugar vb play vb **jugar al mercado** play the
   market
juicio nm opinion n, lawsuit n
junta nf board n **junta anual** AGM (Annual
   General Meeting) abbr **junta de dirección**
   board meeting **junta directiva** board of
   directors **junta extraordinaria**
   extraordinary meeting **junta general**
   ordinaria ordinary general meeting
jurado nm jury n
jurisdicción nf jurisdiction n
justificar vb account for vb, warrant vb
justo adj fair adj
kilo nm kilogram n, kg abbr
kilometraje nm kilometres travelled npl
kilómetro nm kilometre n, km abbr, kilometer
   (US) n
kilovatio nm kilowatt n, kW abbr **kilovatio-**
   hora kWh abbr
Km abbr kilometre n, km abbr, kilometer (US)
labor nf labour n, work n **labor de asesoría**
   consultancy work, consulting work (US)
laboral adj occupational adj
lamentar vb regret vb **lamentamos**
   informarle que we regret to inform you
   that...
lanón nm (LAm) bundle (of money) n
lanzamiento nm eviction n **lanzamiento de**
   un producto product launch
lanzar vb (product) bring out vb, introduce vb,
   launch vb **lanzarse al mercado** hit the market
latifundista nmf landowner n
LBO (compra apalancada de empresas)
   abbr,nf LBO (leveraged buy-out) abbr
legado nm bequest n, endowment n,
   inheritance n, legacy n
legajo nm bundle n
legal adj legal adj
legalización nf probate n, legalisation n
legar vb bequeath vb
legislación nf legislation n
legislar vb legislate vb
legitimidad nf validity n
legítimo adj aboveboard adj, valid adj
lengua nf language n
lenguaje nm language n **lenguaje de**
   ordenador, lenguaje de computadora
   (LAm) computer language

letra nf letter n **letra de cambio** bill of
   exchange **letra grande** large type **letra al**
   propio cargo promissory note **letras**
   descontadas bills discounted **letra a la**
   vista sight draft
levantar vb raise vb, lift vb **levantar un**
   embargo lift an embargo **levantarse**
   adjourn, rise
ley nf law n, statute n **leyes sobre la**
   herencia inheritance laws **Ley**
   Presupuestaria Finance Act, finance bill
   ley sobre la propiedad intelectual
   copyright law **ley que regula la**
   descripción comercial de productos
   Trade Descriptions Act **ley de**
   rendimientos decrecientes law of
   diminishing returns **ley de sociedades**
   anónimas company law
liar vb bundle up vb
libelo nm libel n
liberal adj **las profesiones liberales** the
   professions
libertad nf freedom n **libertad de elección**
   freedom of choice
libra nf (weight) pound n **libra esterlina**
   pound sterling, sterling **libra verde** green
   pound
librar vb wage vb, save vb, (cheque) draw vb
libre adj exempt adj, vacant adj **libre**
   competencia free competition **libre de**
   derechos de aduana (goods) duty-free
   libre de impuestos duty-free, tax-free
librecambio nm free trade n
librería nf bookshop n, bookstore (US) n
librero, -era nm,f bookseller n
libreta nf notebook n
libro nm book n **libro de instrucciones**
   instruction book **libro mayor** ledger **libro**
   mayor de compras bought ledger **libro**
   mayor de la fábrica factory ledger **libro**
   mayor de ventas sales ledger **libro de**
   pedidos order book
licencia nf franchise n, leave n, leave of
   absence (LAm) n, licence n, furlough (US) n,
   permit n **licencia por enfermedad** sick
   leave **licencia por maternidad** maternity
   leave **licencia de obras** building permit
licenciado, -ada, egresado, -ada (LAm)
   nm,f (of university) graduate n
licenciatario, -ria nm,f franchisee n
licitación nf bid n, tender (LAm) n, tendering
   n
licitador, -ora nm,f (LAm) tenderer n
licitar vb bid vb, lodge a tender vb **licitar**
   para un contrato tender for a contract
liderazgo nm leadership n
limitado adj limited adj
limitar vb restrict vb **limitar el tipo de**
   interés, limitar la tasa de interés (LAm)
   cap the interest rate
límite nm (on prices) ceiling n, limit n,
   restriction n **fuera de los límites** out of
   bounds **límite de crédito** credit limit
limpio adj fair adj, clean adj

línea *nf* (of products) range *n* **línea aérea** airline, carrier **línea (de cambio) de fecha** International Date Line **línea directa** hot line **de línea dura** hard-line **línea de fuego** hot seat **línea de montaje** assembly line

liquidación *nf* clearance sale *n*, liquidation *n*, winding-up *n* **liquidación de activo** asset stripping, realization of assets **liquidación por cierre** closing-down sale, closing-out sale (US) **liquidación judicial** winding-up order

liquidar *vb* liquidate *vb*, redeem *vb*, sell off *vb*, wind up *vb* **liquidar una cuenta** settle an account **liquidar una factura** pay a bill, settle an invoice **liquidar una reclamación** settle a claim

liquidez *nf* liquidity *n*

líquido *adj* fluid *adj*, liquid *adj*

lista *nf* index *n*, list *n*, register *n*, schedule *n* **lista de correos, poste restante** (LAm) poste restante **lista de destinatarios** mailing list **lista de espera** hold queue, waiting list, hold line (US)

listo *adj* ready *adj*, clever *adj* **listo para entrega** ready for despatch

litigante *nmf* litigant *n*

litigar *vb* litigate *vb*

litigio *nm* litigation *n*

llamada, llamado (LAm) *nf, nm* call *n* **llamada a cobro revertido, llamado por cobrar** (LAm) reverse-charge call, collect call (US) **llamadas telefónicas gratuitas** Freefone (R) (GB) **llamada telefónica, llamado telefónico** (LAm) telephone call

llamamiento *nm* appeal *n*, call *n*

llamar *vb* call *vb* **llamar a** invite **llamar a alguien para la entrevista** invite sb to interview

llegar *vb* arrive *vb* **llegar a un acuerdo** come to an accommodation, call it a deal, make a treaty **llegar a un acuerdo sobre** (agreement, policy) thrash out **llegar a un acuerdo mutuo / llegar a un arreglo, transar** (LAm) reach a compromise **llegar al conocimiento de alguien** come to the notice of sb

llevar *vb* (premises) occupy *vb* **que lleva mucho tiempo** time-consuming **llevar a cabo** carry out **llevar la contabilidad** keep the books **llevar un negocio** operate a business **llevar un tren de vida que los ingresos no permiten** live beyond one's means

local 1. *adj* local *adj* **2.** *nm* premises *npl* **local comercial** business premises **local de una oficina** office premises

lógica *nf* rationale *n*

logística *nf* logistics *n*

lograr *vb* achieve *vb*, mediate *vb*, win *vb* **lograr un objetivo** reach an objective

logro *nm* accomplishment *n*, achievement *n*

lonja *nf* mart *n*

lote *nm* (of goods) batch *n* (at auction) lot *n*

lucrativo *adj* lucrative *adj*

lugar *nm* place *n* **lugar de la conferencia** conference venue **lugar de trabajo** workplace

lujo *nm* luxury *n*

macroeconomía *nf* macroeconomics *n*

madurar *vb* (business, economy) mature *vb*

mafioso,-osa *nm,f* racketeer *n*

magistratura *nf* magistracy *n* **Magistratura del Trabajo** industrial tribunal

magnate *nmf* magnate *n*, tycoon *n* **magnate de la prensa** press baron

malgastar *vb* waste *vb*

maltratar *vb* abuse *vb*

maltrato *nm* mishandling *n*

malversación *nf* embezzlement *n*, misappropriation *n*

malversador, -ora *nm,f* embezzler *n*

malversar *vb* embezzle *vb*

mandamiento *nm* order *n*, warrant *n* **mandamiento judicial** injunction, writ

mandar *vb* forward *vb*, send *vb*, order *vb* **mandar por correo** post

mandato *nm* term of office **mandato de pago** warrant for payment

mando *nm* command *n* **mando intermedio** middle manager **mandos intermedios** middle management

manejar *vb* gestionar (deal) handle *vb*, manage *vb* **manejar dinero** (money) handle

manejo *nm* (of machine) operation *n* **manejo de datos** data handling

mano *nf* hand *n* **a mano** handy **mano de obra** labour, manpower, labor (US) **mano de obra empleada a base de contrato** contract labour **entre manos** in hand **de primera mano** first-hand

mantener *vb* maintain *vb* **mantener bajos los precios** (prices) keep down

mantenimiento *nm* maintenance *n*, retention *n*

manual 1. *adj* manual *adj* **2.** *nm* handbook *n*

manufacturar *vb* manufacture *vb*

manutención *nf* maintenance *n*

maqueta *nf* working model *n*

máquina *nf* machine *n* **máquina de escribir** typewriter **máquina expendedora automática** vending machine **máquina franqueadora** franking machine

maquinaria *nf* machinery *n*, plant *n*

marca *nf* brand *n*, trademark *n* **marca de calidad**, kite mark (US) **marca comercial** brand name **marca de contraste** hallmark **de marca registrada** proprietary brand **marca registrada** proprietary brand, registered trade name, registered trademark

marcar *vb* mark *vb*

marcha *nf* progress *n*

marchar *vb* walk *vb*, function *vb*, (machine) work *vb*

marcharse *vb* leave *vb*

marco *nm* framework *n*, (deutsche) mark *n* **marco alemán** Deutsche Mark **marco de oportunidad** window of opportunity

margen *nm* margin *n* **margen de beneficio** markup, profit margin **margen bruto** gross margin **margen comercial** trading margin **margen competitivo** competitive edge **margen reducido** narrow margin

marginal *adj* marginal *adj*

marina *nf* navy *n* **marina mercante** merchant marine, merchant navy

marino *adj* marine *adj*

marítimo *adj* marine *adj*

márketing, mercadeo (LAm) *nm* marketing *n* **márketing global** global marketing **márketing de masas, mercadeo de masas** (LAm) mass marketing

materia *nf* **materias** matter, materials **materias primas** raw materials

material *nm* material *n* **materiales de construcción** building materials **material sobrante** waste products

matriz, talón (LAm) *nf, nm* counterfoil *n*

mayor *adj* main *adj*, major *adj*, senior *adj* **al por mayor** at/by wholesale **la mayor parte de** the bulk of

mayoría *nf* majority *n* **mayoría suficiente** working majority

mayorista *nmf* wholesaler *n* **mayorista de pago al contado** cash and carry

mayoritariamente *adv* in the majority *prep*

MBA (Máster en Administración de Empresas) *abbr* MBA (Master of Business Administration) *abbr*

mecánico *adj* mechanical *adj*

mecanismo *nm* machinery *n*, works *npl* **mecanismo de paridades** exchange rate mechanism (ERM) **mecanismo de tasas de cambio** exchange rate mechanism (ERM)

mecanógrafo, -afa *nm,f* typist *n*

mecenazgo *nm* sponsorship *n*

media *nf* average *n* **media general** general average **media hora** half-an-hour **media pensión** half-board

mediación *nf* mediation *n*

mediador, -ora *nm,f* mediator *n*

mediano *adj* medium *adj* **mediano plazo** medium term

mediante *prep* by means of *prep* **mediante negociaciones** by negotiation

mediar *vb* mediate *vb*

médico **1.** *adj* medical *adj* **2.** *nm* doctor *n*

medida *nf* measure *n* **medida financiera** financial measure **medidas antiinflacionarias** anti-inflationary measures **medida de seguridad** safety measure **medidas financieras** financial measures **medidas fiscales** fiscal measures **medidas de reconversión** rationalization measures

medidor *nm* (LAm) meter *n*

medio **1.** *adj* (average) mean *adj* median *adj*, medium *adj* **medio plazo** medium term **medio sueldo** half-pay **2.** *nm* means *npl*, mode *n* **medio de publicidad** advertising medium **medio publicitario** advertising

medium medios ability to pay, means, resources **medios de comunicación** media **medios de comunicación de masas** mass media

medir *vb* measure *vb*

megaocteto *nm* megabyte *n*

mejor *adj* better *adj*, best *adj* **mejor de la gama** top-of-the-range

mejora *nf* amendment *n*, upturn *n* **mejora salarial** wage increase

mejorar *vb* improve *vb*, pick up *vb*, upgrade *vb*

membrete *nm* letterhead *n*

memorándum *nm* memo *n*, memorandum *n*

memoria *nf* (DP) memory *n* **memoria anual** annual report **memoria de lectura** ROM (read only memory) **memoria RAM** (DP) RAM (random access memory)

mencionado *adj* mentioned *adj* **arriba mencionado** above-mentioned

menor *adj* junior *adj*, minor *adj*

mensaje, mandado (LAm) *nm* message *n* **mensaje publicitario, aviso; réclame** (LAm) advertisement

mensajero, -era *nm,f* courier *n*, messenger *n*

mensual *adj* monthly *adj*

mercadeable *adj* marketable *adj*

mercadeo *nm* (LAm) merchandising *n*, marketing *n*

mercaderías *nfpl* freight *n*

mercado *nm* market *n*, mart *n* **de mercado** going **mercado alcista** bull market, buoyant market **mercado amplio** broad market **mercado bajista** bear market **mercado de bonos** bond market **mercado de capitales** capital market **Mercado Común** Common Market **mercado de divisas** foreign exchange market, exchange market **mercado de entrega spot** spot market **mercado de la eurodivisa** eurocurrency market **mercado exterior** foreign/overseas market **mercado de factores (de producción)** factor market **mercado favorable a los compradores** buyer's market **mercado favorable al vendedor** seller's market **mercado financiero** financial/money market **mercado firme** firm market **mercado fluido** fluid market **mercado de futuros** forward/futures market **el mercado se ha desfondado, los precios han caído en picada** (LAm) the bottom has fallen out of the market **mercado inactivo** flat market **mercado inestable** fluid market **mercado inmobiliario** property market, real estate market (US) **mercado libre** free/open market **mercado marginal** fringe market **mercado al por mayor** wholesale market **mercado al por menor** retail market **mercado monetario** money market **mercado mundial** global/world market **mercado nacional/interior** domestic/home market **mercado negro** black market **mercado de oferta** buyer's market

mercado de opciones de compra y venta de acciones options market **mercado de oro** gold market **de mercado popular** (product) down-market **mercado previsto** target market **mercado reducido** narrow market **de mercado selecto** (product) up-market **mercado subsidiario** secondary market **mercado con tendencia a la baja** falling market **mercado con tendencia a subir** bull market **mercado terminal** terminal market **mercado de trabajo** labour market **mercado turístico** the tourist trade **mercado de valores** stock market **mercado de valores de primera clase** gilt-edged market

mercancía nf **mercancías, mercaderías** (LAm) goods, wares **mercancías abandonadas** abandoned goods **mercancías en curso** goods in process **mercancías de exportación** export goods **mercancías a granel** bulk goods **mercancías a prueba** goods on approval **mercancías en tránsito** transit goods **mercancías de venta fácil, mercaderías de venta rápida** (LAm) fast-selling goods

mercantil adj commercial adj, mercantile adj

merecer vb be worth vb

merecido adj earned adj, deserved adj **bien merecido** hard-earned

mes nm month n **del pasado mes** ultimo adj, adv

meta nf target n

metal nm metal n

método nm organization n, method n **método contable para valorar existencias** LIFO (last in first out) abbr **método de producción** production method **métodos de contabilidad** accounting conventions

métrico adj metric adj

metro nm metre n, meter (US) **metro cuadrado** square metre **metro cúbico** cubic metre

metrópoli(s) nf metropolis n

microeconomía nf microeconomics n

microficha nf microfiche n

micrófono nm microphone n **micrófono oculto, peste** (LAm) (listening device) bug

microordenador, microcomputador,-ora (LAm) nm, nm,f microcomputer n

microprocesador nm microprocessor n

miembro nmf member n **miembro de un jurado** juror **miembro vitalicio** life member

mil nm thousand n **mil libras esterlinas** (1000) K, pounds

milla nf mile n **milla marina** nautical mile

millón nm million n

millonario, -ria nm,f millionaire n

mina nf mine n **mina de carbón** coal mine

mineral nm mineral n

minería nf mining n

mínimo adj fractional adj, minimal adj minimum adj **mínima parte** fraction

ministerio, secretaría (LAm) nm, nf government department n, ministry n **el Ministerio de Hacienda** the Treasury Department (US) **Ministerio de Salud** Ministry of Health **Ministerio de Transporte, Secretaría de Transporte** (LAm) Ministry of Transport

ministro, -tra nm,f minister n **ministro, -tra de Economía y Hacienda** Chancellor of the Exchequer (GB)

minoría nf minority n **en minoría** in the minority

minusvalía nf capital loss n

mirar vb look (at) vb

misión nf assignment n

mitad nf half n **mitad de precio** half-price

mítin nm meeting n

mobiliario nm furnishings npl, fittings npl **mobiliario de oficina** office equipment

moda nf trend n **moda actual** current trend

modelo nmf (person) model n

módem nm modem n

moderación nf moderation n **moderación salarial** wage restraint **moderación voluntaria en las reivindicaciones salariales** voluntary wage restraint

moderado adj moderate adj

moderar vb moderate vb

modernización nf modernization n

modernizar vb modernize vb

moderno adj modern adj, up-to-date (LAm) adj

modo nm mode n

módulo nm module n, unit n

molestia nf **molestias** inconvenience, n, nuisance n

moneda nf currency n, coin n **moneda clave** key currency **moneda convertible** convertible currency, hard currency **moneda no convertible** soft currency **moneda de curso legal** legal currency, legal tender **moneda extranjera** foreign currency, foreign exchange **moneda fuerte** hard currency **moneda de oro** gold coin **monedas, sencillo; feria; menudo** (LAm) (coins) loose/small change **moneda verde** green currency

monetario adj monetary adj

monetarismo nm monetarism n

monopolio nm monopoly n

montar vb establish vb (company) set up vb **montar un negocio** set up in business, found a company

montón nm load n

morder vb (LAm) bribe vb

mordida nf (LAm) bribe n, sweetener n

mostrador nm counter n, desk n **mostrador de transbordos** (transport) transfer desk

motivo nm design n **motivo de queja** grievance

movilizar vb mobilize vb **movilizar fondos** raise capital

movimiento nm movement n **movimiento de capital** funds flow **movimiento libre**

de mercancías, movimiento libre de mercaderías (LAm) free movement of goods **movimientos de capitales** capital turnover **mucho movimiento (en la bolsa)** heavy trading

muelle nm (for berthing) dock n quay n **en el muelle** ex quay, ex wharf

muestra nf exhibition n, sample n **muestra de oferta** trial offer

muestreo nm sampling n **muestreo de cuotas** quota sampling

multa nf forfeit n, fine n, penalty n

multilateral adj multilateral adj

multinacional adj multinational adj

multiplicar vb multiply vb

multipropiedad nf timeshare n

multiuso adj multipurpose adj

mundial adj global adj, worldwide adj

mundo nm world n **el mundo de la banca** banking circles **el mundo comercial** the commercial world **el mundo editorial** publishing **el Tercer Mundo** the Third World

municipal adj local adj

municipio nm town council n, town hall n

mutuamente adv mutually adv

mutuo adj mutual adj, reciprocal adj

nación nf nation n **Naciones Unidas (la ONU)** United Nations

nacional adj inland adj, national adj

nacionalidad nf nationality n

nacionalización nf nationalization n

nacionalizar vb nationalize vb

necesario adj necessary adj

necesidad nf (goods) necessity n, requirement n **necesidades materiales** material needs

negar vb withhold vb, deny vb **negarse a aceptar** (goods) reject **negarse a pagar, rehusar pagar** (LAm) refuse payment **negarse a pagar una reclamación** refuse a claim

negativa, plante (LAm) nf, nm refusal n

negligencia nf malpractice n, neglect n, negligence n

negligente adj negligent adj

negociable adj negotiable adj

negociación nf negotiation n, transaction n **en negociación** under negotiation **negociación colectiva** collective bargaining **negociaciones arancelarias** tariff negotiations **negociaciones comerciales** trade talks **negociaciones salariales** wage negotiations

negociador, -ora nm,f negotiator n

negociante nmf merchant n

negociar vb bargain vb, negotiate vb, trade vb

negocio nm deal n **negocio difícil** hard bargain **negocio ilícito** racketeering **negocio en marcha** going concern **negocio en participación** collaborative venture, joint venture **negocio en plena marcha** going concern **negocios** business

negrita nf bold type n

neto adj net(t) adj, after tax adv

neutral adj neutral adj

nivel nm level n **de dos niveles** two-tier **nivel de calidad** quality standard **nivel de cobertura** extent of cover **nivel de desempleo, nivel de cesantía** (LAm) level of unemployment **nivel de empleo** level of employment **nivel de inflación** level of inflation **nivel de precios** level of prices **nivel de producción** flow line production **nivel en el que la tasa de impuestos cambia** tax threshold **nivel de vida** standard of living

no det no det, not adv **no aceptación** non-acceptance **no se admiten agentes** no agents wanted **no aprobar** negative (US) **no asegurable** uninsurable **no asistencia** non-attendance **no colgar, no cortar** (LAm) (phone) hang on **no corresponde** N/A (not applicable) **no cubierto por entero** undersubscribed **no dar a conocer un documento** withhold a document **no discriminatorio** non-discriminatory **no disponemos de los medios para...** we do not have the means to... **no disponible** not available **no finalización** non-completion **no intervención** non-intervention **no negociable** non-negotiable **no perder el hilo de los sucesos** (events) keep up with **no pertinente** not applicable **no podemos correr el riesgo** we cannot afford (to take) the risk **no me puedo permitir el lujo de comprar una nueva impresora** I can't afford to buy a new printer **no rehabilitado** (bankrupt) undischarged **no rentable** non-profitmaking, unprofitable **no retornable** non-returnable **no tener fondos** (cheque) bounce* **no tener más remedio que** resort to **no terminación** non-completion

noción nf notion n **nociones elementales de cálculo aritmético** numeracy

nombramiento nm (to a position) appointment n, nomination n

nombrar, postular (LAm) vb assign vb, nominate vb **nombrar a alguien a un consejo/una comisión, postular a alguien a un consejo/una comisión** (LAm) nominate sb to a board/committee **nombrar a alguien a un puesto** appoint sb to a position

nombre nm name n **de nombre** by name **en el nombre de** in the name of **nombre y apellidos** full name

nómina, planilla (LAm) nf payroll n

nominal adj nominal adj

norma nf norm n **norma de calidad** quality standard **normas comerciales** trading standards

normal adj standard adj

normalización nf standardization n

normalizar vb standardize vb

nota nf memo n, note n, message n **nota de cobertura, póliza provisoria** (LAm) cover

note **nota de crédito** credit note **nota de débito** debit note **nota de entrega** delivery note **nota de envío** dispatch note, forwarding note **nota de expedición, nota de flete** (LAm) dispatch note, forwarding note
notable *adj* noteworthy *adj*
notario, -ria *nm,f* notary *n*
noticia, reporte (LAm) *nf* report *n* **noticias** news **buenas noticias** good news **malas noticias** bad news **noticias financieras** financial news
notificación *nf* advice *n*, notification *n*
notificar *vb* inform *vb*, notify *vb* **notificar de algo** give notice of sth
nuevo *adj* new *adj* **nueva tecnología** new technology **nuevos negocios** new business
nulo *adj* useless *adj*, void *adj* **nulo y sin valor** null and void
numérico *adj* numerical *adj* **numérico-alfabético** alpha-numeric
número *nm* copy *n*, number *n* **número de cuenta** account number **número equivocado** (phone) wrong number **número de pedido** order number **número de referencia** box number, reference number **número de serie** serial number **número de teléfono** telephone number
obedecer *vb* obey *vb*
objeción *nf* objection *n*
objetivo *nm* objective *n*, target *n* **objetivo económico** economic objective **objetivo de producción** production target **objetivo de ventas** sales target
obligación *nf* bond *n*, commitment *n*, debenture *n*, obligation *n* **obligación conjunta** joint obligation **obligación desvalorizada** junk bond **obligaciones contractuales** contractual obligations **obligaciones garantizadas por los activos de la compañia** debenture capital, debenture stock (US) **obligación del Estado** government bond **obligación de fidelidad** fidelity bond **obligación no hipotecaria** debenture bond **obligación registrada** registered bond
obligatoriedad *nf* compulsoriness *n*
obligatorio *adj* binding *adj*, obligatory *adj*
obra *nf* building site *n*, work *n* **obras** works **obras de beneficencia** charity
obrero, -era *nm,f* blue-collar worker, guest worker, labourer, manual worker **obrero no calificado, obrero no calificado; peón** (LAm) unskilled worker **obrero cualificado** skilled worker **obrero especializado** skilled worker **obrero manual, peón** (LAm) manual worker **obreros sindicados** organized labour **obreros** shopfloor
observación *nf* comment *n*, observation *n* **en observación** under observation
observar *vb* observe *vb*
obsolescencia *nf* obsolescence *n* **obsolescencia planificada** built-in/planned obsolescence

obstaculizar, tapar (LAm) *vb* block *vb*
obtener *vb* achieve *vb*, acquire *vb*, gain *vb*, net(t) *vb* **obtener beneficios** make a profit
ocasionar *vb* cause *vb*
octeto *nm* byte *n*
ocupación *nf* employment *n*, occupation *n*, tenure *n*
ocupacional *adj* occupational *adj*
ocupado *adj* busy *adj*
ocupante *nmf* occupant *n*, occupier *n*
ocupar *vb* (premises) occupy *vb* **ocupar un cargo** hold office
oferente *nmf* offeror *n*
oferta, licitación (LAm) *nf* bargain *n*, bid *n*, supply *n*, offer *n*, tender *n*, tendering *n* **oferta combinada** package deal **oferta y demanda** supply and demand **oferta por escrito** offer in writing **oferta final** closing bid **oferta en firme** firm offer **oferta por liquidación, oferta por realización** (LAm) clearance offer **oferta monetaria** money supply **oferta de pago en efectivo** cash offer **oferta provisional, oferta provisoria** (LAm) tentative offer **oferta pública de adquisición (OPA)** tender offer **oferta de rebaja** bargain offer **oferta no solicitada** unsolicited offer **oferta sujeta a confirmación** offer subject to confirmation **oferta superior** higher bid **oferta de trabajo** job offer **oferta válida hasta...** offer valid until...
oficial *adj* formal *adj*, official *adj*
oficina *nf* office *n* **le remitimos a nuestra oficina central** we refer you to our head office **oficina de administración fiduciaria** (bank) trustee department **oficina de cambio** bureau de change **oficina central** HO (head office), headquarters, parent company **oficina de correos, correo** (LAm) post office **oficina de empleo** employment agency, Jobcentre (GB), job shop **oficina de importación** import office **oficina de información** information desk/office **oficina de objetos perdidos** lost-property office **oficina regional** regional office
oficinista *nmf* clerical worker *n*, clerk *n*, white-collar worker *n*
oficio *nm* profession *n*, trade *n* **de oficio** by trade
ofrecer, licitar (LAm) *vb* bid *vb* **ofrecer más** outbid
oído *adj* heard *adj* **de oídas** by hearsay
oleada *nf* (of mergers, takeovers) wave *n*
oligopolio *nm* oligopoly *n*
omisión *nf* default *n*, omission *n*
opción *nf* option *n* **opción de anular** option to cancel **opción de compra** option to buy **opción de compra/venta de acciones a cierto precio para el futuro, beneficios de operación** (LAm) share option, stock option (US)
operación *nf* transaction *n* **operación comercial** business transaction **operación**

al contado cash transaction **operaciones en bolsa** dealing, trading (US) **operaciones de cambio** foreign exchange dealings, foreign exchange trading (US) **operaciones de exportación** export operations **operaciones de iniciado** insider dealing, insider trading (US) **operación financiera** financial operation **operación en el mercado de valores** equity transaction **operación de trueque** barter transaction
operador, -ora, feriante; puestero, -era (LAm) *nm,f, nmf; nm,f* operator *n*, trader *n* **operador de cambios** exchange broker, foreign exchange dealer, money trader **operador de teclado** computer operator
operario, -ria *nm,f* operator *n*
oponerse *vb* object *vb*
oportunidad *nf* opportunity *n* **oportunidad comercial** market opportunity **oportunidades de mercado** market opportunities
oportuno *adj* convenient *adj*
optar *vb* opt *vb*
optativo *adj* optional *adj*
orden *nm* order *n*, rank *n* **orden** *nf* injunction *n*, instruction *n* **orden del día** agenda **órdenes** brief, orders **orden jerárquico** line management **orden judicial** writ **orden permanente de pago** banker's order, standing order **de primer orden** (investment) first-rate
ordenador, computador,-ora (LAm) *nm, nm,f* computer *n* **ordenador central** (DP) mainframe **ordenador personal (PC)** personal computer (PC) **ordenador portátil** laptop computer, portable computer
ordenar, sindicalizar (LAm) *vb* organize *vb*, order *vb*
organigrama *nm* flow chart **organigrama de flujo** flow chart
organismo *nm* organism *n*, body *n* **organismo gubernamental** government body
organización *nf* organization *n* **organización estatal** government body **organización funcional** functional organization **organización internacional** international organization **organización patronal** employers' federation
organizar, sindicalizar (LAm) *vb* organize *vb* **organizar una conferencia** organize/ arrange a conference
órgano *nm* organ *n*
orientación *nf* direction *n*, guidance *n* **orientación profesional, orientación vocacional** (LAm) careers advice
origen *nm* source *n*
oro *nm* gold *n* **oro en lingotes** gold bullion **oro y plata en lingotes** bullion
otorgar *vb* grant *vb* **otorgar crédito** extend credit
PAC (Política Agrícola Común) *nf* CAP (Common Agricultural Policy) *abbr*
pacto *nm* covenant *n*, agreement *n*

paga *nf* pay *n*, wage *n* **paga doble** double time **paga de vacaciones, sueldo gozado durante la licencia** (LAm) holiday pay
pagadero *adj* payable *adj* **pagadero por adelantado** payable in advance
pagado *adj* paid *adj*
pagar *vb* remunerate *vb*, repay *vb* (account) settle *vb* **pagar de más** overpay **sin pagar** (cheque) uncleared **pagar de menos** underpay **pagar por adelantado** pay in advance **pagar con cheque** pay by cheque **pagar al contado** pay in cash **pagar una cuenta** pay a bill **pagar la cuenta y marcharse** (of hotel) check out **pagar una cuota** pay a fee **pagar en efectivo** pay in cash **pagar una factura** pay/settle an invoice **pagar interés** pay interest **pagar a la orden de . . .** pay to the order of . . . **pagar por un servicio** pay for a service **pagar con tarjeta de crédito** pay by credit card
pagaré *n* banknote *n*, debenture *n*, promissory note *n* **pagaré de favor** accommodation bill **pagaré del Tesoro** Treasury bill, open note (US)
página *nf* page *n* **las páginas amarillas** the Yellow pages (R) (GB)
pago *nm* payment *n*, redemption *n* **pago por adelantado** prepayment **pago anticipado** advance payment, cash before delivery, prepayment **pago de compensación** clearing payment **pago al contado** cash payment, spot cash **pago a cuenta** payment on account **pago en efectivo** cash payment **pago en exceso** overpayment **pago ex-gratia** ex gratia payment **pago al hacer el pedido** cash before delivery, cash with order **pago inicial, pie** (LAm) down payment **pago insuficiente** underpayment **pago íntegro** full payment **pago de intereses de una deuda** debt service **pago parcial** part payment **pagos por etapas** staged payments **pago simbólico** token payment **pagos de transferencia** transfer payments **pago total** full payment
país *nm* country *n* **país comerciante** trading nation **país que comercia con otro** trading partner **país desarrollado** developed country **país importador** importing country **país de origen** country of origin, home country **país productor de petróleo** oil state **país anfitrón** host country **país subdesarrollado** underdeveloped country **país del Tercer Mundo** third-world country **país en vías de desarrollo** developing country
palabra *nf* word *n* **palabra clave** (computer) keyword **palabra por palabra** verbatim **palabras por minuto** wpm (words per minute)
palanca *nf* lever *n* **palancas** (LAm) business contacts, influence
paleta *nf* pallet *n*

panorama *nm* prospect *n*
pantalla *nf* screen *n* **pantalla de visualización** visual display unit (VDU)
papel *nm* document *n* (role) function *n* **papel comercial** commercial paper **papel con membrete** headed notepaper, letterhead **papel moneda** paper currency **papel de primera clase** first-class paper
papeleo *nm* paperwork *n*, red tape *n*
paquete *nm* bundle *n*, package *n*, packet *n* **paquete accional autónomo** stake **paquete de software** software package
par *nf* par *n* **por debajo de la par** below par **por encima de la par** above par, at a premium
parado, cesante (LAm) *adj* unemployed *adj*, redundant *adj*
paralización *nf* shutdown *n*
parar *vb* (inflation) halt *vb*
parecer *vb* seem *vb* **parecerle mal a** find fault with
paridad, tasa de cambio (LAm) *nf* parity *n*, exchange rate *n*
parlamento *nm* parliament *n* **Parlamento Europeo** European Parliament
paro, cesantía (LAm) *nm, nf* strike *n*, unemployment *n*, stoppage *n* **en paro, cesante** (LAm) jobless **paro generalizado, cesantía general** (LAm) mass unemployment **paro patronal** (LAm) lockout
parte *nf* block *n*, half *n* **parte contratada** covenantee **parte contratante** covenantor
participación *nf* holding *n*, interest *n*, share *n*, stake *n* **participación mayoritaria** majority holding **participación en el mercado** market share **participación minoritaria** minority holding **participación obrera** worker participation **participación de los trabajadores en la gestión** worker participation
participar *vb* compete *vb*, intervene *vb* **participar en** take part in
partida *nf* batch *n*, entry *n* **de partida doble** (bookkeeping) double-entry
partidario, -ria *nm, f* backer *n*
partir *vb* split *vb* **partir por la mitad** halve
pasaje *nm* ticket *n*, passengers *npl* **pasaje sencillo, boleto sencillo** (LAm) (rail/flight) single/one-way ticket **pasaje de ida y vuelta** return ticket, round-trip ticket (US)
pasajero, -era *nm, f* passenger *n*, traveller *n*, traveler (US) **pasajero en tránsito** (transport) transit passenger
pasar *vb* hand over *vb*, spend *vb* **pasar a** (call) transfer **pasar por alto** overlook **pasar a buscar** call for **pasar a cuenta nueva** carry forward, carry over **pasar por encima** bypass **pasar a máquina, tipear** (LAm) key in, type **pasar la pelota** pass the buck* **pasar la prueba** stand the test
pasivo *nm* debit *n*, liabilities *npl* **pasivo circulante** current liabilities **pasivo a largo plazo** fixed liability

paso *nm* step *n*, pass *n*
pastor, -ora *nm, f* minister *n*
patentado *adj* patented *adj*, proprietary *adj*
patente *nf* patent *n*
patrimonio *nm* wealth *n* **patrimonio nacional** national wealth **patrimonio neto** equity
patrocinador, -ora *nm, f* sponsor *n*
patrocinio *nm* patronage *n*, sponsorship *n*
patrón, -ona *nm, f* boss *n*, employer *n* **patrón oro** gold standard
pauta *nf* indication *n* **pautas de consumo** spending patterns
peaje *nm* (road) toll *n*
pedido *nm* request *n*, demand, order *n*, appeal (LAm) *n*, legal action (LAm) *n* **pedido de pago** request for payment **pedido efectuado por correo** mail order **pedido fijo** standing order **pedido suplementario** repeat order **pedido urgente** rush order
pedir *vb* apply for *vb*, call for *vb* **pedir crédito** request a loan **pedir indemnización** claim compensation **pedir prestado** borrow **pedir una referencia** take up a reference
peligro *nm* hazard *n*, risk *n* **peligro inevitable** natural hazard **peligro para la salud** health hazard
peligroso *adj* hazardous *adj*
penetración *nf* penetration *n* **penetración en el mercado** market penetration
pensión *nf* annuity *n*, pension *n*, retirement pension *n* **pensión de jubilación** retirement pension **pensión proporcional al sueldo** earnings-related pension
pequeño *adj* minor *adj*, small *adj* **pequeño hurto** pilferage
perder *vb* (custom) lose *vb* **perder el derecho a** forfeit **perder valor** depreciate, lose value
pérdida *nf* forfeiture *n*, loss *n*, wastage *n*, waste *n* **pérdida bruta** gross loss **pérdida de ejercicio** trading loss **pérdida de empleo** loss of job **pérdida financiera** financial loss **pérdida de ingresos** loss of earnings **pérdida neta** clear loss, net(t) loss **pérdida sobre el papel** paper loss **pérdidas de estoc** stock shrinkage **pérdida de tiempo** waste of time **pérdida de valor** depreciation
perdido *adj* lost *adj*, missed *adj* **perdido en tránsito** lost in transit
periférico *adj* peripheral *adj*
perimido *adj* (LAm) out of date *adj*
periódico *nm* daily paper *n*, newspaper *n* **periódico de formato grande** broadsheet
periodismo *nm* journalism *n*
período *nm* period *n* **período de aviso** notice period **período de contabilidad** accounting period **período de gestación** lead time **período de gracia** period of grace **período de mayor afluencia** peak period **período de prueba** trial period **período de reflexión** cooling-off period

período de servicio tour of duty **período de vigencia del tipo de interés, período de vigencia de la tasa de interés** (LAm) interest period

perito adj expert adj

permiso nm leave n, leave of absence n, licence n, permit n, furlough (US) **permiso de exportación** export licence **permiso de importación** import licence **permiso de obras** building permit **permiso de residencia y trabajo** (LAm) green card **permiso de trabajo** work permit

permitir vb allow vb, furlough (US), vb

permutar vb barter vb

perro nm dog n **perro guardián** (fig) watchdog

persona nf person n **por persona** per capita, per head **persona en aprendizaje** trainee **persona clave** key person **persona que concede un permiso o una licencia** licensor **persona que da referencias sobre otra** referee **persona mencionada** named person **persona que otorga la concesión** franchisor **persona que trabaja por libre** freelance, freelancer

personal 1. adj personal adj, vested adj **2.** nm manpower n, staff n, workforce n **con demasiado personal** overmanned **personal administrativo** office staff **personal de campo** field personnel **personal cualificado, personal calificado** (LAm) qualified personnel **personal directivo** executive personnel

perspectiva nf prospect n **perspectivas comerciales** business outlook **perspectivas futuras** future prospects

pertinente adj relevant adj

pesar vb weigh vb **pesar ventajas y desventajas** weigh the pros and cons

peseta nf peseta n

peso nm load n, tonnage n, weight n **peso bruto** gross weight **peso muerto** dead weight **peso neto** net(t) weight **pesos y medidas** weights and measures

petición, pedido (LAm) nf, nm demand n, request n **petición final** final demand **petición de informe sobre el crédito** credit enquiry **petición de informes** enquiry

petrodólar nm petrodollar n

PIB (Producto Interior Bruto) nm GDP (Gross Domestic Product) abbr

pichincha nf (LAm) bargain n

pico nm peak n

pie nm foot n, deposit (LAm) n **al pie de la letra** verbatim

pieza nf (of a machine) part n **pieza de recambio, refacción** (LAm) (for machine) spare part

pinchar vb burst vb **pinchar el teléfono, intervenir un llamado** (LAm) bug a call

piquete nm picket n

piratería nf (at sea) piracy n **piratería de programa informático** software piracy

pista nf track n **pista de máxima velocidad** fast track

plan nm (agreement) arrangement n **plan de campaña** plan of campaign **Plan Europeo de Recuperación** European Recovery Plan **plan de inversiones** investment programme, investment program (US) **plan de pensiones** pension scheme **plan piramidal** pyramid scheme **plan provisional, plan provisorio** (LAm) tentative plan **plan de reactivación** recovery scheme **plan de trabajo** work schedule

planear vb design vb, plan vb

planificación nf planning n **planificación económica** economic planning **planificación económica estatal** centralised economic planning **planificación estatal** central planning **planificación financiera** financial planning **planificación a largo plazo** long-term planning **planificación regional** regional planning **planificación de servicios** facility planning

planificar vb plan vbr, design vb

planilla nf (LAm) payroll n

planta nf plant n **planta de almacenaje frigorífico** cold storage plant **planta piloto** pilot plant

plante nm (LAm) refusal n

plantilla, planilla (LAm) nf payroll n, staff n, workforce n **plantilla sindicada** closed shop

plata nf silver n, cash (LAm) n

platal nm (money LAm) fortune n, bundle n

plaza nf square n, place n, job n

plazo, cuota (LAm) nm, nf instalment n, payment n, time limit, n, installment (US) n **a largo plazo** long-haul, long-range, long-term **largo plazo** long term **plazo de entrega** delivery time, lead time **plazo de preaviso** term of notice **plazo de tiempo** time frame

pleito nm legal action n, lawsuit n

plenario adj (assembly, session) plenary adj

pleno adj full adj **plena responsabilidad** full liability **pleno empleo** full employment

plus nm bonus n **plus según rendimiento** performance-related bonus

plusvalía nf capital gain n

PNB (Producto Nacional Bruto) nm GNP (Gross National Product) abbr

población nf population n **población activa** working population

poco adv & adj hardly adv, little adj

poder nm power n **poder adquisitivo** buying power, purchasing power **poderes** (power) proxy **poder notarial** power of attorney

polígono nm area n, zone n **polígono industrial** industrial trading estate

política nf politics n, policy n **Política Agrícola Común** Common Agricultural Policy (CAP) **política arriesgada**

brinkmanship **política de comercio de reciprocidad arancelaria** fair-trade policy **política económica** economic policy **política de la empresa** company policy **política financiera** financial policy **política fiscal** fiscal policy **política del gobierno** government policy **política monetaria** monetary policy **política monetaria expansiva** easy-money policy **política nacional** domestic policy **política de precios** pricing policy **política presupuestaria, política presupuestal** (LAm) budgetary policy **política de reducción de plantilla** LIFO (last in first out) **política salarial** wage policy

político adj political adj

polivalente adj multipurpose adj

póliza nf policy n **la póliza cubre los riesgos siguientes** the policy covers the following risks **póliza dotal** endowment policy **póliza provisional, póliza provisoria** (LAm) cover note **póliza de seguros** insurance certificate, insurance policy

ponencia nf presentation n, proposal n **ponencia de primera categoría** first-class paper

poner vb (manage) run vb (company) set up **poner en circulación** issue **poner con** (call) transfer **poner fecha adelantada, diferir** (LAm) postdate **poner una fecha anterior a un cheque** backdate a cheque **poner fin prematuro a un proyecto** kill a project **poner en marcha, prender** (LAm) (machine) turn on **poner un negocio** set up in business **poner una objeción** make/raise an objection **poner a prueba** carry out trials, try out **poner restricciones** impose restrictions **ponerse en contacto con** contact **poner un servicio** (manage) run **poner un télex** (message) telex ¿**me pone con...?, comuníqueme con...** (LAm) (phone) could you connect me to...?

porcentaje nm percentage n

portacontenedores nm container ship n

portador, -ora nm,f bearer n, holder n, payee n

portátil adj portable adj

portavoz, vocero, -era (LAm) nmf, nm,f spokesperson n

porte nm carriage n **porte debido** carriage forward **porte incluido** carriage included **porte pagado** carriage paid **portes a pagar** carriage forward

poseedor, -ora nm,f bearer n

poseer vb own vb **poseer valores en cartera** have holdings

posesión nf tenure n

posibilidad nf feasibility n, opportunity n, option n, prospect n **posibilidades** potential **posibilidades de ventas** sales potential

posible adj feasible adj **lo antes posible** a.s.a.p (as soon as possible)

posición, ubicación (LAm) nf location n, position n, post n

posponer vb defer vb, postpone vb

póster nm (advertising) poster n

postergar vb postpone vb

postor, -ora, licitador,-ora (LAm) nm,f tenderer n

postulación nf (LAm) nomination n

postulado, -ada nm,f (LAm) nominee n

postular vb (LAm) assign vb

potencia nf power n

potencial nm potential n

potenciar vb (product) promote vb **potenciar la demanda** boost demand **potenciar al máximo** maximise **potenciar la producción** increase output

potentado, -ada nm,f magnate n

potente adj powerful adj **muy potente** high-powered

práctica nf practice n **mala práctica** malpractice **prácticas** work experience **prácticas comerciales leales** fair trading **prácticas restrictivas** restrictive practices **práctica de vender a precio mínimo al público** fair-trade practice

practicar vb practise vb **practicar el pluriempleo** moonlight*

práctico adj businesslike adj, convenient adj, handy adj

preaviso nm advance notice n

precio nm price n, tariff n **bien de precio** (price) reasonable **nuestro precio incluye la entrega** our price includes delivery **de precio alto** high-priced **precio más bajo** bottom price **precio de catálogo** list price **precio al cierre** closing price **precio de compra** buying price, purchase price **precio de coste, precio de costo** (LAm) cost price **precio a cuota fija** flat-rate tariff **precio al detallista** trade price **precio de entrega inmediata** spot price, spot rate **precio en fábrica** factory price **precio de los factores de producción** factor price **precio favorable** favourable price **precio fijo** fixed price, hard price **precio en firme** firm price **precio flexible** flexible price **precio franco fábrica** factory price **precio de futuros** futures price **precio de ganga, precio rematado** (LAm) knockdown price **precio máximo** maximum price **precio al por mayor** wholesale price **precio de mercado** market price **precio mínimo, precio rematado** (LAm) knockdown price **precio mínimo al que pueden venderse en la UE** threshold price **precio neto** net(t) price **precio de ocasión** bargain price **precio de oferta** tender price **precio real** real price **precio de referencia** bench mark price **los precios citados incluyen...** the prices quoted are inclusive **precios fijos** fixed charges **precio simbólico** nominal price **precios de punta** top prices **precios con tendencia a la baja** falling prices **precio de transferencia** transfer price **precio umbral** threshold price **precio por unidad** unit price **precio de venta al**

público retail price **el precio de la vivienda** house prices
precioso adj valuable adj
precisar vb specify vb
precisión nf accuracy n
preciso adj accurate adj, necessary adj
predecir vb forecast vb
predicción nf forecast n
predominio nm predominance n
preferencia nf priority n, right of way n **preferencia comunitaria** community preference
preferencial adj preferential adj
prefijo nm STD code n
pregunta nf enquiry n, question n **pregunta clave** key question
preguntar vb enquire vb, ask vb
prenda nf guarantee n, pledge n
prender vb (LAm) turn on vb
preparación nf preparation n **preparación básica** basic training
preparar vb prepare vb **preparar una campaña** run a campaign **preparar el presupues** to draw up a budget
presenciar vb witness vb
presentación nf fronting n, packaging n, presentation n, introduction n
presentar vb bring forward vb, file vb (motion, paper) table vb **presentar la carta de denuncia** hand in one's resignation **presentar una demanda de indemnización** claim for damages **presentar una factura** (invoice) bill **presentar en forma de tabla** (data) tabulate **presentar un informe, reportear** (LAm) submit/present a report **presentar una oferta, licitar** (LAm) lodge a tender **presentar una queja** make a complaint **presentar una reclamación** claim for damages, put in a claim **presentarse** (at airport) check in **presentar una solicitud** put in a claim
presidente, -nta nm,f chief executive (of company), president n
presidir vb take the chair **presidir una reunión** chair a meeting
prestación nf allowance n **prestación estatal a la familia, asignación familiar** (LAm) family allowance
prestamista nmf lender n
préstamo nm cash advance n, borrowing n, loan n **préstamo de ahorro-vivienda** home loan **préstamo bancario** bank loan **préstamo estatal** government loan **préstamo exterior pagadero en moneda fuerte** hard loan **préstamo extranjero** foreign loan **préstamo financiero** financial loan **préstamo garantizado** secured loan **préstamo garantizado por obligaciones** debenture loan **préstamo hipotecario** mortgage, mortgage loan **préstamo inmovilizado** tied loan **préstamo puente** bridging loan, bridge loan (US) **préstamos** borrowing

prestar vb lend vb **prestar atención** take notice
prestigio nm kudos n, prestige n
presupuestar vb budget for vb
presupuesto nm budget n (price) quotation n **presupuesto de costes, presupuesto de costos** (LAm) estimate of costs **presupuesto fijo** fixed budget **presupuesto flexible** flexible budget **presupuesto de gastos, presupuesto de costos** (LAm) estimate of costs **presupuesto de gastos de capital** capital budget **presupuesto promocional** promotional budget **presupuesto de publicidad** advertising budget **presupuesto publicitario** promotional budget
prevenir vb forestall vb **prevenir a alguien contra algo** warn sb against doing sth
previo adj prior adj, previous adj **sin previo aviso** without warning
previsión nf forecast n, forecasting n **previsión económica** economic forecast **previsión de ventas** sales forecast
prima nf bonus n, premium n **prima por ausencia de siniestralidad** no-claims bonus **prima de enganche** golden hello **prima de seguros, cuota de seguros** (LAm) insurance premium
primera adj first rate **primera clase** first class **primer, -era cliente, -nta** first customer **primera hipoteca** first mortgage **primera letra de cambio** first bill of exchange **primeras entradas, primeras salidas** FIFO (first in first out)
principal adj leading adj, main adj, major adj, senior adj
principio nm principle n, beginning n
prioridad nf priority n **prioridad absoluta** top priority
privatización nf privatization n
privatizar vb denationalize vb, privatize vb
pro nm pro n **pros y contras** pros and cons
probado adj well-tried adj
probar vb sample vb, try out vb
procedencia nf sourcing n, origin n
proceder vb proceed vb **proceder en contra de** take legal action
procedimiento nm process n **procedimiento para presentar reclamaciones** claims procedure
procesador nm processor n **procesador de palabras** word processor
procesamiento nm processing n **procesamiento de datos** data processing **procesamiento por lotes** (DP) batch processing **procesamiento de textos** word processing
proceso nm lawsuit n, process n **proceso de datos** data handling, data processing, information processing **proceso electrónico de datos (EDP)** electronic data processing
producción nf manufacture n, output n,

production n **producción bruta** gross
output
producir vb net(t) vb, produce vb **que
produce intereses** interest-bearing
producir en exceso overproduce
productividad nf productivity n
productivo adj productive adj
producto nm product n **producto básico**
basic commodity **producto interior bruto
(PIB)** gross domestic product (GDP)
producto líder leading product
producto nacional bruto (PNB) gross
national product (GNP) **producto nuevo**
new product **producto primario** primary
product **producto principal** leading
product **producto principal de la marca**
brand leader **productos** goods, produce
productos acabados final products,
finished goods **productos básicos** staple
commodities **productos de desecho**
waste products **productos finales** final
products **productos gratuitos,
mercaderías gratuitas** (LAm) free goods
**productos a prueba, mercaderías a
prueba** (LAm) goods on approval
productos químicos chemical products
profesión nf career n, occupation n,
profession n **de profesión** by trade
programa nm (DP) program n, programme n
schedule n, timescale n, timetable n
programa de asistencia al exterior
foreign aid programme **programa
económico** economic plan **programa
informático** computer program, software
programa de obras públicas public works
programme (GB) **programa de ordenador,
programa de computadora** (LAm)
computer program **programa de
participación en los beneficios** profit-
sharing scheme **programa piloto** pilot
scheme **programa de reciclaje, plan de
recapacitación** (LAm) retraining
programme, retraining program (US)
programa de recuperación recovery
scheme
programación nf (DP) programming n
programador, -ora nm,f (DP) programmer n
**programador de ordenadores,
programador** (LAm) computer programmer
programar vb schedule vb
progreso nm progress n
prohibido adj out of bounds adv, forbidden
adj
prolongado adj long-term adj
prolongar vb prolong vb
promedio nm average n, mean n **promedio
aritmético** arithmetical mean **promedio
ponderado** weighted average
promesa nf pledge n, promise n
promoción nf (of product) promotion n
promoción de las exportaciones export
marketing
promocionar vb (product) promote vb
promotor, -ora nm,f developer n **promotor**

de construcciones property developer
promotor inmobiliario property developer
promotor de ventas merchandizer
pronosticar vb forecast vb
pronto adv promptly adv, soon adv
propensión nf liability n, tendency n
propenso adj liable adj, inclined adj
propiedad nf holding n, ownership n,
property n **co-propiedad** joint ownership
propiedad colectiva workers' collective
propiedades property **propiedad
inmobiliaria** real estate **propiedad
privada** private property
propietario, -ria nm,f landlord n, owner n,
proprietor n **propietario absentista**
absentee landlord **propietario ocupante
de una vivienda** owner-occupier
propietario de una vivienda home owner
propina nf gratuity n, tip n
proponer, postular (LAm) vb nominate vb
proporcionalmente adv pro rata adv
proporcionar vb (supply) provide vb
proporcionar algo a alguien issue sb with
sth
propósito nm (decision) resolution n,
purpose n
prorrata nf pro rata n **a prorrata** pro rata
prorrateo n pro rata n
prórroga nf (of contract) extension n
prosperar vb boom vb, thrive vb
prosperidad nf prosperity n **prosperidad
industrial** industrial health
próspero adj booming adj, prosperous adj
proteccionismo nm protectionism n
proteccionista adj protectionist adj
protestar vb complain vb, make a complaint
vb **protestar por algo** complain about sth
provecho nm benefit n, mileage n, profit n
proveedor, -ora nm,f supplier n **proveedor
principal** main supplier
proveer vb provide vb, equip vb, supply vb
proveer en exceso oversupply vb
provisión nf (stipulation) provision n
provisional, temporario; provisorio (LAm)
adj interim adj, temporary adj
provisorio adj (LAm) interim adj, temporary
adj
proyectar vb design vb, plan vb, schedule vb
proyecto nm project n **proyecto de
contrato** draft contract **proyecto relativo
a la vivienda** housing scheme
prueba nf test n **a prueba** on approval
prueba sobre el terreno field test
publicar vb (policy) issue vb, publish vb
publicidad nf publicity n
publicitario adj promotional adj
público adj public adj
puente nm bridge n **puente aéreo** shuttle
puerto nm harbour n, port n **puerto de
entrada** port of entry **puerto franco** free
port, free trade area
puestero, -era nm,f (LAm) dealer n
puesto nm (job) post n, booth n
puesto nm, **casilla** nf, (LAm) booth n

pujar *vb* push *vb*, bid *vb*
punto *nm* item *n* **punto crítico** break-even point **punto máximo** peak **punto muerto** stalemate **punto de venta** point of sale, sales outlet
quebrar *vb* go out of business *vb*, go to the wall *vb*
quedar *vb* stay *vb*, remain *vb* **quedarse con dinero** (money) keep back
queja *nf* complaint *n*, grievance *n*
quejar *vb* complain *vb* **quejarse de algo** complain about sth
quiebra *nf* bankruptcy *n*, failure *n* (of company), collapse *n*
quincenal *adj* biweekly *adj*
quórum *nm* quorum *n* **con quórum** quorate **quórum de acreedores** quorum of creditors
racionalización *nf* rationalization *n*
racionalizar *vb* rationalize *vb*
RAM *nf* (DP) RAM (random access memory) *abbr*
rama *nf* branch *n*
ramo *nm* branch *n* **ramo profesional** line of business
rango *nm* rank *n* **de alto rango** high-ranking
rápido *adj* prompt *adj*, fast *adj*
ratificación *nf* confirmation *n*, ratification *n*
ratificar *vb* ratify *vb*
ratio *nm* ratio *n* **ratio de facturación, ratio de renovación** turnover ratio
razón *nf* reason *n* **razón social** trade name
razonable *adj* (price) reasonable *adj*
reacción *nf* feedback *n* **reacción negativa** negative feedback
reactivación *nf* (economic) recovery *n*, reflation *n*, upswing *n*
readjudicar *vb* (funds) reallocate *vb*
real *adj* actual *adj*, real *adj*, royal *adj*
realidad *nf* actuality *n*, reality *n*
realizar *vb* accomplish *vb*, carry out *vb* (profit) realize *vb* **realizar ensayos** carry out trials **realizar ganancias excesivas** profiteer
reanudar *vb* (policy, contract) renew *vb*
reasegurar *vb* reinsure *vb*
reaseguro *nm* reinsurance *n*
reasignación *nf* (of funds) reallocation *n*
rebaja *nf* markdown *n*, reduction *n*
rebajado *adj* reduced *adj* **a un precio muy rebajado** at a greatly reduced price
rebajar *vb* (prices) bring down *vb*, mark down *vb*, reduce *vb*, cut *vb*, (employee) demote *vb* **rebajar algo a mitad de precio** reduce sth by half
rebasar *vb* overdraw *vb* **rebasar una cuenta** overdraw on an account
recadista *nmf* messenger *n*
recalentamiento *nm* (of economy) overheating *n*
recargar *vb* mark up *vb*, overcharge *vb*
recargo *nm* additional charge *n*, markup *n*, premium *n* **recargo del impuesto sobre la renta** surtax
recaudación *nf* takings *npl* **recaudación**

neta net(t) proceeds
recaudado *adj* collected *adj*
recaudar *vb* (tax) levy *vb* **recaudar fondos** raise money
recepcionista *nmf* desk clerk *n*, receptionist *n*
receptor, -ora *nm,f* recipient *n* **receptor de la oferta** offeree
recesión *nf* (economic) depression *n*, recession *n*
rechazar *vb* negative (US), (goods) reject *vb*, (contract) repudiate *vb*, (offer) turn down *vb* **rechazar un cheque** bounce* a cheque **rechazar mercancías** refuse goods
rechazo, plante (LAm) *nm* refusal *n*
recibir *vb* receive *vb* **recibir a un cliente** entertain a client
reciclable *adj* (materials) reclaimable *adj* recyclable *adj*
reciclaje *nm* recycling *n* **reciclaje profesional** retraining
reciclar *vb* recycle *vb*
reciente *adj* recent *adj* **recién contratado** newly-appointed
recíproco *adj* reciprocal *adj*
reclamación, reclamo (LAm) *nf, nm* complaint *n* **reclamación de impuestos** tax claim
reclamar *vb* demand *vb*, make a complaint *vb* **reclamar por daños y perjuicios** (legal) claim damages
réclame *nm* (LAm) advertisement *n*
reclamo *nm* (LAm) complaint *n*
reclutar *vb* recruit *vb*
recobrar *vb* repossess *vb*
recogida *nf* collection *n*
recomendación *nf* recommendation *n*, testimonial *n*
recompensa *nf* payment *n*, recompense *n*, compensation *n* **recompensa de directivos** executive compensation
reconocimiento *nm* recognition *n* **reconocimiento de deuda** acknowledgement of debt
recontratación *nf* reappointment *n*
reconversión *nf* rationalization *n*, retraining *n*
reconvertir *vb* restructure *vb*, rationalise *vb*
recordatorio *nm* reminder *n*
recorrido *nm* route *n*, trip *n* **de corto recorrido** short-haul **de largo recorrido** long-distance, long-haul
recortar *vb* (reduce) cut *vb*, (price) knock down *vb*, axe* *vb*, shrink *vb*, ax (US) (spending) squeeze *vb* (investment) trim *vb* **recortar gastos** axe* expenditure
recorte *nm* reduction *n*
recuerdo *nm* (DP) memory *n*
recuperación *nf* repossession *n* **recuperación de datos** information retrieval **recuperación de documentos** document retrieval
recuperar *vb* recover *vb*, recuperate *vb* **recuperar dinero a alguien** recover

money from sb **recuperarse** (improve) pick up

recurrir vb have recourse vb, resort vb **recurrir a** (have recourse) resort to

recurso nm **recursos** ability to pay, means, resources **recursos financieros** financial means/resources **recursos humanos** human resources, manpower **recursos naturales** natural resources

red nf net n, network n **red bancaria** banking network **red de comunicaciones** communication network **red de distribución** distribution network **red de ordenadores, red de computadores** (LAm) computer network

redacción nf wording n, writing-up n

redactar vb write up vb, draft vb **redactar un contrato** draw up a contract **redactar un informe, hacer un reporte** (LAm) draw up a report

redimir vb redeem vb

redistribución nf (of funds) reallocation n

redistribuir vb (funds) reallocate vb

rédito nm earnings yield n

reducción nf abatement n, depletion n, markdown n, reduction n **reducción de costes** cost-cutting, cost trimming **reducción de gastos, reducción de costos** (LAm) cost-cutting **reducción en los impuestos** tax cut

reducir, rematar (LAm) vb (prices) bring down vb, knock down vb, mark down vb, reduce vb **reducir al mínimo** (stocks) run low **reducir al mínimo las pérdidas** minimise losses **reducir a la mitad** halve **reducir la plantilla** (workforce) trim

reelección nf re-election n

reelegir vb re-elect vb

reembolsable adj refundable adj (deposit) returnable adj

reembolsar vb refund vb, reimburse vb, repay vb

reembolso nm rebate n, refund n, reimbursement n (of loan) repayment n **sin reembolso** ex repayment

reemplazar vb replace vb

reexpedir vb (mail) redirect vb

referencia nf reference n **con referencia a** re, with reference to **referencia de crédito** credit reference

referéndum nm referendum n

referir vb refer vb **por lo que se refiere a** regarding

reflación nf reflation n

reflacionario adj reflationary adj

reforma nf reform n **reforma agraria** land reform **reforma arancelaria** tariff reform **reforma monetaria** currency reform

reforzar vb consolidate vb **reforzar la moral** boost morale

refrendar vb countersign vb

regalar vb give vb, (as gift) present vb

regalo nm giveaway n, gift n

regatear vb bargain vb

región nf region n

registrar vb register vb **registrarse** (to hotel) check in vb

registro nm register n, tally n **registro de antecedentes, historial** (LAm) track record **registro catastral** land register **registro de fábricas** factory ledger

reglamento nm regulation n

regulación nf regulation n

rehusar vb refuse vb

reimportación nf reimportation n

reimportar vb reimport vb

reintegrar vb refund vb

reintegro nm refund n **reintegro de fondos, retiro de fondos** (LAm) withdrawal of funds

reinvertir vb (profits) plough back vb, plow back (US), vb

reivindicación, pedido (LAm) nf, nm demand n **reivindicación salarial** wage(s) claim/demand

reivindicar vb demand vb

relación nf list n, ratio n **con relación a** re, with regard to... **relaciones con la clientela** customer relations **relaciones comerciales** business relations **relaciones humanas** human relations **relaciones industriales** industrial relations **relaciones laborales** labour relations **relaciones públicas** customer relations, public relations **con relación a nuestra carta de** we refer to our letter of... **relación de procedencia** statement of origin **relación real de intercambio** terms of trade **relación de trabajo** working relationship

relajar vb (restrictions) relax vb

rellenar vb (form) fill in vb, complete vb

rematar vb (price) knock down vb, bring down vb

remate nm (LAm) auction n

remesa nf consignment n, delivery n, remittance n

remitente nmf consigner/or n, sender n, shipper n

remitir vb send vb **remitir adjunto** enclose **remitir por correo** post

remodelación nf restructuring n, reorganization n **remodelación urbana** urban renewal

remuneración nf remuneration n, salary n

remunerado adj paid adj **bien remunerado** well-paid

remunerar vb remunerate vb

rendimiento nm output n **hay que mejorar nuestro rendimiento** we must improve our performance **rendimiento sobre acciones** yield on shares **rendimiento del capital** return on capital **rendimiento del capital social, plan de recapacitación** (LAm) return on equity **rendimiento económico, performance económico** (LAm) economic performance **rendimiento por hora** per hour output **rendimiento de la inversión** return on capital, return on investment **rendimiento del patrimonio neto, plan de recapacitación** (LAm) return on equity **rendimientos del capital** unearned income **rendimientos decrecientes** diminishing returns **rendimiento de las ventas** return on sales

rendir *vb* yield *vb*

renegociar *vb* renegotiate *vb* **renegociar una deuda** reschedule a debt

renovable *adj* renewable *adj*

renovación *nf* refurbishment *n*, renewal *n*, updating *n*

renovar *vb* refurbish *vb*, (policy, contract) renew *vb*

renta *nf* income *n*, rent *n* **renta anual** yearly income **renta fija** fixed income **renta nacional** national income **renta privada** private income **rentas públicas** revenue

rentabilidad *nf* profitability *n*

rentable *adj* moneymaking *adj*

rentar *vb* (LAm) hire *vb*

renuncia *nf* resignation *n*, waiver *n*

renunciar *vb* abandon *vb*, resign *vb*, waive *vb*

reparar *vb* make amends *vb*, repair *vb*

repartir *vb* allocate *vb* (goods) deliver *vb*

reparto *nm* delivery *n*, distribution *n* **reparto de ganancias** gain sharing **reparto rápido a domicilio** express delivery

repasar *vb* revise *vb*

repatriación *nf* repatriation *n*

repertorio *nm* directory *n*, index *n*

replantear *vb* restructure *vb*

reponer *vb* replace *vb*

reportaje, reporte (LAm) *nm* report *n* **reportaje de las noticias** news coverage **reportaje de prensa** newspaper report

reporte *nm* (LAm) report *n*

representación *nf* representation *n*, delegation *n* **representación falsa** false representation

representante, corredor, -ora (LAm) *nmf, nm,f* agent *n*, representative *n*, salesperson *n* **representante regional** area representative **representante sindical** shop steward, union representative

repudiar *vb* waive *vb*

repunte *nm* (economic) recovery *n* upswing *n*

requerimiento *nm* requirement *n* **requerimiento judicial** injunction

requerir *vb* demand *vb*, require *vb* **que requiere mucha mano de obra** labour-intensive

requisito *nm* requirement *n*, specification *n* **requisitos de la industria** needs of industry

resarcimiento *nm* compensation *n*, repayment *n* **resarcimiento no compensatorio** nominal damages

rescatar *vb* salvage *vb*, recover *vb*

rescate *nm* redemption *n*, rescue *n*

reserva, reservación (LAm) *nf* booking *n*, reservation *n*, supply *n* **con la más**

absoluta reserva in strictest confidence **en reserva** in hand **reserva de divisas** currency reserve **reserva de libras esterlinas** sterling balance **reservas mínimas** fractional reserves **reservas de oro** gold reserves

reservación *nf* reservation *n*

reservar *vb* reserve *vb* **reservar por adelantado** book in advance **reservar una habitación de hotel** book a hotel room **reservar un vuelo** book a flight

residual *adj* residual *adj*

residuos *nmpl* waste *n*

resistir *vb* withstand *vb*

resolución *nf* (decision) resolution n

resolver *vb* (dispute) settle *vb* **resolver hacer algo** resolve to do sth

respaldar *vb* back *vb*, support *vb* **respaldar una empresa** back a venture

respaldo *nm* backing *n*

respectar *vb* be concerned (with) *vb*

respecto *nm* matter *n* **respecto a** regarding, in respect of...

respetar *vb* respect *vb* **respetar las normas** comply with the rules **respetar las reglas** observe the rules

responder *vb* answer *vb*

responsabilidad *nf* accountability *n*, commitment *n*, liability *n* **responsabilidad conjunta/colectiva** joint responsibility **responsabilidad ilimitada** unlimited liability **responsabilidad limitada** limited liability

responsabilizar *vb* make responsible *vb* **responsabilizar a alguien** hold sb liable, hold sb responsible **responsabilizarse de algo** take charge of sth, take responsibility for sth

responsable *adj* accountable *adj*, liable *adj*, reliable *adj*, responsible *adj* **responsable de daños y perjuicios** liable for damages **responsable de la seguridad** safety officer

respuesta *nf* answer *n*, feedback *n* **en respuesta a** in response to . . .

restante *adj* (sum) remaining *adj*

restauración *nf* refurbishment *n*

restricción *nf* restriction *n* **restricciones comerciales** trade restrictions **restricciones de crédito** credit squeeze **restricciones a divisas** exchange restrictions **restricciones a la importación** import restrictions

restrictivo *adj* restrictive *adj*

restringir *vb* restrict *vb* (spending) squeeze *vb*

resultado *nm* balance *n*, consequence *n*, outcome *n* **resultado neto** net(t) result

resultar *vb* (end) turn out *vb* **resultar válido** (withstand scrutiny) hold up

resumen *nm* abstract *n*, summary *n*

resumido *adj* abbreviated *adj*

resumir *vb* abbreviate *vb*, summarise *vb*

retención *nf* retention *n* **retención de título** retention of title

retener vb retain vb, withhold vb **retener algo como garantía** hold sth as security **retener un documento** withhold a document

retirada, retiro (LAm) nf, nm withdrawal n

retirar vb withdraw vb **retirar una oferta** withdraw an offer **retirarse** retire

retiro nm retirement n, withdrawal (LAm) n

retransmisión nf broadcast n

retrasar, demorar (LAm) vb delay vb, hold back vb, hold up vb

reunión nf conference n, meeting n **reunión de la comisión** committee meeting **reunión del comité** committee meeting **reunión del consejo de administración** board meeting **reunión de la junta directiva** board meeting **reunión de negocios** business meeting **reunión de ventas** sales conference, sales talk

reutilizable adj (materials) reclaimable adj

revalorización nf (in value) appreciation n

revalorizar, revaluar (LAm) vb (currency) revalue vb **revalorizarse** gain in value

revaluación nf (of currency) revaluation n

revaluar vb (LAm) revalue vb

reventa nf resale n

revertir vb revert vb **revertir a** revert to vb

revisación nf (LAm) examination n

revisar vb inspect vb, revise vb, examine (LAm) vb

revisión, revisación (LAm) nf examination n (customs) inspection n **revisión de aduana** customs check

revisor, -ora nm,f supervisor n

revista nf journal n, magazine n

revocar vb (offer) revoke vb

riesgo nm hazard n, risk n **de alto riesgo, riesgoso** (LAm) high-risk **de bajo riesgo** gilt-edged **sin riesgo** safe **riesgo del cambio** exchange risk **riesgo natural** natural hazard **riesgo ocupacional** occupational hazard **riesgo de la profesión** occupational hazard **riesgos financieros** financial exposure

riqueza nf wealth n

ritmo nm timing n **ritmo de expansión, tasa de expansión** (LAm) rate of expansion **ritmo de facturación** turnover rate **ritmo de inversiones, tasa de inversión** (LAm) rate of investment **ritmo de reducción de la plantilla** wastage rate

ROM abbr, nf ROM (read only memory) abbr

rompehuelgas, carnero, -ra (LAm) nm, nm,f scab* n, strikebreaker n

romper vb split vb **romper un contrato** break an agreement

rotación nf rotation n, turnover n

rotundo adj total adj

rubro nm (LAm) bill n

rueda nf wheel n **rueda de prensa** press conference

s.r.c. (se ruega contestación), r.s.v.p. (LAm) abbr RSVP (répondez s'il vous plaît) abbr

saber vb know vb **se sabe muy bien** it is

common knowledge **que yo sepa** to my knowledge

sabido adj known adj **bien sabido** well-known **es bien sabido** it is common knowledge

sacar vb (product) bring out vb, introduce vb **sacar algo a licitación** put sth out for tender

sala nf hall n, room n **sala de exposiciones** exhibition hall, showroom **sala de juntas** board room **sala para pasajeros en tránsito** (transport) transit lounge **sala de tránsito** (transport) transfer lounge, transit lounge

salario nm pay n, salary n, wage n **salario de entrada** starting wage **salario justo** fair wage **salario medio** average wage **salario mínimo** minimum wage **salario mínimo indexado** index-linked minimum wage **salario neto** net(t) wage **salario real** real wage

saldar vb liquidate vb (account) settle vb **saldar una cuenta** settle an account **saldar una deuda** pay off a debt

saldo nm balance n **con saldo acreedor** in credit **saldo bancario** bank balance **saldo de cuenta bancaria** bank balance **saldo disponible** balance in hand **saldo final** final balance **saldo deudor/negativo** debit balance, unpaid balance

salida nf departure n, exit n **salida a bolsa** flotation **salida de mercado** market outlet

salir vb (end) turn out vb **salir a la venta** go on sale **salir del trabajo** (finish work) knock off*

salón nm lounge n **salón de exposición** showroom

salud nf health n **salud industrial** industrial health

salvar vb salvage vb, save vb

sanción nf sanction n **sanción económica** economic sanction **sanciones económicas** trade sanctions

sanear vb (company) turn round vb, turn around (US)

sanidad nf health n

satisfacción nf satisfaction n **satisfacción del consumidor** consumer satisfaction **satisfacción laboral** job satisfaction **satisfacción por el trabajo** job satisfaction

sección nf department n, (of company) division n

secretaría nf (LAm) ministry n, Government Department n

secretario, -ria nm,f minister n, secretary n **secretario de la compañía** company secretary **secretario ejecutivo** executive secretary

secreto nm secret n **secreto comercial** trade secret

sector nm sector n **sector primario** primary sector **sector privado** private enterprise/ sector **sector público** government/public sector **sector secundario** secondary industry/sector **sector de los servicios** tertiary industry **sector terciario** tertiary industry/sector

secundario *adj* minor *adj*

sede *nf* headquarters *npl*, HO (head office) *n*, registered office *n* **le referimos a nuestra sede** we refer you to our head office **sede central** head office **sede social** main office

seguir *vb* follow *vb*, continue *vb* **seguir instrucciones** follow instructions

según *prep* in accordance with **según lo establecido en el contrato** under the terms of the contract **según el ministro** according to the minister **según las normas** according to the regulations **según nuestros registros** according to our records **según lo planeado** according to plan **según sus requisitos** in accordance with your requirements

seguridad *nf* security *n* **Seguridad Social** National Health Service (GB), National Insurance (GB), Social Security (GB)

seguro 1. *adj* safe *adj*, secure *adj* **2.** *nm* insurance *n* **seguros** insurance **seguro de automóviles** car insurance **seguro de casco de buque** hull insurance **seguro colectivo** group insurance **seguro de combinación aplazada y decreciente** endowment insurance **seguro contra incendios** fire insurance **seguro contra terceros** third-party insurance **seguro de crédito a la exportación** export credit insurance **seguro de desempleo** unemployment insurance **seguro empresarial contra terceros** employer's liability insurance **seguro de enfermedad** health insurance **seguro de equipaje** luggage insurance **seguro de fidelidad** fidelity insurance **seguro de indemnización** indemnity insurance **seguro marítimo** hull/marine insurance **seguro médico** medical insurance **seguro de responsabilidad** civil third-party insurance **seguro a todo riesgo** all-risks/comprehensive insurance **seguro de viaje** travel insurance **seguro de vida** life assurance/insurance

selección *nf* choice *n*, selection *n* **selección aleatoria** random selection

sellar *vb* seal *vb*

sello *nm* seal *n*

semana *nf* week *n* **semana laboral** working week, workweek (US) **semana de trabajo** working week, workweek (US)

semestral *adj* biannual *adj*

semestre *nm* half-year *n*, semester *n*

semicualificado *adj* semi-skilled *adj*

seña *nf* (LAm) deposit *n*

señal *nf* brand *n*, index *n*, indication *n* **señal de alerta** warning sign **señal de comunicando, tono de ocupado; señal de ocupado** (LAm) engaged signal, busy signal (US)

señalar *vb* indicate *vb*, point *vb*

sensato *adj* well-advised *adj*, sensible *adj*

sentido *nm* direction *n*, way *n* **de doble sentido, de doble mano; de doble vía** (LAm) two-way

sentir *vb* experience *vb*, feel *vb*

ser *vb* be *vb* **ser declarado en quiebra** go to the wall **ser dueño de** own **ser gravemente afectado por** be hard hit by **ser noticia** hit the headlines **ser rechazado** (cheque) bounce* **ser responsable** be in charge **ser testigo de** witness

serio *adj* bona fide *adj*, businesslike *adj*, responsible *adj*, weighty *adj*

servicio *nm* commission *n*, facility *n*, service *n* **servicio de asistencia en carretera** breakdown service **servicio a domicilio** home service **servicio de enlace** shuttle **servicio incluido** service included **servicio post-venta** after-sales service **servicio público** public service **servicios** amenities **servicios postales** postal services **servicio urgente** express service **servicio de veinticuatro horas** twenty-four-hour service

sesión *nf* session *n* **sesión informativa** briefing **sesión de negociaciones** negotiating session **sesión a puerta cerrada** closed session/meeting

signatario, -ria *nm,f* signatory *n*

silicio *nm* silicon *n* **pastilla de silicio** microchip

simulador,- ora *nm,f* malingerer *n*

sindicalizar *vb* (LAm) unionize *vb*

sindicato, gremio (LAm) *nm* syndicate, trade union, union **sindicato industrial** industrial union **sindicato laboral** trade union, labor union (US)

síndico, -ica *nm,f* (bankruptcy) receiver *n*, administrator (US)

sinergia *nf* synergy *n*

síntesis *nf* synthesis *n*

sintético *adj* man-made *adj*, synthetic *adj*

sintonizar *vb* tune *vb* **sintonizar con** be on the same wavelength as

sistema *nm* organization *n*, system *n* **sistema de archivo** filing system **sistema de cuotas** quota system **sistema de dos niveles** two-tier system **sistema experto** expert system **Sistema Monetario Europeo (SME)** European Monetary System (EMS) **sistemas de información** information system **sel sistema de tres turnos** the three-shift system **sistema tributario a tasa cero** zero-rate taxation

sistematización *nf* systematization *n*

sistematizar *vb* rationalize *vb*

situación, ubicación (LAm) *nf* location *n*, position *n*, status *n* **situación económica** financial status **situación financiera** financial situation

sobornar, coimear; morder (LAm) *vb* bribe *vb*

soborno, coima; mordida (LAm) *nm, nm; nf* backhander* *n*, bribe *n*, bribery *n*, payola (US) (bribe) sweetener* *n*
sobrante *adj* residual *adj*
sobre 1. *nm* envelope *n* **2.** *prep* on *prep*, about *prep*
sobrecargar *vb* overload *vb*
sobregirar *vb* **sobregirarse** overdraw *vb*
sobregiro *nm* bank overdraft *n*
sobrepasar *vb* exceed *vb*
sobrepoblación *nf* (LAm) overpopulation *n*
sobreproducción *nf* overproduction *n*
sobrepujar *vb* outbid *vb*
sobrestimar *vb* overvalue *vb*
sobrevalorar *vb* overvalue *vb*
sobrevendido *adj* oversold *adj*, oversubscribed *adj*
sociedad *nf* company *n*, society *n* **sociedad de ahorro y préstamo para la vivienda** building society **sociedad anónima** corporation, joint-stock company **sociedad anónima cuyas acciones se cotizan en bolsa** public limited company **sociedad anónima privada** private limited company **sociedad de ayuda mutua** Friendly Society **sociedad colectiva** partnership **sociedad comercial** trading company **sociedad de consumo** affluent/consumer society **sociedad cotizada en bolsa** public company **sociedad de crédito hipotecario** building society **sociedad cuyas acciones se cotizan en Bolsa** quoted company **sociedad filial** affiliated company **sociedad financiera** credit/finance company **sociedad inmobiliaria** property company **sociedad de inversión** investment trust **sociedad legalmente constituida** registered company **sociedad de primer orden** blue-chip company **sociedad próspera** affluent society **sociedad de responsabilidad limitada** limited company **sociedad tenedora** holding company **sociedad 'holding'** holding company
socio, -cia *nm,f* associate *n*, business associate *n*, member *n*, partner *n*, trading partner *n* **socio en comandita** sleeping partner **socio comanditario** sleeping partner, silent partner **socio general** general partner
solicitante *nmf* claimant *n*, applicant *n*
solicitar, aplicar por (LAm) *vb* apply for *vb* **solicitar un descubierto** request an overdraft **solicitar un mandamiento judicial** take out an injunction
solicitud, pedido (LAm) *nf, nm* request *n*, takeup *n* **solicitud de pago, pedido de pago** (LAm) request for payment
solvencia *nf* ability to pay *n*, creditworthiness *n*, solvency *n*
solventar *vb* pay *vb*, settle *vb* **solventar una reclamación** settle/adjust a claim
solvente *adj* creditworthy *adj*, solvent *adj*
someter *vb* subject *vb*, submit *vb* **someter**

algo a prueba put sth to the test **someter a prueba de mercado** test-market
sondeo *nm* survey *n* **sondeo económico** economic survey **sondeo de opinión consumista** consumer survey
sopesar *vb* weigh the pros and cons *vb*
soportar *vb* withstand *vb*
soporte *nm* support *n*, computerware *n* **soporte físico del ordenador** computer hardware
sospechoso *adj* (dealings) shady* *adj*
standing *nm* standing *n* **de alto standing** high-class, top-level
status *nm* status *n* **statu quo** status quo
suavizar *vb* water down *vb*, soften *vb*
suba *nf* (LAm) rise *n*
subalterno, -rna *nm,f* subordinate *n*
subasta, remate (LAm) *nf, nm* auction *n*
subastador, -ora, rematador, -ora (LAm) *nm,f* auctioneer *n*
subastar, rematar (LAm) *vb* auction *vb* **subastar algo** sell sth at auction
subcontratar *vb* farm out *vb*, subcontract *vb*
subcontratista *nmf* subcontractor *n*
subdirector, -ora *nm,f* assistant manager *n*, deputy director *n*
subempleado *adj* underemployed *adj*
subida, suba (LAm) *nf* rise *n* **subida de precio** price increase
subir *vb* (rise in value) appreciate *vb* (prices) bump up *vb*, increase *vb*, raise *vb*, rise *vb* **subir a bordo** go aboard **subir tarifas** raise tariffs
subproducto *nm* by-product *n*
subsidiar *vb* (LAm) subsidize *vb*
subsidio *nm* benefit *n*, subsidy *n* **subsidio de enfermedad** sickness benefit **subsidio estatal** government subsidy **subsidio familiar, asignación familiar** (LAm) family allowance **subsidio del gobierno**, **subsidio del estado** (LAm) state subsidy **subsidio de paro, subsidio de cesantía** (LAm) unemployment benefit, unemployment pay **subsidios agrícolas** farming subsidies **subsidios sociales** welfare benefits
subvención *nf* subsidy *n* **subvenciones para exportaciones** export subsidies **subvención regional** regional grant
subvencionar, subsidiar (LAm) *vb* subsidize *vb*
sucesión *nf* inheritance *n*
sucursal *nf* branch *n*, branch office *n*, subsidiary *n*, subsidiary company *n* **sucursal de una cadena de grandes almacenes** multiple store
sueldo *nm* pay *n*, salary *n*, wage *n* **sueldo neto** net(t) wage, wage packet, salary package (US) **sueldo semanal** weekly wages
suerte *nf* luck *n* **suerte imprevista** windfall *n*
sufrir *vb* suffer *vb* **sufrir un bajón** slump *vb*
sujetar *vb* (prices) peg *vb*

sujeto *adj* liable *adj*, subject *adj* **sujeto a impuestos** liable for tax
suma *nf* amount *n* **suma bruta** gross amount **suma global** net(t) amount, the grand total **suma simbólica** nominal amount
suministrador, -ora *nm,f* supplier *n*
   suministrador, -ora clave main supplier
suministrar *vb* (supply) provide *vb*
   suministrar algo bajo palabra supply sth on trust
suministro *nm* supply *n*
superable *adj* negotiable *adj*
superar *vb* exceed *vb* **superarse** improve
superávit *nm* surplus *n* **superávit de la balanza de pagos** balance of payments surplus **superávit comercial** trade surplus **superávit de exportación** export surplus **superávit de fondos** funds surplus **superávit percibido** earned surplus **superávit presupuestario** budget surplus
superfluo *adj* redundant *adj*, superfluous *adj*
superior *adj* senior *adj*, higher *adj*, superior *adj*
supermercado *nm* supermarket *n*
superpetrolero *nm* supertanker *n*
superpoblación, sobrepoblación (LAm) *nf* overpopulation *n*
superpotencia *nf* superpower *n*
   superpotencia económica economic superpower
superventas *nm* best seller *n*
supervisión *nf* oversight *n*
supervisor, -ora *nm,f* supervisor *n*
suplementario *adj* extra *adj*, supplementary *adj*
suplemento *nm* additional charge *n*
   suplemento salarial weighting
suplente *nmf* deputy *n* (person) replacement *n*
supresión *nf* abatement *n*, abolition *n*
   supresión de aranceles elimination of tariffs
suprimir *vb* abate *vb*, abolish *vb*, axe* *vb*, ax (US)
suscribir *vb* subscribe *vb* **suscribir un tratado** make a treaty
suscriptor, -ora *nm,f* insurance underwriter *n*, underwriter *n*
suspender *vb* adjourn *vb* **suspender una cita** cancel an appointment
suspensión *nf* adjournment *n*
sustituto, -uta *nm,f* (person) replacement *n*
tablero *nm* (notice) board *n*
tablón *nm* (notice) board *n* **tablón de anuncios** bulletin board
tabular *vb* (data) tabulate *vb*
tácito *adj* tacit *adj*
táctica *nf* tactic *n* **táctica de demora** delaying tactics **táctica de ventas** selling tactics
talla, talle (LAm) *nf, nm* size *n*
taller *nm* shopfloor *n*, workshop *n*
talón *nm* (LAm) counterfoil *n*

talonario *nm* cheque book *n*, receipt book *n* **talonario de cheques** cheque book, checkbook (US)
tamaño *nm* size *n*
tanto *nm* (given) amount *n* **tanto por ciento de los beneficios** percentage of profit
tapar *vb* (LAm) block *vb*
taquilla, boletería (LAm) *nf* box office *n*, ticket office *n*
tara *nf* defect *n*
tardanza, demora (LAm) *nf* delay *n* **sin tardanza, sin demora** (LAm) without delay
tardar *vb* delay *vb*, take one's time *vb*
tarifa *nf* scale *n*, tariff *n* **tarifa horaria** hourly rate **tarifas, tasas** (LAm) (tax) rates
tarjeta *nf* card *n* **tarjeta bancaria** bank card **tarjeta de cajero automático** cashpoint card **tarjeta de crédito** bank card, charge card, credit card **tarjeta de garantía de cheques** cheque card **tarjeta inteligente** smart card **tarjeta profesional** business card **tarjeta de visita** business card
tasa *nf* toll *n*, tax *n*, rate *n*, valuation *n* **tasa de abandono** wastage rate **tasa de acumulación** rate of accrual **tasa base** base rate, base lending rate, basic rate **tasa de beneficios decreciente** falling rate of profit **tasa de cambio flexible** flexible exchange rate **tasa de crecimiento** growth rate **tasa de crecimiento anual** annual growth rate **tasa de inflación** rate of inflation **tasa de interés** bank rate, interest rate **tasa de interés fija** flat rate **tasa de licencia** licence fee **tasa Lombard** Lombard Rate **tasa natural de incremento** natural rate of increase **tasa normal** basic rate **tasa de paro, tasa de cesantía** (LAm) rate of unemployment **tasa de rendimiento** rate of return **tasa de rendimiento justa** fair rate of return **tasa de rentabilidad** rate of return **tasa variable** variable rate
tasación, avalúo (LAm) *nf, nm* appraisal *n*, valuation *n*
tasar *vb* ration *vb*, value *vb*
teclado *nm* keyboard *n*
teclear *vb* key in *vb*
técnica *nf* skill *n* **técnica de ventas** sales technique
técnico, -ica *nm,f* technician *n*
tecnología *nf* technology *n* **de alta tecnología** hi-tech **tecnología avanzada** advanced technology **tecnología de datos** information technology
telebanca *nf* telebanking *n*
telecomunicaciones *nfpl* telecommunications *n*
telecopiadora *nf* telecopier *n*
telefax *nm* facsimile (fax) *n*, telefax *n*
telefonista *nmf* operator *n*, switchboard operator *n*
teléfono *nm* telephone *n*, telephone number *n* **teléfono interno** house telephone **teléfono visual** visual telephone

teleproceso *nm* teleprocessing *n*
telespectador, -ora *nm,f* viewer *n*
teletipo *nm* telecopier *n*
televentas *nfpl* telesales *npl*
televisar *vb* televise *vb*
télex *nm* telex *n*
temporada *nf* season *n* **temporada alta** high season **temporada baja** low season **temporada media** mid season
temporal, temporario; provisorio (LAm) *adj* temporary *adj*
temporario *adj* (LAm) temporary *adj*
tendencia *nf* tendency *n*, trend *n* **tendencia económica** economic trend **tendencia del mercado** market trend **tendencia de precios** price trend **tendencias del consumidor** consumer trends **tendencias de consumo** consumer trends **tendencias económicas** economic trends **tendencias del mercado** market forces, market tendencies
tender *vb* tend *vb*, have the tendency *vb* **tender a** tend toward *vb*
tenedor, -ora *nm,f* holder *n* **tenedor de acciones** shareholder, stockholder **tenedor de libros** book-keeper **tenedor de obligaciones** bondholder
teneduría *nf* (book/account) keeping *n*
tenencia *nf* occupation *n*, tenure *n*
tener *vb* have *vb*, own *vb*, possess *vb* **tener buena reputación** enjoy a good reputation **tener coherencia** (argument) hang together **tener algo en cuenta** take sth into account **tener en existencia** (stock) carry **tener mano de obra excesiva** overman **tener un presupuesto muy limitado** be on a tight budget **tener propiedades** have holdings **tener algo en reserva** hold sth in reserve **tener un saldo positivo** be in the black **tener tendencia a** tend toward **tener trabajo** be in work **¿tendría la amabilidad de...?** would you be so kind as to...?
teoría *nf* theory *n* **en teoría** in theory **teoría cuantitativa del dinero** quantity theory of money
tercero 1. *adj* third *adj* 2. *nm* third person *n*, third party *n*
terminal 1. *adj* terminal *adj* 2. *n* **terminal aérea** air terminal *nf* **terminal del ordenador, terminal de la computadora** (LAm) *nm* computer terminal
terminar *vb* break up *vb*, complete *vb*, wind up *vb* **terminar una reunión** close a meeting
término *nm* term *n*, time limit *n* **bajo los términos del contrato** under the terms of the contract **a término** at term **términos y condiciones** terms and conditions **términos estrictamente netos** terms strictly net(t) **términos ventajosos** favourable terms
terrateniente *nmf* landowner *n*
terreno *nm* plot *n*, ground *n* **terreno**

edificable building site
territorio *nm* territory *n* **territorio de ultramar** overseas territory
tesoro *nm* treasure *n*, Treasury *n* **el Tesoro público** the Treasury
testamento *nm* will *n*
testigo *nm* witness *n*
testimonio *nm* evidence *n*, attestation *n*, witness *n*
texto *nm* text *n*, wording *n*
tiempo *nm* time *n* **a tiempo completo** full-time **a tiempo parcial** part-time **tiempo real** real time
tienda *nf* shop *n*, store *n* **tienda bajo licencia** franchise outlet **tienda de una cadena** chain store **tienda al por menor** retail outlet
tierra *nf* land *n* **por tierra** by road
timador, -ora *nm,f* swindler* *n*
tipificar *vb* standardize *vb*
tipo *m* type *n*, brand *n*, kind *n*, rate *n* **buen tipo de interés, alta tasa de interés** (LAm) fine rate of interest **tipo bancario, tasa de interés** (LAm) bank rate **tipo base** base lending rate, base rate **tipo de cambio** exchange rate **tipo de cambio flexible** flexible exchange rate **tipo de cambio flotante** floating exchange rate **tipo de compra** buying rate **tipo de descuento** discount rate **tipo impositivo** tax rate **tipo de interés** bank rate, interest rate **tipo de interés mínimo establecido por el banco central** minimum lending rate **tipo de paridad, tasa de cambio** (LAm) rate of exchange **tipo preferencial de interés bancario** prime lending rate **tipo variable** variable rate
tiquete *nm* (LAm) ticket *n*
titular *nmf* bearer *n*, holder *n*, occupant *n* **titular del cargo** office holder **titular de una licencia** licence holder, licensee **titular de una póliza de seguros** policy holder
título *nm* (law) deed *n*, bond *n*, heading *n*, qualification *n*, (to goods) title *n* **título académico** academic qualification **título de acción** share certificate, stock certificate (US) **título docente** educational qualification **título del Estado** government bond/security **título nominativo** registered bond **título de obligaciones** bond certificate **título al portador** bearer bond **título provisional** scrip **títulos adecuados** necessary qualifications **títulos de la deuda pública** gilts **títulos del Estado** gilt-edged securities
tocar *vb* affect *vb*, touch *vb* **tocar fondo** bottom out
toma *nf* collecting *n*, taking *n*
tomar *vb* borrow *vb* **tomar apuntes, sacar apuntes** (LAm) take notes **tomar la delantera** take the lead **tomar la determinación** make a resolution **tomar la jubilación anticipada** take early retirement **tomar el mando** take the lead **tomar**

muestras sample **tomar nota de algo** make a note of sth **tomar notas** take notes **tomarse un descanso** take a break **tomarse permiso, estar de licencia** (LAm) take leave **tomarse tiempo** take one's time

tonadilla nf jingle n **tonadilla de un anuncio** advertising jingle

tonelada nf ton n **tonelada métrica** metric ton

tonelaje nm tonnage n **tonelaje bruto** gross tonnage **tonelaje neto** net(t) tonnage

tono nm tone n **tono de marcar, tono de discado** (LAm) (phone) dialling tone, dial tone (US)

tope nm (on prices) ceiling n

total 1. adj absolute adj, total adj **2.** nm total n **total global** the grand total

totalidad nf total n

totalmente adv wholly adv

trabajador, -ora 1. adj hard-working adj **muy trabajador** hard-working **2.** nm,f labourer n **trabajador autónomo** freelance, freelancer **trabajador no cualificado, obrero no calificado; peón** (LAm) unskilled worker **trabajadores por horas** hourly workers **trabajador eventual** casual worker, jobber **trabajador extranjero** migrant worker **trabajador extranjero temporal** guest worker **trabajador itinerante** migrant worker **trabajador manual, peón** (LAm) manual worker **trabajador en paro** (LAm) striker

trabajar vb work vb **que trabaja por cuenta propia** self-employed **trabajar fuera de horas normales** work unsocial hours **trabajar a jornada reducida** be on short time **trabajar a máquina** machine **trabajar a pleno rendimiento** work to full capacity

trabajo nm employment n, labour, labor (US) n, workplace n **sin trabajo, cesante** (LAm) jobless, unemployed **trabajo asignado** workload **trabajo de campo** field investigation/research **trabajo a contrata** contract work **trabajo defectuoso** faulty workmanship **trabajo a destajo** piecework **trabajo eventual** casual work **con trabajo excesivo** overworked **trabajo hecho deprisa** rush job **trabajo manual** factory work **trabajo de oficina** clerical work, office work **trabajo pagado por horas** hourly-paid work **trabajo por teléfono** teleworking **trabajo por turnos** job rotation, shift work

trabajoadicto, -cta nm,f workaholic n

tráfico nm traffic n **tráfico aéreo** air traffic **tráfico de armas** arms trade **tráfico por carretera** road traffic **tráfico por ferrocarril** rail traffic **tráfico marítimo** sea traffic **tráfico de mercancías, tráfico de mercaderías** (LAm) freight traffic

traje nm suit n **traje de oficina, vestido; terno** (LAm) business suit

tramitar vb process vb **tramitar el**

despacho de aduanas de algo clear sth through customs **tramitar el pago de un cheque** clear a cheque

trámite nm business transaction n **trámites aduaneros** customs formalities **trámites burocráticos** paperwork, red tape **trámites legales** legal procedures

transacción nf (business) transaction n **transacción de futuros** forward transaction

transbordar vb transship vb

transcribir vb transcribe vb

transferencia nf transfer n **transferencia bancaria** bank transfer **transferencia de capital** capital transfer **transferencia de divisas** currency transfer **transferencia electrónica de fondos** EFT (electronic funds transfer) **transferencia de fondos** credit transfer **transferencia de moneda** currency transfer **transferencia de tecnología** technology transfer

transferible adj transferable adj

transferir vb carry forward vb, hand over vb **transferir tecnología** transfer technology

transigir, transar (LAm) vb reach a compromise vb

tránsito nm transit n, traffic n **en tránsito** in transit

transmisión nf assignment n, broadcast n

transmitir vb broadcast vb, televise vb, transmit vb **transmitir en cadena** network vb

transnacional adj transnational adj

transporte nm forwarding n, freight n, transportation n **transporte aéreo** air freight/transport **transporte por carretera** haulage, road haulage/transport, freight (US) **transporte por ferrocarril** rail transport **transporte de géneros, transporte de mercaderías** (LAm) goods transport **transporte público** public transport

transportista nmf carrier n, haulier n

trasladar vb relocate vb, (transport) transfer vb, move vb

traslado nm relocation n **traslado temporal** secondment

traspasar vb (ownership) transfer vb

tratado nm treaty n **tratado comercial** commercial treaty **El Tratado de Roma** the Treaty of Rome

tratamiento nm treatment n

tratar vb address vb **tratar con cuidado** handle with care **tratar al personal** (staff) handle **tratar de resolver** (agreement, policy) thrash out

trato nm treatment n, deal n **¡trato hecho!** it's a bargain/deal **trato con información privilegiada** insider dealing, insider trading (US)

tren nm train n **en tren** by rail **tren de mercancías** goods train, freight train (US) **tren de pasajeros** passenger train

tribunal nm tribunal n **ante el tribunal** in court **tribunal agrario** land tribunal

Tribunal de Apelación Court of Appeal,
Court of Appeals (US) **Tribunal Europeo de
Justicia** European Court of Justice (ECJ)
tribunal industrial industrial tribunal
Tribunal Internacional de Justicia World
Court **tribunal penal** criminal court
tributo *nm* tax *n*, testimonial *n*
trimestral *adj* quarterly *adj*
trimestre *nm* (of year) quarter *n*
triplicado *adv* triplicate *adv* **por triplicado**
in triplicate
triquiñuelas *nf* sharp practice *n*
trituradora *nf* shredder *n*
trocar *vb* barter *vb*
trueque *nm* barter *n*
turismo *nm* tourism *n*, the tourist trade *n*
turista *nmf* tourist *n*
turno *nm* shift *n*
ubicación *nf* location *n*
UEO (Unión de la Europa Occidental) (La)
abbr,nf WEU (Western European Union)
abbr
último *adj* last *adj* **última notificación** final
notice **última oferta** final offer
umbral *nm* threshold *n*
unánime *adj* unanimous *adj*
unidad *nf* unit *n* **unidad central,
computadora central** (LAm) mainframe
computer **Unidad de Cuenta Europea
(UCE)** European Unit of Account (EUA)
unidad de despliegue visual visual
display unit (VDU) **unidad de disco** disk
drive **unidad familiar** household **unidad
media** average unit **unidad principal,
computadora central** (LAm) (DP)
mainframe **unidad de proceso central
(UPC)** (DP) central processing unit (CPU)
unidad de producción unit of production
unido *adj* united *adj*
unificación *nf* unification *n*
unilateral *adj* (contract) unilateral *adj*
unión *nf* union *n* **unión aduanera** customs
union **unión económica** economic union
Unión Económica y Monetaria Economic
and Monetary Union **Unión Europea**
European Union **Unión Monetaria
Europea (UME)** European Monetary Union
(EMU)
urbanismo *nm* town planning *n*
urbanización, colonia (LAm) *nf* housing
complex *n*, housing estate *n*, housing
tenement (US) *n*
urgencia *nf* urgency *n*
urgente *adj* urgent *adj*
urgentemente *adv* urgently *adv*
usar *vb* use *vb*, utilize *vb* **usar algo** make use
of sth **de usar y tirar** non-returnable,
disposable
uso *nm* (of machine) operation *n* **para uso
industrial** heavy-duty **uso intensivo**
intensive usage
usuario, -ria *nm,f* user *n* **usuario final** end
consumer, end user **usuario frecuente**
heavy user

usura *nf* usury *n*
usurero, -era *nm,f* shark* *n*
utensilios *nmpl* utensils *npl*, tools *npl*
utensilios domésticos housewares (US)
útiles *nmpl* equipment *n*
utilidad *nf* utility *n* **utilidades** (LAm) profit,
earnings, benefit **utilidad final** final utility
utilidad marginal marginal utility
utilización *nf* utilization *n* **con alta
utilización de mano de obra** labour-
intensive
utilizar *vb* employ *vb*, utilize *vb*, use *vb*
vacación *nf* **de vacaciones, tomando la
licencia** (LAm) on holiday, on leave, on
vacation (US) **vacaciones organizadas**
package tour **vacaciones pagadas** paid
holiday
vacante 1. *adj* vacant *adj* **2.** *nf* vacancy *n*
vaciamiento *nm* asset stripping *n*
vacío 1. *adj* empty *adj* **2.** *nm* gap *n*, void *n*
vacío inflacionario inflationary gap **vacío
poblacional** population gap
vago *adj* idle *adj*
vago, -aga, fiacún, -una; flojonazo, -aza
(LAm) *nm,f* shirker* *n*
vale *nm* coupon *n*, voucher *n*
valer *vb* be worth *vb*
validez *nf* validity *n*
valioso *adj* valuable *adj*
valor *nm* security *n*, share *n*, value *n* **sin
valor comercial** no commercial value
valores no admitidos a cotización
unlisted securities **valores bursátiles** listed
securities **valores emitidos sin aumento
de capital** watered stock **valores del
Estado** gilt-edged securities **valores
inmobiliarios** stocks and shares **valores
seguros** blue-chip securities **valor
extraordinario** extraordinary value **valor
justo de mercado** fair market value **valor
en libros** book value **valor de liquidación**
liquidation value **valor de mercado** market
value **valor nominal** face value, nominal
price, nominal value **valor de primer
orden** gilt-edged security **valor real** real
value **valor de renta variable** equity share
valoración *nf* appraisal *n*, assessment *n*,
estimate *n*, valuation *n* **valoración de
riesgos** risk assessment
valorar *vb* estimate *vb*
varianza *nf* variance *n*
vehículo *nm* vehicle *n* **vehículo comercial**
commercial vehicle **vehículo de gran
tonelaje** heavy goods vehicle
velocidad *nf* speed *n* **de velocidad doble**
two-speed
vencer *vb* expire *vb*, fall due *vb* (business,
economy) mature *vb*
vencido *adj* overdue *adj*, out of date (LAm)
adj
vencimiento *nm* expiration *n*, expiry *n*
vendedor, -ora *nm,f* salesperson *n*, seller *n*,
shop assistant *n*, vendor *n*, trader *n*, joint
vendor *n* **vendedor de periódicos y**

revistas newsdealer (US) **vendedor de seguros** insurance salesperson

vender *vb* market *vb*, sell *vb* **este artículo se vende bien** this article sells well **sin vender** unsold **vender barato** sell off **vender más barato** undercut, undersell **vender en la calle** peddle **vender algo a crédito** sell sth on credit **vender en exceso** oversell **vender algo a granel** sell sth in bulk **vender un inmueble a un mejor postor rompiendo un compromiso** gazump **vender algo al por mayor** sell sth wholesale **vender algo al por menor** sell sth retail **vender un negocio con todas sus existencias** sell up

vendido *adj* sold *adj* **vendido en exceso** oversold

venta *nf* sale *n* **esto nos va a afectar las ventas, esto tendrá implicancias para nuestras ventas** (LAm) this will have implications for our sales **en venta** for sale **venta agresiva** hard sell **venta blanda/ suave** soft sell **venta por concurso** sale by tender **venta al contado** cash sale, cash transaction **venta por correo** mail order **venta domiciliaria** door-to-door selling **venta en efectivo** cash sale **venta ficticia** fictitious sale **venta inmobiliaria** house sale **venta piramidal** pyramid selling **ventas brutas** gross sales **ventas al exterior** export sales **ventas en el mercado interior** home sales **ventas netas** net(t) sales **ventas totales** total sales

ventaja *nf* advantage *n* **ventaja comparativa** comparative advantage **ventaja sobre la competencia** competitive edge **ventaja competitiva** competitive advantage

ventajoso *adj* advantageous *adj*

ver *vb* see *vb* **verse obligado a hacer algo** be obliged to do sth

verdadero *adj* true *adj*, actual *adj*

verde *nm* (LAm) dollar *n*, buck* (US) *n*

verificar, checar; chequear (LAm) *vb* check *vb*

vetar *vb* veto *vb*

veto *nm* veto *n*

vez *nf* time *n* **dos veces a la semana** twice a week

viabilidad *nf* feasibility *n*, viability *n*

viable *adj* feasible *adj*, workable *adj*

viajante *nmf* traveller *n* **viajante comercial** commercial traveller, representative, traveler (US) **viajante de comercio, corredor, -ora** (LAm) commercial traveller, commercial traveler (US)

viajar *vb* travel *vb* **viajar por avión** air travel **viajar al exterior** foreign travel **viajar en grupo** group travel

viaje *nm* journey *n*, trip *n* **viaje de ida y vuelta, viaje redondo** (LAm) round trip

viaje de negocios business trip **viajes al extranjero** foreign travel

viajero, -era *nm,f* passenger *n*, traveller *n*, traveler (US)

vida *nf* life *n* **vida activa** working life **vida laboral** working life

vigente *adj* valid *adj*

vigilancia *nf* vigilance *n* **bajo vigilancia** under observation

vinculante *adj* binding *adj*, legally binding *adj*

violación *nf* violation *n*

VIP *abbr, nmf* VIP (very important person) *n*

visado, visa (LAm) *nm, nf* visa *n* **visado de entrada** entry visa

visión *nf* vision *n* **visión para los negocios** business acumen

visita *nf* visit *n*, visitor *n*

visitar *vb* visit *vb*

visual *adj* visual *adj*

vocero, -era *nm,f* (LAm) spokesperson *n*

voltear *vb* (LAm) turn over *vb*

volumen *nm* bulk *n*, volume *n* **volumen de capital facturado** capital turnover **volumen comercial** trading volume **volumen de negocios** trading volume **volumen de ventas** sales figures, turnover **volumen de ventas acabado** finished turnover

voluntad *nf* will *n*

voluntario *adj* voluntary *adj*

volver *vb* return *vb* **volver a contratar** reappoint **volver a llamar, devolver el llamado** (LAm) (on phone) call back **volver a nombrar** reappoint

votación *nf* vote *n* **votación para decidir si se hace huelga, votación para decidir si se va al paro** (LAm) strike ballot

votar *vb* vote *vb*

voto *nm* vote *n* **voto de censura** vote of no confidence **voto de gracias** vote of thanks

vuelo *nm* (in plane) flight *n* **vuelo chárter** charter flight

vuelta, vuelto; vueltas (LAm) *nf, nm; nfpl* (from purchase) change *n* **dar vueltas** (LAm) turn over

xerografiar *vb* xerox *vb*

yacimiento *nm* deposit *n*, layer *n* **yacimiento petrolífero** oilfield

yen *nm* (currency) yen *n*

zona *nf* zone *n* **zona de comercio** trading area **zona de desarrollo** enterprise zone **zona de exclusión** exclusion zone **zona franca** franco zone, free trade area **zona industrial** industrial region, trading estate **zona de la libra esterlina** sterling area **zona de libre empresa** enterprise zone **zona monetaria** currency zone **zona salarial** wage zone

zonificación *nf* zoning *n* **zonificación fiscal** fiscal zoning

zonificar *vb* zone *vb*

English–Spanish

abandon *vb* abandonar *vb*, renunciar *vb*, dejar *vb*

abandoned *adj* **abandoned goods** *npl* mercancías abandonadas *nfpl*

abate *vb* disminuir *vb*, reducir *vb*, suprimir *vb*

abatement *n* disminución *nf*, reducción *nf*, supresión *nf*

abbreviate *vb* abreviar *vb*, resumir *vb*

abbreviated *adj* abreviado *adj*, resumido *adj*

abbreviation *n* abreviatura *nf*, abreviación *nf*

abeyance *n* **to fall into abeyance** *vb* caer en desuso *vb*

abide by *vb* atenerse (a) *vb*

ability *n* capacidad *nf*, aptitud *nf*, habilidad *nf* **ability to pay** solvencia *nf*, recursos *nmpl*, medios *nmpl*

able *adj* capaz *adj*

aboard *adv* a bordo *prep/adv* **to go aboard** subir a bordo *vb*, embarcarse *vb*

abolish *vb* abolir *vb*, suprimir *vb*

abolition *n* abolición *nf*, supresión *nf*, derogación *nf*

above-mentioned *adj* sobredicho *adj*, antedicho *adj*, arriba mencionado *adj*

aboveboard *adj* legítimo *adj*

abroad *adv* **to go abroad** ir al extranjero *vb*, irse al extranjero *vb*

absence *n* **in the absence of information** a falta de información *prep*, a falta de datos *prep*

absent *adj* ausente *adj*

absentee *adj* ausente *adj* **absentee landlord** propietario, -ria absentista *nm, f*

absenteeism *n* absentismo *nm*

absolute *adj* absoluto *adj*, total *adj*

absorb *vb* absorber *vb* **to absorb surplus stock** absorber existencias sobrantes

abstract *n* resumen *nm*

abundance *n* abundancia *nf*

abuse 1. *n* abuso *nm* **abuse of power/ confidence** abuso de poder *nm*, abuso de confianza *nm* **2.** *vb* abusar (de) *vb*, maltratar *vb*

accelerate *vb* acelerar *vb*

acceleration *n* aceleración *nf*

accept *vb* aceptar *vb* **accept delivery** *vb* aceptar la entrega de *vb*

acceptance *n* aceptación *nf* **consumer acceptance** aceptación por parte del consumidor *nf* **acceptance house** casa

financiera *nf*, banco comercial de negocios *nm* **market acceptance** aceptación de mercado *nf*

access 1. *n* acceso *nm* **2.** *vb* entrar en *vb*, entrar a *vb*

accessibility *n* fácil acceso *nm*, accesibilidad *nf*

accident *n* accidente *nm* **industrial accident** accidente laboral *nm*, accidente de trabajo *nm*

accidental *adj* **accidental damage** daños por accidente *nmpl*

accommodation *n* alojamiento *nm*, espacio *nm* **accommodation allowance** *n* dieta para gastos de alojamiento *nf*

accommodation bill pagaré de favor *nm*

to come to an accommodation llegar a un acuerdo *vb*

accomplish *vb* cumplir *vb*, realizar *vb*, conseguir *vb*

accomplishment *n* logro *nm*, consecución *nf*

accordance *n* **in accordance with** de acuerdo con *prep*, conforme a *prep*, según *prep*

according to *prep* **according to plan** según lo planeado *prep* **according to the minister** según el ministro *prep*

account *n* cuenta *nf* **bank account** cuenta bancaria *nf* **Account Day** (stock exchange) día de liquidación *nm* **expense account** cuenta de gastos de representación *nf* **account-keeping** teneduría de cuentas *nf* **payment on account** pago a cuenta *nm* **profit and loss account** cuenta de pérdidas y ganancias *nf* **savings account** cuenta de caja de ahorros *nf* **accounts receivable** cuentas a cobrar *nf* **statement of account** extracto de cuenta *nm*, estado de cuenta *nm* **to open an account** abrir una cuenta *vb* **to overdraw on an account** girar en descubierto una cuenta *vb*, rebasar una cuenta *vb* **to settle an account** saldar una cuenta *vb*, liquidar una cuenta *vb* **to take sth into account** tener algo en cuenta *vb* **trading account** cuenta de explotación *nf*, cuenta de ejercicio *nf*

account for *vb* dar cuentas de *vb*, justificar *vb*

accountability *n* responsabilidad *nf*

accountable *adj* responsable *adj*

accountancy *n* contabilidad *nf*

accountant *n* contable *nmf*, contador, -ora (LAm) *nm,f* **chartered accountant**

contable colegiado, -ada *nm,f*, censor, -ora
jurado, -ada de cuentas *nm,f*
accounting *n* **accounting conventions**
métodos de contabilidad *nmpl* **financial
accounting** contabilidad financiera *nf*,
contabilidad de finanzas *nf* **management
accounting** contabilidad gerencial *nf*
accounting period período de contabilidad
nm
accredit *vb* autorizar *vb*, reconocer *vb*
accrual *n* acumulación *nf* **rate of accrual**
tasa de acumulación *nf*
accrued *adj* **accrued interest** interés
acumulado *nm*
accumulate *vb* acumular *vb*
accumulated *adj* acumulado *adj*
accuracy *n* precisión *nf*, exactitud *nf*,
fidelidad *nf*
accurate *adj* preciso *adj*, exacto *adj*
accuse *vb* acusar *vb*
achieve *vb* conseguir *vb*, lograr *vb*, obtener
vb
achievement *n* logro *nm*, consecución *nf*,
éxito *nm*
acknowledge *vb* reconocer *vb* **to
acknowledge receipt of sth** acusar recibo
de algo *vb*
acknowledgement *n* **acknowledgement
of debt** reconocimiento de deuda *nm*
acquaintance *n* conocimiento *nm* **business
acquaintance** conocido, -ida de negocios
nm, f **to make the acquaintance of sb**
conocer a alguien *vb*
acquire *vb* adquirir *vb*, obtener *vb*, hacerse
con *vb*
acquisition *n* adquisición *nf*, compra *nf*
acquisitive *adj* codicioso *adj*
action *n* acto *nm*, acción *nf* **industrial
action** acción laboral *nf*, acción industrial *nf*,
huelga *nf*, paro (LAm) *nm* **legal action**
pleito *nm*, demanda *nf* **out of action**
estropeado *adj*, averiado *adj*, inutilizable *adj*,
descompuesto (LAm) *adj*
actual *adj* real *adj*, verdadero *adj*
actuality *n* realidad *nf*
actuary *n* actuario, -ria (de seguros) *nm,f*
acumen *n* **business acumen** visión para los
negocios *nf*
additional *adj* **additional charge**
suplemento *nm*, recargo *nm*
address 1. *n* **home address** dirección
privada *nf*, domicilio particular *nm*
registered address dirección registrada *nf*,
domicilio social *nm* **to change address**
cambiar de domicilio *vb* **2.** *vb* dirigir *vb*,
dirigirse a *vb*, tratar *vb*
addressee *n* destinatario, -ria *nm,f*
adjourn *vb* suspender *vb*, aplazar *vb*,
levantarse *vb*
adjournment *n* suspensión *nf*
adjust *vb* ajustar *vb*, adaptar *vb* **to adjust a
claim** reajustar una reclamación *vb*,
solventar una reclamación *vb* **to adjust the
figures** ajustar las cifras *vb*

adjustment *n* ajuste *nm*
administer *vb* administrar *vb*, dirigir *vb*
administration *n* administración *nf*,
dirección *nf*
administrative *adj* **administrative costs**
gastos de administración *nmpl*, costes de
administración *nmpl*, costos de
administración (LAm) *nmpl*
administrator *n* administrador, -ora *nm,f*
advance 1. *adj* **advance notice** aviso previo
nm, preaviso *nm* **payable in advance**
pagadero por adelantado *adj* **advance
payment** pago anticipado *nm* **2.** *n* (on
salary) avance *nm*, adelanto *nm*, progreso
nm **cash advance** adelanto *nm*, préstamo
nm, crédito *nm* **3.** *vb* (salary) avanzar *vb*,
adelantar *vb*, anticipar *vb*
advanced *adj* **advanced country** país
desarrollado *nm* **advanced technology**
tecnología avanzada *nf*
advantage *n* ventaja *nf* **comparative
advantage** ventaja comparativa *nf*
competitive advantage ventaja
competitiva *nf*
advantageous *adj* ventajoso *adj*
adverse *adj* desfavorable *adj*, adverso *adj*
adverse balance of trade balanza
comercial negativa *nf*
advertise *vb* anunciar *vb*, hacerle
propaganda a *vb*, hacerle réclame a (LAm)
vb
advertisement *n* anuncio *nm*, mensaje
publicitario *nm*, aviso (LAm) *nm*, réclame
(LAm) *nm*
advertising *n* **advertising agency** agencia
de publicidad *nf* **advertising budget**
presupuesto de publicidad *nm* **advertising
campaign** campaña de publicidad *nf*
advertising medium medio publicitario
nm **advertising revenue** ingresos de
publicidad *nmpl*
advice *n* consejos *nmpl*, asesoramiento *nm*,
notificación *nf*
advise *vb* **to advise sb about sth**
aconsejarle a alguien sobre algo *vb*,
asesorarle a alguien sobre algo *vb*
adviser/advisor *n* consejero, -era *nm,f*,
asesor, -ora *nm,f*
advisory *adj* consultivo *adj*
advocate *vb* recomendar *vb*, abogar por *vb*
aerospace *adj* **aerospace industry** industria
aeroespacial *nf*
affidavit *n* declaración jurada *nf*
affiliated *adj* afiliado *adj* **affiliated
company** sociedad filial *nf*
affiliation *n* afiliación *nf*
affluent *adj* **affluent society** sociedad
opulenta *nf*, sociedad de consumo *nf*,
sociedad de la abundancia *nf*
afford *vb* **I can't afford (to buy a new
printer)** no me puedo permitir el lujo (de
comprar una nueva impresora) *vb* **we
cannot afford (to take) the risk** no
podemos correr el riesgo *vb*

after-sales service *n* servicio post-venta *nm*
agency *n* **advertising agency** agencia de publicidad *nf* **employment agency** agencia de empleo *nf*, oficina de empleo *nf* **travel agency** agencia de viajes *nf*
agenda *n* orden del día *nm*, agenda *nf*
agent *n* agente *nmf*, representante *nmf*
AGM (Annual General Meeting) *abbr* junta anual *nf*
agrarian *adj* agrario *adj*
agree *vb* estar de acuerdo *vb*, convenir *vb*
agreed *adj* acordado *adj*, convenido *adj*
agreement *n* acuerdo *nm*, convenio *nm*, consentimiento *nm* **by mutual agreement** de común acuerdo *prep* **verbal agreement** acuerdo verbal *nm*, acuerdo no escrito *nm* **wage agreement** convenio salarial *nm*
agribusiness *n* agroindustria *nf*
agriculture *n* agricultura *nf*
agronomist *n* agrónomo, -oma *nm,f*
aid *n* ayuda *nf*, apoyo *nm*, asistencia *nf* **financial aid** ayuda financiera *nf*
air *n* **by air** por avión *prep*, por vía aérea *prep* **air freight** carga aérea *nf*, transporte aéreo *nm* **air traffic controller** controlador, -ora aéreo, -rea *nm,f*
air-conditioned *adj* climatizado *adj*, con aire acondicionado *prep*
airline *n* línea aérea *nf*
airmail *n* correo aéreo *nm*
airport *n* aeropuerto *nm*
allocate *vb* asignar *vb*, repartir *vb*
allowance *n* complemento *nm*, dieta *nf*, prestación *nf* **family allowance** prestación estatal a la familia *nf*, subsidio familiar *nm*, asignación familiar (LAm) *nf*
amalgamate *vb* integrar *vb*, fusionarse *vb*
amalgamation *n* fusión *nf*
amend *vb* enmendar *vb*, corregir *vb* **to make amends** desagraviar *vb*, reparar *vb*, rectificar *vb*
amendment *n* enmienda *nf*, mejora *nf*
amenities *npl* servicios *nmpl*, instalaciones *nfpl*
amortization *n* amortización *nf*
amortize *vb* amortizar *vb*
amount *n* cantidad *nf*, suma *nf*, importe *nm*
amount to *vb* ascender a *vb*
analysis *n* **cost-benefit analysis** análisis coste-beneficio *nm* **systems analysis** análisis de sistemas *nm*
analyze *vb* analizar *vb*
annual *adj* **annual general meeting (AGM)** junta anual *nf* **annual report** informe anual *nm*
annuity *n* anualidad *nf*, pensión *nf*
annulment *n* anulación *nf*
Ansaphone (R) *n* contestador telefónico *nm*
answer 1. *n* contestación *nf*, respuesta *nf* **2.** *vb* contestar *vb*, coger *vb*, responder *vb*, atender (LAm) *vb*
answering *n* **answering machine** contestador automático *nm*
anti-inflationary *adj* **anti-inflationary**

measures medidas antiinflacionarias *nfpl*
anticipate *vb* anticipar *vb*
antitrust *adj* **antitrust laws** legislación antimonopolista *nf*
appeal 1. *n* interés *nm*, llamamiento *nm*, apelación *nf*, llamado (LAm) *nm*, pedido (LAm) *nm* **2.** *vb* interesar *vb*, apelar *vb*
application *n* **application form** hoja de solicitud *nf*, formulario *nm*, impreso de aplicación (LAm) *nm* **letter of application** carta de solicitud *nf*, carta de aplicación (LAm) *nf*
apply for *vb* solicitar *vb*, pedir *vb*, aplicar por (LAm) *vb*
appoint *vb* **to appoint sb to a position** nombrar a alguien para un puesto *vb*, nombrar a alguien para un cargo *vb*
appointment *n* (to meet) cita *nf*, compromiso *nm*, hora (LAm) *nf*, cita (LAm) *nf* (to a position) nombramiento *nm*, contratación *nf* **to make an appointment** concertar una cita *vb*, pedir una cita (LAm) *vb*
appraisal *n* evaluación *nf*, valoración *nf*, tasación *nf*
appreciate *vb* (rise in value) subir *vb*
appreciation *n* (in value) revalorización *nf*
apprentice *n* aprendiz, -iza *nm,f*
apprenticeship *n* aprendizaje *nm*
appropriate *adj* debido *adj*, adecuado *adj*, apropiado *adj*
appropriation *n* asignación *nf*, apropiación *nf*
approval *n* aprobación *nf*, autorización *nf* **on approval** a prueba *prep*
approve *vb* aprobar *vb*, autorizar *vb*, acreditar *vb*
approximate *adj* aproximado *adj*
approximately *adv* aproximadamente *adv*
arbitrage *n* arbitraje *nm*
arbitrary *adj* arbitrario *adj*
arbitrate *vb* arbitrar *vb*
arbitration *n* arbitraje *nm*
arbitrator *n* árbitro, -tra *nm,f*
area *n* área *nf*, zona *nf*, polígono *nm* **area manager** director, -ora regional *nm,f*, gerente regional *nmf*
argument *n* discusión *nf*, polémica *nf*, argumentos *nmpl*
arithmetic *n* aritmética *nf*
arithmetical *adj* **arithmetical mean** promedio aritmético *nm*
arms *npl* **arms trade** tráfico de armas *nm*, comercio armamentístico *nm*
arrangement *n* (agreement) plan *nm*, arreglo *nm*, disposición *nf*
arrears *npl* atrasos *nmpl* **in arrears** atrasado *adj* **to fall/get into arrears** atrasarse en los pagos *vb*
articulated *adj* **articulated lorry** camión articulado *nm*, camión con remolque *nm*
asap (as soon as possible) *abbr* lo antes posible, cuanto antes
asking *adj* **asking price** precio de oferta *nm*
assembly *n* **assembly line** cadena de

montaje *nf*, cadena de ensamblaje *nf*
assess *vb* evaluar *vb*, calcular *vb*
assessment *n* evaluación *nf*, valoración *nf*, cálculo *nm*
asset *n* activo *nm* **capital assets** activo fijo *nm* **asset stripping** liquidación de activo *nf*, vaciamiento *nmf*
assign *vb* asignar *vb*, destinar *vb*, nombrar *vb*
assignee *n* cesionario, -ria *nm,f*
assignment *n* misión *nf*, transmisión *nf*, cesión *nf*
assistant *n* ayudante *nmf* **assistant manager** subdirector, -ora *nm,f*, ayudante de dirección *nmf*
associate 1. *adj* **associate director** director, -ora adjunto, -nta *nm,f* **2.** *n* socio, -cia *nm,f*, asociado, -ada *nm,f*, colega *nmf*
attend *vb* acudir *vb*, asistir a *vb*, atender *vb* **attendance** *n* asistencia *nf*
attestation *n* testimonio *nm*, autorización *nf*
attorney *n* **power of attorney** poder notarial *nm*
auction 1. *n* subasta *nf*, remate (LAm) *nm* **2.** *vb* subastar *vb*, rematar (LAm) *vb*
auctioneer *n* subastador, -ora *nm,f*, rematador, -ora (LAm) *nm,f*
audit *n* auditoría *nf*
auditor *n* auditor, -ora *nm,f*, censor, -ora *nm,f*, interventor, -ora de cuentas *nm,f*
authority *n* (official) autoridad *nf*
authorize *vb* autorizar *vb*
authorized *adj* **authorized dealer** agente oficial *nmf*, distribuidor, -ora autorizado, -ada *nm,f*
automatic *adj* **automatic cash dispenser** cajero automático *nm*
automation *n* automatización *nf*
automobile *adj* **automobile industry** industria del automóvil *nf*
autonomous *adj* autónomo *adj*
auxiliary *adj* auxiliar *adj*
average 1. *adj* medio *adj* **2.** promedio *nm*, media *nf* **average unit** unidad media *nf*, unidad promedio *nf*
avoid *vb* evitar *vb*, evadir *vb*, eludir *vb*
avoidance *n* **tax avoidance** evasión de impuestos *nf*, evasión fiscal *nf*
axe, ax (US) *vb* recortar *vb*, despedir *vb*, suprimir *vb* **to axe expenditure** recortar gastos *vb*
back *vb* respaldar *vb*, apoyar *vb* **to back a venture** respaldar una empresa *vb*
back pay *n* atrasos de sueldo *nmpl*
backdate *vb* antedatar *vb* **to backdate a cheque** poner una fecha anterior a un cheque *vb*
backer *n* garante *nmf*, capitalista *nmf*, partidario, -ria *nm,f*, patrocinador, -ora *nm,f*
backhander* *n* soborno *nm*, mordida (LAm) *nf*, coima (LAm) *nf*
backing *n* apoyo *nm*, respaldo *nm*, ayuda *nf*
backlog *n* acumulación de trabajo atrasado *nf*
bad *adj* **bad cheque** cheque sin fondos *nm*,

cheque descubierto *nm* **bad debt** deuda incobrable *nf*
bail *n* fianza *nf*
bailiff *n* alguacil *nmf*, administrador, -ora *nm,f*
balance 1. *n* (financial) saldo *nm*, resultado *nm*, balanza *nf* **bank balance** saldo de cuenta bancaria *nm* **final balance** saldo final *nm*, balance final *nm* **balance in hand** saldo disponible *nm* **balance of payments** balanza de pagos *nf* **balance of payments deficit** déficit de la balanza de pagos *nm* **balance of payments surplus** superávit de la balanza de pagos *nm* **balance of trade** balanza comercial *nf* **balance sheet** balance general *nm*, balance de situación *nm* **trade balance** balanza comercial *nf* **2.** *vb* equilibrar *vb* **to balance the books** hacer cuadrar las cuentas *vb* **to balance the budget** ajustar el presupuesto *vb*, equilibrar el presupuesto *vb*
bank 1. *adj* **bank account** cuenta bancaria *nf* **bank balance** estado de cuenta *nm*, saldo bancario *nm* **bank card** tarjeta de crédito *nf*, tarjeta bancaria *nf*, tarjeta de garantía *nf* **bank charges** gastos bancarios *nmpl* **bank clerk** empleado, -ada de banco *nm,f*, bancario, -aria (LAm) *nm,f* **bank details** domiciliación *nf* **bank draft** cheque bancario *nm*, giro bancario *nm* **bank holiday** día festivo *nm*, día feriado (LAm) *nm* **bank loan** préstamo bancario *nm* **bank manager** director, -ora de banco *nm,f* **bank overdraft** descubierto *nm*, sobregiro *nm* **bank payment** domiciliación *nf* **bank rate** tipo bancario *nm*, tipo de interés *nm*, tasa de interés (LAm) *nf* **bank statement** estado de cuentas *nm*, extracto de cuentas *nm* **2.** *n* banco *nm* **3.** *vb* **to bank a cheque** ingresar un cheque *vb*
banker *n* banquero, -era *nm,f* **banker's order** domiciliación bancaria *nf*, orden permanente de pago *nf*
banking *n* banca *nf* **banking circles** el mundo de la banca *nm* **banking hours** horario bancario *nm* **banking system** *n* banca *nf*
banknote *n* billete de banco *nm*, pagaré *nm*
bankrupt *adj* insolvente *adj*, en bancarrota *prep* **to be bankrupt** estar insolvente *vb*
bankruptcy *n* quiebra *nf*, bancarrota *nf*, insolvencia *nf*
bar code *n* código de barras *nm*
bargain 1. *adj* **bargain offer** oferta de rebaja *nf* **bargain price** precio de ocasión *nm* **2.** *n* trato *nm*, ganga *nf*, oferta *nf*, pichincha (LAm) *nf* **it's a bargain** ¡trato hecho! *nm* **3.** *vb* regatear *vb*, negociar *vb*
barrier *n* **trade barrier** barrera comercial *nf*
barrister, lawyer (US) *n* abogado, -ada (que actúa únicamente en el juicio oral) *nm,f*
barter 1. *adj* **barter agreement** acuerdo de trueque *nm* **barter transaction** operación de trueque *nf* **2.** *n* trueque *nm* **3.** *vb* permutar *vb*, trocar *vb*

base *adj* **base lending rate** tipo base *nm*, tasa base (LAm) *nf*

basic *adj* **basic commodity** producto básico *nm* **basic income** ingresos básicos *nmpl* **basic rate** tasa normal *nf*, tasa base *nf* **basic training** preparación básica *nf*

basis *n* **basis of assessment** base de evaluación *nf*

basket *n* **basket of currencies** cesta de monedas *nf*, canasta de divisas (LAm) *nf*

batch *n* (of goods) lote *nm*, serie *nf* **batch processing** (DP) procesamiento por lotes *nm*

bear 1. *adj* **bear market** mercado bajista *nm* **2.** *n* (stock exchange) bajista *nmf* **3.** *vb* **to bear interest** devengar intereses *vb*

bearer *n* portador, -ora *nm,f*, titular *nmf*, poseedor, -ora *nm,f* **bearer bond** título al portador *nm* **bearer cheque** cheque al portador *nm* **bearer share** acción al portador *nf*

bench *n* **bench mark** punto de referencia *nm*, prueba patrón *nf* **bench mark price** precio de referencia *nm*

benefactor *n* bienhechor, -ora *nm,f*

benefit 1. *n* (social security) beneficio *nm*, provecho *nm*, subsidio *nm* **2.** *vb* aprovecharse *vb* beneficiar *vb*

bequeath *vb* legar *vb*

bequest *n* legado *nm*, donación *nf*

best *adj* **best-before date** fecha de caducidad *nf* **best seller** bestseller *nm*, superventas *nm*

biannual *adj* semestral *adj*

bid 1. *n* oferta *nf*, licitación *nf*, intento *nm* **2.** *vb* (auction) licitar *vb*, hacer una oferta *vb*, ofrecer *vb*, licitar (LAm) *vb*

biennial *adj* bianual *adj*

bilateral *adj* **bilateral trade** comercio bilateral *nm*

bill 1. *n* (invoice) factura *nf*, cuenta *nf*, adición (LAm) *nf*, rubro (LAm) *nm* **bill of exchange** letra de cambio *nf* **bill of lading** conocimiento de embarque *nm* **bill of sale** factura de venta *nf* **bills discounted** letras descontadas *nfpl* **to pay a bill** pagar una cuenta *vb*, liquidar una factura *vb* **2.** *vb* (invoice) presentar una factura *vb*

bimonthly *adj* bimensual *adj*

binding *adj* obligatorio *adj*, vinculante *adj* **legally binding** con fuerza jurídica, vinculante *prep*

biweekly *adj* quincenal *adj*

black *adj* **black economy** economía sumergida *nf*, economía informal (LAm), economía paralela (Lam) **black market** mercado negro *nm*, estraperlo *nm* **to be in the black** tener un saldo positivo *vb*

blackmail chantaje *nm*

blank *adj* **blank cheque** cheque en blanco *nm*

block 1. *n* bloque *nm*, parte *nf*, manzana *nf*, cuadra (LAm) *nf* **2.** *vb* bloquear *vb*, impedir *vb*, obstaculizar *vb*, tapar (LAm) *vb*

blockade 1. *n* bloqueo *nm* **2.** *vb* bloquear *vb*

blocked *adj* **blocked account** cuenta bloqueada *nf*

blue *adj* **blue-chip company** empresa de primera clase *nf*, sociedad de primer orden *nf* **blue-collar worker** obrero, -era *nm,f* **blue-chip securities** valores seguros *nm pl*

board *n* junta *nf* **Board of Trade** Departamento de Comercio y Exportación *nm*, Cámara de Comercio *nf* **board meeting** reunión del consejo de administración *nf*, reunión de la junta directiva *nf* **board of directors** (GB) consejo de administración *nm*, junta directiva *nf*, directorio *nm* **board room** sala de juntas *nf*

body *n* cuerpo *nm*, organismo *nm*, masa *nf*

bona fide *adj* de buena fe *prep*, serio *adj*

bond *n* bono *nm*, título *nm*, obligación *nf* **bond certificate** título de obligaciones *nm* **government bond** bono del Estado *nm*, obligación del Estado *nf*, título del Estado *nm* **in bond** en depósito aduanero *prep*

bonded *adj* **bonded warehouse** depósito aduanero *nm*, almacén de depósito *nm*

bondholder *n* tenedor, -ora de obligaciones *nm,f*, bonista *nmf*

bonus *n* prima *nf*, bonificación *nf*, plus *nm*

book 1. *n* libro *nm* **cheque book** talonario de cheques *nm*, chequera (LAm) *nf* **book profit** beneficios contables *nm*, beneficios en libros *nm*, utilidades contables (LAm) *nf* **the books** las cuentas *nf* **book value** valor en libros *nm* **2.** *vb* **to book a hotel room** reservar una habitación de hotel *vb* **to book in advance** reservar por adelantado *vb*

book-keeper *n* contable *nmf*, tenedor, -ora de libros *nm,f*

book-keeping *n* contabilidad *nf*

booking *n* (reservation) reserva *nf*, reservación (LAm) *nf*

bookseller *n* librero, -era *nm, f*

bookshop, bookstore (US) *n* librería *nf*

boom 1. *n* boom *nm*, bonanza *nf* **economic boom** boom económico *nm* **boom in demand** alza de la demanda *nf*, aumento rápido de la demanda *nm* **2.** *vb* prosperar *vb*, aumentar *vb*

booming *adj* próspero *adj*, en fuerte expansión *prep*, en auge *prep*

boost 1. *n* estímulo *nm*, impulso *nm*, aumento *nm* **2.** *vb* **to boost demand** potenciar la demanda *vb*, fomentar la demanda *vb* **to boost morale** reforzar la moral *vb* **to boost production** estimular la producción *vb* **to boost sales** incrementar las ventas *vb*

boot *vb* **to boot a computer** cargar un ordenador *vb*, cargar una computadora (LAm) *vb*

booth *n* (voting) cabina *nf*, puesto *nm*, casilla (LAm) *nf*, caseta (LAm) *nf*

borrow *vb* pedir prestado *vb*, sacar *vb*, tomar *vb*

borrowing *n* préstamo *nm*, deuda *nf*, préstamos *nmpl*

boss *n* jefe, -efa *nm,f*, patrón, -ona *nm,f*, amo, -a *nm,f*

bottleneck *n* atasco *nm*, embotellamiento *nm* **bottleneck inflation** inflación de demanda por cambio de estructura *nf*

bottom 1. *adj* **bottom price** precio más bajo *nm* **2.** *n* **at the bottom** en el fondo *prep* **3.** *vb* **to bottom out** tocar fondo *vb*

bought *adj* **bought ledger** libro mayor de compras *nm*

bounce* *vb* (cheque) ser rechazado *vb*, no tener fondos *vb*

bound *n* **out of bounds** fuera de los límites *prep*, prohibido *adj*

box 1. *n* caja *nf*, apartado *nm*, casilla *nf* **box number** apartado de correos *nm*, número de referencia *nm* **box office** taquilla *nf*, boletería (LAm) *nf* **PO box** apartado de correos *nm*, apartado postal (LAm) *nm*, casilla postal (LAm) *nf* **2.** *vb* **to box sth up** embalar algo *vb*

boycott 1. *n* boicot *nm* **2.** *vb* boicotear *vb*

bracket *n* **tax bracket** banda impositiva *nf*

branch *n* sucursal *nf*, rama *nf*, ramo *nm* **branch company** empresa filial *nf* **branch manager** director, -ora de sucursal *nm,f* **branch office** sucursal *nf*

brand *n* marca *nf*, tipo *nm*, señal *nf* **brand image** imagen de marca *nf* **brand leader** producto principal de la marca *nm*

breach *n* **breach of contract** incumplimiento de contrato *nm*

break 1. *n* **to take a break** descansar *vb*, tomarse un descanso *vb* **2.** *vb* romper *vb* **to break an agreement** romper un contrato *vb*

break even *vb* cubrir gastos *vb*

break up *vb* deshacerse *vb*, desintegrar *vb*, terminar *vb*

break-even *adj* **break-even point** punto crítico *nm*

breakdown *n* (of figures) desglose de estadísticas *nm*, análisis de cifras *nm* **breakdown service** servicio de asistencia en carretera *nm*

breakthrough *n* avance *nm* **to make a breakthrough** hacer un avance importante *vb*

breakup *n* desintegración *nf*, disolución *nf*, división *nf*

brevity *n* brevedad *nf*

bribe 1. *n* soborno *nm*, cohecho *nm*, coima (LAm), mordida (LAm) **2.** *vb* sobornar *vb*, comprar *vb*, coimear (LAm) *vb*, morder (LAm) *vb*

bribery *n* soborno *nm*, cohecho *nm*, coima (LAm) *nf*

bridging *adj* **bridging loan, bridge loan** (US) préstamo puente *nm*, crédito puente *nm*

brief 1. *n* instrucciones *nfpl*, órdenes *nfpl* **2.** *vb* dar instrucciones *vb pl*, informar *vb pl*

briefing *n* informe *nm*, sesión informativa *nf*

bring down *vb* (prices) reducir *vb*, rebajar *vb*

bring forward *vb* presentar *vb*, adelantar *vb*

bring out *vb* (product) sacar *vb*, lanzar *vb*

brinkmanship *n* política arriesgada *nf*

Britain *n* Gran Bretaña *nf*, La Gran Bretaña (LAm) *nf*

British *adj* británico *adj* **British Council** Consejo Británico *nm* **British Isles** Islas Británicas *nfpl*

broad *adj* **broad market** mercado amplio *nm*

broadcast 1. *n* emisión *nf*, transmisión *nf*, retransmisión *nf* **2.** *vb* emitir *vb*, transmitir *vb*, divulgar *vb*

broadsheet *n* periódico de formato grande *nm*

brochure *n* folleto publicitario *nm*

broker *n* agente comercial *nmf*, comisionista *nmf*, corredor, -ora *nm,f*

brokerage *n* corretaje *nm*, comisión *nf* **brokerage firm** agencia de corredores *nf*, agentes de bolsa *nm*

buck* (US) *n* dólar *nm*, verde (LAm) *nf* **pass the buck*** pasar la pelota

budget *n* presupuesto *nm* **to draw up a budget** preparar el presupuesto *vb*, elaborar el presupuesto *vb*

budget for *vb* presupuestar *vb*, asignar *vb*

budgetary *adj* **budgetary deficit** déficit presupuestario *nm*, déficit presupuestal (LAm) *nm* **budgetary policy** política presupuestaria *nf*, política presupuestal (LAm) *nf*

bug 1. *n* virus *nm*, peste (LAm) *nf* (listening device) micrófono oculto *nm*, (computer) error *nm* **2.** *vb* **to bug a call** pinchar el teléfono *vb*, intervenir un llamado (LAm) *vb*

build *vb* **to build a reputation** hacerse conocer *vb*, hacerse buena reputación *vb*

builder *n* contratista *nmf*, albañil *nmf*, empresa constructora *nf*

building *adj* **building contractor** contratista de obras *nmf* **building firm** empresa constructora *nf* **building industry/trade** industria de la construcción *nf* **building permit** licencia de obras *nf* **building site** obra *nf*, terreno edificable *nm* **building society** sociedad de crédito hipotecario *nf*

built-in *adj* fijo *adj*, incorporado *adj*

built-up *adj* **built-up area** zona muy urbanizada *nf*

bulk *n* volumen *nm* **the bulk of** la mayor parte de *nf* **to buy in bulk** comprar a granel *vb*, comprar en grandes cantidades *vb*

bull 1. *n* (stock exchange) alcista *nmf* **bull market** mercado alcista *nm* **2.** *vb* (stock exchange) especular al alza *vb*

bulletin *n* boletín *nm*, anuncio *nm*, comunicado *nm* **bulletin board** tablón/tablero de anuncios *nm*

bullion *n* oro y plata en lingotes *nm* & *nf*

bump up *vb* (prices) aumentar *vb*, subir *vb*

bundle *n* paquete *nm*, legajo *nm*, (financial)

dineral *nm*, platal (LAm) *nm*, lanón (LAm) *nm*

bundle up *vb* liar *vb*

buoyant *adj* **buoyant market** mercado alcista *nm*

bureau *n* **bureau de change** oficina de cambio *nf*, casa de cambio *nf*, cambio *nm* **Federal Bureau (US)** Agencia Federal *nf*, Departamento de Estado *nm*

bureaucracy *n* burocracia *nf*

bureaucrat *n* burócrata *nmf*

bureaucratic *adj* burocrático *adj*

bursar *n* administrador, -ora *nm,f*

bus *n* **bus station** estación de autobuses *nf*, estación de micros (LAm) *nf*, estación de colectivos (LAm) *nf*

business *n* negocios *nmpl*, comercio *nm*, empresa *nf* **to go out of business** quebrar *vb* **business address** dirección comercial *nf* **business associate** socio, -cia *nm,f* **big business** las grandes empresas *nfpl* **business consultant** asesor, -ora de empresas *nm,f* **business expenses** gastos de explotación *nmpl* **family business** empresa familiar *nf* **business hours** horas de oficina *nfpl* **business premises** local comercial *nm* **business studies** ciencias empresariales *nfpl* **business suit** traje de oficina *nm*, vestido (LAm) *nm*, terno (LAm) *nm* **to set up in business** montar un negocio *vb*, poner un negocio (LAm) *vb* **business transaction** operación comercial *nf*, transacción *nf*, trámite *nm* **business trip** viaje de negocios *nm*

businesslike *adj* formal *adj*, serio *adj*, práctico *adj*

busy *adj* ocupado *adj* **busy signal (US)** señal de comunicando *nf*, tono de ocupado (LAm) *nm*, señal de ocupado (LAm) *nf*

buy 1. *n* **a good buy** una buena compra *nf* **2.** *vb* **to buy sth at a high price** comprar algo caro *vb* **to buy sth on credit** comprar algo a crédito *vb* **to buy sth second hand** comprar algo de segunda mano *vb* **to buy sth wholesale** comprar algo al por mayor *vb*

buy out *vb* comprarle su parte a *vb*

buy-out *n* compra *nf*, adquisición *nf*

buyer *n* comprador, -ora *nm,f*, cliente, -nta *nm,f*, encargado, -ada de compras *nm,f* **buyer's market** mercado de oferta *nm*, mercado favorable a los compradores *nm*

buying *n* **buying and selling** compraventa *nf* **buying power** poder adquisitivo *nm* **buying price** precio de compra *nm*, cambio comprador *nm* **buying rate** tipo de compra *nm*, tasa de compra (LAm) *nf*

by-product *n* subproducto *nm*, derivado *nm*

bypass *vb* circunvalar *vb*, pasar por encima *vb*

byte *n* byte *nm*, octeto *nm*

c.i.f. (cost, insurance and freight) *abbr* cif (coste, seguro y flete) *abbr,nm*

CAD (computer-aided or assisted design) *abbr* CAD (diseño asistido por ordenador) *abbr,nm*

calculate *vb* calcular *vb*

calculation *n* cálculo *nm*

calculator *n* calculadora *nf*

call 1. *n* llamada *nf* **call money** dinero a la vista *nm* **person-to-person call** conferencia personal *nf* **reverse-charge call, collect call** (US) llamada a cobro revertido *nf*, llamado por cobrar (LAm) *nm* **2.** *vb* llamar *vb* **to call a meeting** convocar una reunión *vb* **to call it a deal** cerrar un trato *vb*, llegar a un acuerdo *vb*

call back *vb* (on phone) volver a llamar *vb*, devolver la llamada *vb*, devolver el llamado (LAm) *vb*

call for *vb* pasar a buscar *vb*, exigir *vb*, pedir *vb*

call in *vb* (demand the repayment of a loan) exigir el pago inmediato de un préstamo *vb*

campaign *n* campaña *nf* **advertising campaign** campaña publicitaria *nf* **publicity campaign** campaña publicitaria *nf* **sales campaign** campaña de ventas *nf* **to run a campaign** hacer una campaña *vb*, preparar una campaña *vb*

cancel *vb* **cancel a contract** anular un contrato *vb* **cancel an appointment** cancelar una cita *vb*

cancellation *n* cancelación *nf*, anulación *nf* **cancellation charge** cobro por cancelación *nm*

candidate *n* (for job) candidato, -ata *nm,f*, aspirante *nmf*

cap *vb* **to cap the interest rate** limitar el tipo de interés *vb*, limitar la tasa de interés (LAm) *vb*

CAP (Common Agricultural Policy) *abbr* PAC (Política Agrícola Común) *abbr,nf*

capable *adj* capaz *adj*

capacity *n* **earning capacity** capacidad de rendimiento *nf*, grado de rendimiento *nm*, escala de rendimiento *nf* **industrial capacity** capacidad industrial *nf* **in my capacity as chairman** en mi calidad de presidente *prep* **manufacturing capacity** capacidad de producción *nf* **storage capacity** capacidad de almacenamiento *nf* **to expand capacity** ampliar la capacidad *vb* **to work to full capacity** trabajar a pleno rendimiento *vb*

capital *n* (financial) capital *nm*, (city) capital *nf* **capital assets** activo fijo *nm*, bienes de capital *nmpl*, capital disponible *nm* **capital budget** presupuesto de gastos de capital *nm* **capital cost** coste de capital *nm*, costo de capital (LAm) *nm* **capital expenditure** gastos en capital *nmpl*, inversión de capital *nf* **capital exports** exportaciones de capital *nfpl* **fixed capital** capital fijo *nm* **capital funds** fondos para invertir *nmpl*, capital operativo *nm*, capital circulante *nm* **capital gains** ganancias de capital *nfpl*, plusvalía *nf* **capital gains tax** impuesto sobre la plusvalía *nm* **capital goods** bienes de capital *nmpl,* bienes de equipo *nmpl* **initial capital** capital inicial *nm* **invested capital** capital invertido *nm* **capital loss** minusvalía *nf* **capital market** mercado de capitales *nm* **to raise capital** movilzar fondos *vb* **capital turnover** movimientos de capitales *nmpl* **venture capital** capital riesgo *nm,* capital de riesgo *nm* **working capital** capital operativo *nm,* capital circulante *nm*

capitalism *n* capitalismo *nm*

capitalist *n* capitalista *nmf*

capitalize *vb* capitalizar *vb*

card *n* carné *nm,* tarjeta *nf* **bank card** tarjeta de cajero automático *nf* **business card** tarjeta profesional *nf,* tarjeta de visita *nf* **chargecard** tarjeta de cuenta *nf,* tarjeta de pago *nf* **cheque card** tarjeta de garantía de cheques *nf* **credit card** tarjeta de crédito *nf* **identity card** carné de identidad *nm* **smart card** tarjeta inteligente *nf*

career *n* profesión *nf,* carrera *nf,* desarrollo profesional *nm* **careers advice** orientación profesional *nf,* orientación vocacional (LAm) *nf*

cargo *n* carga *nf,* cargamento *nm* **bulk cargo** carga *nf,* carga a granel *nf* **cargo ship** barco de carga *nm,* carguero *nm*

carriage *n* porte *nm* **carriage charge** gasto de transporte *nm* **carriage costs** gasto de transporte *nm,* costes de transporte *nmpl,* costos de transporte (LAm) *nmpl* **carriage forward** porte debido *nm,* portes a pagar *nmpl* **carriage included** porte incluido *nm* **carriage paid** porte pagado *nm,* franco a domicilio *adv,* franco de porte *adv*

carrier *n* transportista *nmf,* empresa de transportes *nf,* línea aérea *nf* **bulk carrier** carguero de graneles *nm* **express carrier** empresa de transportes urgentes *nf*

carry *vb* (stock) tener en existencia *vb*

carry forward *vb* pasar a cuenta nueva *vb,* transferir *vb*

carry out *vb* llevar a cabo *vb,* realizar *vb,* cumplir *vb*

carry over *vb* (to next month) trasladar *vb,* pasar a cuenta nueva *vb*

carrying *adj* **carrying cost** coste de transporte *nm,* costo de transporte (LAm) *nm*

cartel *n* cartel *nm,* cártel *nm*

case *n* caso *nm*

cash 1. *n* dinero *nm,* dinero en efectivo *nm,* efectivo *nm,* plata (LAm) *nf* **cash and carry** autoservicio *nm,* mayorista de pago al contado *nmf* **cash before delivery** pago anticipado *nm,* pago al hacer el pedido *nm* **cash crop** cultivo comerciall *nm* **cash desk** caja *nf* **cash discount** descuento por pago al contado *nm* **cash flow** cash flow *nm,* flujo de caja *nm* **for cash** al contado *prep* **cash machine/dispenser** cajero automático *nm* **cash offer** oferta de pago en efectivo *nf* **cash on delivery (COD)**

cobro a la entrega *nm,* entrega contra reembolso *nf* **cash on receipt of goods** cobro al recibo de mercancías *nm* **cash payment** pago en efectivo *nm,* pago al contado *nm* **cash sale** venta al contado *nf,* venta en efectivo *nf* **to pay in cash** pagar al contado *vb,* pagar en efectivo *vb* **cash transaction** venta al contado *nf,* venta en efectivo *nf* **cash with order** pago al hacer el pedido *nm* **2.** *vb* **to cash a cheque** cobrar un cheque *vb*

cash up *vb* hacer la caja *vb*

cashier *n* cajero, -era *nm,f*

category *n* categoría *nf,* clase *nf*

cater for *vb* atender a *vb,* abastecer *vb*

caution *n* **caution money** fianza *nf,* garantía *nf*

ceiling *n* (on prices) límite *nm,* tope *nm* **to put a ceiling on sth** imponer un límite a algo *vb*

central *adj* **central bank** banco central *nm* **central planned economy** planificación económica estatal *nf* **central planning** planificación estatal *nf* **central processing unit (CPU)** (DP) unidad de proceso central (UPC) *nf*

centralization *n* centralización *nf*

centralize *vb* centralizar *vb*

centre *n* **business centre** centro comercial *nm,* centro financiero *nm* **Jobcentre** oficina de empleo *nf,* agencia de colocaciones *nf,* bolsa de empleo *nf*

certificate 1. *n* certificado *nm* **clearance certificate** certificado de haber efectuado el despacho de aduana *nm* **marriage certificate** certificado de matrimonio *nm* **certificate of employment** certificado de empleo *nm* **certificate of origin** certificado de origen *nm* **certificate of ownership** certificado de propiedad *nm* **share certificate, stock certificate** (US) título de acción *nm* **2.** *vb* certificar *vb*

certified *adj* certificado *adj* **certified cheque** cheque certificado *nm,* cheque conformado *nm*

certify *vb* certificar *vb*

chain *n* cadena *nf* **chain of shops** cadena de tiendas *nf* **retail chain** cadena de minoristas *nf* **chain store** tienda de una cadena *nf*

chair *vb* **to chair a meeting** presidir una reunión *vb*

chamber *n* cámara *nf* **Chamber of Commerce** Cámara de Comercio *nf*

chancellor *n* **Chancellor of the Exchequer (GB)** ministro, -tra de Economía y Hacienda *nm,f*

change *n* (from purchase) cambio *nm,* vuelta *nf,* vuelto (LAm) *nm,* vueltas (LAm) *nfpl* **bureau de change** cambio *nm,* oficina de cambio *nf* **loose/small change** (coins) monedas *nfpl,* calderilla *nf,* sencillo (LAm) *nm,* feria (LAm) *nf,* menudo (LAm) *nm* **charge 1.** *n* **charge account** cuenta de crédito *nf*, cuenta abierta *nf* **bank charges** gastos bancarios *nmpl* **delivery charges** gastos de envío *nmpl*, gastos de transporte *nmpl* **handling charges** gastos de tramitación *nmpl*, costes de manipulación *nmpl*, costos de manipulación (LAm) *nmpl* **legal charges** costes judiciales *nmpl* **2.** *vb* **to charge (a price)** cobrar *vb*, cargar *vb*, encomendar *vb* **to charge commission** cobrar comisión *vb* **to charge for sth** cobrar por algo *vb*, cargar algo *vb* **to charge sth to an account** cargar algo a una cuenta *vb* **to be in charge** estar encargado *vb* **to take charge of sth** hacerse cargo de *vb*, responsabilizarse de algo *vb* **to charge sb with sth** encargar a alguien con algo *vb*

chargeable *adj* cobrable *adj*

charitable *adj* **charitable trust** fundación benéfica *nf*, entidad caritativa *nf*

charity *n* caridad *nf*, obras de beneficencia *nfpl*

chart *n* gráfico *nm* **bar chart** gráfico de barras *nm* **flow chart** organigrama *nm*, diagrama de flujos *nm*, diagrama de secuencias *nm* **pie chart** gráfico sectorial *nm*

charter *n* **charter flight** vuelo chárter *nm*

chartered *adj* **chartered accountant** contable colegiado, -ada *nm,f*, contador, -ora público, -ica (LAm) *nm,f* **chartered bank** banco fundado antiguamente por cédula real *nm* **chartered surveyor** agrimensor, -ora colegiado, -ada *nm,f*

chattels *npl* bienes *nmpl*

check 1. *n* **customs check** control de aduana *nm*, revisión de aduana *nf* **to make a check on sth** verificar algo *vb*, inspeccionar algo *vb*, chequear *vb*, checar (LAm) *vb* **2.** *vb* comprobar *vb*, verificar *vb*

check in 1. *n* (at airport) facturación *nf*, chequeo (LAm) *nm* **2.** *vb* (at airport) presentarse *vb*, facturar el equipaje *vb*, chequear (LAm) *vb* (register in an hotel) registrarse *vb*, inscribirse *vb*

check out *vb* (pay the hotel bill) pagar la cuenta y marcharse *vb*

checkbook (US) *n* talonario de cheques *nm*, chequera (LAm) *nf*

chemical *adj* **chemical industry** industria química *nf* **chemical products** productos químicos *nmpl*

cheque, check (US) *n* cheque *nm* **return a cheque to drawer** devolver un cheque *vb* **blank cheque** cheque en blanco *nm* **cheque book** talonario de cheques *nm*, chequera (LAm) *nf* **crossed cheque** cheque cruzado *nm* **dud cheque** cheque sin fondos *nm*, cheque no cubierto *nm* **a cheque for the amount of £100** cheque por valor de cien libras *nm* **to bounce a cheque** rechazar un cheque *vb* **to cash a cheque** cobrar un cheque *vb* **to make out a cheque** extender un cheque *vb* **to pay by**

cheque pagar con cheque *vb* **to sign a cheque** firmar un cheque *vb* **to stop a cheque** detener el pago de un cheque *vb* **traveller's cheque, traveler's cheque** (US) cheque de viaje *nm*, cheque de viajero *nm*

chief *adj* **chief accountant** jefe, -efa de contabilidad *nm,f* **chief cashier** cajero, -era jefe *nm,f* **chief executive** director, -ora general *nm,f*, jefe, -efa ejecutivo, -iva *nm,f*, presidente, -nta *nm,f* **chief financial officer** jefe, -efa de finanzas *nm,f*

choice *n* selección *nf*

circular *n* (letter) circular *nf*

circulate *vb* (document) hacer circular *vb*, divulgar *vb*

circulation *n* **in circulation** en circulación *prep*

circumstance *n* circunstancias *nfpl* **circumstances beyond our control** circunstancias ajenas a nuestra voluntad *nfpl* **due to unforeseen circumstances** debido a circunstancias imprevistas *prep* **under no circumstances** bajo ningún concepto *prep*

civil *adj* **civil engineering** ingeniería civil *nf*, ingeniería de caminos *nf* **civil servant** funcionario, -ria *nm,f* **civil service** administración pública *nf*

claim 1. *n* demanda *nf*, reivindicación *nf*, reclamación *nf* **claim form** impreso de reclamación *nm* **claims department** departamento de reclamaciones *nm* **claims procedure** tramitación de reclamaciónes *nf* **to put in a claim** presentar una reclamación *vb*, presentar una solicitud *vb* **to settle a claim** liquidar una reclamación *vb* **wage claim** reivindicación salarial *nf*, demanda de aumento salarial *nf* **2.** *vb* **to claim for damages** presentar una demanda de indemnización *vb*, presentar una reclamación *vb*

claimant *n* solicitante *nmf*, demandante *nmf*

class *n* **business class** (plane) clase preferente *nf* **first class** (plane) primera clase *nf*

classification *n* clasificación *nf*

classified *adj* **classified advertisement** anuncio por palabras *nm*, aviso clasificado (LAm) *nm* **classified information** información clasificada como secreta *nf*

clause *n* (in contract) cláusula *nf* **escape clause** cláusula de excepción *nf*, cláusula de salvaguardia *nf* **option clause** cláusula de opción *nf*

clear 1. *adj* **clear loss** pérdida neta *nf* **to make oneself clear** explicarse claramente *vb* **2.** *vb* (a cheque) tramitar el pago de *vb*, compensar *vb* **to clear sth through customs** tramitar el despacho de aduanas de algo *vb*

clearance *n* **clearance offer** oferta por liquidación *nf*, oferta por realizaclón (LAm) *nf* **clearance sale** liquidación *nf*, realización (LAm) *nf*

clearing *adj* **clearing bank** banco comercial *nm*, banco de compensación *nm* **clearing house** cámara de compensación *nf* **clearing payment** pago de compensación *nm*

clerical *adj* de oficina *prep* **clerical error** error de copia *nm* **clerical work** trabajo de oficina *nm*

clerk *n* oficinista *nmf*, empleado, -ada *nm,f*, recepcionista *nmf*, bancario, -ria (LAm) *nm,f*

client *n* cliente, -nta *nm,f*

clientele *n* clientela *nf*

clinch *vb* **clinch a deal** cerrar un trato *vb*

clock in *vb* fichar a la entrada al trabajo *vb*, checar tarjeta al entrar al trabajo (LAm) *vb*

clock out *vb* fichar a la salida del trabajo *vb*, checar tarjeta al salir del trabajo (LAm) *vb*

close *vb* **to close a business** cerrar una empresa *vb* **to close a deal** cerrar un trato *vb* **to close a meeting** terminar una reunión *vb* **to close an account** cerrar una cuenta *vb*

closed *adj* cerrado *adj* **closed session/ meeting** sesión a puerta cerrada *nf* **closed shop** empresa que emplea exclusivamente a trabajadores sindicados *nf*

closing *adj* **closing bid** oferta final *nf* **closing price** precio al cierre *nm* **closing time** hora de cierre *nf*

closure *n* **closure of a company** cierre de una empresa *nm*

co-efficient *n* coeficiente *nm*

COD (cash on delivery), (collect on delivery) (US) *abbr* cobro a la entrega *nm*

code *n* **bar code** código de barras *nm* **professional code of practice** código de práctica *nm* **post code, zip code** (US) código postal *nm* **telephone code** prefijo *nm* **tax code** código fiscal *nm*

collaborate *vb* colaborar *vb*

collaborative *adj* **collaborative venture** empresa conjunta *nf*, negocio en participación *nm*, agrupación temporal de empresas *nf*

collapse *n* (of company) quiebra *nf*, (of economy) desplome *nm*, caída *nf* **on stock market** hundimiento de la bolsa *nm*, caída bursátil *nf*

collateral 1. *adj* **collateral security** garantía colateral *nf* **2.** *n* garantía *nf*, fianza *nf*

colleague *n* colega *nmf*

collect *vb* recoger *vb*, recaudar *vb*, coleccionar *vb* **to collect a debt** cobrar una deuda *vb*

collecting *adj* **collecting agency** banco de cobros *nm*

collection *n* toma *nf*, recogida *nf*, recaudación *nf* **debt collection** cobro de morosos *nm*

collective 1. *adj* **collective agreement** convenio colectivo *nm* **collective bargaining** negociación colectiva *nf* **2.** *n* colectivo *nm*, cooperativa *nf* **workers' collective** propiedad colectiva *nf*

colloquium *n* coloquio *nm*

combination *n* combinación *nf*

command *n* mando *nm*

comment *n* comentario *nm*, observación *nf*

commerce *n* comercio *nm*

commercial *adj* comercial *adj*, mercantil *adj* **commercial bank** banco comercial *nm*, banco mercantil *nm* **commercial traveller, commercial traveler** (US) viajante de comercio *nmf*, corredor, -ora (LAm) *nm,f* **commercial vehicle** vehículo comercial *nm*

commission *n* comisión *nf*, encargo *nm*, servicio *nm*, comisión (LAm) *nf* **commission agent** comisionista *nmf* **commission broker** agente de bolsa *nmf*, comisionista *nmf* **commission fee** cuota de comisión *nf* **to charge commission** cobrar comisión *vb*

commit *vb* cometer *vb*, comprometer *vb*, asignar *vb*

commitment *n* compromiso *nm*, obligación *nf*, responsabilidad *nf*

committee *n* comité *nm*, comisión *nf* **advisory committee** comisión asesora *nf* **committee meeting** reunión del comité *nf*, reunión de la comisión *nf*

common *adj* común *adj* **Common Agricultural Policy (CAP)** Política Agrícola Común *nf* **Common Market** Mercado Común *nm* **common law** derecho consuetudinario *nm*

communication *n* comunicación *nf*, comunicado *nm* **communication network** red de comunicaciones *nf*

community *n* comunidad *nf*

companion *n* compañero, -era *nm,f*

company *n* compañía *nf*, empresa *nf*, sociedad *nf* **holding company** sociedad "holding" *nf* **incorporated company (US)** compañía constituida legalmente *nf* **joint-stock company** sociedad anónima *nf* **company law** ley de sociedades anónimas *nf* **limited company** sociedad de responsabilidad limitada *nf* **parent company** sociedad matriz *nf* **company policy** política de la empresa *nf* **private limited company** sociedad anónima privada *nf* **public limited company** sociedad anónima cuyas acciones se cotizan en bolsa *nf* **registered company** sociedad legalmente constituida *nf* **company secretary** secretario, -ria de la compañía *nm,f* **sister company** compañía asociada *nf* **subsidiary company** filial *nf*, sucursal *nf*

comparative *adj* comparativo *adj*

comparison *n* comparación *nf*, equiparación *nf*

compatible *adj* compatible *adj*

compensate for *vb* compensar por *vb*, indemnizar por *vb*

compensation *n* indemnización *nf*, compensación *nf*, resarcimiento *nm* **to claim compensation** pedir indemnización vb **to pay compensation** indemnizar vb, conceder indemnización vb

compete vb competir vb, hacer la competencia vb, participar vb **to compete with a rival** competir con un(a) rival vb

competing adj **competing company** empresa rival nf

competition n competencia nf, competición nf, concurso nm **cut-throat competition** competencia encarnizada nf **market competition** competencia de mercado nf **unfair competition** competencia desleal nf

competitive adj competitivo adj

competitiveness n competitividad nf

competitor n competidor, -ora nm,f

complain vb quejar vb **to complain about sth** quejarse de algo vb, protestar por algo vb

complaint n queja nf, protesta nf, reclamación nf, reclamo (LAm) nm **to make a complaint** presentar una queja vb, reclamar vb, protestar vb **complaints department** departamento de reclamaciones nm

complete vb terminar vb, acabar vb, rellenar vb

complex 1. adj complejo adj, complicado adj **2.** n **housing complex** complejo habitacional nm, complejo de viviendas nm, urbanización nf, colonia (LAm) nf

complimentary adj elogioso adj

comply vb acatar vb, obedecer vb **to comply with legislation** cumplir con las leyes vb **to comply with the rules** cumplir el reglamento vb, respetar las normas vb

compound adj **compound interest** interés compuesto nm

comprehensive adj amplio adj **comprehensive insurance policy** seguro a todo riesgo nm

compromise n acuerdo mutuo nm, transacción (LAm) nf **to reach a compromise** llegar a un acuerdo mutuo vb, llegar a un arreglo vb, transigir vb, transar (LAm) vb

computer n ordenador nm, computadora (LAm) nf **computer-aided design (CAD)** diseño asistido por ordenador (CAD) nm **computer-aided learning (CAL)** aprendizaje asistido por ordenador (CAL) nm **computer-aided manufacture (CAM)** fabricación asistida por ordenador (CAM) nf **computer centre, center** (US) centro informático nm **computer file** archivo nm **computer language** lenguaje de ordenador nm **laptop computer** ordenador portátil nm **computer literate** con conocimientos de informática prep **mainframe computer** ordenador central nm, unidad central nf **computer operator** operador, -ora de teclado nm,f **personal computer (PC)** ordenador personal (PC) nm **portable computer** ordenador portátil nm **computer program** programa de

ordenador nm, programa informático nm **computer programmer** programador, -ora de ordenadores nm,f, programador, -ora (LAm) nm,f **computer terminal** terminal del ordenador nm **computer ware** n soporte nm

concern 1. n **going concern** negocio en marcha nm, negocio en plena marcha nm **2.** vb (be of importance to) interesar vb, importar vb, incumbir vb, respetar vb

concur vb coincidir vb, concurrir vb

condition n **living conditions** condiciones de vida nfpl **conditions of purchase** condiciones de compra nfpl **conditions of sale** condiciones de venta nfpl **working conditions** condiciones de trabajo nfpl

conduct n conducta nf, comportamiento nm

conference n congreso nm, conferencia nf, reunión nf **conference proceedings** actas de conferencia nfpl **to arrange a conference** organizar una conferencia vb **conference venue** lugar de la conferencia nm

confidence n **in strictest confidence** con la más absoluta reserva prep

confidential adj confidencial adj

confirm vb confirmar vb **to confirm receipt of sth** acusar recibo de algo vb

confirmation n confirmación nf, ratificación nf

conglomerate n conglomerado nm

congress n congreso nm

connect vb **could you connect me to...** (telephone) ¿me pone con...? vb, comuníqueme con... (LAm) vb

connection n conexión nf **business connections** contactos comerciales nmpl, conexiones comerciales (LAm) nfpl

consent 1. n consentimiento nm **2.** vb consentir vb

consequence n consecuencia nf, resultado nm

consideration n (for contract) consideración nf

consignee n consignatario, -ria nm,f, destinatario, -ria nm,f

consigner/or n consignador, -ora nm,f, remitente nmf

consignment n consignación nf, envío nm, remesa nf

consolidate vb consolidar vb, reforzar vb

consolidated adj **consolidated figures** estadísticas consolidadas nf

consortium n consorcio nm

construction n **construction industry** industria de la construcción nf, construcción nf

consul n cónsul nmf

consulate n consulado nm

consult vb consultar vb, asesorar vb **to consult with sb** consultar a alguien vb

consultancy n asesoría nf **consultancy fees, consulting fees** (US) honorarios por asesoría nmpl **consultancy firm,**

consulting firm (US) asesoría *nf*, consultoría *nf* **consultancy work, consulting work** (US) asesoría *nf*, labor de asesoría *nf*

consultant *n* asesor, -ora *nm,f*, consultor, -ora *nm,f*, especialista *nmf*

consumer *n* consumidor, -ora *nm,f* **consumer credit** crédito al consumidor *nm* **consumer demand** demanda de consumo *nf* **consumer habits** conducta del consumidor *nf* **consumer research** investigación sobre el consumo *nf* **consumer satisfaction** satisfacción del consumidor *nf* **consumer survey** estudio de mercado *nm*, sondeo de opinión consumista *nm* **consumer trends** tendencias del consumidor *nfpl*, tendencias de consumo *nfpl*

consumerism *n* consumismo *nm*

contact 1. *n* contacto *nm* **business contacts** contactos comerciales *nmpl*, conocidos de negocios *nmpl*, enchufes *nmpl*, conexiones comerciales (LAm) *nfpl*, palancas (LAm) *nfpl* **to get in contact with sb** ponerse en contacto con alguien *vb* **2.** *vb* contactar (con) *vb*

container *n* contenedor *nm* **container depot** depósito de contenedores *nm* **container ship** portacontenedores *nm* **container terminal** terminal de portacontenedores *nf*

contract *n* contrato *nm* **breach of contract** incumplimiento de contrato *nm* **draft contract** proyecto de contrato *nm* **contract labour** mano de obra empleada a base de contrato *nf* **law of contract** derecho contractual *nm* **the terms of the contract** los términos del contrato *nmpl* **the signatories to the contract** los firmantes del contrato *nmpl* **to cancel a contract** anular un contrato *vb* **to draw up a contract** redactar un contrato *vb* **to sign a contract** firmar un contrato *vb* **to tender for a contract** licitar para un contrato *vb* **under the terms of the contract** según lo establecido en el contrato *prep*, bajo los términos del contrato *prep* **contract work** trabajo a contrata *nm*

contracting *adj* **the contracting parties** las partes contratantes *nf pl*

contractor *n* contratista *nmf* **building contractor** contratista de la construcción *nmf* **haulage contractor** contratista de transporte por carretera *nm*

contractual *adj* **contractual obligations** obligaciones contractuales *nfpl*

contravene *vb* contravenir *vb*, infringir *vb*

contravention *n* infracción *nf*

contribute *vb* contribuir *vb*, aportar *vb*, hacer aportes (LAm) *vb*

contribution *n* contribución *nf*, aportación *nf* **social security contributions** cotizaciones a la Seguridad Social *nfpl*, aportes a la seguridad social (LAm) *nmpl*

control *n* **financial control** control de finanzas *nm*, control financiero *nm* **production control** control de producción *nm* **quality control** control de calidad *nm* **stock control** control de existencias *nm*

convene *vb* **to convene a meeting** convocar una reunión *vb*

convenience *n* **at your earliest convenience** a su mayor brevedad posible *prep*

convenient *adj* oportuno *adj*, práctico *adj*

convertible *adj* **convertible currency** moneda convertible *nf*

copier *n* (photocopier) fotocopiadora *nf*

copy 1. *n* copia *nf*, número *nm* **2.** *vb* (photocopy) copiar *vb*, fotocopiar *vb*

copyright *n* derechos de autor *nmpl*, derechos de reproducción *nmpl*, "copyright" *nm* **copyright law** ley sobre la propiedad intelectual *nf*

corporate *adj* empresarial *adj*, de empresa *prep* **corporate image** imagen pública de la empresa *nf* **corporate investment** inversión de empresa *nf*

corporation *n* sociedad anónima *nf*, empresa *nf*, corporación *nf* **corporation tax** impuesto de sociedades *nm*

correspondence *n* correspondencia *nf*

corruption *n* corrupción *nf*

cosignatory *n* cosignatario, -ria *nm,f*

cost 1. *n* coste *nm*, gasto *nm*, costo (LAm) *nm* **cost breakdown** análisis de costes *nm* **cost centre** centro de coste *nm* **cost-cutting** reducción de gastos/costes *nf* **cost of living** coste de vida *nm* **operating cost** coste de explotación *nm*, costo de operación (LAm) *nm* **cost price** precio de coste *nm* **running cost** coste de explotación *nm*, costo de operación (LAm) *nm* **2.** *vb* **to cost a job** calcular el coste de un trabajo *vb*

counterfeit 1. *n* falsificación *nf* **2.** *vb* falsificar *vb*

counterfoil *n* matriz *nf*, talón (LAm) *nm*

countersign *vb* refrendar *vb*

country *n* **developing country** país en vías de desarrollo *nm* **third-world country** país del Tercer Mundo *nm*

coupon *n* cupón *nm*, vale *nm*, boleto *nm*

courier 1. *n* mensajero, -era *nm,f*, correo *nmf*, guía de turismo *nmf* **by courier service** por servicio de correo *prep* **2.** *vb* entregar por servicio de mensajero *vb*

court *n* corte *nf* **Court of Appeal, Court of Appeals** (US) Tribunal de Apelación *nm* **criminal court** tribunal penal *nm* **in court** ante el tribunal *prep*

covenant *n* pacto *nm*, convenio *nm*

covenantee *n* parte contratada *nf*

covenantor *n* parte contratante *nf*

cover *n* cobertura *nf* **insurance cover** cobertura del seguro *nf* **cover note** póliza provisional *nf*, nota de cobertura *nf*

credit 1. *adj* **credit agency** agencia de informes comerciales *nf* **credit card** tarjeta de crédito *nf* **credit company** sociedad financiera *nf* **credit control** control de crédito *nm* **credit enquiry** petición de informe sobre el crédito *nf* **credit note** nota de abono *nf*, nota de crédito *nf* **credit rating** clasificación crediticia *nf* **credit terms** condiciones de crédito *nfpl* **2.** *n* crédito *nm* **to buy sth on credit** comprar algo a crédito *vb*, comprar algo a plazos *vb* **in credit** con saldo acreedor *prep* **letter of credit** carta de crédito *nf* **long credit** crédito a largo plazo *nm* **3.** *vb* **to credit sth to an account** abonar algo en una cuenta *vb*, ingresar algo en una cuenta *vb*

creditor *n* acreedor, -ora *nm,f*

creditworthiness *n* solvencia *nf*, capacidad de pago *nf*

creditworthy *adj* solvente *adj*

crossed *adj* **crossed cheque** cheque cruzado *nm*

currency *n* moneda *nf*, divisa *nf* **convertible currency** moneda convertible *nf* **foreign currency** moneda extranjera *nf*, divisas *nfpl* **hard currency** moneda convertible *nf*, moneda fuerte *nf* **legal currency** moneda de curso legal *nf* **paper currency** papel moneda *nm* **soft currency** divisa débil *nf*, moneda no convertible *nf* **currency transfer** transferencia de divisas *nf*, transferencia de moneda *nf*

current *adj* **current account** cuenta corriente *nf*

curriculum vitae (CV), résumé (US) *n* currículum (vitae) (CV) *nm*

customer *n* cliente, -nta *nm,f* **customer loyalty** fidelidad a un establecimiento *nf* **regular customer** cliente, -nta de la casa *nm,f* **customer relations** relaciones con la clientela *nfpl*, relaciones públicas *nfpl*

customs *npl* aduana *nf* **customs charges** derechos de aduana *nmpl* **customs clearance** formalidades aduaneras *nfpl* **customs declaration** declaración de aduana *nf* **customs office** despacho de aduana *nm* **customs officer** aduanero, -era *nm,f*, funcionario, -ria de aduana *nm,f* **customs regulations** disposiciones aduaneras *nfpl* **to clear sth through customs** despachar algo por aduana *vb* **customs union** unión aduanera *nf* **customs warehouse** depósito aduanero *nm*

cut 1. *n* recorte *nm* **tax cut** reducción en los impuestos *nf* **2.** *vb* (reduce) recortar *vb*, rebajar *vb*

damage 1. *n* daño *nm*, daños *nmpl* **to cause extensive damage** ocasionar daños graves *vb* **to claim damages** (legal) reclamar por daños y perjuicios *vb* **damage to goods in transit** daños sufridos por mercancías durante el transporte *nmpl* **damage to property** daños materiales *nmpl* **2.** *vb* dañar *vb*, estropear *vb*, perjudicar *vb*

data *n* datos *nmpl*, información *nf* **data bank** banco de datos *nm* **database** base de datos *nf* **data capture** captación de datos *nf* **data processing** proceso de datos *nm*, procesamiento de datos *nm*

date *n* fecha *nf* **delivery date** fecha de entrega *nf* **out-of-date** anticuado *adj*, caducado *adj*, obsoleto *adj*, vencido (LAm) *adj*, perimido (LAm) *adj* **up-to-date** moderno *adj*, actualizado *adj*, al día *prep*

deal *n* trato *nm*, negocio *nm* **it's a deal!** ¡trato hecho! *nm*

dealer *n* comerciante *nmf*, agente mediador, -ora *nm,f* **foreign exchange dealer** agente de cambio *nmf*, operador, -ora de cambios *nm,f*, cambista *nmf*

dealing, trading (US) *n* comercio *nm*, operaciones en bolsa *nfpl* **foreign exchange dealings** cambio *nm*, operaciones de cambio *nfpl* **insider dealing** operaciones de iniciado *nfpl*, trato con información privilegiada *nm*

debenture *n* obligación *nf*, bono *nm*, pagaré *nm* **debenture bond** obligación no hipotecaria *nf* **debenture capital, debenture stock** (US) obligaciones garantizadas por los activos de la compañía *nfpl* **debenture loan** préstamo garantizado por obligaciones *nm*

debit 1. *n* débito *nm*, pasivo *nm*, cargo *nm* **debit balance** saldo negativo *nm*, saldo deudor *nm* **2.** *vb* (account) adeudar *vb*, cargar *vb*

debiting *n* **direct debiting** domiciliación bancaria *nf*

debt *n* deuda *nf*, endeudamiento *nm* **corporate debt** endeudamiento de una sociedad *nm* **to get into debt** endeudarse *vb* **to pay off a debt** saldar una deuda *vb* **to reschedule a debt** renegociar una deuda *vb* **debt service** pago de intereses de una deuda *nm*

debtor *n* deudor, -ora *nm,f*

decline *n* (economic) baja *nf*

decrease 1. *n* disminución *nf* **2.** *vb* disminuir *vb*, bajar *vb*, reducir *vb*

deduct *vb* deducir *vb*, desgravar *vb*

deductible *adj* deducible *adj*, desgravable *adj*

deduction *n* deducción *nf*, desgravación *nf*, descuento *nm*

deed *n* (law) escritura *nf*, título *nm* **deed of sale** escritura de venta *nf* **deed of transfer** escritura de transferencia *nf*

default 1. *n* falta *nf*, omisión *nf* **2.** *vb* incumplir *vb*

defect *n* defecto *nm*, tara *nf*

defective *adj* defectuoso *adj*

defer *vb* (postpone) posponer *vb*, aplazar *vb*

deferment *n* aplazamiento *nm*

deferred *adj* (tax) diferido *adj*, aplazado *adj*

deficiency *n* deficiencia *nf*, escasez *nf*

deficient *adj* deficiente *adj*, insuficiente *adj*

deficit *n* **deficit financing** financiación de déficit *nf*

deflation n deflación nf
deflationary adj deflacionista adj
defraud vb estafar vb
del credere adj **del credere agent** agente que recibe una comisión elevada porque garantiza el pago nmf
delay 1. n retraso nm, tardanza nf, demora (LAm) nf **without delay** sin tardanza prep, sin demora (LAm) prep **2.** vb retrasar vb, tardar vb, demorar (LAm) vb
delegate 1. n delegado, -ada nm,f **2.** vb delegar vb
delegation n delegación nf, delegación de poderes nf, representación nf
deliver vb (goods) entregar vb, repartir vb, cumplir vb
delivery n entrega nf, reparto nm, remesa nf **cash on delivery** entrega contra reembolso nf, cobro a la entrega nm **delivery date** fecha de entrega nf **free delivery** entrega gratuita nf **general delivery (US)** entrega general nf **recorded delivery** correo certificado con acuse de recibo nm **delivery time** plazo de entrega nm
demand 1. n demanda nf, reivindicación nf, petición nf, pedido (LAm) nm **supply and demand** oferta y demanda nf & nf **2.** vb exigir vb, reivindicar vb, reclamar vb
demography n demografía nf
demote vb (employee) rebajar vb
denationalize vb privatizar vb
department n departamento nm, sección nf **government department** ministerio nm, secretaría (LAm) nf **personnel department** departamento de personal nm **department store** grandes almacenes nmpl, tienda de departamentos (LAm) nf
depletion n reducción nf, disminución nf, agotamiento nm
deposit 1. adj **deposit account** cuenta de ahorros nf **2.** n depósito nm, imposición nf, entrada nf, pie (LAm) nm, seña (LAm) nf **3.** vb depositar vb, ingresar vb
depository n depositario, -ria nm,f, guardamuebles nm
depreciate vb depreciarse vb, perder valor vb, amortizar vb
depreciation n depreciación nf, amortización nf, pérdida de valor nf
depression n (economic) recesión nf, crisis nf
deputy 1. adj adjunto adj **deputy director** subdirector, -ora nm,f, director, -ora adjunto, -nta nm,f **2.** n suplente nmf
design 1. n diseño nm, motivo nm **a machine of good/bad design** una máquina bien/mal diseñada nf **2.** vb diseñar vb, proyectar vb, planear vb
designer n (commercial) diseñador, -ora nm,f
devaluation n devaluación nf
developer n promotor, -ora nm,f, promotor, -ora de contrucciones nm,f
digital adj digital adj
diminishing adj **diminishing returns** rendimientos decrecientes nmpl

director n director, -ora nm,f, directivo, -iva nm,f, consejero, -era nm,f **board of directors** consejo de administración nm, junta directiva nf **managing director** director, -ora gerente nm,f, director, -ora ejecutivo, -iva nm,f
disburse vb desembolsar vb
discount n descuento nm, bonificación nf **at a discount** con descuento prep, descontado adj **discount rate** tipo de descuento nm
discounted adj **discounted cash flow (DCF)** "cash flow" actualizado nm, flujo de caja descontado nm
disk n diskette nm, disquete nm **disk drive** unidad de disco nf **floppy disk** disco flexible nm, "floppy" nm **hard disk** disco duro nm **magnetic disk** disco magnético nm
dismiss vb (employee) despedir vb, botar (LAm) vb
dispatch 1. n **date of dispatch** fecha de expedición nf **2.** vb (goods) despachar vb, enviar vb
dispatcher n expedidor, -ora nm,f
display 1. n (of goods) exhibición nf, exposición nf **2.** vb exhibir vb, exponer vb, demostrar vb
disposable adj (not for reuse) desechable adj **disposable income** ingresos disponibles nmpl
dispute n disputa nf, conflicto nm, diferendo (LAm) nm **industrial dispute** conflicto laboral nm
distribution n distribución nf, reparto nm
distributor n distribuidor, -ora nm,f
diversification n diversificación nf
diversify vb diversificarse vb
dividend n dividendo nm, beneficio nm
division n (of company) división nf, sección nf **division of labour** división del trabajo nf
dock 1. n (for berthing) muelle nm **2.** vb (ship) entrar en dársena vb, atracar vb, fondear vb
dockyard n astillero nm
document documento nm, papel nm **document retrieval** recuperación de documentos nf
domestic adj **domestic policy** política nacional nf
door n **door-to-door selling** venta domiciliaria nf
double adj **double-entry** (bookkeeping) de partida doble prep
Dow-Jones average (US) n índice Dow Jones nm
down adv **down payment** entrada nf, pago inicial nm, pie (LAm) nm
downturn n (economic) descenso nm, bajón nm
downward adj & adv hacia abajo prep, a la baja prep, descendente adj
draft 1. n (financial) giro nm, efecto bancario nm, borrador nm **2.** vb redactar vb
draw vb (cheque) girar vb

dry *adj* **dry goods** artículos de mercería *nmpl*

dumping *n* dumping *nm*

durable *adj* **durable goods** bienes duraderos *nm*

duty *n* (customs) derecho *nm*, deber *nm* **duty-free** (goods) libre de impuestos, libre de derechos de aduana *adj, adv*

dynamic *adj* dinámico *adj*

dynamics *npl* dinámica *nf*

early *adj* **early retirement** jubilación anticipada *nf*

earn *vb* ganar *vb*, percibir *vb*, devengar *vb*

earned *adj* ganado *adj*, percibido *adj* **earned income** ingresos en concepto de sueldo *nmpl* **earned surplus** superávit percibido *nm*

earnest *adj* serio *adj* **earnest money** fianza *nf*

earning *adj* **earning capacity** capacidad de ganar dinero *nf*, grado de rendimiento *nm* **earning power** capacidad de ganar dinero *nf*, grado de rendimiento *nm*, escala de rendimiento *nf*

earnings *npl* ingresos *nmpl*, ganancias *nfpl*, beneficios *nmpl*, utilidades (LAm) *nfpl* **earnings drift** deriva de ingresos *nf* **loss of earnings** pérdida de ingresos *nf* **earnings-related pension** pensión proporcional al sueldo *nf* **earnings yield** rédito *nm*

easy *adj* fácil *adj* **easy-money policy** política monetaria expansiva *nf*

EC (European Community) *abbr* CE (Comunidad Europea) *abbr,nf*

econometrics *n* econometría *nf*

economic *adj* **economic adviser** asesor, -ora económico, -ica *nm,f* **economic analysis** análisis económico *nm* **economic crisis** crisis económica *nf* **economic cycle** ciclo económico *nm* **economic decline** declive económico *nm* **economic development** desarrollo económico *nm* **Economic and Monetary Union** Unión Económica y Monetaria *nf* **economic expansion** expansión económica *nf* **economic forecast** previsión económica *nf* **economic geography** geografía económica *nf* **economic growth** crecimiento económico *nm* **economic infrastructure** infraestructura económica *nf* **economic integration** integración económica *nf* **economic objective** objetivo económico *nm* **economic performance** rendimiento económico *nm*, performance económico (LAm) *nm* **economic planning** planificación económica *nf* **economic policy** política económica *nf* **economic sanction** sanción económica *nf* **economic slowdown** desaceleración económica *nf* **economic strategy** estrategia económica *nf* **economic superpower** superpotencia económica *nf* **economic survey** estudio económico *nm*, sondeo económico *nm* **economic trend** tendencias económicas *nfpl* **economic union** unión económica *nf*

economical *adj* económico *adj*

economics *n* economía *nf*

economist *n* economista *nmf*

economy *n* (system) economía *nf* **advanced economy** economía avanzada *nf* **developing economy** economía en vías de desarrollo *nf* **free market economy** economía de mercado libre *nf* **global economy** economía global *nf* **economies of scale** economías de escala *nfpl* **national economy** economía nacional *nf* **planned economy** economía planificada *nf* **underdeveloped economy** economía subdesarrollada *nf*

ECSC (European Coal and Steel Community) *abbr* Comunidad Europea del Carbón y del Acero *nf*

ECU (European Currency Unit) *abbr* ecu (European Currency Unit) *nm*

edge *n* **competitive edge** margen competitivo *nm*, ventaja sobre la competencia *nf*

effect *n* efecto *nm* **financial effects** efectos financieros *nmpl*

efficiency *n* eficiencia *nf*

efficient *adj* eficiente *adj*, eficaz *adj*

EFT (electronic funds transfer) *abbr* transferencia electrónica de fondos *nf*

EFTA (European Free Trade Association) *abbr* EFTA (la) *abbr,nf*, Asociación Europea de Libre Comercio *nf*

elasticity *n* elasticidad *nf* **income elasticity** elasticidad de ingresos *nf* **elasticity of demand** elasticidad de demanda *nf* **elasticity of production** elasticidad de producción *nf*

election *n* elección *nf* **general election** elecciones generales *nfpl*, comicios *nmpl* **local election** elecciones municipales *nfpl*

electronic *adj* electrónico *adj* **electronic banking** banca electrónica *nf* **electronic data processing** proceso electrónico de datos (EDP) *nm* **electronic mail** correo electrónico *nm*

elimination *n* eliminación *nf* **elimination of tariffs** supresión de aranceles *nf*

email *n* correo electrónico *nm*

embargo *n* embargo *nm* **to impose an embargo** imponer un embargo *vb* **to lift an embargo** levantar un embargo *vb* **trade embargo** embargo comercial *nm*

embassy *n* embajada *nf*

embezzle *vb* malversar *vb*

embezzlement *n* malversación *nf*, desfalco *nm*

embezzler *n* malversador, -ora *nm,f*

emergency *n* emergencia *nf* **emergency fund** fondo de emergencia *nm*

emigration *n* emigración *nf*

employ *vb* contratar *vb*, emplear *vb*, utilizar *vb*

employee *n* empleado, -ada *nm,f* **employee recruitment** contratación de empleados *nf*, contratación de personal *nf* **employee**

training formación de empleados *nf*
employer *n* patrón, -ona *nm,f,* empresario, -ria *nm,f* **employer's federation** organización patronal *nf* **employers' liability insurance** seguro empresarial contra terceros *nm*
employment *n* empleo *nm,* ocupación *nf,* trabajo *nm* **employment agency** agencia de trabajo *nf,* agencia de colocaciones *nf,* oficina de empleo *nf* **employment contract** contrato de trabajo *nm* **full employment** pleno empleo *nm* **employment law** derecho laboral *nm*
encashment *n* cobro (en metálico) *nm*
enclose *vb* adjuntar *vb,* remitir adjunto *vb*
enclosure *n* anexo *nm*
end *n* fin *nm,* final *nm,* extremo *nm* **end consumer** usuario, -ria final *nm,f,* consumidor, -ora final *nm,f* **end user** usuario, -ria final *nm,f*
endorse *vb* (cheque) endosar *vb*
endorsement *n* aprobación *nf*
endowment *n* donación *nf,* legado *nm,* dotación *nf* **endowment insurance** seguro de combinación aplazada y decreciente *nm* **endowment policy** póliza dotal *nf*
enforce *vb* (policy) aplicar *vb,* ejecutar *vb*
enforcement *n* aplicación *nf,* ejecución *nf*
engagement *n* (meeting) compromiso *nm,* cita *nf*
engineering *n* ingeniería *nf* **civil engineering** ingeniería civil *nf* **electrical engineering** ingeniería eléctrica *nf* **mechanical engineering** ingeniería mecánica *nf* **precision engineering** ingeniería de precisión *nf*
enhance *vb* (value) incrementar *vb*
enlarge *vb* ampliar *vb,* aumentar *vb*
enquire *vb* preguntar *vb*
enquiry *n* pregunta *nf,* petición de informes *nf,* investigación *nf*
enterprise *n* (project) empresa *nf,* iniciativa *nf* **private enterprise** iniciativa privada *nf,* sector privado *nm,* empresa privada *nf*
entertain *vb* **to entertain a client** recibir a un cliente *vb,* invitar a un cliente *vb*
entrepôt *n* depósito *nm,* centro de almacenaje y distribución *nm*
entrepreneur *n* empresario, -ria *nm,f,* contratista *nmf*
entrepreneurial *adj* empresarial *adj*
entry *n* entrada *nf,* asiento *nm* **entry for free goods** entrada para mercancías exentas de derechos de aduana *nf,* entrada para mercaderías exentas de derechos de aduana (LAm) *nf* **entry into force** entrada en vigor *nf,* entrada a vigor (LAm) *nf* **port of entry** puerto de entrada *nm* **entry visa** visado de entrada *nm,* visa de entrada (LAm) *nf*
equalization *n* **equalization of burdens** equiparación de cargas *nf*
equalize *vb* igualar *vb,* compensar *vb*
equilibrium *n* equilibrio *nm*
equip *vb* equipar *vb,* proveer *vb*

equipment *n* equipo *nm,* útiles *nmpl,* equipamiento *nm,* enseres *nmpl* **equipment leasing** arrendamiento de medios de producción *nm*
equity *n* patrimonio neto *nm,* derechos sobre el activo *nmpl* **equity capital** capital social *nm* **equity financing** financiación de valores *nf,* financiación de acciones *nf* **equity interests** intereses en títulos *nmpl* **equity share** valor de renta variable *nm* **equity trading** comercio de acciones *nm* **equity transaction** operación en el mercado de valores *nf*
ergonomics *n* ergonomía *nf*
escalate *vb* aumentar *vb,* intensificarse *vb*
escalation *n* (prices) escalada *nf*
escalator *n* escalera mecánica *nf*
escudo *n* escudo *nm*
establish *vb* establecer *vb,* montar *vb,* instalar *vb*
establishment *n* establecimiento *nm,* creación *nf,* casa *nf*
estate *n* **estate agency, real estate agency** (US) agencia inmobiliaria *nf* **estate agent, real estate agent** (US) agente inmobiliario, -ria *nm,f*
estimate 1. *n* cálculo *nm,* valoración *nf* **estimate of costs** presupuesto de costes *nm,* presupuesto de gastos *nm,* presupuesto de costos (LAm) *nm* **2.** *vb* calcular *vb,* valorar *vb,* estimar *vb*
eurobond *n* eurobono *nm*
eurocapital *n* eurocapital *nm*
eurocheque *n* eurocheque *nm*
eurocracy *n* eurocracia *nf*
eurocrat *n* eurócrata *nmf*
eurocredit *n* eurocrédito *nm*
eurocurrency *n* eurodivisa *nf* **eurocurrency market** mercado de la eurodivisa *nm*
eurodollar *n* eurodólar *nm*
eurofunds *npl* eurofondos *nm*
euromarket *n* euromercado *nm*
euromerger *n* eurofusión *nf*
euromoney *n* euromoneda *nf*
European *adj* europeo *adj* **Council of Europe** Consejo de Europa *nm* **European Advisory Committee** Comisión Consultiva Europea *nf* **European Commission** Comisión Europea *nf* **European Community (EC)** Comunidad Europea (CE) *nf* **European Court of Justice (ECJ)** Tribunal Europeo de Justicia *nm* **European Development Fund (EDF)** Fondo Europeo de Desarrollo (FED) *nm* **European Investment Bank (EIB)** Banco Europeo de Inversiones (BEI) *nm* **European Monetary Agreement (EMA)** Acuerdo Monetario Europeo (AME) *nm* **European Monetary Cooperation Fund (EMCF)** Fondo Europeo de Cooperación Monetaria (FECM) *nm* **European Monetary System (EMS)** Sistema Monetario Europeo (SME) *nm* **European Monetary Union (EMU)** Unión Monetaria Europea (UME) *nf* **European**

Parliament Parlamento Europeo *nm*
European Recovery Plan Plan Europeo de
Recuperación *nm* **European Regional
Development Fund (ERDF)** Fondo
Europeo de Desarrollo Regional (FEDR) *nm*
European Social Fund (ESF) Fondo Social
Europeo (FSE) *nm* **European Union** Unión
Europea *nf* **European Unit of Account
(EUA)** Unidad de Cuenta Europea (UCE) *nf*
eurosceptic *n* euroescéptico *adj*
evade *vb* evadir *vb*
evasion *n* **tax evasion** evasión fiscal *nf,*
evasión de impuestos *nf,* fraude fiscal *nm*
eviction *n* desahucio *nm,* lanzamiento *nm*
ex *prep* **ex factory/works** en fábrica *prep,*
franco en fábrica, en almacén *prep* **ex
gratia payment** paga voluntaria *nf,* pago
ex-gratia *nm* **ex interest** sin interés *prep,*
sin intereses *prep* **ex quay** en el muelle
prep **ex repayment** sin reembolso *prep* sin
pago *prep* **ex ship** en buque *prep* **ex stock**
de existencias disponibles *prep* **ex store/
warehouse** en almacén *prep* **ex wharf** en
el muelle *prep*
examination *n* examen *nm,* revisión *nf,*
revisación (LAm) *nf*
examine *vb* examinar *vb,* estudiar *vb,* revisar
(LAm) *vb*
exceed *vb* sobrepasar *vb,* superar *vb*
excess *adj* **excess capacity** capacidad
excesiva *nf* **excess demand inflation**
inflación provocada por la demanda
excesiva *nf* **excess profit(s) tax** impuesto
sobre beneficios extraordinarios *nm* **excess
reserves** exceso de reservas *nm*
exchange *n* **exchange broker** operador,
-ora de cambios *nm,f,* cambista *nmf*
exchange cheque cheque en divisas *nm*
exchange clearing agreement convenio
de compensación de cambio *nm* **exchange
control** control de divisas *nm* **foreign
exchange** divisas *nf,* moneda extranjera *nf*
exchange market mercado de divisas *nm*
exchange rate tipo de cambio *nm,* tasa de
cambio (LAm) *nf* **exchange rate
mechanism (ERM)** mecanismo de tasas de
cambio *nm,* mecanismo de paridades *nm*
exchange restrictions restricciones a
divisas *nfpl* **exchange risk** riesgo del
cambio *nm* **Stock Exchange** bolsa *nf,*
bolsa de valores *nf*
excise *n* **excise duty** impuesto sobre la
venta *nm* **the Board of Customs and
Excise** administración de aduanas e
impuestos sobre el consumo *nf*
exclude *vb* excluir *vb*
exclusion *n* **exclusion clause** cláusula de
exclusión *nf* **exclusion zone** zona de
exclusión *nf*
executive 1. *adj* **executive committee**
comisión ejecutiva *nf* **executive
compensation** recompensa de directivos *nf*
executive duties funciones ejecutivas *nfpl*
executive hierarchy jerarquía de dirección

nf **executive personnel** personal directivo
nm **2.** *n* ejecutivo, -iva *nm,f,* director, -ora
nm,f
exempt *adj* exento *adj,* libre *adj* **tax-exempt**
exento de impuestos *adj*
exemption *n* exención *nf,* exoneración *nf,*
desgravación *nf*
exhaust *vb* (reserves) agotar *vb*
exhibit *vb* exponer *vb,* exhibir *vb*
exhibition *n* exposición *nf,* muestra *nf*
exorbitant *adj* excesivo *adj*
expand *vb* expandir *vb,* ampliar *vb,* aumentar
vb
expansion *n* expansión *nf,* ampliación *nf,*
desarrollo *nm* **expansion of capital**
aumento de capital *nm,* incremento de
capitales *nm* **expansion of trade**
expansión del comercio *nf,* ampliación
comercial *nf*
expectation *n* expectativa *nf* **consumer
expectations** expectativas del consumidor
nfpl
expedite *vb* expeditar *vb,* acelerar *vb*
expenditure *n* gasto *nm,* gastos *nmpl,*
desembolso *nm* **expenditure rate**
coeficiente de gastos *nm* **state
expenditure** gasto público *nm*
expenditure taxes impuestos sobre gastos
nmpl
expense *n* gasto *nm* **expense account**
cuenta de gastos de representación *nf*
expense control control de gastos *nm*
entertainment expenses gastos de
representación *nmpl* **travelling expenses,
travel expenses** (US) gastos de viaje *nmpl,*
gastos de desplazamiento *nmpl*
experience 1. *n* experiencia *nf* **experience
curve** curva de la experiencia *nf* **2.** *vb*
experimentar *vb,* sentir *vb*
experienced *adj* con experiencia *prep*
expert 1. *adj* perito *adj* **2.** *n* experto, -rta
nm,f
expertise *n* competencia *nf,* conocimientos
nmpl
expiration *n* expiración *nf,* terminación *nf,*
vencimiento *nm*
expire *vb* caducar *vb,* vencer *vb*
expiry, expiration (US) *n* caducidad *nf,*
expiración *nf,* vencimiento *nm* **expiry date,
expiration** (US) fecha de caducidad *nf,*
fecha de vencimiento *nf*
export 1. *adj* **export bill of lading**
conocimiento de embarque de exportación
nm **export credit** crédito a la exportación
nm **export credit insurance** seguro de
crédito a la exportación *nm* **export
department** departamento de exportación
nm **export-led growth** crecimiento regido
por la exportación *nm* **export licence**
permiso de exportación *nm* **export
marketing** promoción de las exportaciones
nf **export operations** operaciones de
exportación *nfpl* **export strategy** estrategia
de exportación *nf* **export subsidies**

subvenciones dirigidas a fomentar las
exportaciones *nfpl* **export surplus**
superávit de exportación *nm* **export tax**
impuesto a la exportación *nm* **export trade**
comercio de exportación *nm* **2.**
n exportación *nf* **export of capital**
exportación de capitales *nf* **3.** *vb* exportar *vb*
exporter *n* exportador, -ora *nm,f*
express *adj* exprés *adj*, expreso *adj* **express**
agency agencia exprés *nf* **express**
delivery entrega urgente *nf*, reparto rápido
a domicilio *nm* **express service** servicio
urgente *nm*
expropriate *vb* expropiar *vb*
expropriation *n* expropiación *nf*
extend *vb* **to extend a contract** extender
un contrato *vb* **to extend credit** otorgar
crédito *vb* **to extend the range** ampliar la
gama *vb*
extension *n* (of contract) extensión *nf*,
ampliación *nf*, prórroga *nf*
extent *n* **extent of cover** nivel de cobertura
nm
external *adj* externo *adj*, exterior *adj*
external audit auditoría externa *nf*
extortion *n* extorsión *nf*
extra *adj* extra *adj*, adicional *adj*,
suplementario *adj* **extra cost** coste
adicional *nm*, gasto complementario *nm*,
costo adicional (LAm) *nm* **extra profit**
beneficios extraordinarios *nmpl*
extraordinary *adj* **extraordinary meeting**
junta extraordinaria *nf* **extraordinary value**
valor extraordinario *nm*
facility *n* facilidad *nf*, servicio *nm*, instalación
nf **facility planning** planificación de
servicios *nf*
facsimile (fax) *n* facsímile *nm*, telefax *nm*,
fax *nm*
factor 1. *adj* **factor income** ingresos de los
factores *nmpl* **factor market** mercado de
factores (de producción) *nm* **factor price**
precio de los factores de producción *nm*
2. *n* (buyer of debts) agente al por mayor
nmf **limiting factor** factor limitativo *nm*
factor of production factor de producción
nm **3.** *vb* (debts) hacer factoring *vb*
factoring *n* (of debts) factoring *nm*, gestión
de deudas de otras compañías con
descuento *nf*
factory *n* **factory board** comisión de
fábricas *nf*, consejo de la fábrica *nm* **factory**
costs gastos de fábrica *nmpl*, costos de
fábrica (LAm) *nmpl* **factory inspector**
inspector, -ora de fábrica *nm,f* **factory**
ledger libro mayor de la fábrica *nm*, registro
de fábricas *nm* **factory overheads** gastos
generales de fabricación *nmpl* **factory**
price precio en fábrica *nm*, precio franco
fábrica *nm*
fail *vb* (negotiations) fracasar *vb*, fallar *vb*
failure *n* fracaso *nm*, fallo *nm*, quiebra *nf*
fair *adj* justo *adj*, limpio *adj* **fair competition**
competencia leal *nf* **fair market value**

valor justo de mercado *nm* **fair rate of**
return tasa de rendimentio justa *nf* **fair-**
trade agreement convenio sobre los
precios mínimos de venta al público *nm*
fair-trade policy política de comercio de
reciprocidad arancelaria *nf* **fair-trade**
practice práctica de vender a precio
mínimo al público *nf* **fair trading** prácticas
comerciales leales *nfpl* **fair wage** salario
justo *nm*
fall due *vb* vencer *vb*
falling *adj* **falling prices** precios con
tendencia a la baja *nmpl* **falling rate of**
profit tasa de beneficios decreciente *nf*
false *adj* **false representation**
representación falsa *nf*
falsification *n* falsificación *nf* **falsification**
of accounts falsificación de cuentas *nf*
family *n* **family allowance** prestación
estatal a la familia *nf*, asignación familiar
(LAm) *nf* **family branding** identificación
por marca *nf* **family corporation** empresa
familiar *nf* **family income** ingresos
familiares *nmpl* **family industry** industria
familiar *nf*
farm out *vb* subcontratar *vb*, delegar *vb*,
encargar *vb*
farming *n* agricultura *nf*, cultivo *nm*, crianza
nf **farming of taxes** cesión por el gobierno
de la acción recaudatoria a un particular *nf*
farming subsidies subsidios agrícolas
nmpl
FAS (free alongside ship) *abbr* franco en
muelle *adj*, *adv*
fast *adj* **fast-selling goods** artículos de
venta rápida *nmpl*, mercancías de venta fácil
nfpl, mercaderías de venta rápida (LAm) *nfpl*
fast track pista de máxima velocidad *nf*
fault *n* defecto *nm*, culpa *nf*, avería *nf* **minor**
fault defecto menor *nm*, fallo de poca
importancia *nm* **serious fault** defecto grave
nm, avería importante *nf* **to find fault with**
criticar *vb*, parecerle mal a *vb*
faulty *adj* **faulty goods** artículos
defectuosos *nmpl* **faulty workmanship**
trabajo defectuoso *nm*
favour *n* favor *nm* **to do sb a favour** hacerle
un favor a alguien *vb*
favourable *adj* **favourable balance of**
payments balanza de pagos favorable *nf*
favourable balance of trade balanza
comercial favorable *nf* **favourable**
exchange cambio favorable *nm*
favourable price precio favorable *nm*
favourable terms términos ventajosos
nmpl
fax 1. *n* fax *nm*, telefax *nm*, facsímil *nm* **2.** *vb*
enviar por fax *vb*
feasibility *n* viabilidad *nf*, posibilidad *nf*
feasibility study estudio de viabilidad *nm*
feasible *adj* viable *adj*, factible *adj*, posible
adj
federal *adj* federal *adj*
federation *n* federación *nf*

fee *n* honorarios *nmpl*, comisión *nf* **to charge a fee** cobrar honorarios *vb* **to pay a fee** pagar una cuota *vb*

feedback *n* reacción *nf*, respuesta *nf*, información *nf* **to give feedback** comunicar la reacción *vb*

fiat *n* **fiat money** dinero de curso forzoso *nm*

fictitious *adj* ficticio *adj*, falso *adj* **fictitious assets** activos ficticios *nmpl* **fictitious purchase** compra ficticia *nf* **fictitious sale** venta ficticia *nf*

fidelity *n* fidelidad *nf* **fidelity bond** bono de fidelidad *nm*, obligación de fidelidad *nf* **fidelity insurance** seguro de fidelidad *nm*

fiduciary *adj* **fiduciary bond** fianza fiduciaria *nf*, obligación fiduciaria *nf* **fiduciary issue** emisión fiduciaria *nf*

field *n* **field investigation** investigación de campo *nf*, trabajo de campo *nm* **field manager** director, -ora de campo *nm,f* **field personnel** personal de campo *nm* **field research** investigación de campo *nf*, trabajo de campo *nm*, investigación directa *nf* **field test** prueba sobre el terreno *nf* **field work** estudios sobre el terreno *nm*

FIFO (first in first out) *abbr* primeras entradas, primeras salidas *nfpl & nfpl*

file 1. *n* carpeta *nf*, archivo *nm* **2.** *vb* archivar *vb*, presentar *vb*, entregar *vb*

filing *n* **filing cabinet** archivador *nm*, archivero (LAm) *nm* **filing system** sistema de archivo *nm*

final *adj* **final accounts** cuentas definitivas *nfpl* **final demand** petición final *nf* **final entry** asiento final *nm* **final invoice** última factura *nf* **final offer** última oferta *nf* **final products** productos finales *nmpl*, productos acabados *nmpl* **final settlement** acuerdo final *nm*, ajuste definitivo *nm* **final utility** utilidad final *nf*

finance 1. *adj* **finance bill** ley presupuestaria *nf* **finance company** sociedad financiera *nf*, compañía de crédito comercial *nf* **Finance Act** Ley Presupuestaria *nf* **2.** *n* finanzas *nfpl* **3.** *vb* financiar *vb*

financial *adj* financiero *adj*, económico *adj* **financial accounting** contabilidad financiera *nf* **financial assets** activos financieros *nmpl* **financial balance** balance financiero *nm* **financial company** entidad financiera *nf* **financial consultancy** asesoría financiera *nf* **financial consultant** asesor, -ora financiero, -era *nm,f* **financial control** control financiero *nm* **financial crisis** crisis económica *nf* **financial difficulty** dificultad financiera *nf* **financial exposure** riesgos financieros *nmpl* **financial incentives** incentivos financieros *nmpl* **financial institution** entidad financiera *nf* **financial investment** inversión financiera *nf* **financial loan** préstamo financiero *nm* **financial management** gestión financiera *nf*,

dirección financiera *nf* **financial market** mercado financiero *nm* **financial measures** medidas financieras *nfpl* **financial operation** operación financiera *nf* **financial planning** planificación financiera *nf* **financial policy** política financiera *nf* **financial report** informe financiero *nm* **financial resources** recursos financieros *nmpl* **financial risk** riesgo financiero *nm* **financial situation** situación financiera *nf* **financial stability** estabilidad financiera *nf* **financial statement** estado financiero *nm*, balance general *nm* **financial strategy** estrategia financiera *nf* **financial structure** estructura financiera *nf* **financial year** año fiscal *nm*, ejercicio (económico) *nm*

financier *n* financiero, -era *nm,f*

financing *n* financiación *nf* **financing surplus** excedente de financiación *nm*

fine *adj* **fine rate of interest** buen tipo de interés *nm*, alta tasa de interés (LAm) *nf*

finished *adj* **finished goods** productos acabados *nmpl* **finished stock** existencias acabadas *nfpl* **finished turnover** volumen de ventas acabado *nm*

fire* *vb* despedir *vb*, echar *vb*

firm *adj* **firm offer** oferta en firme *nf* **firm price** precio en firme *nm*

first *adj* **first bill of exchange** primera letra de cambio *nf* **first class** primera clase *nf* **first-class paper** papel de primera clase *nm*, ponencia de primera categoría *nf* **first customer** primer, -ra cliente, -nta *nm,f* **first-hand** de primera mano *prep*, directamente *adv* **first mortgage** primera hipoteca *nf* **first-rate** (investment) de primer orden *prep*

fiscal *adj* **fiscal agent** agente fiscal *nmf* **fiscal balance** balance fiscal *nm* **fiscal charges** costes fiscales *nmpl*, costos fiscales (LAm) *nmpl* **fiscal measures** medidas fiscales *nfpl* **fiscal policy** política fiscal *nf* **fiscal receipt** ingreso fiscal *nm* **fiscal year** año fiscal *nm*, ejercicio fiscal *nm* **fiscal year end (fye)** fin de año fiscal *nm* **fiscal zoning** zonación fiscal *nf*

fix *vb* **to fix the price** fijar el precio *vb*

fixed *adj* **fixed assets** activo fijo *nm*, inmovilizado *nm* **fixed asset turnover** facturación de activo fijo *nf* **fixed budget** presupuesto fijo *nm* **fixed charges** precios fijos *nmpl* **fixed costs** costes fijos *nmpl*, costos fijos (LAm) *nmpl* **fixed credit** crédito fijo *nm* **fixed income** ingresos fijos *nmpl*, renta fija *nf* **fixed interest** interés fijo *nm* **fixed liabilities** deudas a largo plazo *nfpl* **fixed price** precio fijo *nm*

fixture *n* **fixtures and fittings** instalaciones fijas y accesorios *nfpl & nmpl*

flat *adj* **flat bond** bono sin intereses *nm* **flat market** mercado inactivo *nm* **flat rate** cuota fija *nf*, tasa de interés fija (LAm) *nf* **flat-rate income tax** impuesto sobre la renta a cuota fija *nm*, impuesto a los réditos a cuota fija (LAm) *nm* **flat-rate tariff** precio a cuota fija *nm*

flexibility *n* (of prices) flexibilidad *nf*

flexible *adj* **flexible budget** presupuesto flexible *nm* **flexible exchange rate** tipo de cambio flexible *nm*, tasa de cambio flexible (LAm) *nf* **flexible price** precio flexible *nm*

flexitime, flextime (US) *n* horario flexible *nm*

flight *n* (in plane) vuelo *nm*, trayectoria *nf*, fuga *nf* **flight capital** capitales de fuga *nmpl* **to book a flight** reservar un vuelo *vb*

float *vb* (currency) dejar flotar *vb*

floating *adj* **floating assets** activo circulante *nm* **floating exchange rate** tipo de cambio flotante *nm*, tasa de cambio flotante (LAm) *nf* **floating rate interest** interés de tipo flotante *nm*, interés de tasa flotante (LAm) *nf*

floor *n* **floor broker** corredor, -ora de bolsa *nm,f*, corredor, -ora de parquet *nm,f* **shopfloor** taller *nm*, obreros *nmpl*

flotation *n* salida a bolsa *nf*, emisión *nf*

flow *n* **cash flow** flujo de caja *nm*, "cash flow" *nm* **flow chart** organigrama *nm*, diagrama de flujos *nm*, diagrama de secuencia *nm* **flow line production** fabricación en cadena *nf*, nivel de producción *nm* **flow of income** flujo de ingresos *nm* **flow production** fabricación en cadena *nf*

fluctuate *vb* fluctuar *vb*

fluctuation *n* fluctuación *nf* **fluctuation in sales** fluctuaciones de ventas *nfpl*

fluid *adj* fluido *adj*, líquido *adj* **fluid market** mercado fluido *nm*, mercado inestable *nm*

FOB (free on board) *abbr* fab (franco a bordo) *abbr*

for *prep* **for sale** en venta *prep*, se vende *vb*

forced *adj* **forced currency** divisas forzosas *nfpl*

forecast 1. *n* previsión *nf*, predicción *nf* **2.** *vb* prever *vb*, pronosticar *vb*, predecir *vb*

forecasting *n* previsión *nf*

foreclose *vb* entablar juicio hipotecario *vb*

foreclosure *n* ejecución *nf*, ejecución de un juicio hipotecario *nf*

foreign *adj* extranjero *adj*, exterior *adj*, extraño *adj* **foreign aid** asistencia económica al exterior *nf* **foreign aid programme** programa de asistencia al exterior *nm* **foreign bank** banco extranjero *nm*, banco exterior *nm* **foreign company** compañía extranjera *nf*, empresa exterior *nf* **foreign competition** competencia extranjera *nf* **foreign currency** divisas *nfpl*, moneda extranjera *nf* **foreign exchange** divisas *nfpl*, moneda extranjera *nf*, cambio de moneda extranjera *nm* **foreign exchange dealer** cambista *nmf*, operador, -ora de cambios *nm,f* **foreign exchange market** mercado de divisas *nm* **foreign currency holdings** cartera de valores extranjeros *nf* **foreign investment** inversión exterior *nf* **foreign loan** préstamo extranjero *nm*, crédito extranjero *nm* **foreign travel** viajes al extranjero *nmpl*, viajar al exterior *nm*

foreman *n* capataz *nmf*, encargado, -ada *nm,f*

forestall *vb* prevenir *vb*, impedir *vb*

forestalling *adj* **forestalling policy** política de acaparamiento *nf*, política de monopolización *nf*

forfeit 1. *n* decomiso *nm*, confiscación *nf*, multa *nf* (shares) confiscación de acciones *nf* **2.** *vb* perder el derecho a *vb*

forfeiture *n* pérdida *nf*, confiscación *nf*

forgery *n* falsificación *nf*

form *n* (document) hoja *nf*, formulario *nm*, impreso *nm*, forma (LAm) *nf*

formal *adj* formal *adj*, oficial *adj* **formal agreement** acuerdo oficial *nm* **formal contract** contrato en firme *nm*

formality *n* **customs formalities** formalidades aduaneras/legales *nfpl*, trámites aduaneros/legales *nmpl* **to observe formalities** cumplir formalidades *vb*

formation *n* (of company) fundación *nf* **capital formation** formación de capital *nf*

forward 1. *adj* **forward contract** contrato a plazo fijo *nm* **forward cover** cobertura a plazo *nf* **forward market** mercado de futuros *nm* **forward transaction** transacción de futuros *nf* **2.** *vb* enviar *vb*, mandar *vb*

forwarder *n* agente de transportes *nmf*, agente fletero (LAm) *nm*

forwarding *n* envío *nm*, expedición *nf*, transporte *nm*, flete de mercancías (LAm) *nm* **forwarding agency** agencia de transporte *nf*, agencia de fletes (LAm) *nf* **forwarding agent** agente de transporte *nmf*, agente de transportes *nmf*, agente de despacho *nmf*, agente de flete de mercancías (LAm) *nmf* **forwarding charges** costes de transporte *nmpl*, costos de flete (LAm) *nmpl* **forwarding note** nota de envío *nf*, nota de expedición *nf*, nota de flete (LAm) *nf*

found *vb* fundar *vb* **to found a company** fundar una empresa *vb*, montar un negocio *vb*

founder *n* fundador, -ora *nm,f*

fraction *n* fracción *nf*, mínima parte *nf*

fractional *adj* fraccionario *adj*, mínimo *adj* **fractional money** dinero fraccionario *nm* **fractional shares** reservas mínimas *nfpl*

franc *n* **Belgian franc** franco belga *nm* **French franc** franco francés *nm* **Swiss franc** franco suizo *nm*

franchise 1. *n* franquicia *nf*, concesión *nf*, licencia *nf* **franchise outlet** franquicia *nf*, tienda bajo licencia *nf* **2.** *vb* conceder en franquicia *vb*

franchisee *n* concesionario, -ria *nm,f*, licenciatario, -ria *nm,f*

franchising *n* concesión de franquicias *nf*, franchising *nm*

franchisor *n* persona que concede la licencia *nf*, persona que otorga la concesión *nf*

franco *adj* **franco domicile** franco a domicilio *adv* **franco price** franco de precio *adv* **franco zone** zona franca *nf*

frank *vb* franquear *vb*

franked *adj* **franked income** ingresos franqueados *nmpl*

franking *n* **franking machine** máquina franqueadora *nf*

fraud *n* fraude *nm*, estafa *nf*

fraudulent *adj* fraudulento *adj*

free *adj* gratuito *adj*, libre *adj*, franco *adj*, gratis *adv* **free agent** dueño, -eña de hacer lo que quiera *nm,f* **free alongside ship (FAS)** franco en el muelle **free competition** libre competencia *nf* **free delivery** entrega incluida en el precio *nf* **duty free** libre de impuestos *adj*, libre de derechos de aduana *adj* **free economy** economía libre *nf* **free entry** entrada gratuita *nf*, entrada libre *nf* **free goods** productos gratuitos *nmpl*, mercaderías gratuitas (LAm) *nfpl* **free market** mercado libre *nm* **free market economy** economía de mercado *nf* **free movement of goods** movimiento libre de mercancías *nm*, movimiento libre de mercaderías (LAm) *nm* **free of charge** gratuito *adj*, gratis *adv* **free of freight** franco de porte *adj*, *adv* franco de flete (LAm) *adj*, *adv* **free of tax** libre de impuestos *adj*, *adv* **free on board (FOB)** franco a bordo *adj*, *adv* **free on quay** franco en muelle *adj*, *adv* **free port** puerto franco *nm* **free trade** librecambio *nm* **free trade area** puerto franco *nm*, zona franca *nf*

freedom *n* **freedom of choice** libertad de elección *nf*

Freefone (R) (GB) *n* llamadas telefónicas gratuitas *nfpl*

freelance 1. *adj* freelance *nmf*, por cuenta propia *prep* **2.** *n* trabajador, -ora autónomo, -oma *nm,f*, persona que trabaja por libre *nf*

freelancer *n* persona que trabaja por su propia cuenta *nf*, trabajador, -ora autónomo, -oma *nm,f*, persona que trabaja por libre *nf*

Freepost (R) (GB) *n* franqueo pagado *nm*

freeze 1. *n* (on prices, wages) congelación *nf* **2.** *vb* (prices, wages) congelar *vb*

freight *n* carga *nf*, transporte *nm*, flete *nm*, mercaderías (LAm) *nfpl*, flete (LAm) *nm* **freight forwarder** agente de transporte *nmf*, agente de transportes *nmf*, fletador (LAm) *nm* **freight traffic** tráfico de mercancías *nm*, tráfico de mercaderías (LAm) *nm*

freighter *n* buque de carga *nm*, avión de carga *nm*, fletador, -ora *nm,f*

frequency *n* frecuencia *nf*

friendly *adj* **Friendly Society** sociedad de ayuda mutua *nf*

fringe *adj* **fringe benefits** incentivos *nmpl*, beneficios extrasalariales *nmpl* **fringe market** mercado marginal *nm*

frontier *n* frontera *nf*

fronting *n* presentación *nf*, dirección *nf*

frozen *adj* **frozen assets** activo congelado *nm* **frozen credits** crédito congelado *nm*

FT Index (Financial Times Index) *n* índice de cotización bursátil del "Financial Times" *nm*

full *adj* **full cost** coste total *nm*, costo total (LAm) *nm* **full liability** plena responsabilidad *nf* **full payment** pago íntegro *nm*, pago total *nm*

full-time *adj* & *adv* a tiempo completo *prep*, a jornada completa *prep*

function 1. *n* (role) función *nf*, papel *nm*, acto *nm* **2.** *vb* marchar *vb*, funcionar *vb*

functional *adj* **functional analysis** análisis funcional *nm* **functional organization** organización funcional *nf*

fund 1. *n* fondo *nm* **funds flow** movimiento de capital *nm*, flujo de fondos *nm* **funds surplus** superávit de fondos *nm* **2.** *vb* financiar *vb*, destinar fondos *vb*

funded *adj* **funded debt** deuda consolidada *nf*

funding *n* financiación *nf*, asignación de fondos *nf* **funding bonds** bonos de financiación *nmpl*

furlough (US) 1. *n* permiso *nm*, licencia *nf* **2.** *vb* permitir *vb*, conceder una licencia *vb*, conceder un permiso *vb*

future *adj* futuro *nm* **future commodity** futuro *nm* **future delivery** entrega futura *nf* **future goods** géneros futuros *nmpl* **futures contract** contrato de futuros *nm* **futures exchange** cambio de futuros *nm* **futures market** mercado de futuros *nm* **futures marketing** comercialización de futuros *nf* **futures price** precio de futuros *nm* **futures trading** comercio de futuros *nm*

fye (fiscal year end) *abbr* fin de año fiscal *nm*

gain 1. *n* **capital gain** plusvalía *nf* **capital gains tax** impuesto sobre la plusvalía *nm* **gain sharing** reparto de ganancias *nm* **2.** *vb* conseguir *vb*, obtener *vb*, ganar *vb* **gain in value** aumentar de valor *vb*, revalorizarse *vb*

gainful *adj* **gainful employment** empleo remunerado *nm*

galloping *adj* **galloping inflation** inflación galopante *nf*

Gallup poll (R) *n* encuesta Gallup *nf*, sondeo Gallup *nm*

gap *n* **population gap** vacío poblacional *nm*, desequilibrio demográfico *nm* **trade gap** déficit comercial *nm*

gas *n* **natural gas** gas natural *nm*

GATT (General Agreement on Tariffs and Trade) *abbr* GATT (Acuerdo General sobre Aranceles Aduaneros y Comercio) *abbr,nm*

gazump *vb* vender un inmueble a un mejor postor, rompiendo un compromiso *vb*

GDP (Gross Domestic Product) *abbr* PIB

(Producto Interior Bruto) *abbr,nm*
general *adj* **general accounting**
contabilidad general *nf* **general agencies**
(US) agencias generales *nfpl* **general agent**
agente general *nmf* **general average** media
general *nf* **general election** elecciones
generales *nfpl* **general management**
dirección general *nf* **general manager**
director, -ora general *nm,f* **general partner**
socio, -cia general *nm,f* **general**
partnership asociación general *nf* **general**
strike huelga general *nf*, paro general
(LAm) *nm*
generate *vb* **to generate income** generar
ingresos *vb*
generation *n* **income generation**
generación de ingresos *nf*
generosity *n* generosidad *nf*
gentleman *n* **gentleman's agreement**
acuerdo entre caballeros *nm*
gilt-edged *adj* de la máxima confianza *prep*,
de bajo riesgo *prep* **gilt-edged market**
mercado de valores de primera clase *nm*
gilt-edged security valor de primer orden
nm
gilts *npl* bonos del Tesoro *nmpl*, títulos de la
deuda pública *nmpl*
giveaway *n* regalo *nm*, obsequio *nm*
global *adj* global *adj*, mundial *adj* **global**
economy economía global *nf* **global**
market mercado global *nm*, mercado
mundial *nm* **global marketing** márketing
global *nm*
globalization *n* globalización *nf*
GMT (Greenwich Mean Time) *abbr* hora de
Greenwich *nf*
gnome *n* **the Gnomes of Zurich** "los
gnomos de Zurich" *nmpl*, los banqueros
suizos *nm*
GNP (Gross National Product) *abbr* PNB
(Producto Nacional Bruto) *abbr,nm*
go-slow *n* (strike) huelga de celo *nf*, huelga
pasiva *nf*, trabajo a reglamento (LAm) *nm*
going *adj* corriente *adj*, de mercado *prep*
going concern negocio en marcha *nm*
gold *n* oro *nm* **gold bullion** oro en lingotes
nm **gold coin** moneda de oro *nf* **gold**
market mercado de oro *nm* **gold reserves**
reservas de oro *nfpl* **gold standard** patrón-
oro *nm*
golden *adj* dorado *adj*, de oro *adj* **golden**
handcuffs prima de permanencia *nf*
golden handshake gratificación por fin de
servicio *nf*, indemnización por despido *nf*
golden hello prima de enganche *nf* **golden**
parachute gratificación por fin de servicio
nf, indemnización por despido *nf*
goods *npl* mercancías *nfpl*, productos *nmpl*,
bienes *nmpl*, mercaderías (LAm) *nfpl* **bulk**
goods mercancías a granel *nfpl*, artículos de
producción en serie *nmpl*, mercaderías a
granel (LAm) *nfpl* **domestic goods** enseres
domésticos *nmpl* **export goods** mercancías
de exportación *nfpl*, mercaderías de

exportación (LAm) *nfpl* **import goods**
artículos de importación *nmpl*, mercaderías
de importación (LAm) *nfpl* **goods on**
approval mercancías a prueba *nfpl*,
productos a prueba *nmpl*, mercaderías a
prueba (LAm) *nfpl* **goods in process**
mercancías en curso *nfpl*, mercaderías en
curso (LAm) *nfpl* **goods in progress**
productos en construcción *nmpl*, mercancías
en curso *nfpl*, mercaderías en curso (LAm)
nfpl **goods on consignment** artículos
consignados *nmpl*, mercaderías en
consignación (LAm) *nfpl* **goods transport**
transporte de géneros *nm*, transporte de
mercaderías (LAm) *nm*
goodwill *n* fondo de comercio *nm*, clientela
nf, crédito *nm*, llave (LAm) *nf*
govern *vb* gobernar *vb*, determinar *vb*,
dominar *vb*
government *n* gobierno *nm*, administración
nf, estado *nm* **government body**
organismo gubernamental *nm*, organización
estatal *nf* **government bond** obligación del
Estado *nf*, acción del Tesoro *nf* **government**
enterprise empresa pública *nf*, empresa
estatal *nf*, iniciativa del gobierno *nf*
government loan préstamo estatal *nm*
government policy política del gobierno *nf*
government sector sector público *nm*
government security título del Estado *nm*
government subsidy subsidio estatal *nm*
graduate 1. *n* (of university) licenciado, -ada
nm,f, egresado, -ada (LAm) *nm,f* **2.** *vb*
escalonar *vb*, graduar *vb*
grant 1. *n* (of a patent) concesión *nf*
regional grant subvención regional *nf* **2.**
vb conceder *vb*, otorgar *vb*
graphics *npl* **computer graphics** gráficos
(de ordenador) *nmpl*
gratuity *n* propina *nf*, gratificación *nf*
green *adj* **green card** carta verde *nf*, permiso
de residencia y trabajo (LAm) *nm* **green**
currency moneda verde *nf* **green pound**
libra verde *nf*
Greenwich *n* **Greenwich Mean Time**
(GMT) hora de Greenwich *nf*
grievance *n* queja *nf*, motivo de queja *nm*
gross *adj* bruto *adj* **gross amount** suma
bruta *nf* **gross domestic product (GDP)**
producto interior bruto (PIB) *nm* **gross**
interest interés bruto *nm* **gross**
investment inversión bruta *nf* **gross loss**
pérdida bruta *nf* **gross margin** margen
bruto *nm* **gross national product (GNP)**
producto nacional bruto (PNB) *nm* **gross**
negligence culpa grave *nf* **gross output**
producción bruta *nf* **gross sales** ventas
brutas *nfpl* **gross weight** peso bruto *nm*
group *n* **group insurance** seguro colectivo
nm **group of countries** grupo de países
nm **group travel** viajar en grupo *vb*
growth *n* crecimiento *nm*, desarrollo *nm*,
expansión *nf* **annual growth rate** tasa de
crecimiento anual *nf* **economic growth**

crecimiento económico *nm*, desarrollo económico *nm* **export-led growth** crecimiento regido por las exportaciones *nm* **market growth** expansión del mercado *nf* **growth rate** tasa de crecimiento *nf* **sales growth** aumento de ventas *nm* **growth strategy** estrategia de desarrollo *nf*, estrategia de crecimiento *nf*

guarantee *n* garantía *nf*, prenda *nf* **quality guarantee** garantía de calidad *nf*

guarantor *n* garante *nmf*, garantía (LAm) *nmf*

guest *n* **guest worker** trabajador, -ora extranjero, -era temporal *nm,f*, obrero, -era *nm,f*

guild *n* gremio *nm*, corporación *nf*

guilder *n* florín *nm*

h *abbr* (hour) h. *abbr*

half *n* mitad *nf*, parte *nf* **half-an-hour** media hora *nf* **half-board** media pensión *nf* **half-pay** medio sueldo *nm* **half-price** mitad de precio *nf* **to reduce sth by half** rebajar algo a mitad de precio *vb* **half-year** semestre *nm*

hall *n* sala *nf* **exhibition hall** salón de exposiciones *nm*, sala de exposiciones *nf*

hallmark *n* contraste *nm*, marca de contraste *nf*

halt *vb* (inflation) parar *vb*, frenar *vb*

halve *vb* reducir a la mitad *vb*, partir por la mitad *vb*

hand *n* **in hand** entre manos *prep*, en reserva *prep* **to hand** a mano *prep*

hand over *vb* entregar *vb*, transferir *vb*, pasar *vb*

handbook *n* manual *nm*, guía *nf*

handle *vb* (deal) encargarse de *vb*, manejar *vb* (money) manejar dinero *vb*, (staff, people) tratar al personal *vb* **handle with care** tratar con cuidado *vb*

handling *n* **handling charges** gastos de tramitación *nmpl*, costos de manipulación (LAm) *nmpl* **data handling** manejo de datos *nm*, proceso de datos *nm*

handmade *adj* hecho a mano *adj*

handshake *n* apretón de manos *nm*

handwritten *adj* escrito a mano *adj*

handy *adj* a mano *prep*, práctico *adj*

hang on *vb* (wait) esperar *vb* (on phone) esperar *vb*, no colgar *vb*

hang together *vb* (argument) tener coherencia *vb*

hang up *vb* (telephone) colgar *vb*, cortar (LAm) *vb*

harbour *n* puerto *nm* **harbour authorities** dirección portuaria *nf* **harbour dues** derechos portuarios *nmpl*, derechos de dársena *nmpl* **harbour facilities** instalaciones portuarias *nfpl* **harbour fees** derechos portuarios *nmpl*

hard *adj* **hard bargain** negocio difícil *nm* **hard cash** dinero en metálico *nm*, efectivo *nm* **hard currency** divisas fuertes *nfpl*, moneda convertible *nf* **hard disk** disco duro *nm* **hard-earned** bien merecido *adj* **hard-**

hit muy afectado *adj* **hard-line** de línea dura *prep* **hard loan** crédito en condiciones desventajosas *nm*, préstamo exterior pagadero en moneda fuerte *nm* **hard news/ information** información concreta *nf* **hard price** precio fijo *nm* **hard sell** venta agresiva *nf* **the hard facts** los hechos puros y duros *nmpl* **hard-working** trabajador *adj*, muy trabajador *adj*

hardware *n* **computer hardware** "hardware" *nm*, equipo *nm*, soporte físico del ordenador *nm*

haul *n* **long-haul** de largo recorrido *prep*, a largo plazo *prep* **short-haul** de corto recorrido *prep*, a corto plazo *prep*

haulage, freight (US) *n* **road haulage** transporte por carretera *nm* **haulage company** compañía de transportes *nf*, empresa de transporte por carretera *nf*

haulier *n* transportista *nmf*, contratista de transporte por carretera *nmf*

hazard *n* peligro *nm*, riesgo *nm*, obstáculo *nm* **natural hazard** riesgo natural *nm*, peligro inevitable *nm* **occupational hazard** riesgo ocupacional *nm*

hazardous *adj* peligroso *adj*

head 1. *adj* **head accountant** director, -ora de contabilidad *nm,f* **head office** oficina central *nf*, sede central *nf*, casa matriz *nf* **2.** *n* **at the head of** a la cabeza de *prep* **head of department** jefe, -efa de departamento *nm,f* **head of government** jefe, -efa de gobierno *nm,f* **per head** per cápita *prep*, por persona *prep* **to be head of** encabezar *vb* **3.** *vb* (department) dirigir *vb*, estar a la cabeza de *vb*

head for *vb* ir camino de *vb*, dirigirse a *vb*

headed *adj* **headed notepaper** papel con membrete *nm*

heading *n* encabezamiento *nm*, título *nm*, acápite (LAm) *nm*

headquarters *n* sede *nf*, oficina central *nf*, domicilio social *nm*

headway *n* **to make headway** hacer progresos *vb*

health *n* salud *nf*, sanidad *nf* **health benefits** compensaciones por enfermedad *nfpl* **health care industry** industria de asistencia médica *nf* **health hazard** peligro para la salud *nm* **industrial health** salud industrial *nf*, prosperidad industrial *nf* **health insurance** seguro de enfermedad *nm* **Ministry of Health** Ministerio de Salud *nm*

healthy *adj* (finances) próspero *adj*, sustancial *adj*

heavy *adj* **heavy-duty** para uso industrial **heavy goods vehicle** vehículo de gran tonelaje *nm* **heavy industry** Industria pesada *nf* **heavy trading** mucho movimiento (en la bolsa) *nm* **heavy user** usuario, -ria frecuente *nm,f*

hedge *n* **hedge against inflation** barrera contra la inflación *nf* **hedge clause (US)**

cláusula de protección *nf*
hidden *adj* **hidden assets** bienes ocultos
nmpl **hidden defect** defecto oculto *nm*
hierarchy *n* (corporate) jerarquía *nf* **data
hierarchy** jerarquía de datos *nf* **hierarchy
of needs** jerarquía de necesidades *nf*
high *adj* **high-class** de alta clase *prep*, de alto
standing *prep* **high finance** las altas
finanzas *nfpl* **high-grade** de alto grado *prep*,
de calidad superior *prep* **high-income** de
altos ingresos *prep* **high-level** de alto nivel
prep **high-powered** dinámico *adj*, muy
potente *adj* **high-priced** de precio alto *adj*
high-ranking de alto rango *prep* **high-risk**
de alto riesgo *prep*, riesgoso (LAm) *adj* **high
season** temporada alta *nf* **high-tech*** de
alta tecnología, high tech* *prep*
higher *adj* **higher bid** oferta superior *nf*
hire 1. *adj* **hire charges** alquiler *nm*,
arriendo (LAm) *nm* **hire contract** contrato
de alquiler *nm*, contrato de arriendo (LAm)
nm **hire purchase** compra a plazos *nf* **2.** *n*
alquiler *nm*, arriendo (LAm) *nm* **for hire** se
alquila *vb*, se arrienda (LAm) *vb*, se renta
(LAm) *vb* **3.** *vb* (person) contratar *vb*,
alquilar *vb*, arrendar (LAm) *vb*, rentar (LAm)
vb
history *n* **employment/work history**
historial de empleo *nm*, historia profesional
(LAm) *nf*
hit *vb* **hit-or-miss** una lotería *nf*, a la buena
de Dios *prep*, a la sanfasón (LAm) *prep* **to
hit the market** lanzarse al mercado *vb* **to
be hard hit by** ser gravemente afectado por
vb **to hit the headlines** ser noticia *vb*
HO (head office) *abbr* sede *nf*, oficina central
nf, domicilio social *nm*
hoard *vb* acumular *vb*, esconder *vb*
hold 1. *adj* **hold area** área de la bodega *nf*
hold queue, hold line (US) lista de espera
nf, cola de comunicantes *nf* **2.** *n* **on hold**
(on phone) esperando para hablar *vb*, sin
colgar *prep* **3.** *vb* **to hold a meeting**
celebrar una reunión *vb* **to hold sth as
security** retener algo como garantía *vb* **to
hold sb liable, responsible** hacer
responsable a alguien *vb*, responsabilizar a
alguien *vb*
hold back *vb* (not release) retrasar *vb*,
contener *vb*, postergar (LAm) *vb*
hold on *vb* (on phone) esperar *vb*, no cortar
(LAm) *vb*
hold over *vb* (to next period) aplazar *vb*,
postergar (LAm) *vb*
hold up *vb* (delay) retrasar *vb*, detener *vb*,
(criminal act) atracar *vb* (withstand scrutiny)
resultar válido *vb*
holder *n* titular *nmf*, portador, -ora *nm,f*,
tenedor, -ora *nm,f* **joint holder** cotitular *nmf*
licence holder titular de un permiso *nmf*,
titular de una licencia *nmf* **office holder**
titular del cargo *nmf* **policy holder** titular
de una póliza de seguros *nmf*
holding 1. *adj* **holding company** holding

nm, sociedad de cartera *nf*, sociedad
tenedora *nf* **2.** *n* participación *nf*, cartera de
valores *nf*, propiedad *nf* **foreign exchange
holdings** cartera de valores en divisas *nf*
majority/minority holding participación
mayoritaria/minoritaria *nf* **to have
holdings** poseer valores en cartera *vb*, tener
propiedades *vb*
holdup *n* demora *nf*, atraco *nm*
holiday, vacation (US) *n* fiesta *nf* **bank
holiday (GB)** fiesta nacional *nf*, día festivo
nm, día feriado (LAm) *nm*, fiesta patria
(LAm) *nf* **on holiday** de vacaciones *prep*,
tomando la licencia (LAm) *vb* **holiday pay**
paga de vacaciones *nf*, sueldo gozado
durante la licencia (LAm) *nm* **tax holiday**
exención fiscal concedida a una nueva
empresa *nf*
home *n* domicilio *nm*, hogar *nm* **home
address** dirección particular *nf*, domicilio
particular *nm* **home buyer** comprador, -ora
de vivienda *nm,f* **home country** país de
origen *nm* **home delivery** entrega a
domicilio *nf* **home industry** industria
nacional *nf* **home loan** préstamo de ahorro-
vivienda *nm* **home market** mercado
nacional *nm*, mercado interior *nm* **home
owner** propietario, -ria de una vivienda *nm,f*
home sales ventas en el mercado interior
nfpl **home service** servicio a domicilio *nm*
home shopping compras hechas sin salir
del hogar *nfpl*
honorary *adj* de honor *prep*
horizontal *adj* **horizontal analysis** análisis
horizontal *nm* **horizontal integration**
fusión horizontal *nf*
host *n* anfitrión, -ona *nm,f* **host country** país
anfitrión *nm*
hot *adj* **hot line** línea directa *nf* **hot money**
dinero caliente *nm*, dinero especulativo *nm*
hot seat línea de fuego *nf* **to be in hot
demand** haber mucha demanda *vb*
hotel *n* hotel *nm* **hotel accommodation**
alojamiento hotelero *nm* **hotel chain**
cadena hotelera *nf* **five-star hotel** hotel de
cinco estrellas *nm* **hotel industry/trade**
industria hotelera *nf*, hostelería *nf* **hotel
management** dirección hotelera *nf* **to run
a hotel** dirigir un hotel *vb*
hour *n* hora *nf* **after hours** fuera del horario
de trabajo *prep* **business hours** horas de
oficina *nfpl*, horas de trabajo *nfpl*, horario de
oficina *nm* **busy hours (US)** horas punta
nfpl, horas pico (LAm) *nfpl* **fixed hours**
horario fijo *nm* **office hours** horario de
oficina *nm*, horas de oficina *nfpl* **per hour**
por hora, a la hora *prep* **per hour output**
rendimiento por hora *nm*
hourly *adj* por hora *prep* **hourly-paid work**
trabajo pagado por horas *nm* **hourly rate**
tarifa horaria *nf* **hourly workers**
trabajadores, - oras por horas *nm,fpl*
house *n* **clearing house** cámara de
compensación *nf* **house duty (US)**

impuesto sobre la propiedad residencial *nm*
house journal/magazine revista interno de
la casa *nf* **mail-order house** compañía de
venta por correo *nf* **packing house (US)**
empresa envasadora *nf* **house prices** el
precio de la vivienda *nm* **publishing house**
editorial *nf* **house sale** venta inmobiliaria *nf*
house telephone teléfono interno *nm*
household *n* casa *nf*, hogar *nm*, unidad
familiar *nf* **household expenditure** gastos
del hogar *nmpl* **household goods** enseres
domésticos *nmpl* **household survey**
encuesta familiar *nf*
householder *n* dueño, -eña de casa *nm,f*
housewares (US) *npl* utensilios domésticos
nmpl
housing *n* **housing estate, tenement** (US)
urbanización *nf*, complejo habitacional *nm*,
colonia (LAm) *nf* **housing industry**
industria de construcción de viviendas *nf*
housing project complejo de viviendas
subvencionadas *nm* **housing scheme**
proyecto relativo a la vivienda *nm*
hull *n* casco *nm* **hull insurance** seguro de
casco de buque *nm*, seguro marítimo *nm*
human *adj* **human relations** relaciones
humanas *nfpl* **human resources** recursos
humanos *nmpl* **human resource
management (HRM)** gestión de recursos
humanos (GRH) *nf*
hundred *n* cien *nm* **one hundred per cent**
cien por cien *nm*
hydroelectricity *n* hidroelectricidad *nf*
hype *n* bombo *nm*
hyperinflation *n* hiperinflación *nf*
hypermarket *n* hipermercado *nm*
hypothesis *n* hipótesis *nf*
idle *adj* inactivo *adj*, desocupado *adj*, vago *adj*
idle capacity capacidad no utilizada *nf*
illegal *adj* ilegal *adj*
implication *n* implicación *nf* **this will have
implications for our sales** esto nos va
afectar las ventas, esto tendrá implicancias
para nuestras ventas (LAm)
import 1. *adj* **import agent** agente de
importación *nmf* **import barrier** barrera a
la importación *nf* **import control** control de
importaciones *nm* **import department**
departamento de importación *nm* **import
duty** derecho de importación *nm* **import
licence** permiso de importación *nm* **import
office** oficina de importación *nf* **import
quota** cuota de importación *nf*, cupo de
importación *nm* **import restrictions**
restricciones a la importación *nfpl* **import
surplus** excedente de importaciones *nm* **2.**
n importación *nf* **3.** *vb* importar *vb*
importation *n* importación *nf*
importer *n* importador, -ora *nm,f*
importing *adj* **importing country** país
importador *nm*
impose *vb* **to impose a tax** gravar con un
impuesto *vb* **to impose restrictions** poner
restricciones *vb*

imposition *n* (of tax) imposición *nf*
impound *vb* confiscar *vb*, embargar *vb*
imprint *n* **to take an imprint** (credit card)
hacer impresión *vb*
improve *vb* mejorar *vb*, aumentar *vb*
perfeccionarse *vb*, superarse *vb* **we must
improve our performance** hay que
mejorar nuestro rendimiento
inadequate *adj* inadecuado *adj*, insuficiente
adj, incompetente *adj*
incentive *n* incentivo *nm*, aliciente *nm*
incidental *adj* **incidental expenses** gastos
menores *nmpl*
include *vb* **our price includes delivery**
nuestro precio incluye la entrega *n* **taxes
are included** van incluidos los impuestos
vb
inclusive *adj* **inclusive of tax and delivery
costs** incluidos impuestos y gastos de
entrega *adj* **the prices quoted are
inclusive** los precios citados incluyen *n*
income *n* ingresos *nmpl*, renta *nf* **gross
income** ingresos brutos *nmpl* **net(t)
income** ingresos netos *nmpl*, renta neta *nf*
private income renta privada *nf* **income
tax** impuesto sobre la renta *nm*, impuesto a
los réditos (LAm) *nm*
inconvenience *n* inconveniente *nm*,
molestias *nfpl*
inconvenient *adj* inconveniente *adj*,
inoportuno *adj*
increase 1. *n* aumento *nm*, auge *nm*,
incremento *nm* **increase in the cost of
living** aumento del coste de vida *nm*,
aumento del costo de vida (LAm) *nm* **price
increase** subida de precio *nf* **wage
increase** aumento de sueldo *nm* **2.** *vb*
(prices, taxes) subir *vb*, incrementar *vb*
incur *vb* (expenses) incurrir en *vb*
indebted *adj* endeudado *adj*
indemnify *vb* indemnizar *vb*, asegurar *vb*
indemnity *n* indemnidad *nf* **indemnity
insurance** seguro de indemnización *nm*
index *n* índice *nm*, lista *nf*, señal *nf* **cost of
living index** índice del coste de la vida *nm*,
índice del costo de la vida (LAm) *nm*
growth index índice de crecimiento *nm*
price index índice de precios *nm* **share
index** índice de acciones *nm*
indicate *vb* indicar *vb*, señalar *vb*
indication *n* indicio *nm*, pauta *nf*, señal *nf*
indirect *adj* indirecto *adj* **indirect cost** coste
indirecto *nm*, gasto indirecto *nm*, costo
indirecto (LAm) *nm* **indirect expenses**
gastos indirectos *nmpl* **indirect tax**
impuesto indirecto *nm*
industrial *adj* industrial *adj* **industrial
accident** accidente laboral *nm* **industrial
arbitration** arbitraje laboral *nm* **industrial
democracy** democracia industrial *nf*
industrial dispute conflicto laboral *nm*,
conflicto colectivo *nm* **industrial
expansion** expansión industrial *nf*
industrial region zona industrial *nf*

industrial relations relaciones industriales *nfpl* **industrial tribunal** tribunal industrial *nm* **industrial union** sindicato industrial *nm*
industry *n* industria *nf*
inefficient *adj* ineficiente *adj*, incompetente *adj*
inferior *adj* (goods) inferior *adj*
inflation *n* inflación *nf* **rate of inflation** tasa de inflación *nf*
inflationary *adj* inflacionario *adj*, inflacionista (LAm) *adj* **inflationary gap** vacío inflacionario *nm* **inflationary spiral** espiral inflacionista *nm*
inform *vb* informar *vb*, notificar *vb*, comunicar *vb*
information *n* información *nf*, datos *nmpl* **information desk** información *nf*, oficina de información *nf* **information management** dirección de información *nf* **information office** oficina de información *nf* **information processing** proceso de datos *nm* **information retrieval** recuperación de datos *nf* **information storage** almacenaje de datos *nm* **information systems** sistemas de información *nmpl* **information technology (IT)** informática *nf*
infrastructure *n* infraestructura *nf*
inherit *vb* heredar *vb*
inheritance *n* herencia *nf*, legado *nm*, sucesión *nf* **inheritance laws** leyes sobre la herencia *nfpl*
inhouse *adj* **inhouse training** *n* formación en el puesto de trabajo *nf*
injunction *n* mandamiento judicial *nm*, requerimiento judicial *nm*, orden *nf* **to take out an injunction** solicitar un mandamiento judicial *vb*
inland *adj* interior *adj*, nacional *adj* **the Inland Revenue, The Internal Revenue Service (IRS)** (US) Hacienda *nf*, fisco *nm*, Dirección General Impositiva (LAm) *nf*, Impuestos Internos (LAm) *nmpl*
insider *n* iniciado, -ada *nm,f* **insider dealing, insider trading** (US) trato con información privilegiada *nm*
insist on *vb* insistir en *vb*, exigir *vb*
insolvency *n* insolvencia *nf*
insolvent *adj* insolvente *adj*
inspect *vb* inspeccionar *vb*, examinar *vb*, revisar *vb*
inspection *n* (customs) control *nm*, revisión *nf*
inspector *n* inspector, -ora *nm,f*, interventor, -ora *nm,f* **customs inspector** aduanero, -era *nm,f*
instability *n* inestabilidad *nf*
instal(l) *vb* instalar *vb*
installation *n* instalación *nf*, investidura *nf*
installment, installment (US) *n* plazo *nm*, cuota (LAm) *nf*
institute *n* instituto *nm*
institution *n* institución *nf*, entidad *nf*,

establecimiento *nm* **credit institution** institución crediticia *nf*
instruction *n* instrucción *nf*, orden *nf*, formación *nf* **instruction book** libro de instrucciones *nm* **instruction sheet** hoja de instrucciones *nf* **to follow instructions** seguir instrucciones *vb*
insurable *adj* **insurable risk** riesgo asegurable *nm*
insurance *n* seguro *nm*, seguros *nmpl* **insurance agent** agente de seguros *nmf*, corredor, -ora de seguros *nm,f* **insurance broker** agente de seguros *nmf*, corredor, -ora de seguros *nm,f* **car insurance** seguro de automóviles *nm* **insurance certificate** certificado de seguros *nm*, póliza de seguros *nf* **insurance company** compañía de seguros *nf*, aseguradora *nf* **comprehensive insurance** seguro a todo riesgo *nm* **insurance contract** contrato de seguros *nm* **fire insurance** seguro contra incendios *nm* **insurance fund** fondo de seguros *nm* **National Insurance (GB)** Seguridad Social *nf* **insurance policy** póliza de seguros *nf* **insurance premium** prima de seguros *nf*, cuota de seguros (LAm) *nf* **insurance representative** agente de seguros *nmf*, asesor, -ora de seguros *nm,f* **insurance salesperson** vendedor, -ora de seguros *nm,f* **third party insurance** seguro contra terceros *nm* **to take out insurance** hacerse un seguro *vb* **insurance underwriter** suscriptor, -ora *nm,f* **unemployment insurance** seguro de desempleo *nm*
insure *vb* asegurar *vb*
intangible *adj* **intangible asset** activo intangible *nm*
intensive *adj* intensivo *adj* **capital-intensive** intensivo en capital *adj* **labour-intensive** con alta utilización de mano de obra, con alto coeficiente de mano de obra *prep*
interest *n* interés *nm*, intereses *nmpl*, participación *nf* **interest-bearing** con interés *prep*, que produce intereses *rel pron* **interest-free** sin interés *prep*, sin intereses *prep*, a bajo interés *prep* **interest period** período de vigencia del tipo de interés *nm*, período de vigencia de la tasa de interés (LAm) *nm* **interest rate** tipo de interés *nm*, tasa de interés (LAm) *nf* **to bear interest** devengar interés *vb*, dar interés *vb*, rendir interés *vb* **to charge interest** cobrar interés *vb*, cargar en concepto de interés *vb* **to pay interest** pagar interés *vb*, abonar interés *vb*
interface *n* interface *nm*, punto de contacto *nm*, interrelación *nf*
interim *adj* provisional *adj*, interino *adj*, intermedio *adj*, provisorio (LAm) *adj*
intermediary *adj* intermediario *adj*, intermedio *adj*
internal *adj* **internal audit** auditoría interna *nf* **internal auditor** censor, -ora de cuentas

interior *nm,f* **the Internal Revenue Service (IRS) (US)** Hacienda *nf*, Hacienda Pública *nf*, el fisco *nm*, Dirección General Impositiva (LAm) *nf*, Impuestos Internos (LAm) *nmpl*

international *adj* internacional *adj* **international agreement** convenio internacional *nm* **international competition** competencia internacional *nf* **International Date Line** línea (de cambio) de fecha *nf* **international organization** organización internacional *nf* **international trade** comercio internacional *nm*

intervene *vb* intervenir *vb*, participar *vb*

intervention *n* intervención *nf*, intercesión *nf* **state intervention** intervención estatal *nf*, intervención del estado *nf*

interview 1. *n* entrevista *nf* **to attend for interview** asistir a una entrevista *vb* **to hold an interview** entrevistar *vb* **to invite sb to interview** llamar a alguien para la entrevista *vb* **2.** *vb* entrevistar *vb*

introduce *vb* (product) introducir *vb*, lanzar *vb*, sacar *vb*, (person) presentar *vb*

inventory *n* inventario *nm* **inventory control** control de inventario *nm*, control público de existencias *nm*

invest *vb* (money) invertir *vb*

investment *n* inversión *nf*, inversiones *nfpl*, investidura *nf* **investment adviser** asesor, -ora de inversiones *nm,f* **investment portfolio** cartera de valores *nf* **investment programme, investment program** (US) plan de inversiones *nm* **investment strategy** estrategia de inversión *nf*

investor *n* inversionista *nmf*, inversor, -ora *nm,f*

invisible *adj* invisible *adj* **invisible exports** exportaciones invisibles *nfpl* **invisible imports** importaciones invisibles *nfpl*

invitation *n* invitación *nf*

invite *vb* invitar *vb*, llamar a *vb*, convidar *vb*

invoice *n* factura *nf* **duplicate invoice** copia de la factura *nf* **to issue an invoice** emitir una factura *vb* **to settle an invoice** pagar una factura *vb*, liquidar una factura *vb*

invoicing *n* facturación *nf*

irrecoverable *adj* (loss) irrecuperable *adj*

irrevocable *adj* irrevocable *adj* **irrevocable letter of credit** carta de crédito irrevocable *nf*

issue 1. *n* **bank of issue** banco emisor *nm* **share issue, stock issue** (US) emisión de nuevas acciones *nf* **2.** *vb* (cheques, shares, notes) emitir *vb*, extender *vb*, (policy) publicar *vb*, (tickets) expedir *vb* **to issue sb with sth** proporcionar algo a alguien *vb*

issuing *adj* **issuing bank** banco emisor *nm*

item *n* artículo *nm*, punto *nm*

itemize *vb* detallar *vb*, desglosar *vb*

itemized *adj* **itemized account** cuenta desglosada *nf*

itinerary *n* itinerario *nm*

jackpot *n* gordo *nm*

jingle *n* tonadilla *nf* **advertising jingle** jingle publicitario *nm*, tonadilla de un anuncio *nf*

job *n* **job analysis** evaluación de puestos de trabajo *nf* **job creation** creación de empleo *nf* **job description** descripción del puesto de trabajo *nf* **job offer** oferta de trabajo *nf* **job rotation** trabajo por turnos *nm* **job satisfaction** satisfacción laboral *nf*, satisfacción por el trabajo *nf* **job shop** oficina de empleo *nf*, agencia de colocaciones *nf*, bolsa de empleo *nf*

jobber *n* trabajador, -ora eventual *nm,f*, intermediario, -ria *nm,f*, agente de bolsa *nmf*

Jobcentre (GB) *n* oficina de empleo *nf*, bolsa de empleo *nf*, agencia de colocaciones *nf*

jobless *adj* desempleado *adj*, sin trabajo *prep*, en paro *prep*, cesante (LAm) *adj* **the jobless** los desempleados *nmpl*, los desocupados *nmpl*, los cesantes (LAm) *nmpl*

joint *adj* conjunto *adj* **joint account** cuenta en participación *nf* **joint obligation** obligación conjunta *nf* **joint ownership** copropiedad *nf* **joint responsibility** responsabilidad conjunta/colectiva *nf*, responsabilidad en común *nf* **joint-stock company** sociedad anónima *nf* **joint venture** empresa conjunta *nf*, negocio en participación *nm*, agrupación temporal de empresas *nf*

jointly *adv* en común *prep*

journal *n* revista *nf*, boletín *nm*

journalism *n* periodismo *nm*

judicial *adj* judicial *adj*

junior *adj* auxiliar *adj*, menor *adj*

junk *n* **junk bond** obligación desvalorizada *nf*

jurisdiction *n* jurisdicción *nf*, competencia *nf*

juror *n* miembro de un jurado *nm*

jury *n* jurado *nm*

K *abbr* (1000) K *abbr*, mil libras esterlinas *nf*, kilobyte *nm*

keen *adj* (competition) afilado *adj*, fuerte *adj*, (price) competitivo *adj*, adecuado *adj*, chévere (LAm) *adj*

keep *vb* (goods) guardarse *vb*, guardar *vb* **to keep an appointment** acudir a una cita *vb* **to keep the books** llevar la contabilidad *vb* **to keep the business running** asegurar la marcha de la empresa *vb*

keep back *vb* (money) quedarse con dinero *vb*, guardarse dinero *vb*

keep down *vb* (prices) mantener bajos los precios *vb*

keep up *vb* (with events) no perder el hilo de los sucesos *vb*, estar al día *vb*

key *adj* **key currency** moneda clave *nf* **key industry** industria clave *nf* **key person** persona clave *nf* **key question** cuestión principal *nf*, pregunta clave *nf*

key in *vb* teclear *vb*, pasar a máquina *vb*

keyboard *n* teclado *nm*

keynote *adj* **keynote speech** discurso en el que se intenta establecer la tónica de... *nm*

keyword *n* (computer) palabra clave *nf*

kg *abbr* Kg *nm*, kilo *nm*, kilogramo *nm*

kill *vb* **to kill a project** acabar con un proyecto *vb*, poner fin prematuro a un proyecto *vb*

kilowatt *n* kilovatio *nm*

kind 1. *adj* amable *adj* **would you be so kind as to...** ¿tendría la amabilidad de...? **2.** *n* clase *nf*, tipo *nm*

king-size(d) *adj* extragrande *adj*, descomunal *adj*

kiosk *n* (phone) cabina (de teléfonos) *nf*

kit *n* (equipment) equipo *nm*

kite *n* **kite mark (GB)** marca de calidad *nf*

km, kilometer (US) *abbr* Km. *abbr*, kilómetro *nm*

knock *vb* (disparage) criticar *vb*, hablar mal de *vb*

knock down *vb* (price) rebajar *vb*, recortar *vb*, reducir *vb*, rematar (LAm) *vb*

knock off* *vb* (finish work) salir del trabajo *vb*

knock-for-knock *adj* **knock-for-knock agreement** acuerdo de pago respectivo *nm*

knock-on *adj* **knock-on effect** repercusiones *nfpl*, efecto secundario *nm*, reacción en cadena *nf*

knockdown *adj* **knockdown price** precio mínimo *nm*, precio de ganga *nm*, precio rematado (LAm) *nm*

know-how *n* conocimientos y experiencia *nmpl & nf*, pericia *nf*, "know-how" *nm*

knowledge *n* conocimiento *nm*, conocimientos *nmpl*, saber *nm* **knowledge base** base de conocimientos *nf* **it is common knowledge** se sabe muy bien *vb*, es bien sabido *vb* **to have a thorough knowledge of sth** conocer algo a fondo *vb* **to have a working knowledge of sth** defenderse bastante bien en algo *vb* dominar los principios básicos de algo *vb* **to my knowledge** que yo sepa *rel pron*

knowledgeable *adj* informado *adj*, culto *adj*

known *adj* sabido *adj* **known facts** hechos ciertos *nmpl*

krona *n* (Swedish) corona sueca *nf*

krone *n* (Danish, Norwegian) corona danesa *nf*, corona noruega *nf*

kudos *n* prestigio *nm*

kW *abbr* kW *abbr*, kilovatio *nm*

kWh *abbr* kwh *abbr*, kilovatio-hora *nm*

label 1. *n* etiqueta *nf* **2.** *vb* etiquetar *vb*, calificar *vb*

labour, labor (US) *n* trabajo *nm*, labor *nf*, mano de obra *nf*, esfuerzos *nmpl* **labour costs** costes de la mano de obra *nmpl*, costos de la mano de obra (LAm) *nfpl* **labour dispute** conflicto laboral *nm* **labour-intensive** con un alto coeficiente de mano de obra *prep*, que requiere mucha mano de obra *rel pron* **labour law** derecho laboral *nm* **labour market** mercado de trabajo *nm* **labour relations** relaciones laborales *nfpl*

labourer *n* trabajador, -ora *nm,f*, obrero, -era *nm,f*, peón (LAm) *nmf*

lack *n* falta *nf*, carencia *nf*, escasez *nf* **lack of investment** falta de inversión *nf*

land *n* **land purchase** compra de tierras *nf* **land reform** reforma agraria *nf* **land register** registro catastral *nm* **land tax** impuesto territorial *nm*, contribución territorial rústica *nf* **land tribunal** tribunal agrario *nm*

landlord *n* arrendador, -ora *nm,f*, propietario, -ria *nm,f*, hacendado, -ada (LAm) *nm,f*

landowner *n* terrateniente *nmf*, latifundista *nmf*

language *n* lenguaje *nm*, lengua *nf*, idioma *nm* **language specialist** especialista en idiomas *nmf*

large *adj* grande *adj* **large-scale** a gran escala *prep*

launch 1. *n* **product launch** lanzamiento de un producto *nm* **2.** *vb* (product) lanzar *vb*, introducir *vb*

law *n* derecho *nm*, ley *nf*, leyes *nfpl* **business law** derecho mercantil *nm* **civil law** derecho civil *nm* **criminal law** derecho penal *nm* **international law** derecho internacional *nm* **law of diminishing returns** ley de rendimientos decrecientes *nf* **public law** derecho público *nm*

lawsuit *n* juicio *nm*, pleito *nm*, proceso *nm*

lay off *vb* (workers) despedir temporalmente *vb*

LBO (leveraged buy-out) *abbr* LBO (compra apalancada de empresas *nf*, adquisición apalancada de empresas *nf*

leader *n* **market leader** empresa líder del mercado *nf*, artículo de mayor venta *nm*

leadership *n* liderazgo *nm*, dirección *nf*

leading *adj* importante *adj*, principal *adj* **leading product** producto líder *nm*, producto principal *nm*

lease *vb* arrendar *vb*, ceder en arriendo *vb*

leasehold *n* arrendamiento *nm*

leaseholder *n* arrendatario, - ria *nm,f*

leave 1. *n* permiso *nm*, vacaciones *nfpl*, licencia (LAm) *nf* **leave of absence** excedencia *nf*, permiso *nm*, licencia (LAm) *nf* **sick leave** permiso por enfermedad *nm*, baja por enfermedad *nf*, licencia por enfermedad (LAm) *nf* **to take leave** tomarse permiso *vb*, estar de licencia (LAm) *vb* **to take leave of sb** despedirse de alguien *vb* **2.** *vb* irse *vb*, marcharse *vb* (resign from) dimitir *vb* dejar atrás *vb*

ledger *n* libro mayor *nm* **bought ledger** libro mayor de compras *nm* **ledger entry** asiento contable *nm*

left *adj* **left luggage** consigna *nf* **left-luggage locker** casilla de la consigna automática *nf*, locker de la consigna (LAm) *nm* **left-luggage office** consigna *nf*, consigna de equipajes (LAm) *nf*

legacy *n* legado *nm*

legal *adj* legal *adj* **legal tender** moneda de curso legal *nm* **to take legal action** entablar un pleito *vb*, proceder en contra de *vb*

legislate vb legislar vb
legislation n legislación nf **to introduce legislation** introducir legislación vb
lend vb prestar vb, dejar vb
lender n prestamista nmf, entidad crediticia nf
lessee n arrendatario, -ria nm,f, inquilino, -ina nm,f
lessor n arrendador, -dora nm,f
let vb (property) alquilar vb
letter n **letter of application** carta de solicitud nf **letter of credit** carta de crédito nf **letter of introduction** carta de recomendación nf
letterhead n membrete nm, papel con membrete nm
level n nivel nm, grado nm **level of employment** nivel de empleo nm **level of inflation** nivel de inflación nm **level of prices** nivel de precios nm
levy vb (tax) imponer vb, recaudar vb, gravar vb
liability n responsabilidad nf, propensión nf **current liabilities** pasivo circulante nm **fixed liability** pasivo a largo plazo nm **limited liability** responsabilidad limitada nf
liable adj responsable adj, propenso adj, sujeto adj **liable for damages** responsable de daños y perjuicios adj **liable for tax** sujeto a impuestos adj
libel n difamación nf, libelo nm
licence n licencia nf, permiso nm, autorización nf **licence fee** cuota de licencia nf, tasa de licencia nf
license vb conceder un permiso vb, autorizar vb
licensee n titular de una licencia nmf, concesionario, -ria nm,f
licensor n persona que concede un permiso o una licencia nf
life n **life assurance/insurance** seguro de vida nm **life member** miembro vitalicio nm
LIFO (last in first out) abbr primeras entradas, primeras salidas nfpl & nfpl, método contable para valorar las existencias nm
limit n límite nm, acotación nf **credit limit** límite de crédito nm
limited adj limitado adj **limited capital** capital limitado nm **limited company** compañía limitada nf **limited liability** responsabilidad limitada nf **limited partnership** asociación limitada nf
line n **above the line** incluido adj **assembly line** cadena de montaje nf, línea de montaje nf **below the line** no incluido adj **line management** orden jerárquico nm, dirección lineal nf **line manager** jefe, -efa de línea nm,f **line of business** ramo profesional nm **product line** gama de productos nf
liquid adj líquido adj **liquid assets** activo disponible nm **liquid capital** capital líquido nm

liquidate vb liquidar vb, cancelar vb, saldar vb
liquidation n liquidación nf **liquidation value** valor de liquidación nm
liquidity n liquidez nf
list 1. n lista nf, relación nf **list price** precio de catálogo nm **2.** vb hacer una lista vb
listed adj **listed share, listed stock** (US) acción cotizada nf
litigant n litigante nmf
litigate vb litigar vb
litigation n litigio nm
load 1. n carga nf, peso nm, montón nm **2.** vb cargar vb
loan n préstamo nm, crédito nm **loan agreement** contrato de préstamo nm **bank loan** préstamo bancario nm **bridging loan, bridge loan** (US) crédito puente nm **personal loan** crédito personal nm, préstamo personal nm **to grant a loan** conceder un préstamo vb **to request a loan** pedir crédito vb
local adj local adj, municipal adj **local taxes** impuestos locales nm
location n posición nf, situación nf, ubicación (LAm) nf
lockout n (of strikers) cierre patronal nm, "lockout" nm, paro patronal (LAm) nm
logistics n logística nf
Lombard Rate n tasa Lombard nf
long adj **long capital** capital a largo plazo nm **long credit** crédito a largo plazo nm **long deposit** depósito a largo plazo nm **long-distance** interurbano adj, de largo recorrido prep **long-range** de largo alcance prep, a distancia prep, a largo plazo prep **long-term** a largo plazo prep, prolongado adj **long-term planning** planificación a largo plazo nf
lose vb (custom) perder vb
loss n pérdida nf **financial loss** pérdida financiera nf **gross loss** pérdida bruta nf **loss leader** artículo de gancho nm **net(t) loss** pérdida neta nf **loss of earnings** pérdida de ingresos nf **loss of job** pérdida de empleo nf **to minimise losses** reducir al mínimo las pérdidas vb
lost-property adj **lost-property office** oficina de objetos perdidos nf
lot n (at auction) lote nm
low adj (price) barato adj, económico adj
lower vb (price, interest rate) bajar vb
lucrative adj lucrativo adj
luggage n **excess luggage** exceso de equipaje nm **luggage insurance** seguro de equipaje nm
lump n **lump sum settlement** ajuste por suma fija nm
luxury n lujo nm **luxury goods** artículos de lujo nmpl **luxury tax** impuesto de lujo nm
machine 1. n máquina nf, aparato nm **2.** vb trabajar a máquina vb, coser a máquina vb
machinery n maquinaria nf, mecanismo nm, aparato nm **machinery of government** aparato estatal nm

macroeconomics *n* macroeconomía *nf*
made *adj* fabricado *adj*, hecho *adj* **made in France** fabricado en Francia *adj*
magazine *n* (journal) revista *nf*
magnate *n* magnate *nmf*, potentado, -ada *nm,f*
magnetic *adj* **magnetic tape** (DP) cinta magnética *nf*
mail order *n* venta por correo *nf*, pedido efectuado por correo *nm*
mailing *n* **mailing list** banco de direcciones *nm*, lista de destinatarios *nf*
main *adj* principal *adj*, mayor *adj*, fundamental *adj* **main office** sede social *nf* **main supplier** proveedor, -ora principal *nm,f*, suministrador, -ora clave *nm,f*
mainframe *n* (DP) unidad principal *nf*, macrocomputadora *nf*, ordenador central *nm*, computadora central (LAm) *nf*
maintenance *n* mantenimiento *nm*, manutención *nf* **maintenance costs** costes de mantenimiento *nmpl*, costos de mantenimiento (LAm) *nmpl*
major *adj* mayor *adj*, principal *adj*, más importante *adj*
majority *n* mayoría *nf* **majority holding** participación mayoritaria *nf* **in the majority** mayoritariamente *adv*
make *vb* **to make a fortune** hacer una fortuna *vb*, hacerse rico *vb* **to make a living** ganarse la vida *vb* **to make money** hacer dinero *vb* **to make use** aprovechar *vb*
malingerer *n* enfermo, -rma fingido, -ida *nm,f*, simulador,- ora *nm,f*
mall *n* **shopping mall** centro comercial *nm*
malpractice *n* negligencia *nf*, mala práctica *nf*
man-made *adj* artificial *adj*, sintético *adj*
manage *vb* dirigir *vb*, administrar *vb*, manejar *vb*, gestionar (LAm) *vb*
management *n* dirección general *nf*, administración de empresas *nf*, gerencia *nf*, gestión (LAm) *nf* **business management** dirección comercial *nf*, gestión de empresas *nf* **management buy-out** adquisición de una empresa por sus propios directivos *nf* **management by objectives** dirección por objetivos *nf* **management consultant** asesor, -ora de empresas *nm,f*, consultor, -ora de empresas *nm,f* **financial management** dirección financiera *nf* **middle management** mandos intermedios *nmpl*, cuadros medios *nmpl* **personnel management** dirección de personal *nf*, gestión de personal *nf* **top management** altos cargos *nmpl*, alta dirección *nf* **management training** formación de directivos *nf*
manager *n* director, -ora *nm,f*, gerente *nmf*, jefe, -efa *nm,f*
manpower *n* recursos humanos *nmpl*, personal *nm*, mano de obra *nf*
manual *adj* **manual worker** obrero, -era *nm,f*, trabajador, -ora manual *nm,f*
manufacture 1. *n* producción *nf*, fabricación *nf* **2.** *vb* manufacturar *vb*, fabricar *vb*
manufacturer *n* fabricante *nmf*
margin *n* margen *nm* **profit margin** margen de beneficio *nm*
marginal *adj* marginal *adj* **marginal cost** coste marginal *nm*, costo marginal (LAm) *nm* **marginal revenue** ingresos marginales *nmpl*
marine 1. *adj* marítimo *adj*, marino *adj* **marine engineering** ingeniería marina *nf* **marine insurance** seguro marítimo *nm* **2.** *n* **merchant marine** marina mercante *nf*
mark *n* marco *nm* **Deutsche Mark** marco alemán *nm*
mark down *vb* (price) rebajar *vb*, reducir *vb*
mark up *vb* aumentar *vb*, recargar *vb*
markdown *n* rebaja *nf*, reducción *nf*
market 1. *adj* **market analysis** análisis de mercado *nm* **down-market** (product) de mercado abajo *prep*, de mercado popular *prep* **market economy** economía de mercado *nf* **market forces** tendencias del mercado *nfpl*, fuerzas del mercado *nfpl* **market leader** empresa líder del sector *nf*, artículo líder *nm* **market opportunity** oportunidad comercial *nf* **market price** precio de mercado *nm* **market research** análisis de mercados *nm*, estudio de mercado *nm*, investigación de mercado *nf* **market research questionnaire** cuestionario para realizar investigaciones de mercado *nm* **market segmentation** división del mercado *nf* **market share** parte del mercado *nf*, cuota de mercado *nf*, participación en el mercado *nf* **up-market** (product) de mercado selecto *prep*, de mercado de élite *prep* **market value** valor de mercado *nm* **2.** *n* mercado *nm* **bear market** mercado bajista *nm* **black market** mercado negro *nm* **bond market** mercado de bonos *nm* **bull market** mercado con tendencia a subir *nm*, mercado alcista *nm* **buyer's market** mercado de oferta *nm* **capital market** mercado de capitales *nm* **Common Market** Mercado Común *nm* **domestic market** mercado nacional *nm*, mercado interior *nm* **falling market** mercado con tendencia a la baja *nm* **firm market** mercado firme *nm* **foreign market** mercado exterior *nm*, mercado extranjero *nm* **futures market** mercado de futuros *nm* **labour market** mercado de trabajo *nm* **money market** mercado monetario *nm*, mercado financiero *nm* **property/real estate (US) market** mercado inmobiliario *nm* **retail market** mercado al por menor *nm* **seller's market** mercado favorable al vendedor *nm* **stock market** mercado de valores *nm*, bolsa de valores *nf* **the bottom has fallen out of the market** el mercado se ha desfondado *vb*, los precios han caído en picada (LAm) *vb* **to play the market**

especular *vb* 3. *vb* vender *vb*, comercializar *vb*

marketable *adj* comercializable *adj*, comercial *adj*, mercadeable (LAm) *adj*

marketing *n* márketing *nm*, mercadeo (LAm) *nm* **marketing consultant** asesor, -ora comercial *nm,f* **marketing department** departamento de márketing *nm*, departamento de comercialización *nm* **marketing director** director, -ora de márketing *nm,f*

markup *n* aumento *nm*, recargo *nm*, margen de beneficio *nm*

mart *n* mercado *nm*, lonja *nf*

mass *adj* **mass marketing** márketing de masas *nm*, mercadeo de masas (LAm) *nm* **mass media** medios de comunicación de masas *nmpl* **mass production** fabricación en serie *nf* **mass unemployment** desempleo masivo *nm*, paro generalizado *nm*, cesantía general (LAm) *nf*

material 1. *adj* **material needs** necesidades materiales *nfpl* 2. *n* material *n* **building materials** materiales de construcción *nmpl* **raw materials** materias primas *nfpl*

maternity *n* **maternity leave** licencia por maternidad *nf*

matrix *n* matriz *nf*

mature *vb* (business, economy) madurar *vb*, vencer *vb*

maximise *vb* potenciar al máximo *vb*

maximum *adj* **maximum price** precio máximo *nm*

MBA (Master of Business Administration) *abbr* MBA (Máster en Administración de Empresas) *abbr*

mean 1. *adj* (average) medio *adj* 2. *n* (average) promedio *nm*, medio *nm*

means *npl* medios *nmpl*, recursos *nmpl* **financial means** ingresos *nmpl*, recursos financieros *nmpl* **to live beyond one's means** llevar un tren de vida que los ingresos no permiten *vb* **we do not have the means to...** no disponemos de los medios para... *vb*

measure 1. *n* medida *nf* **financial measure** medida financiera *nf* **safety measure** medida de seguridad *nf* 2. *vb* medir *vb*, calcular *vb*

mechanical *adj* mecánico *adj* **mechanical engineering** ingeniería mecánica *nf*

media *n* **mass media** medios de comunicación *nmpl*

median *adj* medio *adj*, intermedio *adj*

mediate *vb* mediar *vb*, lograr *vb*

mediation *n* mediación *nf*

mediator *n* mediador, -ora *nm,f*

medical *adj* médico *adj* **medical insurance** seguro médico *nm*

medium 1. *adj* mediano *adj*, medio *adj* **medium-sized firm** empresa mediana *nf*, empresa de tamaño mediano *nf* **medium term** medio plazo *nm*, mediano plazo *nm* 2. *n* **advertising medium** medio publicitario *nm*, medio de publicidad *nm*

meet *vb* conocer *vb*, encontrarse con *vb*

meeting *n* reunión *nf*, encuentro *nm*, mitin *nm* **board meeting** reunión del consejo de administración *nf* **business meeting** reunión de negocios *nf* **to hold a meeting** celebrar una reunión *vb*

megabyte *n* megabyte *nm*, megaocteto *nm*

member *n* miembro *nmf*, socio, -cia *nm,f* **Member of Parliament (MP) (GB)** diputado, -ada *nm,f* **Member of the European Parliament (MEP)** eurodiputado, -ada *nm,f*

memo *n* memorándum *nm*, nota *nf*

memorandum *n* memorándum *nm*, nota *nf*, circular *nf*

memory *n* (DP) memoria *nf*, recuerdo *nm* **memory capacity** capacidad de memoria *nf*

mercantile *adj* mercantil *adj*

merchandise 1. *n* géneros *nmpl*, mercancías *nfpl* 2. *vb* comercializar *vb*

merchandizer *n* promotor, -ora de ventas *nm,f*

merchandizing *n* comercialización *nf*, mercadeo (LAm) *nm*

merchant *n* negociante *nmf*, comerciante *nmf* **merchant bank** banco de negocios *nm*, banco mercantil *nm* **merchant navy**, **merchant marine** (US) marina mercante *nf* **merchant ship** buque mercante *nm*

merge *vb* fusionarse *vb*, unirse *vb*, fundirse *vb*

merger *n* fusión *nf*, unión *nf*

merit *n* mérito *nm* **merit payment** gratificación por méritos *nf*

message *n* mensaje *nm*, nota *nf*, dicho (LAm) *nm*, mandado (LAm) *nm*

messenger *n* mensajero, -era *nm,f*, recadista *nmf*

metal *n* metal *nm*

meter *n* contador *nm*, medidor (LAm) *nm*

method *n* **method of payment** modo de pago *nm*, forma de pago *nf* **production method** método de producción *nm*

metre, meter (US) *n* metro *nm* **cubic metre** metro cúbico *nm* **square metre** metro cuadrado *nm*

metric *adj* métrico *adj*

metrication *n* conversión al sistema métrico *nf*

metropolis *n* metrópoli(s) *nf*

microchip *n* (micro)chip *nm*, pastilla de silicio *nf*

microcomputer *n* microordenador *nm*, microcomputador (LAm) *nm*, microcomputadora (LAm) *nf*

microeconomics *n* microeconomía *nf*

microfiche *n* microficha *nf*

microprocessor *n* microprocesador *nm*

middle *adj* **middle management** cuadros medios *nmpl*, mandos intermedios *nmpl* **middle manager** mando intermedio *nm*

middleman *n* intermediario, -ria *nm,f*

migrant *adj* **migrant worker** trabajador, -ora extranjero, -era *nm,f,* trabajador, -ora itinerante *nm,f*

mile *n* milla *nf* **nautical mile** milla marina *nf*

mileage *n* kilometraje *nm,* provecho *nm*

million *n* millón *nm*

millionaire *n* millonario, -ria *nm,f*

mine *n* mina *nf* **coal mine** mina de carbón *nf*

mineral *n* mineral *nm*

minimal *adj* mínimo *adj*

minimum *adj* mínimo *nm* **index-linked minimum wage** salario mínimo indexado *nm* **minimum lending rate** tipo de interés mínimo establecido por el banco central *nm,* tasa de interés mínima establecida por el banco central (LAm) *nf*

mining *n* minería *nf* **mining industry** industria minera *nf*

minister *n* ministro, -tra *nm,f,* secretario, -ria *nm,f,* pastor, -ora *nm,f*

ministry *n* ministerio *nm,* gestión ministerial *nf,* secretaría (LAm) *nf* **Ministry of Transport** Ministerio de Transporte *nm,* Secretaría de Transporte (LAm) *nf*

minor *adj* menor *adj,* secundario *adj,* pequeño *adj*

minority *n* minoría *nf* **minority holding** participación minoritaria *nf* **in the minority** en minoría *prep*

mint 1. *n* casa de la moneda *nf* **2.** *vb* acuñar *vb* **he/she mints money** hace una fortuna *vb,* hace un dineral *vb*

minutes *npl* **the minutes of the meeting** el acta de la reunión *nm*

misappropriation *n* malversación *nf*

miscalculation *n* error de cálculo *nm*

misconduct *n* (bad management) mala conducta *nf*

mishandling *n* maltrato *nm*

mismanagement *n* mala dirección *nf*

mistake *n* error *nm,* equivocación *nf* **to make a mistake** cometer un error *vb,* equivocarse *vb*

mix *n* **marketing mix** combinación de medios de márketing *nf* **product mix** combinación de productos *nf*

mixed *adj* **mixed economy** economía mixta *nf*

mode *n* (method) modo *nm,* medio *nm*

model *n* (person) modelo *nmf*

modem *n* módem *nm*

moderate 1. *adj* moderado *adj* **2.** *vb* moderar *vb,* aliviar *vb*

moderation *n* moderación *nf*

modern *adj* moderno *adj*

modernization *n* modernización *nf*

modernize *vb* modernizar *vb*

module *n* módulo *nm*

monetarism *n* monetarismo *nm*

monetary *adj* monetario *adj* **European Monetary System (EMS)** Sistema Monetario Europeo (SME) *nm* **International Monetary Fund (IMF)** Fondo Monetario Internacional (FMI) *nm*

monetary policy política monetaria *nf*

money *n* **dear money** dinero caro *nm* **money market** mercado monetario *nm* **money order** giro postal *nm* **public money** dinero público *nm,* fondos públicos *nmpl* **money supply** oferta monetaria *nf* **to raise money** recaudar fondos *vb* **money trader** cambista *nmf,* operador, -ora de cambios *nm,f*

moneymaking *adj* (profitable) rentable *adj*

monopoly *n* monopolio *nm* **Monopolies and Mergers Commission** Comisión de Monopolios y Fusiones *nf*

monthly *adj* mensual *adj*

moonlight* *vb* estar pluriempleado *vb,* practicar el pluriempleo *vb*

moor *vb* amarrar *vb*

mooring *adj* **mooring rights** derechos de amarre *nmpl*

mortgage *n* hipoteca *nf,* préstamo hipotecario *nm* **mortgage deed** contrato hipotecario *nm* **mortgage loan** préstamo hipotecario *nm*

mortgagee *n* acreedor, -ora hipotecario, -ria *nm,f*

mortgagor *n* deudor, -ora hipotecario, -ria *nm,f*

motor *n* **motor industry** industria del automóvil *nf,* industria automovilística *nf*

multilateral *adj* multilateral *adj*

multinational *adj* multinacional *adj* **multinational corporation** empresa multinacional *nf*

multiple *adj* **multiple store** sucursal de una cadena de grandes almacenes *nf*

multiply *vb* multiplicar *vb*

multipurpose *adj* multiuso *adj,* polivalente *adj*

municipal *adj* **municipal bonds** bonos municipales *nmpl*

mutual *adj* mutuo *adj* **mutual fund (US)** fondos mutuos *nmpl*

mutually *adv* mutuamente *adv*

N/A (not applicable) *abbr* no corresponde *vb*

name 1. *n* nombre *nm,* apellido *nm* **brand name** marca comercial *nf* **by name** de nombre *prep* **full name** nombre y apellidos *nm & nmpl* **in the name of** en el nombre de *prep* **registered trade name** marca registrada *nf* **2.** *vb* nombrar *vb*

named *adj* **named person** persona mencionada *nf*

narrow *adj* **narrow margin** margen reducido *nm* **narrow market** mercado reducido *nm*

nation *n* nación *nf* **the United Nations** las Naciones Unidas *nf*

national *adj* **national debt** deuda nacional *nf* **national income** renta nacional *nf* **national insurance (NI) (GB)** seguridad social *nf* **national interest** interés nacional *nm* **National Bureau of Economic Research (US)** Departamento Nacional de

Investigación Económica *nm*
nationality *n* nacionalidad *nf*
nationalization *n* nacionalización *nf*
nationalize *vb* nacionalizar *vb*
nationalized *adj* **nationalized industry** industria nationalizada *nf*
nationwide *adj* a escala nacional *prep,* de ámbito nacional *prep*
natural *adj* **natural rate of increase** tasa natural de incremento *nf* **natural resources** recursos naturales *nmpl*
necessary *adj* necesario *adj,* preciso *adj* **necessary qualifications** títulos adecuados *nmpl,* cualificaciones necesarias *nfpl*
necessity *n* necesidad *nf*
need *n* **needs assessment** análisis de necesidades *nm* **needs of industry** requisitos de la industria *nmpl* **to be in need** estar necesitado de *vb*
negative *adj* **negative cash flow** flujo de caja negativo *nm,* "cash-flow" negativo *nm* **negative feedback** reacción negativa *nf*
negative (US) *vb* rechazar *vb,* no aprobar *vb*
neglect *n* abandono *nm,* negligencia *nf,* incumplimiento *nm* **neglect clause** cláusula de incumplimiento *nf*
negligence *n* negligencia *nf* **negligence clause** cláusula de negligencia *nf* **contributory negligence** culpa concurrente *nf* **gross negligence** imprudencia temeraria *nf*
negligent *adj* negligente *adj,* despreocupado *adj*
negotiable *adj* negociable *adj,* superable *adj* **negotiable bill** factura negociable *nf* **negotiable cheque** cheque negociable *nm*
negotiate *vb* negociar *vb*
negotiated *adj* **negotiated price** precio negociado *nm*
negotiating *adj* **negotiating session** sesión de negociaciones *nf* **negotiating skills** capacidad de negociación *nf*
negotiation *n* negociación *nf* **by negotiation** mediante negociaciones *prep* **to begin negotiations** entablar negociaciones *vb* **under negotiation** en negociación *prep* **wage negotiations** negociaciones salariales *nfpl*
negotiator *n* negociador, -ora *nm,f*
net(t) **1.** *adj* neto *adj,* global *adj* **net(t) amount** importe neto *nm,* suma global *nf* **net(t) assets** activo neto *nm* **net(t) cost** coste neto *nm,* costo neto (LAm) *nm* **net(t) earnings** ingresos netos *nmpl* **net(t) interest** interés neto *nm* **net(t) investment** inversión neta *nf* **net(t) loss** pérdida neta *nf* **net(t) price** precio neto *nm* **net(t) proceeds** recaudación neta *nf* **net(t) profit** beneficio neto *nm* **net(t) result** resultado neto *nm* **net(t) sales** ventas netas *nfpl* **net(t) saving** ahorro neto *nm* **terms strictly net(t)** términos estrictamente netos *nmpl* **net(t) wage** sueldo neto *nm,* salario

neto *nm* **net(t) weight** peso neto *nm* **2.** *vb* obtener *vb,* producir *vb,* embolsar *vb*
network **1.** *n* red *nm* **banking network** red bancaria *nf* **computer network** red de ordenadores *nf,* red de computadoras (LAm) *nf* **distribution network** red de distribución *nf* **2.** *vb* interconectar *vb,* transmitir en cadena *vb*
neutral *adj* neutral *adj*
new *adj* **new account** cuenta nueva *nf* **new business** nuevos negocios *nmpl,* empresa de creación reciente *nf* **new product** producto nuevo *nm* **new technology** nueva tecnología *nf*
newly *adv* **newly-appointed** recién contratado *adj* **newly-industrialised** de reciente industrialización *prep*
news *n* noticias *nfpl* **news agency** agencia de prensa *nf* **bad news** malas noticias *nfpl* **news bulletin** diario hablado *nm* **news coverage** reportaje de las noticias *nm* **financial news** noticias financieras *nfpl* **good news** buenas noticias *nfpl*
newsdealer (US) *n* vendedor, -ora de periódicos y revistas *nm,f*
newsletter *n* boletín informativo *nm*
newspaper *n* periódico *nm,* diario *nm* **newspaper advertisement** anuncio (publicitario) *nm,* aviso (LAm) *nm* **daily newspaper** diario *nm,* periódico *nm* **newspaper report** reportaje de prensa *nm*
nil *n* cero *nm* **nil profit** beneficio nulo *nm*
no *det* **no agents wanted** no se admiten agentes **no-claims bonus** prima por ausencia de siniestralidad *nf* **no commercial value** sin valor comercial
nominal *adj* nominal *adj* **nominal amount** suma simbólica *nf* **nominal assets** capital nominal *nm,* activo nominal *nm* **nominal damages** resarcimiento no compensatorio *nm* **nominal inflation** inflación nominal *nf* **nominal price** valor nominal *nm,* precio simbólico *nm* **nominal value** valor nominal *nm*
nominate *vb* proponer *vb,* nombrar *vb,* postular (LAm) *vb* **nominate sb to a board/committee** nombrar a alguien a un consejo, una comisión *vb,* postular a alguien a un consejo, una comisión (LAm) *vb*
nomination *n* nombramiento *nm,* candidatura *nf,* postulación (LAm) *nf*
nominee *n* candidato, -ata *nm,f,* postulado, -ada (LAm) *nm,f* **nominee shareholder** accionista apoderado, -ada *nm,f*
non-acceptance *n* no aceptación *nf*
non-attendance *n* no asistencia *nf*
non-completion *n* no formalización *nf,* no terminación *nf*
non-contributory *adj* sin aportaciones por parte del empleado *prep*
non-convertible *adj* inconvertible *adj*
non-delivery *n* falta de entrega *nf*
non-discriminatory *adj* no discriminatorio *adj*

non-essential *adj* dispensable *adj*
non-interest-bearing *adj* que no devenga interés *rel pron*
non-intervention *n* no intervención *nf*
non-negotiable *adj* no negociable *adj*
non-payment *n* impago *nm*
non-profitmaking *adj* no rentable *adj*, sin fines de lucro *prep*
non-returnable *adj* no retornable *adj*, de usar y tirar *prep*
non-stop *adj* sin escalas *prep*, sin parar *prep*, directo *adj*
non-transferable *adj* intransferible *adj*
norm *n* norma *nf*
normal *adj* **normal trading hours** horario normal de venta al público *nm*
not *adv* no *adv* **not applicable** no pertinente *adj*, no corresponde *vb* **not available** no disponible *adj* **not dated** sin fecha *prep*
notary *n* notario, -ria *nm,f*
note 1. *n* nota *nf* **advice note** aviso de envío *nm*, aviso de expedición *nm* **cover note** póliza provisional *nf*, nota de cobertura *nf*, póliza provisoria (LAm) *nf* **credit note** nota de crédito *nf* **debit note** nota de débito *nf* **delivery note** nota de entrega *nf* **dispatch note** nota de envío *nf*, nota de expedición *nf* **open note (US)** pagaré del Tesoro *nm* **to compare notes** cambiar impresiones *vb* **to make a note of sth** apuntar algo *vb*, tomar nota de algo *vb* **2.** anotar *vb*
noteworthy *adj* notable *adj*, digno de notarse *adj*
notice *n* antelación *nf*, aviso *nm* **advance notice** aviso previo *nm*, preaviso *nm*, aviso por adelantado *nm* **at short notice** a última hora *prep* **final notice** última notificación *nf* **notice period** período de aviso *nm* **term of notice** plazo de preaviso *nm* **to come to the notice of sb** llegar al conocimiento de alguien *vb* **to give notice of sth** avisar de algo *vb*, notificar de algo *vb* **to take notice** prestar atención *vb*, hacer caso *vb* **until further notice** hasta nuevo aviso *prep*
notification *n* notificación *nf*
notify *vb* notificar *vb*, informar *vb*, avisar *vb*
null *adj* **null and void** nulo y sin valor *adj* + *prep*
number *n* **account number** número de cuenta *nm* **opposite number** homólogo, -oga *nm,f* **order number** número de pedido *nm* **serial number** número de serie *nm* **telephone number** número de teléfono *nm* **wrong number** (phone) número equivocado *nm*
numeracy *n* nociones elementales de cálculo aritmético *nfpl*
numerate *adj* capaz de realizar cálculos aritméticos elementales *adj*
numeric *adj* **alpha-numeric** numérico-alfabético *adj* **numeric character** carácter numérico *nm*
numerical *adj* numérico *adj* **numerical analysis** análisis numérico *nm*

NYSE (New York Stock Exchange) *abbr* Bolsa de Nueva York *nf*
object *vb* oponerse *vb*
objection *n* objeción *nf* **to make/raise an objection** poner una objeción *vb*, expresar una objeción *vb*
objective *n* objetivo *nm* **to reach an objective** lograr un objetivo *vb*
obligation *n* obligación *nf*, compromiso *nm*, deber *nm* **to meet one's obligations** hacer frente a sus obligaciones *vb*, cumplir sus compromisos *vb*
obligatory *adj* obligatorio *adj*
oblige *vb* **to be obliged to do sth** estar obligado a hacer algo *vb*
observation *n* comentario *nm* **under observation** bajo vigilancia *prep*, en observación *prep*
observe *vb* observar *vb* **observe the rules** respetar las reglas *vb*, acatar las normas *vb*
obsolescence *n* caducidad *nf*, obsolescencia *nf* **built-in obsolescence** obsolescencia planificada *nf*
obsolete *adj* anticuado *adj*, caído en desuso *adj*
obtain *vb* obtener *vb*, conseguir *vb* **to obtain credit** conseguir crédito *vb*
occupant *n* ocupante *nmf*, inquilino, -ina *nm,f*, titular *nmf*
occupation *n* ocupación *nf*, profesión *nf*, tenencia *nf*
occupational *adj* laboral *adj*, ocupacional *adj* **occupational disease** enfermedad profesional *nf* **occupational hazard** riesgo de la profesión *nm*
occupier *n* ocupante *nmf*
occupy *vb* (premises) ocupar *vb*, llevar *vb*
off-the-job *adj* **off-the-job training** capacitación fuera del puesto de trabajo *nf*
offence, offense (US) *n* infracción *nf*, delito *nm*, ataque *nm* .
offer *n* **firm offer** oferta en firme *nf* **offer in writing** oferta por escrito *nf* **offer subject to confirmation** oferta sujeta a confirmación *nf* **offer valid until...** oferta válida hasta... *nf*
offeree *n* receptor, -ora de la oferta *nm,f*
offeror *n* oferente *nmf*
office *n* oficina *nf*, despacho *nm*, cargo *nm* **office equipment** equipo de oficina *nm*, mobiliario de oficina *nm* **office hours** horas de oficina *nfpl*, horario de oficina *nm* **office management** dirección de oficina *nf* **office staff** personal administrativo *nm* **to hold office** ocupar un cargo *vb* **to resign from office** dimitir el cargo *vb*
official *n* funcionario, -ria *nm,f*, cargo *nm* **official strike** huelga oficial *nf*, huelga autorizada por el sindicato *nf*, paro oficial (LAm) *nm*
offshore *adj* **offshore company** empresa extraterritorial *nf*, compañía en un paraíso fiscal *nf*
oil *n* **oil industry** industria petrolífera *nf*,

industria petrolera (LAm) *nf* **oil state** país productor de petróleo *nm*

oilfield *n* yacimiento petrolífero *nm*

oligopoly *n* oligopolio *nm*

ombudsman *n* defensor, -ora del pueblo *nm,f*

on-line *adj* en conexión directa con el ordenador central *prep*

on-the-job en el puesto de trabajo *prep* **on-the-job training** capacitación en el puesto de trabajo *nf*

onus *n* **the onus is on us to...** nos incumbe... *vb*, nos corresponde... *vb*

open 1. *adj* **open cheque** cheque abierto *nm* **open credit** crédito abierto *nm* **open market** mercado libre *nm* **open shop** empresa donde los trabajadores no tienen obligación de afiliarse al sindicato *nf* **2.** *vb* **to open an account** abrir una cuenta *vb*

open up *vb* (market) abrir *vb*, flexibilizar *vb*

opening *adj* **opening price** cotización de apertura *nf* **opening times** horario comercial *nm*, horario de atención al público *nm*

operate *vb* operar *vb*, explotar *vb* **to operate a business** llevar un negocio *vb*

operating *adj* **operating expenditure** gastos de explotación *nmpl*, costes de explotación *nm*, costos de operación (LAm) *nmpl* **operating expenses** gastos de explotación *nmpl*, costes de explotación *nm*, gastos de operación *nm*, costos de operación (LAm) *nmpl* **operating income** ingresos de explotación *nmpl*, ingresos de operación (LAm) *nmpl* **operating profit** beneficios de explotación *nmpl*, beneficios de operación (LAm) *nmpl* **operating statement** cuenta de pérdidas y ganancias *nf*

operation *n* (of business) explotación *nf*, dirección *nf*, gestión *nf*, (of machine) funcionamiento *nm*, manejo *nm*, uso *nm*

operator *n* operador, -ora *nm,f*, operario, -ria *nm,f*, telefonista *nmf*

opportunity *n* oportunidad *nf*, posibilidad *nf* **market opportunities** oportunidades de mercado *nfpl* **to seize an opportunity** aprovecharse de la ocasión *vb*

option *n* opción *nf*, posibilidad *nf*, elección *nf* **share option, stock option** (US) opción de compra de acciones a cierto precio para el futuro *nf*, opción de venta de acciones a cierto precio para el futuro *nf* **options market** mercado de opciones de compra y venta de acciones *nm* **option to buy** opción de compra *nf* **option to cancel** opción de anular *nf*

optional *adj* optativo *adj*

order *n* orden *nf*, pedido *nm*, mandamiento *nm* **order book** libro de pedidos *nm* **order form** formulario de pedido *nm* **order number** número de pedido *nm* **pay to the order of...** pagar a la orden de... *vb* **to cancel an order** anular un pedido *vb*, dar orden de no pagar *vb* **to place an order**

hacer un pedido *vb*, encargar *vb*

ordinary *adj* **ordinary general meeting** junta general ordinaria *nf* **ordinary share, ordinary stock** (US) acción ordinaria *nf*

organization *n* organización *nf*, método *nm*, sistema *nm*

organize *vb* organizar *vb*, ordenar *vb*, sindicar *vb*, sindicalizar (LAm) *vb*

organized *adj* **organized labour** (trade unions) obreros sindicados *nmpl*

origin *n* (of a product) fuente *nf* **country of origin** país de origen *nm* **statement of origin** relación de procedencia *nf*

original *adj* **original cost** coste original *nm*, costo original (LAm) *nm*

outbid *vb* sobrepujar *vb*, ofrecer más *vb*

outcome *n* resultado *nm*, consecuencias *nfpl*

outgoings *npl* gastos *nmpl*, desembolsos *nmpl*, salidas *nfpl*

outlay *n* **capital outlay** gastos de capital *nmpl*

outlet *n* **market outlet** salida de mercado *nf* **sales outlet** punto de venta *nm*

outlook *n* **business outlook** perspectivas comerciales *nfpl*

output *n* producción *nf*, rendimiento *nm* **to increase output** potenciar la producción *vb*, aumentar la producción *vb*

outstanding *adj* **outstanding amount** importe a pagar *nm* **outstanding debt** deuda pendiente *nf* **outstanding stock** existencias pendientes *nfpl*

overcharge *vb* cobrar de más *vb* recargar *vb*

overdraft *n* sobregiro *nm* **to request an overdraft** pedir un sobregiro *vb*

overdraw *vb* girar en descubierto *vb*, sobregirarse *vb*, rebasar *vb*

overdrawn *adj* **overdrawn account** cuenta rebasada *nf*

overdue *adj* vencido *adj*, atrasado *adj*

overhead *adj* **overhead costs** gastos generales *nmpl*, gastos indirectos *nmpl*

overheads *npl* gastos generales *nmpl*

overheating *n* (of economy) recalentamiento *nm*

overload *vb* sobrecargar *vb*

overlook *vb* pasar por alto *vb*, dejar pasar *vb*

overman *vb* tener mano de obra excesiva *vb*

overmanned *adj* con demasiado personal *prep*

overmanning *n* (excess staff) exceso de personal *nm*

overnight *adj* **overnight delivery** distribución de noche *nf*

overpay *vb* pagar de más *vb*

overpayment *n* pago en exceso *nm*

overpopulation *n* superpoblación *nf*, sobrepoblación (LAm) *nf*

overproduce *vb* producir en exceso *vb*

overproduction *n* sobreproducción *nf*

overseas *adj* extranjero *adj*, exterior *adj* **overseas market** mercado exterior *nm* **overseas territory** territorio de ultramar *nm* **overseas trade** comercio exterior *nm*, comercio de ultramar *nm*

oversell *vb* vender en exceso *vb*, exagerar los méritos de *vb*

oversight *n* descuido *nm*, supervisión *nf* **due to an oversight** debido a un error *adv*

oversold *adj* sobrevendido *adj*, vendido en exceso *adj*

oversubscribed *adj* sobrevendido *adj*, con demanda que supera a la oferta *prep*

oversupply *vb* proveer en exceso *vb*

overtime *n* horas extra(s) *nfpl*, sobretiempo (LAm) *nm*

overvalue *vb* sobrevalorar *vb*, sobrestimar *vb*

overworked *adj* con trabajo excesivo *prep*, explotado *adj*

owe *vb* deber *vb*

own *vb* poseer *vb*, tener *vb*, ser dueño de *vb*

owner *n* dueño, -eña *nm,f*, propietario, -ria *nm,f*, amo, -a *nm,f*

owner-occupier *n* propietario, -ria ocupante de una vivienda *nm,f*

ownership *n* propiedad *nf*

pack *vb* envasar *vb*, embalar *vb*

package *n* paquete *nm*, embalaje *nm*, envase *nm* **package deal** acuerdo global *nm*, oferta combinada *nf* **package tour** vacaciones organizadas *nfpl*

packaging *n* embalaje *nm*, envase *nm*, presentación *nf*

packet *n* paquete *nm*, dineral *nm*

paid *adj* pagado *adj*, remunerado *adj*, asalariado *adj* **paid holiday** vacaciones pagadas *nfpl*

paid-up *adj* **paid-up capital** capital desembolsado *nm*

pallet *n* paleta *nf*, bandeja *nf*, gama *nf*

palletized *adj* **palletized freight** carga paletizada *nf*, mercaderías empaletizadas (LAm) *nfpl*

paper *n* papel *nm*, documento *nm* **commercial paper** papel comercial *nm*, efectos negociables *nm* **paper loss** pérdida sobre el papel *nf* **paper profit** beneficio ficticio *nm*, beneficio no realizado *nm*

paperwork *n* papeleo *nm*, trámites burocráticos *nmpl*

par *n* par *nf* **above par** por encima de la par *prep* **below par** por debajo de la par *prep*

parent *n* **parent company** oficina central *nf*, empresa matriz *nf*

parity *n* paridad *nf*, igualdad *nf*, tipo de cambio *nm*, tasa de cambio (LAm) *nf*

part *n* (of a machine) pieza *nf* **part payment** pago parcial *nm* **part shipment** envío parcial *nm*, cargamento parcial *nm* **spare part** (for machine) pieza de recambio *nf*, refacción (LAm) *nf*

part-time 1. *adj* a tiempo parcial *prep*, a jornada reducida *prep* **2.** *adv* a tiempo parcial *prep*

participation *n* **worker participation** participación obrera *nf*, participación de los trabajadores en la gestión de la empresa *nf*

partner *n* socio, -cia *nm,f*, asociado, -ada *nm,f* **sleeping partner** socio, -cia comanditario, -ria *nm,f*, socio, -cia en comandita *nm,f*

partnership *n* sociedad colectiva *nf*, asociación *nf* **trading partnership** asociación comercial *nf*

passenger *n* pasajero, -era *nm,f*, viajero, -era *nm,f*

patent *n* patente *nf*

patented *adj* patentado *adj*

patronage *n* clientela *nf*, patrocinio *nm*, influencia *nf*

pattern *n* **spending patterns** pautas de gasto *nfpl*, pautas de consumo *nfpl*

pay 1. *n* (salary, wages) paga *nf*, salario *nm*, sueldo *nm* **equal pay** igualdad salarial *nf* **pay rise** aumento de sueldo *nm*, incremento salarial *nm* **severance pay** indemnización por despido *nf* **unemployment pay** subsidio de paro *nm*, subsidio de desempleo (LAm) *nm* **2.** *vb* pagar *vb*, abonar *vb* **to pay an invoice** pagar una factura *vb* **to pay by credit card** pagar con tarjeta de crédito *vb* **to pay for a service** pagar por un servicio *vb* **to pay in advance** pagar por adelantado *vb* **to pay in cash** pagar al contado *vb*, pagar en efectivo *vb*

payable *adj* pagadero *adj* **accounts payable** cuentas a pagar *nfpl*

payee *n* portador, -ora *nm,f*, beneficiario, -ria *nm,f*

payer *n* pagador, -ora *nm,f* **prompt payer** pagador, -ora puntual *nm,f* **slow payer** pagador, -ora moroso, -osa *nm,f*

payload *n* (of vehicle) carga útil *nf*

payment *n* pago *nm*, plazo *nm*, recompensa *nf*, cuota (LAm) *nf* **down payment** entrada *nf*, depósito *nm*, pago inicial *nm*, pie (LAm) *nm*

payola (US) *n* soborno *nm*, coima (LAm) *nf*, mordida (LAm) *nf*

payroll *n* nómina *nf*, plantilla *nf*, planilla (LAm) *nf* **to be on the payroll** estar en plantilla *vb*, estar en planilla (LAm) *vb*

peak *n* punto máximo *nm*, pico *nm* **peak demand** demanda máxima *nf* **peak period** horas punta *nfpl*, período de mayor afluencia *nm*

pecuniary *adj* **for pecuniary gain** con afán de lucro *prep*

peddle *vb* vender en la calle *vb*

peg *vb* (prices) sujetar *vb*, congelar *vb* **the HK dollar is pegged to the US dollar** el dólar de Hong Kong está vinculado al dólar norteamericano *nm*

penetration *n* **market penetration** penetración en el mercado *nf*

pension *n* pensión *nf* **pension fund** fondo de pensiones *nm* **retirement pension** pensión *nf*, jubilación *nf*, pensión de jubilación *nf* **pension scheme** plan de pensiones *nm*

per *prep* **per annum** al año, por año *prep* **per**

capita per cápita *prep,* por persona *prep*
per cent por ciento *prep*
percentage *n* porcentaje *nm* **percentage of profit** tanto por ciento de los beneficios *nm*
performance *n* (behaviour) actuación *nf* **performance appraisal** evaluación del rendimiento *nf* **performance-related bonus** plus según rendimiento *nm*
period *n* **cooling-off period** período de reflexión *nm* **period of grace** período de gracia *nm*
peripheral *adj* periférico *adj*
perishable *adj* **perishable goods** artículos perecederos *nmpl,* mercaderías perecederas (LAm) *nfpl*
perk *n* gratificación *nf*
permanent *adj* **permanent employment** empleo fijo *nm*
permit *n* permiso *nm,* licencia *nf,* carné *nm* **building permit** licencia de obras *nf*
perquisite *n* ((formal)) beneficio extra *nm,* incentivo *nm*
person *n* persona *nf* **third person** tercero *nm,* tercera persona *nf*
personal *adj* personal *adj*
personnel *n* **personnel department** departamento de personal *nm* **personnel management** dirección del personal *nf*
peseta *n* peseta *nf*
petrodollar *n* petrodólar *nm*
petroleum *n* **petroleum industry** industria petrolera *nf*
pharmaceutical *adj* **pharmaceutical industry** industria farmacéutica *nf*
phoney* *adj* falso *adj,* fingido *adj* **phoney* company** empresa ficticia *nf*
photocopier *n* fotocopiadora *nf*
photocopy 1. *n* fotocopia *nf* **2.** *vb* fotocopiar *vb*
pick up *vb* (improve) mejorar *vb,* recuperarse *vb*
picket *n* (strike) piquete *nm*
piecework *n* trabajo a destajo *nm*
pig iron *n* hierro en lingotes *nm*
pilferage *n* pequeño hurto *nm*
pilot *n* **pilot plant** planta piloto *nf,* fábrica piloto *nf* **pilot scheme** programa piloto *nm*
pipeline *n* conducto *nm,* ducto (LAm) *nm*
piracy *n* (at sea) piratería *nf* **software piracy** piratería de software *nf,* piratería de programa informático *nf*
place 1. *n* lugar *nm,* sitio *nm* **2.** *vb* poner *vb,* colocar *vb* **to place an order** hacer un pedido *vb*
plan 1. *n* **economic plan** plan económico *nm,* programa económico *nm* **plan of campaign** plan de campaña *nm* **to make plans** hacer planes *vb* **2.** *vb* planificar *vb,* planear *vb,* proyectar *vb,* concertar *vb*
planned *adj* **planned economy** economía planificada *nf* **planned obsolescence** obsolescencia planificada *nf*
planning *n* planificación *nf* **regional planning** planificación regional *nf*

plant *n* (machinery) maquinaria *nf* **plant hire** alquiler de maquinaria *nm* **plant manager** director, -ora de fábrica *nm,f,* director, -ora de planta *nm,f*
plastics *npl* **plastics industry** industria del plástico *nf*
pledge *n* promesa *nf,* garantía *nf,* prenda *nf*
plenary *adj* (assembly, session) plenario *adj*
plough back, plow back (US) *vb* (profits) reinvertir *vb*
point *n* **point of sale** punto de venta *nm*
policy *n* **insurance policy** póliza de seguros *nf* **pricing policy** política de precios *nf*
political *adj* político *adj*
politics *n* política *nf*
port *n* puerto *nm*
portable *adj* portátil *adj*
portfolio *n* **investment portfolio** cartera de inversiones *nf*
post 1. *n* (job) puesto *nm* **2.** *vb* mandar por correo *vb,* remitir por correo *vb*
post office *n* oficina de correos *nf,* correo (LAm) *nm*
postal *adj* **postal services** servicios postales *nmpl*
postdate *vb* tener lugar después de *vb,* poner fecha adelantada *vb,* diferir (LAm) *vb*
poste restante *n* lista de correos *nf,* poste restante (LAm) *nm*
poster *n* (advertising) cartel *nm,* póster *nm*
postpone *vb* aplazar *vb,* posponer *vb,* postergar (LAm) *vb*
potential *n* potencial *nm,* posibilidades *nfpl* **sales potential** posibilidades de ventas *nfpl*
pound *n* (weight) libra *nf* **pound sterling** libra esterlina *nf*
power *n* poder *nm,* potencia *nf,* fuerza *nf* **power of attorney** poder notarial *nm*
preference *n* **community preference** preferencia comunitaria *nf*
preferential *adj* preferencial *adj*
premises *npl* local *nm* **office premises** local de una oficina *nm*
premium *n* prima *nf,* recargo *nm* **at a premium** por encima de la par *prep*
prepayment *n* pago anticipado *nm,* pago por adelantado *nm*
president *n* (of company) presidente, -nta *nm,f*
press *n* **press baron** magnate de la prensa *nmf* **press conference** rueda de prensa *nf*
price *n* precio *nm,* cotización *nf* **market price** precio de mercado *nm* **stock exchange prices** cotizaciones de la bolsa *nfpl* **threshold price** precio umbral *nm,* precio mínimo al que pueden venderse en la UE *nm*
pricing *adj* **pricing policy** política de precios *nf*
primary *adj* primario *adj* **primary industry** industria de base *nf*
prime *adj* **prime lending rate** tipo preferencial de interés bancario *nm,* tasa

preferencial de interés bancario (LAm) *nf*
priority *n* prioridad *nf*, preferencia *nf*,
antelación *nf*
private *adj* **private sector** sector privado *nm*
privatization *n* privatización *nf*
privatize *vb* privatizar *vb*
pro 1. *n* **pros and cons** pros y contras *nmpl*
& *nmpl* **2.** *prep* **pro rata** a prorrata *prep*, a
prorrateo *prep*, proporcionalmente *adv*
probate *n* legalización *nf*, trámite para
obtener la legitimación de un testamento
nm
proceeds *npl* beneficios *nmpl*, ganancias *nfpl*
process 1. *n* proceso *nm*, procedimiento *nm*,
curso *nm* **2.** *vb* elaborar *vb*, tramitar *vb*
produce 1. *n* productos *nmpl* **2.** *vb* producir
vb, fabricar *vb*, presentar *vb*
producer *n* fabricante *nmf*
product *n* producto *nm* **primary product**
producto primario *nm*
production *n* producción *nf*, fabricación *nf*,
presentación *nf* **production line** cadena de
montaje *nf*, cadena de producción *nf*
productive *adj* productivo *adj*
productivity *n* productividad *nf*
productivity gains aumentos de
productividad *nmpl*
profession *n* profesión *nf* **the professions**
las profesiones liberales *nfpl*
profit *n* beneficio(s) *nm(pl)*, ganancia(s) *nf(pl)*,
provecho *nm*, utilidades (LAm) *nfpl* **profit
and loss** ganancias y pérdidas *nfpl* & *nfpl*
profit margin margen de beneficio *nm*
net(t) profit beneficio neto *nm* **operating
profit** beneficio(s) de explotación *nm(pl)*,
beneficio(s) de operación (LAm) *nm(pl)*
profit-sharing scheme programa de
participación en los beneficios *nm* **to make
a profit** obtener beneficios *vb*
profitability *n* rentabilidad *nf*
profiteer *vb* especular *vb*, realizar ganancias
excesivas *vb*
program *n* (DP) programa *nm*
programmer *n* (DP) programador, -ora *nm,f*
programming *n* (DP) programación *nf*
progress 1. *n* progreso *nm*, adelanto *nm*,
marcha *nf* **2.** *vb* (research, project) avanzar
vb, desarrollar *vb*
project *n* proyecto *nm*
promissory *adj* **promissory note** pagaré
nm, letra al propio cargo *nf*
promote *vb* (person) ascender *vb*, promover
vb (product) promocionar *vb*, fomentar *vb*,
potenciar *vb*
promotion *n* (of product) promoción *nf* (of
person) ascenso *nm*, promoción *nf*, fomento
nm
promotional *adj* publicitario *adj*
promotional budget presupuesto
publicitario *nm*, presupuesto promocional
nm
prompt *adj* rápido *adj*, pronto *adj*, puntual *adj*
property *n* propiedad *nf*, propiedades *nfpl*,
bienes inmuebles *nmpl* **property company**

sociedad inmobiliaria *nf* **property
developer** promotor, -ora inmobiliario, -ria
nm,f **private property** propiedad privada *nf*
proprietary *adj* patentado *adj*, de marca
registrada *prep* **proprietary brand** marca
registrada *nf*
proprietor *n* propietario, -ria *nm,f*, dueño,
-eña *nm,f*
prospect *n* perspectiva *nf*, posibilidad *nf*,
panorama *nm* **future prospects**
perspectivas futuras *nfpl*
prospectus *n* folleto informativo *nm*, folleto
publicitario *nm*
prosperous *adj* próspero *adj*
protectionism *n* proteccionismo *nm*
protectionist *adj* proteccionista *adj*
provide *vb* (supply) proveer *vb*, suministrar
vb, proporcionar *vb*, disponer *vb*
provision *n* (stipulation) provisión *nf*,
disposición *nf*
proxy *n* (power) poderes *nmpl*, apoderado,
-ada *nm,f*
public *adj* público *adj* **public company**
sociedad cotizada en bolsa *nf* **public funds**
fondos públicos *nmpl* **public relations**
relaciones públicas *nfpl* **public sector**
sector público *nm* **public service** servicio
público *nm*
publicity *n* publicidad *nf*
publishing *n* campo editorial *nm*, mundo
editorial *nm* **desk-top publishing**
autoedición *nf*
purchase 1. *adj* **purchase price** precio de
compra *nm* **2.** *n* compra *nf*, adquisición *nf*
3. *vb* comprar *vb*, adquirir *vb*
purchasing *adj* **purchasing power** poder
adquisitivo *nm*
pyramid *n* **pyramid scheme** plan piramidal
nm **pyramid selling** venta piramidal *nf*
qualification *n* cualificación *nf*, competencia
nf, título *nm*, calificación (LAm) *nf*
academic qualification título académico
nm **educational qualification** título
docente *nm* **professional qualification**
cualificación profesional *nf*
qualified *adj* cualificado *adj*, capacitado *adj*,
calificado (LAm) *adj*, capacitado (LAm) *adj*
qualified acceptance aceptación con
reservas *nf* **qualified personnel** personal
cualificado *nm*, personal calificado (LAm)
nm
qualitative *adj* cualitativo *adj*
quality *n* calidad *nf*, categoría *nf* **quality
control** control de calidad *nm* **quality
report** informe de calidad *nm*, informe
sobre la calidad *nm* **quality standard** nivel
de calidad *nm*, norma de calidad *nf*
quantitative *adj* cuantitativo *adj*
quantity *n* cantidad *nf* **quantity discount**
descuento por grandes cantidades *nm*
quantity theory of money teoría
cuantitativa del dinero *nf*
quarter *n* (of year) trimestre *nm*
quarterly *adj* trimestral *adj* **quarterly**

interest interés trimestral *nm* **quarterly trade accounts** contabilidad comercial trimestral *nf*

quasi-contract *n* cuasicontrato *nm*

quasi-income *n* cuasingresos *nmpl*

quay *n* muelle *nm*

quayage *n* derechos de muelle *nmpl*, espacio disponible en un muelle *nm*

questionnaire *n* cuestionario *nm*, encuesta *nf* **questionnaire design** diseño de cuestionarios *nm*

queue *n* cola *nf*

quick *adj* **quick assets** activo disponible *nm*

quiet *adj* **quiet market** mercado poco móvil *nm*

quit *vb* (resign) abandonar *vb*, dejar de *vb*

quittance *n* descargo *nm*, compensación *nf*

quorate *adj* (meeting) con quórum *prep*

quorum *n* quórum *nm* **quorum of creditors** quórum de acreedores *nm*

quota *n* cupo *nm*, cuota *nf* **quota agreement** acuerdo de cuotas *nm* **quota buying** compra de cupos *nf* **import quota** cupo de importación *nm* **sales quota** cupo de ventas *nm* **quota sampling** muestreo de cuotas *nm* **quota system** sistema de cuotas *nm*

quotation *n* (price) cotización *nf*, presupuesto *nm*

quoted *adj* **quoted company** sociedad cuyas acciones se cotizan en Bolsa *nf* **quoted investment** inversión cotizada *nf* **quoted share, quoted stocks** (US) acciones que se cotizan en Bolsa *nfpl*

racket *n* chanchullo *nm*, estafa *nf*, timo *nm*

racketeer *n* estafador, -ora *nm,f*, mafioso, -osa *nm,f*

racketeering *n* crimen organizado *nm*, negocio ilícito *nm*

rag *n* **the rag trade** (informal) el comercio textil *nm*, la industria del vestido *nf*

rail *n* **by rail** en tren *prep*

railway, railroad (US) *n* ferrocarril *nm*

raise *vb* (price, interest rate) subir *vb*, aumentar *vb*, incrementar *vb*, (capital, loan) subir *vb*, elevar *vb*

RAM (random access memory) *abbr* (DP) RAM *nf*, memoria RAM *nf*

random *adj* **at random** al azar *prep* **random selection** selección aleatoria *nf*

range *n* (of products) gama *nf*, alcance *nm*, línea *nf*

rate *n* **base rate** tipo base *nm*, tasa base (LAm) *nf* **rate of exchange** tipo de cambio *nm*, tipo/tasa de paridad *nm/f*, tasa de cambio (LAm) *nf* **rate of expansion** ritmo de expansión *nm*, coeficiente de expansión *nm*, tasa de expansión (LAm) *nf* **rate of growth** tasa de crecimiento *nf* **rate of inflation** tasa de inflación *nf* **rate of interest** tipo de interés *nm*, tasa de interés (LAm) *nf* **rate of investment** ritmo de inversiones *nm*, tasa de inversión (LAm) *nf* **rate of return** tasa de rendimiento *nf*, tasa

de rentabilidad *nf* **rates** (tax) tarifas *nfpl*, contribuciones municipales *nfpl*, tasas (LAm) *nfpl*

ratification *n* ratificación *nf*

ratify *vb* ratificar *vb*

ratio *n* ratio *nm*, relación *nf*

rationale *n* lógica *nf*

rationalization *n* racionalización *nf*, reconversión *nf* **rationalization measures** medidas de reconversión *nfpl*

rationalize *vb* racionalizar *vb*, sistematizar *vb*

raw *adj* (unprocessed) crudo *adj*, sin analizar *prep*

re *prep* con referencia a *prep*, con relación a *prep*, Asunto *nm*

re-elect *vb* reelegir *vb*

re-election *n* reelección *nf*

ready *adj* listo *adj*, dispuesto *adj* **ready for despatch** listo para entrega *adj*

real *adj* **real estate** propiedad inmobiliaria *nf*, bienes raíces *nmpl* **real price** precio real *nm* **real time** tiempo real *nm* **real value** valor real *nm* **real wages** ingreso real *nm*, salario real *nm*

realization *n* **realization of assets** liquidación de activo *nf*

realize *vb* (profit) realizar *vb*

reallocate *vb* (funds) redistribuir *vb*, readjudicar *vb*

reallocation *n* (of funds) redistribución *nf*, reasignación *nf*

realtor (US) *n* agente inmobiliario *nmf*, agente de la propiedad inmobiliaria *nmf*, corredor, -ora de propiedades (LAm) *nm,f*

reappoint *vb* volver a nombrar *vb*, volver a contratar *vb*

reappointment *n* recontratación *nf*

reasonable *adj* (price) razonable *adj*, bien de precio *adv*

rebate *n* desgravación *nf*, reembolso *nm*, descuento *nm* **to grant a rebate** conceder una desgravación *vb*

receipt *n* **to acknowledge receipt** acusar recibo *vb* **to issue a receipt** expedir un recibo *vb*, extender un recibo *vb*

receive *vb* recibir *vb*, cobrar *vb*

receiver, administrator (US) *n* (bankruptcy) síndico, -ica *nm,f*

recession *n* recesión *nf*

recipient *n* receptor, -ora *nm,f*, destinatario, -ria *nm,f*, beneficiario, -ria *nm,f*

reciprocal *adj* recíproco *adj*, mutuo *adj*

reclaimable *adj* (materials) reciclable *adj*, reutilizable *adj*

recommend *vb* recomendar *vb*, aconsejar *vb*

recommendation *n* recomendación *nf*

recompense *n* indemnización *nf*, recompensa *nf*

record 1. *n* archivo *nm*, acta *nm*, antecedentes *nmpl*, historial (LAm) *nm* **according to our records** según nuestros registros *prep* **2.** *vb* anotar *vb*

recover *vb* **to recover money from sb** recuperar dinero a alguien *vb*

recovery *n* (of debt) cobro *nm* (economic) reactivación *nf*, repunte *nm*

recruit *vb* reclutar *vb*, contratar *vb*

recruitment *n* contratación *nf* **recruitment campaign** campaña de reclutamiento *nf*

recyclable *adj* reciclable *adj*

recycle *vb* reciclar *vb*

red *adj* **red tape** burocracia *nf*, trámites burocráticos *nmpl*, papeleo *nm* **to be in the red** estar en números rojos *vb*, entrar en déficit *vb*

redeem *vb* amortizar *vb*, liquidar *vb*, redimir *vb*

redeemable *adj* **redeemable bond** bono amortizable *nm*

redemption *n* amortización *nf*, pago *nm*, rescate *nm* **redemption fund** fondo para amortizaciones *nm*

redirect *vb* (mail) reexpedir *vb*

reduce *vb* (prices) reducir *vb*, rebajar *vb* (taxes) recortar *vb*

reduced *adj* rebajado *adj* **at a greatly reduced price** a un precio muy rebajado *prep*

reduction *n* reducción *nf*, rebaja *nf*, recorte *nm*

redundancy *n* despido *nm*, cese *nm*, baja *nf*

redundant *adj* desempleado *adj*, excesivo *adj*, superfluo *adj*, parado (LAm) **to make sb redundant** despedir a alguien por reducción de plantilla *vb*

refer *vb* referir *vb*, hacer referencia *vb* **we refer to our letter of...** hacemos referencia a nuestra carta de *vb*, con relación a nuestra carta de *prep* **we refer you to our head office** le remitimos a nuestra oficina central *vb*, le referimos a nuestra sede *vb*

referee *n* evaluador, -ora *nm,f*, persona que da referencias sobre otra *nf*, árbitro *nm* **to act as referee** estar dispuesto a dar referencias sobre *vb*

reference *n* referencia *nf*, informe *nm* **credit reference** referencia de crédito *nf* **reference number** número de referencia *nm* **to take up a reference** pedir una referencia *vb* **with reference to** con referencia a *prep*

referendum *n* referéndum *nm*

reflation *n* reflación *nf*, reactivación *nf*

reflationary *adj* reflacionario *adj*

reform *n* reforma *nf* **currency reform** reforma monetaria *nf*

refund 1. *n* reembolso *nm*, reintegro *nm* **2.** *vb* reembolsar *vb*, devolver *vb*, reintegrar *vb*

refundable *adj* reembolsable *adj*

refurbish *vb* renovar *vb*, hacer reformas en *vb*

refurbishment *n* renovación *nf*, restauración *nf*

refusal *n* negativa *nf*, rechazo *nm*, plante (LAm) *nm*

refuse *vb* rehusar *vb*, negarse a *vb*, denegar *vb* **to refuse a claim** negarse a pagar una reclamación *vb* **to refuse goods** rechazar mercancías *vb* **to refuse payment** negarse a pagar *vb*, rehusar pagar (LAm) *vb*

regard *n* **with regard to...** en cuanto a *prep*, con relación a *prep*

regarding *prep* respecto a *prep*, por lo que se refiere a *prep*

regional *adj* **regional office** oficina regional *nf*, dirección general *nf*

register *n* registro *nm*, lista *nf*, archivo *nm*

registered *adj* **registered bond** obligación registrada *nf*, título nominativo *nm* **registered capital** capital certificado *nm*, capital nominal *nm* **registered company** compañía registrada *nf*, sociedad legalmente constituida *nf* **registered letter** carta certificada *nf*, carta registrada (LAm) *nf*, carta recomendada (LAm) *nf* **registered mail** correo certificado *nm*, correo recomendado (LAm) *nm* **registered office** domicilio social *nm*, sede *nf* **registered share** acción nominativa *nf* **registered trademark** marca registrada *nf*

regret *vb* **we regret to inform you that...** lamentamos informarle que *vb*

regular *adj* **regular customer** cliente, -nta habitual *nm,f*

regulation *n* regulación *nf*, reglamento *nm* **according to the regulations** según las normas *prep*, de acuerdo con las disposiciones *prep*

reimburse *vb* reembolsar *vb*

reimbursement *n* reembolso *nm*

reimport *vb* reimportar *vb*

reimportation *n* reimportación *nf*

reinsurance *n* reaseguro *nm*

reinsure *vb* reasegurar *vb*

reject *vb* (goods) rechazar *vb*, negarse a aceptar *vb*

relations *npl* **business relations** relaciones comerciales *nfpl* **industrial relations** relaciones industriales *nfpl*

relationship *n* **working relationship** relación de trabajo *nf*

relax *vb* (restrictions) relajar *vb*, flexibilizar *vb*

relevant *adj* pertinente *adj*, apropiado *adj*

reliability *n* fiabilidad *nf*, formalidad *nf*

reliable *adj* fidedigno *adj*, responsable *adj*, formal *adj*, fiable (LAm) *adj*, confiable (LAm) *adj*

relocate *vb* trasladar *vb*, trasladarse *vb*

relocation *n* traslado *nm*

remaining *adj* (sum) restante *adj*

reminder *n* recordatorio *nm*, advertencia *nf*

remittance *n* remesa *nf*, envío *nm*, giro *nm* **remittance advice** aviso de expedición *nm*

remunerate *vb* remunerar *vb*, pagar *vb*

remuneration *n* remuneración *nf*

renew *vb* (policy, contract) renovar *vb*, reanudar *vb*

renewable *adj* renovable *adj*

rent 1. *n* alquiler *nm*, arrendamiento *nm*, renta (LAm) *nf*, arriendo (LAm) *nm* **2.** *vb* (house, office) alquilar *vb*, arrendar *vb*, rentar (LAm) *vb*

rental n alquiler nm, arrendamiento nm, renta (LAm) nf, arriendo (LAm) nm
repair 1. n **costs of repair** costes de reparación nmpl, costos de reparación (LAm) nmpl **2.** vb reparar vb, arreglar vb
reparation n indemnización nf
repatriation n repatriación nf
repay vb reembolsar vb, devolver vb, pagar vb
repayment n (of loan) reembolso nm
repeat adj **repeat order** pedido suplementario nm
replace vb reemplazar vb, reponer vb
replacement n (person) sustituto, -uta nm,f, suplente nmf
reply n **in reply to your letter of...** en contestación a su carta de prep
report n informe nm, noticia nf, reportaje nm, reporte (LAm) nm **annual report** memoria anual nf **to draw up a report** redactar un informe vb, elaborar un informe vb, hacer un reporte (LAm) vb **to submit/present a report** presentar un informe vb, reportear (LAm) vb
repossess vb confiscar vb, recobrar vb
repossession n recuperación nf, confiscación nf
representative n representante nmf, agente nmf, viajante nmf **area representative** representante regional nmf **sales representative** agente comercial nmf
repudiate vb (contract) cancelar vb, rechazar vb
reputation n fama nf **to enjoy a good reputation** tener buena reputación vb
request n solicitud nf, petición nf, pedido (LAm) nm **request for payment** solicitud de pago nf, pedido de pago (LAm) nm
requirement n necesidad nf, requisito nm, estipulación nf **in accordance with your requirements** según sus requisitos prep, de acuerdo con sus estipulaciones prep **it is a requirement of the contract that...** exige el contrato que vb
resale n reventa nf
rescind vb anular vb, cancelar vb
research n investigación nf, estudio nm **research and development (R&D)** investigación y desarrollo (I y D) nf & nm **market research** investigación de mercado nf, estudio de mercado nm
reservation n reserva nf, reservación (LAm) nf **to make a reservation** hacer una reserva vb, hacer una reservación (LAm) vb
reserve 1. adj **reserve currency** divisa de reserva nf **reserve stock** existencias de reserva nfpl **2.** n **currency reserve** reserva de divisas nf **to hold sth in reserve** tener algo en reserva vb **3.** vb reservar vb
residual adj residual adj, sobrante adj
resign vb dimitir vb, presentar la dimisión vb, renunciar vb
resignation n dimisión nf, renuncia nf **to hand in one's resignation** presentar la carta de renuncia vb

resolution n (decision) resolución nf, propósito nm **to make a resolution** tomar la determinación vb, decidirse vb
resolve vb (sort out) resolver vb, aclarar vb **to resolve to do sth** resolver hacer algo vb, optar por hacer algo vb
resort to vb (have recourse) recurrir a vb, no tener más remedio que vb
resources npl recursos nmpl, medios nmpl
respect n respeto nm **in respect of...** respecto a prep
response n **in response to...** en respuesta a prep
responsibility n **to take responsibility for sth** asumir responsabilidad vb, responsabilizarse de algo vb
responsible adj responsable adj, formal adj, serio adj
restrict vb restringir vb, limitar vb
restriction n restricción nf, límite nm **to impose restrictions on** imponer restricciones a vb
restrictive adj restrictivo adj **restrictive practices** prácticas restrictivas nfpl
restructure vb remodelar vb, reconvertir vb, replantear vb
retail adj **retail outlet** comercio al por menor nm, tienda al por menor nf **retail price** precio de venta al público nm **retail sales tax** impuesto sobre las ventas al detalle nm **retail trade** comercio al por menor nm, comercio minorista nm
retain vb retener vb, conservar vb, contratar vb
retention n retención nf, mantenimiento nm **retention of title** retención de título nf
retire vb jubilarse vb, retirarse vb
retirement n jubilación nf, retiro nm **to take early retirement** tomar la jubilación anticipada vb
retrain vb hacer un curso de reconversión vb, hacer un curso de recapacitación (LAm) vb
retraining n reciclaje profesional nm, reconversión nf **retraining programme, retraining program** (US) programa de reciclaje nm, curso de reciclaje nm, plan de recapacitación (LAm) nm
return 1. n vuelta nf, rendimiento nm, retorno (LAm) nm **in return** a cambio prep **return on capital** rendimiento del capital nm, rendimiento de la inversión nm **return on equity** rendimiento del capital social nm, rendimiento del patrimonio neto nm **return on investment** rendimiento de la inversión nm **return on sales** rendimiento de las ventas nm **returns** cifras nfpl, datos nmpl, resultados nmpl **2.** vb volver vb, regresar vb, retornar vb
returnable adj (deposit) reembolsable adj
revaluation n (of currency) revalorización nf, revaluación (LAm) nf
revalue vb (currency) revalorizar vb, revaluar (LAm) vb
revenue n ingresos nmpl, rentas públicas nfpl

reverse *vb* invertir *vb*, cambiar radicalmente *vb*

revert *vb* revertir *vb*

revert to *vb* volver a *vb*, revertir a *vb*

revise *vb* revisar *vb*, repasar *vb*

revocable *adj* **revocable letter of credit** carta de crédito revocable *nf*

revoke *vb* (offer) revocar *vb* (licence) revocar *vb*

right *n* derecho *nm*, derecha *nf* **right of recourse** derecho a recurrir *nm* **right of way** derecho de paso *nm*, preferencia *nf* **the right to do sth** el derecho a hacer algo *nm* **the right to sth** el derecho a algo *nm*, el derecho de algo *nm*

rights *npl* **rights issue** emisión de derechos *nf* **sole rights** derechos exclusivos *nmpl*

rise, raise (US) **1.** *n* (in earnings) subida *nf*, aumento *nm*, suba (LAm) *nf* (in inflation) subida *nf*, aumento *nm*, incremento *nm* (in unemployment) subida *nf*, aumento *nm*, crecimiento *nm* **2.** *vb* subir *vb*, levantarse *vb*, aumentar *vb*

risk *n* riesgo *nm*, peligro *nm* **all-risks insurance** seguro a todo riesgo *nm* **risk analysis** análisis de riesgos *nm* **risk assessment** valoración de riesgos *nf* **at the buyer's risk** por cuenta y riesgo del comprador *prep* **risk capital** capital de especulación *nm* **risk management** gestión de riesgos *nf* **the policy covers the following risks...** la póliza cubre los riesgos siguientes *nf*

road *n* **by road** por carretera *prep*, por tierra *prep* **road haulage** transporte por carretera *nm* **road haulage company** empresa de transportes por carretera *nf*, compañía de transportes *nf* **road traffic** circulación en la carretera *nf*, tráfico por carretera *nm*, tránsito en la carretera (LAm) *nm* **road transport** transporte por carretera *nm*

ROM (read only memory) *abbr* ROM *abbr,nf*, memoria de lectura *nf*

Rome *n* **the Treaty of Rome** El Tratado de Roma *nm*

room *n* **room for manoeuvre** espacio para maniobrar *nm*

royal *adj* real *adj* **the Royal Mint** (GB) casa real de la moneda *nf*

RSVP (répondez s'il vous plaît) *abbr* s.r.c. (se ruega contestación) *abbr* R.S.V.P. (LAm) *abbr*

run *vb* correr *vb* (manage) dirigir *vb*, poner *vb*, poner un servicio *vb*

run down *vb* (stocks) ir recortando *vb*

run low *vb* (stocks) ir agotándose *vb*, reducir al mínimo *vb*

running *adj* **running costs** gastos de explotación *nmpl*, costes corrientes *nmpl*, costos de operación (LAm) *nmpl*

rush *n* **rush hour** hora punta *nf*, hora pico (LAm) *nf* **rush job** trabajo hecho de prisa *nm* **rush order** pedido urgente *nm*

sack, fire* (US) *vb* despedir *vb*, echar del trabajo *vb*, botar del trabajo (LAm) *vb*

safe *adj* seguro *adj*, fiable *adj*, sin riesgo *prep*

safety *n* **safety officer** responsable de la seguridad *nmf*

salary *n* sueldo *nm*, remuneración *nf*, salario *nm* **salary scale** escala salarial *nf*

sale *n* venta *nf* **closing-down sale, closing-out sale** (US) liquidación por cierre *nf* **sales** *npl* ventas *nfpl* **sales campaign** campaña de ventas *nf* **sales conference** reunión de ventas *nf* **sales department** departamento de ventas *nm* **export sales** ventas al exterior *nfpl* **sales figures** cifras de ventas *nfpl*, volumen de ventas *nm* **sales forecast** previsión de ventas *nf* **home sales** ventas nacionales *nfpl*, ventas en el mercado interior *nfpl* **sales ledger** libro mayor de ventas *nm* **sales management** gestión de ventas *nf*, dirección comercial *nf*

salesperson *n* dependiente, -nta *nm,f*, vendedor, -ora *nm,f*, representante *nmf*, corredor, -ora (LAm) *nm,f*

salvage *vb* salvar *vb*, rescatar *vb*

sample 1. *n* muestra *nf*, ejemplo *nm* **2.** *vb* probar *vb*, tomar muestras *vb*

sampling *n* muestreo *nm*

sanction *n* sanción *nf* **trade sanctions** sanciones económicas *nfpl*

saving *n* ahorro *nm*, economía *nf* **savings bank** caja de ahorros *nf*

scab* *n* rompehuelgas *nmf*, esquirol *nm*, carnero, -era (LAm) *nm,f*

scale *n* escala *nf*, balanza *nf*, tarifa *nf*, banda *nf*

scarcity *n* escasez *nf*, carestía *nf*

schedule 1. *n* programa *nm*, horario *nm*, lista *nf* **2.** *vb* programar *vb*, proyectar *vb*

scheme *n* **pension scheme** plan de pensiones *nm* **recovery scheme** plan de reactivación *nm*, programa de recuperación *nm*

scrap *n* (metal) chatarra *nf*

scrip *n* acción gratuita *nf*, título provisional *nm*

SDRs (special drawing rights) *abbr* DEG (derechos especiales de giro) *abbr*

sea *n* mar *nm* & *nf* **by sea** en barco, por vía marítima *prep* **sea freight** flete marítimo *nm*, carga marítima *nf*

seal 1. *n* sello *nm*, cierre *nm*, aprobación *nf* **2.** *vb* sellar *vb*, cerrar *vb*

sealed *adj* cerrado *adj*, sellado *adj* **sealed bid** oferta en pliego cerrado *nf*

season *n* temporada *nf*, estación *nf*, época *nf* **high season** temporada alta *nf* **low season** temporada baja *nf*

seasonal *adj* estacional *adj*

SEC (Securities and Exchange Commission) (GB) *abbr* Comisión de Valores y Cambios (La) *nf*, Comisión de Bolsa y Valores *nf*

secondary *adj* **secondary industry** sector secundario *nm* **secondary market** mercado subsidiario *nm*

secondment n traslado temporal nm
secretary n secretario, -ria nm,f **executive secretary** secretario, -ria ejecutivo, -iva nm,f
sector n sector nm **primary sector** sector primario nm **secondary sector** sector secundario nm **tertiary sector** sector terciario nm
secure adj seguro adj
secured adj **secured loan** préstamo garantizado nm
securities npl valores nmpl, titulos nmpl, acciones nfpl **gilt-edged securities** títulos del Estado nmpl, valores del Estado nmpl **listed securities** valores bursátiles nmpl, acciones cotizables en bolsa nfpl **unlisted securities** valores no admitidos a cotización nmpl
security n seguridad nf, valor nm **Social Security (GB)** Seguridad Social nf
self-assessment n autoevaluación nf
self-employed adj autónomo adj, que trabaja por cuenta propia rel pron
self-financing adj autofinanciado adj
self-management n autogestión nf
self-sufficient adj autosuficiente adj
sell 1. n **hard sell** venta agresiva nf **soft sell** venta blanda/suave nf **2.** vb vender vb **to sell sth at auction** subastar algo vb, rematar (LAm) vb **to sell sth in bulk** vender algo a granel vb **to sell sth on credit** vender algo a crédito vb **to sell sth retail** vender algo al por menor vb **this article sells well** este artículo se vende bien **to sell sth wholesale** vender algo al por mayor vb
sell off vb liquidar vb, vender barato vb
sell up vb liquidar vb, vender un negocio con todas sus existencias vb
seller n vendedor, -ora nm,f
semi-skilled adj semicualificado adj
send vb enviar vb, mandar vb, remitir vb
send back vb devolver vb
sendee n destinatario, -ria nm,f
sender n remitente nmf
senior adj mayor adj, superior adj, principal adj **senior management** alta dirección nf
seniority n antigüedad nf
service n **after-sales service** servicio postventa nm **civil service** administración pública nf **service included** servicio incluido nm **service industry** industria de servicios nf, sector servicios nm **National Health Service (GB)** Seguridad Social nf
set up vb (company) montar vb, fundar vb, poner vb
settle vb (dispute) resolver vb (account) pagar vb, saldar vb, solventar vb
severance n **severance pay** indemnización por despido nf
shady* adj (dealings) sospechoso adj, turbio adj
share 1. n participación nf, cuota nf, acción nf **share in the profits** una parte de las ganancias nf **market share** participación en

el mercado nf, cuota de mercado nf **ordinary share** acción ordinaria nf **2.** vb compartir vb **to share the responsibilities** compartir las responsabilidades vb
shareholder n accionista nmf, tenedor, -ora de acciones nm,f
shark* n usurero, -era nm,f, explotador, -ora nm,f
sharp adj **sharp practice** triquiñuelas nf
shift n cambio nm, turno nm, desplazamiento nm **the three-shift system** el sistema de tres turnos nm **shift work** trabajo por turnos nm
shipbuilding n construcción naval nf
shipment n (consignment) carga nf, consignación nf
shipper n expedidor, -ora nm,f, remitente nmf
shipping n **shipping agent** consignatario, -ria nm,f, agencia de transportes nf **shipping broker** agente expedidor nm, corredor marítimo nm **shipping line** compañía naviera nf
shipyard n astillero nm
shirker* n vago, -aga nm,f, flojo, -oja nm,f, fiacún, -una (LAm) nm,f, flojonazo,-aza (LAm) nm,f
shoddy* adj de baja calidad
shop n **shop assistant** dependiente, -nta nm,f, vendedor, -ora nm,f, empleado, -ada de tienda (LAm) **closed shop** plantilla sindicada nf **shop steward** representante sindical nmf, enlace sindical nmf, delegado, -ada sindical nm,f **to shut up shop** (informal) cerrar vb, cerrar la tienda vb, dar por terminado un asunto vb **to talk shop** (informal) hablar del trabajo vb
shopping n **shopping centre** centro comercial nm
short adj breve adj, corto adj **short delivery** entrega insuficiente nf **to be on short time** trabajar a jornada reducida vb
shortage n falta nf, escasez nf
show n (exhibition) exposición nf, exhibición nf, feria nf
showroom n salón de exposición nm, sala de exposiciones nf
shredder n trituradora nf
shrink vb recortar vb, contraerse vb
shrinkage n **stock shrinkage** pérdidas de estoc nfpl, fugas de existencias nfpl
shutdown n cese nm, paralización nf
shuttle n servicio de enlace nm, puente aéreo nm
SIB (Securities and Investment Board) (GB) abbr Comisión de Bolsa y Valores nf
sick adj **sick leave** baja por enfermedad nf, licencia por enfermedad (LAm) nf
sickness n **sickness benefit** subsidio de enfermedad nm
sight n **sight draft** letra a la vista nf, efecto a la vista nm
sign vb firmar vb, fichar vb
signatory n firmante nmf, signatario, -ria nm,f

signature n firma nf
silent adj **silent partner** socio, -cia
comanditario, -ria nm,f
sinking n hundimiento nm, amortización nf
sinking fund fondo de amortización nm
sit-in n (strike) encierro en señal de protesta
nm
size n tamaño nm, talla nf, talle (LAm) nm
skill n habilidad nf, técnica nf
skilled n (worker) cualificado adj,
especializado adj, capacitado (LAm) adj
slackness n (laxity) falta de actividad nf, falta
de movimiento nf
sliding adj **sliding scale** escala móvil nf
slogan n consigna nf, eslogan nm
slow down vb desacelerar vb, frenarse vb
slowdown n desaceleración nf, reducción nf,
huelga de celo nf
slump 1. n depresión nf, caída repentina nf
2. vb caer en picado vb, sufrir un bajón vb
slush adj **slush fund** fondo para sobornos
nm, fondo de reptiles nm
small adj pequeño adj **small ads** anuncios
clasificados nmpl, avisos clasificados (LAm)
nmpl **small scale** pequeña escala nf
smuggle vb contrabandear vb
society n sociedad nf **building society**
sociedad hipotecaria nf, sociedad de crédito
hipotecario nf, sociedad de ahorro y
préstamo para la vivienda nf **consumer
society** sociedad de consumo nf
socio-economic adj **socio-economic
categories** grupos socioeconómicos nmpl
software n software nm, programa
informático nm **software package** paquete
de software nm
sole adj exclusivo adj, único adj **sole agent**
representante en exclusiva nmf
solicitor, lawyer (US) n abogado, -ada nm,f
solvency n solvencia nf
solvent adj solvente adj
source n fuente nf, origen nm, raíz nf
sourcing n aprovisionamiento nm,
procedencia nf
specialist n especialista nmf
speciality n especialidad nf
specialize vb especializar vb
specification n especificación nf, requisito
nm
specify vb precisar vb, indicar vb
speculate vb especular vb
speculator n especulador, -ora nm,f
spend vb gastar vb, pasar vb, emplear vb
spending n gastos nmpl
spendthrift adj despilfarrador adj
sphere n ámbito nm, campo nm, esfera nf
sphere of activity ámbito de actividad
profesional nm
spin-off n efecto indirecto nm
split 1. adj **split division** fraccionamiento
nm **2.** vb escindirse vb, desintegrar vb,
dividir vb, partir vb, romper vb
spoilage n desechos nmpl, desperdicios nmpl
spoils npl botín nm

spokesperson n portavoz nmf, vocero, -era
(LAm) nm,f
sponsor n patrocinador, -ora nm,f, espónsor
nmf
sponsorship n patrocinio nm, mecenazgo nm
spot adj **spot cash** pago al contado nm,
dinero en mano nm **spot market** mercado
de entrega spot nm **spot price** precio de
entrega inmediata nm, tarifa de entrega
inmediata nf **spot rate** precio de entrega
inmediata nm, tarifa de entrega inmediata nf
spread vb (payments) distribuir vb
spreadsheet n hoja de cálculo nf
squander vb despilfarrar vb, derrochar vb
squeeze 1. n **credit squeeze** restricciones
de crédito nfpl **2.** vb (spending) restringir vb,
recortar vb
stable adj (economy) estable adj
staff n personal nm, plantilla nf, empleados
nmpl
staffing n dotación de personal nf
stage n etapa nf **in stages** por etapas prep
staged adj **staged payments** pagos por
etapas nmpl
stagger vb (holidays) escalonar vb
stagnation n estancamiento nm
stake n participación nf, inversión nf, paquete
accional autónomo nm
stakeholder n inversor, -ora nm,f, apostador,
-ora nm,f
stalemate n punto muerto nm
standard 1. adj normal adj **standard
agreement** contrato-tipo nm **2.** n **gold
standard** patrón-oro nm **standard of
living** nivel de vida nm
standardization n estandarización nf,
normalización nf
standardize vb normalizar vb, tipificar vb
standing 1. adj **standing charges** cuotas
fijas nfpl **standing order** orden permanente
de pago nf, pedido fijo nm **2.** n standing nm
staple adj **staple commodities** productos
básicos nmpl, artículos de primera
necesidad nmpl
start-up n inicio nm **start-up capital** capital
de puesta en marcha nm
state n **state-owned enterprise** empresa
estatal nf, empresa de propiedad pública nf
statement n afirmación nf, declaración nf,
instrucción nf **bank statement** estado de
cuentas nm
statistics n estadísticas nfpl, cifras nfpl
status n **financial status** situación
económica nf **status quo** statu quo nm
statute n estatuto nm, ley nf
steel n **steel industry** industria del acero nf
sterling n esterlina nf, libra esterlina nf
sterling area zona de la libra esterlina nf
sterling balance reserva de libras
esterlinas nf **pound sterling** libra esterlina
nf
stock, inventory (US) n (goods) existencias
nfpl, estoc nm, stock nm **stock control**
control de existencias nm **stock exchange**

bolsa *nf* **in stock** en almacén *prep*, en estoc *prep* **stock market** mercado de valores *nm*, bolsa de valores *nf* **out of stock** con las existencias agotadas **stocks and shares** acciones *nfpl*, valores inmobiliarios *nmpl*

stockbroker *n* corredor, -ora de Bolsa *nm,f*, agente de Bolsa *nmf*, corredor (LAm) *nm*

stockholder *n* accionista *nmf*, tenedor, -ora de acciones *nm,f*

stocktaking *n* inventario de existencias *nm*, balance *nm*

stoppage *n* (strike) paro *nm*, cese *nm*

storage *n* almacenaje *nm*, almacenamiento *nm* **storage capacity** capacidad de almacenaje *nf* **cold storage plant** planta de almacenaje frigorífico *nf*

store 1. *n* (shop) almacén *nf*, tienda *nf* **chain store** tienda que forma parte de una cadena *nf* **department store** grandes almacenes *nmpl* **2.** *vb* guardar *vb*

stowage *n* gastos de estiba *nmpl*, bodega *nf*

strategic *adj* estratégico *adj*

strategy *n* estrategia *nf*

stress *n* **executive stress** estrés profesional *nm*

strike 1. *adj* **strike action** acción laboral *nf*, huelga *nf*, paro (LAm) *nm* **strike ballot** votación para decidir si se hace huelga *nf*, votación para decidir si se va al paro (LAm) *nf* **2.** *n* huelga *nf*, paro (LAm) *nm* **wildcat strike** huelga salvaje *nf*, paro incontrolado (LAm) *nm*, paro imprevisto (LAm) *nm* **3.** *vb* declararse en huelga *vb*, hacer huelga *vb*, ir al paro (LAm) *vb*, declararse en paro (LAm) *vb*

strikebreaker *n* rompehuelgas *nmf*, carnero, -era (LAm) *nm,f*

striker *n* huelguista *nmf*, trabajador, -ora en paro (LAm) *nm,f*

subcontract *vb* subcontratar *vb*

subcontractor *n* subcontratista *nmf*

subordinate *n* subalterno, -rna *nm,f*

subscribe *vb* contribuir *vb*, suscribir *vb*

subsidiary *n* empresa filial *nf*, sucursal *nf*

subsidize *vb* subvencionar *vb*, subsidiar (LAm)

subsidy *n* subvención *nf* **state subsidy** subvención estatal *nf*, subsidio del gobierno *nm*, subsidio del estado (LAm) *nm*

suburb *n* afueras *nfpl*, colonias (LAm) *nfpl* **outer suburbs** barrios residenciales de las afueras *nmpl*

supermarket *n* supermercado *nm*, autoservicio *nm*

supertanker *n* superpetrolero *nm*

supertax *n* impuesto elevadísimo *nm*

supervisor *n* supervisor, -ora *nm,f*, revisor, -ora *nm,f*, director, -ora *nm,f*

supervisory *adj* **supervisory board** comité de supervisión *nm*

supplementary *adj* suplementario *adj*

supplier *n* suministrador, -ora *nm,f*, proveedor, -ora *nm,f*, abastecedor, -ora *nm,f*

supply 1. *n* oferta *nf*, suministro *nm*, reserva

nf **supply and demand** oferta y demanda *nf* & *nf* **2.** *vb* proveer *vb*, abastecer *vb*

surplus *n* excedente *nm*, exceso *nm*, superávit *nm* **budget surplus** superávit presupuestario *nm* **trade surplus** superávit comercial *nm*

surtax *n* recargo del impuesto sobre la renta *nm*

survey *n* encuesta *nf*, sondeo *nm* **market research survey** estudio de mercado *nm*, investigación de mercado *nf*

swap 1. *n* canje *nm*, cambio *nm*, intercambio *nm* **2.** *vb* canjear *vb*, intercambiar *vb*

sweetener* *n* (bribe) soborno *nm*, coima (LAm) *nf*, mordida (LAm) *nf*

swindle* *n* estafa *nf*

swindler* *n* estafador, -ora *nm,f*, timador, -ora *nm,f*

switchboard *n* centralita de teléfonos *nf*, conmutador (LAm) *nm* **switchboard operator** telefonista *nmf*

syndicate *n* agrupación *nf*, sindicato *nm*, consorcio *nm*

synergy *n* sinergia *nf*

synthesis *n* síntesis *nf*

synthetic *adj* sintético *adj*

system *n* sistema *nm* **expert system** sistema experto *nm* **systems analyst** analista de sistemas *nm*

table *vb* (motion, paper) presentar *vb*

tabulate *vb* (data) tabular *vb*, presentar en forma de tabla *vb*

tabulated *adj* **tabulated data** datos tabulados *nmpl*

tacit *adj* tácito *adj* **by tacit agreement** por acuerdo tácito *prep*

tactic *n* táctica *nf* **delaying tactics** táctica de demora *nf* **selling tactics** táctica de ventas *nf*

tailor *vb* (adapt) adaptar *vb*

take *vb* **to take legal action** entablar un pleito *vb* **to take notes** tomar apuntes *vb*, tomar notas *vb*, sacar apuntes (LAm) *vb* **to take part in** participar en *vb* **to take the chair** presidir *vb* **to take the lead** tomar la delantera *vb*, tomar el mando *vb* **to take one's time** tomarse tiempo *vb*, tardar *vb*

take over *vb* (company) adquirir *vb*

takeover *n* adquisición *nf*, absorción *nf*

takeup *n* solicitud *nf*, interés *nm*

takings *npl* ingresos *nmpl*, recaudación *nf*, entrada *nf*

talk 1. *n* **sales talk** argumentos de venta *nmpl*, reunión de ventas *nf*, conversación sobre ventas *nf* **2.** *vb* hablar *vb* **to talk business** hablar de negocios *vb*, hablar en serio *vb*

tally 1. *n* cuenta *nf*, registro *nm* **2.** *vb* coincidir *vb*, cuadrar *vb*

tally up *vb* hacer la cuenta *vb*, cuadrar *vb*

tally with *vb* concordar con *vb*, coincidir con *vb*

tangible *adj* **tangible asset** activo tangible *nm*, activo material *nm*

tap *vb* **to tap a market** aprovechar un mercado *vb* **to tap resources** explotar recursos *vb*

target *n* objetivo *nm*, meta *nf* **target date** fecha objetivo *nf* **target market** mercado previsto *nm* **production target** objetivo de producción *nm* **sales target** objetivo de ventas *nm* **to set a target** fijar una meta *vb*

targeted *adj* **targeted campaign** campaña dirigida *nf*

tariff *n* arancel *nm*, tarifa *nf*, precio *nm* **tariff barrier** barrera arancelaria *nf* **tariff negotiations** negociaciones arancelarias *nfpl* **tariff quota** cupo arancelario *nm* **tariff reform** reforma arancelaria *nf* **to raise tariffs** incrementar aranceles *vb*, subir tarifas *vb*

task *n* tarea *nf*, faena *nf* **task management** gestión de tareas *nf*

tax *n* impuesto *nm*, tributo *nm* **after tax** después de deducir impuestos *prep*, neto *adj* **tax allowance** desgravación fiscal *nf*, deducción impositiva *nf* **before tax** antes de deducir impuestos *prep*, bruto *adj* **capital gains tax** impuesto sobre las plusvalías *nm* **tax claim** reclamación de impuestos *nf* **tax-deductible** desgravable *adj* **direct tax** impuesto directo *nm* **tax-free** libre de impuestos *adj*, exento de impuestos *adj* **income tax** impuesto sobre la renta personal *nm* **indirect tax** impuesto indirecto *nm* **tax liability** deuda fiscal *nf* **tax rate** tipo impositivo *nm* **to levy taxes** cobrar impuestos *vb* **value-added tax, sales tax** (US) impuesto sobre el valor añadido/agregado (IVA) *nm* **tax year** año fiscal *nm*, ejercicio fiscal *nm*

taxable *adj* **taxable income** ingresos gravables *nmpl*

taxation *n* imposición *nf*, cargas fiscales *nfpl* **corporate taxation** imposición de sociedades *nf*

taxpayer *n* contribuyente *nmf*

team *n* **research team** equipo de investigación *nm*

technical *adj* **technical director** director, -ora técnico, -ica *nm,f*

technician *n* técnico, -ica *nm,f*

technique *n* **sales technique** técnica de ventas *nf*

technology *n* tecnología *nf* **information technology** informática *nf*, tecnología de datos *nf* **technology transfer** transferencia de tecnología *nf*

telebanking *n* telebanca *nf*

telecommunications *npl* telecomunicaciones *nfpl*

telecopier *n* telecopiadora *nf*, teletipo *nm*

telefax *n* telefax *nm*

telephone *n* teléfono *nm* **telephone box, telephone booth** (US) cabina de teléfonos *nf* **telephone call** llamada telefónica *nf*, llamado (LAm) *nm* **telephone directory** guía telefónica *nf*, directorio telefónico

(LAm) *nm* **telephone number** número de teléfono *nm*

teleprocessing *n* teleproceso *nm*

telesales *npl* televentas *nfpl*

televise *vb* televisar *vb*, transmitir *vb*

teleworking *n* trabajo por teléfono *nm*

telex 1. *n* télex *nm* **2.** *vb* (message) poner un télex *vb*

teller *n* cajero, -era de banco *nm,f*

temporary *adj* temporal *adj*, provisional *adj*, temporario (LAm) *adj*, provisorio (LAm) *adj* **temporary employment** empleo eventual *nm*, trabajo temporario (LAm) *nm*

tenant *n* inquilino, -ina *nm,f*, arrendatario, -ria *nm,f*

tend *vb* **to tend toward** tender a *vb*, tener tendencia a *vb*

tendency *n* tendencia *nf*, propensión *nf* **market tendencies** tendencias del mercado *nfpl*

tender *n* oferta *nf*, concurso *nm*, licitación *nf* **tender offer** oferta pública de adquisición (OPA) *nf* **tender price** precio de oferta *nm* **sale by tender** venta por concurso *nf* **to lodge a tender** presentar una oferta *vb*, licitar (LAm) *vb* **to put sth out for tender** sacar algo a licitación *vb*

tenderer *n* postor, -ora *nm,f*, licitador, -ora (LAm) *nm,f*

tendering *n* licitación *nf*, oferta *nf*

tentative *adj* **tentative offer** oferta provisional *nf*, oferta provisoria (LAm) *nf* **tentative plan** plan provisional *nm*, plan provisorio (LAm) *nm*

tenure *n* tenencia *nf*, ocupación *nf*, posesión *nf*

term *n* **at term** a término *prep* **long term** largo plazo *nm* **medium term** medio plazo *nm* **term of office** mandato *nm* **terms and conditions** términos y condiciones *nmpl & nfpl* **short term** corto plazo *nm* **terms of reference** atribuciones y responsabilidades *nfpl & nfpl*, competencia *nf*, ámbito *nm* **terms of trade** relación real de intercambio *nf*

terminal 1. *adj* terminal *adj*, final *adj* **terminal bonus** bonificación recibida al concluir un seguro *nf* **terminal market** mercado terminal *nm* **2.** *n* **air terminal** terminal aérea *nf* **computer terminal** terminal de ordenador *nm*

termination *n* caducidad *nf*, cese *nm* **termination date** fecha de caducidad *nf* **termination of employment** baja *nf*, cese *nm*, despido *nm*

tertiary *adj* **tertiary industry** sector terciario *nm*, sector de los servicios *nm*

test *n* prueba *nf*, ensayo *nm* **test case** caso que sienta jurisprudencia *nm* **test data** datos de prueba *nmpl* **to put sth to the test** someter algo a prueba *vb*, poner algo a prueba *vb* **to stand the test** pasar la prueba *vb*

test-market *vb* someter a prueba de mercado *vb*

testimonial n recomendación nf, tributo nm, homenaje nm

textile n **textile industry** industria textil nf

theory n **in theory** en teoría prep, teóricamente adv

third adj **third party** tercero nm, tercera parte nf **third-party insurance** seguro contra terceros nm, seguro de responsabilidad civil nm **the Third World** el Tercer Mundo nm

thirty adj **Thirty-Share Index (GB)** índice de cotización de acciones nm

thrash out vb (agreement, policy) tratar de resolver vb, llegar a un acuerdo vb

three adj **three-way split** división triple nf

threshold n umbral nm **tax threshold** nivel en el que la tasa de impuestos cambia nm

thrive vb prosperar vb, crecer vb

through prep **to get through to sb** (phone) comunicarse con alguien vb, entenderse con alguien vb **to put sb through (to sb)** (phone) conectar vb

tick over vb ir tirando vb

ticket n billete nm, ticket nm, entrada nf, pasaje (LAm) nm, boleto (LAm) nm, tiquete (LAm) nm **ticket agency** agencia de venta de localidades nf **ticket office** taquilla nf, despacho de billetes nm, boletería (LAm) nf, taquilla (LAm) nf **price ticket** etiqueta del precio nf **return ticket, round-trip ticket** (US) billete de ida y vuelta nm, pasaje de vuelta nm **season ticket** billete de abono nm, boleto de abono (LAm) nm **single/one-way ticket** (rail/flight) billete de ida nm, pasaje sencillo nm, boleto sencillo (LAm) nm

tide over vb ayudar a salir de un apuro vb

tie up vb (capital) inmovilizar vb

tied adj **tied loan** préstamo inmovilizado nm

tier n **two-tier system** sistema de dos niveles nm

tight adj **to be on a tight budget** tener un presupuesto muy limitado vb

time n tiempo nm, vez nf **time and a half** paga y media nf **double time** paga doble nf **time frame** plazo de tiempo nm **lead time** plazo de entrega nm, período de gestación nm **time limit** plazo nm, término nm, fecha tope nf **time management** gestión del tiempo nf

time-consuming adj que lleva mucho tiempo rel pron

time-saving adj que ahorra tiempo rel pron

timescale n programa nm, calendario nm, escala de tiempo nf

timeshare n multipropiedad nf, copropiedad nf

timetable n horario nm, programa nm, agenda nf

timing n ritmo nm, cronometraje nm

tip n (suggestion) consejo práctico nm, aviso nm **market tip** información confidencial acerca del mercado nf

title n (to goods) título nm **title deed** escritura de propiedad nf

token n **token payment** pago simbólico nm **token strike** huelga de advertencia nf

toll n peaje nm, tasa nf, efecto nm, cuota (LAm) nf

ton n tonelada nf **metric ton** tonelada métrica nf

tone n tono nm **dialling tone, dial tone** (US) (phone) tono de marcar nm, tono de discado (LAm) nm

tonnage n tonelaje nm, peso nm **bill of tonnage** declaración de tonelaje nf **gross tonnage** tonelaje bruto nm **net(t) tonnage** tonelaje neto nm

top adj **top management** alta dirección nf **top prices** precios de punta nmpl **top priority** prioridad absoluta nf

top-level adj de primera categoría prep, de alto standing prep

top-of-the-range adj mejor de la gama adj

total 1. adj total adj, absoluto adj, rotundo adj **total sales** ventas totales nfpl **2.** n total nm, totalidad nf **the grand total** total global nm, suma global nf

tough adj **tough competition** competencia fuerte nf, competencia intensa nf

tour n **tour of duty** período de servicio nm

tourism n turismo nm

tourist n turista nmf **the tourist trade** la industria del turismo nf, turismo nm, el mercado turístico nm

town n **town centre** centro ciudad nm **town council** ayuntamiento nm, municipio nm **town hall** ayuntamiento nm, municipio nm, presidencia municipal (LAm) nf, intendencia (LAm) nf **town planning** urbanismo nm

TQM (Total Quality Management) abbr gestión total de calidad nf

track n pista nf **track record** antecedentes nmpl, registro de antecedentes nm, historial (LAm) nm **to be on the right track** ir por buen camino vb

trade 1. adj **trade agreement** acuerdo comercial nm **trade balance** balanza comercial nf **trade barrier** barrera comercial nf, barrera arancelaria nf **trade cycle** ciclo económico nm **trade directory** guía comercial nf, guía de fabricantes y comerciantes nf **trade fair** feria de muestras nf **trade figures** estadísticas de la balanza comercial nfpl **trade name** nombre comercial nm, razón social nf **trade price** precio al detallista nm **trade restrictions** restricciones comerciales nfpl **trade secret** secreto comercial nm **trade talks** conversaciones comerciales nfpl, negociaciones comerciales nfpl **Trade Descriptions Act** ley que regula la descripción comercial de productos nf **Trades Union Congress** Confederación de Sindicatos nf **trade union** sindicato nm, gremio (LAm) nm **2.** n comercio nm **balance of trade** balanza comercial nf **by trade** de profesión prep, de oficio prep **fair trade** comercio con reciprocidad arancelaria

nm **foreign trade** comercio exterior *nm,* comercio de ultramar *nm* **retail trade** comercio al por menor *nm* **to be in the trade** (informal) dedicarse al negocio de *vb* **3.** *vb* comerciar *vb,* negociar *vb* **to trade as** (name) comerciar como *vb* **to trade with sb** comerciar con alguien *vb*
trademark *n* marca *nf* **registered trademark** marca registrada *nf*
trader *n* comerciante *nmf,* vendedor, -ora *nm,f,* operador, -ora *nm,f,* feriante (LAm) *nmf,* puestero, -era (LAm) *nm,f*
trading *adj* **trading area** zona de comercio *nf* **trading capital** capital de explotación *nm,* capital circulante *nm* **trading company** sociedad comercial *nf* **trading estate** zona industrial *nf,* polígono industrial *nm* **trading loss** pérdida de ejercicio *nf* **trading margin** margen comercial *nm* **trading nation** país comerciante *nm* **trading partner** empresa que comercia con otra *nf,* país que comercia con otro *nm,* socio, -cia *nm,f* **trading standards** normas comerciales *nfpl* **Trading Standards Office (US)** departamento de control de prácticas comerciales *nm* **trading year** ejercicio comercial *nm*
traffic *n* tráfico *nm,* tránsito *nm* **air traffic** tráfico aéreo *nm* **rail traffic** tráfico por ferrocarril *nm* **road traffic** tráfico por carretera *nm* **sea traffic** tráfico marítimo *nm*
train 1. *n* **goods train, freight train** (US) tren de mercancías *nm* **passenger train** tren de pasajeros *nm* **2.** *vb* (staff) formar *vb,* capacitar *vb*
trainee *n* aprendiz *nmf,* persona en aprendizaje *nf* **trainee manager** aspirante a un puesto directivo *nmf*
training *n* formación *nf,* capacitación *nf,* aprendizaje *nm* **advanced training** capacitación avanzada *nf* **training centre** centro de formación *nm* **training course** cursillo de actualización *nm*
transaction *n* transacción *nf,* operación *nf,* negociación *nf* **cash transaction** operación al contado *nf* **transaction management** gestión de transacciones *nf*
transcribe *vb* transcribir *vb*
transfer 1. *adj* **transfer desk** (transport) mostrador de transbordos *nm* **transfer duty** impuesto de transferencia *nm* **transfer lounge** (transport) sala de tránsito *nf* **transfer payments** pagos de transferencia *nmpl* **transfer price** precio de transferencia *nm* **transfer tax** impuesto sobre transferencias *nm* **2.** *n* **bank transfer** transferencia bancaria *nf* **capital transfer** transferencia de capital *nf* **credit transfer** transferencia de fondos *nf* **3.** *vb* (call) pasar a *vb,* poner con *vb* (ownership, technology) transferir *vb,* traspasar *vb* (transport) trasladar *vb,* hacer transbordo *vb*
transferable *adj* transferible *adj*

transit *n* **transit goods** mercancías en tránsito *nfpl* **in transit** en tránsito *prep* **lost in transit** perdido en tránsito *adj* **transit lounge** (transport) sala de tránsito *nf,* sala para pasajeros en tránsito *nf* **transit passenger** (transport) pasajero en tránsito *nm*
transmit *vb* transmitir *vb,* emitir *vb,* comunicar *vb*
transnational *adj* transnacional *adj*
transport *n* **transport agent** agente de transportes *nm* **fair transport** transporte aéreo *nm* **transport company** compañía de transportes *nf,* empresa de transportes *nf* **public transport** transporte público *nm* **rail transport** transporte por ferrocarril *nm* **road transport** transporte por carretera *nm*
transportation *n* transporte *nm*
transship *vb* transbordar *vb*
travel 1. *adj* **travel agency** agencia de viajes *nf* **travel insurance** seguro de viaje *nm* **2.** *n* **air travel** viajes en avión *nmpl,* viajar por avión *vb* **business travel** viajes de negocios *nmpl* **3.** *vb* viajar *vb,* desplazarse *vb*
traveller, traveler (US) *n* viajero, -era *nm,f,* pasajero, -era *nm,f,* viajante comercial *nmf* **traveller's cheque, traveler's check** (US) cheque de viajero *nm,* cheque de viaje *nm*
travelling, traveling (US) *n* **travelling expenses, travel expenses** (US) gastos de viaje *nmpl*
treasurer *n* **treasurer check** (US) cheque de tesorero *nm* **company treasurer** director, -ora de finanzas de la empresa *nm,f*
treasury *n* tesoro *nm* **Treasury bill** pagaré del Tesoro *nm* **the Treasury** el Tesoro público *nm,* la Hacienda Pública *nf* **the Treasury Department (US)** Departamento del Tesoro *nm,* el Ministerio de Hacienda *nm*
treaty *n* tratado *nm,* acuerdo *nm,* convenio *nm* **commercial treaty** tratado comercial *nm,* acuerdo comercial *nm* **to make a treaty** suscribir un tratado *vb,* llegar a un acuerdo *vb*
trend *n* tendencia *nf,* coyuntura *nf,* moda *nf* **trend analysis** análisis de tendencias *nm* **current trend** moda actual *nf* **economic trend** tendencia económica *nf* **market trend** tendencia del mercado *nf* **price trend** tendencia de precios *nf* **to buck a trend** ir contracorriente *vb* **to set a trend** iniciar una moda *vb*
trial *n* **trial and error** ensayo y error *nm* & *nm* **trial offer** muestra de oferta *nf* **trial period** período de prueba *nm* **to carry out trials** poner a prueba *vb,* realizar ensayos *vb*
tribunal *n* tribunal *nm,* comisión *nf* **industrial tribunal** Magistratura del Trabajo *nf*
trim *vb* (investment) recortar *vb* (workforce) reducir la plantilla *vb*
trimming *n* **cost trimming** reducción de costes *nf*

trip *n* viaje *nf*, recorrido *nm* **business trip** viaje de negocios *nm* **round trip** viaje de ida y vuelta *nm*, viaje redondo (LAm) *nf*
triplicate *n* **in triplicate** por triplicado *prep*
trust *n* **trust agreement** acuerdo fiduciario *nm* **trust company** compañía fiduciaria *nf* **trust estate** herencia fiduciaria *nf* **trust fund** fondo de fideicomiso *nm*, fondo de custodia *nm* **investment trust** sociedad de inversión *nf* **to hold sth in trust** estar encomendado de algo *vb* **to set up a trust** establecer un fideicomiso *vb* **to supply sth on trust** suministrar algo bajo palabra *vb*, abastecer algo a crédito *vb* **unit trust** sociedad inversora por obligaciones *nf*, fondos mutuos *nmpl*, fondo de inversión mobiliaria *nm*
trustee *n* fideicomisario, -ria *nm,f* **trustee department** (bank) oficina de administración fiduciaria *nf*
trusteeship *n* fideicomiso *nm*, cargo de administrador *nm*
try out *vb* probar *vb*, poner a prueba *vb*
turn *vb* (market) cambiar *vb*, fluctuar *vb*
turn down *vb* (offer) rechazar *vb*
turn on *vb* (machine) poner en marcha *vb*, conectar *vb*, prender (LAm) *vb*
turn out *vb* (end) salir *vb*, resultar *vb*, acabar *vb*
turn over *vb* facturar *vb*, dar la vuelta a *vb*, voltear (LAm) *vb*, dar vuelta (LAm) *vb*
turn round, turn around (US) *vb* (company) sanear *vb*
turnabout *n* giro *nm*, cambio *nm*
turning *adj* **turning point** vuelta de la marea *nf*, momento decisivo *nm*
turnover *n* volumen de ventas *nm*, cifra de facturación *nf* **capital turnover** volumen de capital facturado *nm* **turnover rate** ritmo de facturación *nm*, índice de rotación de existencias *nm* **turnover ratio** ratio de facturación *nm*, ratio de renovación *nm* **turnover tax** impuesto sobre el volumen de ventas y negocios *nm*
twenty-four *adj* **twenty-four-hour service** servicio de veinticuatro horas *nm*
two *adj* **two-speed** de velocidad doble *prep* **two-tier** de dos niveles *prep* **two-way** de doble sentido *prep*, bilateral *adj* de doble mano (LAm) *prep*, de doble vía (LAm) *prep*
tycoon *n* magnate *nmf*
type 1. *n* **bold type** negrita *nf* **italic type** cursiva *nf* **large type** letra grande *nf* **small type** caracteres pequeños *nmpl* 2. *vb* escribir a máquina *vb*, pasar a máquina *vb*, tipear (LAm) *vb*
typewriter *n* máquina de escribir *nf*
typing *adj* **typing error** error tipográfico *nm*
typist *n* mecanógrafo, -afa *nm,f*
ultimo *adj* del pasado mes *prep*
unanimous *adj* unánime *adj*
uncleared *adj* (customs) sin despachar *prep*, (cheque) sin pagar *prep*
unconditional *adj* incondicional *adj*

unconfirmed *adj* sin confirmar *prep*
undeclared *adj* (goods) sin declarar *prep*
undercapitalized *adj* infracapitalizado *adj*
undercharge *vb* cobrarle de menos a *vb*
undercut *vb* vender más barato *vb*
underdeveloped *adj* **underdeveloped country** país subdesarrollado *nm*
underemployed *adj* subempleado *adj*, infrautilizado *adj*
underinsured *adj* infrasegurado *adj*
underpay *vb* pagar de menos *vb*
underpayment *n* pago insuficiente *nm*
undersell *vb* vender más barato *vb*
understanding *n* comprensión *nf*, entendimiento *nm*, acuerdo *nm*
undersubscribed *adj* no cubierto por entero *adj*
undertake *vb* emprender *vb*, comprometerse *vb*, encargarse *vb*
undertaking *n* empresa *nf*, compromiso *nm*
undervalue *vb* infravalorar *vb*
underwrite *vb* (risk) asegurar *vb*
underwriter *n* suscriptor, -ora *nm,f*, asegurador, -ora *nm,f*
undischarged *adj* (bankrupt) no rehabilitado *adj*
unearned *adj* **unearned income** rendimientos del capital *nmpl*, renta no salarial *nf*
unemployed *adj* desempleado *adj*, parado *adj*, sin trabajo *prep*, cesante (LAm) *adj*
unemployment *n* desempleo *nm*, paro *nm*, cesantía (LAm) *nf* **unemployment benefit** subsidio de paro *nm* **unemployment insurance** seguro de desempleo *nm* **level of unemployment** nivel de desempleo *nm* **rate of unemployment** tasa de paro *nf*
unexpected *adj* inesperado *adj*
unfair *adj* **unfair dismissal** despido improcedente *nm*, despido injustificado *nm*, despido injusto *nm*
unforeseen *adj* **unforeseen circumstances** circunstancias imprevistas *nfpl*
unification *n* unificación *nf*
unilateral *adj* (contract) unilateral *adj*
uninsurable *adj* no asegurable *adj*
union *n* sindicato *nm*, unión *nf*, asociación de estudiantes *nf*, gremio (LAm) *nm* **union membership** afiliación sindical *nf* **union representative** representante sindical *nmf*, delegado, -ada sindical *nm,f* **trade union, labor union** (US) sindicato laboral *nm*
unit *n* unidad *nf*, módulo *nm*, conjunto *nm* **unit cost** coste unitario *nm*, costo por unidad (LAm) *nm*, costo unitario (LAm) *nm* **unit of production** unidad de producción *nf* **unit price** precio por unidad *nm* **unit trust** fondos mutuos *nmpl*, fondo de inversión mobiliaria *nm*
united *adj* unido *adj* **United Nations** Naciones Unidas (la ONU) *nfpl*
unlimited *adj* **unlimited company** empresa ilimitada *nf* **unlimited credit** crédito ilimitado *nm* **unlimited liability**

responsabilidad ilimitada *nf*
unload *vb* descargar *vb*, deshacerse de *vb*
unmarketable *adj* invendible *adj*
unofficial *adj* **unofficial strike** huelga no autorizada *nf*, huelga ilegal *nf*
unpack *vb* deshacer *vb*, desembalar *vb*, sacar *vb*, desempacar (LAm) *vb*
unpaid *adj* **unpaid balance** saldo deudor *nm*, saldo negativo *nm*, importe a pagar todavía *nm* **unpaid bill** factura sin saldar *nf* **unpaid cheque** cheque impagado *nm*
unprofessional *adj* contrario a la ética profesional *adj*
unprofitable *adj* no rentable *adj*, no lucrativo *adj*, infructuoso *adj*
unsaleable *adj* invendible *adj*, no comerciable *adj*
unsatisfactory *adj* insatisfactorio *adj*, deficiente *adj*
unsecured *adj* **unsecured bond** bono no garantizado *nm* **unsecured credit** crédito sin garantía *nm*
unskilled *adj* **unskilled worker** trabajador, -ora no cualificado, -ada *nm,f*, obrero, -era no especializado, -ada *nm,f*, obrero,-era no calificado,-ada (LAm) *nm,f*, peón (LAm) *nmf*
unsold *adj* invendido *adj*, sin vender *prep*
unsolicited *adj* **unsolicited offer** oferta no solicitada *nf*
up-to-date *adj* actual *adj*, al día *prep*, moderno (LAm) *adj* **to bring sth up-to-date** actualizar algo *vb*, poner algo al día *vb*, modernizar algo *vb*
update *vb* (records) actualizar *vb*
upgrade *vb* mejorar *vb*, ascender *vb*
upswing *n* reactivación *nf*, repunte *nm*
upturn *n* mejora *nf*, reactivación *nf*, giro positivo *nm*
upward *adj* & *adv* alcista *adj*, hacia arriba *prep* & *adv*
urban *adj* **urban renewal** remodelación urbana *nf* **urban sprawl** expansión urbana descontrolada *nf*
urgency *n* urgencia *nf* **a matter of urgency** asunto urgente *nm*
urgent *adj* urgente *adj*, apremiante *adj*
urgently *adv* urgentemente *adv*
usage *n* **intensive usage** uso intensivo *nm*
use *n* **to make use of sth** usar algo *vb*, hacer uso de algo *vb*
user-friendly *adj* fácil de utilizar *adj*, amigable *adj*
usury *n* usura *nf*
utility *n* utilidad *nf* **marginal utility** utilidad marginal *nf* **public utility** empresa de utilidad pública *nf*
utilization *n* utilización *nf*, empleo *nm*
utilize *vb* utilizar *vb*, usar *vb*, emplear *vb*
vacancy *n* vacante *nf*, habitación libre *nf*
vacant *adj* vacante *adj*, libre *adj*, desocupado *adj*
valid *adj* vigente *adj*, legítimo *adj*
validate *vb* convalidar *vb*
validity *n* validez *nf*, legitimidad *nf*

valuable *adj* valioso *adj*, precioso *adj*
valuation *n* valoración *nf*, tasación *nf*, evaluación *nf*, avalúo (LAm) *nm*
value *n* valor *nm* **face value** valor nominal *nm* **market value** valor de mercado *nm* **to gain value** aumentar de valor *vb*, revalorizarse *vb* **to get value for one's money** conseguir buen precio *vb* **to lose value** depreciarse *vb*, perder valor *vb*
variable *adj* **variable costs** costes variables *nmpl*, costos variables (LAm) *nmpl* **variable rate** tasa variable *nf*, tipo variable *nm*
variance *n* varianza *nf*, discrepancia *nf*, variación *nf* **budget variance** variación presupuestaria *nf*
VAT (value added tax) *abbr* IVA (impuesto al valor agregado, impuesto sobre el valor añadido) *abbr,nm*
vendee *n* comprador, -ora *nm,f*
vending machine *n* máquina expendedora automática *nf*
vendor *n* vendedor, -ora *nm,f* **vendor capital** capital de vendedor, -ora *nm,f* **joint vendor** vendedor, -ora *nm,f*, asociado, ada *nm,f*
verbatim *adv* palabra por palabra *nf*, al pie de la letra *prep*
vertical *n* **vertical integration** integración vertical *nf*
vested *adj* personal *adj*, adquirido *adj* **vested interests** interés personal *nm* **vested rights** derechos adquiridos *nmpl*
veto **1.** *n* veto *nm* **2.** *vb* vetar *vb*
viability *n* viabilidad *nf*
video *n* vídeo *nm* **video facilities** equipo de vídeo *nm*
viewer *n* telespectador, -ora *nm,f*
VIP (very important person) *abbr* VIP *abbr,nm*
visa *n* visado *nm*, visa (LAm) *nf*
visible *adj* **visible exports** exportaciones visibles *nfpl*
visit **1.** *n* visita *nf* **2.** *vb* visitar *vb*, hacer una visita *vb*
visitor *n* visita *nmf*, invitado, -ada *nm,f*
visual *adj* visual *adj* **visual display unit (VDU)** unidad de despliegue visual *nf*, pantalla de visualización *nf* **visual telephone** teléfono visual *nm*
vocational *adj* profesional *adj*
volatile *adj* (prices) inestable *adj*, fluctuante *adj*
volume *n* volumen *nm*, cantidad *nf*, capacidad *nf* **volume discount** descuento por volumen *nm* **trading volume** volumen comercial *nm*, volumen de negocios *nm*
voluntary *adj* voluntario *nm* **to go into voluntary liquidation** entrar en liquidación voluntaria *vb* **voluntary wage restraint** moderación voluntaria en las reivindicaciones salariales *nf*
vote **1.** *n* voto *nm*, votación *nf* **vote of no confidence** voto de censura *nm* **vote of thanks** voto de gracias *nm* **2.** *vb* votar *vb*, aprobar *vb*

voting *adj* **voting right** derecho de voto *nm*
voucher *n* vale *nm*, bono *nm*, comprobante *nm*
wage 1. *adj* **wage demand** reivindicación salarial *nf* **wage earner** asalariado, -ada *nm,f* **wage increase** aumento de sueldo *nm*, incremento salarial *nm*, mejora salarial *nf* **wage negotiations** negociaciones salariales *nfpl* **wage packet, salary package** (US) sueldo neto *nm* **wage policy** política salarial *nf* **wage restraint** moderación salarial *nf* **wage rise** aumento de sueldo *nm*, incremento salarial *nm* **wage(s) agreement** acuerdo salarial *nm* **wage(s) bill** coste total de los salarios *nm* **wage scale** escala salarial *nf* **wage(s) claim** reivindicación salarial *nf*, demanda salarial *nf* **wage(s) freeze** congelación salarial *nf* **wage(s) settlement** convenio salarial *nm*, acuerdo salarial *nm* **2.** *n* salario *nm*, sueldo *nm*, paga *nf* **average wage** salario medio *nm* **minimum wage** salario mínimo *nm* **net(t) wage** sueldo neto *nm*, salario neto *nm* **real wage** salario real *nm* **starting wage** salario de entrada *nm* **3.** *vb* librar *vb*, hacer *vb* **to wage a campaign** hacer una campaña *vb*
waiting *n* **waiting list** lista de espera *nf*
waive *vb* renunciar *vb*, repudiar *vb*
waiver *n* renuncia *nf*, exención *nf* **waiver clause** cláusula de renuncia *nf*
wall *n* **tariff wall** barrera arancelaria *nf* **to go to the wall** quebrar *vb*, ser declarado en quiebra *vb* **Wall Street (US)** Wall Street *n*, centro financiero de Nueva York *nm*
war *n* **price war** guerra de precios *nf* **trade war** guerra comercial *nf*
warehouse *n* almacén *nm*, depósito *nm*, bodega (LAm) *nf* **bonded warehouse** depósito aduanero *nm*, bodega aduanera (LAm) *nf*
warehousing *n* almacenaje *nm*, depósito *nm*
wares *npl* mercancías *nfpl*, mercaderías (LAm) *nfpl*
warn *vb* avisar *vb*, advertir *vb*, aconsejar *vb* **to warn sb against doing sth** prevenir a alguien contra algo *vb*
warning *n* aviso *nm*, advertencia *nf* **due warning** debido aviso *nm* **warning sign** señal de alerta *nf* **without warning** sin previo aviso *prep*
warrant 1. *n* orden *nf*, autorización *nf*, derecho de suscripción de nuevas acciones *nm* **warrant for payment** mandato de pago *nm* **2.** *vb* justificar *vb*, garantizar *vb*, asegurar *vb*
warranty *n* garantía *nf* **under warranty** bajo garantía *prep*
wastage *n* pérdida *nf*, desgaste *nm*, desperdicio *nm* **wastage rate** tasa de abandono *nf*, ritmo de reducción de la plantilla *nm*
waste 1. *adj* **waste products** material sobrante *nm*, productos de desecho *nmpl*,

desechos *nmpl* **2.** *n* desperdicio *nm*, pérdida *nf* **industrial waste** residuos industriales *nmpl*, desechos industriales *nmpl* **waste of time** pérdida de tiempo *nf* **to go to waste** echarse a perder *vb* **3.** *vb* malgastar *vb*, despilfarrar *vb*
wasting *adj* **wasting asset** activo amortizable *nm*
watch *vb* **to watch developments** seguir de cerca los sucesos *vb*
watchdog *n* (fig.) perro guardián *nm*, guardián, -ana *nm,f* **watchdog committee** comisión de control *nf*
water down *vb* diluir *vb*, suavizar *vb*
watered *adj* **watered capital** acciones emitidas sin aumento de capital *nfpl* **watered stock** valores emitidos sin aumento de capital *nmpl*
watertight *adj* (fig.) infalible *adj*, hermético *adj*
wave *n* (of mergers, takeovers) oleada *nf*
wavelength *n* **to be on the same wavelength** sintonizar con *vb*
weaken *vb* (market) debilitarse *vb*, caer *vb*, aflojar *vb*
wealth riqueza *nf*, patrimonio *nm*, abundancia *nf*, fortuna *nf* **national wealth** patrimonio nacional *nm* **wealth tax** impuesto sobre el patrimonio *nm*
week *n* **twice a week** dos veces a la semana *nfpl* **working week** semana laboral *nf*
weekly *adj* **weekly wages** salario semanal *nm*
weigh *vb* pesar *vb* **to weigh the pros and cons** pesar ventajas y desventajas *vb*, sopesar *vb*
weight *n* **dead weight** peso muerto *nm* **excess weight** exceso de peso *nm* **gross weight** peso bruto *nm* **net(t) weight** peso neto *nm* **weights and measures** pesos y medidas *nmpl* & *nfpl*
weighted *adj* **weighted average** promedio ponderado *nm* **weighted index** índice ponderado *nm*
weighting *n* suplemento salarial *nm*, bonificación *nf*
weighty *adj* importante *adj*, serio *adj*
welfare 1. *adj* **welfare benefits** subsidios sociales *nmpl* **welfare state** estado asistencial *nm*, estado benefactor *nm* **2.** *n* bienestar *nm*, asistencia social *nf*
well-advised *adj* sensato *adj*
well-informed *adj* muy al corriente *prep*, muy interiorizado (LAm) *adj*
well-known *adj* conocido *adj*, bien sabido *adj*
well-made *adj* de buena fabricación *prep*, fuerte *adj*
well-paid *adj* bien remunerado *adj*
well-tried *adj* probado *adj*
WEU (Western European Union) *abbr* UEO (Unión de la Europa Occidental) (La) *abbr,nf*
white *adj* **white-collar worker** administrativo, -iva *nm,f*, empleado, -ada de oficina *nm,f*, oficinista *nmf*

wholesale *n* **at/by wholesale** al por mayor *prep* **wholesale price** precio al por mayor *nm* **wholesale trade** comercio al por mayor *nm*

wholesaler *n* mayorista *nmf,* comerciante al por mayor *nmf*

wholly *adv* totalmente *adv,* completamente *adv* **wholly-owned subsidiary** filial de entera propiedad *nf*

wide-ranging *adj* amplio *adj,* diverso *adj,* de gran alcance *prep*

will *n* voluntad *nf,* testamento *nm*

win *vb* ganar *vb,* conseguir *vb,* lograr *vb* **win customers** hacerse con clientes *vb* **to win support** ganarse apoyo *vb*

wind up *vb* terminar *vb,* concluir *vb,* liquidar *vb*

windfall *n* suerte imprevista *nf* **windfall profit** beneficio inesperado *nm*

winding-up *n* conclusión *nf,* liquidación *nf* **winding-up arrangements** disposiciones de liquidación *nfpl* **winding-up order** liquidación judicial *nf*

window *n* **window of opportunity** marco de oportunidad *nm*

withdraw *vb* retirar *vb,* sacar *vb,* cancelar *vb* **to withdraw an offer** retirar una oferta *vb*

withdrawal *n* retirada *nf,* abandono *nm,* retiro (LAm) *nm* **withdrawal of funds** reintegro de fondos *nm,* retiro de fondos (LAm) *nm*

withhold *vb* retener *vb,* negar *vb* **to withhold a document** retener un documento *vb,* no dar a conocer un documento *vb*

withstand *vb* resistir *vb,* soportar *vb*

witness 1. *n* testigo *nm,* testimonio *nm* **2.** *vb* atestiguar *vb,* ser testigo de *vb,* presenciar *vb* **to witness a signature** atestiguar una firma *vb*

word *n* palabra *nf* **word processing** procesamiento de textos *nm* **word processor** procesador de palabras *nm* **to give one's word** dar su palabra *vb,* comprometerse *vb* **to keep one's word** cumplir su palabra *vb*

wording *n* texto *nm,* redacción *nf*

work 1. *adj* **work experience** experiencia laboral *nf,* prácticas *nfpl* **work permit** permiso de trabajo *nm* **work schedule** plan de trabajo *nm* **work study** estudio del trabajo *nm* **2.** *n* **casual work** trabajo eventual *nm* **day off work** día libre *nm* **day's work** jornada *nf* **factory work** trabajo manual *nm* **office work** trabajo de oficina *nm* **works** obras *nfpl,* fábrica *nf,* mecanismo *nm* **works committee** comité de la empresa *nm,* comité de empresa *nm* **works council** consejo de obreros *nm* **works manager** jefe, -efa de taller *nm,f,* director, -ora de fábrica *nm,f* **public works programme (GB)** programa de obras públicas *nm* **to be in work** tener trabajo *vb* **to be out of work** estar desempleado *vb,*

estar en paro *vb,* estar en cesantía (LAm) *vb* **to look for work** buscar trabajo *vb* **3.** *vb* trabajar *vb* **to work to rule** hacer huelga de celo *vb,* hacer huelga de trabajo lento *vb,* trabajar a reglamento (LAm) *vb* **to work unsocial hours** trabajar fuera de horas normales *vb*

workable *adj* factible *adj,* viable *adj*

workaholic *n* trabajoadicto, -cta *nm,f*

workday (US) *n* día laborable *nm*

worker *n* **casual worker** trabajador, -ora eventual *nm,f* **clerical worker** oficinista *nmf,* administrativo, -iva *nm,f,* empleado, -ada de oficina *nm,f* **worker-director** director, -ora obrero, -era *nm,f* **manual worker** obrero, -era manual *nm,f,* trabajador, -ora manual *nm,f,* peón (LAm) *nmf* **worker participation** participación obrera *nf* **skilled worker** obrero, -era especializado, -ada *nm,f,* obrero, -era calificado, -ada *nm,f* **unskilled worker** obrero, -era no cualificado, -ada *nm,f,* peón *nmf,* obrero, -era no calificado, -ada (LAm) *nm,f*

workforce *n* personal *nm,* plantilla *nf,* fuerza laboral *nf*

working *adj* **working agreement** acuerdo laboral *nm* **working area** área de trabajo *nf,* campo de trabajo *nm* **working capital** capital circulante *nm* **working conditions** condiciones de trabajo *nfpl* **working environment** ambiente laboral *nm* **working hours** horario de trabajo *nm* **working knowledge** conocimientos básicos *nmpl* **working language** idioma de trabajo *nm* **working life** vida activa *nf,* vida laboral *nf* **working majority** mayoría suficiente *nf* **working model** maqueta *nf* **working paper** documento de trabajo *nm* **working party** equipo de trabajo *nm* **working population** población activa *nf* **working week (GB)** semana laboral *nf,* semana de trabajo *nf*

workload *n* trabajo asignado *nm,* carga de trabajo *nf*

workmate *n* compañero, -era de trabajo *nm,f*

workplace *n* lugar de trabajo *nm,* trabajo *nm*

workshop *n* taller *nm,* estudio *nm*

workweek (US) *n* semana laboral *nf,* semana de trabajo *nf*

world *n* mundo *nm* **the commercial world** el mundo de los negocios *nm,* el mundo comercial *nm* **world consumption** consumo global *nm* **world exports** exportaciones mundiales *nfpl* **world fair** exposición universal *nf* **World Bank** Banco Mundial *nm* **World Court** Tribunal Internacional de Justicia *nm*

worldwide *adj* mundial *adj,* global *adj*

worth 1. *adj* que vale *rel pron* **to be worth** valer *vb,* merecer *vb* **2.** *n* valor *nm*

wpm (words per minute) *abbr* palabras por minuto *nfpl*

wreck *vb* destrozar *vb,* echar por tierra *vb*

writ *n* orden judicial *nf*, mandato judicial *nm*, mandamiento judicial *nm* **to issue a writ** dictar un mandato judicial *vb*

write down *vb* (depreciation) depreciar *vb*, amortizar *vb*

write off *vb* (debts) anular *vb*, dar por perdido *vb*, (vehicle) declarar siniestro total *vb*

write-off *n* anulación *nf*, depreciación *nf*, fracaso *nm*

wrongful *adj* **wrongful dismissal** despido injusto *nm*

xerox *vb* fotocopiar *vb*, xerografiar *vb*

Xerox (R) *n* (machine) fotocopiadora *nf*

year *n* año *nm* **year-end dividend** dividendo de fin de año *nm* **year-end inventory** inventario por cierre de ejercicio *nm* **financial year** ejercicio financiero *nm* **fiscal year** ejercicio fiscal *nm*, año fiscal *nm* **tax year** año fiscal *nm*, ejercicio fiscal*nm*

yearly *adj* anual *adj* **yearly income** renta anual *nf*

yellow *adj* **the Yellow pages (R) (GB)** las páginas amarillas *nfpl*

yen *n* (currency) yen *nm* **yen bond** bono de yen *nm*

yield 1. *adj* **yield curve** curva de rendimiento *nf* **2.** *n* **yield on shares** rendimiento sobre acciones *nm* **3.** *vb* rendir *vb*, devengar *vb*, ceder *vb*

young *adj* **young economy** economía nueva *nf*

zenith *n* cenit *nm*, apogeo *nm*

zero *n* cero *nm* **zero address** sin dirección *prep* **below zero** bajo cero *prep* **zero defect** sin defecto *prep* **zero growth** crecimiento cero *nm* **zero hour** hora cero *nf* **zero rate/rating** imposición del 0% *nf*, exento de impuestos *adj* **zero-rate taxation** sistema tributario a tasa cero *nm* **to be zero-rated for VAT** estar exento de IVA *vb*

zip code (US) *n* código postal *nm*

zone 1. *n* zona *nf*, polígono *nm* **currency zone** zona monetaria *nf* **enterprise zone** zona de libre empresa *nf*, zona de desarrollo *nf* **postal zone** distrito postal *nm* **time zone** huso horario *nm* **wage zone** zona salarial *nf* **2.** *vb* zonificar *vb*

zoning *n* zonificación *nf*, división por zonas *nf*

Index

Index

Business Correspondence

Spanish Commercial Correspondence, notes on 114

Business Practice

Grammar

Glossary